VOLUME THREE

CONTROL OF
HUMAN BEHAVIOR
BEHAVIOR MODIFICATION IN EDUCATION

Roger Ulrich
Western Michigan University

Thomas Stachnik
Michigan State University

John Mabry
Porterville State Hospital
Porterville, California

SCOTT, FORESMAN AND COMPANY

The opinions or conclusions stated in this volume are those of the editors and are not to be construed as official or as necessarily reflecting the policy of the Department of Health, State of California.

Library of Congress Catalog Card Number: 73-88912
ISBN: 0–673-07621–0
Copyright © 1974 Scott, Foresman and Company, Glenview, Illinois.
Philippines Copyright 1974 Scott, Foresman and Company.
All Rights Reserved.
Printed in the United States of America.

Regional offices of Scott, Foresman and Company are located in Dallas, Texas; Glenview, Illinois; Oakland, New Jersey; Palo Alto, California; Tucker, Georgia; and Brighton, England.

PREFACE

The *Control of Human Behavior* series has grown along with the field of behavior modification. This third volume turns its attention to education, a field that is a current and important focus of behavior modifiers. Although the topic is narrower than those of preceding volumes, this volume is somewhat longer. Its greater size reflects the exponential increase in activity by behavior modifiers in education as in other fields. In education especially, behavior modifiers have been busy building programs for all ages from infancy to adulthood, establishing nursery schools, training teachers, revamping college and special education programs. The technological advance resulting from the involvement of behavioral psychologists in education has been tremendous. Programmed instruction, behavioral objectives, precision teaching, accountability, and numerous techniques for controlling classroom behavior have been generated. By sampling these achievements, this volume presents a comprehensive view of behavior modification as its now functions in education.

Several individuals performed essential work in the course of compiling this book. Sylvia Dulaney helped with early planning. Galen Alessi made numerous valuable suggestions based on his expert knowledge of the literature. Kay Mueller assisted in the final compilation of the manuscript, and Marie Harris deciphered and typed the interstitial material.

Of course, the people who really made the volume possible are those who built the programs and developed the technology reported. The editors hope that their own efforts have produced a collection that correctly represents the work of these individuals.

Roger Ulrich
Thomas Stachnik
John Mabry

CONTENTS

INTRODUCTION

Part I.   *INTRODUCTION TO BEHAVIORAL EDUCATION - 1*

1. *Two Views of Behavioral Education - 2*

How I Spent My Christmas Vacation - *3*
H. S. Pennypacker

Behavior Modification Techniques for the Educational Technologist - *18*
Richard B. Stuart

Part II.   *NEW PROGRAMS OF BEHAVIORAL EDUCATION - 41*

2. *In the Education of Infants - 42*

Infant Day Care - *44*
M. F. Cataldo and Todd R. Risley

An Educational Day-care Program for Infants - *50*
D. B. Spates, G. J. Alessi, A. Gutmann, S. Ellsworth, K. L. Mueller,
and R. E. Ulrich

3. *In Early Education - 61*

The Use of a Token System in Project Head Start - *62*
L. Keith Miller and Richard Schneider

The Effectiveness of Direct Verbal Instruction on IQ Performance
and Achievement in Reading and Arithmetic - *69*
Siegfried Engelmann

4. *In Elementary-School Education - 85*

Operant Conditioning in the Classroom Setting: A Review of Research - *86*
Karl I. Altman and Thomas E. Linton

The Use of Behavior Modification by Individual Classroom Teachers - *96*
Thomas J. Stachnik

The Learning Village Elementary School - *106*
C. Hren, K. Mueller, C. R. Spates, C. Ulrich, and R. E. Ulrich

5. *In Adolescent and Secondary Education - 115*

Use of Group Activities and Team Rewards to Increase Individual
Classroom Productivity - *116*
Barbara B. Sloggett

Effective Behavior Change at the Anne Arundel Learning Center Through Minimum
Contact Interventions - *124*
Shlomo I. Cohen, J. Michael Keyworth, Richard I. Kleiner, and William L. Brown

6. *In College and University Education* - *143*

Contingency Management in University Courses - *144*
Kenneth E. Lloyd

An Experimental Approach to Learning: Introduction for Students - *153*
Philip N. Hineline

An Experimental Approach to Teaching: Introduction for Teachers - *155*
Philip N. Hineline

I've Got Blisters on My Soul . . . - *161*
R. W. Malott, Patricia Hartlep, and Stuart Hartlep

7. *In the Education of Adults* - *169*

Reinforcing Self-help Group Activities of Welfare Recipients - *170*
L. Keith Miller and Ocoee L. Miller

The Use of Contingency Management to Affect Learning Performance
in Adult Institutionalized Offenders - *177*
John M. McKee

Universal Parenthood-Training: A Proposal for Preventive Mental Health - *187*
Robert P. Hawkins

8. *In Special Education* - *193*

Nonreinforcement for Teachers: Penalties for Success - *194*
Maryanne Q. Brown

The School Adjustment Program: A Model Program for Treatment of Severely
Maladjusted Children in the Public Schools - *197*
Robert P. Hawkins and J. Eric Hayes

9. *In Personal Education* - *209*

On Developing Personally Competent Individuals: A Behavioral Perspective - *210*
Carl E. Thoresen

The View from the Inner Eye: Personal Management of Inner and
Outer Behaviors - *213*
Ann Dell Duncan

Social Control of Form Diversity and the Emergence of New Forms
in Children's Blockbuilding - *217*
Elizabeth M. Goetz and Donald M. Baer

10. *In Community Settings* - *225*

Public Access Learning: Experimental Studies in a Public Museum - *226*
C. G. Screven

Exercises in the Design of Learning Environments - *234*
Richard Allen Chase, M.D. Michael Williams, and John J. Fisher, III

Part III. *A BEHAVIORAL TECHNOLOGY OF EDUCATION* - *253*

11. *Behavioral Objectives* - *254*

   Measurable Objectives for Educational Programs - *255*
   Jerry Short

   Linguistics, Communication, and Behavioral Objectives: A Remedial
   Curriculum - *265*
   Richard R. Lee

12. *Programmed and Automated Instruction* - *274*

   The Basic Programming Principles - *275*
   Susan Meyer Markle

   Problems of Applying Computer Technology to Teacher Education - *289*
   Alfred Ellison

   Teaching Classification by Computer - *295*
   James G. Holland and Judith Doran

13. *Structuring Antecedent Stimuli* - *298*

   Teaching Concepts and Operations, or How to Make Kids Smart - *299*
   Wesley C. Becker

   Some Principles of Instructional Design at Higher Cognitive Levels - *312*
   Susan M. Markle and Philip W. Tiemann

14. *Techniques for the Modification of Group Behavior* - *324*

   Effects of Group Contingent Events upon Classroom Noise - *325*
   Gilbert W. Schmidt and Roger E. Ulrich

   Group Contingencies, Peer Tutoring, and Accelerating Academic Achievement - *333*
   Robert L. Hamblin, Craig Hathaway, and John Wodarski

15. *Techniques for the Reduction of Problem Behaviors* - *341*

   The Modification of Several Classroom Behaviors of an Emotionally Disturbed Child
   in a Regular Classroom - *342*
   Moira McArthur and Robert P. Hawkins

   Good Behavior Game: Effects of Individual Contingencies for Group Consequences
   on Disruptive Behavior in a Classroom - *353*
   Harriet H. Barrish, Muriel Saunders, and Montrose M. Wolf

   The Functions of Time-out for Changing the Aggressive Behaviors
   of a Preschool Child: A Multiple-baseline Analysis - *359*
   Judith M. LeBlanc, Karen Haney Busby, and Carolyn L. Thomson

16. *Assessment, Accountability, and Performance Contracting - 365*

A Source of Disorder in the Schools and a Way to Reduce It:
Two Kinds of Tests - *367*
Roy A. Moxley, Jr.

The Effect of Internal Accountability on the Development of
a Bilingual Program - *372*
Robert M. Offenberg

How We *ALL* Failed in Performance Contracting - *378*
Ellis B. Page

17. *Precision Teaching - 383*

". . . and a Child Shall Lead Them": Stephanie's Chart Story - *384*
Stephanie Bates and Douglas F. Bates

Precision Teaching in Perspective: An Interview with Ogden R. Lindsley - *387*

Precision Techniques in the Management of Teacher and Child Behaviors - *391*
Marie Gaasholt

**Part IV. *THE FUTURE OF BEHAVIORAL EDUCATION:
ISSUES AND POSSIBILITIES - 399***

18. *Some Issues in Behavioral Education - 400*

Tangible Reinforcers: Bonuses or Bribes? - *401*
K. Daniel O'Leary, Rita W. Poulos, and Vernon T. Devine

Guidelines for Using Behavior Modification in Education - *408*
Roger W. McIntire

Political Implications of Applying Behavioral Psychology - *413*
James G. Holland

19. *Some Possibilities in Behavioral Education - 420*

Student Applications of Behavior Modification to Teachers and Environments or
Ecological Approaches to Social Deviancy - *421*
Paul S. Graubard, Harry Rosenberg, and Martin B. Miller

The Challenge of Youth - *432*
Henry S. Pennypacker

REFERENCES - 437

INTRODUCTION

The first volume of *Control of Human Behavior* presented some basic principles of behavior control and their application in a variety of settings. The second volume projected a movement in behavioral control away from remediation, or cure, toward the development of preventive strategies that can preclude remediation. The subject of this third volume of the series is education.

Education was one of the first areas in which results obtained from the laboratory analysis of behavior were applied to human beings. Education is a natural area of application, since the central subject matter of behavior analysis is learning. Learning, in behavior analysis, is defined as a change in behavior. This definition fits the field of education, since it is primarily interested in the acquisition of new behaviors. In the laboratory, behavioral psychologists had arranged conditions under which many different organisms acquired a wide variety of behaviors. Justifiably, these psychologists felt that they would also be able to arrange conditions under which human students could acquire new behavior.

Decades ago, B. F. Skinner was suggesting possible applications of behavior analysis to education. The most publicized of his suggestions was programmed instruction and its handmaiden, the teaching machine. Although programmed instruction has by no means replaced traditional teaching practices, it is in widespread use today. Teaching machines, with the advance of technology, have evolved into computers. The research conducted today in computer-assisted instruction is largely a continuation of Skinner's early interest in teaching machines.

Another application of behavior analysis to education grew with the area known as "behavior modification." In the late 1950s, work in behavior modification began to accelerate. In early behavior modification studies, psychologists would enter a mental hospital, a home for the retarded, or a school and choose a few individuals and a limited number of their behaviors for modification. The individuals chosen were generally ones with problem behaviors; society had labelled them "mentally ill," "retarded," or "hyperactive." The behavior dealt with also involved a problem; often it was too much of an undesirable behavior. The psychologists designed programs that would decrease rates of destroying property, physical self-injury, eating, hoarding, or grossly inappropriate speech. In schools, popular target behaviors were being out of one's seat and talking out in class. Some additional problems early behavior modifiers dealt with involved long-standing deficits. Among other behaviors, psychologists taught people to walk, use the toilet, dress themselves, speak, and interact cooperatively with other people.

Most of these early behavior modification studies were carefully designed and controlled. Responses were explicitly defined and recorded by an independent observer. Control procedures, such as reversals and multiple baselines, were used. Research of this sort continues today in an increasingly sophisticated form.

Tightly controlled behavior modification research has limitations. First, the psychologist works with a small number of behaviors of a small number of individuals for a short period of time. Although measurements are made of phenomena such as "generalization" or "group effects," usually the projects are not designed to achieve far-reaching results. Second, the psychologist usually works within an institution established by nonpsychologists. He is often seen as an unwelcome interloper; his behavior may be arrogant, and he may inadvertently stress the threatening rather than the helpful aspects of his technology. He may make some limited changes, but he usually makes no lasting impression on the institution. When he leaves, the institution may close over him like water over a falling stone. A third problem with traditional behavior modification projects is their "cure" orientation. As suggested by Volume II of *Control of Human Behavior*, the goal of psychology should be to move away from remediating problems toward preventing them. Preventive programs, however, cannot be piecemeal. Setting up a single reinforcement contingency for a single person will do little to prevent future problems. Prevention must involve the redesign of institutions so that the milieu in which a person lives—the total of all contingencies set by his environment—leads to his growth and happiness.

Indeed, psychologists have moved away

from piecemeal remediation and have attempted to design environments. Behavioral psychologists have been put in charge of extensive segments of mental hospitals, homes for the retarded, and prisons. Perhaps most importantly, behavioral psychologists have established their own educational programs.

Of all the areas touched by behavior modification, education offers the best possibilities for the fruitful, preventive use of behavior modification techniques. Education, by definition, is the development of behaviors. If educational institutions can be designed to teach adaptive, constructive behaviors, many problem behaviors will be precluded. Also, many behavior problems find their origin in childhood, and educational institutions can influence this behavior. Education, therefore, is in a position to make preventive use of behavior modification in the area in which it can be most effective and with the individuals for whom it can be most effective.

Many of the papers included in this volume describe education programs established by behavior modifiers. The reader accustomed to work written up in strict scientific format will find them different. Designing and setting up a program is not the same as designing and setting up an experiment. Although they describe programs, these papers are full of ideas that can be used by the individual teacher or researcher with more specific interests.

The papers that describe programs represent behavioral psychologists coming in contact with the reality of long-term commitments. No longer are they visiting magicians, arriving, doing their trick, and leaving, perhaps shaking their fist at recalcitrant administrators or workers. Now the behavioral psychologists *are* the administrators and workers in permanent residence. Their function is not to correct but to design and construct. For most psychologists, it is a humbling experience. Working in education is particularly humbling. Education is an extremely complex and wide-ranging task, fraught with responsibility. Tricks will not work. Psychologists have a lot to offer, but they will not displace educators who have been at it a long, long time. The programs described in this book, then, represent some of the first attempts of psychologists to really come to grips with education—to learn enough about education to be able to apply their own knowledge to it.

Besides accounts of programs, this book contains other types of material. Part I will orient the reader who is unfamiliar with behavior modification. It should give him a "feel" for behavior modification in the classroom and introduce him to some terminology. Part II presents vignettes and small-scale studies, as well as the descriptions of programs already mentioned. Part III contains papers on what is often called "educational technology." Some of the sections within this part cover useful behavior modification techniques, such as those used to treat problem behaviors or regulate group behavior. Others deal with areas of current interest to educators such as behavioral objectives, programmed instruction, automated instruction, assessment, accountability, performance contracting, and precision teaching. Part III also presents a glimpse of what behavior analysis has to offer the traditional educational field of curriculum design. Part IV, the final part in the book, deals with questions specific to the future of behavioral education.

In compiling this book, the editors have continually tried to keep the future in mind. When the first volume of *Control of Human Behavior* was published, behavioral psychology was regarded by many as the black knight of the psychological world. Now behavioral psychologists are respected, and how they use their skills remains to be seen. Hopefully, some of their greatest achievements will be in education, in the direction indicated by this volume.

INTRODUCTION
TO BEHAVIORAL EDUCATION

1

1

TWO VIEWS OF BEHAVIORAL EDUCATION

Two views of behavioral education are presented in this section, one concrete and one conceptual. The first, by Pennypacker, is a humorous account of a professor of psychology finally practicing what he professes. The document parallels some of the equally charming testimonials heard from teachers after their first experiences with contingency management techniques. Pennypacker's article reminds us that behind the rate charts, behavioral objectives, contingency management systems, and other techniques of behavioral education are real teachers teaching real students in real classrooms.

In the second introduction, Richard Stuart sets forth systematically the concepts and techniques used in behavioral education. The concepts and techniques were derived ultimately from laboratory work in behavior analysis. However, the conceptual framework of "operant conditioning" has been modified slightly to suit the educational situation. Stuart's system is well known, and many teachers have found it useful.

How I spent my Christmas vacation

H. S. PENNYPACKER

INTRODUCTION

Many years have passed since John Dewey observed that the science of psychology found its first and most natural application in the public school classroom, and that from the classroom could come questions and problems of unique and fundamental interest to the psychological scientist. Many things have happened in the interim. Psychology and education have grown up, at least in size, as professions. They have, for a variety of historical and sociological reasons which we shall not attempt to enumerate here, become more or less estranged.

The academic and applied communities within both psychology and education have been equally alienated. Thus, experimental psychologists have diligently inquired into the phenomena of human learning with the aid of the memory drum and the nonsense syllable while almost totally ignoring the daily opportunity to study the same phenomena *in situ* as they taught their undergraduate courses. Meanwhile, those faculty members in Colleges of Education having any interest in empirical research at all have almost universally sought to advertise the "purity" of their research endeavors. They presumably legitimatize their claim to full academic citizenship by designing and studying simulated educational environments such as carefully populated laboratory schools or demonstration classrooms. Small wonder that most public school teachers report that their formal training, whether in psychology or education, did little to prepare them for the realities of classroom teaching in the contemporary public school. Moreover, they relate that relatively little value is gained from the numerous in-service short courses, workshops, and seminars that university personnel are fond of conducting.

In the face of this mounting irrelevance of the university enterprise to the problems and challenges of public education, a small but growing group of serious students of human behavior have rediscovered the importance of Dewey's observation of over half a century ago. These people come from both psychology and education and attach very little importance to this distinction. They enthusiastically share the conviction that there is still much of basic importance to be learned in the public school classroom, and that, through diligent and rigorous application of the principles and tactics of that discipline known as the experimental analysis of behavior, there almost certainly will result consequences for the technology of education that will be of enormous social and humanitarian value. Such consequences have already appeared in other areas of human concern with treatment of the mentally ill being perhaps the most conspicuous example.

My own personal and professional history parallels almost exactly that of psychology and education which I have so summarily described in the foregoing paragraphs. I was trained as an experimental psychologist, and my area of particular competence was learning. Instead of the nonsense syllable, I concentrated on the blinking eyelid of both man and monkey, not wishing to become overspecialized too early in my career.

Like most of my academic contemporaries, I regarded educational research as soft-headed and sloppy and the resulting technology as necessarily trivial. So ingrained were these attitudes, that in spite of the fact that I received considerable formal training in behavior analysis as a graduate student, I had been out of graduate school nearly seven years before it occurred to me to apply these principles and tactics to my own courses in an effort not only to improve my teaching but to acquire data of fundamental relevance to the study of human learning. The results of that insight are now a matter of public

Reprinted by permission of the author.

record (Johnston and Pennypacker, 1971) and have indeed been gratifying.

At about the same time, largely as a result of stimulation and encouragement I was receiving from education students in my revamped psychology courses, I began to realize the full implications of the infusion of these principles and techniques into public education in general. An enormous undertaking, to be sure, but, as I have already indicated, I was not alone in this enterprise. A small group of pioneers from both psychology and education had been struck by the same vision and were already acting upon it.

The most notable of these pioneers happened to be a close personal friend since my days as a graduate student through the unlikely coincidence of our having both been professional country musicians much earlier in our respective careers (O. R. Lindsley, personal communication, 1961). I am referring to Dr. Ogden R. Lindsley who, under the descriptive rubric "precision teaching," had systematically translated the principles, philosophy, and tactics of the experimental analysis of behavior into a working technology of education by 1967. It was immediately suitable for use either as a research tool or for direct application by the classroom teacher.

I at once became steeped in all facets of precision teaching and like Lindsley began attempting to export it to what I naively assumed would be an enthusiastic and eager group of consumers—public school teachers. I borrowed upon the goodwill I had created with a few former students and began conducting in-service workshops as well as private night classes for parents and teachers in various homes. Although this activity met with sufficient success and publicity so that I was able to extend my workshop activities throughout Florida and Georgia, it was not until September 1970 that I was presented with an opportunity to conduct continuous in-service training at a public school in my home area. Thus, when Mr. William Cliett, Assistant Principal of Duval Elementary School in Alachua County, agreed to contract for such an in-service program, I knew the moment of truth had finally arrived. For the first time outside of the uni-

versity course, I would be able to attempt to teach precision teaching to teachers. I could use its own methods and procedures and be unhampered by the temporal limitations of a one- or two-day workshop. This would be the ultimate test, if not of the system, at least of my ability to use it in teaching others. So, ably assisted by my devoted wife, Sue—an accomplished precision teacher—I enthusiastically launched our program at Duval Elementary School.

Objectively, our efforts at Duval have been far more successful than any of my previous undertakings. By the end of November more than half of the faculty were in regular voluntary attendance at the weekly sessions, had mastered the fundamentals of charting, and were presenting meaningful and orderly data. Many also were able to show evidence of successful and sometimes dramatic changes in the behavior of individual children. This compared favorably with the 5 or 10 percent of an audience of general teachers who might be urged to this level of accomplishment by a short workshop.

Somehow, though, something was missing. After two and a half months, I knew all too well what it was. I was still a university professor, an outsider who couldn't possibly know what it is *really* like. How could I know the sheer physical strain that results from standing on your feet for six hours every day while between 100 and 150 eleven- and twelve-year-olds pass through your room in groups of 30 every forty minutes or so, each challenging you to provide a better reason for what you want him to do than he already has for doing what he wants to do. I talked of individualizing curriculum based upon analysis of daily charts, but had I ever tried to individualize curriculum for a hundred students every day in two or three different subjects, with or without the aid of charts? If so, when did I find time to do it along with playground duty, bus duty, lunchroom duty, parent conferences, faculty meetings, and PTA get-togethers? And with all this charting, when did I find time even to chart the individual performance of a hundred or so kids in two or three different subjects? The teachers at Duval were either too wise or too polite to ask these questions directly; they didn't have to. Teachers have been asking me these questions for the past two years; the time had come to find the answer!

Sue and Mr. Cliett arranged the details. My last class at the University was to be Friday, December 4. I had to be in Washington for an APA committee meeting on Sunday, December 6, and in Tallahassee on December 7 to visit one of our precision college teaching programs. Returning to Gainesville that Monday afternoon would give me one day to get my affairs in order so that on the morning of Wednesday, December 9, I would be able to enter Room 21 at Duval Elementary School and have a go at public school teaching. Since the Christmas recess for the public schools would begin Friday, December 18, I would have an eight-day taste of what happens in the life of a public school teacher for 180 days each year.

On Tuesday, December 8, I spent most of the morning with Mrs. Ellis, the teacher who had graciously agreed to let me be her substitute, as she went through her usual routine. She introduced me to each class and explained only that I would be their teacher until Christmas.

What follows is a daily account of my eight days in Room 21 at Duval Elementary School. Each afternoon I would come home, collapse on my bed, and relive the day's events into the dictaphone. Here is how it went.

FIRST DAY: DECEMBER 9, 1970

This was my first day as a public school teacher. Surprisingly, I slept well last night; the bourbon must have had something to do with it. After sitting numbly through our usual Wednesday morning in-service workshop on precision teaching, run capably by Sue from 8 to 9 A.M., I went into the pit to greet my homeroom. They knew I would be coming and were expecting me. Mrs. Ellis asked if she should stay and I told her no. I figured I might as well dive in with both feet.

The kids came in somewhat noisily, took their seats, and looked at me expectantly. I reminded them who I was and explained to them that all I got to do at the University was teach teachers, and that I always had wanted to see what it would be like to teach real live kids. I explained further that Mr. Cliett had assured me that if I did a good job during the fall with his teachers he would let me teach for a week or two, and so here I was.

This news was imparted while I circulated among the seats dispensing M&M's for sitting quietly, raising hands before talking out, and generally emitting behavior necessary for orderly academic progress. This tactic worked beautifully for five minutes when I discovered that, although I had announced along with each M&M the behavior which had earned it, I had failed to announce the schedule. I discovered that failure to announce the schedule implies to sixth-graders that the schedule is CRF. In the absence of laboratory manipulandum, activated counters, a child readily assumes the role: "Hey, I said the same thing! Don't I get one too?" or "Hey, I've been quiet for two minutes, where's my M&M?" At this point, I realized that a concurrent VR-EXT schedule would be the best I could manage. I announced that not every instance of good behavior would automatically earn an M&M, but every out-of-seat, talk-out, or physical assault would insure no M&M's. This did nicely; I continued to dispense M&M's, contingent on appropriate behavior, to individuals who I thought had not earned one yet and tried my best to refrain from rewarding blatant holding out of hands no matter what the concurrent verbal behavior.

We proceeded through the morning exercises: We sang the "Star-Spangled Banner," but my voice cracked badly on the phrase about rockets' red glare, and there was the not unexpected tittering. Next we pledged allegiance to the flag, and as is the custom, we had a moment of silent meditation during which the decibel level did, indeed, drop by several JND's.

This behind us, I introduced the first curriculum. The lesson plan called for handwriting. Since I subscribe to the principle that one must practice what one preaches, and since my handwriting is legible to only the chosen few, I decided this particular portion of the lesson plan would be satisfied if some handwriting were emitted by all students. It was my intention to implement a modified token-economy in the eight days I would spend in the classroom. I decided that a reinforcement menu should be prepared, and that the kids should dictate its contents. I therefore passed out Standard Behavior Charts and instructed in the proper filling in of names, ages, classes, etc. Without further elaboration, I instructed the class to turn the chart over and form two columns: "things I like" and "things I like to do." In the next ten minutes, they wrote their individual menus on the backs of their charts. Sometime tonight, I will collate these data, make some fundamental economic decisions, and God willing, produce a menu by nine o'clock tomorrow morning.

I must hasten to add that this homeroom activity involved all but a select few who, for reasons that escape me at this moment, had art at this hour. The full consequences of this administrative decision were not realized until later in the day. At the moment, however, it was clear that accurate attendance taking was in the hands of the Almighty. We did what we could with the list on the blackboard of those who had signed out for art, but many names not on the blackboard were, judging by the class's unanimous statement, indeed in art instead of at my feet receiving precise Socratic instruction in the mysteries of the reinforcement contingency.

The homeroom hour, all in all, went well. At this moment, I am tempted to ascribe this to the M&M's, my university status, or possibly my beard. Tomorrow will tell. At the appointed moment, they lined up and departed for their next scheduled activity which, if my memory serves, was P.E.

I welcomed their departure for it gave me thirty minutes of "planning time" during which Mrs. Ellis and I scored two sets of science papers and chatted about what might be happening during the rest of the day. From here on in, I was to do my thing: Teach science with the aid of the behavior chart.

The first-period science class appeared on schedule. They, too, had been advised of my appearance, so my introduction to them was similar to that of the homeroom group. I anticipated the M&M problem and announced the concurrent schedule in advance.

With this class, and with all succeeding science classes, my patter was essentially the same. All of science, whether pure or applied (they had just learned the distinction) depended upon data, but did they know that yesterday while reading about copper and writing down its various uses they were collecting data? If we were going to be scientists, we must know how to represent these data in chart form. Thus, we introduced the behavior charts. Each kid plotted his own performance from the previous day on the appropriate day and number line. (The top three cycles of the behavior chart were used for instructional purposes with number rather than rate emphasized—little steps for little feet. Time will tell whether this tactic precludes effective transfer to rate charting.)

The remaining science classes were pretty much like the first period science class. After the introductory patter, we settled down to the charting problem; within the twenty or thirty minutes available every kid accurately charted his first data point! There is absolutely no question that sixth-graders, regardless of their IQ or what have you, can be taught to chart their own performance on the Standard Behavior Charts. This news, while theoretically gratifying, means that I have to develop new curriculum for tomorrow!

Our thirty-minute lunch period was eventful. I elected to eat with the kids, which had two effects. There was a moment of amazement since most teachers escape to the lounge at that time. This was followed by vigorous contesting for the privilege (?) of sitting by me. I went through the line, bought my lunch, and sat next to the first person, a shy little Caucasian girl, who requested the honor of my presence at her side. I endured the din and chaos of the lunchroom for twenty minutes and answered only those questions and acknowledged only those comments which I thought betrayed some serious intent. At 12:20, I excused myself, took my uneaten banana, and retreated to the teachers' lounge where I poured a cup of coffee too hot to drink and took a few puffs on a cigar.

Twelve-thirty came all too quickly. Back to the pit and a new crop—this time fifth-graders. Since they had the same curriculum the day before as the sixth-graders, I again taught the chart with reference to their performance on the uses of copper. The fifth-graders were, in general, much more orderly and placid; however, it was necessary to be much more explicit with them while teaching the chart. Nevertheless, they all successfully charted their first day's performance.

My homeroom returned for their science class. By now, they had gone four hours without any M&M's, and they made it known that any charting behavior, or any other behavior that I expected, would be M&M dependent. I reiterated the VR schedule and proceeded, as with the other classes, to teach the chart with reference to their previous day's performance. All in all, at this point in the day, the homeroom class presented the most obvious behavior problems. From 1:45 to 2:45, I had a total of twelve substantive outbursts: physical assaults, shrieks, and "rumbles." The announcement that a deceleration in this behavior would earn ten minutes out-of-doors at the end of the day had a good effect, but I was unable to count because the last forty minutes were supposed to be devoted to Group IV individual reading. This was accomplished while the remainder of the homeroom pursued individual activities: putting up Christmas decorations, working on their "Lost on the Moon" problem (see Figure 1) which I had introduced earlier, reading silently, or raising hell in inconspicuous ways.

Individual reading gave an opportunity to involve the kids in a second phase of charting. They each read for one minute from their assigned readers, and error rate based on long hesitations or mispronunciations was recorded, charted, and explained to them. This involved them to a surprising degree; when it was time to go out the two kids who had not yet read virtually insisted that they be allowed to perform so their reading could be charted. With my heart in my throat I accommodated them while the

others, who had earned the privilege of going outside, were released. I decided that my first duty was to teach and my second duty was to patrol the playground, so everyone in Group IV read aloud and was charted.

By the time I had arrived at the playground, the members of my homeroom had scattered to the four winds. An occasional familiar face was to be seen, but I despaired of ever getting them all back into the room before they were to leave at 3 P.M. Those who were within earshot rejoined me at the homeroom and departed for their homes. I assume the others made it, because I have yet to be telephoned by an anxious parent inquiring as to the whereabouts of his child.

So ended the first day. I withdrew to the teachers' lounge, finished the cup of coffee I had poured at noon, and chatted with a number of teachers who appeared genuinely solicitous about my first day's experiences. I assured them that one day there is the equivalent of a week of teaching at the college level, but that they were to be envied because they had a shorter history of educational mistakes to try to overcome than we did at the college level.

I must now return to the task of preparing tomorrow's curriculum. If I don't, I am assured that my failure tomorrow will reverberate in the years to come.

SECOND DAY: DECEMBER 10, 1970

For some reason, I woke up at five o'clock this morning and could not get back to sleep. After finally going to bed at midnight, this meant facing the second day with only five hours' sleep.

Things were far easier today than yesterday, perhaps because in retrospect nothing could have been worse. After our initial display of mechanized patriotism, the homeroom group and I completed the NASA "Lost on the Moon" problem-solving project including the discussion of the answers. This is an excellent piece of curriculum for the contemporary sixth-grader. It captures his interest and permits him to share his wealth

DECISION FORM

by Jay Hall

<u>INSTRUCTION</u>   You are in a crew originally scheduled to rendezvous with a mother ship on the lighted surface of the moon. Due to mechanical difficulties, however, your ship was forced to land at a spot some 200 miles from the rendezvous point. During re-entry and landing, much of the equipment aboard was damaged and, since survival depends on reaching the mother ship, the most critical items available must be chosen for the 200-mile trip.

Below are listed the 15 items left intact and undamaged after landing. Your task is to rank order them in terms of their importance in allowing your crew to reach the rendezvous point. Place the number <u>1</u> by the most important item, the number <u>2</u> by the second most important, and so on through number <u>15</u>, the least important.

____ Box of matches

____ Food concentrate

____ 50 feet of nylon rope

____ Parachute silk

____ Portable heating unit

____ Two .45 caliber pistols

____ One case dehydrated Pet milk

____ Two 100-pound tanks of oxygen

____ Stellar map (of the moon's constellation)

____ Life raft

____ Magnetic compass

____ 5 gallons of water

____ Signal flares

____ First aid kit containing injection needles

____ Solar-powered FM receiver-transmitter

Figure 1. *Lost on the Moon exercise.*

of lunar knowledge acquired from the televised moon shots while teaching him some of the implications for practical human survival in the lunar environment.

Next period was P.E. for the homeroom groups. We retired to the outdoor basketball area where I began by getting the girls organized into lay-up lines which some boys elected to participate in as well. As soon as that appeared to be functioning smoothly, I joined the boys who were involved in a fairly good game of half-court basketball. Just as I approached the group a fight between David and Eddie reached the cocked fist and threatening gesture stage. I stepped between them, taking both by the arm, and advised the apparent aggressor that his behavior was quite unsportsmanlike. He replied to the general effect that it was his intention to "show that black motherfucker that for me sport begins and ends with my fist." I told him that that was fine, but he would be doing it on his own time, not on the taxpayer's. There was mutual agreement between the combatants to reopen the issue at some other time. Later, during lunch, I saw them sitting side by side happily chatting, so perhaps an alternative solution was found. I next attempted to referee the resurrected basketball game, but soon found that with no whistle I was more in the way than anything else. Tomorrow, I'll bring a whistle.

Routine for the four science classes was uniform and quite gratifying. We reviewed the charting procedures in unison. Then the kids took turns at the overhead projector charting data points, by day and number, that were supplied by other kids in the room. Following this, they did their first charted assignment again by reading a comic book about copper and writing down all the things that are made from copper. They were told that this performance also would be charted, and that they should try to make their charts go up as much as possible. I am sure that without the incentive of the chart consequence there would have been considerable grumbling about doing the same thing a second time. Fortunately, I won't have that problem again.

Mrs. Ellis rejoined me for the short homeroom period just before lunch. She worked with the majority of the class on decorations for the room Christmas party next Friday, while I took the three people in the lowest reading group off into a corner for individualized reading instruction. We are charting a rather unusual accuracy pair of lines read and errors based on words mispronounced, omitted, or repeated. Two- or three-minute time samples are taken with the aid of a Lux Minute Minder purchased last night. (We must stock these; they are indispensable.) While I count errors on a wrist counter, the nonreaders are counting lines while following along so that everybody has a sense of participation as each child is reading. We shall continue this on a daily basis with the lowest reading group.

Lunch today was delicious! I had two pieces of chicken, two scoops of mashed potatoes, two rolls, some string beans, nuts, and half an orange. Oh, yes, and milk. Not bad for fifty-five cents. As usual, I forgot my napkin, but I was doubly fortunate in that I ate my chicken before I ate my rolls and was able to wipe my fingers on my rolls before eating them. I was sitting again next to my diminutive Caucasian girlfriend who had taken two napkins and cheerfully gave me one. Thus, I was able to avoid the embarassment of a hundred pairs of staring eyes watching as I wiped my greasy fingers on my socks, hair, or beard. Eight minutes before the next class, I dashed into the teachers' lounge, ate my orange, took a few puffs on a cigar, washed my face, and strode back into the pit.

Two more science periods after lunch went very well under the procedure described above. The last period of the day was homeroom reading. I decided to test the effect of yesterday's M&M delivery on my status as an announcer of working contingencies. As the chaos developed, I recorded eleven out-of-seats in about ten minutes while people were getting organized into the groups and getting their work passed out. I called their attention to the counting, read the count, and advised them that if it exceeded twenty they would lose ten minutes of the Christmas party. Thereafter, only six more out-of-seats were counted, and these were clearly of the accidental variety such as people getting up to get a drink of water or going to the bathroom without remembering to ask.

That worked so well, I decided to try it tomorrow all day for a day-end consequence. I announced that if, throughout the entire day, the homeroom kept their out-of-seats below twenty-five, we would spend the last fifteen minutes having a dance. This was chosen because many of the kids had indicated dancing as one of their preferred activities. Later, I discovered that only folk dancing was permitted by the rules. I would be surprised, however, if these children are schooled in anything but folk dancing as that term is now defined by musicologists.

Thus, the reading period went quite well. We sampled and charted the individual reading of one group while the remainder of the class worked on a special reading curriculum, ingeniously provided by Sue, consisting of want ads from yesterday's paper which they were to read while writing down words they did not know. After selecting the one they felt most desirable, they were to reply to the ad by letter. This engaged them enthusiastically. A number who were off doing other things returned with only a few minutes to go and asked if they could take the materials home that night. I assured them they could, finished the last individual reading performance five minutes after the bell, and sank with satisfied exhaustion into the hard wooden chair.

THIRD DAY: DECEMBER 11, 1970

Today was Friday. Everyone knows what that means in a public school. This, however, was probably the easiest day I will have at Duval because of a scheduling quirk that I will try to describe in a moment. Nonetheless, I felt today would be the real test. The novelty of my presence would have worn off by now, and I·would be judged from here on out on the basis of what I did, not on who I was.

As the homeroom assembled at 9 A.M. and the usual portion immediately disappeared for art, I reiterated the announcement of the previous day that twenty-five or less out-of-seats would earn a special activity of dancing for the girls and basketball for the boys in the last fifteen minutes. The reaction was prompt and perfect. No one so much as twitched as we sang "America," pledged allegiance, and had our moment of silence. My magazine training had been effective!

We departed for P.E. where, with my plastic whistle, I refereed thirty minutes of basketball among the boys while trying to ensure that the girls were engaged in something more vigorous than gossiping about the fact that my fly had been open all yesterday afternoon. After P.E., I was on top of the world because the next forty minutes were "planning time," and I had already done my planning.

Now a word about the scheduling quirk. As near as I can tell, during the last quarter of every other moon, there is one day when all but ten of the members of each sixth-grade science class have art and the fifth-grade science class does not show at all. I checked with Mrs. Ellis against the outside possibility that this was a regular feature of Friday, and she assured me that it was not. It would not happen again until some time in January or February.

Now, under these circumstances, there absolutely would be no point in introducing any serious curriculum intended for the entire science class. It would only have to be repeated on Monday for all but the ten whom fate had cheated. So,. falling back on my dear wife's bag of tricks, I had decided to read aloud a few of the little who-done-its in *Encyclopedia Brown*. I divided the small group into two teams and rewarded those who successfully used the data in the story to deduce a conclusion from which they could induce a theory which would solve the mystery. This worked pretty well, although by the second class, I was beginning to get hoarse from so much dramatic reading. I really blew it with the first class by M&Ming the team which solved the first mystery. The losers were outraged, and only the most theatrical oral reading of my career on the second problem averted disaster. With the second problem, I virtually shaped the correct response from the previous losers so that everybody had had one M&M. The third problem was to be solved, not for the booty of an M&M, but for the glory of the old team! The solution was forthcoming from the team which had solved the first problem, but we all knew our hearts were not in it. Educational policy notwithstanding, these kids will work their tails off for something that doesn't melt in their hand.

This observation was confirmed with the second-period science class for whom no M&M's were offered. They had a great deal more trouble attending to the relevant facts and required a good deal more prompting before the correct response was jointly emitted. (There is a good experiment here: prompts necessary to solution as a function of solution consequence. But today was not my day to do research, however applied. I'll pass this along to a student.)

The most gratifying experience of my first three days occurred in the homeroom period just before lunch. Elaine, a little black girl who calls herself Cassandra, was in the lowest reading group with whom I have daily individual contact. She almost doubled her yesterday's rate of lines read and decreased her error rate to approximately one-fifth of the previous day. This growth, though ascribable to a million factors based as it was on only two days' data, brought what I am sure was the first smile of satisfaction in accomplishment that this girl has ever experienced in public school. Her chart told her something that no teacher, black or white, probably ever guessed—she could achieve!

There is little to be said about lunch except that today's fishcakes were no match for yesterday's chicken. One could directly validate this observation by merely counting the number of bits of each commodity that were thrown on the two successive days. The fish would win in a walk. I sat with the boys today and contributed feebly to a thoroughly expert discussion on the relative merits of the various dragsters in the Southeast. If anybody wants reading or math curriculum that would reach David, he would need only buy a program from any drag race.

After lunch I finished the individual reading work with Group I while Mrs. Ellis supervised construction of Christmas decorations. Everyone's chart improved today

though none with quite the drama of Elaine's.

Since my fifth-graders were unavailable because of the scheduling mentioned above, my next teaching experience was my homeroom science class. Only a handful were present, and they urged that the period be devoted to free play. Thus, *Encyclopedia Brown* had an uphill fight and probably earned a draw. David kept score for the first round, but his lack of impartiality made it necessary to change this arrangement for the second problem. We successfully solved three problems, again with numerous prompts, but without the aid of M&M's. Since this was homeroom, out-of-seats were counted and were virtually no problem.

The last period of the day was the conglomerate of Group II reading, free activity, or productive activity for those who had not yet done yesterday's want ad problem. The out-of-seats count rose to fourteen during these twenty minutes. The total was well below the magic twenty-five since David and Angela's three-rounder behind the teacher's desk only counted as two out-of-seats. They had indeed earned their special activity (see Figure 2). My devoted wife appeared on schedule and managed the dancing portion while I refereed another basketball game. The dancing must have been a powerful consequence. Nearly every kid within earshot tried to break down the door and participate. I think we will drop the required count to fifteen on Monday.

FOURTH DAY: DECEMBER 14, 1970

Today was rough! Many of the boys spent the weekend watching pro football. I knew this because the first fight I broke up in homeroom had as the major issue of contention the final score of the San Francisco game. They were well rested when they came to school this chilly Monday morning. Also, today was the first day we had the entire homeroom group for the opening period. The art activity which made attendance taking impossible last week turned out to occur only once every so often, so we had the

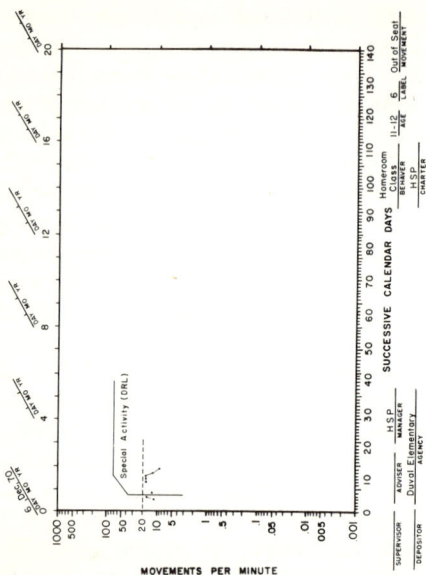

Figure 2.

whole gang for opening period and handwriting.

The curriculum I chose for handwriting emerged from an idea I borrowed from Nancy Johnson in Kansas City: I thought it would be nice to have the kids write short stories, either from fact or fiction. With a little editing, we will assemble them into booklets for some of the kids whose taste for the standard reading curriculum obviously is very slight. I still think the idea is a good one, but I must talk to Nancy and get some tips on handling the production problems. At 9:15 this Monday morning, the muses evidently had deserted my would-be authors. Although they loudly endorsed the idea, we have a dearth of finished manuscripts at this point.

The four science periods all went well although the curriculum I had prepared was evidently a bit more stimulating than I had anticipated. The noise level rose in each period to almost deafening levels. Putting last Thursday's copper performance on the charts went very smoothly. They all even managed to carry out the instructions of paper clipping their chart to their worksheet and turning these back in to me.

The fun began when we introduced the unit on the solar system. We were going to take an imaginary trip from the sun outward to Pluto and, of course, we would have to have a map. Crayons were distributed. I took my position at the overhead, and we all produced, in four colors, a schematic representation of the nine planets, their orbits, the sun, and the asteroid belt. Technical problems were minimal although I now realize that if the overhead had been a little closer to the screen I would not have encountered the difficulties inherent in projecting Neptune and Pluto on the ceiling with the sun slowly setting past the towel dispenser into the sink. No, those problems were minor. But I assure the reader that there is no sound on earth to compare with the riveting noise produced by thirty sixth-graders drawing their asteroid belts. Again, my fault! I made little sharp dotting motions at the overhead, and they made big sharp dotting motions at their seats causing crayons to break, papers to tear, and tempers to fly. All this occurred amid a sound that seemed like the result of thirty riveters each attacking his own Chinese gong inside the same abandoned quonset hut.

I was able to read with only about six individuals today. Elaine (Cassandra) again showed progress, and her reaction to the appearance of this fact on her chart made the whole day worthwhile. Another moment of gratification came when Anita and Angela absolutely spontaneously advised me that they had been timing and counting each others' reading and they wanted me to look at their data! I hugged them both! Perhaps I shouldn't have done that, because by that time of the day my Hai Karate had long since yielded to the basic odors of a male primate under stress. I know this, because when I got home my family insisted that I burn my socks. I had put them on clean this morning!

By 2:20 in the afternoon, I had finally had it. My homeroom science period had just ended, and we were about to fade into reading, etc. With my voice cracking, I yelled for order and delivered a short speech which went approximately as follows: "You will remember that I told you last week that I thought it would be fun, for a change, to come and teach real live kids. It was fun until about ten minutes ago. But the noise and racket in here has made it stop being fun. Now you all know that I don't have to do this. Therefore, whether or not I come back tomorrow is entirely up to you. You decide! If you can act like ladies and gentlemen for the next forty minutes, I will see you again in the morning. If you can't, I will walk out that door at three o'clock today and hope I never see you again. Now it is up to you. You can have either. Which do you want?"

I had thought about this move as carefully as one can under the circumstances before making it. I felt I could predict their decision, but certainly not with the confidence that I can predict the behavior of a pigeon or college student. Either way, I would get information, and the kids would ultimately benefit.

As it turned out, my prediction was accurate. A hush fell over the room that was positively funereal. A sob or two was heard together with a barely audible "Oh shit, David. Now look what you've done!" I called my reading group together while the remainder of the class quietly worked on their stories or the Christmas decorations. At 2:45, because the out-of-seat count miraculously had risen only to eighteen, we went outside for fifteen minutes of basketball.

As every teacher knows, the limits have to be tested. They were tested today. I, at least, learned a great deal!

FIFTH DAY: DECEMBER 15, 1970

Today was as different from yesterday as day from night. By and large, the outrageous behavior of all the classes yesterday which we ascribed to the weekend rest was missing today. Not that we did not have our little problems. We did.

The first of these occurred during morning P.E. for the homeroom which occurs right after the opening exercises. A group of black girls appropriated what turned out to be the white girls' basketball. Prior to this, I had observed no overt racial difficulty. I called the black girls together, explained that color made no difference, etc., and tried to form them into two lines for lay-ups. No good!

The black girls refused to play with the white girls, hurled a number of racial insults which were returned in kind, and strode off as a unit to loiter around the jungle jim. I decided I would accomplish nothing by paying attention to this sullen withdrawal on the part of the black group. I turned the basketball over to the remaining girls, one or two of whom were black, and finished refereeing the boys' game. I kept an eye out for further trouble, but there was none on the playground.

Later, I heard that fallout from this incident erupted in the music class to which our group went after P.E. This occasioned one of our most energetic black girls being banished from music class and sent to the disciplinary bench where I passed her on my way to the lounge for my "planning time." I stopped and had a little supportive chat with her as she experienced the consequences of whatever misbehavior she had emitted in music. Later in the day, she became the first of my homeroom class to give me a Christmas card.

The science classes were a sheer delight today! I had planned to read the "Guide Book" to the solar system and then pass out the first question sheet so that tomorrow we could chart our first performance on this unit. I didn't get further than reading and explaining the Guide Book with any of the classes. Their enthusiasm and eagerness to contribute information, however faulty, made it clear that the time was well spent in stimulating them with this material. The enthusiasm of a sixth-grade class when confronted by topical, though relatively abstract, curriculum is a wondrous thing. I have seen it all too rarely at the college level.

By the time I did my act four times, I was hoarse and exhausted but relaxed and satisfied. My act consisted not only of dramatic reading but of attempting to illustrate every point I could using the overhead projector as the sun, the globe as the earth, and a kick ball as any of the other planets. The explanation of revolution and rotation become quite animated particularly in the case of the planet Mercury where the periodicity of these two motions is the same, causing one side of the planet to forever face the sun.

In every science class, even the homeroom after lunch, excitement was high but well controlled. I feel an odd sense of fulfillment.

Elsewhere through the day, I managed to pick up charted reading behavior on a few of the kids who I had not yet heard read aloud. In addition, my lowest reading group again performed individually. Randy made the greatest progress and led out a whoop of delight when we charted his data. Elaine went on to a new story and both her rates changed in the expected direction. This was explained to her, but I think unsuccessfully. In the most serious tone I have heard her use in the five days I have been at Duval, she promised she would try harder tomorrow. I left school today forty minutes after the last child had departed. As I was unlocking my car Elaine ran across the street, just to say "hey!"

Today marked the occurrence of perhaps the most profound validation of a fundamental principle of precision teaching: The child is always right. Just before we went out to P.E. this morning, I called David aside and showed him a copy of the *Road and Track Test Annual* for 1970. I told him that if he could go through the entire day without shouting, pushing, or fighting, he could have that as his reading curriculum for our late afternoon reading session. Further, I told him that if he could maintain this behavior until the end of the week, the magazine was his to keep!

David was a different young man today. Even during basketball, when Raymond fell on him, he displayed hardly a trace of his usual combativeness. He easily earned the right to read *Road and Track* during the last half hour. While doing that, he produced his first requested written work, a list of words he did not know.

Tomorrow, I must without fail chart a sample of his reading from this material. I have an idea it will be very different from the data he has given us under the stimulation of his assigned curriculum.

SIXTH DAY: DECEMBER 16, 1970

When the alarm rang at 7 o'clock this morning I knew this would be less than an outstanding day. I had been awake, smoking cigars, since 4 o'clock. I simply was unable to sleep in spite of the fact that I knew how rotten I would feel. My guess is that the sugar in the rum sours I drank last night was the culprit. I can't eat rich desserts without suffering the same problem.

Today being Wednesday, we had our regular precision teaching workshop which again was handled very capably by Sue. She awarded prizes for the first three finishers in the total number of charts competition that had been going on since September. First prize went to Barbara Minter whose 140 math charts were indeed impressive.

Since I am viewed by most as a faculty member at Duval, I took my turn and showed only the charts of the homeroom's performance on the unit on copper. With these data I was able to suggest the possibilities for curriculum analysis that were clearly evident. The most growth on this particular curriculum was shown by the kids who had started badly whereas the "bright" kids with good work habits were victims of ceiling effect.

Mrs. Ellis handled the first homeroom period in order to help plan the Christmas party, an activity in which I readily confessed absolutely no skill and only slightly more interest. I observed her intently as she managed their behavior through the necessarily noisy procedure, and I must say the control she exerts with her soft voice and gentle manner is truly magnificent.

After our planning period, Mrs. Ellis came in and watched while the science group gave a demonstration of their charting progress. We again used the procedure of having kids take turns standing at the overhead, plotting problems given by kids out in the audience. I was pleased with their performance!

The science classes today went very well. I have learned that allowing too much help with the passing out and taking up of materials contributes to the pandemonium and ultimately slows the whole process down. We performed on the question sheets based on the guide book to the solar system using the guide book and map for information. I have not yet evaluated their performance, but my impression is that very few were errorless in the allotted twenty minutes. Most will have gotten about half of them right, and the remainder, owing largely to their reading handicaps, will have gotten very few right. I am most distressed that I will be unable to chart a second performance on this curriculum for any but a handful of students because of tomorrow's Christmas programs and Friday's parties. First things first, I guess!

Yesterday, Mrs. Ellis had expressed some disappointment in the low rate of story production of three stories in two days from the homeroom group. I asked her if she would be interested in seeing the effects of a tangible consequence on story production, and she said indeed she would. This morning I announced that any story produced during the day would earn two M&M's. By day's end, we had twenty with more promised in the morning.

Just before lunch, Tommy, who had not caused a single problem, absolutely flattened a black girl from another room. She rose at the count of one and dealt Tommy a staggering blow. I caught him as he was going for her throat, grabbed her by the arm and hurled her out the door, and marched Tommy to his seat where I held his arm until I could feel his pulse begin to recede. I pointed out to him that he would get more M&M's sooner by writing stories than by smashing girls, and he rather begrudgingly began to work.

Individual reading today, as usual, produced my greatest satisfactions. As she had promised yesterday, Elaine did indeed accelerate her lines read and decelerate her errors on her new curriculum. Her reaction to this fact was as touching as it has been on previous occasions. I watched her a little more closely throughout the day and observed essentially no other academic performance. She is being considered for special education. Her reading chart shows unequivocally that for Elaine achievement is not a matter of ability but of patient and careful shaping of work and study habits which hitherto evidently have been completely ignored. This is the function of public education, not special education!

David, our pugilist of some days ago, again maintained his combative behavior at zero

rate and read for me from *Road and Track Test Annual* in preference to going outside for basketball during the earned special activity. The data show that his lines per minute in *Road and Track* are nearly equal to his regular reader, and that his error rate is slightly higher. Tomorrow, however, I hope to take a second measure from *Road and Track*; his two reading performances last week were characterized by an acceleration in errors. Somehow, I think this week will be different.

SEVENTH DAY: DECEMBER 17, 1970

I had a very good night's sleep last night and the effect on today was magnificent. I knew, of course, that these last two days would not be massively productive. Yet I still felt that, in spite of the schedule disruptions, I had to leave all the kids proficient in charting rates. More on that later.

During our homeroom period this morning, I picked up the last few stragglers on the reading charts while the remainder of the class worked with Mrs. Ellis decorating the table for the Christmas party or sat at their desks hammering out stories and poems for M&M's. I have carefully preceded each M&M delivery with a good deal of praise. This morning, a couple of kids turned in their papers, received their praise, and walked away before I could get the M&M's out.

At the end of the scheduled homeroom period, we had no idea how long it would be until our sixth-graders were to assemble in the cafeteria for the Christmas program. Our best guess was that it would be some time around 10:15, so we elected to give them a portion of their scheduled P.E. No sooner had we gotten organized on the playground than word was sent that we were late for the sixth-grade portion of the program. We herded them into a semi-organized mass and funneled ourselves into the cafeteria.

I must say that the music teacher had accomplished a miracle of mass behavior management. Not only did each class emit their vocal renditions in a very close approximation to unison, but the behavior of the audience was not unlike an audience at a performance of the West Point Glee Club. Such management evidently was not achieved without some reliance on techniques of aversive control. On the way out to P.E. before the program, Freanta ran by me and said, "Let's all go get dirty so we don't have to go to the program." The reader will recall Freanta—she had been banished to the bench from rehearsal two days before.

The program did not run quite as long as expected so I had the regular second-period science group on schedule. As expected, they taught me how to teach sixth-graders to chart rates. The transition from number lines to rate lines posed no problem. Indeed, the only problem I encountered with any of the classes arose from the need to interpolate numbers to the right of the decimal. Somehow, to a sixth-grader who does not know about decimals or who is a little shaky on division in general, there is little similarity between the charting of .25 and 25. I corrected this in subsequent classes by explicitly instructing for it.

The fifth-graders, as usual our most orderly and attentive group, caught on with absolutely no difficulty, perhaps because I anticipated their problem and broke the instruction into smaller steps. Later Mrs. Ellis was helping with the homeroom, and she and a number of students made an important discovery: In charting rate, the first thing we must do is locate the cycle that the first number goes in. The problem of charting a rate like 1.23 had become extremely tedious until this observation was offered and validated.

Our individualized reading today went largely as expected. In particular, David's performance in *Road and Track*, although the data are admittedly scant as yet, indicates that that this journal is capable of promoting more growth in his reading skills than *Actors to Astronauts*.

Tomorrow is my last day, and I anticipate it with an odd mixture of relief and sadness. We are going to the annual Duval Faculty Christmas Party tonight, so that by 8 o'clock tomorrow morning these anticipatory emotions may be reduced to simple dread. Tomorrow afternoon will see the staging of the

Christmas party, so no science will be taught. Consequently, in order to get data points on the solar system unit from our homeroom, we will surprise them in the morning by eliciting a second performance on their worksheets as a substitute for a handwriting curriculum and then letting them have P.E. just before the party. The expected results of this unorthodox scheduling will be the opportunity to relate acceleration on the science curriculum to reading performance which, I suspect, will show a tremendous functional relationship to science achievement. By tomorrow night, this suspicion will be either confirmed or denied. Precision teaching will have yielded an answer from the ultimate source: the kids.

EIGHTH DAY: DECEMBER 18, 1970

Last night's faculty party at the Hutchinsons' was terrific. Almost the entire Duval faculty was there with spouses, and the atmosphere of swinging congeniality that we have detected in the school was suitably amplified. We contributed about three gallons of last Saturday night's artillery punch which, to coin a phrase, was a smashing success. The covered dish dinner included some delectables that would have been the envy of master chefs everywhere: Yates' Exotic Peas come readily to mind as does Minter's Chicken Dish, Hutchinson's Cheese Puffs, and Mary Lou's Chicken.

But enough of last night. Today was to be my last day, at least for a while, as a public school teacher. I must confess there was, and will be for some time to come, a small lump in my throat. I experienced many emotions as the day passed, but dread was certainly not one of them.

As expected, the kids grumbled at our procedure for switching the periods with the homeroom, but they fell to the task of their second performance on the solar system worksheet with a good deal more enthusiasm than we anticipated. Nearly half completed in less than the allotted twenty minutes. The analysis to be done this weekend will reveal whether this haste reflects increased mastery or the pressure of the impending Christmas party.

First and second science periods were pretty chaotic. Since we had not met the first-period group yesterday, they had to begin at the beginning with rate charting. With the exception of a handful for whom the request for any productive work on this day was the paramount insult, most people seemed to catch on and successfully chart their first data point from the solar system performance sheet. Again, the biggest problem was with interpolation. I suspect that if I were to do it again, or if I had longer, I would segment the process out and at first require only approximate charting on the existing rate lines and save interpolation for a later date. This is why I went to Duval in the first place—to learn from the kids how to teach the chart. This has been accomplished, although I do not believe I was totally successful with the first-period science group.

The second-period science group, having been introduced to rate charting yesterday, had a somewhat different curriculum today. I passed out fresh charts, told them to write their names on them, and put the word "practice" in the movement space. We then set up a procedure whereby the kids took turns calling out problems of day and rate which I would solve at the overhead with a towel taped over the magnifying glass. When each one indicated he had plotted his point, I would flip the towel back so he could check it. This procedure worked much better than having the kids take turns at the overhead and created far less movement and commotion. With this method everybody participated and everybody got immediate feedback. Why it takes us so long to make these discoveries I'll never know!

After about twenty minutes of this, there were evident signs of restlessness: A group of girls slunk out of their seats and began playing jacks behind the sink. I feigned disapproval, collected the balls, and did only two more problems making sure the offending girls charted accurately. For the balance of the hour, we worked on the NASA moon problem which fared no better than the charting. By the end of the hour, things had pretty well deteriorated although the serious students were absorbed by the task and would like to have been allowed the necessary peace and quiet to complete it. Such was not to be on the day of the Christmas party.

Just before lunch, the homeroom came in and began emptying out the desks so that the custodial staff could take fire hoses to the place over the Christmas break without ruining the books. During this melee, David and I retired to the corner for a last reading from Road and Track. Both rates were down, but no one could read orally with much precision on the fringes of a howling mob.

The cleanup activity was completed after lunch. Then the cute little fifth-graders came in. I count it as evidence of divine mercy that the schedule had given me the fifth-graders rather than sixth-graders for this period. By now, with the parties only about an hour away, the slightest show of determination at teaching would have been met by most sixth-graders with threats of violence to my person. So we did the moon problem, and they thoroughly enjoyed it and each other though not necessarily in that order. Nevertheless, most of them finished it, a few had time to justify their choices, and we even got nearly through the NASA key before the bell rang.

The homeroom reappeared, and we quickly organized them for P.E., hoping to run off a little steam before the party. With no control group, we will never know if this tactic was successful. From the amount of steam that was exhausted at the party, if it was successful, no human could have survived the control group anyway.

Actually, things went pretty well. There was a slight miscalculation in the distribution of presents, and we came up one or two short. We had inadvertently left the door unlocked and unattended for a few minutes earlier in the day, and the presents under the tree were temptingly close to the door. As Mrs. Ellis was bravely coping with the inequity thus created, all but the present-less were gleefully throwing wrapping paper around the room and trading gifts. Behind the shield of my briefcase cover, I hastily wrapped a 3M pen, labeled it "girl," and slipped it to my confederate. I will never know whether this satisfied the entire shortage or not, because at that moment the group bolted for the food. I went out to the car and with Eddy and Raymond's help brought in my guitar and amplifier. The musical selections were a curious mixture of Christmas carols and heavy soul. There was a variety of tastes to satisfy in our homeroom.

The festivities were abruptly concluded when the bell rang at 2:55. There was a general winding down, a few kids stayed to help swamp out, and then it was suddenly quiet. For some reason, it took me forty minutes to gather my belongings and leave.

EPILOGUE

Several weeks have passed. I am again meeting my university classes, fumbling with minor problems of academic administration, traveling a good deal to give lectures and workshops on precision teaching, and, most importantly, continuing our Wednesday morning training sessions at Duval. But I am not the same person I was when I entered Room 21 on December 8, 1970, and I doubt that I ever shall be again. I have now been where the action is, where the problems are very real and very human, and where the rewards for progress in their solution are very rich. In short, I have had a taste of what it means to be a teacher rather than a professor.

The major accomplishment of these eight days has been to verify the value of directly recorded behavioral data to educational decision making and evaluation. Permitting the kids to keep individual daily charts makes such evaluation as routine as the practice of a physician who makes daily checks on the medical charts of a whole ward of patients. The picture may not always be pretty, but it is accurate. The analogy holds all too well for educational decision making. The ultimate validation of a medical decision is defined in terms of recordable changes in the patient's physiology; while the ultimate validation of an educational decision is, or should be, defined in terms of recordable changes in the student's behavior. Failure to base such decisions, either medical or educational, upon the most precise and objective data available will not alter the consequences of a bad decision. Unlike the situation in medicine, however, a single bad educational decision is rarely fatal. Moreover, because human behavior is far more amenable to alteration than is human physiology, there is always hope for complete recovery. I saw this hope in Elaine's face when we charted her progress in reading, and I shall never forget it.

Behavior modification techniques for the education technologist

RICHARD B. STUART

As evidenced by the rising rates of school dropout and student rebellion, parent protest, and legal challenge, American education must be said to be in a state of crisis. Compounding the problem, teachers, psychologists, school social workers, and school administrators appear to be suffering from a technological lag, making efforts to apply the (at best) partially successful solutions of the 1940s and '50s to current problems. It is only when professionals in the education field and its ancillary services include present-day advances in their practice that even a partial solution to the current crisis may be expected....

In the past, failures in education have been blamed on the individual student, rather than the school environment. The child has been

Reprinted with permission of the National Association of Social Workers, from **The School in the Community,** edited by Rosemary C. Sarri and Frank F. Maple (New York, 1972).

held accountable for any deficit in his functioning while the school has been credited with success in producing whatever positive changes are observed. In fact, however, the school carries the burden of responsibility for the success or failure of the child with respect to both academic and social performance. The teacher is assumed to have acquired the skills necessary to "teach" his students to make new responses in the presence of increasingly complex stimuli. The teacher is also assumed to have acquired the skills necessary to create an environment suitable to the acquisition of new skills by students. And yet Patterson, Shaw, and Ebner (1969) have observed:

"In many respects the classroom is a barren wasteland when one compares it to other, normally reinforcing interactions. Most of the reinforcers in the system are highly formalized, such as grades and test scores. The control of social behavior is achieved more as a function of threatened or applied aversive consequences than by positive social reinforcers [p. 15]."

In such an environment it is no wonder that children develop learning deficits and become socially disruptive. It may be that this is the behavior that is most rewarded!

In view of the defects observed within the schools, it is strongly suggested that the professional (whether teacher, psychologist, or school social worker) view the present problems of students as reasonable reactions to deficient environments. Granted, the social worker who makes this assumption runs the risk that he might be ignoring a pressing problem of some other etiology. If this is the case, however, the early, measurable failure of his efforts will alert him to this possibility.

On the other hand, the worker who seeks to change the individual rather than the classroom runs the following risks: (1) iatrogenic illness (that is, illness caused by the treatment) may well result from his efforts (Stuart, 1970a), (2) if effective, there is a distinct probability that his efforts will not generalize into the classroom and the behavioral problems may quickly recur, and (3)

defects in the educational system will be permitted to persist without change. Unlike the possible negative consequences of shorter term behaviorally oriented treatment, the ill effects of individually oriented treatment are slower to appear and—what is more often the case—do not permit remediation.

STUDIES OF STUDENT BEHAVIOR

Most requests by teachers for outside help center on behavioral rather than presumed dynamic problems. Repeated studies both in Europe (Cummings, 1944: Wall, 1955) and America (Rogers, 1942; Walsh and O'Conner, 1968; Woody, 1964) have shown that teachers generally refer students for help with problems related to poor study habits or poor social relationships. While cultural differences (including differences in professional cultures) are naturally reflected in these referrals, teachers' requests for help apparently stress concerns with objectifiable target behaviors within the classroom.

Teachers also request aid in handling responses that occur with greater intensity or frequency in problem children but that occur in nonproblem children as well. For example, one series of studies has shown that hyperactivity—high rates of inattention, moving about the room, talking out of turn, or wriggling in one's seat—is manifested by "normal" students about once per minute and by "problem" students about five times per minute (Patterson et al., 1969). Thus the subjects of the teacher's concern are typically quantitative rather than qualitative in nature. Other studies have shown that the rate of task-oriented behavior—for example, visual focusing, reading, writing, and other responses previously determined as necessary prerequisites for task completion (Hammerlynck, Martin, and Rolland, in press)—varies from 20 to 80 percent of class time, but nontask-oriented behavior typically does *not* disrupt the attention patterns of neighboring students (Hammerlynck, 1968).

In addition to stressing the actual response of the student, another approach to the selection of a target behavior includes the teacher's evaluation of the behavior. For example, one such approach (Abbott, Howard, and Walter, 1969) uses the following three categories:[1]

"Appropriate behavior—any behavior which is proper and acceptable given the situation.

Inappropriate behavior—any behavior which is not proper or appropriate, given the situation, but can be ignored. Examples include: removing one's shoes and walking in stocking feet; tapping lightly on the table during a language or reading activity; leaving the table quietly during a table activity; or whispering to one's neighbor during an activity or when students are expected to remain silent and pay attention to the teacher.

Unacceptable behavior—any behavior which is harmful to the child or others around him, any behavior which . . . disrupts the class or a proportion of other students, and any behavior which involves breaking a rule the consequences of which have been clearly stated by the teachers. Examples include: eating paint or other toxic art material; leaving the table during a table activity and running around the room disturbing the other children; . . . [p. 4]."

The advantages of this approach, which was used also by Wasik, Senn, Welch, and Cooper (1969), are its ability to reflect differing social demands and its immediate cueing of the teacher as to his appropriate response. It should be pointed out, however, that this system makes reference to social behavior; specification of academic or task behavior would require greater precision.

Finally, it should be indicated that in addition to individual students, entire classes might be the subject of observation and assessment. A wide range of observational systems is possible, depending on the values and intentions of the observer (Amidon and Hough, 1967; Medley and Mitzel, 1963; Werry and Quay, 1968). For example, investigators might be interested in fine-category observation of a single child and his teacher on a time-sampling basis (Ray, Shaw, and Patterson, 1968) or coarse-category observation of the rule-testing and enforcing

behavior of an entire class and its teacher (Research and Development Center, undated).

One criterion for a useful system is its specification of student and teacher behavior. In addition Patterson and Harris (1968) have suggested that the system should permit observer reliability and generalization of observational data, be relatively free from observer bias, permit reliable sampling of behavior, and control for the effect of the observer on the data. Both Patterson and Harris (1968) and Surratt, Ulrich, and Hawkins (1969) have shown that the mere presence of an observer materially affects the nature of the data presented for observation.

Response Specification

Hyperactivity and nontask-oriented behavior are relatively imprecise terms because children could engage in any of an enormous array of responses compatible with either behavior. It is therefore necessary to identify precisely the target of behavioral change in a process termed "response specification."

Reflexive behaviors that are under autonomic control are termed respondents. Operant responses are classes of behavior that produce some change in the environment (Millenson, 1967). For example, a child might raise his hand (response), and the teacher might grant permission for him to speak (a change in the environment). Most teachers are primarily concerned with operant responses. This paper will deal with their specification and control.

The second requirement of response specification is the selection of responses that occur in excess of once every ten to fifteen minutes (Ackerman, 1969).[2] This is necessary because effective behavior modification is often expedited by the chance to provide repeated learning opportunities. When target behaviors occur at intervals of several weeks

1 This approach appears in Appendix A (see p. 37) as part a schema for planning behavior modification in the classroom.

2 A simple method for calculating rates has been the use of a "nomogram." See Branch and Sulzbacher (1968).

or even several hours, it is often necessary to wait for a long time before sufficient experience has been accumulated to facilitate new learning, and experiences intervening between training periods may mitigate the cumulative effect of this training.

Moreover, Patterson (1969a) has suggested that behaviors occur in predictable chains with the more serious behavior taking place after a series of less disturbing premonitory responses. Unpublished data by Stuart, for example, have shown that shouting by a six-year-old brain-damaged child occurred at the rate of one episode per ninety minutes, but that he stamped his feet once in fifty-five minutes, said "no" in a loud voice once in seven minutes, and shook his head vigorously from side to side once in seventy-five seconds. Identification of this behavioral chain permitted early intervention in the behavioral cycle with two distinct advantages: Repetition of control efforts permitted radical behavioral change without removing the child from the classroom, and the amount of disruption of the class diminished as his outbursts decreased.

The third requirement of response specification is that it be a definite behavioral action rather than a nonaction. Lindsley (1968) has termed this the "dead man test," implying that dead students are best at "not talking out in class," while their live counterparts excel at "talking only when recognized" or "talking without recognition" (see also Ackerman, 1969). This requirement is essential because the nonoccurrence of an event cannot be counted.

The final requirement of response specification is the selection of a positive action to count in association with any negative action. There are two main reasons for this. First, teachers and others tend to concentrate spontaneously on the problem behavior of children identified as deviants. The clinician should avoid reinforcing this negative tracking. Second, as will be shown shortly, the technology for accelerating behavior is more powerful, as a general rule, than that available for deceleration. It is therefore essential to select as a behavior target those responses amenable to acceleration.

It is desirable to establish a target rate at which the response is expected to occur when intervention is terminated. This decision is always "political" in the sense that it involves some compromise between the behavioral patterns emitted by the individual and the expectations of those judging his behavior—parents, teachers, and administrators, among others. If the rate is at the criterion level, no further action is needed. If the rate is below the criterion level, this rate constitutes a baseline, and the evaluation of behavior must continue.

In evaluating the need for treatment based on rate data, as well as evaluating the changes mediated by treatment, Patterson et al. (1969) have developed an ingenious technique. They measure the behavior of a so-called problem child, but at the same time measure the behavior of one other randomly selected child in the class. This gives a general measure of the behavioral climate of the class, facilitating interpretation of the observed rates by supplying a context for their evaluation.

Antecedent Conditions[3]

If a response is an action that produces changes in the environment, then antecedents set the occasion for the response to occur. Management of antecedents is the province of behavioral engineers, architects, and professionals with a wide range of concerns. Some antecedents are favorable to the occurrence of a desired response; these are designated A+. Others, designated A−, are either unfavorable to the occurrence of the desired response or conducive to the occurrence of problem responses in the same situation. It is obvious, for example, that a well-constructed school (A+) will be more likely to be associated with good student performance than a dimly lit, cold, and poorly ventilated building (A−). In the same vein it is clear that loud music or noise in the halls is likely to interfere with effective study responses (hence A−).

There are four classes of antecedents. The first class is *instructional stimuli*—verbal or

---

3 See Table 1 in Appendix A., p. 36.

symbolic stimuli, such as rules or facial expressions, that serve to cue a response. If it is true that a well-managed class is (1) "a predictable one" (Smith and Smith, 1968, p. 4) and (2) one in which the teacher controls more of the consequences than students (Semmelroth, 1969), then the teacher must have a stable rule system composed of contingent rather than absolute rules. Contingent rules stress acceleration of positive responses and specify that if a desired response is emitted, a prescribed consequence will follow. Nonoccurrence of the desired response leads to absence of the consequence. In contrast, absolute rules stress deceleration of negative responses and specify that if negative behavior occurs, then a negative consequence will follow. Contingent rules lodge the responsibility for producing positive consequences with the student; absolute rules lodge responsibility with the teacher. Contingent rules are a more effective means of controlling behavior.

Smith has observed that rules must be enforced on at least 80 percent of the relevant occasions if they are to be at all effective (Research and Development Center, undated). In addition Madsen, Becker, and Thomas (1968) have shown that mere mention of rules is less effective than rule enforcement backed by positive attention to appropriate behavior. Therefore it is clear that rules should be kept small enough in number and should be simple enough to permit teachers to use enforcement procedures readily. In addition rule systems should be free of contradictions and should provide an effective means by which both student and teacher may determine when desirable behavior has occurred.

Anyone who would generate a rule system must be aware that rule-testing is an inevitable consequence of rule-making. Smith and Smith (1968) have shown that rules will be tested at least twice in an effort to establish a basis for reasonable predictions of the consequences. This means that teachers and others must be prepared to make appropriate responses in the face of possible apparent failure of rule systems, knowing that once the consequences of rule-testing are established,

the rate of compliance with rules will increase.

A second class of antecedent conditions is *facilitating stimuli*—the essentials necessary if the response is to occur. For example, facilitating stimuli for the solution of algebraic problems are the tools for studying (such as a table, good light, and a quiet room), study materials, and the prerequisite skills (that is, arithmetic skills).

A great deal has been written about the effects of environment on learning (Ebner, 1967) and the design of effective learning environments (Cohen, Goldiamond, Filipczak, and Pooley, 1968). Similarly a great deal has been written about the value of such instructional aids as computers (Atkinson, 1968), teaching machines (Cleary and Packham, 1968), and programmed instruction (Birnbauer, Bijou, Wolf, and Kidder, 1965; Hendershot, 1967; Keller, 1968, 1969; Lloyd and Knutzen, 1969) for selective use (Eldred and Brooks, 1966) with students at all levels of education. The advantages of these approaches are that they permit individualized instruction and provide immediate feedback about the accuracy of responses so that all members of a large class can work simultaneously on different materials at different levels, while avoiding the practice of errors.

The third class of antecedent stimuli is *potentiating stimuli*—events manipulated by the behavior modifier in an effort to maximize the value of the consequences that will follow a response (Goldiamond, 1968). For example, a teacher might schedule a game period for midafternoon when students are most likely to want a break, or he might read the first chapter of an adventure story [termed "reinforcer sampling" by Ayllon and Azrin (1968)] that he plans to use as a reward for the completion of task behavior throughout the day. In either case the likelihood that the student will work to attain the reinforcer is increased.

The fourth class of antecedents includes *discriminative stimuli*, which are indications that a positive consequence will follow a response, and *stimulus deltas*, which indicate that responses are unlikely to be followed by a positive consequence. For example, a student might know that asking his regular teacher for permission to leave school early will be refused while such requests are likely to be granted by substitutes; the regular teacher is a stimulus delta for making such requests, the substitute teacher, a discriminative stimulus.

For some children good grades may be an indication of pleasant things to come. Superior papers might be posted on the bulletin board or read to the class or school staff; other students might expect to be granted money or extra privileges at home. Grades thus serve as a discriminative stimulus for approaching certain potentially reinforcing persons or situations. Will all children work to achieve good grades? Only those who in the past have enjoyed positive consequences associated with grades. Thus a discriminative stimulus or stimulus delta controls a response that has been learned through past experience. If a given child has not had experiences that add meaning to these events, he will not work to produce them.

Consequent Conditions

Antecedent conditions set the occasion for responses, increasing the likelihood that they will occur initially. If they are to recur, however, they must produce favorable consequences. If an operant response is a response that produces some change in the environment, then the changes or consequences produced by a given response must be regarded as the conditions exercising primary control over it (Skinner, 1953). Some consequences accelerate the likelihood that the rate of a response will increase: expressions of encouragement, payment for work completed, or an end to nagging. Other consequences decelerate the probability that a given response will be emitted: criticism, being ignored, punishment, loss of something of value, or being temporarily enjoined from engaging in a positive activity. In order for these consequences to exercise their control, however, they must occur; behavior is controlled by realities, not by expectations. For example, a child will work to achieve good grades if he receives some recognition for his efforts. If he has merely been promised this recognition without ever having received it, his behavior is unlikely to be controlled by it.

The manipulation of consequences is a powerful means of behavioral control. When consequences follow solely on the occurrence of a given response, they are termed contingencies, and their manipulation is termed contingency management (Homme, 1969). A teacher may use recess as a contingency if recess is restricted to those who put away their materials properly or perform whatever the desired behavior is. Conversely, he may use recess noncontingently if he allows every child to go to recess regardless of whether he has put away his materials.

Two studies have evaluated the effect of contingent as opposed to noncontingent consequences in classroom settings. Each of these studies has followed a six-step procedure common to current research in operant behavior:

1. A given response is specified, in the present instances, study behavior (Bushell, Wrobel, and Michaelis, 1968) and cooperative play (Hart, Reynolds, Baer, Brawley, and Harris, 1968).

2. A baseline measurement is taken, reflecting the rate at which these responses occur in the environment prior to any manipulation.

3. The first experimental condition is instituted—noncontingent use of tokens in the first study and teacher attention in the second study, with measurement of the dependent variables (study and cooperative play) being continued.

4. The first experimental condition is terminated and the second condition—contingent use of tokens and teacher attention—is instituted, with continued measurement of the dependent variable.

5. The second condition is terminated and is replaced by a return to the first condition (a reversal that might equally have been a return to the original baseline condition), with measurement of the dependent variable continuing.

6. Finally, the second experimental condition is reinstituted, associated with a final measurement of response rates.

Both of these studies have shown that the rates of both study and cooperative play increase when consequences are applied contingently and actually *decrease* when consequences are applied noncontingently. These studies strongly support the suggestion that the many accelerative consequences available in normal classrooms—for example, attention, preferred seating locations, privileges such as use of special materials, or participation in trips and games, among many others—should be made available on a purely contingent basis in order to maintain or augment the teacher's positive control of the class.

Consequences may have either of two characteristic forms: They may be informational or material. Information is anything that "removes or reduces uncertainty" (Attneave, 1959, p. 1). Feedback—"information about the effects of one's own behavior"—has great value (Stuart, 1970a, p. 191). Its function is to facilitate the planful control of the individual's behavior by "feeding back" to him the results of his own behavior (Wiener, 1956). In a real sense every operant consequence evokes behavior-regulating feedback in the sense that when a child learns that he may go to recess regardless of whether he has completed his work, this information will be useful to him in planning his next efforts (Skinner, 1953, p. 59). However, some consequences are informational secondary to their material characteristics—as when we know that our work is appreciated when we receive an unexpected bonus check. Although it is recognized that there is a distinct overlap between informational and material consequences, they nevertheless will be discussed separately in the interest of clarity.

Informational consequences. Social reactions are a prime source of feedback because of their evaluative component and because they are often associated with eventual access to material reinforcers (Hill, 1968). This is another way of saying that they have acquired or secondary value by virtue of having been associated with valued material consequences. For example, when a teacher tells a child that he may sit anywhere in the room he chooses (privilege, a material consequence as used here), this permission is typically associated with smiles, attention, and positive words. The teacher's gestures and words in the future are likely to be accelerative consequences for the child.

Feedback may be used either to accelerate or decelerate responses. Implicitly, whenever one aspect of a response is praised, other aspects are neglected. It is to be expected that the praised aspect will be strengthened while the neglected, ignored, or extinguished aspects will be weakened. Beyond this, however, behavior modifiers may choose deliberately to remove positive feedback following certain responses, such as a sixth-grade child's solutions to fifth-grade problems, in an effort to motivate the child to undertake more complex sixth-grade problems. While decisive research on the subject cannot be cited, it is believed wise to avoid the use of simple extinction procedures because, as will be shown later, the control exercised by the behavior modifier may be weakened if such an approach is relied on. Instead it seems invariably wise to begin with the acceleration of a desired response, preferably one that is incompatible with the problem response, and only later resort to decelerative techniques to do away with any problem behavior that persists.

The use of positive attention has controlled a variety of behaviors in schoolchildren. Among preschool children, positive teacher attention has been shown to increase climbing (Buell, Stoddard, Harris, and Baer, 1968), cooperation (Hart et al., 1968), crawling (Harris, Johnston, Kelley, and Wolf, 1964), and speech. In one study (Brison, 1966) a five-year-old kindergartner who had not spoken in over a year spoke within four weeks when the teacher was attentive to him following each successive step toward effective speech (termed shaping or reinforcement of successive approximations). Among older schoolchildren teacher attentiveness has been used to increase rates of study and acceptable social responses (Hall, Lund, and Jackson, 1968; Hall, Panyan, Rabon, and Broden, 1968a; Madsen, Becker, Thomas, Kosar, and Plager, 1968).

Unfortunately, both teachers and peer groups may serve to maintain problem behavior as well as desirable behavior (Baer and Wolf, 1968; Harris, Wolf, and Baer, 1964; Wahler, 1967). For this to be true, the amount of attention offered to the child for negative behavior must almost equal or exceed the attention paid to positive behavior; Charlesworth and Hartup (1966) have shown that even nursery-school children may exert a similar negative influence. Much of this strengthening of problem responses is undoubtedly unintentional. For example, it has been shown that reliance on simple commands such as "Sit down!" may actually accelerate the rate of out-of-seat behavior and attention to crying may accelerate the rate of crying (Madsen et al., 1968; Hart, Allen, Buell, Harris, and Wolf, 1964). Faced with a class of perhaps twenty-five students and constrained by reliance on absolute rule systems, teachers may find it difficult to do other than pay attention to negatives; the need to reverse this tendency is clear.

The use of positive attention to increase the rate of a behavior incompatible with a problem response in order to extinguish that response has been convincingly demonstrated in several studies. In one, a child whose temper tantrums continued when she was held on the teacher's or principal's lap was brought under positive control within four weeks by reinforcement of appropriate social behavior and ignoring of inappropriate behavior (Carlsen, Arnold, Becker, and Madsen, 1968). In another demonstration a socially isolated child was brought to a pattern of social approach behavior by withdrawing efforts to encourage him to join groups (which rewarded his isolation) and paying attention only to social approach responses (Allen, Hart, Buell, Harris, and Wolf, 1964). This procedure has been used to accelerate the rate of task-oriented behavior while decreasing hyperactivity (Allen, Henke, Harris, Baer, and Reynolds, 1967), aggression (Brown and Elliott, 1969), and other socially disruptive responses of normal students as well as a variety of behaviors of brain-injured children (Becker, Madsen, Arnold, and Thomas, 1967; Hall et al., 1968; Hall et al., 1968a; Hall and Broden, 1967).

It is important to note that these changes have been achieved in work with individual children alone or in class, as well as with groups of children and entire classes. It is important to note that while some of these dramatic effects have been achieved with no increase in the overall amount of teacher attentiveness (Ward and Baker, 1968), it is clear that the teacher's attention must be radically redirected from negative to positive behavior. Hall, Panyan, Rabon, and Broden (1968b) have shown that in a class in which students studied 43 percent of the available time and teachers used positive feedback 1.4 times per session, the rate of studying increased to 77 percent of the available time following an increase to 17 teacher comments per session. The total professional cost of this change was minimal, having been held to fifteen to thirty minutes with each teacher to introduce the procedure and several minutes with each on a weekly basis to review the results.

When efforts are made to use attention to accelerate a behavior incompatible with problem responses, Ackerman (1969) suggests as a general rule that the rate of attention for desirable behavior should equal 110 percent of the attention previously given for both positive and negative behaviors. For example, if a child received two teacher comments per day for positive behavior and eight positive comments per day for negative behavior, the accelerated positive behavior should occur at the rate of eleven comments per day $(1.1 \times 2 + 8)$. While data in support of this rule have not yet been published, it would appear at this time to be a reasonable guide.

Other than providing social feedback to children—a process that may make troublesome demands on the teacher—several investigators have used a variety of simple devices to transmit this information. Working with a physically handicapped eleven-year-old boy, McKerracher (1967) used a light to indicate positive behavior and a buzzer to signify negative behavior; Quay, Werry, McQueen, and Sprague (1966) used lights to signal positive behavior with normal elementary-school children. Several other investigators also used visual and auditory signals with normal and brain-damaged children, backing up the signals for positive behavior with reinforcements such as candy (Addison and Homme, 1966; Patterson, Jones, Whittier, and Wright, 1965). In addition Patterson (1969b) has developed a "workbox" that contains a counter that can be reset and a light activated by a pushbutton controlled at some distance by a teacher. The workbox has been used successfully to modify the behavior of a number of children. Even more complex light signal systems have been used to modify the behavior of groups of students or even entire classes (Surratt et al., 1969; Walker, Mattson, and Buckley, 1969). In each of these instances lights have signaled the eventual provision of a variety of material reinforcers. The dual advantages of this approach are that (1) the teacher is able to give increased amounts of feedback to students without disrupting his normal teaching routines, and (2) feedback can be provided immediately following a desired response. Thus there is no danger of a teacher's forgetting to respond positively and there is no delay in the student's receipt of information necessary for his continued performance.

Another means of transmitting feedback from teachers to students is through the use of traditional grading procedures. In theory grades represent a reflection of the value of student output and should be associated with positive consequences in proportion to the value of the work done. In practice, however, there are five limitations to the value of grades.

1. Smith and Smith (1968) contend that grades can only be useful if they are positive. They state:

"Information feedback serves to increase motivation and stimulate change if the information is positive. But if it is negative, it can discourage both learner and teacher. In fact, evidence of failure is so punishing that people have built up effective techniques for ignoring information that might be negative [p. 52]."

The techniques to which the authors refer include attacking the adequacy or relevance of the information, ignoring the information, or claiming that the essential aspects of performance have not been measured. In a partial test of this view, this author offered positive examination grades to one half of a large graduate social work class; the other half of the class received negative grades. Seven days later he asked the class to identify their scores on the examination. Controlling for the level of grades, students who received positive information were significantly more accurate in their recall than were students who received negative information. Despite general knowledge of this tendency, positive grades are given infrequently.

2. A second limitation of grades is that grades should be secondary reinforcers because of their association with positive consequences. In point of fact, grades are typically used as a means of avoiding negatives rather than as a means of achieving positives. Skinner (1968) has observed, for example:

"The commonest practice in high school as well as college is still 'assign and test.' We tell the student what he is to learn and hold him responsible for learning it by making a variety of unhappy consequences contingent upon his failure. In doing so we may give him some reason to learn but we do not teach [p. 707]."

Unless positive incentives are associated with grades, grades will not acquire the property of secondary reinforcement. Some parents attach desirable consequences—such as money and extra free time—to good grades, but schools should not depend on parents to supply reinforcement for school-related behavior. Instead, schools should provide positive consequences such as the privilege of taking elective classes or coming to school at a later hour.

3. A third limitation is that grades typically are offered too late for either the student or teacher to make use of their information value. When tests come at the end of a unit of work, little can be done to overcome the deficits they reflect. If instead grades were offered at many intervals during a study activity, they could serve a regulatory function in the teaching process.

4. One explanation for the perpetuation of terminal grading is the assumption that

grades are a reflection of student performance. This is the fourth limitation of grading procedures. In point of fact, the student's "learning" is a dependent variable that varies as a function of the teacher's skill in the management of the teaching situation. Traditionally students may fail, but teachers always pass (Gideonse, 1968).

"The existing practice of grading students assumes at bottom that the student is responsible for his learning and that his failure or success is a tribute to or a consequence of factors intrinsic to him. This idea of grading a school on the basis of its outputs assumes that all students can learn that the responsibility of the schools is to make that happen . . . [p. 544]."

At the present time the person who occupies the relatively weaker position in an educational setting—the student—receives feedback. If the tradition were reversed—if teachers' reinforcement were made contingent on the grades earned by students—then teachers could use their relative position of strength to modify instructional conditions and thereby improve student performance.

5. Another limitation of grading procedures is the use of absolute rather than achievement ratings. Absolute ratings are measurements of student performance in comparison either to an arbitrarily determined ratio scale (grades are commonly assigned on the basis of the proportion of correct answers, the total number of questions being arbitrarily determined by teachers) or to the performance of other students. This curve grading introduces a double artifact: Not only is the ratio scale arbitrarily determined, but students are denied exact information about the expected criteria for their performance prior to an examination, as a means of protecting the teacher from setting objective standards for measurement of his own performance as a teacher. In contrast to this approach, achievement ratings would compensate students according to the extent to which their performance improves from one test period to the next. The danger in a system that uses the student as a standard for his own evaluation is that students might

unintentionally perform poorly at the outset. But if this approach were combined with traditional procedures, implying that students could receive certain privileges (for example, exemption from attendance at a given class or from homework assignments), this obstacle could be overcome.

If grades are (1) offered positively, (2) associated with accelerative consequences, (3) offered promptly, (4) understood to be indications of teacher achievement first and student performance second, and (5) offered as consequences for absolute and relative changes, then they can serve a useful function as a medium of feedback. If these criteria are not met, then it is doubtful that grades can be useful.

A final form of feedback in school settings is information about teacher functioning. Beyond grades, teachers may benefit greatly from information about their management of classes. Flanders (1967) has noted:

"As a group, teachers are isolated from systematic information about their own behavior. However, research indicates that teaching performance depends upon the range of behavior a teacher can produce, the self-control required to provide particular patterns of influence, a teacher's sensitivity in diagnosing the requirements of the moment, and his ability to predict the consequences of alternative actions. . . . Considerable improvement probably can be brought about by any program that provides reasonably intelligent teachers of average emotional adjustment with systematic information about their classroom behavior [p. 24]."

To the extent that specific nuances of teacher behavior are associated with the differential performance of students, it would seems as though information about teacher behavior would be vitally essential to effective classroom behavior.

Several studies have contributed information about the criteria that differentiate highly effective from less effective secondary school teachers. (It is probable that quite different patterns are associated with primary- and college-level teaching). For example, Flanders (1960, 1963) has shown that two thirds of classroom time is occupied with talk, and two thirds of this time is typically occupied with talk on the part of the teacher. But Amidon and Giammatteo (1967) contrasted thirty-three teachers rated as superior with 120 not-so-rated by noting that superior teachers spoke 40 percent of the time in comparison to normative teachers who spoke 52 percent of the time. Qualitative differences between the two groups showed that superior teachers used greater amounts of contingent praise and offered half as much direction and criticism. It has also been shown that student teachers talk more than experienced teachers and that effective teachers are more consistent in rule enforcement than ineffective teachers (Kirk, 1967; Research and Development Center, undated). Thus the three principal factors that have been identified are the overall rates of verbal behavior by teachers versus that of students, positive versus negative comments, and rule enforcement versus rule neglect.

Three approaches have been used in efforts to bring teacher behavior into closer approximations to these objectives. First, teachers have been offered guidance outside the classroom as a means of improving student performance. This approach was illustrated by by the work of Hall et al. (1968a). Second, teachers have been provided with feedback and their behavior has even been cued during class sessions. Assuming that verbal behavior of teachers and students is a valid index of other teacher actions, Amidon and Flanders (1963) have developed a system of classifying teacher behavior, including such indirect categories as acceptance of feeling or giving praise or encouragement and such direct categories as lecturing and giving directions. When baselines have been established for teacher behavior, this information is fed back to the teacher, who seeks to modify his performance to coincide with criterion levels of performance. While the criterion levels are not fully documented, the success of such an approach utilizing feedback mediated by others is being demonstrated (Kirk, 1967). A third approach to the use of feedback to modify the teacher's behavior in class, developed by Smith and

his associates, relies on self-shaping (Research and Development Center, undated). Teachers are asked to identify appropriate, inappropriate, and unacceptable classes of student behavior as well as the response they feel they should make to these behaviors. They are then merely asked to count the rate at which these behaviors occur. Smith has shown that the rule-enforcement responses of teachers can be accelerated from 50 to 80 percent of the relevant occasions by this method, with corresponding decreases of rule tests from a level forty to fifty per quarter-hour to a level of ten to twenty per quarter-hour.

Similar changes have been observed elsewhere in a study demonstrating that teachers using self-shaping could radically modify the behavior of brain-injured kindergarten children (Abbott et al., 1969). Self-shaping is perhaps the least costly procedure and may well be the most generally useful because the teacher can resort to self-shaping whenever he believes it might be helpful. The tools of self-shaping are as simple as a chalk mark on the blackboard or a hash mark on an index card taped to a desk. More elaborate procedures might call for utilization of a counter.

Many of the foregoing approaches have depended on the provision of positive feedback to accelerate responses incompatible with poor performance, with a consequent withdrawal of attention from negative responses. In some instances this feedback has been self-produced, as in the self-shaping systems, while in the socially produced feedback conditions, normal social relationships, behavioral observers, signal systems, or grades have been the medium of feedback.

In essence these approaches have rested heavily on the manipulation of positive feedback. Negative feedback, while of questionable value, may be used in two additional procedures. First, negative feedback may be provided until desirable behavior occurs, at which time it is terminated. This is well represented by the teacher who stands in front of a class censoriously berating students until they come to order. The weaknesses in this approach are obviously that the teacher may become so aversive that he loses his influence or the students may be wise enough not to accelerate the teacher's negative behavior by compliance (Stuart, 1969). By the same token the primary use of negative feedback is subject to the danger that the person attempting to modify behavior might suffer a loss of influence and in addition run the risk of failing to provide necessary behavioral prescriptions for desirable responses. More will be said about the limitations of these procedures in the following section, in which material decelerative techniques will be discussed.

Positive reinforcement. Material consequences may be either concrete—such as candy, money, or an affectionate pat on the back—or privileges. Another term for accelerative consequences is positive reinforcement, which implies that when an event is followed or reinforced by a given consequence, its rate will be affected positively. This is a purely functional definition and suggests that events are positive when they work, not merely when the behavior modifier expects them to work. For example, candy offered contingently on the emission of correct reading responses by a young child might accelerate the rate of such responses, but it might also interfere with reading if the child interrupts his reading to eat his reinforcers. The determination of which consequences are accelerative is therefore an empirical matter.

There is strong suggestion that informational consequences may not be sufficient to compensate children for positive behavior. Millenson (1967, pp. 251–254) suggests that whereas teachers might be adequately reinforced by changes in their students' behavior (a fact that should be withheld from the attention of school administrators at bargaining sessions), students may need more tangible and immediate reinforcement. Using the research methodology described, Reynolds and Risley (1968) demonstrated that the verbal behavior of a preschool child could not be accelerated through the mediation of social reinforcement alone, but that marked changes did occur when social and material reinforcers were used in combination. Similar observations have been repeated elsewhere

with preschool (Risley, 1968), elementary (Patterson et al., 1965), and high-school students (Miller, 1964). Other than the obvious money and candy, a wide range of reinforcers is available in the classroom. Recess has been used most effectively (Osborne, 1969), as have classroom games (Barrish, Saunders, and Wolf, 1969; Hall et al., 1968b). Other reinforcers include being permitted to give recitations in class, work with higher level academic materials, tutor slower learning or younger students, listen to records, attend special events, and participate in an endless series of other privileges common to virtually all classrooms. Table 1 (See Appendix A, pp. 36.) presents a reinforcement menu, showing the range of reinforcers available to the teacher.

Two difficulties encountered in the use of material consequences are the facts that (1) all children are not reinforced by the same things at the same time and (2) it is often not possible to deliver large reinforcements after small responses. To overcome these problems, Ayllon et al. (1968) have developed a token system of reinforcement. This approach requires (1) specification of desirable behaviors, (2) development of a range of reinforcers formulated into a "reinforcement menu" (Addison et al., 1966), (3) assignment of values to the reinforcers in terms of the responses required to earn them, (4) development of a token or point medium to be given to the student following completion of the required tasks and to be exchanged by the teacher when the student chooses his reinforcer, and (5) rules for how and when reinforcing events may be used. Sherman and Baer (1969) have pointed out that the effective use of token systems depends both on training the recipient to value the tokens and the value he places on the selection of reinforcers ultimately provided. They further note that the long-term effectiveness of token-aided behavioral change programs depends on the assumption by other agents in the environment (e.g., parents) of responsibility for reinforcing the behavior. They conclude, however, that on balance the advantages of token systems increasingly seem to outweigh their disadvantages and are steadily increasing in application.

Indeed, the range of successful demonstrations of token systems with normal children in nursery school (Bushell et al., 1968), elementary school (Quay et al., 1966; Wood, 1968), and junior high school settings (Giles, 1969) has been impressive. In addition, success has been met in applying token systems to the problems of disturbed children in special settings (McKensie, Clark, Wolf, Kothera, and Benson, 1968; O'Leary and Becker, 1967; Rabb and Hewett, 1967; Wolf, Giles, and Hall, 1968) and with retardates in special settings (Birnbauer and Lawler, 1965; Birnbauer, Wolf, Kidder, and Tague, 1965; Nolen, Knuzelmann, and Haring, 1967; Perline and Levensky, 1968; Zimmerman, Zimmerman, and Russell, 1969). What is especially impressive about these token systems is that they may be effectively administered by nonprofessionals (Staats, Minker, Goodwin, and Landeed, 1967), parents, and peers (Patterson, Shaw, and Ebner, 1969), and their cost relative to more elaborate systems [which, incidentally, have a lower probability of success (Stuart, 1970c)] is quite low. For example, Wolf et al. (1968) report a total average cost of $225 per child per year in contrast to a possible institutional cost approaching $100 per diem (Stuart, 1970a).

Teachers, parents, and others who use token reinforcement can gain precise control over the behaviors with which they are concerned. They can immediately provide amounts of reinforcement directly proportional to the emitted responses. Three additional procedures have been used to further augment the potency of the system. First, "fines" have been levied against tokens earned as a way of decelerating undesirable behaviors. Following Wiener's (1962) demonstration of this response-cost technique, Giles (1969) has demonstrated that it may not be useful with all persons, and Hall et al. (1968a) demonstrated that the proportion of task-oriented responses escalated from 47 percent to 65 percent when tokens redeemable for recess time were introduced, but the rate again spurted to 81 percent when students suffered fines for intervals of nontask-oriented behavior.

A second technique that may be used is the mobilization of group support for the teacher's goals by giving tokens to the group for the positive behavior of one person, a few individuals, or the entire group. Lindsley (1963) originally described four formats for reinforcement: (1) individual reinforcement, (2) mutual reinforcement, in which all individuals in a group receive the same reinforcement at the same time, (3) joint reinforcement, in which each individual receives one portion of a reinforcement that must be pooled with others in order to realize a complete reinforcer for the group, and (4) communal reinforcement, in which one group reinforcement is given, requiring individuals to compete for its complete control or agree to subdivide or share it. Drawing on Lindsley's alternatives, it is possible to give an individual points that are redeemable as reinforcements for the entire group.

Patterson, Shaw, and Ebner (1969) have effectively demonstrated that the behavior of several hyperactive children was well controlled by allowing them to earn the privilege of distributing to the class candy or ice cream donated by their parents. In a second alternative, a variety of contingencies were made available to entire classes depending on the number of tokens earned (Bushell et al., 1968). Other investigators have divided classes in half; the half of the class that receives the fewest chalk marks on the board for undesirable behavior is given such positive reinforcements as extra recess time (Barrish et al., 1969). The technique has also been used in work with retardates with whom the goal was to reduce the rate of obscene gestures made in class (Sulzbucker and Houser, 1968). In this application, one of ten cards was flipped over each time any child made a gesture, indicating a loss of one minute of recess time for the entire class. The daily rate of occurrence of the gesture was reduced from sixteen to two within two weeks.

The full range of Lindsley's procedures has not been reported yet in the literature, although it seems most likely that their effectiveness will soon be demonstrated. The advantage of group reinforcement is that it gives the teacher allies among the students. Without group reinforcement, the misbehavior of selected children in the class might provide an entertaining diversion for the remaining students, leading them both to stimulate and try to maintain the problem behavior. When some cost, whether in the form of a delay or loss of reinforcement, is imposed, every child in the class has a stake in the good behavior of the problem child, and all will assist the teacher in control efforts if the reinforcement has a value greater than relief from monotonous routine.

The third technique for increasing the effectiveness of token systems has been termed "contingency contracting" by Homme (1969). The approach begins by development of a reinforcing menu that contains a potpourri of the things students are most likely to do when they are permitted to do whatever they want (Addison et al., 1966).[4] The second step is to limit access to these events so as to increase their value. Then a series of task cards is prepared that contains assignments such as reading a number of pages in a schoolbook and answering questions about the reading. The student may select cards containing assignments that interest him or contingencies that he especially desires (naturally, interesting assignments will carry less reinforcement value than undesirable assignments). This enables the student to work at his own pace. By keeping track of the contracts completed by each child in a master record (Brethower, 1969), the teacher has access to instant information about the educational status of every student in the class while also ensuring the maximum output of each student.

Negative reinforcement. In the foregoing section it was shown that responses can be accelerated through positive reinforcement using several techniques. It is also possible to accelerate the rate of responses by removing an aversive event following a desired response. This is termed negative reinforcement. Laboratory demonstrations of its effectiveness have generally been confined to the treatment of sexual abnormalities, but teachers have taken such action as keeping problem students after school until they publicly repent.

There is a problem in the use of negative reinforcement that is common to aversive strategies in general. The person attempting to manage behavior may·acquire such an undesirable image that his subject will not be influenced by his disapproval.

Punishment. A punishing consequence is any stimulus that reduces the rate of responses that produce it. This is a functional definition, empirically defined. Punishment is typically associated with such "unpleasant" events as spanking or electric shock. These associations are often quite misleading, however. For example, penny arcades have for years offered electric shocks as reinforcers in games that people pay to play.

There are at least two broad classes of punishment: corporal and programmatic events. The use of corporal punishment in public schools has had an episodic history in which there has been a tendency to advance its use following each step in the "liberalization" of education. While punishments such as spanking have been used as an adjunct to a variety of effective therapeutic procedures with children demonstrating extreme behavioral problems (Birnbauer, 1968; Lovaas and Simmons, 1969; Tate and Baroff, 1966), its use with schoolchildren has not been studied extensively.

Apart from the legal ramifications that must be considered, there are several reasons for seriously questioning the use of punishment in such settings:

1. Many of the conditions that Azrin and Holz (1965) describe as necessary prerequisites for the use of punishment are often not met in natural settings. For example, it is frequently impossible to punish problem responses immediately, severely, consistently, and without associating punishment with certain socially desirable consequences such as attention.

2. It has been shown that while punishment may lead to immediate suppression of a problem response, it is also true that when the conditions associated with punishment have been removed, the problem response is likely to recur (Risley, 1968).

3. The delivery of a punishment is typically a fairly aggressive response. When a person in authority acts as a punisher, he

---

4 See Table 1.

models the use of aggressive interpersonal strategies that may then be imitated by the person being punished.

4. Further, the use of punishment is likely to disrupt the learning situation markedly because of the child's physical and emotional response to that punishment or because of the high probability that he will reflexively attack either the punisher or innocent by-standers.

Program may be used in preference to corporal punishment as a decelerative event, as has been suggested by Lindsley (1968). As an illustration, teachers have sought to use repetition of arduous tasks such as writing sentences a specified number of times as a means of decelerating the rate of a child's problem behavior. While this use of program has certain advantages over corporal punishment, it shares the disadvantages of reducing the attractiveness (and potential influence) of the teacher, and it also may lend an unpleasant quality to the programmatic task. In place of repetitive tasks the teacher might require the student to emit an above-average number of less negative but more productive responses such as solutions to several set-theory problems or the writing of fiction.

Time-out. If a desirable response is being maintained by an accelerative consequence, then time out from the opportunity to earn that consequence may be an effective way of decelerating the rate of any undesirable response that may become associated with the desirable response. For example, Baer (1962) demonstrated that once nursery-school children were positively reinforced by being allowed to watch cartoons, temporary inter-ruption of the cartoons contingent on thumb-sucking could reduce the rate of the latter behavior. The same procedure has been used to modify the tantrum behavior of young children (Wolf, Risley, and Mees, 1964), the gross antisocial behavior of adolescents in in-stitutional settings, and the disruptive behav-ior of schoolchildren. Brown and Shields (1967) demonstrated that children sent home from school following specific rule violations —termed "systematic exclusion"—showed a radical decrease in the rate of these viola-tions over a period of several months.

The use of time-out procedures is a com-plex process. First, some of the child's be-havior, such as playing with others in a group, must be maintained by a positive con-sequence. Second, a disruptive response must occur, such as hitting another child. Third, the positive consequence must be withheld for a definite time, such as removing the child from the group.

Patterson and White (undated) suggest that the time out must be mildly aversive. This is brought about by (1) making certain that the individual has no access to rein-forcing stimuli while undergoing time-out, which is possible only when supervision is available during that time, and (2) prolong-ing time-out as a consequence of disruptive behavior that takes place during the time-out period. As Baer (1961) has suggested, this removal of a positive reinforcer is in effect a decelerative consequence following disrup-tive behavior. Further, positive reinforcement is restored when the child behaves as desired in the group setting.

The use of time-out offers some decided advantages over extinction and punishment in that the behavior modifier can avoid the negative cast associated with the latter two strategies. In addition, negative interpersonal responses are not modeled, and there is minimal disruption of the teaching-learning environment.

In school settings it is essential to apply consequences in a manner governed by rules rather than allowing them to be applied arbitrarily by the teacher. It is also essential to make certain that the environment in which the child is placed is not rich with reinforcement. The principal's office, where the child can overhear the school's adminis-trative business, and the hall, where he can speak with his friends, are obviously positive rather than aversive environments. On the other hand, placement behind a screen in the classroom or in a special room designated for the purpose may be highly effective.

It has been shown that the broad classes of informational and material consequences available in all social situations may be divided into techniques that can accelerate or decelerate the rate of occurrence of the responses that produce them. It has also been shown that accelerative techniques offer distinct operational advantages over decelerative techniques, although the two are frequently used in combination. Two questions that have not been discussed pertain to the broader consequences of the use of behavior modification in the classroom: maintenance and generalization of behavioral effects.

Maintenance. A behavior that has been therapeutically or experimentally manipulated is said to be maintained if its rate does not appreciably diminish following termination of the interventive procedure. Conventionally determined through an evaluation of the follow-up procedures, virtually all of the studies cited in this paper include such considerations.

The critical issues in follow-up evaluations are unfortunately somewhat arbitrary. For example, the amount of "drift" in the response rate that is tolerable within the "success" class is defined by the individual researcher and varies from study to study. The amount of time that must elapse before a response can be said to have been maintained is also arbitrary. Patterson (1969b) has noted that many behavioral changes disappear six months after the termination of treatment. This would suggest the need to use somewhat longer intervals.

The maintenance of behavioral change is never coincidental. In one set of behavioral therapy techniques, the patient or others in his immediate social environment is "instigated" to modify his behavior (Kanfer and Phillips, 1969). If the patient is the subject of instigation, he is responsible for reprogramming others with whom he interacts to reinforce him positively for a new set of positive responses. This is frequently difficult because, for example, a teacher is likely to have a negative set toward a troublesome child and is therefore unlikely to attend to his positive responses; the result is that these may be extinguished. On the other hand, if the teacher is instigated to change his behavior vis-à-vis the child, the child's environment can be reprogrammed to strengthen the desired responses (Patterson, Hawkins, McNeal, and Phelps, 1968). In this case the behavior is more likely to be maintained. This reasoning affords a strong argument for the use of consultative services with teachers in place of direct services to children.

When direct treatment is used, the patient is placed in a "prosthetic environment" that intensifies the conditions conducive to the learning of new responses. For example, the behavioral therapist might carefully cue verbal responses and immediately reinforce these responses in much the same manner that the psychotherapist encourages reflective discussion of selected issues and reinforces a given class of verbal responses. When treatment is approaching the point of termination, the therapist must seek to weaken the client's dependence while strengthening the behavioral control found in the natural environment. This is achieved through the process of "fading."

In effect fading seeks to replace one set of controlling conditions with another. The procedure (Sherman et al., 1969) has been described in the following terms:

"Fading is used to develop new discriminations, i.e., to change the discriminative stimulus conditions controlling the behavior. Initially the behavior is maintained with reinforcement in those stimulus conditions where the behavior is already highly probable. Gradually, at a rate which produces no disruption in performance, the desired changes are introduced in these stimulus conditions (the behavior will come under the control of these new discriminative stimuli) [p. 196]."

Risley and Baer (undated) have described fading as a two-way procedure. They describe the efforts of a therapist to reinforce imitative vocal responses in a retarded child who had already imitated the experimenter's motor responses. The therapist first faded in vocalizations by gradually associating vocal responses with motor responses; he then faded out the motor responses, leaving only vocal imitations, by reducing the complexity of the stimuli used to prompt the child. This left the child with a set of responses that more closely resembled those of "normal" children, thereby increasing the probability that the adults he will encounter outside of the experimental situation will respond to him as if he were normal. That in turn will increase the likelihood that he will receive positive reinforcement in these encounters.

The same goal—gradually reducing the special qualities of intervention procedures so as to make them more comparable to natural controlling conditions—can be achieved through fading other aspects of the intervention procedure. For example, Kale, Kaye, Whelan, and Hopkins (1968) trained schizophrenic patients to greet an experimenter, reinforcing greetings with cigarettes. They then increased the interval between the cueing and reinforcement of greetings, fading the temporal proximity of the two events. Gratifications rarely follow social responses immediately; by training their subjects to expect a delay, the experimenters enhanced the social repertoires of their patients.

In addition to fading the complexity of stimuli or their temporal association, behavior modifiers can also fade the intensity of reinforcement. When responses are initially induced to occur they are typically richly rewarded. For example, a first-grade teacher may reinforce every response approximating a correct approach to a given problem. Over time, the teacher may offer these reinforcements only following more work or may offer less reinforcement. By so doing the teacher "thins" the schedule or quality of reinforcement. Most social and task responses are cumulatively reinforced—that is, they are reinforced after increasing numbers have been accumulated. To expect reinforcement following every response would be to invite disappointment: To be prepared to work for reinforcements earned over time is to display some of the equipment needed for social survival.

Ackerman (1969) suggests that when social responses are desired, the rate at which these are reinforced should never fall below the rate at which deviant responses were previously reinforced. This is a sound recommendation, since it accentuates the behavior modifier's control over positive responses. Ackerman also offers as a guideline for instituting a thinning of schedules ten successive intervals of constructive behavior at a criterion level. While this is an arbitrary determination, it appears to be reasonable.

Behavioral therapy that neglects the problem of fading may result in a schoolchild who has been changed in the treatment situation but who is underequipped to deal effectively with the normal stresses and strains of classroom life. To the extent that behavior modification techniques are behavioral prostheses, they must be faded to bring the individual under the control of those events that comprise his normal social environment. A child who learns to talk reasonably only to his therapist may have accumulated an isolated positive experience, but he has not developed social survival skills.

Generalization. If maintenance is concerned with the problem of sustaining a response under conditions closely related to the original learning situation, generalization is concerned with accelerating the rate of the response under conditions related to, although not identical with, conditions under which it originally occurred. For example, the concept of roundness may be learned in association with small, perfect circles printed in black ink. Larger, less perfect, and differently colored circles will also be identified as round through the process of abstraction that is one illustration of generalization. The social worker who assists a teacher in changing the behavior of a child in one class may quite properly be concerned with the likelihood that this change will be carried over to other classes as well. Studies that have attended to this issue have given strong indication that this may reliably occur (Buell et al., 1968; Surratt et al., 1969; Walker and Buckley, 1968).

A certain amount of generalization will occur naturally. For example, a child might greet a substitute teacher as he greets his regular teacher. If he is reinforced positively for this, the response will recur and generalization from one teacher to another may be said to have taken place. This same effect may be deliberately achieved. Several investigators have sought to promote generalization of positive behavior through use of peers and parents as primary or adjunctive forces in treatment (Evans and Oswalt, 1967; Hartup, 1964; Patterson, 1969b; Patterson, Ebner, and Shaw, 1969; Patterson et al., 1965; Tiktin and Hartup, 1965). The value of such therapeutic allies lies in the fact that their presence may set the occasion for desired responses and these responses may then occur in a variety of environments.

In addition to concern with the range of environments in which a client emits a desired behavior, a behavior modifier might also be interested in tracking the effect on other individuals of his efforts to modify the behavior of one person. This has been studied in classrooms as the "ripple effect" (Kounin and Gump, 1958). Some evidence suggests that favorable consequences may be observed when other children watch the positive reinforcement of one of their peers (Boudin, 1967; Gnagey, 1960; Ryan, 1959). On the other hand, data collected by Patterson, Ebner, and Shaw (1969) for other purposes suggests that the behavioral change efforts directed toward one child may be essentially unrelated to the responses of another. Definitive evaluations of the ripple effect have not been published, but the question remains one of great importance.

Summary. The process of behavioral change is orderly. It begins with specification of a response or identification of an objective positive response that occurs at a comparatively high rate. The rate of occurrence of the response is measured and recorded, and a decision is made about whether to attempt to modify the rate. A sample form for recording the rates of appropriate, inappropriate, and unacceptable behaviors is presented in Appendix B (see pp. 38–39).

If a decision is made to go further, the antecedent conditions that set the occasion for the response are identified as a second step. Falling into four classes—instructional (rules), facilitating (tools and skills), potentiating (increasing the value of the consequences), and discriminative (indicating the probability of certain consequences)—certain antecedent events set the occasion for positive responses (A+) while other antecedents set the occasion for problem behaviors (A−). An effort is naturally made to strengthen the A+ conditions and to weaken the A− conditions.

As a third step, the consequent conditions that ultimately determine the rate of the response are examined. Consequences may be informational or material, may be applied contingently or noncontingently, and may accelerate or decelerate the rate of the response. In summary fashion, accelerative consequences may be identified as C+ conditions, decelerative consequences as C− events. Again the behavior modifier's goal would be to strengthen the conditions conducive to positive response while weakening those conducive to problem behaviors.

The fourth step is complex. It calls for the fading of the prosthetic techniques while seeking to generalize their effects. Fading implies the systematic removal of therapeutic techniques and is achieved, for example, through reducing the schedule of reinforcement from extremely high response to reinforcement ratios to much lower ratios. Generalization refers to the efforts to make certain that the desired behaviors occurs in the natural environment as well as the therapeutic environment. In many instances the processes of fading and generalization rival the complexity of the original response induction procedures and failure in these efforts may vitiate the effectiveness of the entire behavioral change process.

*   *   *

APPENDIX A. Table 1. Classroom reinforcement menu.

Extra Time out of Class

1. Go to rest room
2. Get drink
3. Run errands to office
4. Go to library
5. Early dismissal
6. Day off
7. Reduce homework
8. Hall monitor
9. Go to principal's office

Assistance to Teacher

1. Pass out/collect papers, books, etc.
2. Take attendance
3. Help to put up bulletin board displays
4. Grade papers
5. Escort visitors
6. Enter grades in markbook
7. Safety patrol
8. Class officer
9. Class monitor
10. Tutor other children

Reinforcers Given in School —Valued at Home

1. Favorable progress note
2. Making gifts
3. Conference with parent
4. Parent invited to visit
5. Photo of child working
6. Certificates of merit
7. Test scores

Extrinsic Reinforcers

1. Token system
   a. in which tokens are given or removed
   b. on an individual or group basis
   c. redeemable from menu or store
2. Parties
   a. for own class
   b. host for other class
3. Trips
   a. picnics, parks
   b. museums, zoos
   c. movies
   d. sports events, skating
   e. newspapers
4. Free time in recreation area
5. Candy, gum, fruit, etc.
6. School supplies, erasers, etc.
7. Toys, comics, coloring books, etc.
8. Extra time with teacher, principal
9. Jacks, marbles, trading cards, etc.
10. Check out extra library books
11. Clown, magician
12. Puzzles, dominos, checkers, etc.
13. Eligibility for sports

Inherent in Class Activity

1. Teacher read, continue story
2. Student read, continue story
3. Choose own instrument to play, song to sing
4. Use of telescope, microscope, TV, etc.
5. Choice of own reading material
6. Participation in plays
7. Chance to write letters
8. Chance to select workmate
9. Choice of seat
10. First in line
11. Art, cutting, coloring, etc.
12. Arts and crafts
13. Bake, cook, etc.
14. Choice of class games
15. Team captain
16. Discussion period of child's choice
17. Recess outside in warm weather, inside in colder weather
18. Free time for all other active games
19. Movies
20. Assembly

Feedback—Evaluative

1. Grades
2. Competitive ranking
   a. seats
   b. charts
   c. work displays
3. Praise from class
4. Class performance graph
5. Individual performance graph
6. Teacher praise

Antecedents	Behavior	Consequences
Facilitating Stimuli	*Response Specification*	*Acceleration Techniques*
Physical environment: Would any change increase the likelihood of a positive response or decrease the likelihood of a negative response?	Categorize behavior as to: appropriate—social and task inappropriate—but tolerable because it does not interfere with the safety or productivity of others unacceptable—requiring a deceleration procedure because if continued response would materially interfere with the safety or well-being of others.	Contingent attention
		Token, point contingencies
		Schedule change—e.g., drh, ratio vs. interval, variable vs. fixed
Skills: Does the child have all requisite skills?		Use of high probability behavior
Tools: Does the child have all of the tools required by the response?		Shift in reinforcement from informational to material
		Negative reinforcement
Instructional Stimuli	Who?—designation of child or group.	Contingency contracts for:
Have the rules been made (a) explicit, (b) positive, (c) contingent, (d) reasonable, (e) feasible, (f) consistent, (g) few, and (h) fair?	Is to do what?—a response which is (a) positive (dead man test), (b) monitorable, (c) compatible with rules and other desirable behaviors, and (d) likely to occur under natural conditions.	individual responses
		group homogeneous responses
		group heterogeneous responses
		makkarenko—e.g., group reinforced for individual behavior or individual reinforced for group behavior
Potentiating Stimuli	How often per what unit?—e.g., time.	Shaping
Has access to the consequence been controlled?	To be measured how and by whom?—e.g., by self-monitoring form or peer signaling positive and negative responses.	Modeling, vicarious reinforcement
Has the gap between response and consequence been bridged?		Peer monitoring
Has the range of consequences been provided?	Under what conditions?—e.g., when academic work is in progress and alarm sounds.	Self-shaping
Have the consequences been scheduled so as not to conflict with desired responses?	And at what criterion level of frequency?— e.g. to what level should the response be	Change in physical environment
Has the child been exposed to the consequence with all of its detail, or has he sampled it directly himself?	(a) accelerated, (b) decelerated, (c) maintained, (d) fluctuated—include conditions; or (e) stabilized—include conditions.	*Deceleration Techniques*
		Time-out
		Negative practice
		Token, point loss
Discriminative Stimuli/Stimuli Delta		Negative attention (very problematic)
Has the positive response been associated with this positive consequence in the past?		Schedule change—e.g., drl, dro
Has the negative response not been associated with the positive consequence in the past?		Shift in reinforcement from material to informational
		Use of acceleration techniques such as contingency contracting, etc. Negative reinforcement (very problematic)

[5] The following people aided in the development of Table 1 and Appendix A and B: Kathleen Faller, Margaret Fleming, Robert Hill, James McCabe, James McGloin, Nan Meldrum, Susan Schwartz, and Marilyn Viccaro.

APPENDIX B.   *Classroom interaction assessment form.*

It is best if observational forms are designed individually to suit the idiographic demands of each experimental or therapeutic situation. The form which is presented here was designed for data collection for a project evaluating varying forms of token systems in the modification and maintenance of the behavior of individual children in elementary classrooms.

This form was designed to structure the observation of both a "target" or problematic child and one other randomly selected child whose activities took place in the vicinity of the target child. This follows the precedent set by Patterson, Shaw, and Ebner (1969) which yields data descriptive of both the target and approximations of the general behavioral environment in the classroom.

The first column headed "A" refers to the antecedent conditions which set the occasions for the child's behavior. The study for which this form was designed basically was interested in collecting data about teacher-pupil interaction, and therefore the principal categories of antecedent events pertain to teacher actions. One might, in another study, have been more concerned with peer interactions, the effect of program variables, or other events which might functionally set the occasion for specific behaviors.

The second column headed "B" refers to the child's behavior. This study was concerned with the general rates of appropriate ($+1, 2, 3$), inappropriate ($0\ 1, 2, 3$) and unacceptable ($-\ 1, 2, 3$) behaviors.

The observations were not restricted necessarily to the nine named-behaviors but rather these served as anchoring illustrations for coders. In this procedure, the recorded responses were those which occurred immediately following the elapsed time of fifteen seconds with no records being kept of intervening behaviors. Another study might wish to secure continuous behavioral records in place of the time-sampling procedure used in this study.

The third column headed "C" permits recording of the consequences of the student's behavior. All of the possible consequences are not noted: Rather provision has been made for recording only those consequences which are pertinent to the hypotheses of the present study. One special set of consequences was considered to be so important that provision was made for a fourth column headed "T" for the recording of therapeutic alternatives: Points could be given or removed from individuals or from groups contingent upon individual behavior. Accordingly four therapeutic events were stressed.

Once a behavior-assessment form has been designed it must, of course, be pretested. There is no alternative to multiple observations for determining the reliability of the form. There is no alternative to projecting data from the form in an effort to determine the validity of the form with respect to the objectives of a particular therapeutic or experimental activity.

| Date: | Time Started: | Time Stopped: | Minutes Observed: |

School: Grade: Activity: Observer:

Child's initials: Child's initials:

Teacher: Teacher:

	A	B	C	T
15				
45				
15				
45				
15				
45				
15				
45				
15				
45				
15				
45				
15				
45				
15				
45				
15				
45				
15				
45				
15				
45				
15				
45				
15				
45				
15				
45				
15				
45				
15				
45				
15				
45				
15				

Antecedents:

Teacher

  TC   command
  TQ   question
  T+   attention
  T−   attention
  0   other

Peer

  P+   attention
  P−   attention
  Ph   physical

Behaviors:

+1 _____

+2 _____

+3 _____

01 _____

02 _____

03 _____

−1 _____

−2 _____

−3 _____

Consequences:

Teacher

  No   no response
  A+   positive attention
  A−   negative attention
  P   praise
  D   disapproval
  C   compliance
  NC   non-compliance
  Ph+ positive physical
  Ph− negative physical
  0   other

Peer

  +   positive
  0   neutral/none
  −   negative

Therapeutic Consequences:

PI+ points individually given
PI− points individually removed
PG+ points group given
PG− points group removed
0   other

	A	B	C	T
30				
60				
30				
60				
30				
60				
30				
60				
30				
60				
30				
60				
30				
60				
30				
60				
30				
60				
30				
60				
30				
60				
30				
60				
30				
60				
30				
60				
30				
60				
30				
60				
30				

NEW PROGRAMS
OF BEHAVIORAL EDUCATION

11

2

IN THE EDUCATION OF INFANTS

Part II of this volume presents examples of the application of behavioral principles to various areas of education. Some of these areas are characterized by the ages of the students. Programs are described for the education of infants, preschoolers, elementary-school children, adolescents, college and university students, and adults. Programs are also described in the areas of special education, personal education, and education in nonschool community settings. Some characteristics of programs are peculiar to their mission. Infants, because of their helplessness, require unique physical-care procedures; adolescents, because of their unique subculture, benefit from certain reinforcement contingencies. However, programs in all areas use techniques that can be useful in other areas. The elementary-school teacher may find techniques developed in special or secondary education useful in dealing with the problem behaviors she encounters. Some of the techniques developed for education in nonschool settings may inspire classroom teachers. Anyone involved in education should benefit from the following descriptions of behavioral education.

The first area to be described is also the newest: the education of infants. Few programs for infants are available; those programs that do exist have had to develop their own curricula and even physical-care procedures. The first article, by Cataldo and Risley, discusses some techniques that might be used to meet infants' physical needs. They recommend a type of organization Risley has elsewhere called a "zone defense" (as opposed to a "man-to-man defense"). In zone defense, physical care is divided up by task rather than by child. A teacher, for example, is responsible for diapering all children rather than seeing that several children are fed, diapered, dressed, etc. Physical care is far more complicated and critical to the education of infants than to the education of any other age group. Cataldo and Risley correctly point out that without systematic, efficient procedures, the physical care of infants cannot be guaranteed.

The program described by Cataldo and Risley also takes data on its effects (Cataldo and Risley, 1972). For example, in order to be in full view of staff, sleeping cribs are placed in an open area. Since the surrounding activity could possibly rob infants of sleep, Cataldo and Risley measured the amount infants sleep in both closed and open areas. They found no difference. Also, one rationale for zone-defense physical-care procedures is that they give the staff free time to develop the infants' affective, cognitive, and motor skills. The assumption is that the more efficient the physical-care procedures, the more adults will be available for interaction with infants, and the more contact infants will have with adults. To check out this assumption, Cataldo and Risley collected data on the amount of adult-infant contact that occurred when between one and five adults were present in the play area, which ordinarily contained from twelve to fifteen infants. Surprisingly, they found that, as the number of adults in the play area increased, the percentage of their time spent interacting with the infants actually decreased. Apparently, left to themselves, the staff interacted with each other rather than the children. However, when specific activities were planned, the interaction between staff and children did increase as the number of staff increased. Apparently a high staff-to-student ratio, required by many states, can actually be detrimental to infants' care. The critical factor is a well-planned, structured program. Hopefully other insights will emerge from future data taken in the program described by Cataldo and Risley.

The second paper in this section describes a behavioral program for infants that has been operating for several years as part of the Kalamazoo Learning Village. The program includes physical-care procedures, behavioral objectives, and programs for teaching self-care, cognitive, affective, and motor skills. Eventually the Learning Village program hopes to follow children from the age of two or three months to the age at which they begin public school. By providing a structured behavioral-educational program during all the preschool years, the program hopes to help children develop without many of the behavioral deficits and inappropriate responses now encountered by public school and even by preschool teachers.

In American society, motherhood is notoriously sacrosanct. Especially during infancy, children are expected to spend all their time in the nuclear family. However, the nuclear family may not be the best possible environment for infants. As Stevenson and Fitzgerald (1971) have pointed out, the work of anthropologists has shown that, in many societies, children spend their time in large extended families or among unrelated community members. Indeed, in this country, the women's liberation movement has suggested that the sanctity of motherhood may be a myth designed to keep women out of the job market. Alternatives to the nuclear family deserve consideration.

Infant day care

M. F. CATALDO AND TODD R. RISLEY

Several factors, present and predicted, make new objectives in early childhood research imperative. Work-training programs, family economics, and feminine equality are producing an exponential rise in day-care centers for young children. The day-care center, unlike most intervention preschools, involves extensive periods of each child's life, including most of his waking hours. The paucity of knowledge of living environments and child-rearing practices appropriate to groups of children, the spectre of the bleak existence of children in most of the residential centers currently in existence in our society (those for retarded and disturbed children), and the massive destructive effects attributed to maternal and stimulus deprivation should warn us of the severe, potential danger involved when an increasing proportion of our nation's children are being reared in day-care centers.

To avoid this danger, we must conduct research to make explicit what is now usually implicit in good programs for young children. We must empirically examine how activities are organized, how materials are selected and presented, and how facilities are designed so that children may be better served in group-care situations.

Too often we have tended to talk about learning and teaching activities in a preschool as if the children were sitting on a shelf, to be taken down at our convenience and "taught." In reality, of course, the formal teaching activities we described are a very small part of a preschool program, and the children spend more time in, and can be more influenced by, the activities which we consider mere "fillers."

Basic to the operation of most preschools is the assumption that in play, when a child concentrates upon a particular object or event for a period of time, he gains skill and understanding. Preschool teachers are therefore trained to provide, display, and regulate the use of a wide variety of materials and activities in such a way as to maximize the probability of the child's prolonged engagement with them during play.

Although the objectives of this training are unformalized in the preschool literature, the actual practice of most preschools provides the outlines of a technology for maintaining a living environment which will engage groups of children in constructive activities. At the Juniper Gardens Children's Project, we have been active in developing convenient and reliable procedures for measuring the engagement of groups of preschool-aged children with materials, people, and events throughout the day in a day-care center. We are using this measure to study the effects of various schedules, routines, activities, types of materials, and methods of displaying and presenting materials. We continue to find that our objective data usually confirm the effectiveness of the techniques which most preschool teachers are trained to use. We have also done extensive work on how the materials and events in the free-play periods of a well-organized preschool can be used to teach particular pre-academic skills (Risley, 1968; Jacobson, Bushell, and Risley, 1969), and a variety of language skills (Reynolds and Risley, 1968; Hart and Risley, 1968; Risley and Hart, 1968; Risley, Reynolds, and Hart, 1970; Risley, Hart, and Doke, 1971; Hart and Risley, in press). Thus, we are rapidly proceeding with our program to empirically examine and formalize existing preschool technology for maintaining a living environment for groups of toddlers and preschool-age children and to develop procedures to use such living environments to teach pre-academic skills.

There exists no comparable technology, however, for maintaining a living environ-

Reprinted by permission of the authors.

This is one of a series of projects conducted by the Living Environments Group at the University of Kansas under the direction of Todd R. Risley. This program is supported in part by grants from the U.S. Office of Education to the National Program on Early Childhood Education and to the University of Kansas' Kansas Center for Research on Early Childhood Education.

ment for groups of infants. We must develop that technology. We must develop the same sort of "flexible routines" and repertoires of materials and activities for infants that we have for preschoolers.

Fortunately, our procedures for measuring children's engagement with their environment need only minor adjustment to be applied to infants. Such measures enable us to examine a variety of devices for infant care, such as a bathing-diapering device and low, lightweight baby barriers, the position of cribs in the room, the placement of the infant (on front or back) in the crib, the type and variety of crib toys, and the other objects and events which are normally associated with a solicitous and attentive mother's care of her infant. Our goal is to maximize the proportion of each infant's waking hours which he spends attending to and manipulating his physical and social environment.

To this end, the Living Environments Group at the University of Kansas is conducting an Infant Day-Care Center. The Center was established in 1970 and provides care for up to nine hours each day, Monday through Friday, for children four weeks to twelve months of age. The Infant Center is based on a model of day care for up to twenty infants with the equivalent of five full-time staff members. Through the operation of the Infant Center, we have made a beginning; we have developed routines and materials that are efficient for the staff and enable increased time for adult-child interaction.

Design of Environments for Infants

In addition to feeding and health care, we must have special concern for time spent in interaction and playing with the infants. Previous research (LeLaurin and Risley, 1972; Doke and Risley, 1972) has shown that children are more profitably engaged with their environment when staff responsible for the care of children are assigned to specific areas of the environment rather than to specific children. Accordingly, the Infant Center was designed so that the total space was

divided into activity areas for receiving/departing, diapering, sleep, feeding, and play. Staff members are assigned individually to the feeding area, the diapering area, and the play area. The sleep area does not require the constant supervision of a full-time staff member because the physical design of the Center permits this area to be monitored from any point in the Center. The supervisor manages the receiving/departing area as well as oversees the operation of all other areas. This arrangement allows all staff members to interact with children in the large play area when not actually needed in their own area.

Each of these activity areas, although discrete in function, is separated from the others only by low, easy-to-step-over barriers. Thus the Infant Center is actually one large open space, not a series of separate rooms. The

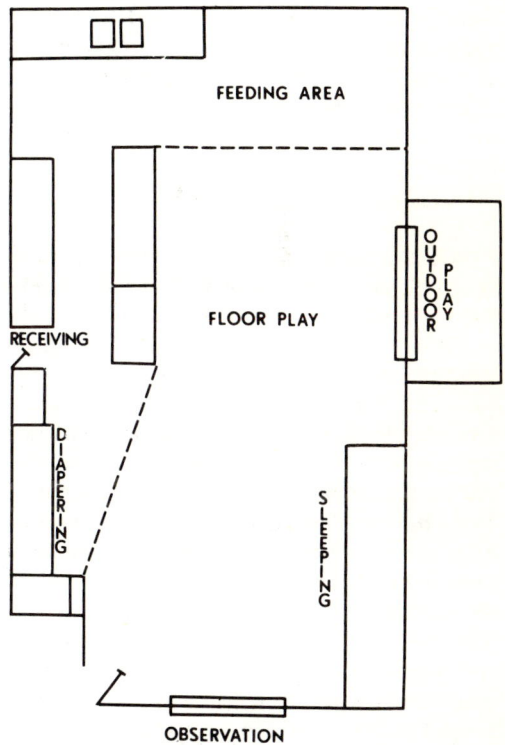

Figure 1. *Floor plan of infant day-care center.*

open environment of the Infant Center facilitates the transfer of responsibilities and permits continual monitoring of all activity areas. Because there are no walls, every child is always visible to every staff member.

The open arrangement of the Infant Center and the assignment of staff duties by areas means it is possible for up to twenty infants to be cared for by the equivalent of a full-time staff of five. At some times during the day, for example when a number of infants must be fed at once, more staff members are needed than at other times, such as when six or seven children are asleep. The Infant Center has therefore utilized several part-time staff members along with a supervisor and two other full-time staff members.

The organization of the Infant Center is also based on individualized care for each child. Each day, parents provide schedules and information about the care of their child for the day. Individualized scheduling also affects the physical arrangement of the Infant Center; because infants tend to eat and sleep at different times during the day, as few as eight to ten cribs and four to five feeding chairs will suffice for up to twenty infants.

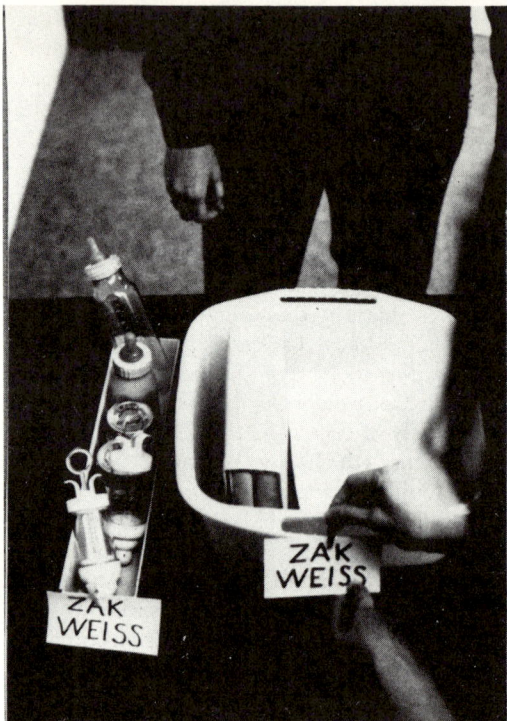

Figure 2. *Food trays and diaper bins are used at the Receiving Area to facilitate the transfer of the child's belongings.*

Receiving/Departing Area

When infants are involved, even outwardly simple activities, if not well organized, can take a good deal of both the child's and the staff's time. Upon arrival in the morning, for example, not only the child but all his supplies for the day including diapers, extra clothing, food, bibs, medicines, powders, and ointments must be transferred from the parent to the center and must be kept separate from the supplies of other infants. Additionally, the center must receive the instructions and information from the parent necessary to provide the high level of individualized care which denotes quality infant care. At the receiving area the child must also be given a quick health check and then must be moved safely into the appropriate activity area. Again at the end of the day all the child's belongings and information about his day must accompany the child's return to the parents.

At the Infant Center efficient staff routines and the physical design of the receiving/departing area allow all necessary materials and information to be transferred quickly and easily. As with all the activity areas in the open environment of the Infant Center, the receiving/departing area is visible throughout the center, yet arriving parents never enter the center proper and therefore do not disrupt any other areas. The supervisor greets parents on their arrival, transfers the child, usually to the play area, and records the arrival time. Meanwhile, parents place the child's diapers and clothing in a diaper bin and his food in a food tray. Both the diaper bin and food tray are labeled with the child's name for quick, sure identification. Parents also fill out a daily data sheet with the child's feeding and sleeping schedule and special instructions, if any. The location of the area, between the feeding and diapering areas, makes it convenient to transfer the child's supplies to the appropriate area. Thus in the process of receiving the child and his belongings, the Infant Center has carefully organized all supplies and information from the parents, insuring that the child will receive appropriate individualized care for the rest of the day.

Before each child leaves, the supervisor gathers his belongings, returns them to the parent's diaper bag, and checks to be sure all the child's activities have been recorded on the parent's data sheet. When parents arrive, the supervisor is able to discuss the child's day, make suggestions for schedule changes, or share a new achievement or favorite toy with the parents.

Diapering Area

It is easy enough for a parent caring for her child at home to be sure her child's diaper is changed often during the day. When dealing with fifteen or twenty infants, however, each of whom may need a diaper change six to eight times a day, it is clear that a specific diaper-checking procedure is necessary. After experimentation with a variety of time-interval checking procedures, it has been found that checking each child's diaper each time he moves from one Infant Center activity area to another is a more efficient method. In addition, to be sure, children who have not changed areas for a while are not overlooked; once each hour the diapering-area manager checks the diapers of all infants who have not been changed in the past hour.

The mechanics of diapering fifteen to twenty children six to eight times a day can also be a problem if efficient staff routines are not employed. The safety of the child demands that he never be left unattended in the diapering area. Therefore, a routine which allows the diapering-area manager to keep one hand on the child at all times is necessary. At the Infant Center first the child's supplies are set out from his diaper bin and placed on the diapering table within easy reach. Then the child is brought to the area, cleaned, and changed. The child is returned to another area before his supplies are put away and the area is cleaned.

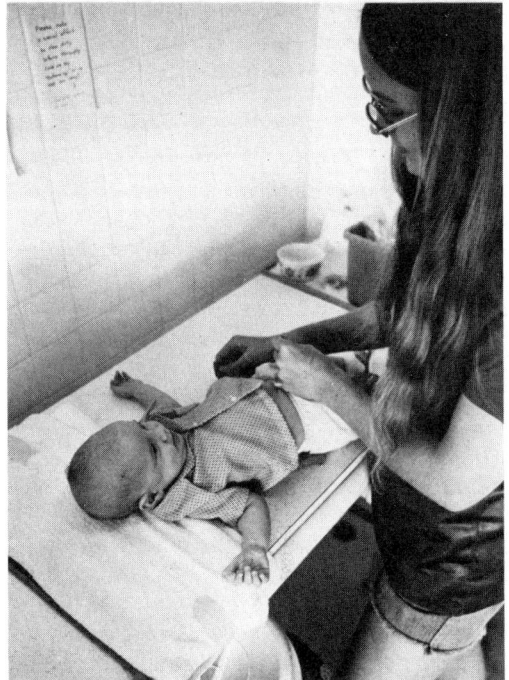

Figure 3. *Children are diapered on a specially designed table secured in a bathtub and which can be used for both changing and bathing the child.*

Routine health care in an all-day child-care facility often includes bathing the children. Here, as with diapering, the safety of the child is of paramount importance, along with materials and routines that increase staff efficiency. The specially designed diapering-bathing table in use at the Infant Center promotes both safety and efficiency. The table is attached in a bathtub and cradles the infant being bathed in a net hammock. With the use of a telephone-type shower extension, a child can be bathed quickly and easily, and the staff member need not fear losing her grip on a soapy, slippery child. When not in use for bathing, the table has a solid surface that closes over the net hammock.

Sleep Area

Naps are an essential component of an infant's day. However, individual children's sleep patterns vary. Therefore, while infant day-care environments must provide a sleep area, it is not necessary to have a separate crib for each child, for all children will never be asleep at one time.

By the use of parents' suggested nap times and the children's individual indicators (i.e., rubbing face, lying down in the play area, etc.), it can be determined that a child is ready for a nap before he reaches the fussy, disruptive behavior stage.

The sleep area at the Infant Center is part of the open environment; that is, the cribs are not physically or visually separated from the rest of the center. Cribs are raised to adult eye level and sides are of see-through nylon mesh, making it easy for all staff members to see the children in cribs. This easy visibility greatly reduces the amount of time an awake child spends in the relatively isolated environment of a crib.

Because children at the Infant Center are kept on their individual schedules, it is not necessary to provide a crib for each child. As few as ten cribs are sufficient for a center occupied by twenty infants. This not only increases the economic feasibility of infant day care, but facilitates the arrangement of space to provide a maximum area for play.

Feeding Area

In a group of twenty infants, it is likely that no two will have the same schedule for feedings. A very important aspect of infant day care, therefore, is organizing feeding so that each infant is fed the appropriate amount and kinds of food at the appropriate times. From information provided by parents, a master feeding schedule can be prepared and displayed so the feeding-area manager can easily determine when children need to be fed. To ensure the safety of the child, he is never left unattended in the feeding area. When the feeding-area manager notes that a particular child's mealtime is approaching, she prepares his food and arranges his bib and other necessary items before bringing the child to the area. After the child is fed, burped, and played with, he is returned to another area before his equipment and the area are cleaned.

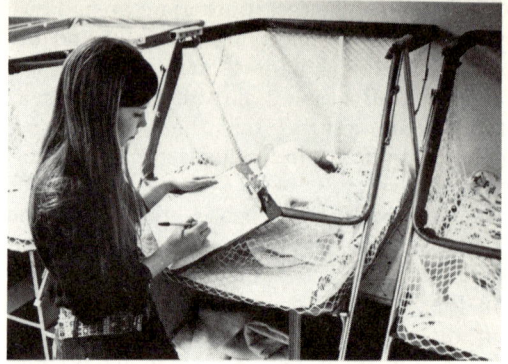

Figure 4. Cribs are see-through netting, with a collapsible side, and are secured on shelves at adult height.

How children are fed (i.e., held or seated in a chair) is an issue that requires additional investigation. In a group situation it is obvious that holding children will require a great deal of staff time for each child. For an infant center then, an economical procedure is to feed children while they are seated in small groups. However, holding is often considered a preferable method, at least for young children. The effects on children's eating behavior while being held vs. being seated should be investigated.

Another area about which little is known is the type of feeding chair that is most suitable for developing infants. The Infant

Figure 5. The Feeding Area is designed for meeting children's individual feeding schedules.

Center presently has a variety of feeding chairs in use—infant seats, high chairs, and low walker-chairs—and has developed plans for a group-feeding table. Study is required to determine the most efficient and effective type of feeding chair for infants.

Play Area

Not much is known of appropriate play materials and activities for very young children. As part of the Infant Center project, efforts are being made to evaluate the children's interaction with the toys available to them. Often toys which appeal to adults and which are being marketed as appropriate toys for infants are not attractive to the children. Sometimes toys designed for older children are preferred over "infant" toys. For very young infants it is possible to create manipulative crib toys by combining mobiles and other toys presently available separately. Children at the Infant Center who are crawling or beginning to walk have a large selection of toys available to them, displayed on low shelves around the play area.

Cleanliness and safety of the play area are important considerations. The Infant Center's play area is simply a large expanse of carpeted floor space. The carpet is frequently sanitized, and hospital slippers are worn in the Center. Toys are washed in an antiseptic solution after each child uses them.

Older infants who are crawling or walking often fall over younger children who cannot move out of the way. A special area for the younger ones not only protects all children but increases the possibility of the younger infants' interaction with play materials by providing toys they can easily reach and that cannot be pushed out of range.

The design of the Infant Center and its staff assignments were intended primarily to free staff members from spending all their time in routine chores so they could spend more time interacting with children in the play area. It has been found that more appropriate use is made of this time when the staff are expected to contribute to scheduled and planned play activities.

Recording Procedures

During each day the child's activities in each area are recorded, and the times the child eats, sleeps, and is diapered are noted and returned to the parents at the end of the day.

These recording procedures serve a number of purposes. They provide parents with an accurate record of their child's activities and behavior each day. They provide a normative reference of the average length of time each activity takes as well as a baseline against which to compare later manipulations in day-care procedures. In addition, this data can be used to guide others using this model in evaluating the effectiveness with which they carry out the procedures.

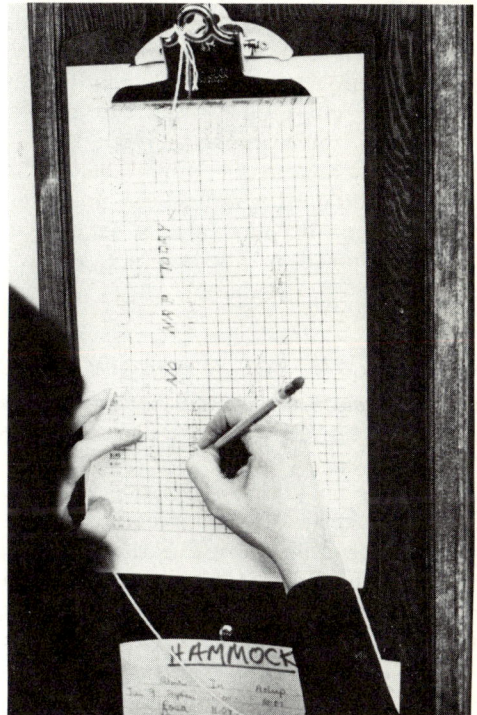

Figure 6. *The prominent display of area duties and the use of reliable recording procedures are employed to insure the standards for care at the center.*

Summary

It is clear that caring for infants in groups is not the same as caring for them at home. The Infant Center has demonstrated that it is possible to develop efficient care routines for groups of infants and has also shown that the efficiency of these routines is heavily dependent upon the proper arrangement of adequate facilities. Happily, the results to date indicate that the proper use of facilities and routines makes needed quality infant care possible and economically feasible. Finally, from the development of infant-care routines and reliable measurement procedures, a technology of infant day care can be prepared in a form that can be used effectively by other centers.

The Infant Center is a start toward the development of a technology of infant group care; it has produced a set of staff routines and definite procedures, measurement devices, recording forms, and ideas for the more effective and efficient arrangement of the infant-care environment. Currently in the preparation and testing stages are training materials on the planning and operation of each activity area in the Infant Center that relatively untrained personnel can utilize, ensuring that quality day care for infants can be a widespread reality and not a rarity.

Future plans include development of additional equipment more adequate for group care than traditional types, more precise play routines and toy evaluation, and an overall measurement system to evaluate the major components of the system.

The Infant Center has considered the development of a technology for a program of group infant day care. Behavior modification, on the other hand, while having been shown to be successful in the control of human behavior in numerous areas (education, training, remediation of undesired behavior, etc.), has been shown to be successful in these areas when implemented within the framework of an already existing program (classroom, workshop, MR institution, etc.). This becomes clear when dealing with a population with which we have not worked before and for which there is little in the way of a formal program or specification of activities or behaviors to engage in. Thus, with infants we have found it necessary to consider not techniques for the modification of infant behavior toward specific criteria, but as an initial step the development of a technology for a program to provide and maintain acceptable group infant care. It is, then, in such a program that specific curricula and developmental and remedial techniques can be implemented.

An educational day-care program for infants

D. B. SPATES, G. J. ALESSI, A. GUTMANN, S. ELLSWORTH, K. L. MUELLER, AND R. E. ULRICH[1]

The educational day-care program for infants at the Kalamazoo Learning Village began as an effort to focus on prevention in education. In 1966, a group of psychologists in Kalamazoo, Michigan, began working in preschool and elementary school education. They worked as consultants in the public schools and began their own preschool program (Ulrich, Wolfe, and Bluhm, 1968; Ulrich, Surratt, and Wolfe, 1969; Ulrich, Wolfe, and Cole, 1970). They noticed that teachers and psychologists in the public schools centered much of their attention on

problems: children who could not read, hyperactive children, and classroom nuisances

Reprinted by permission.

1 Over the past several years, many people have contributed to the success of the Learning Village infant program. Names that immediately come to mind are Joe Auffrey, Ruth Auffrey, Kathy Bowen, Jan Brown, Anton Colosacco, Judy Donovan, Jonathan Hinde, Madelon Lewis, Dan Mandel, Lynne Peters, Bob Pierce, Martha Potter, Jim Scherrer, Duane Shields, Carol Siep, Bruce Williams, Kathy Williams, Mary Williams, and Mary Ann Zender. Presently working in the program are Fran Zimmerman, Susy Stein, Lilly Anderson, Emmy Donaldson, Boyce McDole, Ted Williams, Diana Wedig, and Dorathy Marine, who directs the program.

such as being out-of-seat and talking out. Even at the preschool level, teachers spent too much of their time dealing with problems. Children would come to the preschool who had had virtually no contact with other children. They, in essence, had to be socialized before they could be taught anything. Others had adopted aggression as a major way of dealing with people; the aggressive behavior had to be reduced. Still others didn't seem to have the attention span or basic cognitive skills needed to begin instruction. As the preschool teachers faced these problems, they continually wished they had been able to work with the children earlier in their lives.

When the Learning Village (Ulrich, Louisell, and Wolfe, 1971) was established as an outgrowth of these efforts, its founders wanted to include an infant program. They encountered enormous difficulties in obtaining a license (Wolfe, Ulrich, and Ulrich, 1970). The Michigan Department of Social Services was not sympathetic to the idea of taking infants out of the nuclear family. Work in orphanages (Bowlby, 1953) and homes for unwed mothers (Spitz and Cobliner, 1965) suggested that group care can slow the development of infants and cause permanent affective damage. In addition, the founders were behavior modifiers and looked at developmental processes differently than the social workers who controlled licensing. Furthermore, the founders weren't advocating the program simply as an unpleasant necessity for working mothers. They believed that a well-designed group care situation would be *preferable* to the usual home care situation.

Eventually, however, in 1969, a license was granted that allowed children to begin at the Learning Village as young as two months of age. Soon after licensing, the staff found themselves with responsibility for the care of fifteen children between two months and two years of age. They had few resources; nothing existed at the time that would serve as a curriculum. Procedures had to be worked out for caring for the children physically, for teaching skills, and for fostering the normal progression of development. Since that time, various staff members have developed procedures and objectives. Their use has varied from time to time; they have seldom been functioning perfectly all at once. However, they hopefully will provide useful ideas and information for others hoping to work with infants in a day-care setting.[2]

PHYSICAL CARE PROCEDURES, ESPECIALLY FOR YOUNG INFANTS

As LeLaurin and Risley (1971) have emphasized, physical care is critical to the success of an infant program. Physical well-being seems to dominate the lives of young infants, and they are totally dependent on adults for that care. The main areas of concern are in feeding the infant, in keeping him clean, and in seeing that he gets the right amount of sleep.

Feeding

For each infant, a daily chart is kept. The basic chart is shown in Figure 1. When the mother brings a young infant to school, she is asked when he last ate. The staff then has an idea of when the next feeding should occur. Infants are fed more or less on demand, although an attempt is made to establish a schedule comfortable for the infant. Baby food is supplied by the program, but, until the baby drinks whole milk, the parents supply formula and bottles. Parents generally let the staff know when the baby begins eating solids, although staff do suggest to the parents that cereal should be started at two months and vegetables and fruit soon thereafter. Pediatricians seem to feel that early introduction of solids helps later eating habits become more flexible, which is understandable from a behavioral viewpoint. Finger foods and other table foods also are added in consultation with the parents. Until an infant learns to feed himself, an individual staff member remains responsible for his

2 The Learning Village infant program is also described in a film entitled, "One Step at a Time," published by CRM Films, Del Mar, California.

Child's Name _____

Special Instructions: _____

All-day behavior pinpoint to count: _____

Date: _____

Year _____ Month _____ Day _____

#	Specific Room and/or Event Change	Time Start	Time Stop	specific pinpoint(s) verb -- object	# counts	Staff Init.	Toilet Train.	Staff Init.
1.	Arrived	9:00				SS	9:10 / WET	SS
2.	Playroom	9:00	10:00	worked on standing up. 9:45 Bottle.		SS	10:00 / WET + SOILED	ED
3.	Nap	10:00	11:30			ED	11:30 / WET	ED
4.	Lunch	11:30	11:50	½ jar Beef ½ jar Sweet Pot. ½ jar Applesauce 11:50 Bottle		SS	12:45 / WET	SS
5.	Playroom	11:50	2:00	worked on playing w/another child. practiced walking in a walker.		ED	2:00 / WET	ED
6.	Nap	2:00	3:00			ED	3:05 / SOILED WET	ED
7.	Home	3:10						
8.								
9.								
10.								

Figure 1. Daily record chart kept for an eight-month-old child enrolled in the Learning Village infant program. Feedings, naps, eliminations, and activities are recorded.

feeding. That staff member becomes familiar with the baby's usual eating habits and his current progress in self-feeding.

Keeping Clean

Each staff member is also responsible for diapering certain children (not necessarily the same children that they feed). Diapering and the type of elimination are recorded on the daily record sheet. Having a certain person diaper a child is particularly helpful when the child begins toilet training, since that teacher is familiar with the child's habits.

Sleeping

In the morning, parents of young infants are asked when the child last slept. That information, combined with the child's behavior, helps the staff decide when the babies should be put in their cribs for naps. Naps, like feedings and diaperings, are recorded on the record sheet.

In general, the physical care procedures work quite well. Occasionally some confusion arises from the multiple caretaker situation. On the other hand, some of the staff have had extensive experience in taking care of infants; they are certainly more expert than most first-time parents. Overall, the physical care received by infants at the Learning Village is probably similar to the care received by infants in most large families.

OBJECTIVES OF THE PROGRAM

The program, of course, has many intangible objectives. Hopefully the children will be happy, outgoing, spontaneous, uninhibited, irrepressible, conscientious, creative, and loving. The more tangible objectives for the program have been derived from two sources. One is the list of prerequisite behaviors drawn up by the nursery program to which the children will "graduate" when they are about two and one-half years old. The second is a more detailed list of objectives gleaned from the developmental literature.

Prerequisites for the Nursery Program

The nursery program at the Learning Village has listed some behaviors it considers necessary for entrance into that program. The behaviors fall into four areas: self-care skills, motor skills, social skills, and language skills. The requirements are not rigid; they serve as goals for the infant program and as a guide for placement of incoming children. The list of prerequisites is as follows:

I. Self-Care Skills
    A. Toilet Skills—Child should be able to exhibit control over excretory functions by:
        1. Informing a teacher that he needs to "go to the bathroom" (with prompt, if necessary).
        2. Traveling to and from bathroom unaccompanied.
        3. Eliminating in the toilet.
    B. Dressing Skills—Child should attempt, with assistance, to put on or remove any article of clothing.
    C. Washing Skills—Child should be able to wet hands and face, apply soap to hands, then dry.
    D. Eating Skills—Child should be able to eat with a spoon and drink from a cup.

II. Motor Skills
    A. Child should be able to walk unassisted, including up and down stairs.
    B. Child should be able to run a distance of fifty feet without falling in an area free from obstructions.
    C. Child should be able to sit in a child-size chair with both feet on the floor for a period of five minutes.
    D. Child should be able to lie down on a cot in a naptime environment for a period of one hour.
    E. Child should be able to pick up a penny with his fingers from the floor.
    F. Child should be able to grasp a cup and a spoon with his hands.
    G. Child should be able to hold a pen-

cil or a crayon and make random marks on paper with either.

H. Child should be able to remove and replace lightweight objects from surfaces within reach of the child's arms.

III. Social Skills
A. Basic Play Skills
1. Child should be able to play in a cooperative manner with other children as defined by the following behaviors:
   a) Child should demonstrate ability to share by allowing other children access to objects or activities with which he is involved (with prompt, if necessary).
   b) Child should demonstrate ability to play in a nonaggressive manner, i.e., without hitting, biting, pushing, kicking, etc. (with prompt, if necessary).
2. Child should be able to select and replace playthings (with prompt, if necessary).
3. Child should be able to select and play with a variety of toys.
4. Child should be able to play with toys, etc., in a nondestructive manner.
B. Interactions
1. Child-Child Interactions
   a) Child should be able to communicate desires to other children (nonverbally or in semi-sentence form).
   b) Child should engage in playroom activities with other children (with prompt, if necessary).
   c) Child should be able to aid another child in a task (with prompt, if necessary).
2. Child-Adult Interactions
   a) Child should engage in activities with an adult (games, etc.).
   b) Child should be able to ex-change verbalizations with an adult.
   c) Child should be able to make desires known to an adult in a verbal or nonverbal manner.
   d) Child should aid an adult in task when prompted.
   e) Child should be able to respond correctly to simple directions from an adult.
C. Self-Control
1. Child should be able to maintain a level of noise in verbalizations appropriate to the condition.
2. Child should exhibit an absence of unprovoked, spontaneous, aggressive behaviors (i.e., aggression occurring without observable provocation).
3. Child should be able to be subjected to situations where access to an "attractive object" (attractive to that child) is denied temporarily without "tantrumming," crying, etc.

IV. Language Skills
A. Child should be able to verbally construct simple sentences with prompt.
B. Child should be able to state own first name when asked.
C. Child should be able to meet verbal criteria as stated in previous objectives.

Developmental Objectives

More detailed objectives were written by searching the developmental literature. Although other sources were surveyed, the principal sources used were Cattel (1940), the Vineland Social Maturity Scale (Doll, 1965), and the Preschool Attainment Record (Doll, 1966). Objectives were listed separately for cognitive, affective, and motor skills, although these areas overlap considerably.

Cognitive skills include verbal behavior and basic conceptual behavior. Some examples are:

The child should be able to vocally make crowing sounds and laugh (12 weeks).

The child should be able to follow a ball two inches in diameter rolling across a table (16 weeks).

The child should be able to vocally imitate sounds made by an adult, e.g., ba, ga, a (28 weeks).

The child should be able to attain a toy that is under a cup by removing the cup (47 weeks).

The child should be able to recognize the parts of a doll by pointing to the part when named by instructor, e.g., arms, legs, head, eyes, nose, mouth, ears, feet, hands, hair (78 weeks).

Given seven objects the child encounters frequently in the environment, the child should be able to verbally identify two of them (96 weeks).

The child should be able to match familiar objects by color, shape, size, and thickness (104 weeks).

Affective skills include those behaviors that indicate an awareness of self and others, affection towards self and others, happiness, creativity, and independence. Some examples are:

The child should be able to indicate that he recognizes a person he encounters frequently in the environment by smiling in that individual's presence, extending his arms toward the individual as he approaches, and not crying in the individual's presence (16 weeks).

The child should be able to pat and smile at his reflection in a mirror (30 weeks).

The child should be able to wave bye-bye upon request (39 weeks).

The child should be able to drink from a cup or glass unassisted (73 weeks).

The child should be able to scribble, given a crayon or pencil and a piece of paper (78 weeks).

The child should be able to approach an adult or peer he encounters frequently and hug him (130 weeks).

Motor skills include both gross and fine motor skills. Some examples are:

The child should be able to grasp a rattle that is placed on his chest (16 weeks).

The child should be able to grasp an 8½×11" sheet of paper and tear it (30 weeks).

The child should be able to stand unassisted (52 weeks).

The child should be able to remove a ¼-inch peg from a hole and replace it (60 weeks).

A child should be able to draw a circle, given a picture of a circle from which to copy (156 weeks).

These objectives represent what developmental psychologists have considered normal development. The goal of the infant program is that every child, *minimally*, should develop normally and perform at age level.

BASIC INSTRUCTIONAL PROCEDURES

The instructional procedures used in the infant program consist principally of the reinforcement of successive approximations. Reinforcement is usually social or edible. Children can be praised, hugged, or given a piece of sugar-coated cereal. The reinforcement is tailored to the individual child. Some children don't care about edible reinforcers, although most do. Some prefer certain kinds of social reinforcers to others, and the reinforcers must be adjusted to their preferences.

The behaviors that are reinforced sometimes occur "spontaneously." Young infants, in particular, seem to be under strong developmental control—they continually try to make sounds, locomote, and manipulate objects. Reinforcement of these spontaneous behaviors enhances them. In some cases the child is physically led through the behavior, as a prompt, then reinforced. He may be "walked" by an adult holding on to his hands; his spoon may be guided to his mouth; the puzzle piece may be guided to the correct slot. In still other cases, behavior is evoked by modeling. Speech and motor skills such as hand-clapping are taught through imitation of models.

In this paper, instructional procedures are sometimes loosely described as "encouraging the child to...." "Encourage" simply means "use reinforcement of successive approximations appropriate to the individual child." Other vague terms can be similarly translated.

SELF-CARE PROGRAMS FOR OLDER INFANTS

Programs have been worked out for teaching infants to rely increasingly on themselves to meet their own physical needs. In general, self-care skills are taught at the earliest possible age. Learning these skills gives a child a feeling of self-confidence and also lessens the discomforts inherent in waiting for others to attend to his physical needs. The skills, however, are not pushed on a child but rather taught when he is developmentally ready. Positive reinforcement is used to shape and maintain them.

Toilet Training

Toilet training is begun when a child has gained enough control of his bladder to remain dry a substantial amount of the time. Much attention and praise are given to a child when he starts wearing training pants at the beginning of the training procedure. For the sake of consistency, one staff member trains a particular child. She checks the child for dryness at intervals she feels are appropriate to the child's bladder control. (The intervals range in length from ten to thirty minutes.) If the child is dry, he is given a reinforcer and asked if he wants to "go potty." If he then uses the toilet, he is given another reinforcer and praised. Later, reinforcers are faded. Reinforcers are selected according to the individual child. One little

girl liked having her hair in pigtails and also liked potato chips. When she was dry, her hair was either put up in pigtails or left in pigtails; if she used the toilet, she received a potato chip. Eventually the potato chips given to her after using the toilet were faded and finally the pigtails for being dry.

Self-feeding

When they are able to sit unassisted during feeding, the children are encouraged to use their fingers to feed themselves. They are also allowed and encouraged to play with spoons. As their coordination improves, the teachers physically help them fill their spoons and carry them to their mouths. The assistance is then gradually faded. Help with putting the food into the mouth is the first to go, and loading the food on the spoon is the last. Putting the food on the spoon seems to be the most difficult part of self-feeding.

After self-feeding is established, the child eats at the table with the older children and is reminded to use his spoon. His plate is quietly removed for a short time (say, ten seconds) if he plays excessively in his food. If a spill occurs, the child helps clean it up. After eating, each child throws the remains of his own lunch in the garbage.

Self-dressing

Initially, children are encouraged to do the easiest parts of self-dressing themselves. Even babies as young as nine or ten months of age can help push their arms into shirts and can lift their legs to help in putting on pants. These initial movements are expanded until the staff member helps only with the most difficult parts of self-dressing: getting the first arm out of the sleeve or the last arm in, getting in and out of tight clothes, working difficult fasteners. The staff help the children to learn to work fasteners by partially zipping zippers and letting the child finish, by putting buttons half-way through and letting the child push them the rest of the way, and so forth. For practice, toys are available that button, snap, zip, tie, and hook.

Napping

The older infants (twelve to thirty months) all nap on separate cots, in the same room, from about 12:30 to 2:30 P.M. When a child moves from his crib to a cot or when an older infant enters the program, he is shaped to lie down at the beginning of naptime and remain quiet. First the child is asked to get on his cot and then is praised and/or given a small edible reinforcer when he complies. Next, he is asked to lie down and reinforced when he complies (if he does not comply, the teacher lays him down and then reinforces him). The teacher then rubs the child's back and tells him that his back is being rubbed because he is lying quietly. If the child fusses, the teacher ignores him as much as possible and again begins to rub his back as he quiets down. Edibles and reinforcement of intermediate steps are later faded, but back-rubbing remains a permanent part of naptime routine. As children get on their cots and lie quietly, the teachers come by and rub their backs.

Hand-washing

Each of the steps involved in hand-washing is added in turn. First the teacher washes the child's hands but asks him to turn off the water. Then the child turns off the water and dries his hands. Next the child rinses his hands, turns off the water, and dries his hands. Then he soaps his hands, rinses, turns off the water, and dries his hands, and so forth.

PROGRAMS TO MEET OBJECTIVES IN COGNITIVE, AFFECTIVE, AND MOTOR AREAS

From time to time teachers have developed methods of teaching the cognitive, affective, and motor objectives gleaned from the developmental literature. Some of these programs are described below. In addition, exercises from two excellent books are used. These "textbooks" are *Teach Your Baby* (Painter, 1971) and *Baby Learning Through Baby Play* (Gordon, 1970).

Cognitive Skills

Cognitive skills can be roughly divided into language and conceptual skills. For both kinds of lessons the child's attention span must be developed. As lessons progress, children are reinforced for sitting quietly, attending, and responding appropriately; the length of lessons is gradually increased from five to twenty minutes. Lessons are usually given on a one-to-one basis, although a teacher will teach two or several children if the staff-to-student ratio or progress of the children demands it. Depending on available personnel, lessons are given in a scheduled fashion or at the discretion of the teacher.

Language. Some important bases of language learning are vocal play and exploration and imitation of environmental models. Through vocal exploration, as in crying and wailing, young babies discover articulatory movements of the lips, jaws, and tongue and the breathing patterns used in speech. Through vocal play, they discover simple phonemic and syllabic vocal productions such as /a/, /ma/, /pa/, /dæ/, and /ga/. Through modeling, teachers encourage infants to imitate motor responses, such as head-turning and arm-waving, and simple vocal productions. As the children progress, responses presented for imitation become more and more complex; they involve sequences of motor responses, words, sentences, and songs.

Object identification is another area that contributes to language development. The teacher, first using objects in the environment and later pictures on SRA object identification cards, points to an object and says, "This is a ball—point to the ball." She then helps the child point to the ball if he does not do so by himself. Later she teaches the child to pick out a named object from an array of two or three objects. Still later the teacher will say, "This is a ball—say it," at which time the child is expected to say "ball," "a ball," ". . . is a ball," and "This is a ball," through a backward chaining procedure. Finally the teacher encourages the child to make statements about items.

Of course, language is also developed outside of the lesson periods, for expressive development of concepts essential to the syntactical structure of language. During lunch, the children are encouraged to say, "Bread, please," or "Milk, please," and so forth. Teachers converse with children as they play and ask them to name or make statements about the objects they play with.

Concept Learning. Many of the exercises in *Teach Your Baby* (Painter, 1971) and *Baby Learning Through Baby Play* (Gordon, 1970) are designed to teach concepts. Painter suggests teaching spatial relationships to six-month-olds by first putting a toy close to the baby and then moving it farther away. Gordon suggests a problem-solving game in which a toy is placed out of reach but on a blanket; by pulling the blanket the child gains access to the toy. Painter and Gordon both point out that toys are useful in teaching many concepts such as comparative size, same and different, color, categorization, and polarity. Toys that make noises when manipulated teach cause and effect relationships.

A Fit-A-Shape set is sometimes used to teach shapes, colors, and sizes and to build perceptual-motor skills. It contains rectangular rubber molds of different colors with a small, medium, and large shape cut in each of them, making spaces and shapes that fit into the spaces. The children are taught to select the correct shape and put it in the correct space. Later they are taught to name and identify the color of the shapes as they fit them in place. In addition, the children are taught to count to ten by first counting to three, then four, etc. They are also taught the concept of one-to-one correspondence by making sets that match the teacher's.

Affective Behavior

Affective skills include behaviors that indicate independence, a positive self-image, self-awareness, positive interpersonal relations, and creativity. Learning the self-care skills described earlier is an important part of gaining a sense of independence, competence, and self-awareness. Self-awareness also is taught by encouraging children to look at themselves in a mirror and later by teaching

them the names of body parts. Until they are eighteen to twenty-four months of age, infants ordinarily do not interact with their peers to a great extent. Affectionate interaction is encouraged by reinforcing a moderate amount of kissing and hugging. (Some children become "kissing freaks.") Teachers sometimes reinforce children with edibles for playing "catch," "ring around the rosie," or other simple games in small groups. The infants are also praised when they share and take turns.

Grabbing toys is a frequent behavior among infants; it is consequated with response cost. Aggression is consequated with time-out. Some children, when they are learning to talk, have trouble substituting words for crying when they need help. The teachers encourage them to ask for help rather than emit tantrum behaviors. Creativity is also encouraged by arranging for the children to finger paint, color, listen to music, scribble, or play simple musical instruments.

Motor Skills

Most infants, especially those from economically disadvantaged families, are very active and need relatively little encouragement to develop gross motor skills. Sometimes, however, it is beneficial to help children perform a skill. For example, infants are helped to sit up and walk as they become physically capable of learning those behaviors. Infants can be encouraged to locomote by placing an object they like just out of reach. Some motor skills can be taught by modeling; examples are hand-clapping, jumping, and hopping. The infant nursery also contains play equipment scaled for very small children; it includes a slide, a tube to crawl through, and stairs. The children appear to enjoy this equipment and play on it with minimal encouragement.

RESULTS

Children in a program such as the Learning Village should be tested comprehensively and repeatedly; unfortunately, the money needed to do such testing has not been available. At

BAYLEY SCALES
OF INFANT DEVELOPMENT
MENTAL DEVELOPMENT INDEX

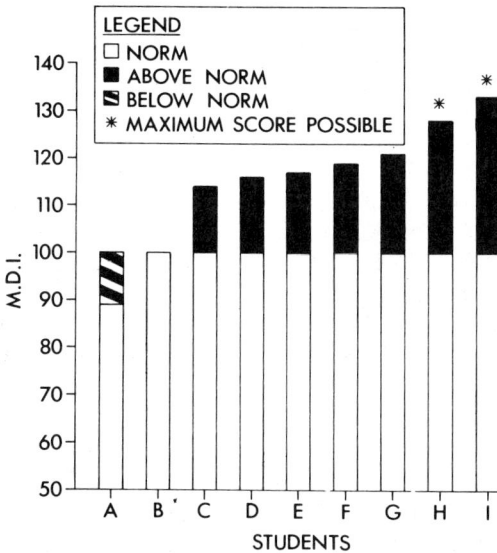

LEGEND
- □ NORM
- ■ ABOVE NORM
- ▨ BELOW NORM
- ＊ MAXIMUM SCORE POSSIBLE

Figure 2. Scores, on the Mental Development Index of the Bayley Scales of Infant Development, obtained by children who had been enrolled in the program at least six months.

one point, however, the children who had been in the program at least six months were given the Bayley Scales of Infant Development. Figure 2 shows the scores of the children on the Mental Development Index— all children scored above average, and two children obtained the maximum possible score. These results certainly are not conclusive, but they are promising.

SOME FRINGE BENEFITS

Parents and teachers of children in the Learning Village infant program have reported, anecdotally, some benefits that seem to result more from the group-care situation than from the explicitly planned educational programs. One benefit is a reduction in hesitancy to interact with new people. Young infants are said to go through periods when

they are characteristically afraid of strangers; these "stages" are not as pronounced in the Learning Village infants. When a visitor enters the room, older infants will often approach him and say "Hi!" and attempt to interact with him. One imagines, in observing the children, that they will be able to face social situations with greater confidence than children who have been raised in a nuclear family.

The group-care situation also provides the children with a rare thing for their age: a peer group. Most infants spend their time among adults or older children. When they are given the opportunity to be around children their own age, they seem fascinated by them. Toddlers seem to love babies, and babies seem to prefer other children to adults. Only in a group-care situation can very young children be with people who are not necessarily bigger and better at things than themselves. No one knows how much an infant can benefit from a peer group, but it seems worthwhile to provide them with one.

Group care also seems to contribute positively to the relationship between mothers and their infants. Mothers of the Learning Village infants rarely have the feeling of being at their "wit's end." Infants can be very annoying when there is no escape from their activity, crying, and needs for care. On the other hand, babies can be the most reinforcing creatures in the world. When mothers are not continually exposed to the positive and negative aspects of caring for an infant, they seem better able to appreciate the positive and be patient with the negative. Although some readers may feel that this is a rationalization designed to make separation of the mother and her baby more palatable, parents report that they really do feel happy with the group-care arrangement.

Group-care situations can also supply a physical environment that is relatively free of "no-no's." The nursery environment at the Learning Village is not luxurious but is relatively free of tables with sharp edges, cabinets full of harmful substances, doors that can pinch fingers, valuable possessions that can be destroyed, things that can be turned into messes, and so forth. The environment mostly consists of toys, furniture, and play equipment made especially for infants.

The children at the Learning Village also seem to be unusually free of problems: Very few of the children suck their thumbs or are attached to "Linus" blankets, there is relatively little tantrumming, and the children, for the most part, seem to accept toilet training matter-of-factly. The only children who cry on separation from their parents are older children who are just beginning in the program or children who present other abnormalities on a given day. None of the children appear particularly timid or fearful. In other words, the program does seem to have prevented some of the problems it was hoping to prevent.

FUTURE PLANS: PERFORMANCE CONTRACTING WITH INFANTS

Like many educational programs, the Learning Village infant program has suffered from several inconsistencies. Staff have come and gone, each, to an extent, bringing and taking with her a unique approach. Children have also come and gone. Some of the children who enrolled as small babies have later withdrawn for several months and still later reentered. Very often children enroll when they are eighteen months or older. Also, evaluation has been sparse.

Currently a new program is getting under way that should correct some of these deficiencies.[3] The Learning Village has contracted with the Michigan Department of Education to work with ten infants beginning at ages younger than six months. The children have been drawn from economically disadvantaged families and from families in which a sibling or a parent has failed in public school. The infants will stay in the Learning Village until they are five years old. To help assure continuity, parents are paid bonuses for keeping their children in the program. The children will be given the Bayley Scales of Infant Development semi-annually, and the Village will receive payment only for children who score at least in the normal range on the Bayley Scales. Eventually the children will attend public school and hopefully will have a more successful school experience than did other members of their families. This program should provide an opportunity to see what long-term group care for infants can accomplish.

IN SUMMARY

The Learning Village infant program provides a setting in which shaping and reinforcement techniques can be used to help children develop without many of the problems sometimes observed in older children. Procedures have been established for the physical care of the children, objectives have been written in the areas of self-care and cognitive, affective, and motor skills, and programs have been written to meet these objectives. Test results, although sparse, have indicated that the program has been successful; parents and teachers have also reported satisfaction with the program. An improved program, including long-term attendance and repeated testing, is now under way.

3 The program is directed by Marshall Wolfe and Dorathy Marine.

3

IN EARLY EDUCATION

Several years ago, early education was held to be a panacea for educational ills. Public school personnel attributed the failure of many children to their preschool environment. A change in that environment was therefore expected to solve many problems. Head Start Programs were funded, and many private and semiprivate day-care programs begun. Many of the educational failures were poor children who, it was said, lacked the normal middle-class, enriched, preschool experience. Therefore, most preschool programs concentrated on "enrichment." They took the children to zoos and art galleries and gave them an opportunity to play in an environment different from the one at home. Unfortunately, as the report on Head Start by the Westinghouse Learning Corporation (1969) showed, the results of preschool programs were variable. The most successful programs, not surprisingly, were those that went beyond enrichment and taught structured academic material. Other work, by Weikart (1972) and by Hawkridge, Chalupsky, and Roberts (1968), has similarly found that children given a structured, academically oriented preschool experience do far better than those simply exposed to an enriched environment.

This section presents two structured approaches to early education. The first, by Miller and Schneider, shows how a Head Start or any preschool program can be organized around a token economy to include academic, as well as enrichment, activities. The second approach is one of the most effective structured preschool programs in existence. Originated by Engelmann and others, it has produced academic achievement and IQ gains in disadvantaged preschool children that surpassed gains made by middle-class children in a Montessori program.

The idea of using preschool programs to prevent school failure was a good one. The misdirection of some programs should not prevent increased implementation of other, successful programs. Preschool programs are expensive. However, it is far less expensive to give a child two or three years of high-quality preschool experience than it is to give him years of special education, unemployment compensation, or even incarceration. The human cost of neglecting preschool education is even greater.

The use of a token system in project Head Start

L. KEITH MILLER AND RICHARD SCHNEIDER

Token systems provide an effective method for generating socially important behaviors in a wide variety of settings (Ayllon and Azrin, 1965; Birnbrauer, Wolf, Kidder, and Tauge, 1965; Cohen, Filipczak, and Bis, 1965; Giradeau and Spradlin, 1964; Clark, Lachowicz, and Wolf, 1968; Staats and Butterfield, 1965; Wolf, Giles, and Hall, 1968). The present paper describes a token system designed to develop and maintain writing skills in a group of underprivileged children in a summer Head Start program. The function of the token system in generating these skills was assessed by individual experiments with each of the children in the experimental token class. The overall effect of the program was evaluated by comparing the pretest and the posttest scores of the token class with a matched control class.

METHOD

Subjects

Thirty students, 4 to 5 years old, who were enrolled in the regular Head Start Program of a small midwest city, served as subjects with the explicit agreement of their parents. Students were randomly assigned to an experimental token class and a control class. For reasons of health and irregular attendance 4 children in each class were dropped from the experiment. Of the remaining 22 children, 19 were black and 3 were white. All children came from low-income families as defined by the Office of Economic Opportunity scale.

Staff

The staff for each class consisted of a teacher and two teacher's aides. The junior author, who had received training in behavior modification, served as the teacher in the token class. A local public school teacher taught the control class. The other staff members were welfare recipients and had no training in behavior modification.

Control Group

The control group consisted of 11 children. Their teacher was a state certified grade-school teacher in the local system who had taught in the Head Start program the previous year. Although she was not instructed on how to teach her class, she was provided with the same instructional and reinforcing materials provided to the experimental group to use as she saw fit. A writing achievement test was administered to her class during the first week of the program, and she was informed that it would be administered again during the final week. It was suggested that she teach the children these skills as one goal of her summer program. However, no effort was made to force her to teach these skills, whether in her own way or by using the writing program developed for the experimental class. Furthermore, no systematic observation was made of her attempts to use it. Her own reports and casual observation indicated that several attempts to use the program met with no cooperation from the children.

Experimental Group

Experimental room. The experimental space consisted of a room approximately 25 by 40 feet and an additional outside play area

From *Journal of Applied Behavior Analysis,* Fall 1970, Vol. *3*(3), 213-220. Copyright © 1970 by the Society for the Experimental Analysis of Behavior, Inc. Reprinted by permission of the authors and the *Journal of Applied Behavior Analysis.*

This is a revised version of a paper presented at the meeting of the American Psychological Association, San Francisco, 1968. The investigation and preparation for this paper was supported in part by a grant from the Mental Health Fund of the Illinois Department of Mental Health to the Behavior Modification Program of the Rehabilitation Institute of Southern Illinois University, Carbondale, Illinois, and in part by Office of Economic Opportunity Grant CG 8719 A/O.

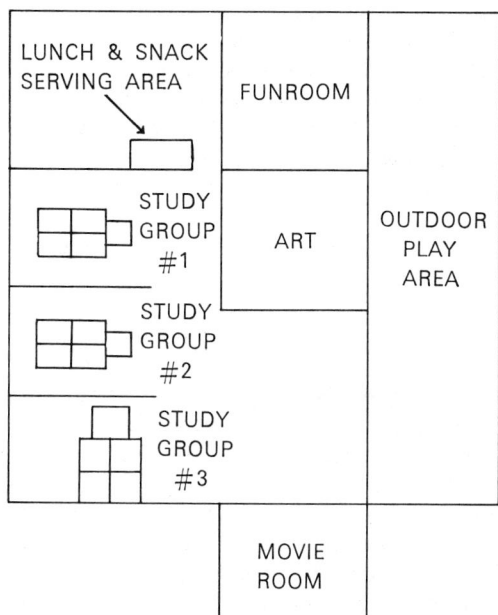

Figure 1. *Floorplan of the Head Start classroom.*

(Figure 1). This space was divided into six functional areas. Five of the areas were associated with reinforcement and had restricted entrances; the sixth area was associated with the opportunity to study. The areas were:

(1) *Food area:* snacks of cookies and Kool Aid were served here. Lunch plates, dessert cups, and milk glasses were dispensed as children earned them before lunch. Lunch was served to the children from this area.

(2) *Funroom:* this area contained a wide variety of toys that the children could play with. The toys included blocks, cars, dolls, dress-up clothes, a piano, blackboard, and record player.

(3) *Art:* this area contained such art supplies as paints, crayons, rubber ink, stamps, paste-on pictures, and paper.

(4) *Outdoor play area:* this area contained outdoor toys such as a beachball, rocking horse, climbing bar, pedal car, and several water guns.

(5) *Movie room:* this area contained a strip film projector and a small library of educational films obtained through the school system.

(6) *Study area:* this area contained three groups of five children's school desks. Each desk was separated from the other four in that same group by plywood partitions (Figure 2). Each group was separated from the other groups by folding partitions. Visual access between children required standing on their chair or table, or walking away from their desk.

Response definition. A program was prepared that was designed to teach the children the necessary skills prerequisite to learning freehand printing. These skills included: (1) how to hold a pencil, (2) how to draw a

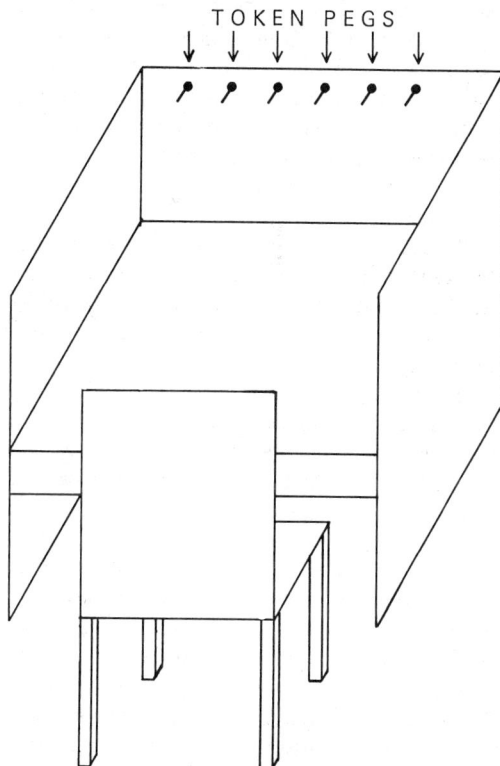

Figure 2. *Individual cubicle in which each child worked during study period.*

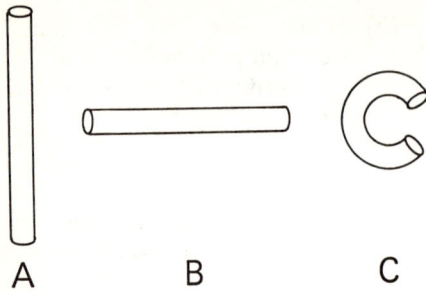

A   B   C

Figure 3. *Samples from writing program.*

straight line at different angles, (3) how to draw curved lines at different angles, (4) how to draw freehand lines, and (5) how to draw a variety of different shapes in which lines joined and crossed at specified points. The entire program contained 15 distinct steps, several examples[1] of which are shown in Figure 3. Each step was duplicated between 24 and 48 times on a single sheet of paper. Each child in the token class worked on each step until he produced one perfect paper. He was then allowed to progress to the next step in the program. Both classes were provided with as many copies of the program as they requested.

A correct response was judged by the teacher's aides. If the child's response started at the correct point, did not cross the guidelines, and ended at the correct point, it was to be graded as correct. Each aide was supplied with a different colored marker so that her grading responses could be readily identified at any time. Her responses consisted of an "X" next to each incorrect response and a dot or short line next to each correct response.

Constant assessment of grading accuracy was required because of the volume of work required of the aides; they graded an average of 20 responses per minute, delivered tokens, and administered the reinforcing activities immediately after the work sessions. In addition, grading many responses at the very end of the work period was often done in a "crisis" atmosphere conducive to mistakes. It must be added that the aides were also somewhat more sympathetic toward near misses

than was the teacher. In order to maintain a reasonable level of accuracy, the teacher checked each aide's grading as soon as possible and gave her further instruction until the grading was at least 95 percent accurate. Spot checking of accuracy was maintained for the duration of the experiment.

Procedure. The children in the token class were introduced to the token system during the first eight days. At the beginning of the first day, the aides were given explicit instructions on their duties. After this instruction period, the children were permitted to sample each of the play activities if they first repeated its name to one aide, for which they received a token, and then gave the token to another aide. During the second day, access to the snacks and activities required one token. The children were permitted to earn tokens at any time by working on the writing program; they could immediately exchange the tokens for 5 minutes of access to the reinforcer. During the next six days, tokens could be earned only during formal study periods, which alternated with brief play periods. Initially, the study periods were 5 minutes long; they were progressively increased during the six-day period until there

Table 1. *Number of tokens required for lunch materials, snacks, and access to different activities.*

Reinforcer	Price
LUNCH MATERIALS	
Lunch Plate	5
Second Plate	5
Dessert Cup	5
Milk Glass	5
SNACKS	
Kool Aid	5
Cookie	5
ACTIVITIES	
Fun Room	10
Playground	10
Art	10
Movies	10

1 This program has been expanded and perfected by Dr. Donald Bushell.

were four 30-minute study periods and four 20-minute play periods. Once this change had been introduced, the children were permitted to buy play activities only during play periods.

Table 1 lists 10 reinforcers and their prices that were available to the children in exchange for tokens.

When the study periods were introduced, a response chain and a conditioned reinforcer system were developed to bridge the delay between the child's response and his access to the reinforcers. The response chain consisted of completing a fixed number of writing responses designated by the teacher and then raising his hand. When a child raised his hand, the teacher would go to that child's desk and grade each response. Tokens were given for correct responses according to a small fixed-ratio schedule. After receiving his tokens, the child could apply them to one or more tickets, which depicted the different reinforcers. He bought a ticket by filling up a peg in his study booth that also held the ticket. The peg was adjusted in length so that the number of tokens that could fit onto it equalled the price of the reinforcer. This system had the advantages of (1) not requiring counting, (2) displaying a wide variety of reinforcers, and (3) not requiring any intervention or assistance by the aides.

The effectiveness of the token system in maintaining responding was experimentally evaluated after a seven-day baseline period. The evaluation used four study periods of one day. Before the first and third periods of that day, the children were given 25 tokens noncontingently and instructed to complete 8 responses. After they completed those responses, the teacher graded them, praised their work, and informed them that there were no more tokens available to give out. The children were then informed that they could complete more writing responses if they wished. During the second and fourth work periods, the children were given tokens contingent upon their completion of correct responses. Each work period was 30 minutes long and was separated from the next work period by a 20-minute play period during which tokens could be spent. The design was duplicated during a second day.

In addition to this basic experiment, the effect of different work durations was also evaluated. On subsequent days, 20-minute, 30-minute, and 60-minute work sessions were scheduled with the token system in effect.

Finally, the overall effect of the token system was evaluated by an achievement test given during the first three days of the program (pretest) and again at the end of the six-week program (posttest). The test covered each target behavior of the writing program. This test was given to both the token class and the control class. The test was shown to the control class teacher before the start of classes as one target for her teaching.

RESULTS

Figure 4 shows the day-by-day variation in response rates during the seven-day baseline

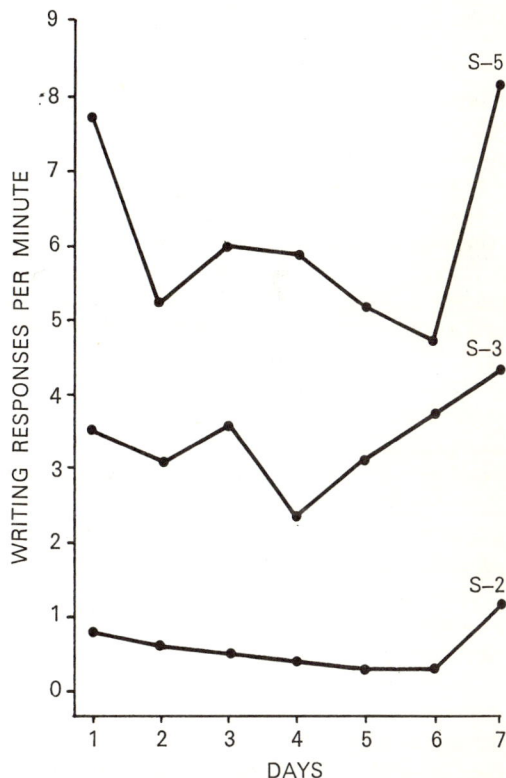

Figure 4. *Writing responses per minute for a high, medium, and low-rate child during first seven days of token reinforcement.*

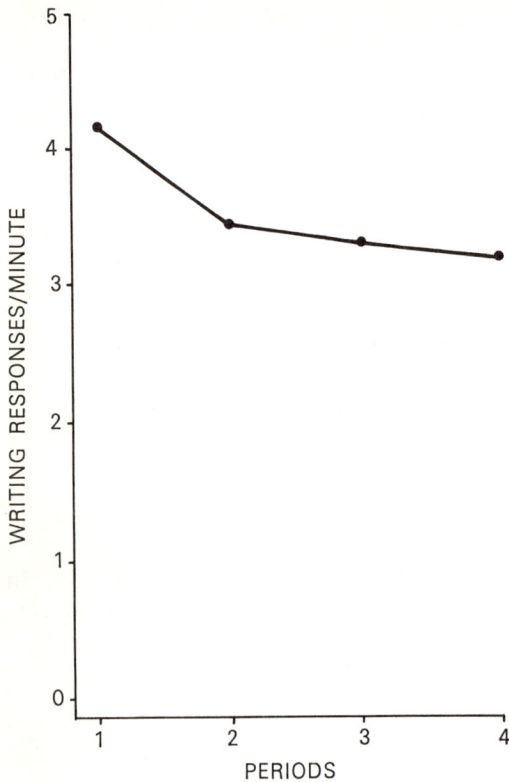

Figure 5. *Mean writing responses per minute for the four daily work periods for the first seven days of token reinforcement.*

uniform rate of responding within each day, with some tendency for a decrease in rate after the first period.

Figure 6 shows the average response rate for the 10 children present during the four study periods of the experimental session. In general, the students worked at a much higher rate during the two periods when the tokens were contingent. During those periods, they averaged about 5 responses per minute. During the periods when 25 tokens were given non-contingently and social attention was the only event contingent upon responding, they averaged about 0.8 and 0.2 responses per minute. T-tests were computed for each adjacent period. The differences between periods were significant at approximately the 0.0005 level or beyond for each comparison. Two subjects deviated from this statistical pattern. S-6 did not recover a high response rate during the first period. However, she showed comparable rates when tokens were delivered contingently during the other periods. S-10 worked at a high rate during the first period of non-contingent delivery of tokens but otherwise showed a pattern comparable to the other children. Six children made no responses after the 8 responses they were instructed to complete. Two children maintained low rates, but still

period for a child with a high, medium, and low rate. S-5 showed considerably more variation than the other children. Most children maintained a fairly uniform daily rate during the baseline period. Two children did not, both increasing from a low rate of about two responses per minute to about seven responses per minute. In general, these data suggest a relatively stable day-to-day rate of responding during baseline.

Figure 5 shows the variation within days during the baseline period. The average number of responses in each period decreased from about 4.2 responses per minute in the first period to about 3.3 responses per minute in the fourth period. These averages are not a precise measure of the individual children, however. For example, Period 4 is the slowest work period for only 3 of the 11 children. These data suggest a relatively

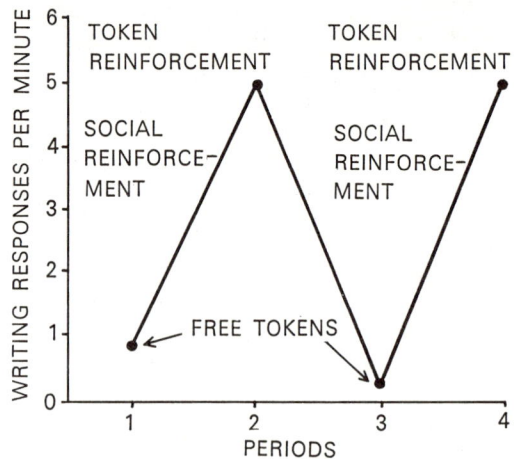

Figure 6. *Mean rate of responding with and without contingent token reinforcement. Each point represents the mean rate for 10 children during a 30-minute study period.*

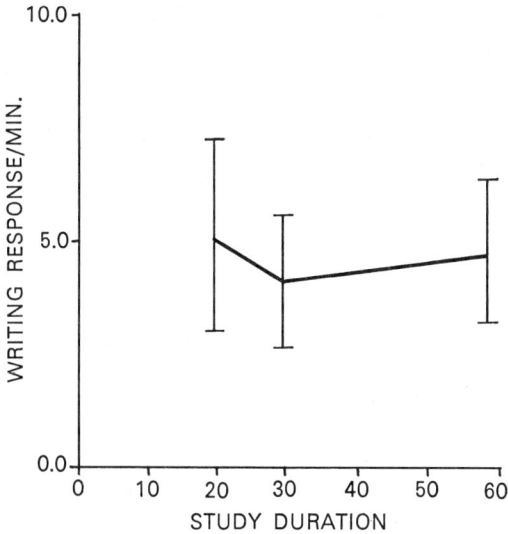

Figure 7. *Mean rate of responding during study periods of different durations. Each point represents mean rate for seven children during four 20- and 30-minute study periods and during one 60-minute study period. Vertical bars show ranges for the 7 children at each duration.*

ment is that there is no evidence to suggest that the children's response rate decreased even when hour-long study sessions were used. This contrasts with the intuitive notion that 4- to 5-year-old children have a very short attention span, particularly for formal educational behaviors. This experiment suggests that children can work at educational activities for long periods of time with no necessary reduction in response rate—if their behaviors are adequately reinforced.

Figure 8 shows the results of the pretest and the posttest. Both groups made about 35 percent correct responses on the pretest. On the posttest, the control group showed a small gain of about 3 percent to a score of about 38 percent correct responses. The token group showed a very large gain to almost 100 percent correct responses on the posttest. These results indicate that the token class made very large gains on the writing achievement test while the control group made only slight gains.

showed considerably higher rates during the periods when tokens were contingent. Virtually identical differences in rate between the reinforced and non-reinforced periods were obtained during the second experimental day. These differences between periods during the experimental days contrast sharply with the small variability between periods obtained during the baseline period. These results indicate that the tokens were effective in maintaining a high response rate among the children during the experimental days.

Figure 7 shows the effect of different study period durations on the children's rate of emitting writing responses. On the average, the children maintained a response rate of between 4 and 5 responses per minute whether the study period was 20, 30, or 60 minutes long. The rates for the individual children are similar to this average; 4 children showed a slight increase in rate when comparing the 20- and 60-minute study periods, and 3 showed a slight decrease in rate. The interesting thing about this experi-

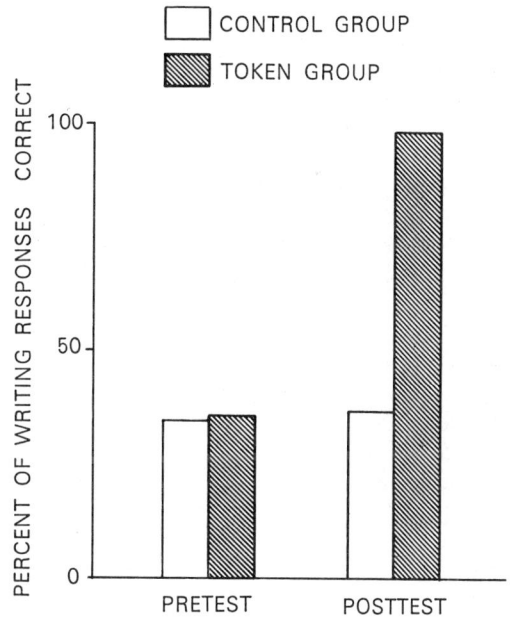

Figure 8. *Comparison of pretest and posttest achievement scores for the token group and the control group. Token group bars are average for 7 children present at both tests; control group bars are averages for 11 children present at both tests.*

DISCUSSION AND CONCLUSIONS

The differences in rates between periods with and without reinforcement contingencies suggest that the tokens were effective in maintaining writing responses. This conclusion is further strengthened by the relative lack of differences between periods during baseline when all responses were reinforced.

The data also suggest that the token system can maintain writing behavior over a period of several weeks. Counting the seven baseline days, the two experimental days, and the three days during which different durations of work periods were studied, writing behavior was maintained during the reinforced portion of twelve days. This suggests that the present reinforcing procedure has some durability.

This research indicates that token systems can be adapted to the Head Start situation. It may be that the ease with which token control was developed over these children resulted from several fortuitous features of the system. First, the development of an explicit response chain beginning with a writing response and ending with hand-raising may have effectively bridged the inevitable time delay between writing responses and token delivery. Without the hand-raising response, the aides would have had to move continually from child to child to see if they had completed their work. Not only would this have permitted unauthorized social reinforcement to occur, but it would have introduced a non-discriminated time delay between responding and token delivery. Second, the use of tickets containing a picture of the reinforcing activity may have effectively bridged the gap between token delivery and the actual access to the "back-up" reinforcing activity. It also made it possible to display a wide variety of reinforcers to subjects with no reading ability. Third, the use of token pegs adjusted in length to count the children's tokens for them permitted the children to select their reinforcers with no intervention from the teacher or the aides. Not only might this have taught them to make responsible choices, but, by eliminating the teacher's influence, it may have heightened the probability that the tokens were ex-changed for the most reinforcing events. The pegs also permitted the use of a differential pricing system without first requiring the children to learn how to count. Fourth, the fact that the children could begin to apply their tokens toward a variety of back-up reinforcers while the study period was in process may have reduced the tendency of the children to satiate on tokens. In any event, the token system reported here did rapidly develop token control in the Head Start situation. This control also produced large and measurable gains in the writing skills of these children. This success suggests that we should explore methods for applying token systems to such basic skills as vocabulary improvement, counting and adding, and reading readiness.

It should be noted that the present token system is practical as well as successful. The reinforcers used are commonly available in Head Start classrooms without additional cost. Perhaps even more important is that the token system can be administered by untrained teacher's aides. This made it practical to hire the most needy Head Start mothers: those on welfare. One of the mothers serving as a teacher's aide could not read; yet she was an excellent teacher within this system. Thus, this system was used without raising either materials or personnel costs.

Informal observations suggest that the token system had several unanticipated effects. First, the token system required intense interaction between the children and the teacher's aides. Children had to learn new words in order to follow instructions successfully; the fact that the situation was relatively objective made it possible for the aides readily to observe whether instructions were understood and take corrective measures if they were not. Second, the children appeared to develop a favorable attitude toward school. Several children were kept home for a day due to a minor misunderstanding. All of them cried for several hours because they wanted to go to school. This led the parents to investigate the misunderstanding and return the children to school. Third, children gained a great deal of experience playing cooperatively with other children. One very shy child with a deformed face initially refused to play with other children. But a brief shaping period encouraged her to try playing with them. After she had tried, she rapidly overcame her shyness and became a full participant in the play periods. These and other unanticipated effects suggest that token systems may provide an environment far more suitable to developing many of the less specified behavioral changes of interest to child development specialists than one might guess. It would be of value in future token studies systematically to investigate such changes. Perhaps objective methods could be developed to increase the rate of such changes deliberately. Even if these methods could not be developed, objective data demonstrating that such changes are not incompatible with token systems would be of considerable interest.

A major failing in the present experiment was the lack of community—in particular, parent—control over the program. While a parent advisory committee was involved in all decisions from the initial hiring to the selection of teaching goals, interest and participation tended to be low. Perhaps the extension of a token system to the parents, similar to that used to maintain participation in self-help clubs (Miller and Miller, 1970), could be introduced.

The effectiveness of direct verbal instruction on IQ performance and achievement in reading and arithmetic

SIEGFRIED ENGELMANN

INTRODUCTION

The performance of a child on an IQ test is taken by some as an indication of the child's intelligence. It is suggested that the child's performance indicates something about the child's ability to learn and retain information and skills. On the surface, this interpretation has a certain face-value appeal; however, if it is analyzed more carefully, it becomes something of an absurd position. There is no learning in the abstract. The child who is learning is always taught. He is provided with models of behavior; he is corrected if his performance is incorrect; he is reinforced for appropriate behavior. In other words, the term "learning" is not a very accurate description of what happens in a "learning situation," since the child is always being taught. Even if he is working alone, with no "teacher" present, he is still being taught by the physical environment. The physical environment provides rather clear demonstrations of what can be done and what can't.

Since there can be no learning (except in trivial, autistic instances) without teaching, we can categorically assert that if a child performs appropriately on an IQ item, he has been taught the skills needed to handle that item. This does not mean that the item on which he is tested has been presented to the child. It means, however, that he has learned the words, the operations, and concepts that would allow him to handle that item or similar items dealing with the problem (assuming that the words used in the item are within the child's repertoire). The amount of teaching that has been required for two different children to achieve a particular criterion of performance on an IQ item may vary considerably. One child may have required only a minimum of "teaching" while another child may have required a considerable amount of instruction. The performance on the item provides for no inference about the amount of teaching that has been provided; therefore, the item cannot be seriously considered as an indicator of the child's innate capacity or genetic endowment. Two 6-year-old children may score

From **Disadvantaged Child, Vol. 3, Compensatory Education: A National Debate,** edited by Jerome Hullmuth. Copyright © 1970, pp. 339-361. Reprinted by permission of Brunner/Mazel Publishers.

correctly on the same set of IQ items. One child may have received three times the amount of instruction that the other child received. Yet, the IQ score tells us nothing about the environment. Therefore, the IQ test can in no way be a very reliable indicator of the genetic composition of these children.

It may be argued that the children who respond to an IQ test appropriately are not actually taught the skills that would lead to correct performance. Such would be an ill-conceived argument. We could test the limits to see what the child had been taught. If we were to present the same item using a foreign language, such as Pali, the chances are that the child who responded appropriately when the task was presented in English would not respond appropriately. We could therefore conclude that successful performance on the item is contingent upon an understanding of the English language. How does a child acquire an understanding of this language? He is taught. To say that he learns it begs the question. The language is not a whole. It is the sum of various meanings and operations. He does not acquire the "language" as a whole. He acquires it as he is taught it, a meaning and operation at a time.

What if we were to change the IQ item so that it involved English, but a very anfractuous English. Would the child perform on the item? Probably not, simply because he has not been taught the meanings we refer to with the revised item. On the other hand, we could construct a number of items that are similar to the original that do not involve "difficult" language, but do involve different responses. (We may require the child to produce a verbal response, in which he answers a what question, a response to a yes-no question, a pointing response, etc.) We could also change the examples used in the original item. Through these procedures, we would be able to make some kind of strong statement about what the child has been taught about the operation being tested. Again, however, it would tell us precisely nothing about the child's genetic endowment, merely about the *effective* instruction that he has received.

It may be that some children are taught analogies, for example, through very oblique teaching demonstrations. It is quite probable that the teacher demonstrations of analogies that are effective for some children would not be effective for others. Unless, however, there are precise statements about the type of instruction that has been provided to teach the operations that underlie basic analogies, it is impossible to make precise statements about the nature of the child's genetic capacity. Two children may exhibit the same successful performance on Stanford-Binet analogies; yet, they may have received rather drastically different degrees of instruction. To attempt to derive conclusions about their genetic endowment, therefore, would be something verging on the absurd.

The work that has been conducted at the University of Illinois (formerly under the direction of Carl Bereiter, and currently under the direction of Wesley Becker) was based on the simple proposition that if disadvantaged or "normal" children are taught a wide variety of concepts at a faster-than-normal rate, they will become relatively "smart." Their smartness should be reflected in both performances on IQ tests and on achievement tests that deal with the specific skills taught in the program. These measures are admittedly poor, since they do not articulate precisely what has been taught. At best, they sample, and the sampling is sometimes obscured by items that test operations that the children have been taught but involve language that may not have been taught.

Note that the goal of the program is to teach specifics. The notion of nonspecific operations is rejected. An operation is applicable only to certain concrete problems. The subject must somehow be able to see that certain aspects of the problem imply a particular operation. Without this assumption, the operation would be used either universally or randomly. If it is used in a discriminated manner, there must be a basis for discrimination, which means that the operation is specific to a certain set of cues. The operation can be applied to a wide variety of situations, but the operation still remains quite specific.

Also note that the idea of long-range effects of the program is rejected as a legitimate measure of the program's effectiveness. Granted, it is quite possible, even probable, that if children who receive an intensive preschool and kindergarten instruction are tested four years later, there should be a *tendency* for the children in the experimental program to perform better than the children who received no such intensive training. However, the argument is based on the idea that all things are equal. And when we deal with questions of intellectual growth, the question becomes a very troublesome one at best. It is one thing if we mean by "all things are equal" that the children are allowed to progress from the point at which they are and are taught according to the skills that they have at any given time. The "all things are equal" means something quite different if the children, regardless of the skills that they have at the time, are put through a lockstep program, which may in fact attempt to teach skills that have been taught or skills for which adequate preparation has not been provided. One would expect that the differences between the experimental children and the controls would be lessened—either because the experimental children are being relatively held back and are not receiving the opportunity to "develop" at an accelerated rate, or because both the controls and the experimental children would have an "equally" inadequate base for performing or "developing."

The measure of the "long-range" effectiveness of an approach, unfortunately, is not a clean test of the program. It is a test of the program plus a host of intervening variables. Unless the nature of these variables is clearly specified, one would be at a loss to make strong inferential statements about the effectiveness of the experimental program. The results may lead the investigator to a number of spurious conclusions, such as: "The program shows a slight tendency to be better than the traditional program...." "The gains that are realized through the program do not hold up over time...." These conclusions may be spurious in the sense that different programs that intervene between the termination of the experimental program and the test of long-range effectiveness may change the outcomes astronomically, even if

the same program is provided for both the control and experimental children.

In short, the position is this. Children get relatively smart if you teach more than they would be expected to be taught under "normal" conditions during a given period of time. Similarly children become relatively less smart if the rate of effective instruction is slowed. When children begin to regress, it means only one thing. They are not being taught at relatively the same rate that they had been taught before. It can mean nothing else. This is not to say that all of the instruction a child receives goes on in school. But it is axiomatic that if his performance begins to slow, he is not being taught at the rate that he previously had been taught. No statement of the child's genetic composition or capacity is implied. This statement is strictly one about what he is taught.

As an indication of what can be done with middle-class and disadvantaged children, I refer to the disadvantaged and middle-class children who graduated from the Bereiter-Engelmann kindergarten program in 1967. In one sense, this group received the most concerted instruction of any experimental classes from 1965–1969. Our best teachers were assigned to these children. We had no trainees working with the children (the instruction of whom tends to reduce by about one-third the rate at which the children are taught). Finally, there was a concerted attempt to make sure that the lowest performing children were taught. Program improvements were introduced. These were based on the performance of the low-performing children who had graduated the preceding year. Also during the school years of 1966–1967 the program was continuously revised, based on the difficulties the lowest performing children were having.

The hypotheses investigated were:

1) effective instruction can dramatically increase the rate at which children are taught new behaviors that are relevant both to specific achievement tests (such as reading achievement) and more general achievement tests (such as the Stanford-Binet);

2) the children will achieve gains both in the first and second year of instruction if the instruction continues to teach skills at a

faster-than-expected rate. The IQ drop noted during the second year of many preschool programs (after a 4–8 point first-year gain) is a function of poor instruction, not of the genetic capacity of the children;

3) any child can be accelerated to at least "average" if the instruction is effective.

The goal of the program was not to achieve mere statistical differences between experimental and control groups, while demonstrating no obvious differences in performance between the groups. Rather it was to achieve changes of such magnitude that there could be little doubt (statistically or otherwise) that the changes were a function of instruction. The basic goal was to bring all of the children to "average" on some of the more common measures of achievement, such as IQ measures.

METHOD

Subjects

The disadvantaged subjects for the present experiment were 4-year-old culturally disadvantaged children who would be eligible for Head Start. The selection criteria were as follows:

1) according to Warner ratings of occupations (1949) and housing ratings obtained through the City Planning Commissioner's office, subjects were from low socioeconomic homes (mean weighted S.E.S. in the low 40's);
2) subjects were 4 years old by December 1, in keeping with public school entrance policies;
3) subjects did not have previous preschool experience;

4) children with gross physical handicaps and severely retarded children were excluded.

Subjects received Stanford-Binet tests and were divided into three groups—high intelligence, middle intelligence, and low intelligence. Children were assigned to the experimental and comparison classes, each class receiving the same proportion of highs, middles, and lows. Adjustments were made so that each class had approximately the same proportion of Negro-whites, and a nearly equal number of male and female subjects. Fifteen children were assigned to the experimental group and 28 to the comparison group. The composition of both groups is summarized in Table 1.

In addition to the disadvantaged subjects, 18 middle-class 4-year-old children were selected for a 2-year program. These subjects were not given IQ tests upon entrance. They were introduced into the experiment to demonstrate the differential effects of the experimental program on children who might be considered developmentally impaired and those considered normal. The control for the middle-class children was a group of middle-class 4-year-olds in a Montessori preschool. The middle-class subjects in the experimental program were referred by parents of the Montessori children as children whose parents would be interested in a Montessori type of education (or a relatively intensive preschool education). Some of the experimental children were on the Montessori waiting list. The selection criterion was adequate, it was felt, to identify children who should be roughly comparable to the Montessori children. The Montessori controls were the same age as the experimental children although the Montessori children had already had 1

Table 1. *Characteristics of disadvantaged subjects.*

Subjects	Mean CA	Mean Binet IQ	White	Negro	Male	Female	Mean Weighted S.E.S.
Experimental N = 15	4-3	95.33	6	9	8	7	41.93
Comparison N = 15	4-3	94.50	11	17	15	13	42.50

year of schooling at the time the experimental children began their program.

Evaluation of Performance

The disadvantaged children were given Stanford-Binet IQ tests after the first and second year of instruction. The middle-class children received Stanford-Binets only after the second year of instruction. These tests were taken as a measure of "general achievement," primarily in language concepts. The disadvantaged and middle-class subjects in the experimental program also were tested on reading, arithmetic, and spelling achievement with the Wide-Range Achievement Test (1965). This test was selected for evaluating the subjects because:

1) There are fewer potential sources of extraneous difficulty. The instructions are uncomplicated, and the tests are clearly tests of relevant content. For a child to achieve a given score in reading, he has to read—not circle words or follow complicated instructions.

2) No multiple-choice items appear in the Wide Range, which means that the children cannot receive a spuriously high score because they happened to guess correctly.

3) The Wide Range is capable of measuring achievement below the first-grade level.

The disadvantaged children in the comparison group were not given achievement tests, because they were not taught skills in reading, arithmetic, or spelling. The Montessori group was given the Wide-Range Test once, after they had finished their pre-kindergarten year.

Procedure

The subjects in the disadvantaged comparison class received a traditional preschool education. During the first year, they attended a 2-hour-a-day preschool based as closely as possible on the recommendations of child development authorities. The emphasis of the program was on play, self-expression, developing a positive self image through role playing, and typical nursery-school activities. The preschool was outfitted with a sand table, dress-up corner, and a variety of toys. The child to teacher ratio was about 5 to 1. During the second year, comparison subjects went to public-school kindergartens.

The middle-class comparison group attended a Montessori program which operated for 3 hours a day. The emphasis of the program was on nonverbal manipulative activity. The child to teacher ratio was about 10 to 1.

During the first year (1965–1966) 15 disadvantaged children and 19 middle-class children were enrolled in experimental programs for 2 hours a day. Three of the disadvantaged children were not continued in the program the second year, and 12 middle-class children were not continued. The 12 remaining disadvantaged children and 7 middle-class children were integrated in a single class and received a second year of 2-hours-a-day instruction. Throughout the 2-year treatment, the child to teacher ratio was about 5 to 1.

The Experimental Program

The emphasis of the experimental program was on rapid attainment of basic academic concepts. The children attended three 20-minute classes daily—a language concept class, an arithmetic class, and a reading class. For these classes, the children were divided into small (4–7 children) relatively homogeneous groups (based on performance in the classroom). For the remaining hour the children engaged in a period of semi-structured activities (writing, drawing, working reading-readiness problems), a music period (in which the songs were geared to the concepts presented in the language-concepts program), and a juice-and-toilet period.

Both the content and the style of teacher presentation used in the language, arithmetic, and reading sessions derived from a relatively simple principle: Teach in the fastest, most economical manner possible. In language, the children were taught how to use a "minimum" instructional language. The language was derived from the requirements of future teaching situations. In future teaching situations, the teacher would present physical objects of some kind and call the children's attention to some aspect of the objects—perhaps the color, perhaps the relative size, perhaps the position in relation to another object. The teacher would also "test" the children, primarily by asking a child (or the group) questions. The basic language that is needed for all such instructional situations is one that adequately describes the objects presented, that adequately calls attention to the conceptual dimension to which the teacher is directing the children, and that allows for unambiguous "tests" or questions.

The language that satisfies the requirements of the teaching situation consists of the two statement forms,

This is a ....
This .... is ....

with plural and *not* variations (This is not a ....), with *yes-no* questions (Is this a ball?), and with the *what* question (What is this?).

The basic language of instruction was taught during the first year. The language teachers did not use a rich variety of expressions; rather, they confined themselves to the basic patterns noted above until the children had demonstrated through performance that they understood the statements and the relationships between statements and questions.

The content that was taught in connection with the basic language consisted of names of common objects, polars (hot-cold, wet-dry, big-little, long-short, etc.), colors, prepositions, and hierarchical classes (vehicles, buildings, tools, clothing, weapons, etc.). After the children mastered the basic language they were introduced to tense variations, action verbs, conditional statements, *and, or, if-then,* and *only.* Finally, during the second year, the children were taught methods for defining words (through genera and differentia), and for describing complex figures and events.

In arithmetic, the children were taught

how to count both objects and events (Tell me how many times I clap). They were then shown how addition, subtraction, and multiplication reduce to counting operations. For example, the children were shown how to translate such a problem as

$$5 + 3 = b$$

into the counting operation: start out with 5; get more; get 3 more; and you end up with .... ; we have to count them to find out.

All addition problems were reduced to this operation. The children were taught some rote facts, such as the series

$$1 + 1 = 2$$
$$2 + 1 = 3$$
$$3 + 1 = 4$$
etc.,

which articulates the relationship between counting and adding. There was, however, no attempt to teach the children an exhaustive set of arithmetic facts. Rather, the emphasis was on the operations that would lead to a correct solution.

The children were introduced to algebra and story problems early. To work algebra problems, the children used a variation of the translation they were taught for handling regular problems. For example, the operation for handling the problem

$$5 + b = 8$$

was: start out with 5; get more; we don't know how many more, but we know we end up with 8. By starting out with 5 and getting more until he ends up with 8, the child discovers how many more he has to get.

The initial story problems were quite similar to the statement operations taught in connection with each type of problem. For example: A man starts out with 5 balls; then he gets more; he gets three more; how many does he end up with? The problem translates directly into the arithmetic statement:

$$5 + 3 = b.$$

Problems were then systematically destructured. That is, synonymous expressions were systematically introduced. After the children had learned to handle the basic story problems, the children were introduced to problems in which a man *has* so many balls, in which he *finds* so many balls, in which he *makes* so many balls.

The children were taught to read according to a modified ITA approach (the first version of DISTAR reading, 1969). The innovations which were introduced into the experimental program (primarily with the low performing children) had to do with the formation of long-vowel sounds and the convention for blending words. The following symbols were introduced to designate long-vowel sounds: $\bar{a}$, $\bar{e}$, $\bar{i}$, $\bar{o}$. The rationale for these symbols was that they could be introduced to help the child "spell" or sound out a variety of long-vowel words; after the children learned these words ($s\bar{o}$, $g\bar{o}$, $n\bar{o}$, $h\bar{e}$, $sh\bar{e}$, $m\bar{e}$, $s\bar{a}ve$, $f\bar{i}ne$, etc.), the diacritical mark could be dropped without grossly changing the total configuration of the word.

To help the children learn how to blend words, a skill disadvantaged children often fail to master after years of reading instruction, only continuous-sound words (*fan*, not *ban* or *tan*) were introduced initially. The children were taught how to proceed from letter to letter *without pausing*. In sounding out words in this manner, the children were actually saying the words slowly and could see the relationship between the slowly produced word and the word as it is normally produced. To assure adequate performance in blending, the children were given say-it-fast drills with spoken words. "Say it fast, and I'll show you the picture: te-le-phone."

As early as possible, the children were introduced to controlled-vocabulary stories. After reading the stories, the children took them home. Taking stories home functioned as an incentive.

In each of the three study areas, the teachers proceeded as quickly as possible, but only after the children had demonstrated through performance that they had mastered the skills that they would be expected to use on higher-level tasks.

The above description of the curriculum is very rough. In each of the major subject areas, there are many subtasks. To teach each of the subtasks, the teacher had to take a number of steps. For example, to teach the

children to blend words that are presented orally (a subtask reading), the teacher first presented two-part words, each part of which is a word—ice-cream, motor-boat, snow-man. Next, the teacher introduced relatively long words the parts of which were not "words," sit-ting, shov-el, mon-ey, etc. Next, the teacher broke the words that had been presented into more than one part—mo-tor-boat, snow-ma-n, sh-ov-el. The teacher then introduced shorter words, broken into two parts: si-t, bea-t, c-ream, m-an. Finally, the teacher introduced short words that were divided into individual phonemes—m-a-n, s-i-t, sh-o-v-e-l. (A more detailed description of the arithmetic and language programs is contained in *Teaching Disadvantaged Children in the Preschool* [1966].)

The Teacher's Behavior

The teacher had three primary roles in the experimental program:

1) she managed the group of children, keeping them on task;
2) she taught concepts;
3) she tested the children's knowledge of concepts before either providing a remedy or proceeding to the next task.

The general rules that guided her behavior in all three areas were:

1) don't assume that the children know anything unless they have demonstrated that they do;
2) get as many correct responses and as few incorrect responses out of the children during the allotted time as possible;
3) teach the behaviors necessary for successful classroom performance.

Since the goal of the program was to induce learning at an above-average rate, procedures that induce learning at a normal rate were rejected. The teacher did not first "shape" behavior and then introduce academic content. She simultaneously introduced academic content and the rules of behavior associated with the content. The focus was always on the behavior related to the task, never on behavior in the abstract.

The sanctions that were used were:

Negative:

Loss of food reinforcers (raisins, juice);

Additional work ("If you keep that up, you'll have to work when the other children are singing. You're here to work.");

Physical manipulation (tugging on an arm to secure attention, tapping leg, physically turning children around in seat, turning face toward presentation);

Scolding, usually in loud voice ("Cut that out! Sidney! Look here!");

Repetition of task ("Do it again... Again ... Again... Again. Now, after this when I tell you to do it, you do it.").

Positive:

The use of reinforcing objects in presentations ("Look at that silly number. That's 7. I can't stand a 7. I have to erase it. Oh, there's another 7. I can't stand a 7...");

The use of personalization ("Here's a story about, guess who! Sidney!");

The use of mock shock ("Everybody knew the answer. And I just said nobody will know the answer. You guys really fooled me.");

The use of praise ("Now, did you hear Sidney? He's a smart boy. Let's clap for him. He is smart; and he's working hard.");

Dramatic change of pace (After having the children repeat a series of statements in unison, the teacher stops. The room is dead silent. The children look at each other and smile. Then they laugh. The teacher interrupts in a loud voice, "Okay, let's hear it: 4 plus 0 equals 4.");

A dynamic presentation of objects (During a 2-minute segment, the teacher may present as many as 30 objects—some repeated—and as many questions. "Tell me about this... What about this... And this ... And this...");

Positive speculations ("Boy, will your mother ever be surprised when she finds out that you can read. She'll say, 'I never knew you were so smart.' That's what she'll say.");

Exercises with a reinforcing payoff ("Everybody likes to erase numbers, right? So I'll point to it and you can erase it.");

Relating positive comments of others—both real and fictitious ("Do you know what the man who watched you read said to me? He said, 'These are the smartest kids I've ever seen in my life.' And you want to know something? He's right.");

Food rewards ("If you do a good job on this problem, I'll give you some raisins. So work hard.");

Fooler games (The children say that when they add 3 to 4, they end up with 7. The teacher says, "So I write a 7." She writes a 4. The children object, and the teacher pouts, "I guess I just can't fool you guys." The children laugh.);

Hand shakes ("Sidney did such a good job that I'm going to shake his hand. Good boy, Sidney.");

Special privileges ("Sidney is working so hard I'm going to let him be the teacher.");

Singling out a member of the group for praise ("Debby did it that time. I didn't hear the rest of you guys, but I sure heard Debby. Let's do it again; see if anybody else can say it like Debby does.");

Presenting take-homes ("Tell me this sound, and you can take it home.").

The teacher had a full range of social and physical reinforcers at her disposal to use as the situation demanded. Some of the reinforcers listed as positive reinforcers are "acquired." Once taught, however, they proved to be quite effective in influencing behavior, increasing attention, and maintaining the kind of concerted participation that might be called "working hard."

Note that the primary reinforcing emphasis was on positive reinforcement. The teacher used herself as a model, "I'm smart. I can do this stuff." She used other children in the group as models. "Did you hear Sidney? He and I are the only ones who can do this. We're smart." She always tried to acknowledge the correct responses of every child in the group. "Hey, everybody did it that time. Boy, you are smart kids. Good work, Tyrone. You too, Lisa."

Whenever the teacher taught, she utilized some of the reinforcing techniques noted above. She moved quickly so that the children were not confronted with a static presentation. She spoke loudly one moment, softly the next. She presented interesting examples of the concept, when the interesting aspects of the objects did not interfere with the concept being taught. She structured the presentation so that the children had a pay-off—perhaps playing a fooler game, perhaps a hand-out for correct responses.

In addition to the reinforcing aspects of the presentation, however, the teacher followed a basic rule in presenting any new concept: *The presentation must be consistent with one and only one concept.* When the teacher presented the concept big, for example, she used the statement forms, "This ... is big," and "This ... is not big," to describe a variety of object pairs—cups, circles, figures, men. Each of the objects in the pair was identical except for size. Through this type of presentation, the teacher demonstrated what the invariant *big* means. She further demonstrated the type of statement that is used to describe the invariant. "This cup is big; this ball is big; this man is big ..."

Because of the presentational requirements necessary to demonstrate a concept, the teacher presented a great many examples, usually 10–15 times more than are used by the average classroom teacher (a judgment based on the presentational suggestions of instructional programs designed for children in the early primary grades).

The teacher tested the children on various levels of performance. The first test of a concept was whether the children could find (or point to) the appropriate example. "Find the man that is big."

The next test was whether the children could answer *yes-no* questions about an object the teacher pointed to. "Is this ball big? ... Is this ball big?"

The next test was whether the children could answer *what* questions. These are more difficult than *yes-no* questions because the children must supply the content word. "This ball is what? ... Yes, this ball is *big.*"

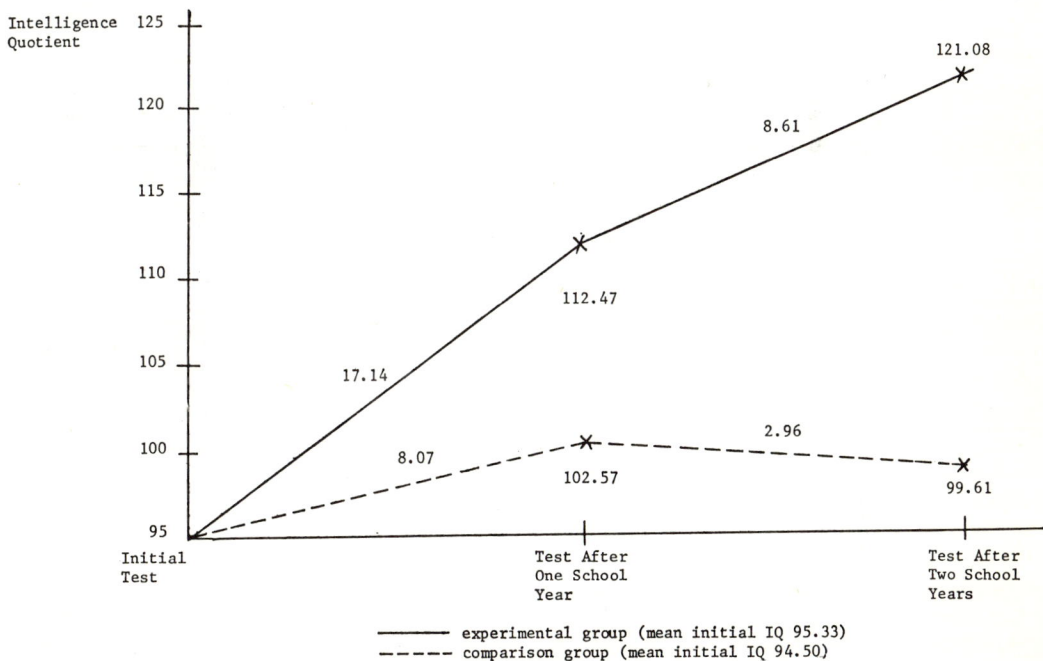

Figure 1.

The teacher usually introduced the various tests rapid fire, in no particular order. However, if the children had difficulty with a *what* question, the teacher would restructure the tasks, starting with the *finding* task and working up to the *what* task. "Sidney, find the ball that is big . . . Good. This ball is big. Is this ball big? . . . Yes, this ball is big. This ball is what? . . . Yes, this ball is big."

While the rate at which questions were presented to the group and to individuals in the group varied with the tasks, the teacher often introduced as many as 20 questions a minute. She used the children's responses to these questions as indications of whether or not they had learned the concepts she was presenting. She geared her presentation *to the lowest performer in the group*, because the goal of instruction was to teach every child each criterion skill. (If a child consistently lagged behind the others in the group, he was moved to a slower group in which his performance was more consistent with that of the other members.)

IQ Performance of Disadvantaged Subjects

The disadvantaged subjects in the experimental program achieved significantly greater Stanford-Binet IQ gains than the subjects in the comparison program. More important, the mean IQ of the experimental subjects after 2 years of instruction was 121.08, well above the mean of normal, middle-class children. The mean of the comparison group was 99.61 after 2 years of instruction.

Figure 1 shows the IQ performance of the experimental and comparison groups after 1 and 2 years of instruction. The comparison group achieved an 8.07 gain after the first year of instruction, but had a loss of 2.96 points after the second year (which is typical of early compensatory programs). The experimental group showed a 17.14 gain after the first year and an 8.61 gain after the second year.

Table 2 shows the performance of the in-

Table 2. *Stanford-Binet IQ performance of disadvantaged experimental subjects after one and two years of training.*

Subject*	Entering IQ	IQ after One Year	First-Year Gain	IQ after Two Years	Second-Year Gain	Total Gain
MA	92	113	+21	123	+10	+31
TA	93	94	+1	103	+9	+10
TB	105	112	+7	121	+9	+16
MB	89	101	+12	131	+30	+42
(DB)	(82)	(112)	(+30)	—	—	(+30)
RC	99	116	+17	119	+3	+20
MC	86	105	+19	112	+7	+26
(NC)	(70)	(89)	(+19)	—	—	(+19)
BG	119	130	+11	139	+9	+20
BP	90	107	+17	112	+5	+32
SV	85	101	+16	108	+7	+23
RV	109	127	+18	138	+11	+29
DD	99	118	+19	129	+11	+30
DW	101	123	+22	118	−5	+17
(BW)	(111)	(139)	(+28)	—	—	(+28)
X Total	95.33	112.47	17.14	—	—	24.20
X One-Year Subjects	87.66	113.33	25.67	—	—	25.67
X Two-Year Subjects	97.25	112.25	15.00	121.08	8.83	23.83

* One-year subjects in parentheses.

Table 3. *IQ performance of disadvantaged comparison subjects.*

Subject	Entering IQ	IQ after Two Years Training	Change
AB	94	115	+21
AC	118	115	−3
AD	83	94	+11
BA	90	92	+2
BB	88	´74	−14
BC	76	93	+17
BD	92	90	−2
CR	101	87	−14
CS	82	95	+13
DB	85	100	+15
BC	79	83	+4
DF	107	97	−10
DJ	113	114	+1
DK	107	120	+13
EA	97	109	+12
EE	97	88	−9
EM	89	94	+5
EP	93	93	0
MA	92	107	+15
MB	88	87	−1
MC	79	87	+8
MR	93	89	−4
NB	94	104	+10
NS	91	106	+15
NT	101	109	+8
PA	109	127	+18
PB	111	117	+6
PR	97	103	+6
X	94.50	99.61	+5.11

experimental subjects experienced an overall loss. The lowest gain was 10 points. The largest total gain was 42. The lowest IQ score after 2 years of instruction was 103 (subject TA). The highest IQ score after 2 years of instruction was 139 (subject BG).

Table 3 shows the IQ performance of the disadvantaged children in the comparison group after 2 years of instruction. Only 12 of the 28 control subjects scored higher than 103, the score of the lowest IQ performer in the experimental group. Eight control subjects had overall IQ losses compared to no IQ losses for the experimental group. The highest IQ gain for the control group was 21 points, whereas the *mean* gain for the experimental group was 24 points.

Achievement Performance of Experimental Disadvantaged Subjects

Table 4 shows the achievement performance in reading, arithmetic, and spelling of the 12 subjects who finished 2 years of the experimental program. The mean reading achievement was grade level 2.60 with a

Table 4. *Achievement of disadvantaged experimental subjects after two years of instruction.*

Subject	Grade Level on Wide-Range Achievement Test			
	IQ	Reading	Arithmetic	Spelling
MA	123	2.7	2.2	1.8
TA	103	1.6	2.3	1.7
TB	121	3.1	3.3	2.2
MB	131	3.7	3.1	2.1
RC	119	2.7	2.9	2.0
MC	112	3.6	2.5	2.3
BG	139	3.1	3.3	2.1
BP	112	1.6	1.4	1.0
SV	108	2.0	2.2	1.7
RV	138	3.1	2.7	2.0
DD	129	1.7	2.2	1.9
DW	118	2.3	2.0	1.6
	121.08	2.60	2.51	1.57

dividual disadvantaged subjects after 1 and 2 years of instruction. The mean first-year gain of those children who were retained in the program for 2 years was 15.00 (IQ 112.25). The mean gain of those who were not continued a second year was 25.67 (IQ 113.33). The total mean gain for the 2-year subjects after the second year of instruction was 23.83.

There was only one instance of an IQ loss in either the first or second year of the experimental program. Subject DW had a second-year loss of 5 IQ points. None of the

Table 5. *Achievement and IQ scores of middle-class subjects after one and two years of instruction.*

Subject	First-Year Achievement on Wide Range			Second-Year Achievement on Wide Range						IQ Stanford-Binet
	Read.	Ar.	Sp.	Read.	Gain	Ar.	Gain	Sp.	Gain	
MC	2.0	1.4	1.8							
M	3.5	2.0	2.0							
G	1.4	1.2	1.0	3.3	+1.9	2.2	+1.0	2.2	+1.2	113
H	2.0	1.2	1.9							
H	2.7	1.4	1.8							
H	2.7	1.2	1.9	3.9	+1.2	3.9	+2.7	2.3	+1.4	125
H	1.7	1.6	1.6	3.0	+1.3	2.9	+1.3	1.9	+.3	118
SK	2.7	1.2	1.9							
VK	3.4	2.0	2.1							
JL	1.8	1.4	1.5	3.4	+1.6	2.7	+1.3	1.8	+.3	121
KM	2.0	1.5	1.6							
BO	2.6	1.4	2.2							
CP	1.9	1.4	1.5	2.9	+1.0	3.1	+1.7	2.1	+.6	140
MP	2.2	1.4	1.8							
GS	1.7	1.4	1.2	3.5	+1.8	2.5	+1.1	2.0	+.8	110
KT	2.7	1.5	1.8							
T	3.0	1.4	2.1	3.9	+.9	3.1	+1.7	2.1	—	137
SW	3.7	1.6	1.3							
M of Two yr. sub.	2.03	1.37	1.54	3.41	+1.4	2.91	+1.5	2.06	+.66	123.43
M of One yr. sub.	2.68	1.51	1.84							
M of Total	2.43	1.46	1.72							

range of 1.6–3.7. The mean arithmetic performance was 2.51 with a range of 1.4–3.3. The mean spelling performance was 1.87 with a range of 1.0–2.3. As Table 4 indicates, the correspondence between IQ scores and achievement scores is not perfect. Subject MC had the second highest reading achievement score and the highest spelling achievement score; yet, he had an IQ of only 112. Similarly, subject TB had achievement scores of 3.1, 3.3, and 2.2 in reading, arithmetic, and spelling; however, TB's IQ was only "average" for the group—121.

The Middle-Class Subjects

Table 5 summarizes the performance of the middle-class experimental subjects. After the end of the first year of instruction, the mean achievements of the middle-class subjects in reading and spelling had nearly reached the level that was achieved by the disadvantaged subjects after 2 years of instruction. The middle-class children had achieved a mean grade level of 2.43 in reading and 1.72 in spelling (compared to 2.60 and 1.87 for the disadvantaged children after 2 years of instruction). At the end of the first year, the achievement of the 7 children who continued in the program for 2 years was below the mean of those who did not continue for a second year in all achievement areas, but most noticeably in reading achievement. The mean reading achievement for the continuing children was 2.03 (compared to 2.68 for the 1-year subjects); however, during the second year, continuing subjects progressed a full year and a half in reading achievement, terminating the program with a mean reading achievement score of 3.41 (.8 of a year above the mean of the disadvantaged children).

Interestingly enough, the IQ performance of the middle-class children was only about 2 points higher than that of the disadvantaged subjects, after 2 years of instruction. Both middle-class and disadvantaged subjects seem to be regressing toward a mean, but this mean is not IQ 100; it is considerably higher than that. This mean would be an operational indicator of the effective rate of "cognitive development" induced by the program in which these subjects were placed.

Table 6 shows the achievement scores of the middle-class comparison children after they had 2 years of instruction (having finished pre-kindergarten). The mean grade levels of achievement for the Montessori-trained children in reading and arithmetic (1.04 and 1.21) were well below the means of the middle-class experimental children after 1 year of Bereiter-Engelmann training (2.43 and 1.46). Significantly, the Montessori-trained children did not "burst into reading."

DISCUSSION

Performance of the Disadvantaged Children

The performance difference between the experimental and control disadvantaged children is most economically explained as a function of different training. The experimental children were taught new skills at a much higher rate than the children in the comparison program. The children in the comparison group were taught at a rate only slightly higher than the rate at which they would have been taught if they had not attended the preschool-kindergarten program. The experimental children, on the other hand, were taught at a rate substantially higher than they would have been taught if they had not been enrolled in the program.

There is a tendency in evaluating the effectiveness of instructional programs to look at the long-range effects of the program. While such effects are relevant, they are not of primary concern. The primary issue is: Can a program meet the educational objectives to which it addresses itself? In the case of the present experiment, can the program teach disadvantaged preschool and kindergarten children basic skills in reading, arithmetic, and the logical use of language? The IQ scores of the children reflect the effectiveness of the language program. The achievement scores in reading, arithmetic, and spelling indicate the effectiveness of the arithmetic and reading programs. Not one experimental child scored below 100 in IQ after 2 years of instruction (compared with 14 children in the comparison group who scored below 100). Not one experimental child scored below 1.6 grade level in reading or below 1.4 grade level in arithmetic. In other words, there were no instructional failures. All of the children were taught. The mean performance in arithmetic and reading

Table 6. *Performance of middle-class comparison five-year-olds on Wide-Range Achievement Test after two years of instruction (Test, May 1966).*

Subject	Reading	Arithmetic
DA	1.1	.7
SA	2.6	2.3
JD	.9	1.2
KD	.3	1.4
CE	1.3	1.0
CG	.5	1.0
MH	1.8	1.6
FJ	1.5	1.2
MK	1.3	1.4
EL	1.2	1.5
RM	1.2	1.5
JP	0	.3
LS	.9	1.2
AS	1.3	1.4
DV	.9	1.4
MV	.7	1.1
MW	.3	.6
X̄	1.04	1.21

indicates that the experimental subjects, after finishing their kindergarten year, performed as well as "average" disadvantaged children 2 or 3 years older. Mean achievement scores of 2.5 in reading and arithmetic are not unusual for fourth-grade disadvantaged children. If children can be accelerated by 3 years (as the present experiment indicates), the general failure in the public schools is not necessarily a result of the children's innate inferiority or lack of aptitude. It is a function of inadequate instruction.

Middle-Class Children

At the end of the first year of reading instruction, the middle-class children performed on the 2.43 grade level, which means that they had progressed nearly a year and a half during the first year. Those children who continued for a second year in the program had progressed 1 year (achieving a mean reading score of 2.03 at the end of the first year). During the second year, however, the children who continued gained nearly a year and a half in reading. These children, in other words, were progressing at a faster rate than older children in the public schools.

By the end of the second year, 2 disadvantaged children scored above grade 3.4 in reading, the mean of the middle-class children, and interestingly, both of these children were Negroes who entered with IQ's in the 80's (MB and MC). Four disadvantaged children scored on or above the middle-class mean in arithmetic. By the end of the second year, there were disadvantaged children in the top-performing study group and there were middle-class children in the B and C groups.

The middle-class children did not have to be taught many of the sub-skills that had to be programmed for the disadvantaged children, especially in reading. For example, the middle-class children did not have to be taught how to blend the letters of a word. The disadvantaged children required a great deal of practice in this skill. By the end of the second year, the advantaged children were almost a full year ahead of the disadvantaged children in reading, although the

disadvantaged children made more than 1 year's progress during the second year.

The reading performance of the middle-class and disadvantaged children was achieved with only about 96 hours of classroom instruction. The amount of time devoted to reading in the regular school program during the first 2 years of instruction is probably 3–6 times greater. It seems evident, in terms of the performance of children, that the public schools do not utilize their available time to good advantage.

The performance of the experimental children may be viewed as an example of the "hawthorne" effect. However, in the program there was very little interaction with the parents and correspondingly little attempt to change the patterns of behavior in the home. There was a total of 3 parent meetings over a 2-year period. During these meetings, the staff members emphasized the good performance of the children and tried to persuade the parents that their children were smart. Beyond this, however, nothing was done to change the conditions which affected the outside-school learning of the children. The changes that took place in these children were changes that resulted primarily from the experimental treatment in the classroom.

The Effects of "Pressure" on Younger Children

One of the traditional encumbrances to early formal education is the belief that the pressure resulting from such instruction will developmentally malform the children. While it is difficult to evaluate the effects of the present program on the children's personalities, interviews with parents and observations of the children disclosed no ill effect. In the program there were virtually no tantrums or behavior problems beyond the second week, although at least 2 of the disadvantaged children were considered emotionally disturbed. The children participated, and they seemed to enjoy participation. All children engaged in the music period. All complied with the rules—but not as automatons. If the program failed in any respect, it did not adequately prepare the children for the kind of behavior-for-behavior-sake rules which they would encounter in school. During free time or semi-structured activities, the children talked freely to each other. They made observations and asked questions. When given the slightest opportunity, they would relate personal experiences and engage in conversations that were sophisticated for 4- and 5-year-old children. In short, they showed no engrams from the "pressure" of the program. They worked hard; but the parents noted no regressive behavior, bed wetting, thumb sucking, nightmares, etc. In fact, if the parents' reports are to be taken seriously, the children had fewer emotional problems than any sample of "unpressured" children.

Perhaps the most noticeable characteristic of the children after 2 years of instruction was their confidence. The easiest way for the teacher to capture their interest was to announce a difficult task. "This is so hard I shouldn't even be giving it to little kids like you. You'll never be able to do it." The children would respond to this type of challenge by insisting, "We can do it! You'll see." Their confidence had been programmed through fooler games in which the children proved to be "smarter" than the teacher. The children exhibited confidence because they had received many demonstrations that they were competent and could succeed in challenging situations. They had surprised— even crushed—the teacher with their smartness. This is not to say that the children would be confident in *all* situations or even all instructional situations. But they had firm and realistically based confidence about their capacity to perform in new-learning situations of the type presented in the B-E program.

SUMMARY

A group of disadvantaged 4-year-olds and a group of middle-class 4-year-old children were taught intensively in the Bereiter-Engelmann program for 2 years (the preschool and kindergarten years). The group of disadvantaged children was comparable in IQ and race-sex composition to a group of 28 children assigned to a traditional nursery-school and kindergarten program. The middle-class children were roughly comparable to a group of Montessori-trained 4-year-olds. The major hypothesis tested by the program was that children are taught at different rates; if the effective rate at which disadvantaged and middle-class children are taught is increased substantially, these children will perform at an above-normal level, which means that the disadvantaged subjects may become "superior" in specific areas of achievement.

The hypothesis was confirmed. The disadvantaged children in the comparison group showed no particular advantage over children in similar compensatory programs, such as Head-Start programs. The program failed to bring half of the children up to an IQ of 100. The mean for the group was 99.6. The experimental program, however, brought the IQ's of every child to above 100. The mean IQ after two years of instruction was 121, with a range from 103 to 139. The mean achievements of the experimental group were: reading, 2.6; arithmetic, 2.5; and spelling, 1.9. The scores are what one would expect from 8- to 10-year-old disadvantaged children; the experimental subjects, however, were 6 years old at the end of the program.

After one year of instruction, the middle-class subjects had achievement scores of 2.4 in reading, 1.5 in arithmetic, and 1.7 in spelling. The comparison group did not score as well in any of these achievement areas, although the comparison children had been in a Montessori program for two years at the time of testing. By the end of the second year, those middle-class children who continued in the program scored 3.4 in reading, 2.9 in arithmetic, and 2.1 in spelling. The mean IQ of the group after the second year was 123, only several IQ points higher than the mean IQ of the disadvantaged experimental children.

The present experiments seem to indicate, rather strongly, that the reason disadvantaged children fail in public schools is not necessarily that they are genetically inferior or developmentally impaired but that they receive poor instruction. If younger children with initially lower mental ages can achieve at an above-normal rate, school-age disadvantaged children (who usually learn more rapidly) should have little trouble achieving at the rate of normal children in specific achievement areas if instruction is adequate.

The results of the experiment cast rather serious doubt on the validity of IQ measures as indicators of genetic endowment. The children in the experimental program were changed rather dramatically during the two years of instruction. Unless one knew what went on in the environment during these two years, one would be at something of a loss to describe these children. If we were to take their terminal IQ scores as indications of genetic endowment, then we would be faced with the difficult problem of explaining how the genetic composition of the children changed over the two-year period. Was it something that they ate?

The fact that some of the children made relatively little progress compared to others may be taken as an indication of differential genetic influence. But again, this conclusion would be quite hasty. Before we can intelligently discuss what happened to individuals, we would have to know what went on in that individual's environment (his total waking environment and not merely the 2½ hours a day that he was in school) before we could presume to talk about the relative influence of the "environment" on intelligence. Probably everyone would agree that genetic endowment makes a difference, but the extent of that difference is far from obvious. At best, genetic influence seems to be a minor factor among the overwhelming majority of children.

4

IN ELEMENTARY-SCHOOL EDUCATION

Most of the first applications of behavior modification to education occurred in elementary-school classrooms. They involved "studies" in which a psychologist would come into the classroom, suggest to the teacher modifications that followed standard experimental design, and leave after collecting his data. The first article in this section, by Altman and Linton, reviews much of this early work. The review also suggests that large-scale use of such techniques and designs is far from meeting reality. One reason is the presence of existing public schools. Innovators in preschool education have been able to construct new programs to suit their methodology, whereas the behavior modifier who wishes to work in elementary education must change practices that have been previously established in the public schools.

One way to break into the public schools is through teacher training programs. The second article, by Stachnik, shows the results of one course in behavior modification for teachers. For all of the teachers involved, this course was the first experience they had with the theory or practice of behavior modification. After relatively little instruction, the teachers designed and carried out projects that dealt with social behaviors as well as academic skills and group as well as individual behavior. These studies show that the elementary-school classroom teacher can effectively utilize behavior management techniques with minimum training and without day-to-day supervision.

Some elementary schools have been established whose total operation is based on principles derived from the experimental analysis of behavior. The third article, by Hren, Mueller, Spates, Ulrich, and Ulrich, describes one such program. This paper is dedicated to all those who have expended great effort to establish behavior modification programs in the public schools and who ordinarily have been limited to isolated, often bootleg kinds of projects. Although financial difficulties have constrained development, there are many aspects of this program that public-school teachers and administrators would do well to emulate.

Operant conditioning in the classroom setting: A review of research

KARL I. ALTMAN AND THOMAS E. LINTON

Within the last two decades several psychologists have moved from an experimental analysis of behavior toward a concern for the applied implications of their laboratory work. This move might be viewed as one from a laboratory study of operant conditioning to behavioral engineering in various community institutions. Both the operant conditioner and the behavioral engineer are cognizant of the theory and applied principles of behavior modification. The operant conditioner, however, is concerned with the advancement of the basic laboratory science and is interested in variables that relate to behavior, while the behavioral engineer has left the laboratory in order to make systematic applications of the principles of operant conditioning to problem behaviors as determined by society (Homme, Baca, Cottingham, and Homme, 1968). This change in direction has been accompanied by a new research strategy, i.e., the applied analysis of behavior and a new body of knowledge.

Some of the current dimensions of an applied behavior analysis have been described by Baer, Wolf, and Risley (1968). Many of these dimensions are common to an experimental analysis of behavior as well, e.g., the quantitative characteristics of the target behavior and an experimental manipulation to determine the variables responsible for behavioral change. The major difference between the strategies of experimental and applied behavior analyses lies in their focus (Baer et al., 1968).

"Nonapplied research is likely to look at any behavior, and at any variable which may conceivably relate to it. Applied research is constrained to look at variables which can be effective in improving the behavior under study [p. 91]."

The purpose of this review is to summarize the findings of the behavioral engineers in their attempts to improve contingency management in the public school classroom. The review will also present some of the problems and issues involved in an applied behavioral analysis of classroom behavior.

There are three major reasons why teachers and classrooms are ideal targets for behavioral engineering. First, the classroom is the traditional place where children's social and academic behavior is modified (Whelan and Haring, 1966).

"Teachers have traditionally been assigned to change or modify the behavior of children entrusted to them for several hours a day [p. 288]."

The desired objectives are generally accomplished by the use of praise, grades, and criticisms contingent upon student classroom behavior. By definition, the teacher is a contingency manager, i.e., the teacher knowingly or not reinforces behavior. Given time and experience, most teachers determine which techniques are most effective for them in managing classroom behavior (Hall, Panyan, Rabon, and Broden, 1968b). Such trial and error learning by teachers is not only unnecessary but inefficient and often unsuccessful.

Writers such as Bergan and Caldwell (1967) and Homme (1967) have suggested that the behavioral engineers have already developed a technology which could provide a more effective and empirically based approach to the school-learning process. The latter is probably an overstatement of the present status of behavioral engineering theory. But whether or not it is an overstatement, the theory and technology of behavioral engineering provide a means of developing a more effective and scientific learning model for the public schools.

The schools are ideally suited for behavioral engineering in that the necessary en-

From *The Journal of Educational Research,* February 1971, *64*(6). Reprinted by permission of the authors and *The Journal of Educational Research.*

vironmental controls are feasible in this setting. That teachers could become contingency managers and would be able to reinforce the desired, and recognize and reinforce approximations to that behavior, however, is not a sufficient condition (Homme et al., 1968). The contingency manager must be able to set, specify, and to some extent control the environmental variables so that a response by the learner can be reinforced or not as the occasion demands. Public-school classrooms are amenable to such control since the students are captive audiences in what is perhaps an already overly controlled environment.

EARLY IDENTIFICATION
AND PREVENTION
OF LEARNING DISORDERS

Another reason for the application of behavioral analysis to the classroom is that these techniques offer much promise for the prevention of those behavior problems which have traditionally led to special class placement and eventual rejection by the school system. Studies by Cohen (1967) and Martin, Burkholder, Rosenthal, Tharp, and Thorne (1968) have shown that some students are not susceptible to the behavioral controls which are usually employed in the public-school classroom. However these students can be shaped so that they are able to respond to the usual classroom reinforcement techniques.

The extent of shaping necessary for the disadvantaged and the handicapped child would be greatly reduced if early identification procedures were utilized. Studies have indicated that early identification is possible (Zax, Cohen, Rappaport, Beach, and Laird, 1968). An alternative approach to prevention lies in utilizing more effectively, or extending, the behavioral controls usually exercised in the classroom in order to deal with a wider range of behaviors.

EMPHASIS ON CLASSROOM
BEHAVIORAL CONTROL

This review is primarily concerned with the management of those student behaviors usu-

ally considered as prerequisites for classroom learning. The concern here is not with the nature and structure of the material to be learned. For this reason, programmed instruction has not been included. The research in that area has recently been reviewed by Leib, Cusack, Hughes, Pilette, Wertner, and Kintz (1967). Those studies concerned mainly with special class, institutionalized, or pre-school populations will be presented only when they have relevance for the public school classroom. By relevance is meant the presentation of new techniques or the underscoring of old techniques which upon empirical assessment have shown promise for effective application in the usual classroom setting.

For the sake of orderly discussion, it appeared worthwhile to group the studies under the headings of teacher attention, peer attention, token reinforcement, and vicarious reinforcement, based upon the nature of the reinforcement contingency employed and assessed.

TEACHER ATTENTION

Teacher attention in the form of praise, smiles, and reprimands, when made contingent upon the behaviors of students in a classroom, may serve to increase the rate those behaviors are emitted regardless of the nature, positive or negative, of that attention. Studies of nursery-school children summarized by Baer and Wolf (1967, 1968) have lent support to this assumption and have subsequently led to its investigation in public-school classrooms.

Holmes (1966) reported the case study of a boy who chronically disrupted the classroom, initiated fights, and was under-achieving academically. An evaluation of the situation indicated that the teacher was reprimanding the child in the classroom and that this served to maintain or accelerate the deviant behavior. A reversal of the strategy by the teacher was initiated. The teacher punished the child by isolating him from the class and attended to appropriate behavior while the child was in the class. This procedure resulted in an apparent elimination of the student's problem behavior in the classroom. As Holmes has indicated, this study has little value other than providing an illustration of the principles of behavior modification in action in a school setting. Since systemic recording of behavior was not carried out by Holmes, we cannot be assured that change did occur.

A preliminary study by Becker, Madsen, Arnold, and Thomas (1967) demonstrated a reliable technique for recording teacher-student behavior in the classroom. Ten children whose behaviors could reliably be rated by trained observers, and who also displayed frequent problem classroom behaviors were selected for study. The children were drawn from 5 different classrooms each with a different teacher. Following the 5-week baseline period, teachers were instructed to provide rules of good classroom conduct, dispense reinforcement, e.g., smiles and praise, only for behaviors compatible with learning and teaching, and to generally ignore behaviors incompatible with these goals. When teacher approval was made contingent upon appropriate behavior, the rate of such behavior increased significantly. The average deviant behavior for the 10 children during the baseline period was 62.13 percent while the deviant behavior during the experimental phase was 29.19 percent. The follow-up study (Madsen, Becker, Thomas, Koser, and Plager, 1968b) attempted to institute controls which were lacking from the earlier study by Becker et al. (1967). By instituting rules and praise, ignoring conditions separately, and employing a reversal to baseline, it was possible to determine the relative effectiveness of each condition by comparing them against a common baseline. Attending to the rules and ignoring inappropriate behavior exerted no substantial decremental effects upon the base rate of inappropriate behavior, but when praise for appropriate behavior was added, inappropriate behavior decreased significantly.

Further support for the effectiveness of praise contingent upon appropriate and not inappropriate classroom behavior in decreasing the rate of disruptive classroom behavior has been gathered by Carnine, Becker, Thomas, Poe, and Plager (1968). The rate of disruptive behavior was assessed for students when the teachers used only disapproval (baseline) and approval for appropriate behavior and ignored inappropriate behavior for one group of students (B), but did not use approval for another group (A). They then withdrew praise for group A, and instituted the prior group A condition for group B. The dispensing of praise in the classroom was found to affect decreases in disruptive behavior only for those students for whom it was response contingent at that time. Approval, consequated with appropriate behavior, and the absence of approval, consequated with inappropriate behavior, appeared to be the necessary conditions for maintaining classroom behavioral control in this case.

Of those studies discussed thus far, only Madsen, Becker, and Thomas (1968a) ·and Carnine et al. (1968) made any attempt to reverse experimental conditions. Neither of these reversals consisted of switching the positively reinforced behavior. If teacher praise is indeed a positive reinforcer, it should increase the rate of whatever behavior it consequates. Hall, Lund, and Jackson (1968a) provided a test of that notion. From 3 different classrooms, a total of 5 students were selected by their teachers as manifesting problem behaviors. After base rates for student study and nonstudy behaviors were established and teacher attention to each was tabulated by reliable observers, teachers were instructed to pay attention only to study behaviors. This procedure resulted in an increase in study behavior for all 3 classes.

The next experimental condition called for a reversal in the form of attending only to nonstudy behaviors. The results of this contingency reversal revealed consequent decrements in the study behaviors and, of course, increases in nonstudy behaviors of the students. These data then confirm the hypothesis that attention functioned as a positive reinforcer for whatever behavior it followed.

The studies mentioned up to this point have dealt with problem behaviors in public-school classrooms with typical pupil-teacher ratios. None of these studies has attempted to assess the effectiveness of teacher attention on all students in a single classroom. Instead, the target population of children with problem behaviors was selected for study. In one of a series of experiments reported by Hall et al. (1968b), study and nonstudy behavior of an entire first-grade class and consequent attention to each of these conditions by their teacher was recorded. Following the establishment of a base rate, the teacher was instructed to increase positive comments following study behavior, and a concomitant increase in study behavior occurred. Study behavior sharply decreased in a brief reversal when almost no reinforcement for it was provided. The return of reinforcement brought the study behavior back up to a rate slightly above that for the first reinforcement condition. Up to this point, negative comments following nonstudy behavior were only assessed but not manipulated. Such comments, when made contingent upon nonstudy behavior remained nearly constant throughout all prior conditions. Following the second reinforcing condition, the teacher was instructed to discontinue all comments following nonstudy behavior, but to continue her positive comments contingent upon study behavior. As a result, no noticeable change in study behavior or consequently nonstudy behavior occurred relative to the rates present during the prior reinforcement period. These results shed doubt upon the interpretation that it is merely the amount of attention which is the most important variable influencing the amount of study behavior. If amount of attention alone was the determining factor, a deceleration in study behavior would have been expected when the comments following nonstudy behavior were discontinued.

A second study which focused upon the entire class rather than target students is that of Madsen et al. (1968b). This study systematically investigated the contention made by Holmes (1966) that some behavioral consequences that were regarded by the teachers as punishing or negative may, in fact, have been positive reinforcers for the behaviors they were intended to punish. Prior to this experiment, these teachers had unsuccessfully tried several methods to lessen classroom talking and out-of-seat behavior for their 48 "lower-primary" students. The teachers recorded the number of times the students were out of their seats as well as the frequency of "sit-down" commands and praise they gave for appropriate behavior. After these base rates were established, a condition was initiated where the teachers were asked to triple the frequency of their "sit-down" commands. This experimental condition was conducted twice. Following the second condition of frequent sit-down commands, teachers were instructed to give praise for in-seat and ignore out-of-seat behaviors. Each time the frequency of sit-down commands was increased, the out-of-seat behavior increased relative to the base rates. But when praise was made contingent upon appropriate behavior and inappropriate behavior was ignored, the out-of-seat behavior decreased to a level below both of the prior base rates. Technically, these results do not indicate that punishment accelerated the frequency of the behavior it was intended to decelerate. Instead, these data point out that what is considered a punisher by the reinforcing agent may actually be a positive reinforcer for the student. Theoretically, if sit-down commands originally became aversive by being paired with a primary punishment, they would lose their aversiveness when such punishment no longer was paired. In order to keep the sit-down command enforced, periodic pairing of the commands with aversive stimulation may have to be accomplished.

Each study mentioned has attempted to remove or decelerate behaviors of particular students or entire classes designated as a problem by the teacher involved. Such deceleration was said to have been achieved through systematically varying teacher behavior. It could be argued that such techniques are effective only for restricted populations, i.e., those where "problem" behavior exists. If true, such a criticism would only curtail the generality of the principles involved and not render them invalid or unreliable. But the validity of this criticism is quite doubtful in light of a study of Thomas, Becker, and Armstrong (1968a). Here, by systematically varying teacher disapproval (e.g., physical restraint, verbal reprimands) and approval (e.g., smiles, praise), an initially "good class" became disruptive. Base rates of teacher approval and disapproval and student disruptive behavior (e.g., noise-making and being out-of-seat) and appropriate behavior (e.g., reading) were established. Then the condition of no approval (i.e., only disapproval) was instituted followed by a base rate. These conditions were then followed by those of no approval, frequent disapproval, no approval, and base rate. Such manipulation suggested that the consequence of withdrawing teacher approval and increasing teacher disapproval results in a concomitant increase in disruptive student behavior. Although the frequency of disruptive behavior was highly variable under most conditions and two independent variables were simultaneously manipulated, the fact that disruptive behavior reached new heights under frequent disapproval is of interest. This finding and those of Hall et al. (1968b), Holmes (1966), and Madsen et al. (1968b) support the tenability of the hypothesis that "negative" consequation in the form of teacher disapproval may function as a positive reinforcer for some disruptive classroom behaviors.

In retrospect, studies of the systematic variation of teacher attention appear to indicate: (a) that teacher approval functions as a positive reinforcer for those student behaviors it is contingent upon; and (b) teacher disapproval, physical or verbal, may also serve as a positive reinforcer or have no effect upon those behaviors, usually disruptive classroom behaviors, with which it is made contingent upon.

PEER ATTENTION

Thomas et al. (1968a) have suggested another interpretation of the increases in disruptive behavior following withdrawal of teacher approval. It may have been that such behaviors were positively reinforced by peer attention. Patterson, Jones, Whittier, and Wright (1965) offer some support for the effectiveness of the classroom peer group in controlling the behavior of a classmate. Comparing this study with an earlier one (Patterson, 1965), Patterson speculated that

"the one variable which seems to account for the difference (a more dramatic effect) among studies is the greater involvement of the peer group..." (Patterson et al., 1965, p. 224). Although these studies both effected acceleration in hyperactive children's appropriate behavior in a classroom situation, peer group influence was not systematically studied.

One such study has appeared in the literature, i.e., Evans and Oswalt (1968). Two students were selected from fourth-grade spelling and arithmetic classes and 1 student from fifth- and sixth-grade social-science classes. All of the Ss were considered academic underachievers by their teachers. For all of these experimental students and their classmates, used as controls, discontinuance of regular classroom activities in the form of story reading or early class dismissal was made contingent upon gains in weekly test performance for the experimental Ss.

Performance gains were assessed relative to base rates and classmate controls. Overall analysis showed that for the 6 experimental Ss mean gain was significantly greater than that of their classmates. Although this study tends to support the contention that peer influence may have positive reinforcing effects for the behavior of individuals, it is possible that access to the reinforcing events alone was the influential variable. Future studies should contrast the effectiveness of group and individual performance with individual reinforcement contingent upon individual performance.[1] Such an analysis would clarify whether peer influence is an effective variable in affecting individual performance in the classroom. No conclusions regarding the efficacy of peer influence seem warranted.

TOKEN REINFORCEMENT

Many public-school classrooms have traditionally been operated so that the behavioral consequences set up to maintain appropriate behavior are social reinforcement, e.g., in the form of teacher attention, and token rein-

1 This study (Barrish, Saunders, and Wolf, 1969) has been performed since December 1968, when the present article was completed.

forcement. Token reinforcement has been defined as "... tangible objects or symbols which attain reinforcing power by being exchanged for a variety of other objects such as candy and trinkets which are back-up reinforcers" (O'Leary and Becker, 1967). For some, and perhaps most children, doing well in school signified by stars, grades, and points is already a desirable consequence when they enter school. For others they may become incentives by being exchanged for other reinforcers such as access to responsible positions, earlier dismissal from school, and teacher or parental approval. But there may be some children for whom none of the usual reinforcers found in public schools are effective. It has been found that for delinquents (Cohen, 1967), retardates, and conduct problem children "generalized social reinforcers such as praise, teacher attention, and positive feedback, often have minimal effects or negative effects upon their classroom behavior" (Meichenbaum, Bowers, and Ross, 1968, p. 343). For these children, it appears that the traditional social reinforcement is inadequate to establish and/or maintain appropriate behavior. Suggestions for improving the effectiveness of their education is necessary and the research which follows may possess that potential.

Bushell, Wrobel, and Michaelis (1968) investigated the effectiveness of token reinforcers in accelerating the study behaviors of preschoolers. Access to special events was indirectly made contingent upon study behavior by providing tokens required to purchase such events directly contingent upon study behaviors. During the second phase tokens and praise were still dispensed for study behavior, but the purchasing power of the tokens was eliminated by permitting all children to engage in special events regardless of the amount of study behavior displayed. The contingent phase was then reinstituted. For 10 of the 12 children studied, the results indicated that study behaviors were highest when the special events were contingent and lowest when they were not contingent. It should be noted that only the value of the tokens changed in the noncontingent phase, indicating that the social reinforcement paired with the tokens throughout all phases could not alone maintain or achieve the same rate of study behavior reached by contingent redeemable tokens plus social reinforcement. In the public school, tokens and special events such as museum trips and access to snack times are available reinforcers which usually are not made contingent upon student performance in any systematic manner.

In the Becker et al. (1967) study discussed earlier, differential social reinforcement from the teacher for appropriate classroom behavior did not seem to effect behavior change in one student until the addition of a daily half-hour of remedial reading. To assess the effect of remediation, Thomas, Nielsen, Kuypers, and Becker (1968b) observed the frequency of disruptive behavior of a single child in a public-school classroom under the following: (a) ongoing conditions (87.6 percent), (b) low teacher approval (69.1 percent), (c) high approval (51.1 percent), (d) low approval (64 percent), (e) high approval and 6 weeks of tutoring (33.4 percent), and (f) throughout an 8-week follow-up period (11 percent). The numbers in parentheses show the percent of observation intervals during which the S displayed disruptive behavior. It appears that although teacher approval of nondisruptive behavior decelerated the rate of disruptive behavior, tutoring was instrumental in reducing it even further. It is important to note that the tutoring procedure employed entailed the use of redeemable token reinforcers, marks on a card, paired with praise for academic progress in the tutoring session. Thus, further deceleration in disruptive behavior may have been due to an increase in the efficacy of social reinforcers by virtue of being paired with "back-up" reinforcers. An expansion of the student's academic repertoire thereby increased his potential for emitting appropriate responses and consequently also increased the probability that he will be reinforced socially in class, or both. Although the validity of these interpretations is an empirical question as far as the results of the Thomas et al. (1968a) study are concerned, each provides a different approach to remediation and each may be differentially effective with different students' problems.

Before continuing with the discussion of

the efficacy of token reinforcement in controlling classroom behavior, it is important to answer the question regarding the feasibility of this technique in public schools which has been posed by Quay, Werry, McQueen, and Sprague (1966). Bushell et al. (1968) have demonstrated the feasibility of token reinforcement in a preschool classroom setting. O'Leary et al. (1967) demonstrated a significant reduction in the "daily mean of deviant behavior" from a baseline range of 66 to 91 percent to a range of 3 to 32 percent during the token program. The class had one teacher and 17 nine-year-old boys who had been assigned to the class because they exhibited such "undesirable" classroom behaviors as temper tantrums, uncontrolled laughter, and fighting. During the token period each child received points, ranging from 1–10, in a booklet and approval which reflected the extent to which the child had exhibited the appropriate behaviors was listed on the blackboard. Points could be redeemed for a variety of small prizes. The teacher doled out ratings from 3 to 5 times daily at the end of the lessons. The teacher's time involved in giving the ratings never required more than 3 minutes. In fact, the authors noted that the reduction in deviant behavior during the token phase concomitantly increased the amount of time the teacher had to provide more individual attention. This may have contributed in an unknown degree to the lessening of deviant behavior during the token phase. An added feature of this study (O'Leary et al., 1967) lies in the finding that the time lapse between the token and back-up reinforcer was gradually extended to 4 days without adversely affecting the level of disruptive behavior. Transfer of behavioral control from tangible tokens to teacher attention adds to the value and feasibility of token systems for use in public-school settings. The successful use of a token system·in a normal-sized classroom with a more than average number of conduct-problem children answers the criticism of Quay et al. (1966).

A search of the available literature has resulted in only two studies which have systematically investigated the effects of token reinforcers, as previously defined, on the classroom performance of the entire class in a public-school setting. Hall et al. (1968b) were able to increase the mean rate study behavior in a seventh-grade classroom with 30 students from 47 to 65 percent by having the teacher increase the frequency of her attention to "appropriate" behavior, and decrease the frequency of her attention to "inappropriate" study behavior. In an attempt to further decelerate inappropriate and accelerate appropriate classroom behaviors, a token reinforcement system was implemented in addition to the previous contingency of teacher attention. The procedure entailed a point system which determined whether the entire class would receive their usual 5-minute break between periods. If any student disrupted the class or was out of seat inappropriately for 5 seconds a chalk mark was placed on the blackboard. Each mark decreased the duration of the break by 10 seconds, and 24 marks eliminated the break. Study behavior increased to 76 percent under this condition, which might be called token punishment instead of reward. Two days of reversal when break-time was no longer contingent upon behavior resulted in a drop in study behavior of approximately 16 percent. Return of the contingency raised the study rate to 81 percent where it remained until the end of this investigation.

The second systematic study of token reinforcement in a public-school classroom was done by Schroer and Johnson (1968). This experiment examined "The Effects of Curtailed and Delayed Lunchtime Upon Fifteen Sixth-Grade Pupils' Arithmetic Performance." The entire class was subjected to the following experimental phases: baseline, curtailed lunchtime, delayed lunchtime, baseline. In all phases students were presented with 10 arithmetic problems to solve in 10 minutes. The problems varied from day to day. During the consequated phases, i.e., curtailed and delayed lunchtime, 5 minutes of lunchtime were awarded for each correct problem. The rate of correct problems per minute was .6, 1.2, 1.6, and .8 for baseline 1, curtailed and delayed lunchtime, and baseline 2, respectively. Acceleration of rate correct from baseline 1 to curtailed and delayed lunchtime phases as well as deceleration from these lunchtime contingent phases to baseline 2 were significant. The authors concluded that consequation of arithmetic performance was essential to accelerate and maintain that performance at a relatively high level. It is noteworthy that the increase in rate of incorrect problems per minute was not accompanied by an increase in rate of incorrect problems. Thus, quantity of productivity was increased without sacrificing quality. When academic performance is the target behavior, it is especially important to note whether the gains made were substantial on a pass-fail basis. In this study, only 2 of the 15 students remained at a failing level in spite of showing some improvement.

SUMMARY OF TOKEN REINFORCEMENT STUDIES

In spite of the dearth of directly pertinent studies, it appears that public-school situations do possess the essential requirements for a token economy system, i.e., potential reinforcing events and point systems to buy access to the necessary reinforcers. Although tokens are employed in the classroom to establish and maintain behavior, they are either not dispensed immediately nor are they backed up by potential reinforcing events which are readily available and apparently essential to control the behavior of some students. Events which are reinforcing to students may vary considerably, but the events available should be more than adequate to account for the differences between individual students. Homme (1966) and Addison and Homme (1966) have demonstrated the value of utilizing reinforcing event menus to establish control of academic and other behaviors. Although some items on these menus are novel, they are available in most educational settings. Some adolescent high-school dropouts worked through 20 frames of an arithmetic program when consequated with access to working on Russian for 10 minutes (Homme, 1966). The potential of token reinforcement appears to be an as yet largely untapped resource for behavior control in the public-school classroom.

VICARIOUS REINFORCEMENT

Vicarious reinforcement has been defined "as a strengthening of behavior which occurs as a function of observing another being reinforced for that behavior" (Carnine et al., 1968). The existence of a vicarious reinforcement effect in a multitude of different laboratory settings has been demonstrated by Bandura (1966). Thus far the only attempt to investigate the effect of reinforcing the appropriate behavior of one student in a classroom upon the frequency of such behavior on the other students was made by Carnine et al. (1968). This study has already been discussed under the section entitled "Teacher Approval." Briefly, that study failed to uncover much deceleration of inappropriate classroom behavior in pupils unless teacher praise, the independent variable, was made directly contingent upon a student's behavior. In fact after contingent praise was withdrawn from Group A and instituted in Group B, increases in disruptive behavior for Group A were more often the case than decreases. Recognizing the inconclusive nature of their findings Carnine et al. (1968) concluded:

"The results of the present investigation suggest, but not conclusively, that changes induced by such a procedure (vicarious reinforcement) are either weak or short lived. It is our best guess at this point that praising Tommy serves as a discriminative stimulus for Johnny to behave in a similar way, but that unless some direct reinforcing consequence follows Johnny's improved behavior it will not be maintained."

An experimental laboratory study by Mithaug and Burgess (1968) offers some support for the "best guess" of Carnine et al. (1968). These authors found that individual feedback was essential to accelerate an individual's response rate in a group situation.

Not enough research has been done to pass any verdict on the efficacy of vicarious reinforcement for classroom behavior control. However, the appeal of such a technique in terms of economy of teacher time certainly warrants future investigation. Even if it does turn out that the effect occurs only when backed up by occasional contingent attention, the economy of the technique might still be a productive one.

DISCUSSION

Having summarized the findings of attempts by behavioral engineers to improve contingency management in the public schools, we shall now look at some of the problems and important considerations involved in instituting an applied behavioral analysis in the classroom. A discussion of these problems is deemed a more worthwhile pursuit than a premature critique of the research methodology since all of the studies have been recently completed and most are part of long-range research programs.

Gaining Teacher Cooperation

In working within a classroom setting several investigators have encountered the problem of gaining teacher cooperation, e.g., Becker et al. (1967) and Hall et al. (1968a, 1968b). The following comments from one of the teachers in the Becker et al. (1967) study concerning cooperation is most indicative of the problem:

"The plan of the experiment was a bit nebulous, since too much knowledge of what was to be done would affect the results. To add to all this, these people were psychologists! My reinforcement history of working with psychologists need not be discussed here [p. 288]."

Some of the early investigations in order to obtain cooperation sacrificed some experimental control, e.g., by not using or using only brief reversals (Becker et al., 1967; Hall et al., 1968a). Once the teachers were convinced of the effectiveness of the technique and the necessity for reversal, future studies employed reversals, e.g., Madsen et al. (1968a). An additional means of gaining cooperation has been to provide daily feedback to the teachers in the form of graphs illustrating their differential effectiveness under the different experimental conditions. The value of daily teacher-recorded performance rates for their students has been demonstrated by Johnson, Davis, and Lindsley (1968). In general, once the teachers realize that such analyses are beneficial to understanding what techniques are most effective in controlling behavior, they in turn are reinforced by the evidence of improvement in the students' behavior. Lindsley (1967) has found that it is possible for teachers to successfully utilize behavioral analysis and management techniques after 10 to 20 hours of instruction. The most dramatic illustration of generating teacher enthusiasm for the techniques comes from Hall et al. (1968b). In that study, one teacher was saved from being dismissed because the techniques helped the teacher to gain control of a noticeably disruptive classroom group.

Assessment of Stimulus Control: Validity, Reliability, and Experimental Design

A valid applied behavioral analysis is dependent upon a reliable technique for measuring behavior. Becker et al. (1967) have presented in detail the steps involved, and the technique they used in assessing classroom behavior. In general, the categories for scoring which fit the situation, i.e., specific or general, and which define the stimulus and the behavioral events in observable terms, are assembled. Observers familiar with the derived scoring categories and their symbols then attempt to use them in the test situation to determine their feasibility and reliability. Agreement between independent observers is taken as evidence of the technique's reliability. Disagreement may indicate that the code is invalid or that different categories are not mutually exclusive. Disagreement may also indicate the faulty training of observers. Inadequacy in the method of assessing agreement is measured in terms of total frequency of behavior instead of the frequency of occurrence on individual segments of the record. Since time sampling is always used, synchronization between observers as to who as well as what behaviors are being observed at a particular point in recorded time is imperative. Time sampling could be done away with if video tapes are used. Every study mentioned in this review employed a time sampling technique. Yet, the assumption of time sampling, that the behavior observed at certain times in a situation is representative of behavior that occurs at other times in that situation, is usually taken for granted. Only Bushell et al. (1968) made an attempt to assess the validity of the time sample technique by comparing time samples with continuous behavioral ratings. This technique was found to be highly valid in that situation. However, as Bijou, Peterson, and Ault (1968) have noted, such situational idiosyncrasies as frequency of the target behavior necessitate changes in the size of the time sampling interval necessary for valid measurement. The time sampling interval determines the upper as well as lower limits of behavior frequency. For example, if a 10-second interval is used, the maximum response frequency per minute would be 6. "Thus in studies with a high frequency of behavioral episodes, small time intervals are employed to obtain high correspondence between the actual and recorded frequencies of occurrences" (Bijou et al., 1968, p. 180). To help insure validity, as well as reliability of measurement, many of these studies hold constant the time and type of tasks performed when manipulations are assessed. Continuing reliability has been insured through periodic spot checks by an additional observer.

The possibility that the teacher or other contingency manager in such situations may also profit from these measuring techniques has been explored by Johnson (1967), Johnson et al. (1968), and Koenig (1967). Briefly, these investigations indicate that it is practical and informative for teachers to assess their students' performances in terms of daily rate plotted graphically for target Ss as well as for the entire class. Johnson (1967) found that achievement as measured by standardized tests is not the same as when measured by daily performance rates. Daily performance rate would seem to be a more meaningful measure of student performance since it permits immediate and frequent evaluation of progress and is more sensitive

to detect specific directions for alternation and/or remediation of curriculum.

Following the method of an applied and experimental analysis of behavior, the majority of studies discussed employed what has become known as an A B A B design. Specifically, such a design entails assessing the base rate, instituting some contingency, removing the contingency in an attempt to return to baseline, and then reinstituting the contingency. Control over target behaviors is said to have been gained when rates of such behaviors reflect manipulations of the independent variables. Replications of such parallel effects are attempted because as Baer et al. (1968, p. 95) stated "... replication is the essence of believability." Aside from the problem of teacher cooperation, reversals sometimes are difficult to obtain because control of the established behavior, for example, by teacher attention, may be maintained by peer attention (Baer et al., 1967). An alternative design suggested by Baer et al. (1968) which has not been taken advantage of by researchers in this area entails simultaneous assessment of several behaviors, while "consequating" only one or two at a time. Both of these research designs are powerful in that they depict causal variables and permit analysis both between and within Ss across several conditions. A within-Ss design which does not obscure individual differences is most important when one of the goals of the study is application of the techniques involved. One design that has not yet been employed could be termed an A A B A B design. Madsen et al. (1968a) mentioned that the training of teachers in the use of operant techniques in the Becker et al. (1967) study may have caused some target children to improve during the baseline as a result of premature teacher application of the experimental contingencies. Madsen et al. (1968a) precluded such an effect by training teachers after the baselines had been taken. The suggested A A B A B design could assess the effect of training teachers by taking two baselines, i.e., one before and one after teacher training. Such a design may also be more effective in interpreting the results of reversals to baseline attempted later. It may be argued that once a teacher has added these techniques to her repertoire it would be impossible to revert to former traditional teaching methods, and hence, any baseline taken prior to such learning may not be replicable.

CONCLUSION

In summary, it appears that the entry of the behavior modifiers into the public-school classroom has shown that the techniques and designs developed for behavioral control in the laboratory are applicable in natural settings. The ultimate test of the techniques' efficacy will lie in the extent to which they are understood and employed by those in natural settings. As Quay et al. (1966) have pointed out, there are essentially three major learning situations for the child: the school, the peer group, and the family. This review has concentrated upon the school.

Holmes (1966) has illustrated how behavior modification can be carried out when parents and teachers simultaneously apply the techniques. Baer et al. (1967) and Ferster (1967) have pointed out that the key to generalization of the efficacy of a behavior probably rests in the natural community of reinforcement. Certainly a combination of efforts where school, peer group, and family are included in the program for behavioral change would seem a worthwhile goal. As the review has shown, more research is necessary to determine the efficacy of peer influence and vicarious reinforcement in effecting behavioral change. The effects of each of the reinforcement techniques discussed need to be studied on a larger scale. Usually observations account for about 1 percent of a child's behavior during a school day. Video-tape recordings, as Madsen et al. (1968a) have pointed out, would extend the scope of the investigation by including more student observations over longer periods of time. This would also provide access to more valid and reliable data gathering.

This review has attempted to demonstrate both the need for and the value of applied behavioral analysis in the public-school classroom. It has been demonstrated that teachers can become more effective contingency managers. The immediate and contingent usage of reinforcing events was shown to be a crucial element for effective classroom control. Problems have arisen in securing teacher cooperation, reliable and valid measurement of behavior, feasible and adequate designs and reinforcers, and solutions have either been found or were suggested.

The use of behavior modification by individual classroom teachers

THOMAS J. STACHNIK

During the fall term of 1969, I taught a masters'-level course at Oakland University in Rochester, Michigan, titled, Mental Health of School Children. The class met one evening a week since virtually all the participants had full-time teaching positions, mostly in elementary and junior high school settings. The course began with some discussion about what constituted "mental health," followed by considerable debate as to what role teachers should play in promoting the mental health of their students. Initially, a few of the teachers felt that they should do little more than make referrals to psychiatric professionals when a child exhibited some deviant behavior. But as the discussion progressed, it became more apparent that mental health could be defined behaviorally (the presence of certain behaviors and the absence of others), and that a child's teacher was perhaps in a better position than anyone else to help strengthen appropriate behaviors and weaken others.

At that point substantial interest arose

about acquiring techniques which would enable the teacher to intervene effectively. Therefore, the balance of the course was designed to meet two objectives: (1) to introduce the teachers to the principles of behavior upon which behavior modification strategies are based, and (2) to give the teachers some experience in adapting those principles into effective classroom behavior management techniques.

The first objective was met in a traditional, didactic fashion which included readings, discussions, films, etc. The second objective was met largely through a classroom behavior modification project assigned to each teacher. The guidelines for the project were clear: Identify, objectively measure, and record the behavior of an individual student or the entire class, and then modify that behavior in an appropriate direction. At the end of the term, each teacher orally described his project and submitted a written report. The balance of this paper contains a sampling of those reports.

In reviewing the reports and reflecting upon the discussion which occurred during the course of the term, the following conclusions seem warranted:

1. The teachers enrolled in the course were very receptive to learning the rudiments of behavior modification. They also showed considerable skill in translating the principles they learned into useful classroom techniques.

2. Teachers can be made to readily recognize that their historical role of automatically referring troubled children to mental health professionals can be improved upon. They can be made to see that deviant social behavior in the classroom or unsuccessful academic performance is often the precursor to more serious problems, and that the classroom is often the chosen intervention setting.

3. Although all the teachers in the course had received bachelor degrees from accredited teacher-training institutions, they were woefully unprepared to deal effectively with problem behaviors in any specific way. The implication is obvious: Undergraduate teacher-training programs must begin to include the technology of contingency management in their curricula. That addition would insure the production of more competent action-oriented teachers and simultaneously contribute toward the prevention of a variety of mental health problems among their students.

A PROBLEM IN MATHEMATICS
BY
CAROL BLUMENSTOCK

Problem

One of the problems a classroom teacher is faced with is what to do about the child who understands the concepts presented, knows how to do the work, but never seems to complete his daily work. It was this problem that led me to select Leigh, a student in my class, as the subject for my project.

Leigh is a "normal" seven-year-old child, who seems to be very well adjusted. She possesses an average intelligence and has no apparent learning disabilities. But, since Primary I, she has had difficulty completing each day's work.

Procedure

After careful observation of Leigh's daily work, I discovered that she very seldom completed her math assignment. She would leave the page unfinished or haphazardly fill in any answer. There were two behaviors that I wanted to establish:

(1) complete each day's assignment;
(2) discontinue the practice of filling in any number for an answer to a math problem.

I established a baseline by keeping a record of Leigh's daily math assignments and the progress she made. I kept a record of the following items:

(1) whether or not the assignment was finished;
(2) the number of problems per day;
(3) the number of correct answers per day;
(4) the number of errors per day;
(5) the number of unfinished problems per day.

These are my findings:

	(X) Finished assignments	Number of problems	Number correct	Number of errors	Number unfinished
Monday		14	3	3	8
Tuesday	X	18	11	7	0
Wednesday		27	13	4.	10
Thursday	X	14	6	8	0
Friday		32	11	9	12

Before intervening with a behavior modification technique, I wanted to discover whether Leigh had difficulty knowing what to do or how to do it. I found that she understood the concepts presented and knew how to do the problems. The technique I chose to use was the token system. I chose this technique for two reasons. From past experience, I learned that Leigh was a child who needed to be highly motivated and that what once served as motivation often did not work if used again. I explained the token system to Leigh in the form of a game, and she agreed that she would like to play. We decided that one token would be given for every correct answer. Leigh selected what were to be her rewards by naming activities she liked to participate in if given a free choice. The rewards that Leigh chose for herself were:

(1) to have recess on gym day;
(2) to have five extra minutes of recess;
(3) to have show-and-tell for the class;
(4) to cut-out and draw using colored paper;
(5) to choose a game or a puzzle to play with for ten minutes at the end of the day;
(6) to bring a snack for the class;
(7) to have no boardwork for a day;
(8) to help make things for the bulletin boards;
(9) to play a math game at the end of the day with the class.

I assigned a token value to each of the above rewards and made a copy of these items for Leigh and taped the list to her desk.

Results

At the end of the first day I checked Leigh's math assignment. There were 23 problems and she had 5 correct, 11 errors, and 7 unfinished problems. Needless to say, I was not impressed with the results of the first day, and so at this time I added another dimension to the experiment. Leigh was told she would be awarded two extra tokens for each page of math that she completed. This contingency should have been included in the beginning, since it applied to one of the behaviors to be modified. I continued to record Leigh's progress for the next seven days. Here is the information that I obtained.

	(X) Finished assignments	Number of problems	Number correct	Number of errors	Number unfinished
Monday		23	5	11	7
Tuesday	X	36	36	' 0	0
Wednesday		29	16	6	7
Thursday	X	20	17	3	0
Friday	X	32	26	6	0
Monday	X	34	33	1-	0
Tuesday	X	30	28	2	0
Wednesday	X	25	25	0	0

Of course, I am very pleased with the results, but of more importance is the great pride Leigh now takes in completing her math pages. I intend to continue using this technique with Leigh and gradually move from using the tokens to using social reinforcers.

THE REDUCTION OF CHAIR-TIPPING BEHAVIOR
BY PEGGY LABELLE[1]

When experimenting for the first time on the management of classroom behavior, a

1 The author wishes to gratefully acknowledge the helpful cooperation and ingenuity of Mrs. Betty Peters, classroom teacher. Her classroom management helped to make the study a success.

school psychologist always has many reservations in mind. After several weeks of lecture and the reading of several interesting articles on the subject, I wondered whether the seemingly simple techniques outlined would really prove successful for me. The articles indicated that if the behavior in question was evaluated realistically and the management of this behavior was likewise realistically evaluated and consistently carried out, I could anticipate some degree of success. With this philosophy in mind I consulted with the classroom teacher about the management of the subject in this study.

Method

The project was conducted on a seven-year-old boy who was a student in a regular second-grade classroom. This child's record showed an increasing accumulation of academic problems as each year passed. His work was far below grade level in all areas. This was complicated by his inability to sit quietly and work for more than one or two minutes at a time. The subject's poor showing in school had certainly been evidenced by his kindergarten and first-grade records. However, it was clear that these classroom difficulties could not be separated from the fact that within a fifteen-month period the family had suffered the loss of two sons due to accidents. The first, a boy of fifteen years, was hit by a car while riding his bicycle; the second, a boy of thirteen, incurred a broken neck by swinging into a clothes pole in his own yard. The second accident happened six weeks prior to the beginning of the study. Although classroom behavior had remained essentially the same since the beginning of the year, there were subtle comments and behavioral instances that showed the effects of these traumatic experiences. The teacher was aware of the problem and tried to be supportive in her relationship with this child.

The subject seemed to be generally inattentive. He would go from a pencil-chewing reverie to poking the child in the next seat, or to standing to gaze around the room. However, the most disruptive behavior was a constant habit of chair-tipping which resulted in considerable reinforcement from the teacher and other students in the classroom. The teacher and I decided to try using behavior modification techniques to eliminate the child's chair-tipping.

Establishment of a Baseline

The seven-year-old was observed for two different ten- or twenty-minute periods a day during the six-day baseline. Figure 1.1 shows baseline and other data on chair-tipping taken during the study. The subject was observed only during structured work periods which included math, writing, social studies, and group reading. At these times either the teacher was teaching a unit to the whole class which involved listening or working problems at the desk or she was at a table with the subject's reading group of six children. Chair-tipping always appeared at some time during each baseline observation. Every whole tip of the chair was counted during the given observation time. The total number was then divided by the number of minutes of observation. Chair-tipping consistently averaged from four to eight times per minute. Approximations of tipping or times spent suspended back on two legs were not counted. During baselines the reading group was observed while seated on the floor at two different times. Complete changes in position were counted as one chair-tip. Leg, arm, or partial body movements were not counted. These observations are marked on baseline; however, there was very little variation in the count.

Procedure

We decided that the teacher would discuss the chair-tipping with the child. We knew that he was very aware of the habit because of the teacher's reminders to "quit tipping so you can do your work," and the "it's not quiet" complaints of other children in the reading group when the banging into the table interfered with their work.

The teacher explained to the boy that we

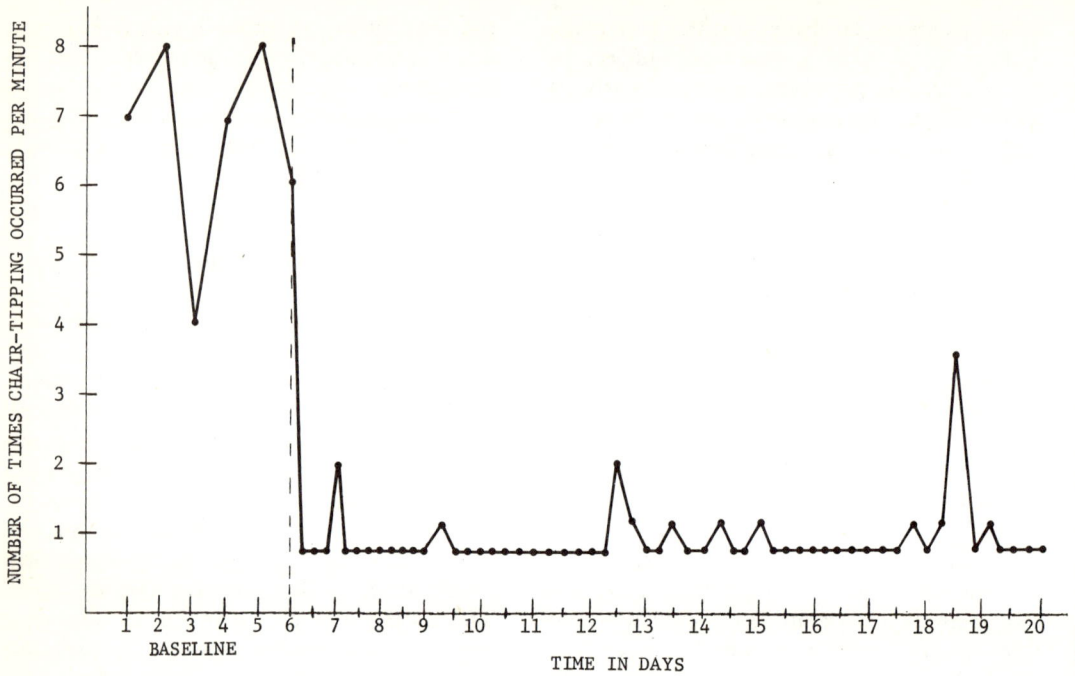

Figure 1.1. *Chair-tipping per minute by a 7-year-old boy during a baseline period in which he was reinforced for not tipping his chair.*

had been counting the times he had tipped his chair. Our subject also was shown the counter we had been using. He and a number of the children had expressed curiosity in the counter several days before. The teacher then asked our subject if he thought he would like to try to remember not to tip his chair in class. The question was met with an enthusiastic nod of assent.

We immediately rewarded the child's cooperative attitude with a small, brand-new, red notebook. The pages in the notebook were divided into four equal sections. It was taken to the teacher before morning recess, at noon, before afternoon recess, and before going home; if the tipping behavior did not occur in that quarter of the day, a star was placed in the notebook. If tipping had occurred the child was not scolded or reproached but given the simple explanation that, since he had tipped in his chair, no star would be added.

During the fifteen-day management period, care was given to accurately record instances of tipping. The quarters of the day that stars were given far outnumbered the

quarters when tipping occurred, and only on one occasion did tipping go up to three times a minute. It is probably not coincidental that this was the third rainy day, which meant the children had not been able to go outside for recess. Needless to say, the general tone of the whole school was one of controlled chaos.

At the end of the first day of the experiment, the subject was told to think of something special at school that he would like to do or something he would like to have that the teacher could give or do for him. A few suggestions or alternatives were given by the teacher, but the subject was encouraged to think of a reward on his own. He was told that he would receive this reward every time he received four stars for two days in a row. This requirement was lowered to seven stars on the eighth day of the study. The interesting part of this portion of the experiment was that it took the subject six days and two accumulated rewards to decide what special thing he wanted. He settled for stick candy that the teacher kept in her desk. With this momentous decision I breathed a sigh of relief. I had feared that he would ask for a new striped pencil. During baseline the blue striped pencil that he had been chewing on since September 5 had collapsed. Although not documented, pencil chewing had diminished, and we hoped it would stay that way!

Conclusion

The purpose of the experiment was to alter the chair-tipping behavior of a seven-year-old boy. The alteration of this behavior could have many positive implications for the subject. Because of the emotional problems encountered by the whole family, it was especially important for school to be a secure rewarding situation. The graph indicates that the management procedure was successful. The child's schoolwork has improved, and his reading group is certainly more congenial since the table no longer jiggles. The reward system will continue until the tipping no longer exists. The teacher already has plans for instituting a system of rewards for assignments completed. Hopefully this will be another step in the direction of making school a successful venture for this child.

MODIFICATION OF SOBBING BEHAVIOR BY BEVERLY BLESSINGER

Problem

A second-grade teacher, a friend who works in another school system, requested my aid as a reading clinician in a reading-discipline problem. One of the children in her class, Kirman, sobbed daily throughout the reading period. This behavior did not particularly disturb the other children since Kirman stayed in her seat with her head on her desk, sobbing softly. But her behavior was disturbing the teacher. Besides the annoyance of the actual sobbing, the teacher knew that Kirman was not doing her work at this time, and she was troubled that the child appeared so unhappy.

Kirman's teacher explained to me how she already had attempted to modify the child's behavior. At first, she had gone to the sobbing Kirman and attempted to find out why she was crying. The child said that the work was too hard for her. Although her teacher thought that the assignments were at Kirman's instructional level, she gave her easier work to do. But the sobbing continued. Then the teacher tried what she called punishment. When Kirman sobbed instead of doing her work, Kirman had to stay in the room during recess. But the sobbing continued.

Method

First, I asked the teacher to observe the amount of time Kirman sobbed each day and to report the result at the end of each day. I recorded these times for five days; this and subsequent records of sobbing appear in Figure 2.1. The average sobbing time was thirty minutes. This behavior only occurred during the forty minutes Kirman was supposed to be doing independent-reading seatwork while the teacher was holding directed reading lessons with the other two reading groups. When Kirman's reading group was called, she came to the reading table quietly and did adequate work.

Thinking that the teacher's attention was the reinforcing agent for Kirman's behavior, I told Kirman's teacher to ignore her completely during the sobbing. I explained that Kirman, wanting the teacher's attention, was not being punished but rewarded when allowed to stay with the teacher during recess. (This was especially true since the teacher tended to chat with her during the "punishment.") Paying attention to Kirman while she sobbed was actually strengthening the sobbing behavior. I suggested that the teacher reward Kirman whenever she was working without sobbing by giving her some small, overt form of attention: smiling at her, glancing approvingly over her work, or by giving her a word or two of praise. This, hopefully, would reinforce the working, non-sobbing behavior.

For fifteen days, Kirman's teacher ignored Kirman's sobbing. On the first day, when another child informed her of Kirman's crying, the teacher quietly told the class not to

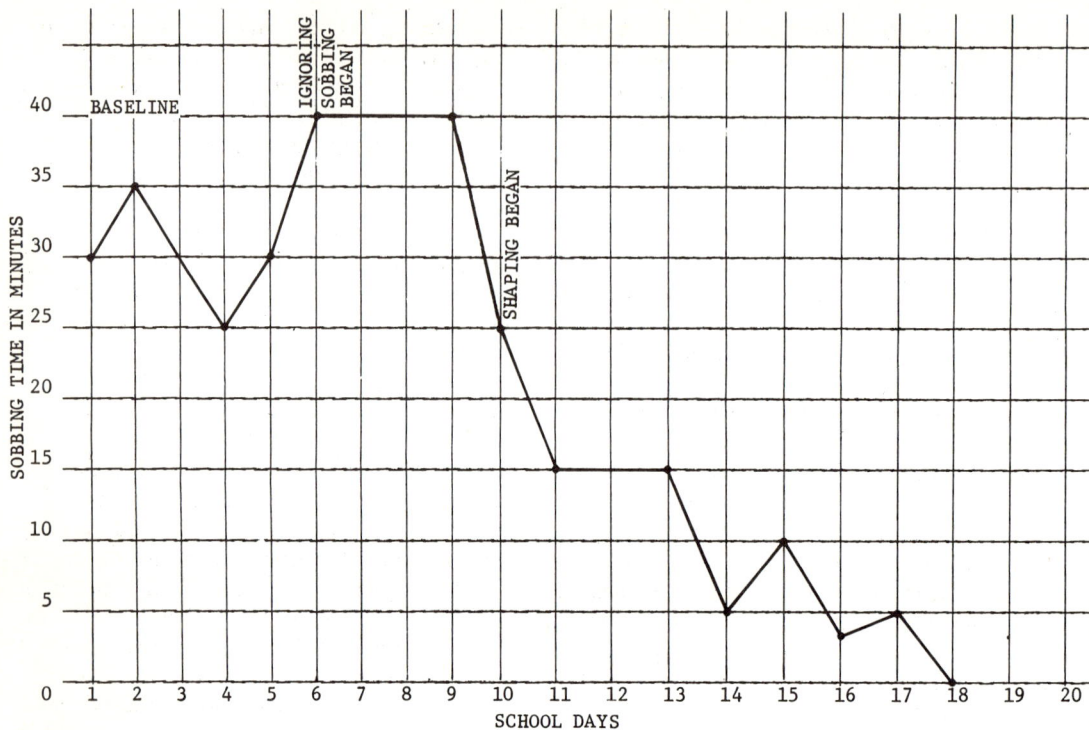

Figure 2.1. *Number of minutes a second-grade girl spent sobbing during baseline, ignoring of sobbing, and attention for not sobbing.*

pay attention to it and not to tell her about it. At the end of each day, the teacher reported the amount of time Kirman sobbed.

For the first four of the fifteen days, Kirman sobbed for the entire forty minutes of independent reading. There seemed to be no opportunity to reward her with attention since she cried the entire time. Kirman's teacher began hinting that she was not going to "put up with this much longer" but was going to attend to Kirman when she was crying. Rather than attempting to explain to the teacher how reinforcing this would be, I tried to think of some way to shape Kirman's behavior. Using successive approximations, I told the teacher to attend to Kirman at the very start of the forty minutes, right before Kirman began whimpering. With this encouragement, Kirman started her work; the teacher praised her, and smiled at her about three minutes later. Kirman cried for only twenty-five minutes that day. From then on, there was always an opportunity to pay attention to Kirman. Each day, Kirman's teacher rewarded her with a smile or praise

after she had worked without sobbing a little longer than she had the day before.

Results and Discussion

The effects of these procedures are shown on the graph (see Figure 2.1). After fifteen days during which Kirman's sobbing was consistently ignored and her nonsobbing behavior reinforced, Kirman spent the entire forty minutes working without sobbing. For the first four days of the modification attempt, Kirman's sobbing behavior actually increased. Perhaps this increase was due to the teacher's previous unwitting intermittent reinforcement of Kirman's behavior; the teacher periodically had paid attention to Kirman's sobbing behavior. Perhaps Kirman felt that now she had to "cry harder" to be rewarded with attention. If I had suggested shaping Kirman's working behavior at the start of the experiment, the sobbing behavior might have been extinguished earlier.

Although the experiment was officially over on the twentieth day and the teacher no longer reported to me, I suggested to her that Kirman would not have to be reinforced every day. Instead, Kirman could be reinforced "every once in a while" or more intermittently. A few days later, Kirman's behavior was not only work-oriented, but, as an extra benefit, the other children were friendlier to her since she was no longer a "crybaby." Thinking that the new friends' attitudes would also reinforce Kirman's non-sobbing behavior, I heartily agreed with Kirman's teacher that everything was "just great."

REDUCING DISRUPTIVE OUTBURSTS
BY
CAROL CALLAHAN

Problem

My second-grade (Team 2) class of 13 boys and 6 girls were grouped according to the Gesell performance test. Their overall social and academic performance in September indicated they were working at a first-grade level. Two of the boys in the group had loud overpowering voices. They blurted out anything at anytime and rarely raised their hands or awaited a turn to speak. In September, I began ignoring them when they talked without raising their hands and immediately smiled and called on them when their hands were up. When I decided to record their talking-out-of-turn episodes in October, I discovered that they had begun to raise their hands. This allowed quieter-speaking children to talk out and, in fact, I even reinforced that behavior by acknowledging their questions. Thus, I decided to try to reduce the frequency of disruptive outbursts of the entire class.

Procedure

For five consecutive half-day sessions (both morning and afternoon) I kept a tally of the number of times the children talked without raising their hands in all but very small group work, talking while someone else was talking, or loudly calling out to me or another student. The children's arithmetic teacher also kept a tally of outbursts.

As I occasionally kept the tally on the board, the children began to guess why and would often stop to count the marks. (On the fifth day, I verified what they had guessed, and they agreed they sure talked out an awful lot!) The frequency of outbursts ranged from 35 to 45 per half-day session.

Since some children preferred recess more than others and most of the class valued having free time to play or socialize before the tardy bell rang, I decided to use both activities to help reduce the frequency of disruptive outbursts. I explained that, beginning the next morning, the class would have 40 points to work with each half-day. Each time they talked out, talked while someone else was talking, or were shouting or loudly talking while I was working with others, I would "X out" a number. If their outbursts exceeded 20, they would lose their free time before the bell the next session, and if they exceeded another 20 (total of 40 for a half-session), they would lose recess the next session. In other words, the activities they earned depended upon the appropriate behavior exhibited in the preceding session.

Under the circumstances, it was difficult to reinforce appropriate behavior immediately. Therefore, I displayed two charts, numbered from 1 to 20, with a sign attached to each which indicated the activity on one side and the loss of the activity on the other (Figure 3.1). By looking at the charts and the signs, the children knew before they went home each session which activity they had earned for the next session. If the children were able to keep the outbursts below 20 each session, they would not lose either activity. After losing one free-time period, their outbursts dropped considerably. At point A (see Figure 3.2), I lowered the criterion for each activity to 10 points per half-day session, and strengthened the desirability of these activities by allowing the children to bring their favorite games to play during free time and recess if they desired.

At point B (see Figure 3.2), I again lowered the criterion for each activity to 5 points per half-session. By this time, the children had sufficiently lowered their voices and raised their hands so frequently that I counted only loud or disturbing outbursts, and thus did not feel the criterion was too stiff. I also

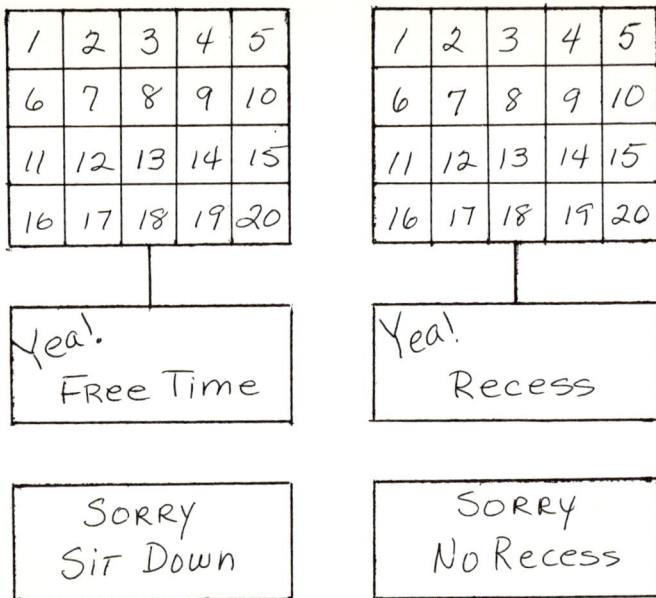

Figure 3.1. *Charts that illustrate a point system and consequences used to control disruptive behavior of a second-grade class. When disruptive behavior occurred, the teacher would "X" out a number. When all numbers were "X-ed" out, the reversible sign at the bottom would be turned from the positive to the negative consequence.*

added Reinforcing activities at this time by asking the children to suggest things they would like to do if they could. These suggestions included: taking walks, having longer recesses, getting drinks without asking, having surprise treats hidden around room (this was done before), playing a game in the gym when it was free, listening to records using earphones, and playing their favorite games when their work was finished. These suggestions were written on small pieces of paper, combined with a few blank pieces, and placed in what we called "The Special Box." Using the idea of intermittent reinforcement, they could draw a slip from the box and would have a chance to do one of the desired activities. If the paper was blank, they could have another chance the next time outbursts totaled less than 10 per day.

Results and Discussion

The effects of this technique are dramatically indicated in Figure 2. The children did not earn free time on several occasions, but they never lost recess. Most significant was the low frequency of disruptive outbursts.

There also were many other equally good effects. The children were pleased to earn special activities and liked the fact that they rarely lost free time or recess. I rarely needed to single out any one person or raise my voice. When I witnessed disruptive behavior, I would calmly and quietly mark off a number. The child who caused the disruption did not become angry or sullen—common in the case of being reprimanded—but usually smiled or indicated a "whoops, I goofed" reaction. On the whole, the children appeared to be more attentive in large-group discussions, awaiting their turn to speak, or listening rather then talking to someone. There were no incidents in which anger was directed at one child in particular who might have caused more than his share of disruptions. The class was extremely honest about the number of outbursts made. They kept their own record in arithmetic class and during unit-study, which in-

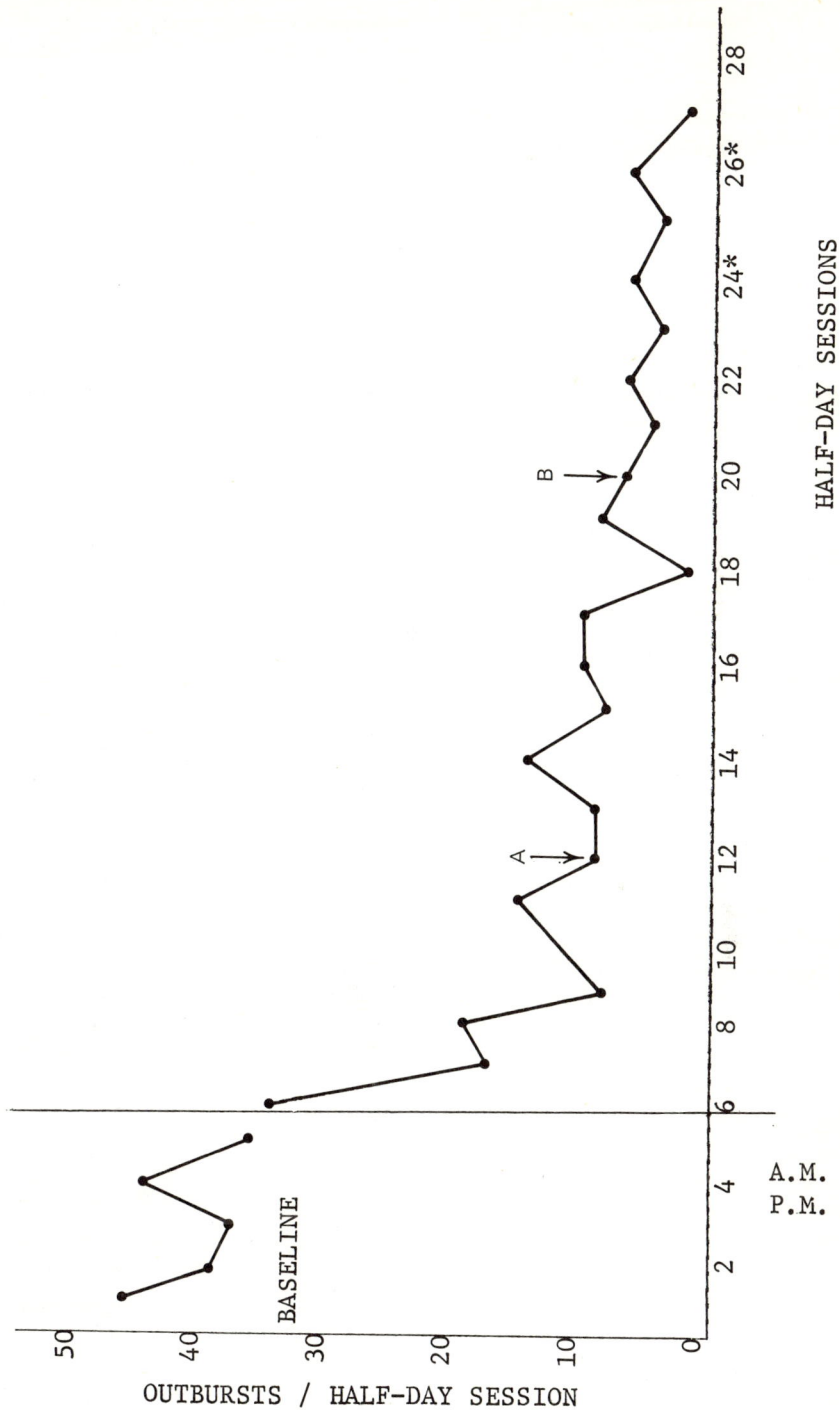

* Total of A.M. and P.M. sessions below 10.

Figure 3.2. *Frequency of outbursts of a second-grade class during baseline and loss of points for disruptive behavior.*

cluded all 90 children in the Team. Thus, hopefully they learned to identify disruptive behavior.

The decline of disruptive behavior enabled the children to participate in many more small-group experiences, to work individually, to use audio-visual aids, and to work with a partner. The technique, I feel, was effective. Besides, I haven't even had laryngitis yet this year.

The Learning Village elementary school

C. HREN, K. MUELLER, C. R. SPATES, C. ULRICH, AND R. E. ULRICH[1]

Newspapers, magazines, and professional publications currently are full of accounts of attempts to rescue public grade schools from apparent ineffectiveness and even harmfulness. Industrial contractors have been called in, computers have been introduced, and parallel instructional systems established. These attempts are of inestimable social value. Our society is facing the consequences of schools turning out people who haven't the intellectual skills or the behavioral history necessary to function adaptively in society. Having wasted at least one generation, we are now trying to recoup our losses. Many of the large-scale attempts to change our schools probably represent the biggest first-aid measure ever applied to our society, and as such many attempts are successful. They are judged successful (and rightly so) if children make average gains for the school year. Some programs achieve this goal; they successfully confront the problem, as indeed they must if our society is to survive at all.

The long-term survival of our society will require more of educational products than *not* being illiterate or *not* being disruptive. It will require people with intellectual and social skills beyond what we can even imagine today. If we continue to approach education as we have in the past, we are unlikely to produce such people. We must not wait until our society is in terrible trouble and desperate need of skills that few of its people possess. We must begin now to develop techniques that can later be used on a large scale to fulfill the needs of future human beings.

We need laboratories for the development and testing of educational techniques under conditions that will allow us to go beyond remediation. The elementary-school program to be described here was established for that purpose. It is part of the Learning Village; the infant program of the Village has been described elsewhere in this volume. The Learning Village elementary school enrolls not hundreds, thousands, or tens of thousands of students, but eighteen. It spends not $300, nor $800, nor $1200 per pupil per year, but over $2500. It has a student-to-teacher ratio of about seven to one. Although the Learning Village cannot claim conditions or performance even close to ideal, it has provided a unique opportunity to try out behavioral educational techniques on a long-term program-wide basis.

The Learning Village is a private school that operates ten hours each school day, all year round. It is now approximately four

Reprinted by permission.

The data collection system described here for the token economy, daily class records, and infant data sheets were developed and implemented and improved upon by a cooperative and energetic Learning Village staff. This program has been supported financially by the Kalamazoo Valley Intermediate School District, the Michigan Department of Mental Health, the Michigan Department of Social Services, the Michigan Department of Education, and the National Institute of Mental Health.

1 These names were selected more or less arbitrarily for authorship. The names of the entire staff of the Learning Village and its parent organization, the Behavior Development Corporation should be included.

years old. Most of its elementary school children have been in behavioral education programs for at least that amount of time. Many began as preschoolers. About half of the children come from middle-class or upper-middle-class backgrounds; about half of the children are on scholarships; about half are black. The three teachers who work in the program also have children enrolled.

THE CURRICULUM

The curriculum of the Learning Village elementary school is similar to that of ordinary grade schools. The children have lessons primarily in reading, language, and mathematics. When possible, classes are added in science, social science, music, art, and physical education. When good program materials and the funds to purchase them are available, they are used. *Distar* (Engelmann and Bruner, 1969) and the *SRA Reading Laboratory* (Parker, Covell, LaForge, Paternoster, Quinn, and Fisher, 1959) are used in reading. *Handwriting with Write and See* (Skinner and Krakower, 1968) is used to teach cursive writing as part of the language program. In other areas, standard text books are used with behavioral objectives: In math, the *Sets and Numbers* math series (Suppes and Suppes, 1962) is used, in language, *English for Meaning* (McKee and Harrison, 1968), and in science, the Scott, Foresman science series (Marshall and Beauchamp, 1968; Marshall, Challand, and Beauchamp, 1968; Blough, Marshall, Bailey, and Beauchamp, 1968b, 1968c, 1968a).

In social sciences, teachers have attempted to develop their own curriculum. Traditional grade-school social science programs have taught that coffee beans are grown in Brazil and that the President's term of office is four years. The Learning Village social science program has concentrated on three areas: behavior analysis, social studies, and social behavior.

Behavior Analysis

Since the children should learn a realistic view of their own and others' behavior, the concepts of behavior analysis are introduced

as soon as possible. A simple program has been written to introduce those concepts to the children; fifth- and sixth-grade children have worked through the programmed text *The Analysis of Behavior* (Holland and Skinner, 1961) and one has even enrolled (for credit) in a behaviorally oriented college psychology course. The children visit local psychological laboratories and are exposed daily to behaviorally oriented psychologists at the Learning Village.

The children also conduct their own "experiments" at the Village. Students in the elementary school frequently work with children in the infant and nursery-school programs. Some of this work takes place during free-play periods when the students assist the regular teachers in their work. In addition, students have given lessons to infants as part of the regular infant-program curriculum. In one case, students first took a baseline count of how many pictures of objects their "subjects" could identify. Then the "teachers" named each object and reinforced the student with praise and edibles for echoing the name. Later the students were asked to, and reinforced for, naming the objects without prompting. Finally, the "experimenter" counted the number of objects the infant could identify after his lessons. Such experiments show the student the value of reinforcement and collecting data. They also give the student the satisfaction of having taught something to someone.

Most people today grow up with the view of behavior that permeates our culture. They believe that individuals are basically "good" or "evil" and that their behavior is controlled mainly by their "will." Even people trained as adults in behavioral psychology tend to think this way. When in a calm, rational mood, they may be able to analyze the behavior of others, to control their own behavior, and to avoid blaming others for undesired behaviors; however, when the emotional level of behaviorists rises, they behave like most other people. They get angry; they get vengeful; they blame the other person; they act as if their own behavior had no effect on the other person and as if that person's behavior were simply a result of his willing it.

Hopefully, when people, as children, are

given exposure to a scientific view of man, they will be freer from these lapses into superstition. Of course, "behavioral" teachers probably will inadvertently teach their superstitions as well as their ideas. Nevertheless, these children might be less likely to blame or become angry with another person because of his behavior. They may have fewer "blind spots" and be better able to analyze their own behavior and the behavior of others.

Social Studies

The heading, social studies, subsumes topics such as social structure, social problems, and social practices. The children have readings and discussions to help them understand the experiences of other human beings. Discussions include the experiences of people imprisoned, of people who live in poverty, and of people of different races. Topics such as overpopulation, war, aggression, crime, and pollution are discussed. Films such as *Essay on War* (Essay Productions, undated) are seen and discussed. Political processes are described as realistically as possible. An unrealistic picture of a perfectly functioning society is not presented. An effort is made to help the children understand the problems —and advantages—of living in a complex, modern society.

Social Behavior

Not as part of the formal curriculum, but as a part of all Village activities, an attempt is made to teach adaptive social behaviors. "Adaptive" social behaviors have been identified somewhat arbitrarily by Village staff. Hopefully, they include behaviors that contribute to the long-range survival of the individual and society. Such behaviors include cooperation, sharing, helping others, affectionate behavior, honesty, trust, conflict resolution, reinforcing others, and finding alternatives to aggression. Although these behaviors seem desirable, they must not be approached in a naive fashion. For example, some black parents have stated that nonag-

gression in the past has been of dubious value to black people. Black children, they feel, must be taught to use aggression. Honesty is another behavior that is often advocated and, sometimes with reason, not practiced. For example, people sometimes are unable to tolerate the truth, and their behavior must be appropriately shaped. Similarly, trust is not always wise, and its effective use must include the ability to discriminate when trust is appropriate.

Those social behaviors identified as appropriate are reinforced by the teaching staff. Far too often children are ignored when they are "good" and punished when they are "bad." Reinforcement of good behaviors, by strengthening behaviors incompatible with "bad" ones, helps break out of the syndrome. When undesirable behaviors do arise, they are either ignored (put on extinction) or mildly punished. In the elementary school, punishment usually involves loss of tokens in the token economy, to be described below. Occasionally time-out is used. In summary, then, the social studies program both helps children to understand social behavior and helps them to behave toward one another in desirable ways.

THE TOKEN SYSTEM

The token system used in the Learning Village elementary school was developed both to consequate behavior systematically and to record that consequation. Through each school day, each child carries with him a "distribution sheet" such as that shown in Figure 1. The first column lists the classes and activities in the school day. The "antecedent" column refers to behaviors that must occur before the behavior of concern can take place. In classes, antecedent behaviors include sitting attentively at one's desk, having the necessary materials ready, etc.; at lunch, antecedent behaviors include finding one's way to the table and sitting in an orderly fashion. "Academic" behaviors include completing lessons, responding in class, asking appropriate questions, doing extra reading, etc. "Social" behaviors include the cooperative, nonaggressive, and altruistic behaviors already discussed.

THE LEARNING VILLAGE   Token Economy Daily Distribution Sheet

Student_____ Date ___/___/___
                                        Mo.   Day   Year

Cumulative Savings_____

BEHAVIOR CAT.	ANTECEDENTS	ACADEMIC	SOCIAL	TOTAL
9:00 BUS & BEFORE SCHOOL			(A2)	
9:45 Reading	cu	cu	cu	
10:30 Math	cu		cu	
10:45 RECESS I	(E2)			
11:30 Science	(E2)	(E2)	(E2)	
12:00 LUNCH	(A2)		(A2)	
12:30 RECESS II	(A2)		(A2) (A2)	
1:15 Music	(A2)	(A2)	(A2)	
2:00 Printing	(A2)	(A2) (A2) (A2)	(A2)	
2:15 Recess	✗ ✗		✗ ✗	
3:00 Lit Read	✗	✗ ✗	✗ ✗ ✗	
TOTALS				

Figure 1. *Daily token sheet used in the Learning Village elementary school. Tokens (circled letters and initials) are given for antecedent, academic, and social behavior. Letters and initials indicate the person dispensing the tokens. Tokens are crossed out as a response-cost technique to control undesirable behavior.*

The letters on the sheet are the tokens; teachers place a token in the appropriate cell by initialing it or stamping it with a self-inking stamp they carry with them on the end of a pencil. The stamps are coded, and each teacher has his or her own stamp. Thus the distribution sheet provides a record of how many reinforcements were received, ap- proximately when they were received, for what type of behavior they were received, and from whom they were received.

Tokens also can be lost as a consequence of aggressive or extremely disruptive behavior. To remove a token the teacher simply crosses off one and writes "rc" (response cost) beside it. Any type of token may be forfeited;

"antecedent" tokens may be lost for aggressive social behavior, and "social" tokens may be lost for disruptive antecedent behavior. Removal of tokens is conducted with as little emotion as possible. In fact, it serves as an important substitute for the negative social control that teachers must ordinarily use. Teachers don't have to "nag" the students; the students know what behaviors are expected of them, and they understand the consequences of producing or not producing those behaviors. The teachers also do not have to show anger or blame or scold the students. Loss of tokens is part of the system; it reflects only on the student's behavior, not on him as an individual. At one time, because of financial problems and subsequent reorganization of the Learning Village, the elementary school was temporarily without a token system. Both the teachers and the students were happy to have it return.

OTHER CONSEQUENCES

Social and behavioral reinforcements also are used. Social reinforcement involves the praise used by teachers everywhere. It may also involve physical contact, such as a pat on the back or a hug. Since social reinforcement probably is used more frequently at the Village than in most school situations, the teachers have to be sophisticated in their use of praise. Possibly because of their long history of behavioral education, the students do not find mechanical praise very reinforcing. Praise must be imaginative and sincere.

Behavioral consequences are also built into the school day. At present, the children save their tokens for roller-skating parties held on Fridays. Occasionally the children may take field trips to community institutions, to parks, or to lake-front property purchased for a future site of the Learning Village. As the children complete each lesson or block of lessons, they may go to a reinforcement room that contains games and toys, or they may choose to read a library book as many do. The use of behavioral reinforcement helps do away with the inactivity and rigidity that make school a boring and frustrating experience for many children.

Two types of data are collected at the Learning Village: (1) daily records, and (2) the results of standardized testing. The latter is the traditional method of evaluation in education. However, standardized tests have several disadvantages. First, the tests do not directly sample the child's academic behavior. For a variety of reasons, a child who does well in class may do very poorly on a standardized test. In such cases, the child's classroom performance, if adequately measured, should be taken as a more accurate indicator of his achievement. Second, standardized tests involve a time lag that reduces their usefulness. They are given infrequently, and, in some cases, results take some time to arrive; thus the child may have spent months in the classroom before the teacher gleans whatever useful information she can from test results. Finally, a skilled teacher or classroom observer, equipped with the necessary measuring procedures, can do a better job of analyzing a child's performance than can standardized tests. Poor reading performance may be due to anything from motor restlessness to failure to grasp concepts. Conversely, relatively high reading performance may be due to a very high rate of both correct and incorrect responses or to a moderately high rate of correct responses. Some form of direct observation of the child's behavior must be made to obtain an accurate picture of his achievement.

Standardized tests are useful, however. They can identify children who need special work and indicate areas of the program that are weak. For example, math scores at the Village have never been as good as reading scores, so efforts to choose and develop curricula and to train teachers have been focused on the math program. Finally, standardized tests provide a means for the rough comparison of educational programs. The results of some standardized tests used at the Learning Village will be given below.

Daily Records

One daily record-keeping procedure has already been mentioned. The token system

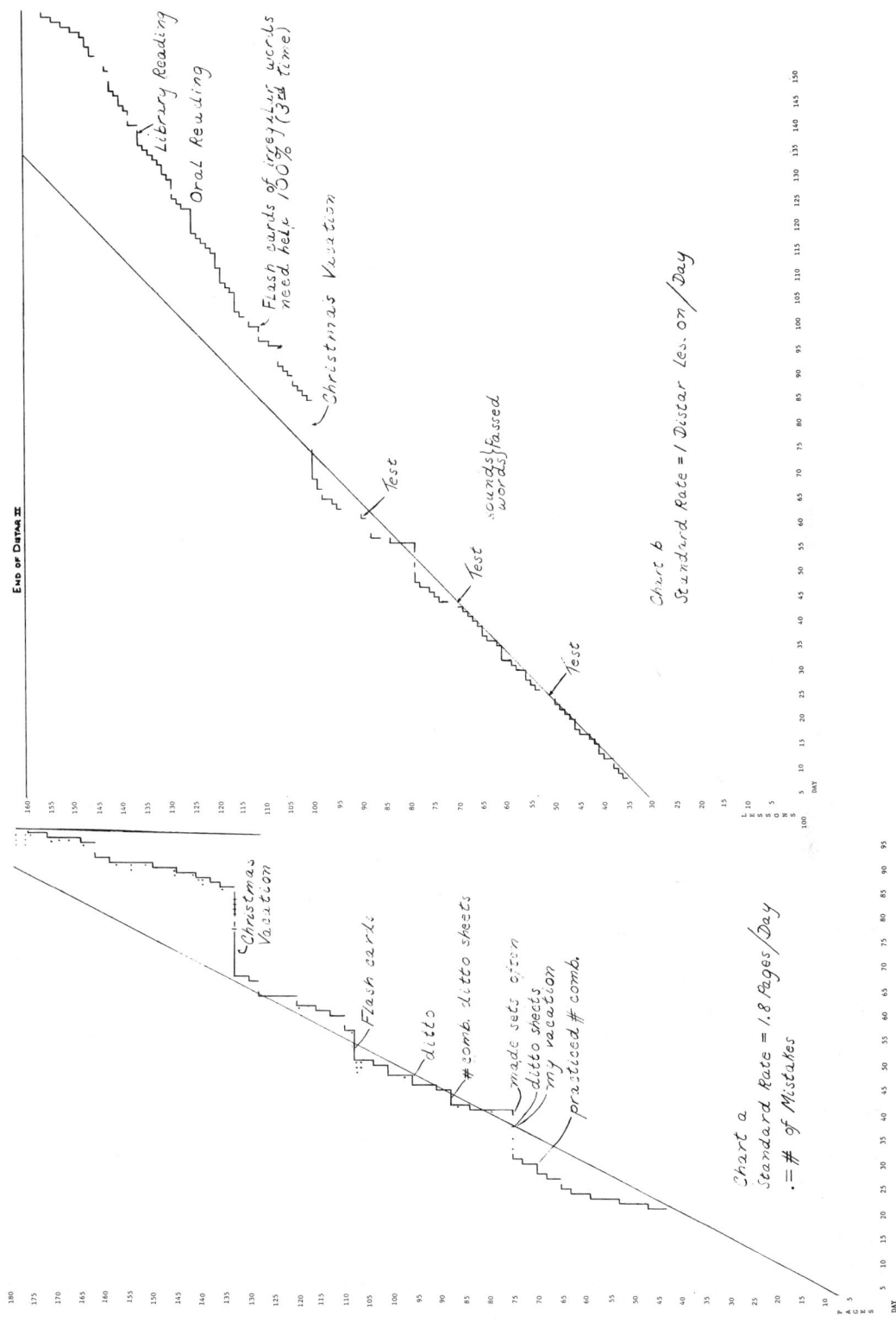

Figure 2. Daily progress charts kept for each child in the Learning Village elementary school. Figure 2a shows the progress of a child in the **Sets and Numbers** math series. Each upward step represents 1.8 pages completed. Figure 2b shows the progress of a child in the **Distar II** reading program. Each upward step represents a lesson completed.

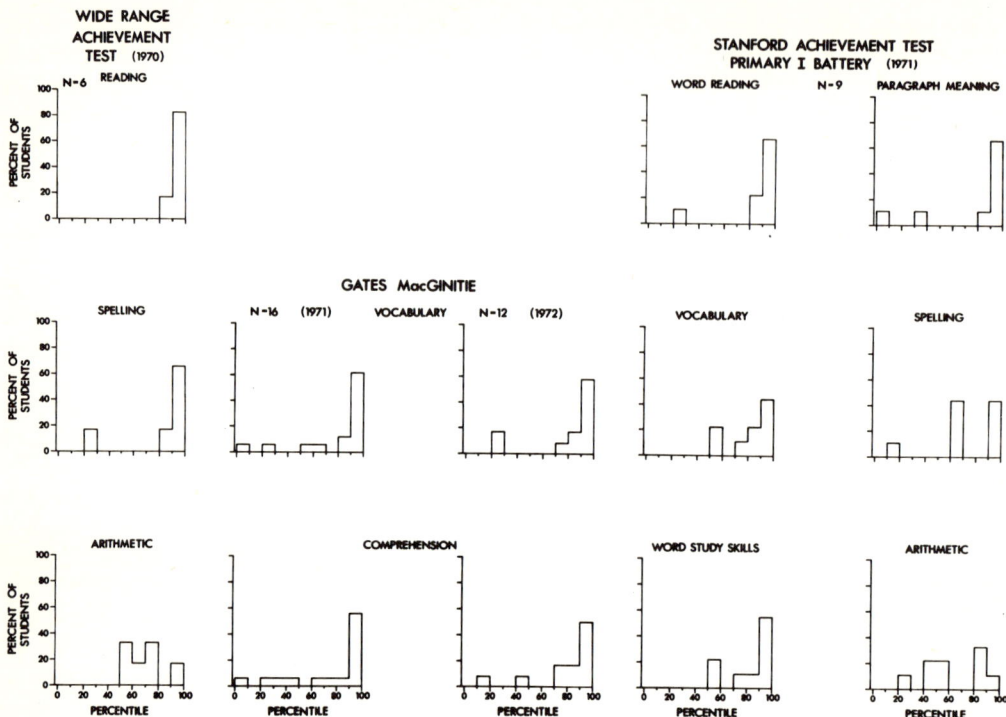

Figure 3. *Scores of Learning Village elementary school children on the Wide-Range Achievement Test, the Gates MacGinitie Reading Test, and the Primary I battery of the Stanford Achievement Test.*

automatically provides a daily record of how many tokens were received, who dispensed the tokens, the category of behavior that was reinforced, and approximately the time of day reinforcement occurred. The token sheets are retained in binders for future reference. Each day the number of tokens earned, lost, spent, and saved is totalled and recorded for each child. If a child has earned or saved few tokens, or if he has lost an exceptional amount, the system assures that the teacher will be alerted. In practice, teachers usually "track" the children's behavior well enough to be aware of problems; however, the token-recording system may help the teacher pinpoint a situation. If a child has earned relatively few tokens, the teacher may check back and see if a low rate of learning occurred in any particular class or activity or for any particular type of behavior. Special work

with the child can then be undertaken to accelerate his learning rate.

Charts of academic behavior are made in various subjects for each child. Two charts are shown in Figure 2. School days are represented along the abscissa and lesson units along the ordinate. The straight diagonal line shows the rate of progress of a student who completes one lesson unit every day. Units may be defined in terms of lessons in a programmed sequence, pages in a text book, or lessons in a text book. The diagonal lines represent an ideal or, in some cases, a more than ideal rate of progress. For each lesson unit completed, the child's line is drawn up a notch; for each school day, the child's line is drawn over a notch. Each dot to the left of a step represents an error in whatever active behavior was required. Gaps in the line represent absences.

Chart a in Figure 2 shows the progress of a student in the *Sets and Numbers* math series. Each lesson unit is approximately 1.8 pages long. Except for pauses for vacation, the student worked steadily and at a satisfactory rate. Chart b shows the progress of a child through the lessons in the Distar II reading series. Although the child's record shows decelerations, they are mainly due to absences, Christmas vacation, or the introduction of supplemental materials, such as flash cards and library reading. The charts, then, are simply a convenient way of providing a record of the child's recent progress on some aspect of the curriculum.

Results of Standardized Testing

Figure 3 shows the distributions of scores on the standardized achievement tests that have been given the Learning Village elementary school children. The reading-related scores have a J-shaped distribution that is very much in contrast with the "normal" curve anticipated by most educators. The Learning Village especially stresses reading, and the scores reflect this emphasis. Math scores are not as striking, but they are better than usual. Clearly the program at the Learning Village led to exceptional achievement, especially in verbal skills.

The Vineland Social Maturity Scale also was given to the children. Figure 4 shows the results of that test. All but two children scored above the norm for their age, and most placed years above their norm.

Although, as discussed earlier, the significance of standardized-test results is questionable, the Learning Village does expect its children to score *at least* at average levels on standardized tests. When a child does not, an effort is made to change his educational program. The change may involve more intensive academic work in some areas or emphasis on nonacademic behaviors such as

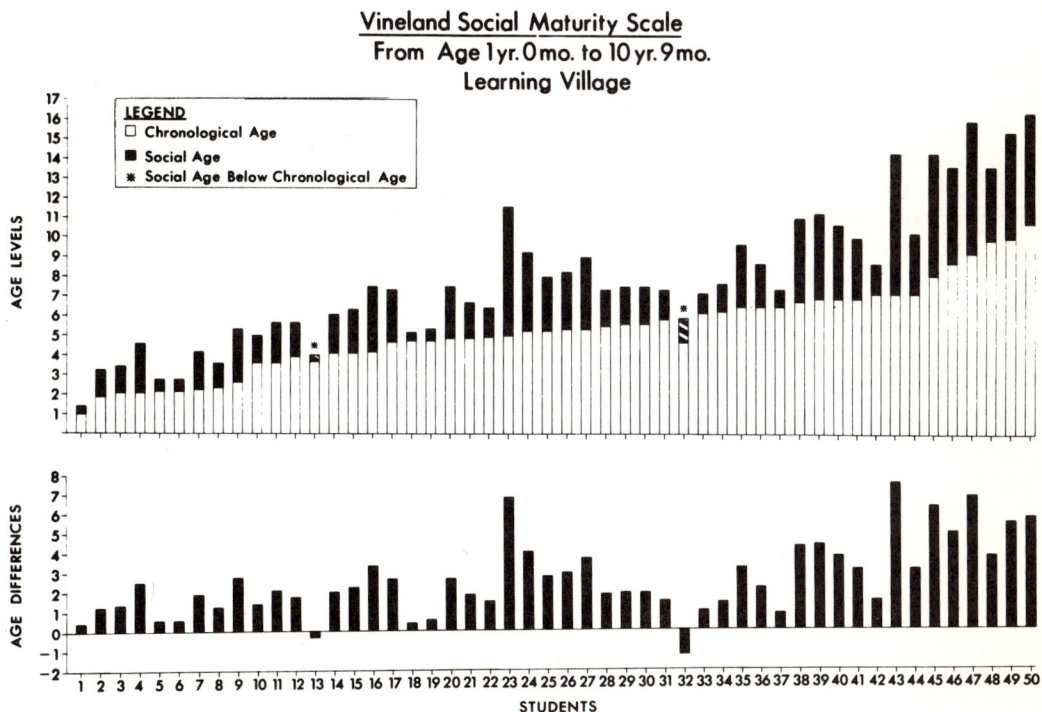

Figure 4. *Performance of all Learning Village children on the Vineland Social Maturity Scale.*

staying "cool" under pressure. Apparently though, the Learning Village has done a fair job of meeting its goals.

ROUND-THE-CLOCK EDUCATION

Several of the parents of Learning Village children have formed a 24-hour-a-day child-care group. The parents rotate five days a week in caring for the children and try to apply Learning Village principles in non-school hours. The group extends the exposure to the social values of the Learning Village and to behavioral methodology. It also supplies for the children an alternative to watching television in after-school hours. Because it isn't just another evening at home with the family, the parent currently caring for the children is able to be more tolerant, consistent, and innovative in his relationships and is more likely to provide special after-school experiences for the children.

FUTURE PLANS

Plans currently are being made to expand the Learning Village and the child-care group into an experimental community centered on education. Land has been purchased, and a few people now live on it; however, most community members are commuters as yet. Nevertheless, some of the problems inherent in setting up an experimental community already have been experienced. It is never easy to get agreement from a number of highly individualistic people.

Unfortunately another plan for the immediate future is to close down the grades above grade two in the Learning Village. Since only twenty children of various ages are enrolled, it is impossible, financially, to provide the staff necessary to plan lessons for five grades and five subjects a day. Aid-to-Dependent-Children tuition payments for economically disadvantaged children cease when they reach first grade; these children must be carried on scholarship. Even the tuition charged is not adequate to pay for such small-scale individualized instruction. Financial assistance from foundations and government agencies has not been adequate. Until these conditions change, operations must be limited. The original "vision" of the Learning Village was to provide children with a comprehensive program of behavioral education from infancy until college or beyond, but so far funding has not made this possible. The results that have been obtained suggest that such a program could produce some unusual individuals.

The true potential of behavioral education will be seen only when it can be applied not to one behavior in one classroom for a finite period of time but to the entire education of people. More experiments like the Learning Village are needed to discover the problems and possibilities inherent in comprehensive behavioral education.

5

IN ADOLESCENT AND SECONDARY EDUCATION

The two articles in this section deal with the special problems of educating adolescents. The first study, by Sloggett, discusses some techniques that may be effective with adolescents in public-school settings. This paper points out that special forms and systems of reinforcement may be necessary in dealing with some adolescent groups because of their unique subculture.

The second article, by Cohen, Kleiner, and Brown, describes a special program, outside the regular public schools, designed to educate delinquent and predelinquent children. The program features an elaborate token economy and utilization of parents through contingency contracting and "home-based reinforcers." Such techniques for integrating parents into school programs are needed if the effects of school treatment are to transfer to home situations.

The fact that the best programs now operating for adolescents are remedial testifies to failure in educational programs for younger children. Adolescence is a special time for intellectual and social growth, as well as problems. Perhaps, in the future, programs can be established that will tap this growth and build on earlier educational progress. Such programs may be able to draw attention to the potential rather than the problems of adolescence.

Use of group activities and team rewards to increase individual classroom productivity

BARBARA B. SLOGGETT

National attention is currently directed toward changing our middle-class-oriented educational system to one which would work with minority-group children. The need for change has been most apparent with children who are socially disadvantaged, potential school dropouts, or low-achieving students (Bloom, 1966; Grotberg, 1965; Hunt, 1966; Miller, 1963, 1964; Pressman, 1969). On the U.S. Mainland, the focus of attention is on urban ghettos. In Hawaii interest centers on rural Hawaiians.

This article describes how a token reinforcement system was used to reward group rather than individual behavior in order to promote academic development among low-achieving adolescent Hawaiian boys. The program described was based on a classroom field experiment conducted in an economically depressed Hawaiian community.

Background of the Experimental Class

Twenty-four boys whose ages ranged from fourteen to seventeen were enrolled in a self-contained class in an intermediate school. The principal and vice-principal made all class assignments. All of the boys chosen for the experimental class demonstrated poor academic achievement and disruptive classroom behavior.

Academic problems demonstrated. Although the boys had been in eighth- and ninth-grade classes, they achieved considerably below their grade levels in every academic subject. Most were doing fourth-grade work in arithmetic and second-grade work in reading.

At the beginning of the project, which was conducted during the spring semester, only six students were doing any academic work at all. None had succeeded in course work, and, in general, they viewed themselves as school failures.

Social behaviors demonstrated. Many of the boys were chronic absentees, several had spent time in a boys' correctional facility, and all were potential school "push-outs," i.e., chronically disruptive students who were no longer welcome in the school system. One boy was openly defiant toward everyone, another was completely withdrawn. The remaining students spent most of their class time in small groups talking among themselves or drawing elaborate doodles, allowing the teacher a maximum of ten minutes of their attention during any class period and devoting, at most, fifteen minutes of the period to assigned work. Class periods lasted from sixty to ninety minutes.

In the beginning of the semester the classroom atmosphere was chaotic. It was a bewildering experience to be confronted by twenty-four boisterous teenage boys, all engaged in rowdy behavior, such as bouncing a basketball around the room, throwing chalk and erasers, tipping over chairs, and writing obscene words on the blackboard.

Why Use a Token Reinforcement System?

What is a token reinforcement system? A token reinforcement system rewards those behaviors to be promoted by giving the learner a token, e.g., bus tokens, poker chips, trading stamps, or even money, which can be exchanged for material items of value such as food, toys, or privileges. Items for which tokens can be exchanged are referred to as back-up reinforcers. After frequent pairings with back-up rewards, tokens, as conditioned reinforcers, may acquire value for their own sake, just as money acquires value. Within

From **Teaching Exceptional Children**, Winter 1971, 54-66.
Reprinted with permission of The Council for Exceptional Children.

the classroom tokens can be earned for desirable behaviors, and their use provides the teacher with a limitless source of reinforcement. She can generously dispense tokens without exhausting the limited supply of back-up reinforcements (Staats, 1968).

The use of token reinforcement systems with non-middle-class learners. There is a substantial body of experimental evidence concerned with the psychology of learning which shows that the use of rewards is instrumental in the process of making work (or striving for achievement) self-satisfying. Many students who appear to enjoy academic work for its own sake have probably received considerable reinforcement (e.g., praise) for achievements in the past (Staats and Staats, 1963).

"A child raised in a situation where middle-class achievement is not reinforced will not work for these consequences. The individual who has been deprived of a history where achievements have been consistently reinforced, is frequently described as lazy, stupid, constitutionally inferior, and so on. Actually, however, this individual would not aspire to middle-class achievements—would not find them reinforcing—because he had not been so trained [p. 296]."

Why rewarding individual behavior might not work with the experimental class. There is evidence that Hawaiians are seldom concerned with the pursuit of success for the purely personal satisfactions involved (Gallimore and Howard, 1968; Gallimore, 1969). For example Hawaiians scored significantly below local Japanese and Filipinos, as well as lower-class Mainland Negroes and Caucasians, on a test of achievement motivation (Sloggett, Gallimore, and Kubany, 1970). In addition, Hawaiians apparently derive little personal pleasure from competing successfully against others and, in fact, avoid individual competition. According to Gallimore and Howard (1968), Hawaiians are motivated primarily by peer pressure, affiliation, and avoidance of social disapproval.

As an illustration, many children in the school refused to accept material rewards (e.g., cokes or candy) for high grades or successful competition unless the rewards could be shared with their friends. With the exception of the aggressive and withdrawn students, members of the experimental class engaged in continuous social interaction, usually carried on in a friendly though boisterous manner.

Such observations suggested that if the boys could be placed in groups in which their interactions were directed toward mutually meaningful goals then the use of a token reinforcement system might serve to convert the initially disorganized classroom situation into a more productive environment. If peer approval could be channeled, it could serve as a powerful motivator to work for rewards.

The Use of Teams

The problem was how to establish a cooperative peer-sanctioned climate that at the same time would be conducive to classroom achievement. It was decided that the boys would work as teams rather than as individuals. Through the establishment of group goals, it was to one team member's advantage for another to complete his work; at the same time the possibility of individual failure was removed.

Constituting the teams. The boys were divided into four matched groups of six members each on the basis of academic ability (grades and I.Q.) and social competence (e.g., passivity-aggressiveness) as judged by teachers familiar with the students. The groups were physically separated within the classroom by clustering desks into four distinct areas. Typically, at the end of a period each boy handed in an assignment with his own name and team number on it. Each student contributed to a team score, and each team received rewards as a unit. The boys worked together in their groups and were encouraged to help one another. Peer interaction was not discouraged in any way—in fact, within-team cooperation greatly facilitated goal attainment.

Using token reinforcement in a team-oriented context. Points were used as token reinforcers. Students earned points and approval for various achievement-related activities throughout the day, and, at the end of each week, the total points were translated into letter grades. The boys earned points daily in a team-participation context; each member of a team contributed his points to the team's total and in return achieved the grade his team earned as a unit.

How the Point System Worked

The boys could earn points for their team by their individual performances and by their group-oriented activities.

Individual points. For individual performance, each member of a team could contribute to his team a maximum of 300 points daily in each subject area. The 300 points could be earned as follows:

50 points for presence or excused absence,
50 points for appropriate classroom behavior (as defined later under Student Participation in Decision-Making),
100 points for having materials (pencils, paper, etc.) and participating,
100 points for accurate work.

The points earned by each team in each of the five subject areas (in-service, English, math, social studies, and P.E.) could be translated into letter grades. ("In-service" refers to an activity in which the boys were allowed to tutor kindergarten pupils with behavior problems or to assist in classrooms where teachers were having discipline problems.) Each team that earned an average of 250–300 points per member in a given subject area during a one-week period received an "A" for that subject; each team earning between 185–249 points received a "B," and so on. In this way every team had an opportunity to earn an "A" at the conclusion of each weekly session.

It is important to emphasize that the boys earned points not only for accurate work but also for a wide variety of other behaviors. For example, coming to class, being on time, bringing supplies, and paying attention are certainly important to academic progress but

are frequently taken for granted and left unrewarded. In the present study, however, achievement behaviors were "shaped" by reinforcing these "approximations"—that is, if the teacher had withheld reinforcement until these boys consistently came to school on time, were well prepared, and performed at ninth-grade level, the boys might have had an endless wait before receiving their first reward. By making the initial criteria relatively easy to attain, reinforcement was readily available for these boys, who in the past seldom found anything reinforcing about the classroom.

In a long-term program the strategy would be to raise the level of performance required prior to reinforcement progressively, with the expectation that behaviors such as coming to school on time and paying attention would become so well established that reinforcement for these behaviors could eventually be phased out. Emphasis could then be primarily on academic achievement.

Team points. Each team could earn additional points for certain group oriented activities not specifically related to task performance but intended to encourage the boys to help one another. Such group effort or "pulling together" was rewarded in the following manner:

100 points for contacting remiss students about school attendance, tardiness, or misbehavior,
50 points for contacting students about other school or behavioral matters (e.g., notifying absent members concerning class activities or helping classmates with home or personal problems).

Weekly payoff. At the end of each week the point count of each team was computed. Each team that achieved an average of at least 1,000 points per member could earn a grade of "A" and an award—for example, an excursion off school grounds during the following school week. Each team was competing against a standard of known value, and all, a few, or none could obtain the highest reward—in other words, grading was not on a curve basis.

It should be added that, in addition to the points and material back-up rewards, the boys were praised *liberally* for all behaviors that earned points. However, the boys were not praised indiscriminately in a "shower them with love" manner; praise was given only following appropriate behavior.

Maintaining Discipline

Maintaining order is one of the major concerns of any teacher. When requests for order are disobeyed, many teachers typically resort to threats and punishments.

Negative attention may maintain undesirable behavior. Previous research has demonstrated that "negative attention" (e.g., scolding bad behavior) may in fact have reinforcing properties and actually maintain inappropriate behavior rather than eliminate it (Gallimore, Tharp, and Kemp, 1969; Ayllon and Michael, 1959; Williams, 1959; Madsen, Becker, Thomas, Koser, and Plager, 1968). For example, Madsen et al. (1968) obtained clear evidence that the more frequently first-grade teachers asked their children to sit down, the more frequently they stood up. In addition, repeated use of punitive measures often involves a large expenditure of teacher energy and can result in exhaustion and frustration, especially if these techniques don't work. As far as the punished student is concerned, school may come to represent a hostile environment, and when his parents or the law no longer require him to stay in school, he may become an early drop-out.

Ignoring negative behavior and rewarding positive behavior. In the present study, a concerted and continuing effort was made to completely avoid threats and punitive reprimands. Disruptive behavior was simply ignored. Rather than emphasize classroom violations, attention was focused on the performance of acceptable responses *incompatible* with misbehavior. For example, a student cannot be on time and late for class at the same time; rather than punish or simply ignore tardiness, the incompatible behavior of being on time was rewarded with points.

The usual school procedure for tardiness involved sending the student to the office for a cut slip; students with frequent tardiness were given verbal reprimands and occasionally suspended from school. It was believed that such actions would more likely lead to avoidance of the classroom entirely than to increased punctuality. Therefore, emphasizing the positive, punctuality was rewarded and tardiness was ignored. As additional examples, the boys were rewarded for bringing materials rather than being criticized for forgetfulness, and were rewarded for their academic accomplishments rather than disciplined for failure to do the assignments. In all cases attempts were made to gain classroom control by reinforcing desired behaviors rather than trying to "stamp out" undesired behaviors.

Developing Student Participation in Decision-making

Several studies have shown that performance improves as participation in decision-making increases (Coch and French, 1948; Lovitt and Curtiss, 1969; MacDonald, 1967). Therefore the program was not arbitrarily imposed on the boys. They were given the opportunity to help decide on ways to implement the experimental program and were encouraged to make suggestions for improvements.

Describing the program to the boys. The entire program was described to the boys at the beginning of the semester, and they were asked specifically to suggest changes. The boys made the following major decisions which were incorporated into the program: (a) choice of academic subjects to study, (b) definitions of appropriate classroom behavior, and (c) selection of rewards.

Selecting academic preferences. Concerning their academic preferences, the boys selected mathematics as their first choice for study. Other areas they selected were social studies, English, P.E., and the in-service program. Further, the boys selected the sub-areas within a given academic subject—for in-of being on time was rewarded with points. stance, they expressed an interest in learning how to do fractions and long division.

Defining appropriate behavior. Regarding definitions of appropriate behavior, the boys were asked how they thought they should behave in the classroom, and they listed the following rules on the blackboard:

1. Don't fight.
2. Don't throw chalk and erasers or spitballs.
3. Don't yell—raise your hand if you want to talk.
4. Don't break the furniture.

It is interesting to note that they stated every rule in negative terms; a fact which strongly suggests that in the past their teachers had focused on bad rather than good behavior.

Selecting rewards. Perhaps most importantly, the students were allowed to choose, within limits, what they wanted as rewards (back-up reinforcers). Parents and teachers often assume that they know what children like; this assumption may not always be valid, as evidenced by the fact that several of the reinforcers selected by the boys in the experimental class would not have occurred to the author—girl-watching in Waikiki, for example. Interestingly, the boys made virtually no unreasonable or impossible requests, although preferences changed frequently. Their initial requests were for cokes, candy, and doughnuts; other choices included playing basketball during class time, a picnic in the park adjoining the school grounds, and permission to play their transistor radios in class. Surprisingly, the boys also requested that they be given letter grades for their earned points. The back-up reinforcer of the highest value was an excursion during school hours to various island locations, ranging from surfing at Waimea Bay and Makapuu to movies and girl-watching at Waikiki. In fact, excursions became the most popular back-up reinforcer during the last half of the semester.

Where the Class Was at the Close of the Project

Arithmetic achievement. Of the several academic subjects selected for instruction, pre- and post-semester achievement data were obtained only in the area of mathematics. The pre-post tests included subtests in subtraction, multiplication, division, and fractions and were at the sixth-grade level of difficulty. There were dramatic improvements made over the course of the semester. In each of the sub-areas and in total score, there were highly significant mean differences between the number of problems correct on the pretests and posttests ($p > .001$ in each of the four test comparisons). At the beginning of the year, many of these teenage boys could not add or subtract well enough to count their change from a simple transaction in a retail store; only one student could do long division and fractions. At the end of the semester nearly every boy was able to do both.

Increased productivity. A four-day mid-semester experiment revealed that class productivity was far superior under reinforcement than nonreinforcement conditions, i.e., no points or approval ($p > .001$). Inasmuch as there was no suitable control group available, the specific contribution of the team arrangement could not be determined unequivocally, although some direct and much indirect evidence suggested that it, as well as the token system, had a strong influence in shaping classroom habits.

Reduction in disorderly behavior. As mentioned previously, the boys initially demonstrated highly chaotic behavior. They ignored requests to sit down and be quiet. Verbal reprimands and scoldings also were ineffectual. When negative sanctions were removed and inappropriate behavior first was ignored, misbehavior actually increased temporarily. As the semester proceeded, however, misbehavior decreased markedly, and by the end of the semester the amount of destructive behavior was almost negligible. When working in their groups, the boys never did become highly restrained or orderly and typically were noisy, but it should be noted that no attempt was made to reduce peer interaction during group activities. On the other hand, the boys were quiet and attentive while the instructions were being given for the daily assignments. Further, the school vice-principal reported a dramatic decline in the number of problem referrals he ordinarily received, although smoking, gambling, and occasionally glue-sniffing continued to be problems outside the classroom. It should be mentioned that there are few "perfect" classrooms—even in model classrooms, problem behavior is seldom reduced to zero. The goal of education, however, is not to make children into academic robots; even the most well-behaved children transgress now and then, and an infrequent disruption seldom interferes significantly with the ongoing academic process.

Increased self-imposed peer pressure for good conduct. Accompanying the decline in classroom misconduct, there appeared to be an increase in self-imposed peer pressure for good conduct. As a surprising example, class members periodically requested the teacher to take disciplinary action in response to individual misconduct. When the teacher continued to ignore the misbehavior, other students occasionally stepped in and requested order. Behavior such as this suggests that potential peer pressure for appropriate behavior exists within the classroom. Such observations also lend support to the notion that, among Hawaiians at least, affiliation and peer-approval motives can operate in the direction of self-regulation in the classroom. An experiment by Patterson (1965) demonstrated that it was possible to enlist students to control each other in the classroom. In Patterson's study the teacher rewarded an entire class if a particularly hyperactive and aggressive boy behaved himself. As a result, his classmates no longer reinforced him with laughter or social approval for his disruptive behavior which subsequently diminished.

Improved attendance. While the attendance for the school as a whole dropped between the fall and spring semesters (an expected occurrence), attendance of the experimental class members actually improved in the spring. Not only did attendance increase, but in the spring attendance in the experimental class surpassed the class average for the entire school—in spite of the fact that these statistics included two boys who were absent almost from the first day; one boy was in jail and another was residing in the hospital with his injured brother. As an interesting sidelight, one of the boys, Scott, inevitably was absent when the surf was "up," but in order not to lose his points he would send his brother, Ron, to take his place in class. Ron, who also was a poor student and chronic absentee but was not selected initially for the experimental class, eventually became a regular member of the class and subsequently demonstrated an excellent attendance record. There also were occasional "drop-in" students from other classes who apparently were curious about the experimental classroom. These boys never were disruptive and frequently sat with their friends and did some work themselves.

Other improvements. A number of other incidental observations are of interest. For example, it frequently happened that a boy who had been absent would ask to make up any work he had missed, providing, of course, that he and his team received points for the work. If a boy missed class because of cafeteria work, he rarely failed to pick up the class assignment and complete it during recess or overnight. Further, it was not uncommon for teammates to fill out a problem sheet for absent members along with the absent members' signatures. After the point system had been in operation for a few weeks, several of the boys asked if they could do extra work in order to earn additional points. Accordingly, "bonus problems" were made available with bonus points contingent on correct solutions.

The individual behavior of a number of boys also changed dramatically. For instance, the defiant boy mentioned earlier became one of the better students academically; he frequently did the most accurate work on his team and "tutored" those who had difficulty. In addition, the completely withdrawn boy eventually started participating in team activities and made an effort to contribute his share of points.

The boys' conduct while on excursions deserves comment. What is interesting is that these boys caused no disciplinary problems during the excursions—they were polite, helpful, and respectful at all times. As a matter of fact, after the first surfing expedition they insisted on cleaning the sand out of the author's car, and they never failed to share their lunch or treats whenever they had them. There was no question about the boys having the appropriate behaviors in their repertoire—the situation simply had to be designed to elicit them.

Follow-up Findings

The experimental class was terminated in June, and in September, eighteen of the boys were assigned to the tenth grade in the local high school while six were placed in a newly organized community classroom designed to employ techniques similar to those reported here. In the spring of the following year, only four of the eighteen were still attending classes, while all six placed in the community classroom were maintaining good attendance. Interestingly, the boys assigned to the local high school frequently were seen on the campus during school hours visiting with their friends. The opportunity to affiliate with their peers apparently attracted them to the campus but not into the classroom.

Factors to Consider in Implementing a Similar Program

The cost of using a token reinforcement system. It is recognized that, while the use of a token reinforcement system may involve additional expenditures to school budgets, the costs should be considered situation-specific and may be moderate in some cases. For unusual or severe problems, effective reinforcers may not be readily apparent or available; in such cases, relatively large expenditures for effective rewards or professional consultation may be indicated. On the other hand, many reinforcers are a naturally

occurring part of most school settings, but ordinarily are not made contingent on specified behaviors—these include games, recesses, toys, snacks, rest periods, play periods during regular class time, television, and, of course, social approval (smiles, praise, physical proximity, physical contact, etc.). Recess, for example, is typically on a fixed-schedule (the same time every day) regardless of classroom behavior. Aside from administrative hurdles, it would be a relatively simple matter to require students to "earn" their recess or other free time.

Does a peer team always work? The major innovation of the present study was the incorporation of the team concept into the classroom structure. The use of teams promises to be a potentially effective means of capitalizing on the affiliative habits of Hawaiian schoolchildren, although this conclusion must remain tentative at present. This view is strengthened by the preliminary findings of a recent, well-controlled experiment in which team goals facilitated classroom performance and attendance of socially disadvantaged delinquents in Hawaii (Test, 1969). In regard to the implementation of the team system, one further point should be made. In Test's study several of the more intelligent team members did not like working for team goals, because they contributed a disproportionate amount of the team's points; they were dissatisfied with their share of the reward (money), which was divided equally among the team members. In his study the team members worked individually, and only correct answers earned points. In contrast, in the present study the poorer students were still able to contribute a large share of the team's points simply by going through the motions of being a good student (arriving on time, bringing materials, avoiding misconduct, working on the assignment). As a result, none of the better students complained that they were contributing more than their fair share. And by working together, the better students actually served as tutors for the poorer students in order to gain a few extra points for correct answers. In fact, the most productive team included both the best and (from the academic viewpoint) the worst students in the class.

Summary

An experimental classroom was conducted in a rural intermediate school with a group of twenty-four low-achieving Hawaiian adolescent boys. The class was divided into four six-student teams in an attempt to capitalize on the importance of peer affiliation among Hawaiians. Disruptive and other inappropriate behaviors were ignored. Reinforcement systems were used with a wide variety of student-selected back-up reinforcements, ranging from cokes to excursions. Thus the approach was twofold: (a) to arrange a classroom environment compatible with the peer approval system of the Hawaiian culture, and (b) to provide meaningful reinforcers.

Rather than force the boys into the mold of an educational system that typically emphasized competition and individual achievement, it was believed that the use of teams was a logical way of utilizing the natural pressures of a highly interactive peer group. The traditional educational system for middle-class Mainland Caucasians may be inappropriate for Hawaiians (or other cultural minorities), and it would seem unfair to tamper with the rich Hawaiian heritage for the sake of academic achievement alone. The fact that most Hawaiians are poorly educated, according to Mainland standards, may be less the fault of the Hawaiian people than it is of the educational system imposed on them. In fact: "Where the reigning philosophy of education is that it is the student's responsibility to learn, attention may not be directed to the inadequacy of the program of training even in the face of many educational failures" (Staats & Staats, 1963,
p. 428). It would seem preferable to change the educational system to fit and preserve the culture than to change the culture to fit the system.

Although there were numerous indications that the twelve-week program was a substantial success, a long-term program would be necessary to thoroughly evaluate the various components of the project and their implications. Returning the students to the traditional system after only one semester or year amounts to experimental extinction, and in most cases one might expect them to return to their previous school habits. Staats (1969) recently recommended the establishment of a self-contained experimental school operated on the basis of experimentally derived learning principles. Such a school would not be handicapped by teacher resistance to change of existing programs. The staff of school systems, deeply rooted in tradition, frequently resent and resist innovations, even temporary experimental ones isolated from the school at large. John Paul Scott (1969) made a relevant point when he stated that ". . . organization inhibits reorganization. To alter the school curriculum involves reorganizing an already highly organized social system. It is often easier to set up an entirely new experimental school than to change an established one."

Conclusion

Several of the procedures employed in the experimental classroom do represent a significant departure from typical methods of classroom operation. However, if the efficacy of innovations such as these can be unequivocally demonstrated in long-term experimental programs, school administrators may become more enthusiastic about accepting them as a new part of the curriculum.

Effective behavior change at the Anne Arundel Learning Center through minimum contact interventions

SHLOMO I. COHEN, J. MICHAEL KEYWORTH, RICHARD I. KLEINER, AND WILLIAM L. BROWN

The initial section of this paper describes the overall program which existed at the Anne Arundel Learning Center (AALC) during 1970–71. The latter section describes three minimum contact intervention procedures which involved the parents of Learning Center students in helping their children improve performances at school.

THE AALC PROGRAM

The AALC is a public school for students ejected from other public schools in Anne Arundel County, Maryland. About 150 students aged twelve to seventeen years are enrolled at the Learning Center. All of the students have academic and/or social deficits, and many have had interactions with psychiatric and/or psychological agencies as well as with the juvenile courts. All of the students have been ejected from other county schools; most also are potential dropouts who could be described as delinquent or predelinquent.

The Learning Center campus at Fort Meade is divided into a work area consisting of three army barracks and a reinforcer area (Student Activities Center) consisting of two additional barracks. The academic curriculum is individualized and includes the IPI Math Continuum, a language arts curriculum developed by AALC staff based on the IPI model, a reading program utilizing Distar and the Reading Attainment Series, and an ecology unit requiring math, science, language arts, and social studies skills.

These programmed materials are broken down into units called tasks which are designed to require approximately thirty to sixty minutes of work from the individual student using the materials. Because the materials are clearly sequenced a student may easily begin a new task following the successful completion to 80 percent criterion of the preceding task. The student may complete as many or few tasks as he chooses, but, of course, he is reinforced accordingly.

At the beginning of each month, the Learning Center accepts ten new students who have recently been ejected from other schools. Upon entry, the new student completes the orientation-curriculum package, a programmed curriculum unit of several tasks which explains the operation of the Learning Center. In this way, a student participates in the school program as soon as he enters. During the entry procedures, students are tested and assigned either to the basic-skills program or to the secondary-skills program.

The Learning Center program emphasizes positive control of student behavior and provides several options to the students. Students are allowed free exit from the work and reinforcer areas (Student Activity Center) at any time. A student may enter his work building at the beginning of a period, work on his individualized package of material for ten minutes, and then go outside to the loafing area. At any time of the school day, a visitor might see students working at their desks in the work buildings, other students participating in the Student Activities Center (SAC), and still other students outside in the loafing area. A basic assumption underlying the free-exit policy is that each student participates in the academic program to the extent that the curriculum is appropriate to his skill level and to the extent that the activities in SAC are reinforcers for him. When the ongoing data indicate that a student is spending large amounts of time in the loafing area, we are, in effect, being informed that the environment designed for that student is inappropriate, and curriculum and/or reinforcer changes are required.

Reprinted by permission of the authors.
This research was performed at the Anne Arundel County Learning Center and was partially supported by a grant from the Maryland State Department of Mental Hygiene to the Anne Arundel County Board of Education.

CARRY OVER TOTAL [   ]

NAME _____ BLDG. # _____
WEEK _____

		CHECKS					TASK COMPLETED			
DATE	PERIOD	PEN/PENCIL	ASSIGNED AREA	GOOD WORK	GOOD BEHAVIOR		TASK 1	TASK 2	TASK 3	TASK 4	
THURS.	1										
	2										
	3										
	4										
	5										
	CUM. CHECK TOTAL						CUM. T.C. TOTAL				
FRI.	1										
	2										
	3										
	4										
	5										
	CUM. CHECK TOTAL						CUM. T.C. TOTAL				
MON.	1										
	2										
	3										
	4										
	5										
	CUM. CHECK TOTAL						CUM. T.C. TOTAL				
TUES.	1										
	2										
	3										
	4										
	5										
	CUM. CHECK TOTAL						CUM. T.C. TOTAL				
WED.	1										
	2										
	3										
	4										
	5										
	CUM. CHECK TOTAL						CUM. T.C. TOTAL				

Figure 1. *The Student Check List placed on each student's desk. Students may receive four teacher's signatures by fulfilling the four requirements during a work period.*

In the work areas, each student has a Student Check List (SCL) on his desk. The SCL can be seen in Figure 1. The SCL specifies four behaviors which are antecedents for academic task completion. During each period (fifty minutes) that the student is in his work building, he may earn a teacher signature for (1) having a pen or a pencil, (2) being in an assigned area—usually his desk, (3) having curriculum materials on his desk, and (4) not disturbing other students. Previous work at the AALC has suggested that when a student fulfills the above four requisite antecedent behaviors (RABS) (Hawkins, 1971), the probability of task completion is increased. During each period, these checks are given out at varying intervals averaging about every twelve minutes. To earn all four checks the student must emit desirable behaviors for the duration of the period. The student in his work area for all five periods of a school day could possibly earn twenty signatures on that day. When a student earns fifty-two signatures, which requires at least thirteen complete periods (of twenty-five in the school week) in the work building, he may exchange the signatures for a booklet of twelve tickets of admission, each good for one period in the Student Activities Center. Figure 2 shows a ticket of admission to the SAC.

The school program is designed so that a student could spend thirteen periods per school week in his work building, and the remaining twelve periods per week in SAC. Most students tend to mix work-time and reinforcer-time on any given day rather than participate in work or SAC in large blocks. When a student receives his SAC tickets, he writes his name on each ticket in ink, and then the tickets are stamped to expire two weeks from the date received. Thus the student may save any ticket only for a two-week period. Any erasure on a SAC ticket invalidates the ticket.

When the SAC tickets are first received, they may not be used to gain admission into SAC activities. Each ticket becomes useable only after validation by a teacher in the work building. The validation of a ticket occurs when a teacher completes the bottom

First Name _____

Last Name _____

Expires on _____

Today's Date _____

SAC ACTIVITY COUPON

Period   Activity Choice

1 2 3 4 5   1._____

(circle one)   2._____

Validated on_____by_____

Work Completed
page_____task_____

Figure 2. *Ticket of admission for one period in the Student Activities Center.*

two lines of the SAC ticket (see Figure 2). Validation occurs only after a student completes an academic task. The presentation of SAC tickets in exchange for SCL checks serves to reinforce the requisite antecedent behaviors, while validation of SAC tickets reinforces task-completions.

The behaviors involved in the completion of most tasks are reading, writing answers to questions, and/or checking off answers to questions, and/or orally answering questions from teachers, and/or performing mathematical operations. As a student's skills gradually improve, a task gradually includes more work to be completed within the thirty to sixty minutes. The validation of a SAC ticket might occur at any time of the day in a work building.

If a student requires teacher assistance while completing his task, he does not raise his hand but places his name card in a centrally located box. Teachers respond to a

ANNOUNCEMENTS

1. STUDENTS WHO HAVE RETURNED TO SCHOOL FROM AN ABSENCE MAY
   PARTICIPATE IN SAC ACTIVITIES ON THE DAY THEY RETURN (IF THERE
   IS ROOM) BY BRINGING VALIDATED COUPONS TO THE WINDOW OF THE
   OFFICE IMMEDIATELY UPON THEIR RETURN TO SCHOOL.

2. ANY QUESTIONS ABOUT THE SPL OR TODAY'S SCHEDULE WILL BE
   ANSWERED AT THE WINDOW UNTIL 9:40 - NO CHANGES WILL BE MADE
   AFTER THIS TIME.

3. SIX PERIODS OF BASKETBALL PRACTICE CAN BE BOUGHT FOR FIVE
   COUPONS.

4. TO EARN A GOOD-FRIDAY LETTER THIS WEEK, YOU MUST HAVE COMPLETED
   A TOTAL OF 12 TASKS AND SAC ACTIVITIES BETWEEN THURSDAY, MAY 20
   AND WEDNESDAY, MAY 26. TO EARN AN EXCELLENT-FRIDAY LETTER, YOU
   MUST COMPLETE A TOTAL OF 18 TASKS AND SAC ACTIVITIES.

5. TO EARN A GOOD-READING LETTER EACH WEEK, YOU MUST COMPLETE 4
   READING TASKS AND COME TO READING AT LEAST THREE TIMES.

SAC SCHEDULE FOR WEDNESDAY, MAY 26, 1971

TIME	ACTIVITY	LIMIT	PLACE	LEADERS
9:30	CRAFTS	10	B	ANN, MARY
FIRST	INDOOR GAMES	10	C	SAM
PERIOD	FIELD TRIP 4			
	or 5 COUPONS			
10:25	"COLUMBIA SWIM-			
	MING POOL"			ELLEN, JOHN,
	(Bring Your Lunch)	15	OFFICE	GEORGE
10:30				
SECOND	INDOOR GAMES	10	C	SAM
PERIOD	CRAFTS	10	B	MARY
11:20				
VENDING 11:00-11:25	CANDY &		SHACK	ANN
	DRINKS			
11:25	SOFTBALL TEAMS 1 VS 4	20	FIELD	ANN, SAM
THIRD	CRAFTS	10	B	MARY, NANCY
PERIOD	WATCH THE GAME	10	FIELD	GEORGE, SUE
12:15	WATCH THE GAME			
12:20				
FOURTH	INDOOR GAMES	10	C	ANN, SAM
PERIOD	CAFETERIA	8	B	MARY, NANCY
1:10				
VENDING 12:45-1:10	CANDY &		SHACK	ANN
	DRINKS			
1:10				
FIFTH	CARD PARTY	10	B	ANN, NANCY
PERIOD	INDOOR GAMES	10	C	MARY, SAM
2:00				

Figure 3. *SAC schedule indicating to students what activities will be offered during the next school day.*

FIRST PERIOD 9:30 - 10:25

INDOOR GAMES		APPLIED ECOLOGY	CRAFTS	MOVIE
Larry M.	Ron M.	Delroy B.	Charles P.	Jackie O.
Lemon O.	Derwin R.	Randy C.	Sharon R.	Brenda B.
Nat S.	Al S.	Kevin C.	David H.	
Richard S.	Donald B.		Dwight H.	
Madison W.	Ron M.		Greg J.	
			Tyrone J.	
FULL!				

SECOND PERIOD 10:30 - 11:20

INDOOR GAMES		BIKING	CRAFTS	DRAMA CLUB
Ron M.	Derwin R.	Larry M.	Charles P.	
Lemon O.	Nat S.	Jerry W.	Sharon R.	
Al S.	Richard S.		Donald B.	
Madison W.	Kevin C.	FULL!	Johnny J.	
Ron M.	David H.		Tyrone J.	
			Greg J.	
FULL!				

THIRD PERIOD 11:25 - 12:15

TV	SOFTBALL TEAMS		CRAFTS	COOKING
David H.	4 VS 5		Lemon O.	Larry M.
Dwight H.	Gary P.	Nat S.	Donald B.	Sharon R.
Derry K.	Charles P.	Jerry W.	Kevin C.	Derwin R.
	Jose P.	Madison W.	Greg J.	
	Ross R.		Tyrone J.	FULL!
	Ron M.			

FOURTH PERIOD 12:20 - 1:05

INDOOR GAMES		OPEN SOFTBALL	CAFETERIA
Larry M.	Lemon O.	Gary P.	Jackie O.
Ron M.	Derwin R.	Ron M.	Jerry W.
Madison W.	Nat S.	Dwight H.	Phyllis W.
Donald B.	Al S.	Clyde J.	Brenda B.
Johnny J.	Kevin C.	Derry K.	Tyrone J.
FULL!			

FIFTH PERIOD 1:10 - 2:00

INDOOR GAMES		CARD PARTY	KITE-FLYING & FRISBEE
Ron M.	Madison W.	Jackie O.	Jerry W.
Lemon O.	Donald B.	Phyllis W.	
Gary P.	Kevin C.	Brenda B.	
Derwin R.	Dwight H.	Johnny J.	
Al S.		Greg J.	
		Tyrone J.	

VENDING - 11:00 - 11:25	CANDY & DRINKS	SHACK
VENDING - 12:45 - 1:10	FOOD, CANDY, & DRINKS	SHACK

Figure 4. *Student Participation List indicating which students may participate in SAC activities.*

card in this box by having a short interaction with the student who has requested help. Attention also is given to students when they have not requested help. This occurs when the SCL checks are given out approximately once every twelve minutes, and on-task behavior is reinforced.

After a student receives a validation he may use the validated SAC ticket to sign up for an activity by filling in the date, the period, and choice of activity and depositing the ticket in a SAC coupon box located in the SAC Information Centers around the Learning Center. In each of the SAC Information Centers is a schedule of SAC activities for the following school day. The schedule describes which activities will be offered, during which period, which staff member will lead the activity, and the number of students to be admitted to any activity. Figure 3 shows a SAC schedule with typical SAC offerings.

A student with a validated ticket checks the SAC schedule in a SAC Information Center and fills in his validated SAC coupon to sign up for a scheduled SAC activity on the following school day. SAC staff members collect the filled-in SAC coupons at the end of the school day, and based on student preferences, assign students into SAC activities on the

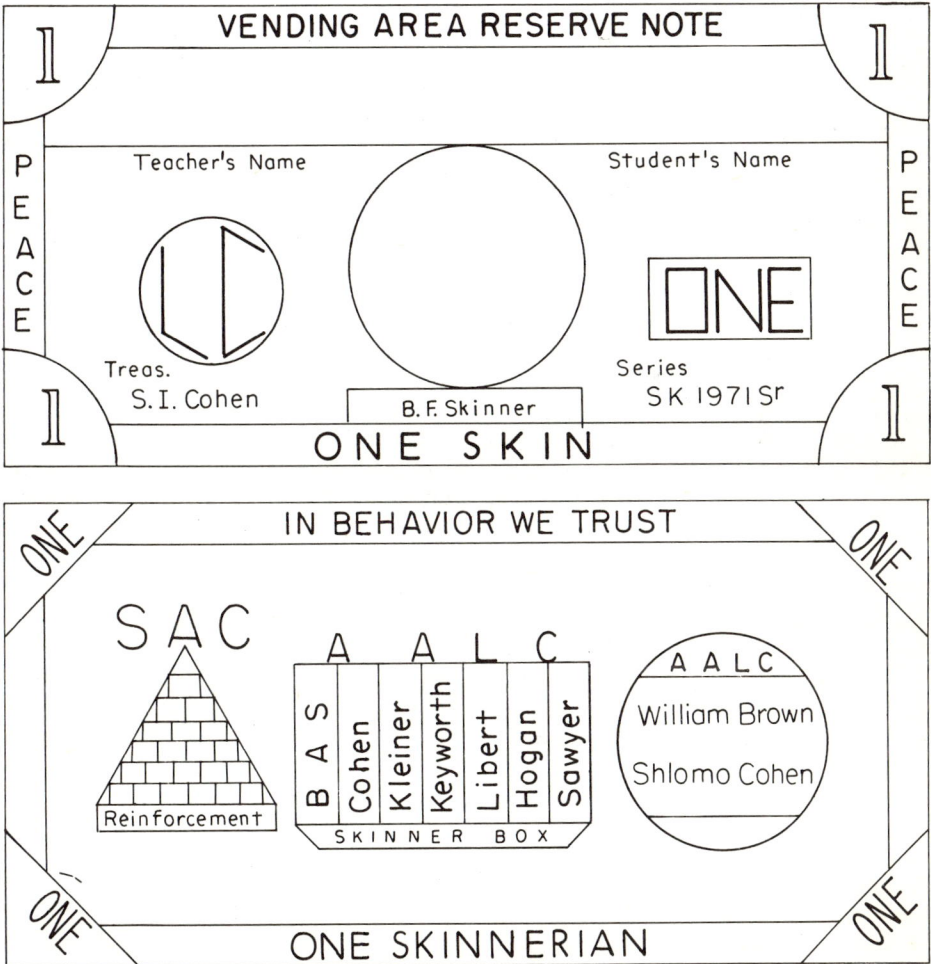

Figure 5. *Front and back views of a Skinnerian token redeemable in the student store.*

LEARNING CENTER
BOARD of EDUCATION
Anne Arundel County

Week of   /To/

Dear

This is a "Good Friday Letter" To inform you That your child has been doing very good work This week. We are pleased To See doing so well.

Sincerely yours,

William L. Brown

Shlomo Cohen

Figure 6. *A Good-Friday Letter which a student may earn by accounting for twelve periods of the school week by task completion and participation in SAC activities.*

following school day. The list of students scheduled to participate in SAC is published daily. This Student Participation List (SPL) is placed in the SAC Information Centers each morning, so students are informed regarding their participation in SAC activities. Figure 4 shows a Student Participation List. Thus, each student at the Learning Center assumes responsibility for scheduling his own day at the school. He may participate in SAC if he has previously signed up, he may work on his academic curriculum package, or he may spend his time in the loafing area.

The work buildings are viewed as the environment designed primarily for the development of academic skills, whereas the SAC buildings are viewed as the environment in which the development of social skills occurs. In order to shape desirable social skills in the SAC, the SAC staff designed a curriculum of social behaviors and developed a token called the Skinnerian (see Figure 5).

"Skins" are given out by SAC staff, contingent on desirable social behaviors of students at SAC activities. These tokens can be redeemed in the school store during scheduled

"vending periods." Back-up reinforcers in the school store are edibles such as soda and candy. The success of the SAC staff in shaping desirable social behaviors of the students is evidenced by the complete absence of staff members' asking students to leave SAC activities. Since the rate of desirable social behaviors emitted by students in SAC has increased and created conditions allowing for more social reinforcement to occur, the SAC staff has been able to systematically fade out the use of Skinnerians without associated decrements in desirable social behaviors.

A student who completes twelve academic tasks, or participates in twelve SAC activities, or who accounts for twelve school periods by a combination of task completions and SAC participation, earns a "Good-Friday" letter. Thus a student who completes nine tasks and attends three SAC activities or a student who completes five tasks and attends seven SAC activities receives a Good-Friday letter to take home. Figure 6 shows a Good-Friday letter.

Students who account for eighteen school periods by task-completions and/or SAC participation, earn an "Excellent-Friday" letter. A Good-Friday letter-earner receives ten Skinnerians, and an Excellent-Friday letter-earner receives twenty Skinnerians. In addition, Good-Friday letters have been assigned a value of one point and Excellent-Friday letters a value of one and one-half points toward end-of-the-year reinforcers. These reinforcers are highly valued prizes including three-day sightseeing or camping trips. Earning a Good-Friday letter signifies a successful week at the Learning Center. A successful year at the Learning Center is defined as receiving 50 percent of the Good-Friday letters potentially available during enrollment at the AALC. As stated earlier, students are reinforced commensurate with the amount of work they complete, although they are not hassled should they choose not to work.

In addition to letters home we have used other techniques of contacting the home with minimal professional time requirements. These techniques have included contingency contracting between parents and their children, telephone calls home, and daily brief reports to the home on student performance.

PARENT CONSULTATION PROGRAM

Parents of Learning Center students are invited to attend weekly parent meetings which occur from 7:30 P.M. to 9:00 P.M. on Thursday evening. About ten families are represented at any given meeting. The purposes of the parent group are to help parents in the application of behavior modification techniques for altering the behaviors of their children at home, in school, or in both environments and to provide the school with access to strong home-based reinforcers for its students. Some of these home-based reinforcers have been money, opportunity to drive the family car, parent signatures on work permits and driver's education applications, opportunity to work in a neighborhood store, buying food for the family pet, records, days off from school, and even a trip to Europe. The contingencies of reinforcement between student, parent, and school are arranged via a contract signed by parent and child. Not all parents who attend parent meetings enter into contracts with their children.

Contingency Contracting

A contingency contract essentially is a written agreement between two or more parties specifying behavioral requirements for each signatory of the contract. It clearly states the behavior to be emitted by one individual and the consequences to be provided for these behaviors by a second individual. The contract serves to specify (and hopefully to control) the behaviors of those who sign it.

Homme (1969) suggested the following conditions to maximize the effectiveness of contingency contracting in the classroom.

1. The contract payoff (reward) should be immediate.
2. The initial contract should call for and reward small approximations.
3. Reward should be frequent and in small amounts.
4. The contract should call for and reward accomplishments rather than obedience.

5. The performance should be rewarded after it occurs.
6. The contract should be fair.
7. The terms of the contract should be clear.
8. The contract should be honest.
9. The contract should be positive.
10. Contracting as a method should be used systematically.

Homme considered the contracting a technique essentially the same as other behavior modification procedures. Several generally accepted procedures such as specifying target behaviors, shaping, using positive control, etc., are included in Homme's suggestions for contracting.

In his description of contracting with the families of delinquents, Stuart (1970) emphasized that a contract is a means of scheduling the exchange of positive reinforcement among two or more persons. In Stuart's view, five essentials for effective contracts are:

1. precise statements of privileges;
2. precise statements of responsibilities;
3. precise statements of sanctions;
4. precise statements of bonuses;
5. a means of monitoring events relevant to the agreement.

Stuart also did not treat contracting as a separate behavioral technique. In essence, he suggested that the basic elements crucial to successful contracting were specification of target behaviors (responsibilities), specification of reinforcers (privileges and bonuses), specification of possible punishers (sanctions), and methods of objective data collection.

MacDonald, Gallimore, and MacDonald (1970) described "deals" which were made between school counselors and adults who controlled possible reinforcers for chronic nonattenders at school. A "deal" was an agreement made by an adult that promised to provide a target student with a reinforcer contingent on school attendance according to a prearranged schedule. The authors emphasized that adults in the student's natural environment could effectively use contingency management techniques through "deals" to improve the school attendance of chronic nonattenders.

Parents of Learning Center students generally experience difficulty in specifying reinforcers for their children. To a large extent, their attempts to develop the behaviors of their children have been extinguished, and their child-rearing behaviors need careful rebuilding.

Tharp and Wetzel (1969) suggested that when the relationship between parents and child deteriorated into punitive interactions as was the case in many Learning Center families, it was useful to depersonalize some of those interactions through contingency contracting. The process of negotiating the contract also could be useful in teaching more appropriate parent-child interactions. With the aid of the Learning Center staff, parents were helped to specify behaviors and positive reinforcers for their children. Because the students were teen-aged and fairly independent, controlling relevant aspects of their environments was a difficult and often unsuccessful task.

The designing of a contract generally occurs at the parent meeting. Once the outline of the contract is complete, the student adds his reactions on the following school day. After input from the parents and child is completed, the contract is typed and taken home for review and signatures. Contracts generally are effective for a period of two weeks, after which they may be renegotiated. Once the contract is signed by parent, child, and a Learning Center staff member, if required, it is binding until its expiration date. Each party may register opposition to the agreement by withholding his signature.

Contingent Phone Calls

Contingent positive feedback was given to parents via the telephone. At the end of the school day, a phone call was made to the home informing the parents of the progress made during that school day.

Noncontingent Notes Home

Feedback was also provided to parents via a short form filled in at the end of the school day. The communication was carried to the parent by the child, and the parent was required to return a short note on the following school day.

As part of standard operations at the Learning Center, data are collected on the ongoing performances of the students. The data provide information on several vari-

Table 1. Summary data of Bartholomew during baseline and contract periods.

	Checks/ Day	Checks/ Work Period	Work Periods/ Day	Tasks/ Period	Tasks/ Day	SAC Periods/ Day	Attendance	Rate of Suspensions
Baseline 1/18–2/12	6.72 (80%)	3.18	2.11	.39	.83	1.44	18/20–.90	0
			Reading Tasks/Day		.056			
			Reading Tasks/Period		.03			
Contract 2/15–2/26 3/1–3/19	7.2 (80%)	3.2	2.25	1.18	2.65	1.3	20/24–.83	0
			Reading Tasks/Day		2.0			
			Reading Tasks/Period		.44			
Baseline 3/24–4/6	7.0 (80%)	3.18	2.2	.36	.8	.8	5/12–.42	1
			Reading Tasks/Day		.60			
			Reading Tasks/Period		.27			

<u>CONTRACT</u>

DATE   <u>February 12, 1971</u>

CONTRACT #   <u>1</u>

1) Bartholomew may earn <u>25¢</u> for each task that he completes in reading. He may earn up to $2.50 per week. To pick up his money, Bartholomew should bring a note to the office from the reading teacher stating how many tasks he has completed.

This contract will expire February 26, 1971, at which time it may be renegotiated.

I, Bartholomew, agree to the terms of the agreement as stated above.

_____
Bartholomew

We, the undersigned, agree to the terms of the contract as stated above.

_____   _____
Father   Mother

(Contract #2 same as above, negotiated March 1, 1971, expired March 19, 1971)

Figure 7. *Contract negotiated twice between Bartholomew and his parents.*

ables such as school attendance, SCL checks (teacher signatures) earned in the work buildings, tasks completed, reading tasks completed (for students with entry skills below fourth-grade level), and percentages of time in work area, in a reinforcer area, and by subtraction, in the loafing area. When the ongoing data indicate that a student is not functioning well in the school environment, efforts are made to involve the parents (or guardians) by contingency contracts, through phone calls, or through daily notes home.

METHODS AND RESULTS

Bartholomew

Bartholomew was fifteen years old when he was referred to the Learning Center as an alternative to incarceration in the State Detention Center. He came to the Learning Center with a history of suspensions from school, charges of possession of lethal weapons, and several previous incarcerations in detention centers. He had been implicated in auto theft and arson and had physically assaulted his father on several occasions. Both of his parents worked, and even minimal contact with the family was extremely difficult.

During the four weeks prior to the establishment of a parent-child contingency contract, baseline data indicated that performances of the student were minimally acceptable except in the completion of reading

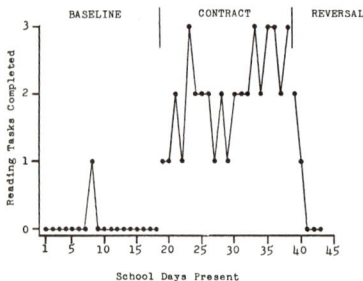

Figure 8. *Reading tasks completed by Bartholomew under contract and baseline conditions.*

tasks. (Baseline data in all cases presented were collected under conditions of the behavior modification program described previously.) Reading tasks during baseline were completed at the rate of .056 tasks per day (see Table 1).

A reading task for Bartholomew consisted of reading a booklet on the third level of the Reading Attainment Series. Completing a booklet generally required reading a 250–400 word story, answering ten multiple choice questions concerning the reading, writing approximately eight glossary words with their meanings on 3 × 5 index cards which were placed in the student's personal dictionary, answering ten multiple-choice questions from the skill card associated with the reading passage, and passing an oral quiz concerning the reading. During all phases of the program, Bartholomew earned 80 percent of the SCL checks potentially available to him.

Since overall functioning indicated that each day the student spent about three and one-half periods out of five in desired activity, a short meeting was held between a Learning Center staff member and the boy's mother. A contract (see Figure 7) was negotiated, specifying money as a reinforcer for the completion of reading tasks. Two weeks later, the contract was renegotiated during a telephone conversation. The contract period endured from February 15 to March 19, a period of twenty-four school days.

During the contract phase, task-completions in reading increased from an average of .056 per day in the baseline to an average of 2.0 per day during the contract phase. Upon return to baseline conditions, rate of reading-task completions decreased to an average of .60 per day. Although this rate was lower than the rate during the contract phase, it did not indicate a return to the extremely low rate of reading-task completions during the first baseline. Possibly once involved in the reading program, the student was reinforced by some of the natural reinforcing consequences provided in and by the reading program. A graphical presentation of reading tasks completed by this subject during the days he was in attendance can be seen in Figure 8.

Table 2. *Summary data of Donovan during baseline and treatment periods.*

	Checks/ Day	Checks/ Work Period	Work Periods/ Day	Tasks/ Period	Tasks/ Day	SAC Periods/ Day	Attendance	Rate of Suspensions
Baseline 2/25–3/23	7.43 (74%)	2.97	2.50	.26	.64	.50	14/18–.78	1/14
Calls Made 3/24–4/6	9.40 (76%)	3.03	3.10	.39	1.20	1.30	10/10–1.00	0
Baseline 4/12–4/28	7.92 (79%)	3.17	2.50	1.00	2.50	.92	12/12–1.00	0

Donovan

Donovan was a fifteen-year-old male referred to the Learning Center with a history of frequent altercations with other students, truancy, threats to school personnel, an informal court hearing, and treatment by a psychiatrist. His IQ was 100 on the Lorge-Thorndike.

During a baseline period of eighteen school days, the subject was present fourteen days. During the fourteen days, Donovan spent an average of 2.5 periods per day in the work building and his average potential check earnings were 10 SCL checks per day. During the baseline period he earned an average of 7.43 SCL checks per day or 74.3 percent of the checks available to him. Tasks were completed at an average rate of .64 per day, and SAC participation was at an average of .50 activities per day (see Table 2).

The telephone call procedure was instituted for ten days. See Figure 9 for the standardized telephone feedback to parents. Donovan was present during all ten treatment days. Check earnings increased from an average of 7.43 per day in the baseline to an average of 9.40 checks per day during treatment. Work periods per day, however, also increased from an average of 2.5 during baseline to an average of 3.1 during treatment. Therefore Donovan's potential check earnings during the treatment phase increased to an average of 12.4 SCL checks per day. Thus, the average of 9.4 checks earned per day during treatment represents

a slight increase from 74 percent to 76 percent of potential checks earned. Task-completions increased from an average of .64 tasks per day during the baseline to an average of 1.20 tasks per day in the treatment period. SAC participation increased from an average of .50 SAC periods per day in the baseline to an average of 1.30 SAC periods per day during the treatment period (see Table 2).

During a return to baseline of twelve school days, Donovan was present during all twelve days. This represents a higher rate of attendance than in the first baseline period during which attendance was at 78 percent. Check-earnings decreased to an average of 7.92 per day, but work periods per day also decreased to an average of 2.5. In the return to baseline, Donovan actually was earning a higher percentage (79.2 percent) of the potential checks available to him than during the treatment (see Table 2). Also during the return to baseline, average rate of task completions increased markedly to one task per work period. Graphical presentations of checks earned and tasks completed are presented in Figure 10.

Eugene

Eugene was a fifteen-year-old male when referred to the Learning Center. His behavior was described as bizarre and unusual and included depression, poor interpersonal relationships, involvement in sexual perversions,

DATE _____

TELEPHONE NO. _____

Hello! Mr. or Mrs. _____

This is _____ at the Learning Center.

I called to let you know that _____ was in

school today, and:

      He earned   _____ checks.

      He completed _____ tasks.

      He went to   _____ SAC activities.

We think that he did well today. We are glad to see him doing

so well.

Thank you! Good bye!

Figure 9. Standard format used for telephone feedback to parents.

and talking to animals. His medical history indicated that tranquilizers were prescribed as a result of violent temper tantrums in school. His school record showed a long history of truancy, classroom disruptions including jumping out of a schoolroom window, parent conferences, and suspensions. Testing indicated an IQ of 78 on the Lorge-Thorndike.

Eugene was present eight days out of a sixteen-school-day baseline period. During this time, Eugene did not enter his work area or the reinforcer area. Data on all performance measures except attendance were zeros (see Table 3).

During a seventeen-day treatment period, Eugene carried home a standardized brief note (see Figure 11) each day. At a brief meeting to explain the procedures, his parents agreed to respond in writing to the note. The data show (see Table 3) that attendance increased from 50 percent in the first baseline to 100 percent during treatment. Checks per day increased to an average of 7.06 per day during treatment. With an average of 2.29 periods per day in the work building, an average of 9.16 checks were available to Eugene each day of the treat-

ment. During the treatment he received 77 percent of the checks available to him. Rate of task-completions accelerated because of increases in entering and remaining in the work building.

For both Donovan and Eugene, specific kinds of tasks (e.g., reading) were not targeted. Increases in number of tasks completed per day were a function of faster rates of task-completion and/or longer periods of time in the work building. The tasks included completing IPI math booklets and their posttests to 80 percent criterion, writing paragraphs of gradually increasing length with a decreasing number of spelling and/or grammatical errors, completing the reading of science booklets of about four pages in length, answering questions on the associated quiz cards, and answering four of five questions in an oral quiz given by the teacher following the reading. The format of the ecology tasks was similar to the science tasks —reading followed by written and oral posttests.

Toward the end of the "note-home" treatment, a letter and a gift of books for the school were sent by the parents in appreciation for "special interest in Eugene and improvements in his behavior." During the return to baseline for fourteen school days,

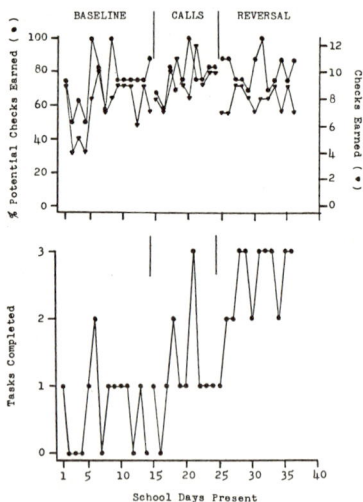

Figure 10. Check earnings and task completions by Donovan under calls-home and baseline conditions.

Table 3. *Summary data for Eugene during baseline and treatment periods.*

	Checks/ Day	Checks/ Work Period	Work Periods/ Day	Tasks/ Period	Tasks/ Day	SAC Periods/ Day	Attendance	Rate of Suspensions
Baseline 4/1–4/28	0	0	0	0	0	0	8/16–.50	0
Notes Sent 4/29–5/21	7.06 (77%)	3.08	2.29	.56	1.29	.29	17/17–1.00	0
Baseline 5/24–6/11	1.86 (81%)	3.25	.57	.50	.29	0	7/14–.50	0

Eugene attended seven days. Performance on checks per day and tasks per day decreased primarily as a function of the reduction in the amount of time spent in the work area —approximately half a period per day.

During the return to baseline, Eugene received an average of 1.86 checks per day, which represented earnings of 81 percent of the checks potentially available when in the work building an average of only .57 periods per day. Task-completions decreased to .29 per day although task completions per period remained about the same. Although decreases in performance did occur during the return to baseline, performance did remain above the zero level of the initial baseline period. Graphical presentation of checks earned and tasks completed are presented in Figure 12.

DISCUSSION

General Issues

Several general issues deriving from the design of the Learning Center and the work performed there require elucidation. Since the total ongoing program at the AALC is based on behavior modification principles, why are there students who are not performing well and who require special programs? The answer to this question is related primarily to the availability of strong reinforcers. For several of the Learning Center students, the potential reinforcers provided in the SAC do not function as reinforcers in actuality. These students do not complete tasks in order to play football or pool, go to McDonald's, or participate in arts-and-crafts activities. Because of this lack of response to reinforcers for some of the AALC students, continuing efforts are made to add new activities to the SAC program as well as to gain access to home-based reinforcers. Of the "special programs" described, contracting, in particular, reflects the attempts to locate and use strong reinforcers from the homes of AALC students.

Reliability of observations was not discussed in any of the procedures described, because the data presented were not based directly on observations of teacher-student interactions but on behavioral products such as completed answer sheets, written paragraphs, completed IPI booklets, checkmarks on the SCL, and filled-in SAC coupons. It was assumed that in a continuing program of extensive training in behavior modification including occasional monitoring and feedback, and after clearly defining guidelines for acceptable staff interactions with students (particularly the behaviors of the SCL checker), the staff would adhere to the criteria for giving task completions and SCL checks. Possibilities certainly exist that the size of tasks (although not the criteria for completing them) may have been slightly enlarged as skills of the students improved during the studies described. The opportunity for a student to complete tasks varied directly with the number of times the student entered the work building. The opportunity to enter the work building remained constant from day to day.

Contracting procedures focused on contingencies of reinforcement related to one or a few individual behaviors specified by parents and teachers. Standardized phone calls and notes home were related to performances relevant to all students at the Learning Center. Because the contracts focused on specific individual behaviors, they were useful in multiple baseline designs (Cohen et al., 1972). Notes and phone calls home were not useful in multiple baseline designs since these procedures simultaneously affected all of the baselines observed. Although the daily notes and phone calls were standardized, there do not seem to be any reasons why they also, like the contracts, could not focus on specific behavior problems of individual students. The effectiveness of these procedures might be increased if, indeed, they were related to specific behavior problems of specific students. All of the described procedures emphasized positive feedback. The contracts utilized positive reinforcement and the notes and calls provided feedback only on the progress of the students.

There were several advantages and problems common to the three minimum contact-intervention techniques described. Defining, but especially controlling reinforcers for relatively independent teen-age children with

Date_____

To: _____

From: _____

_____ was in school today and completed the following behaviors:

1. Completed _____ academic tasks.

2. Earned_____ teacher checks for desirable behavior in his work building.

3. Attended _____ supervised activities in the Student Activity Center.

4. Remained the entire day in the authorized areas of the school. - - - YES   NO

5. Please return a short note indicating you have read this.

Figure 11. Standardized note carried home by student each day during treatment.

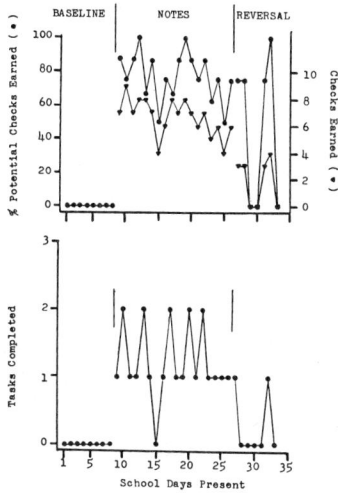

Figure 12. *Check earnings and task completions by Eugene under notes-home and baseline conditions.*

very sophisticated although highly undesirable survival skills was difficult and occasionally not successfully accomplished. Almost all AALC students had access to sources of money other than their parents. These sources were friends, relatives, local supermarkets where students could earn tips by carrying bags, and other small job opportunities in their neighborhoods. Secondly, each of the three techniques relied directly or indirectly on some parental behavior, although only the contracting procedure specified parental behaviors. Of the three procedures, contracting was the most effective for controlling parent behavior since the contracts clearly specified the behaviors of the parents. The phone-call and note-home procedures did not provide instructions regarding parent-child interactions, and it is not known what changes in parent-child interactions occurred as a function of these techniques. In addition to some lack of control over parent behavior and to some lack of control over sources of reinforcers for students, a third factor was related to the behavioral programs described in the present studies. Only small behavior changes were specified in the contracts or calls home. The note-home procedure did not require a minimum performance to earn the note but simply was

a statement of student progress contingent on attending school.

During the treatment phases of the contract and phone-call procedures, performances increased just enough to meet the criteria for success. When Bartholomew earned $.25 for each completed reading task with a maximum of $2.50 per week, the average rate of completed reading tasks increased to 2 per day which resulted in $2.50 a week. When Donovan earned a call home by earning five SCL checks per day, completing one task per day, and attending one SAC activity per day, the rate of checks earned increased to 9.4 per day, which was already above criterion in the baseline. Task-completions increased to an average of 1.2 per day, and SAC attendance increased to an average of 1.3 per day, slightly more than enough to meet the criterion.

Most likely the effectiveness of all three of the treatments was facilitated by clearly defined academic tasks and SCL behaviors built into the AALC design. It was possible that the effectiveness of these procedures would have been diminished had the behaviors of concern not been clearly specified.

Specific Issues

Contracting. Many of the child-rearing behaviors of the parents of AALC students, particularly those whose children are involved in "special programs," were suppressed and extinguished. At initial parent meetings, parents of "special program" children generally reported that when they responded to their children, they were more likely to punish undesirable behaviors of their children than reinforce desirable ones. Tharp and Wetzel (1969) and Cohen et al. (1972) pointed out that when the relationship between parent and child became punitive and mutually debilitating, contracting was a relatively effective procedure for regaining some control over the behaviors of the children as well as for rebuilding the parent-child relationship on a more positive basis.

Contracting is the most general of the three procedures described. There is little question that the notes or phone calls could be incorporated into a formalized written contingency contract. A major difference between contingency contracting and other procedures for behavior change is that the conditions of the behavior-change program are documented and signed in a contract, whereas the formalized document and signatures are usually lacking in other procedures. However, the development, negotiation of, and imposition of contingencies of reinforcement are aspects of most behavior-change programs. The major advantages of the written document seem to be that it exerts antecedent control over parent and child behaviors, serves as a record and reminder to both, and depersonalizes previously harmful parent-child interactions.

The contracting procedures were also helpful in teaching parents to apply contingency management techniques to the behaviors of their children. Before contracting was an integral part of the AALC parent program, parents were trained to sit and listen, to fill in blanks, and to verbalize in other ways about behavior modification in a rather traditional lecture educational program. They were not, however, successfully modifying the behaviors of their children. With the move toward contracting, the theoretical and didactic aspects of the parent-education program were diminished and replaced by more applied activities.

Instead of verbalizing about reinforcers, etc., parents were instructed to help design conditions of contracts and then perform the operations of changing behavior as defined in the contract. Parents became skillful at systematically imposing contingencies on the behaviors of their children. A common occurrence for staff members attending parent meetings was to learn that parents independently arranged less formal "deals" with their children to support behaviors at school or at home.

Little difficulty was experienced at parent meetings in helping parents and children enter into contracts. School behaviors were not difficult to pinpoint, and parents were helped to identify home behaviors and reinforcers. Although usually somewhat reluctant to "pay" their children for doing better in school and at home, most parents eventually agreed to "try anything" as a last resort. A frequently used persuader was: "Parents have jobs and receive pay, and children have jobs at school and at home and should also receive pay accordingly." Reversals of contracted contingencies posed no problems since a contract was allowed to lapse after a two-week period. To perform the reversal, staff members took no initiative to reinstate an elapsed contract when parents did not attend a parent meeting. There were several sets of parents whose attendance at meetings was such that contracts did not lapse but were continuously effective. After some time, parents were encouraged to renegotiate a contract if reinstatement of the special contingencies seemed necessary.

During the last two and one-half years, contingency contracts were negotiated with thirty-five to forty AALC families. Procedures for contract negotiation and renegotiation were essentially the same as described in the present study. Data from Bartholomew's case were characteristic of most of the systematic contracting which occurred. Behaviors generally improved during contract phases and dropped to levels not as low as in the initial baselines during the reversals. Several contracts were negotiated but never really initiated since the reinforcers specified were beyond parental control from the outset.

Phone calls. The phone-call procedure generated several problems. Most bothersome were busy signals and other problems which necessitated more than one attempted call (e.g., no one at home). These problems were compounded since all calls had to be routed through the Fort Meade switchboard. There were no discussions with parents about the phone-call procedures or instructions to parents concerning how to interact with their children. Effects of the phone calls on parent behaviors are not known; parents who did not attend any parent meetings were selected to receive the calls. Very simply, parents started to receive phone calls one day, and eventually the phone calls stopped.

After the first phone call occurred, Donovan mentioned the call to a staff member and was told the criteria for earning a phone call. Obviously the parents had at least told him that the call had occurred. Although very mechanical in nature, the standardized phone call was adhered to as written. Had the parents made inquiries after the termination of the calls, office staff were prepared to inform them that an unusually heavy workload in the office made calling impossible. In actuality, the parents did not inquire about the calls although they generally seemed pleased during the treatment itself.

Donovan's improved performance during the return to baseline was somewhat puzzling. Perhaps the phone-call procedure became mildly aversive to Donovan and, therefore, its termination was followed by increase in performance. Donovan, however, could have avoided the phone calls during treatment by showing performance decrements to a level below the criterion required to earn a phone call. The hypothesis that the phone-call procedure was aversive seemed untenable. A more likely speculation was that parent behavior was changed during the treatment, and the behavior changes were maintained by improvements in Donovan's performance at school. Possibly these unknown changes in parent behavior became even more reinforcing to Donovan during the return to baseline when his behavior was no longer under the antecedent control of phone calls from school but "honest" expressions of parental pride.

The phone-call procedure was used with one other student at the AALC. Performances improved during treatment and decreased slightly below initial baseline levels during the reversal. This treatment was not attempted with additional students because problems unique to the Fort Meade telephone switchboard made calling unduly difficult.

Notes home. No problems specific to the notes-home procedure were noted. This procedure was discussed at a special meeting between the principal of the school, the parents, and Eugene. The parents agreed to read the note each day and return a short note indicating they had received the school note. No other instructions regarding parent behavior were made. It was decided that the notes would stop at some time in the future.

Because of this meeting, it was unlikely that Eugene would fail to carry the notes to and from school. If he did not bring a note from school, he would in effect be informing his parents that he had not attended school that day. In actuality, Eugene carried the notes throughout the procedures. It was possible that Eugene's parents were punished for gifting the school with books since this was closely followed by the termination of the note-home procedure. A multiple baseline procedure which might have avoided this possible punishment of the parents was not possible since the notes reported on all of Eugene's performances.

Of the three minimum contact procedures, the notes-home procedure was the simplest to implement. It did not require a discussion to pinpoint problem school behaviors but specified all relevant school behaviors. It did not necessitate a discussion of reinforcers available to parents; it was simply an agreement by the parents to respond to daily progress reports from school.

The notes-home procedure had a major impact on the current design (1971–72) of the AALC program which was different than that described (1970–71). This procedure was modified and expanded such that a daily "successful day card" which is a progress report to parents is available to each student at the AALC contingent on the completion of two academic tasks. The preliminary results, since this procedure was institutionalized in the AALC design, seem to indicate improvements in performances of most students. The performance of many students is now steady at two task-completions per day, rather than scalloped with most (but occasionally not sufficient) task-completions coming toward the end of a marking period.

Follow-up. Just prior to Bartholomew's withdrawal from the AALC, he completed a seventy-seven page level-three book entitled *How the Human Body Works.* Bartholomew's career at the AALC was terminated, however, when he was incarcerated in the Maryland Training School for Boys as a result of severe violence at home. As he had passed his sixteenth birthday, he was permanently withdrawn from the rolls of the public schools upon incarceration. He held various low-level jobs in his home neighborhood and was a leader among a group of teen-age youths over whom he exerted considerable influence. The treatment was successful, but the patient died.

Donovan continued to do acceptable work at the AALC for approximately five school months following the described study. He withdrew from the AALC upon his sixteenth birthday and enrolled in a vocational rehabilitation program. He was successful in that program for the two months since his enrollment.

Eugene also is no longer at the AALC but has completed the requirements of a transfer contract to his neighborhood junior high school. Immediately prior to his transfer he functioned as a task-checker (teacher-aide), evaluating other student's work, which he had previously successfully completed. He received full credit for the time he was at the Learning Center and was doing well in the two months since his return to a "regular" junior high school in Anne Arundel County.

6

IN COLLEGE AND UNIVERSITY EDUCATION

Most behavioral psychologists also are teachers in colleges and universities. As the principles of behavior began to be applied to human beings, some of these psychologists realized that those principles were being neglected in their own teaching and began to devise more scientifically based techniques of "higher" education. Fred Keller was the most notable pioneer. His system featured programmed instruction completed at the student's own pace, supervision by student teaching assistants, and use of lectures as reinforcers. Numerous modifications were made to accommodate Keller's method to the exigencies of fixed academic terms and some realities of student life. The first paper in this section, by Lloyd, presents one such modification. A problem in the Keller method is the go-at-your-own-pace feature. Probably because of competing pressures on students' time, "go-at-your-own-pace" resulted in a very slow pace. Lloyd's paper describes the manipulation of contingencies to keep the rate of student behavior high and steady.

Another method of college instruction developed by behavioral psychologists is the "interview technique," a method of requiring active teaching and recitation behavior from the student. The second and third papers, by Hineline, serve as guides, for the student and teacher, to the use of that technique. Hineline also effective presents some of the reasons behavioral psychologists do not favor traditional university instruction.

As part of the efforts of behavioral psychologists to shape college teaching, new instructional materials have been produced. A small portion of one textbook is presented as the fourth item in this section. The title of the book is *Contingency Management in Education and Other Equally Exciting Places or I've Got Blisters on My Soul and Other Equally Exciting Places*. The book teaches the principles of behavior as the learner follows the exciting exploits of Captain Contingency Management (Con Man), Behaviorman, and Behaviorwoman, all presented in pop-art format. In spite of the levity, the material is not treated lightly. The book is as solid and comprehensive as it is refreshing and fun. Nevertheless, it is a book that students will choose to read. It is, if you will, an excellent example of intrinsically reinforcing educational material.

Contingency management in university courses

KENNETH E. LLOYD

This paper is divided into five sections. The first section summarizes the characteristics of contingency management systems in university classes. The second describes briefly one such system employed by the author. The third presents data from students enrolled in these courses. The fourth outlines decisions that must be made by the instructor who would teach such a course, and the fifth answers some questions that have frequently been asked about these courses.

CONTINGENCY MANAGEMENT SYSTEMS IN UNIVERSITY COURSES

Contingency management in the university classroom is another application of the experimental analysis of behavior (Honig, 1966; Verhave, 1966) to a relevant social problem. Like contingency management programs employed in nursery schools (e.g., Risley and Hart, 1968), elementary schools (e.g., Schmidt and Ulrich, 1969), psychological clinics (e.g., Ullman and Krasner, 1965) and psychiatric hospital wards (e.g., Ayllon and Azrin, 1968; Lloyd and Garlington, 1968), the programs in a university classroom also involve a contingency, or a relationship between a response and a subsequent event. The first step in such a program is to select responses whose frequencies are to be altered. The second step is to specify the contingency between the response and the reinforcer; that is, to specify how the reinforcer will be available, eliminated, or postponed after the student makes certain responses. These steps are similar to those involved in the more familiar programmed textbooks (Lumsdaine, 1964; Gagne, 1965). Contingency management systems differ from programmed textbooks in that they typically encompass a wider variety of behaviors.

The responses which are selected depend upon which terminal behaviors the instructor seeks to establish in his students. Some instructors have emphasized verbal fluency with the course material (e.g., Ferster and Perrott, 1968), others have stressed written mastery (e.g., McMichael and Corey, 1969), and certain instructors have required a variety of responses (e.g., Malott, 1968). Lloyd and Knutzen (1969) designed their course so that the students would sample those behaviors most frequently engaged in by psychologists working in the content area of the course. These included reading the psychological literature, talking about the course topics with other students and with psychologists, performing laboratory tasks, and writing reports of what had been done or read.

Although the potential reinforcers for student behavior available at a university are undoubtedly much greater in number than those which have so far been put to use, the final grade for a given course is not only widely used but effective as well. Final grades, like most social rewards, however, are events that are awarded after long delay and not in any specified relation to easily identifiable responses. In order to be useful within a contingency management system the final grade must be divided into smaller parts which can be made available to students throughout the semester. Lloyd et al. (1969) accomplished this by defining each letter grade in terms of total accumulated points (an A was 600 points, a B was 450 points, and so on). Students could obtain points by completing assignments; each assignment was given a point value. Points from different assignments were added together during the semester and the resulting final total determined a student's final course grade. Keller (1968) and McMichael et al. (1969) divided courses into units of work (e.g., a test on a chapter in the textbook). One unit must be completed at a specified minimum accuracy level before the student may begin work on the next unit. Final grades are determined by the number of units completed.

From *Educational Technology,* 1971, *11*(4), 18-23. Reprinted by permission of *Educational Technology Magazine.*

Selecting responses and specifying contingencies between responses and subsequent events result in additional characteristics of these courses. Some of these are outlined below (see Keller, 1968, as well). The course requirements for the student are clearly defined. What he must do to complete a given assignment or to receive a given grade is specified in detail at the beginning of the course. Most, if not all, assignments must be completed at a specified level of mastery. This is accomplished by permitting students to repeat or re-do inadequate parts of an assignment. At the end of the course students vary in the amount of work completed, rather than how well they have done it. A D student, for example, may only have read two chapters in the textbook but scored as well on a test of that material as an A student. The emphasized responses are the written and spoken words of the students, that is, what the students themselves have done, not lectures or demonstrations by the instructor. Due dates for assignments have been omitted (Keller, 1968; Lloyd et al., 1969; McMichael et al., 1969) or set by the instructor (Malott, 1968; Lloyd, 1969). In the former case the course is self-paced by the student, and grades of incomplete are freely given. Finally, a relatively large teaching staff is involved, including the instructor, a graduate teaching assistant, and several undergraduate proctors, all of whom share in the interactions with students. Proctors have taken the course previously and receive credit in a reading course for their services.

AN EXAMPLE OF A CONTINGENCY MANAGEMENT SYSTEM AT THE UNIVERSITY LEVEL

Lloyd et al. (1969) have described their first contingency-managed course in detail. Since then several additional courses have been taught and several changes in course outlines have been made. A brief description of a typical course outline will be presented here. The reader who is interested in additional detail may consult Lloyd et al. (1969) or Lloyd (1969). Table 1 contains a list of assignments for an Introductory Psychology course. For each letter grade shown in Column 1 there are four or five assignments shown in Column 2, along with the number of points it was possible to obtain each time that assignment was completed (Column 3). Column 4 indicates which assignments were required as well as the number of points that must have been obtained on that assignment before it was considered complete. The Required Points for each letter grade are also listed in Column 4 (e.g., 250 for a D, 350 for a C, etc.).

For example, in order to obtain a final course grade of D the student could attend class (2 points each meeting), ask or answer questions during class or outside of class (up to 4 points per question), obtain 80 of 90 points on two tests covering material in the textbook, and write a summary of three or four journal articles (10 points per summary) selected from a book of readings.

Many of the D, C, and B assignments were components or approximations of the A assignments. For example, one choice for an A was to write a term paper (100 points). Assignments for the lower grades included behaviors that are part of writing a term paper. For a D (10 points) the student read a journal article and answered four questions which required him to explain the purpose of the experiment, to identify the independent variables, to describe the results, and to evaluate the experiment. For a C (25 points) the student read two similar journal articles. These were selected from the same chapter in the text, or after reading one article, the student could select the second from the references listed in the first article. His report was evaluated on appropriateness of the articles, how well he incorporated the four questions required for the D report, how he integrated the two articles, and his use of the psychological concepts involved. For a B (40 points) the student read two articles selected from different chapters in the text or dissimilar topics in the course. Again he submitted a written report which was evaluated according to the previous criteria as well as how he specified a relationship between the articles. All of these articles could have dealt with the same general topic and could have been included in the term paper, or

Table 1. *Possible points and required points for each assignment associated with each grade in an introductory psychology course.*

Grade	Assignment	Possible Points	Required Points
	Attend a class	2	
	Participate in class	4	
	Test I and Test II	90 each	80 each
	Read a journal article	10	10
D			250
	Tape record a group discussion	20	15
	Test III	60	55
	Similar readings	25	20
	Review a movie	10	
	Condition a rat to bar press	30	20
C			350
	Discussion with a psychologist	30	
	Test IV	60	55
	Dissimilar readings	40	35
Choose	Write a question for class, or	5	
one	summarize a public lecture, or	10	
	wire an electrical circuit	20	
	Extinguish and recondition the rat	30	20
	Field Trip and Test VI (Optional)	65	230 by eighth week
B			450
	Test V (Optional Chapter)	60	400 by tenth week
Choose	Symposium or lecture in class, or	100	to be eligible
one	write a term paper, or	100	90
	design and conduct an experiment	100	
Choose	Observe staff member's research, or	20	
one	arrange personal field trip	20	
A			600

they could have all been on different topics.

Another choice for an A assignment was to present a symposium or lecture in class. Again assignments for the lower grades included behaviors that were part of a class presentation. For a D, students participated in class discussion; for a C, they discussed a course topic with two or three other students and turned in a tape recording of this discussion for evaluation. For a B, two or three students arranged an appointment with a faculty member not connected with the course and discussed an agreed-upon topic. The cooperating faculty member then turned in a rating of their performance. Similarly the conditioning assignments with a rat for a C and a B were component behaviors of conducting an experiment for an A.

Tests based on the textbook were given, but the students were provided, ahead of time, a list of items from which the test items would be sampled. The students were required to obtain scores of 90 percent on each test. If they failed to do so on their first try, they answered the missed items a second or third time, if necessary, to obtain the minimum score before trying the next test.

Students generally worked at their own pace. They could complete the requirements for a given grade before the end of the semester, or they could elect an Incomplete grade and continue working beyond the end of the semester. However, in order to attend a field trip students must have been working at a B level by midsemester (230 points by the eighth week), and in order to work for an

A students must have completed most of the B requirements by the tenth week of the semester.

When a student turned in an assignment, the work was dated and graded by a member of the teaching staff. The teaching staff included the instructor, a graduate teaching assistant, and up to six or seven undergraduate proctors. All members of the teaching staff graded all of the papers turned in during the first few weeks in order to establish common grading criteria. The undergraduate proctors talked with students, operated the laboratory, graded papers, and read articles.

THE BEHAVIOR OF THE STUDENTS: DATA RESULTING FROM CONTINGENCY-MANAGED COURSES

Much of the behavior of students in these courses is readily observable to the teaching staff. Part of the evaluation of the method is an examination of how students do respond under the imposed contingencies. Several courses have been completed using variations of the method described above. This section of the paper will examine data obtained from students in these courses.

The basic response measure has been the rate at which students accumulated points. After a student turned in an assignment the number of points earned was recorded on a grade sheet that specified the two-week interval during which he submitted the completed work. There were eight two-week intervals during the semester. Points were summed for each interval, and these sums were cumulated to obtain the rate at which students completed assignments.

The first course taught by this method was a course in the experimental analysis of behavior (Lloyd et al., 1969). The assignments were similar to those in Table 1. The thirty-five students enrolled were mostly sophomores and juniors. They were given a course outline on the first day of class; printed instructions for the different assignments were also given to them as needed. These instructions have been condensed in the preceding section of this paper and have been printed in detail in Lloyd and Knutzen (1969).

Histograms showing the number of students in each of five grade categories (A, B, C, D, F) at the end of each two-week interval were constructed by noting how many points a student should have accumulated after, say, two weeks if he were working steadily (linearly) toward any of the four grades. These histograms revealed that over half or nineteen of the students had done little or no work by the end of the twelfth week. At the end of the semester seven students obtained A's, eight obtained B's, seven obtained C's, two obtained D's or F's, and nine requested Incompletes.

Figure 1 contains individual cumulative point curves for typical students from each grade category. The data were plotted at two-week intervals. The curves are labeled with a number and a letter; the number is the student's rank in the class after sixteen weeks, and the letter is the grade he received. The mean cumulative point curve for the thirty-five students is plotted with open circles on the scale at the right of Figure 1. This mean curve remained below the D level until the twelfth week of the semester, after which it rose to a C level.

These curves indicate two important features of student performance. First, there is a direct relationship between the time at which the student began to turn in appreciable amounts of work and the final grade he received. The A students began working within two weeks, the B students began after four weeks, the C and D students started several weeks later. Student Number 34 never started. Student 27 would have received a D, but he requested an Incomplete and fourth months later completed the requirements for a C. Second, although different students began working at different times, once they did begin to work they all worked at approximately the same rate. Students 18 and 34 represent extremes in response rates. The remaining students all performed more similarly to Student 18 than to Student 34. When they worked, their response rates exceeded the linear rate for an A grade.

It is doubtful if any teacher could look at the curves in Figure 1 without thinking of ways to try to alter them (i.e., the behaviors

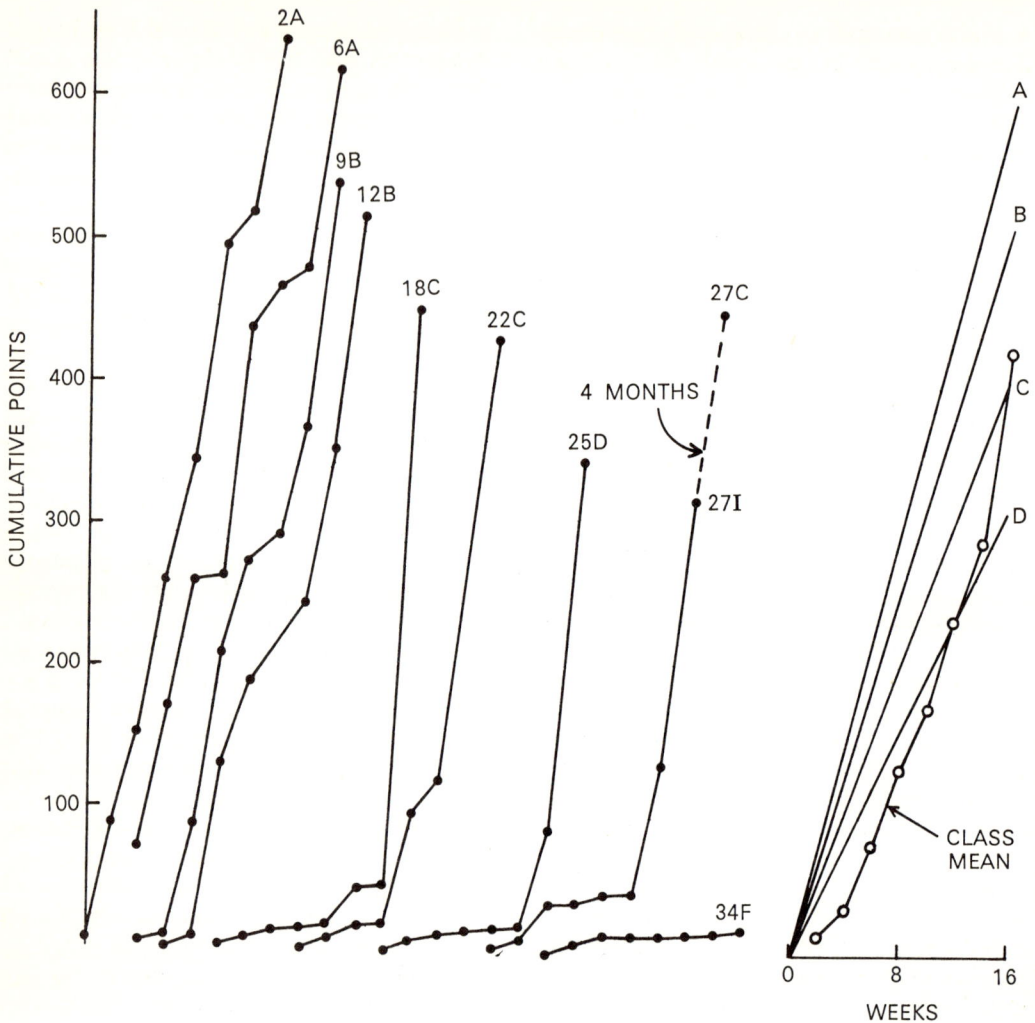

Figure 1. *Cumulative point curves at two-week intervals for typical students from each grade category. The scale on the right indicates linear response rates for the different grades. The class-mean cumulative-point curve is plotted with open circles.*

the curves represent). Perhaps the most obvious change would be to induce more students to begin working sooner. Once students began to work they worked at a high and steady rate, and once started no students arbitrarily quit working part way through the semester. Therefore it should follow that if the students began working sooner, they would complete more assignments.

Three different procedures have been employed in order to affect the response rates shown in Figure 1. Two of these procedures were evaluated by comparing the performance of students in two sections of the same course taught concurrently by the same instructor. The third procedure involved a comparison of the performance of different assignments under different kinds of contingencies by the same students in one section of a course.

The first procedure involved offering bonus points to students in one of two sections of an introductory psychology course. Students in the second section did not receive bonus points. Bonus points were awarded on a percentage basis depending upon when assignments were completed during the semester, e.g., work turned in during the first two weeks received a 60 percent bonus, work turned in during the second two weeks received a 30 percent bonus, and so on. The bonus reached zero by the tenth week. In order to equate the total required work in the two sections, the point requirements for the bonus section were increased by 30 percent. There were sixteen freshmen students in each section. After two weeks eleven students in the bonus section, as compared to one student in the no-bonus section, had turned in work. The students in the bonus section began working immediately and continued to do so throughout the semester. The students in the no-bonus section paused initially, and then some of them began turning in work by the fourth week. The performance of the latter section was similar to that of the students shown in Figure 1. As in the prior course, once students began to work they continued to do so throughout the semester. At the end of the semester nine students in the bonus section received an A, and none received an F or D. In the no-bonus section there were six A's, one F, and two D's. These frequency differences were not statistically different, but the bonus students had a clear head start and avoided the rush at the end of the semester.

In the second procedure different amounts of work were required for grades of D, C, and B in two sections of another introductory psychology course. The amount of work required for an A (665 points) was identical in both sections. In one section very little work was required to obtain a D (85 points), but the requirements for the higher grades demanded progressively more work, that is, a C was 215 points, a B required 415 points, and an A required 665 points. In the second section considerable work was required to obtain a D (250 points), but the requirements for the higher grades demanded progressively

less work than in the first section, that is, a C was 450 points, a B required 580 points, and an A required 665 points. Students were asked to state which grade they would work toward. A bonus-point system was in effect for both sections throughout the semester. This bonus system differed from the prior system in that the percentage basis remained constant throughout the semester but differed in terms of which grade a student said he was working toward. Students committed to an A were eligible for a larger absolute bonus than students committed to a B, and so on.

The original purpose of this manipulation was to learn if making it easy to achieve a D would induce students to begin working sooner and (as had been the case previously) to continue working steadily, so that the first section would produce more A's. However, this did not happen. The grade distributions for the two sections (N = 37 in both sections) were similar throughout the semester. At the semester's end there were 7 A's, 7 B's, 18 C's, 4 D's and 1 F in the first section and 6 A's, 11 B's, 12 C's, 5 D's, and 3 F's in the second. The only differences in these final grades seemed to be fewer B's and more C's in the first section. An examination of the individual cumulative-point curves of all students indicated what had happened.

First, the majority of the students got off to an early start, that is, thirty students in the first section and thirty-three in the second section turned in work steadily during the first four weeks. Second, although the students who received A's or B's continued to work steadily as had been observed in prior classes, the students who received C's or lower grades paused in the middle of the semester and then turned in large amounts of work at the end. Third, this pausing was more pronounced in the first section than in the second. Stated more precisely, the proportion of C students who, after accumulating at least one hundred points, obtained less than twenty points in either a four- or six-week period was greater in the first section (Xs^2 greater than 11.0, df = 2, $p < .01$). These three observations of the individual response-rates suggested that the bonus points were effective in establishing early responding, but that setting relatively easy requirements for a C encouraged midsemester pausing.

These two comparisons of student performance between concurrent sections were not definitive for several reasons. Although the teaching staff made every effort to treat students in the paired sections alike, a bias could have operated. The students in the two sections knew that the rules differed between sections. Other variables could have altered performance. Despite these shortcomings, which can be corrected in future work, there were recurrent consistencies in the data. In addition it became obvious that it would be possible to change the rate at which students worked.

An experimental design in which possible differences between students in different sections were eliminated would be an improvement. Studies in the experimental analysis of behavior typically examine in detail the effects of a variable on the behavior of a single subject, and this type of design was followed in the third procedure. In this last procedure (presented in detail in Lloyd, 1969) some assignments (twelve weekly quizzes) had to be completed within each two-week period, that is, two quizzes had to be completed within each two-week period. The remaining assignments had no specific due dates except for the usual criteria for attending the field trip (week 8) and for being eligible for an A (week 10). Figure 2 contains individual cumulative point curves for sixteen students selected from this course. The data were plotted at two-week intervals. The curves are labeled with a number and a letter. The number is the student's rank in the class after sixteen weeks. The letter is the grade he received.

There are two rows of cumulative-point curves in Figure 2. The bottom row contains cumulative-point curves for the twelve weekly quizzes. The top row contains cumulative-point curves for all other course assignments. There is a curve for each student in each row. The quizzes had to be completed within each two-week period, and response-rates of different students were similar regardless of the final grade they received. The other assignments had no specific due-dates, and response-rates of different students varied

with the grade they received, much as in Figure 1. The top row of curves in Figure 2 shows students procrastinating until the final moment. The bottom row of curves in Figure 2 shows no procrastination, as a result of the contingency that two of the twelve weekly quizzes had to be completed within each two-week period. The curves in the top row, in which this contingency was not in effect, do show this procrastination.

Differences in response-rates between the instructor-paced quizzes and self-paced assignments were consistent and clear cut for all students. Differences in response-rates between students were much less for instructor-paced assignments than for self-paced assignments. The conclusion that instructor-paced assignments were successful in inducing students to begin working early seems reasonable. However, the assignments themselves were different for the instructor-paced and the self-paced assignments. The former were quizzes, the latter were primarily reading reports and discussions. Preparation time for these assignments differed. A needed control procedure would be to reverse contingencies on the different assignments during the semester or to vary the kind of pacing imposed on different parts of the same assignment.

Like the earlier results, the data in Figure 2 strongly suggest that response rates of students can be readily changed by a change in contingencies. Many questions of procedure in these courses remain to be answered. The data presented above only indicate that empirical answers to the questions are possible. In the meantime the instructor who wishes to employ a contingency management system must make some immediate decisions based on less than complete information.

DECISIONS TO BE MADE BY INSTRUCTORS OF CONTINGENCY-MANAGED COURSE

This section will consider some of the decisions that must be made by the instructor setting up a course similar to those described above. The first decision concerns which terminal behaviors are to be established and

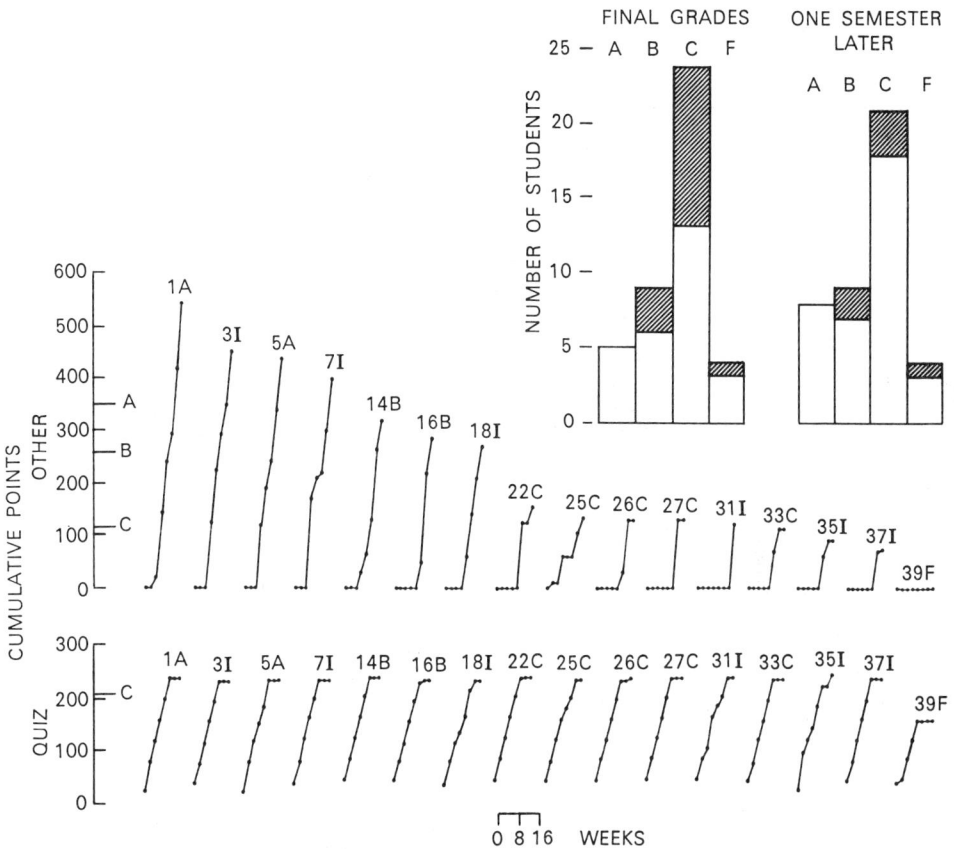

Figure 2. *Cumulative point curves from sixteen selected students plotted at two-week intervals for two differently paced assignments. There are two cumulative curves for each student. The histograms indicate grade distributions at the end of the semester and one semester later.*

which responses or assignments are likely to lead to these terminal behaviors. For example, the sequencing of assignments described in the second section above has not been validated. The component assignments at the lower grades may or may not be necessary for adequate performance at the A level.

There are decisions as to how many assignments to require for each grade and how to weight different assignments. The courses described here were difficult ones, but students responded favorably to the course and they suggested changes in the point system (see course critique in Lloyd et al., 1969). As noted above, when the lower grades were easy to obtain, students paused during mid-

semester. Some instructors have eliminated this difficulty by offering students only two grades, A or F (Malott, 1968), on the assumption that all students are capable of excellent work. But if the instructor indicates that lower standards are acceptable, then some students will perform accordingly.

The instructor must also decide upon a reinforcer. Grades remain the most readily manipulated reinforcer although Keller (1968) and McMichael et al. (1969) have used lectures and demonstrations. At periodic intervals during their courses lectures were given by the instructors. Admission to the lecture was contingent upon having completed a certain number of units. The authors did not report their attendance data from the lectures, so it is not possible to evaluate the effectiveness of these events as reinforcers.

Finally the instructor is faced with a decision about pacing the students. Permitting the student to work at his own pace (Keller, 1968) seems reasonable, unless it means that he does nothing until the last minute. If two students worked steadily but at different rates, then they could be given different periods of time in which to complete the same assignments. The data do not indicate that this happens during the course, however. The students of Lloyd et al. (1969) stated in a questionnaire that they wanted the instructor to set deadlines for them. These authors assigned a grade of Incomplete to anyone who requested it. Students who had been working at high rates when they received the Incomplete grade abruptly stopped working. However, within one year, seven had improved their grade and two had not. If this ratio of success is generally found, then go-at-your-own-pace may be more effective after a course is over than during the time the course is offered.

Frequently Asked Questions

Many questions are asked by readers or listeners encountering this material for the first time. Some of these questions along with current answers are presented below.

Question 1. Does the system reinforce quantity of work at the expense of quality? The answer depends upon the fourth column in Table 1. How the instructor has specified the minimum requirements determines what quality of work he will receive. For example, in summarizing a journal article four questions were asked. Students were responsible for answers to these four questions only. If they could answer them without reading the article from beginning to end, then there was little point in their reading the entire article. If an instructor wants students to read an entire article, then he must ask questions which require that behavior. Quantity of work is certainly reinforced but not necessarily at the expense of quality. In addition to the contingencies controlling quality of work which the instructor can manipulate, there seems to be another less-explicit contingency operating. Namely, the student knows that he has had ample time to prepare an assignment, knows exactly what he must do, knows he is capable of doing the work, and knows the work will be returned to him if it is unsatisfactory—all of these factors contribute to a job well done.

Question 2. Do students understand the material, or are they just doing the work? What do you do about creativity? These questions are related to the first question. The answer depends upon what behaviors the instructor must observe the student emit before the instructor will say that the student understands the material, or that the student is creative, or that the student does work of high quality, and so on. Sometimes observing a student emit several responses to one stimulus is the occasion for an instructor to say the student understands. At times observing a student emit a response infrequently emitted in his verbal community will be sufficient for the instructor to say he is creative. On occasion additional criteria are required. The point is that all of these behaviors can be specified for and required of students.

Question 3. Is the meaning of a grade changed? Yes. An A means that a specified amount of work has been completed at a specified level of competence. A lower grade means that some lesser percentage of this amount of work has been completed but at the *same* level of competence as A work. Just what percentage of A work represents B work or C work is arbitrary at the moment, but the results of the study cited above suggest that some grade percentage arrangements encourage more work than others. The best arrangement may be to offer only two grades as Malott (1968) has done. If more than two grades are offered, there will be students who will take them.

Question 4. Would the system work for a graduate course as well as for an under-

graduate course? The instructors who have tried it are enthusiastic (e.g., Professors Robert Chapman and Jack Michael, personal communications). Graduate students have been given weekly quizzes which consist of eight or ten questions chosen from a list of perhaps fifty questions covering that week's assignment. The author offers a graduate seminar in which students may register for variable credit. Only grades of A or F are given. To receive one semester hour of credit the student must attend 90 percent of the meetings and must show some evidence (e.g., notes) of having read the material before attending class. For two-hours' credit the student must do the above plus present an oral report, and for three-hours' credit the student must also collect some data relevant to his seminar topic.

Question 5. Do students do any better in these courses than in lecture courses? If they do better, then does having taken a course like these affect their work in other courses?

McMichael et al. (1969) have presented data showing better learning with contingency management. The author has computed several rank order correlations of total points with ranked grade point averages for all university work as well as for only the prior semester's work. These correlations were uniformly positive, low, and insignificant (i.e., there was little relationship between these measures).

The effect of these courses on other courses must be investigated. Within three years after the author introduced the first course at Washington State University, there were thirteen courses taught in a similar manner. Students who later took a second course under a contingency management system reported that the second course was much easier than the first. One student who took three such courses concurrently complained about the amount of work. Keller (1968) suggested that an instructor should probably limit himself to, at most, two such courses per semester.

An experimental approach to learning: Introduction for students

PHILIP N. HINELINE

For a college course to be of value, something special must happen to those who experience it. They must learn—which is to say, they must change; there must be things that they can do after taking the course that they could not do beforehand. A course is effective to the extent that this happens. Further, when you, as a student, register for a course, you are contracting with a teacher to induce or facilitate these changes in you, yourself.

If the course in question were swimming or underwater basket weaving, the desired changes would be obvious: At the end of the course, your ability to swim or to weave baskets underwater should be measurably improved. The course could be considered effective to the extent that this was accomplished. In light of this, consider the following:

"This, ladies and gentlemen, is Swimming 321, a course in swimming techniques for beginners. It will meet in this classroom on Monday and Friday from 10:00 to 11:00 A.M., during which I shall lecture, and you will take thorough, accurate, and excellent notes. There will be a midterm examination and a final examination. The midterm will be conducted in the 25-meter pool; you will jump into the deep end and swim to the shallow end. For those who do not reach the

From *Behavioral Adaptation Manual: Methods and Materials for Student Interview Teaching with Psychology Today: An Introduction,* CRM Books, 1971. Reprinted by permission.

other end, notice will be sent to the dean, expressing our concern at your slow progress. For the final examination, you will be taken, by boat, to the center of Lake Winnibigoshish, where you will jump out and swim to shore. Those reaching the beach within two hours will pass the course; the rapidity and elegance with which you reach the shore will determine your exact grade. . . ."

"Welcome to the advanced course, Underwater Basket Weaving 696, offered Tuesday and Thursday from 10:00 to 11:30. Please note that Swimming 321 is a prerequisite for this course. Class meetings will be devoted to guided group discussions on the role of the basket in our society. There will be a midterm examination, multiple-choice, based on the footnotes of the assigned textbook, *Der Unterdemwasserbasketgewever* by U. M. Basquet. For the final examination you will be required to take apart a two-liter basket while submerged with your materials, under eight inches of water. Students not completely demolishing a basket within two hours will fail the course."

These courses appear ineffective, unfair, and somewhat implausible. But they seem implausible mainly because swimming and basket weaving are usually more effectively taught. The activities usually scheduled in such courses are much more closely related to skills that the students are supposed to acquire from the course. The fare described above, steady diets of lectures or teacher-directed discussions, would contribute little to one's ability to swim or to weave baskets. Yet, the methods described above are based on teaching methods that are common to many, if not most, of today's college courses. The teachers using them could claim to be in the mainstream of college education, even though few of their classroom activities contributed to the desired changes in students' abilities.

But, it might be argued, in more academic, book-learning-type courses, the objectives are not always quite so clear and certainly not definable in terms of specific skills. True, most course objectives are usually described vaguely as "knowledge," and the courses are defined solely in terms of topics of subject matter. But here, at least, we can do better than that. In our course in psychology we are concerned with every student's ability to do things—that is, his ability to discuss and explain, and to use terms and concepts in psychology; to deal with experimental, clinical, or theoretical problems in ways that take advantage of proven facts and principles of psychology. For facilitating these skills, the traditional lectures and the like are not much more appropriate than they would be in a course in swimming.

Consider what commonly occurs in a college course. First, you and your teacher have been allotted fixed scheduled times for use of a classroom. The room has chairs all facing front, perhaps even bolted to the floor. Your teacher has experienced countless hours of lectures, both as student and as teacher, so it will seem to him a natural way to proceed. And you probably expect lectures, too. After all, you paid your tuition and should get something tangible in return. So he lectures, and you listen. There may be occasional discussions, but these usually are dominated by three or four people.

During lectures, or discussions for that matter, the whole class moves in lock-step. If the speaker moves slowly, or digresses, the whole class moves slowly and digresses with him. Your time would be much better spent in reading. On the other hand, if the lecturer moves very quickly, supplying large amounts of information, you can listen only as a passive transcriber, writing down an imperfect record of what was said, and understanding or remembering little at the time. No matter how your teacher paces his lectures, he will always be either too fast or too slow for a sizeable group of students. And if anyone stops him for clarification, the whole class stops together.

The examinations determine many of the remaining features. If they cover mainly the lectures, most of your active studying (where the actual learning occurs) is over your notes, which are quite imperfect as a textbook. If the examinations cover mainly the book, usually little indication is given regarding just what you are to know. The result is, particularly in preparation for multiple-choice examinations, that you are obliged to spend more time on minor facts than on important concepts.

And where does this leave us with respect to the stated objectives of the course? When were you encouraged to explain anything in class? When did you address a problem that involved relating several concepts, or designing an experiment, or evaluating an explanation? When were you, and everyone else, actively involved in the course?

The present materials ... are designed to facilitate these kinds of activities. The materials can be used for study on your own, but they were designed to be used with others, providing the basis for your actively explaining and discussing concepts and experiments from the text. If your instructor so chooses, these materials could form the basis for a course in which class time was spent with all students actively learning and lectures took a secondary supplementary role.

In brief, questions are provided which serve as a basis or "guide" for "interviews" concerning material in the textbook. The questions indicate the important concepts in the text and can be used as guides for study. To best use them, find a friend who also studied the material you wish to cover. Then flip a coin to decide who interviews whom. The interview which follows should be a one-sided conversation, with the interviewee discussing ... point by point. Both participants may follow the guide, but additional notes should not be used except when specifically indicated. During the interview the interviewer should say very little, merely indicating approval of good answers, indicating approval of good answers, indicating when a good topic has been adequately covered and nothing which topics will require further review. When a section or chapter has been completed, discuss the topics that were troublesome, and then decide whether to review or proceed.

You will find that some of the questions are difficult; the answers cannot always be lifted directly from the text. Those questions were intentionally devised to give you practice at manipulating and reorganizing material in the book and at applying, rather than parroting, the concepts of psychology.

Effective learning requires active involvement. We hope that these materials help you become actively involved with psychology today.

An experimental approach to teaching: Introduction for teachers

PHILIP N. HINELINE

"An effective way to learn something thoroughly is to teach it." We can put this old saw to work in college courses by contriving situations in which everybody spends his time in active teaching, one way or another. A good vehicle for this is "interviewing," an activity in which students explain to one another and evaluate one another's explanations of concepts and facts presented in the textbook. During the actual interviewing, the classroom resembles a sit-down cocktail party. The instructor helps from the sidelines, assisting with points of ambiguity or difficulty in the interviews, and helping students who encounter undue difficulty with particular concepts. ...

If you prefer, the interviewing can be introduced as an occasional supplement to lectures. Later, if you become more confident in the effectiveness of the interviews and can pull yourself from the limelight, the lectures may eventually be restricted to supplementing the interviews. In short, the balance between these activities can vary with the style of the individual instructor or with other considerations. The truly experimental or innovative part of this approach has to do with how the program of interviewing is

From **Behavioral Adaptation Manual: Methods and Materials for Experimental Teaching with Psychology Today: An Introduction,** CRM Books, 1971. Reprinted by permission.

enacted. There are many options regarding:

a) specific format of the interviews,
b) controlling who interviews whom,
c) arrangements for maintaining rigor in interviews,
d) the extent to which the students pace themselves, and
e) the subject matter and types of questions that produce best interviews.

We shall consider each of these in its turn.

Format of the Interview

For our purposes, an interview should be a one-sided conversation in which a student explains definitions and concepts in psychology and illustrates them by describing experiments and facts. The topics covered by an interview are determined by a written interview guide which is a list of questions that indicates what should be emphasized in a particular portion of the textbook. The guide is, functionally, an outline of a portion of the textbook. Both interviewer and interviewee keep a copy of the interview guide in view. The interviewee discusses and explains it point by point. During most of the interview the interviewer should say very little, merely indicating approval of good answers, indicating when a given topic has been adequately covered, and ensuring that the interviewee's presentation touches on each topic of the guide. His main job during most of the interview is to evaluate the interviewee's presentation and fill out a form noting topics covered especially well, topics missed, and material that was ambiguous either in the textbook or in the interview guide.

When the interviewee's main presentation is completed, the two can discuss topics that gave trouble: If there were only one or two minor points missed, these can be explained by the interviewer, after which the interviewee must explain it back—simply saying that he understands is not enough. Finally, the interviewer indicates whether the interviewee has passed or must repeat all or part of the interview. If only one or two main points were missed, it would be appropriate to recommend a few minutes' study with the textbook, after which these specific points could be covered again in a "partial repeat." If several topics are missed, then the interviewee must repeat the whole interview. There is no penalty for repeating, other than the extra time and work involved.

It may be desirable, with especially difficult material, to precede the actual interviews with a "small-group review" in which groups of four or six students discuss the parts of the interview that are likely to give trouble. If an adequate answer to some question cannot be achieved within this group, the instructor should be called in to help. Use of this small-group format serves nicely to introduce variety into the interview situation, but previous use does show that the small-group discussion is not an adequate substitute for one-to-one interviewing. It provides preparation for the interview, but cannot substitute for it since even in a small group, some students talk a great deal while others remain quiet. We are concerned that every student acquire practice in explaining and describing topics in psychology.

Who Should Be the Interviewer?

In some applications of this method, the interviewers have been either paid graduate teaching assistants or undergraduates who previously did well in the course. The main advantage is obvious: Such individuals are well qualified to ensure rigorous interviewing. Some disadvantages are equally obvious. One must have rather special support from the department chairman and perhaps the dean to obtain permission (and/or funds) to use these assistants. But the most important disadvantage of teaching assistants as interviewers is that they don't need the experience, and they're depriving someone who does need this opportunity.

If a student in the class serves as interviewer, he gets an extra review of the material and is exposed to alternative answers or points of view that he may not have considered. It provides redundancy in the course without mere repetition. It involves the student in a second activity of teaching—as interviewee he explains the material; as interviewer, he is called upon to evaluate someone else's explanations.

If the students themselves are to be interviewers, we must use some arrangement to ensure that the interviewer is qualified. If permitted, many students would gladly serve as interviewers before even having read the textbook. This can be handled with a set of "ground rules." For example, if the course is completely self-paced, a pyramid arrangement can be used whereby the instructor interviews the student who is ready first. That student, and perhaps the instructor, too, interviews one or two others; those in turn interview two or more students as they become ready, and so on. Eventually everyone is interviewed, and no one is allowed to be an interviewer before passing as interviewee. A main disadvantage of this method is its penalizing of students who progress slowly and hence have very few opportunities to serve as interviewers. Another approach which produces adequate rigor if there are other contingencies that support it, is that of requiring both interviewer and interviewee to be prepared to be interviewee before arranging to do an interview together. It is best to formalize this; either the instructor determines which of the pair will be interviewer, or when ready to begin the interview they must flip a coin to decide who takes which role. Once the first round of interviews occurs on a given interview guide, there will be a plentitude of qualified interviewers around who can be used to advantage. The ground rules also can require that, whenever possible, an interviewee must use an interviewer who has already passed the material to be covered. This set of rules gives the opportunity for interviewing to a much larger number of students. It can be improved further by requiring that no one may serve as interviewer twice without having first passed an interview as interviewee and by prohibiting back-to-back interviews. (If John interviewed Joyce on the fifth interview, then Joyce cannot interview John on the fifth interview.) When such back-to-back interviewing is permitted, it works superbly for the best students, but the slowest students gravitate toward each other, sharing their ignorance without realizing it. For similar reasons it may be useful to add additional constraints: Two people can jointly participate in no more than four interviews during the semester. This all sounds very complicated in the explaining, but it is quite simple in practice.

Interviews Can Contribute Directly to Grades

Grades, as well as course credit itself, can be based on students' participation, both as interviewers and as interviewees. In an open-ended course—such as, for example, if all thirty-five chapters of a textbook were used for a one-semester introductory course—the grades could be based simply on how many interviews a student completed. This would be most appropriate in cases where the interviewers were teaching assistants rather than students in the course, since it would provide neither credit for interviewing nor for quality control of the interviews. Serving as interviewer can contribute to course credit if some sort of point system is used. One that has proved satisfactory is to give five points for passing an interview (as interviewee), and two points per interview for serving as interviewer, whether the interview results in pass or repeat. It is possible that increased rigor could be obtained by giving the interviewer three points for an interview resulting in repeat—counteracting the tendency of students to "go easy" on each other—but this would probably complicate interpersonal relations within the class. There are other kinds of contingencies, or arrangements, which ensure rigorous interviewing without undesirable side effects. Of course, participation in interviews need not determine the entire course grade; one could still retain examinations, papers, and the like as partial determiners of credit or final grade.

Ensuring Rigorous Interviewing

The provision for students to evaluate their peers' interviews is the strongest, but also, potentially, the most troublesome feature of the learning formats proposed here. Its strength lies in what the interviewer reviews and learns during an interview. Its potential weakness lies in the possibilities for superficial interviewing; the interviewer largely determines the standards that the interviewee must meet in order to pass. We dealt with one aspect of this problem when we considered ways to ensure that a student is qualified to function adequately as interviewer. But we must also ensure that a qualified student will function adequately as interviewer. In short, we are concerned that rigorous standards be maintained for passing an interview.

The procedures to be used for this are amenable to experimentation. They involve variables to be manipulated with care, for they determine the extent to which all the other arrangements will be effective. These procedures are devised to make the performance of the interviewee important to the interviewer. Specifically, the interviewee's performance on examinations contributes to the interviewer's grade. For this to be defensible and valid, the examinations must cover the same material that was covered in the interviews with essentially the same stress on different topics. We must eliminate "surprise" or obscure questions on examinations; that is not to say that the examinations must be easy or superficial. Rather, we must indicate, through the interview guides, what is important in the course and address our examinations to the important material. The examinations should require thorough preparation but should not entail unnecessary uncertainty. Uncertainty constitutes harassment and is inconsistent with the other methods that are advocated here.

The most potent arrangement for producing rigorous interviewing would be one in which the interviewer's grade was entirely determined by the examination performance of the students he interviewed. The problem with this, other than the insurrection it might produce, is that there would be few consequences maintaining diligent examination writing.[1] It would also require extensive and complicated bookkeeping.

A less radical arrangement that has been used with some success is one in which an interviewer's grade is only partially determined by the performance of other students. The class is divided into groups of five or six students each, on the basis of a preliminary questionaire dealing with the students' backgrounds. Each group contains an equal number of students with minimal backgrounds in psychology, biology, and other supporting courses. The interview format, and the reasons for it, are first explained with considerable emphasis on the fact that the purpose of the course is to teach not just "knowledge" in an abstract sense but also skill at explaining and discussing concepts in psychology. Given this explanation, it makes sense that one must examine how well the "explainee" knows what was explained. Hence, since interviewing—that is, being the interviewer—is part of the course, it makes sense to grade or give credit for this interviewing on the basis of how effective it is. To accomplish this, an individual's grade on the hour examinations is determined partly on his own performance on the examination and partly by the mean examination grade for his group. The students are regrouped after each examination.

The first question that arises is: How much of an individual's grade should depend on the performance of his group? In preliminary work, informal comparisons were made of different formulas for computing an individual's grade by observing the extent to which interviewing was confined to fellow group members. The students were not explicitly required to interview only with people in their own groups; it was merely pointed out that interviewing one's own group members had a distinct advantage.

When 25 percent of each grade was determined by the mean score for one's group, the students tended to interview outside their groups to a considerable extent—especially after the first hour exam when regrouping

---

1 Although in this context we should note that in a recent controlled test of a teaching format resembling the present one, but using teaching assistants, the students on the experimental procedure did much better on a final examination than students in a lecture-discussion course using the same materials—even though, unlike the latter group, the interview students' final examination performance contributed nothing to their grades.

occurred. They continued to interview with members of their previous groups. In contrast, when 50 percent of a student's grade was based on the mean for his group, most interviews occurred within groups. It also produced a considerable number of complaints, particularly from the better students. With other things being relatively constant, 33 percent proved to be a reasonably good compromise; this is the value presently in use, and most interviews occur within groups.

Another possible variation is that of allowing interviews outside of class. This is an attractive option to those of us with long histories of reinforcement for lecturing; it allows time for both lectures and interviews. The difficulty is that if uncertainties arise in an interview outside of class, the instructor is not present to clear things up, and by the next class period, the question loses its poignancy. If the students complain of being pressed for time in getting all the interviews done in class, an option of doing them outside of class could be used, but extra credit would be received for doing them inside of class.

To date, the group contingency procedures are used in conjunction with hour examinations given every four or five weeks, each examination covering ten or twelve interviews. It is quite possible that the group contingency would be more effective if examinations based on smaller blocks of material were taken more frequently. This needn't involve more paper grading: An hour exam with six essay questions could just as well be given as three shorter exams with two questions each. If the exam questions are based on interview questions (usually requiring combinations of material from two interview questions), the atmosphere of harassment that usually accompanies standard weekly quizzes could be avoided. This testing procedure would provide effective feedback on the quality of interviewing; however, it remains to be seen whether this would make the course aversive.

Another approach for the group contingencies would be to combine it with a study of descriptive statistics. For example, the first time around, 33 percent of an individual's grade would be determined by the mean for

his group; the second time by 33 percent of the median; the third time, by the lower extreme of the range; the fourth time by 33 percent of the lower quartile for the group, and so on. By the time this was completed, everyone would know his descriptive statistics! Perhaps one of these other measures would prove more useful than the mean, for our purposes.

Pacing

With teaching assistants doing the interviewing, there is no difficulty in using the interview method in a completely self-paced program in which each student proceeds entirely at his own rate. With the group contingencies this is more difficult, but it still can be accomplished by forming groups simply on the basis of who is ready to proceed on to the next unit of material. Self-pacing, however, often results in inefficient performance: Little work is done early in the semester until examination time draws near, which results in severely massed practice and, consequently, poor retention. An effective modification of self-pacing is to set a minimum pace, with a due-date for each interview. Students may work ahead of this pace if they wish, but any interviews done after their due-dates result in only half-credit.

The pace, in terms of number of interviews per week, of course, depends heavily on how much material is to be covered in each interview. Preliminary work with interviews based on the textbook indicates that three chapters every two weeks is a fairly rapid pace. In terms of the size of reading assignments that we give out in standard course formats, this is not very much. However, the interview techniques ensure coverage of the book in considerable depth; a student is, in a sense, preparing a small lecture for each interview to be taken.

The Interview Guides:
What Kinds of Questions?

The choice of interview questions, since it defines what is to be stressed in the course, is very critical and is probably the part of this program where disagreement can occur. Nevertheless, at least two basic strategies can be specified, each with its advantages and disadvantages. Most of the questions are designed with one or the other of these two strategies in mind, so it is best that they be made explicit.

The first, and most prosaic of the two, is to ask questions that follow the organization of the textbook. These questions ask the student to accurately present the text's argument or description, the interview question giving some indication of the specific points that should be emphasized. For this kind of question there is a readily identifiable right answer, given that one has read and understood the book. It is consistent with the philosophy of the interview procedures—mastery before proceeding; one student should not pass another on a given interview until he is convinced that the interviewee answered each question adequately. The main disadvantage of this kind of question is that it is usually dull. It asks for a "laundry list" of items to be recalled: three parts of this, four facts that prove that, two experiments that show this. Unfortunately, some of these questions are unavoidable.

The other strategy is to write problem-oriented questions. The basic definitions and facts are applied to a question that cannot be answered with a mere repeat of the material presented in the textbook. The question may require the student to relate two concepts presented in different chapters; it may require the student to decipher an illustration that is not fully explained in the text; it may require him to explain how a given graph would change if the conditions of the experiment were changed; it may ask him to relate two graphs or concepts that appear to be quite independent.

The advantage of these questions is that they generate more thought; they effectively hold the student's interest. Facts and definitions are acquired as tools for explaining phenomena or for answering meaningful questions which is much closer to the behavior we wish the student to emit. However, a negative aspect of this strategy is that it is not always clear what is a right answer; there may be more than one correct answer. When the students come to recognize this, they tend to pass the interviewee for a less-than-complete answer on some of the more straightforward questions that should be answered completely and concisely. The instructor can resolve the difficulties raised by the problem-oriented questions, if the students are encouraged to ask for help when they are unable to evaluate a response. The activity generated by the best of these questions is exciting to see; at the end of a class period the students leave in twos and threes, talking and arguing about psychology.

R. W. MALOTT, PATRICIA HARTLEP, AND STUART HARTLEP

From **Contingency Management in Education and Other Equally Exciting Places or I've Got Blisters on My Soul and Other Equally Exciting Places.** Reprinted by permission of Behaviordelia.

I DON'T KNOW WHY, BUT I CAN'T RESIST SWEETS. EATING SWEETS IS JUST A HABIT!

OVEREATING IS A COMMON PROBLEM, AND BEHAVIORAL SCIENCE IS NOT SURE WHAT THE CAUSE IS.

THERE ARE CERTAIN SITUATIONS WHERE FOOD IS A REINFORCER, ALTHOUGH THE PERSON IS CLEARLY NOT DEPRIVED OF FOOD.

WE JUST DON'T KNOW ENOUGH ABOUT THOSE SITUATIONS YET.

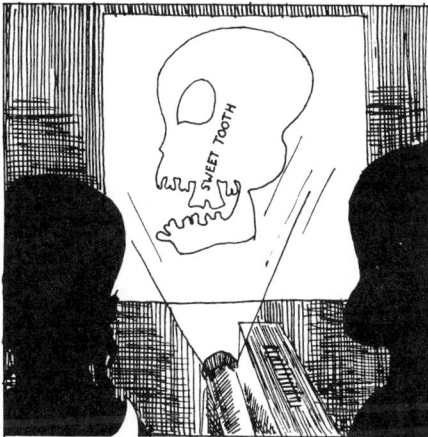

SWEET TOOTH

HOWEVER, WE DO KNOW HOW TO DEAL WITH THE PROBLEM. YOUR MAIN PROBLEM IS THAT YOUR "SWEET TOOTH" MAKES YOU OVEREAT, SO YOU'RE GETTING FAT.

LET'S CONCENTRATE PRIMARILY ON YOUR WEIGHT.

SOUNDS GOOD TO ME.

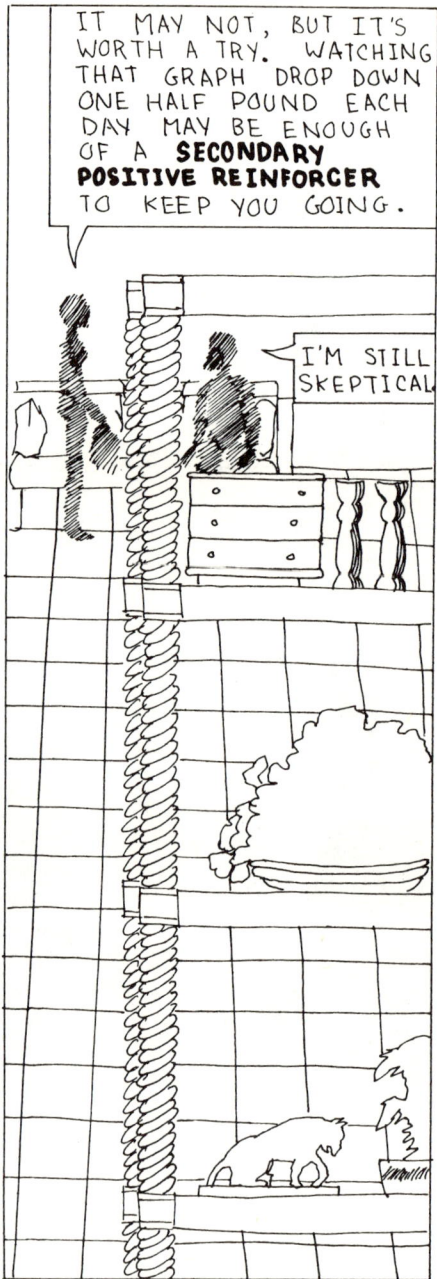

7

IN THE EDUCATION OF ADULTS

Few adults sit on the students' side of the classroom after they complete their formal education. Most of their learning takes place in their homes or on the job, and that learning is controlled by the contingencies in force. This section presents examples of more explicit educational programs for adults. Two adult populations often cited as needing education are welfare recipients and prison inmates. The first article, by Miller and Miller, describes a program for strengthening responses that will improve welfare recipients' lives. This program relies, not on threats of withdrawing money, but on the introduction of positive reinforcers.

Because prisons exert a high degree of control over inmates and because many inmates badly need new alternative behaviors, prisons are likely settings for behavior modification programs. The second paper in this section describes the Draper Project, a program employing contingency management in an Alabama prison. Various reinforcement strategies are used to increase the inmates' rate of working on academic tasks. Such an application of behavior modification to the personal growth of prison inmates probably would be considered ethical by most people. Because of the extreme deprivation of the inmates and the extensive control exerted by the prison, it is important to use behavior control techniques not simply to make prisoners more submissive but to increase the behaviors that will be of long-range benefit to them.

One of the major dislocations in our techno-society is in child-rearing traditions. Sociologists such as Toffler (1970), in *Future Shock,* document many of the changes and migrations occasioned by superindustrialization. Such futurists predict the demise of "dilettante" parents in favor of professional child-care workers. However, the issue does not focus on whether the child-rearing agent is the biological parent or a hired professional but rather on whether the agent is effectively trained in the techniques of child-training and care. The final article by Hawkins, stresses the importance of training parents. He suggests that everyone should have training in child care before they have children. He also feels that training should include the supervised practice of parental skills rather than simply the studying of textbooks.

As McIntire points out in an article presented later in this volume, adults are the least likely objects of behavior control techniques. Adult behavioral scientists, in dealing with other adults, quickly forget their training. They bring flowers home to their wives after arguments, blame their colleagues, and punish their assistants. If adults would finally agree to include themselves in the family of living creatures, conditions could be arranged that would maximize their happiness, intellectual growth, and effectiveness.

Reinforcing self-help group activities of welfare recipients

L. KEITH MILLER AND OCOEE L. MILLER

Applied behavior analysis has been defined as the application of behavior analysis to the solution of socially relevant problems (Baer, Wolf, and Risley, 1968). Socially relevant situations thus studied have included mental hospital wards (Ayllon and Azrin, 1968), classrooms (Hall, Lund, and Jackson, 1968), preschools (Bushell, Wrobel, and Michaelis, 1968), autistic children (Lovaas, Schaeffer, and Simmons, 1965), and a variety of individual behavior problems. In these situations it has been found that reinforcement procedures can be used to increase the occurrence of "desirable" behaviors. This provides some evidence that behavior analysis can be successfully applied to a wide variety of socially relevant problems.

With its strong emphasis on socially relevant problems, it is not surprising that behavior analysis has begun to be applied to the behavioral components of poverty. For example, a number of studies have been directed at improving the educational attainment of low-income youths (Wolf, Giles, and Hall, 1968; Bushell and Jacobson, 1969; Jacobson, Bushell, and Risley, 1969; Clark, Lachowicz, and Wolf, 1968; Miller, 1968; Hart and Risley, 1968). Another study has been directed at increasing the rate of "desirable" behaviors among institutionalized juvenile offenders (Phillips, 1968). These studies provide some evidence that behavior analysis can be successfully applied to some of the problems posed by poverty conditions.

However, poor persons are increasingly rejecting approaches to poverty based solely on changing their behavior to conform to existing institutions. They are demanding that existing institutions be changed and even that new institutions be invented. This demand requires not only behavioral changes on the part of poor persons but also changes on the part of other segments of our society. Thus, a more complete approach to the conditions that cause and maintain poverty may require changing the behavior of both poor persons and others in ways that do not conform to existing institutional requirements.

Part of this more complete approach to poverty has focused on creating new organizations composed of poor people, governed exclusively by them, and directed toward planning and executing programs for their own benefit (Clinard, 1966). Self-help programs sponsored by these groups include self-improvement through education, cooperatives and other business enterprises, the organization of pressure groups, and the development of groups to improve neighborhood and housing conditions. The successful establishment of self-help groups requires behavioral change among both the poor and the rest of the community. However, these groups can be a potent force for creating the social change necessary to deal with poverty conditions.

If self-help groups are to be successful agents for social change, they must be capa-

From *Journal of Applied Behavior Analysis,* Spring 1970, *3*(1), 57-64. Copyright © 1970 by the Society for the Experimental Analysis of Behavior, Inc. Reprinted by permission of the authors and the *Journal of Applied Behavior Analysis.*

This paper was supported in part by grant CG-8719A-0 from the Office of Economic Opportunity.

ble of attracting and maintaining the participation of poor persons. In behavioral terms, this would mean that participation must result in reinforcement if it is to be maintained. One might guess that the long-range and often indirect benefits produced by these groups —such as cleaner neighborhoods, educational improvement, progressive government— would not be sufficiently strong reinforcers to maintain the participation of poor persons. However, there is some evidence from questionnaire and interview surveys that poor persons participate less frequently than the middle class in such voluntary groups as unions, political associations, and churches (Berelson and Steiner, 1964). This suggests that such long-range benefits may not be sufficiently strong reinforcers to maintain the participation of poor persons. If self-help groups are to provide a successful approach to poverty, a method for maintaining participation must be found.

A behavioral approach to maintaining participation requires that "participation" be specified in behavioral terms. However, this is an almost impossible task because participation is a catch-all term including attending meetings, speaking, listening, carrying out assignments, keeping minutes, and negotiating with other groups. An alternative behavioral approach is to select a particularly relevant aspect of participation that can be simply specified and investigate methods for maintaining just that aspect. In the present experiment, attendance at meetings was chosen for investigation. It is a particularly relevant aspect of participation because it is an "entry" behavior for most other aspects of participation. If a person attends meetings he can also talk, listen, keep minutes, chair the meeting, and receive assignments. Furthermore, meeting-attendance is methodologically convenient in that it has a physically specifiable definition and can be directly observed.

In the present experiment, the use of supplementary reinforcement was examined as a method for maintaining meeting attendance. During two experimental periods, supplementary reinforcement was delivered. In order to assess the effect of this procedure, two control periods were instituted during which no

supplementary reinforcement was delivered. Thus, the present experiment evaluated the effectiveness of supplementary reinforcement in maintaining meeting attendance in comparison with the effectiveness of the reinforcers inherent in self-help groups.

METHOD

Membership

Membership in the self-help group was restricted to current recipients in the Aid to Families with Dependent Children (ADC) program of a small midwestern city. In the beginning of the experiment, 94 families received ADC; by the end of the study 120 families received ADC. Of these, 52 family members participated in the self-help groups; 50 were women, 2 men; they ranged in age from 18 to 57 years.

Personnel

One author served as a welfare counselor, providing assistance and information to about 50 welfare recipients in the eight months before the experiment. As a result, she was familiar with welfare problems, the welfare agency's response to such problems, and many of the relevant regulations of the agency.

Self-Help Groups

Two self-help groups were formed. The membership of each group was determined by its members, who elected a president from among themselves. All meetings except the first one were held in a member's home at a time designated by the president. Members were notified by mail of the date, time, and place of the meeting. Meetings were scheduled monthly.

Meeting Procedures

All meetings followed a formal agenda. First, roll was taken and the $.25 dues collected and recorded. Second, the president, using the notes of the previous meeting, found out if all outstanding individual problems had been solved. Each person was specifically asked about any problem that had been described at the previous meeting. If a problem had not been solved, the group decided what further steps to take. Third, the president went over a checklist of welfare problems with each member. This checklist included questions about whether the members received all checks on time last month, received their medical card, and received any increases or decreases in their allowances. Fourth, the members discussed new problems revealed by the checklist or brought up by members. A specific strategy for solving any new problems was arrived at through discussion. Fifth, a general discussion of other community affairs that affected group members was initiated. This ranged over such areas as urban renewal, school-board policy, police problems, and city government. If members decided there was a problem, a strategy for dealing with it was decided upon. Finally, additional resources were described. These included services and used goods. Quarterly meetings of all presidents were scheduled in addition to monthly membership meetings. These meetings were designed to exchange information about strategy, agency response, and membership reaction and to coordinate the different self-help groups.

Procedure

During the first phase of the experiment, all ADC recipients were notified by mail before each of three meetings designed to form self-help groups. The welfare counselor was present to explain the purpose of the groups, but there was no supplementary reinforcement for attending these meetings. This phase lasted for three meetings.

At the beginning of the second phase, each recipient was informed in writing of another meeting to form self-help groups. This time, however, they were offered the opportunity to select two free Christmas toys for each child in their family if they attended the meeting. At subsequent meetings of the individual

self-help groups, the members in attendance were permitted to ask for any of the types of items listed in Table 1. If the item was available it was given to the recipient on the spot or arrangements were made for its delivery. If the item was not available, the member was permitted to continue making selections. If a member did not select an item, or if no acceptable items were available, then she received nothing for attending that meeting. Less than 10 percent of the requests were for unavailable items. The goods were solicited from the "concerned" middle-class community by the welfare counselor. Many items were maintained in a storage facility. Services and information were similarly sought out by the counselor. To the extent that the counselor was unsuccessful these items were unavailable. The second phase lasted eight meetings.

The third phase was introduced when the welfare counselor discontinued attendance at meetings due to major surgery and supplementary reinforcers were not available for

Table 1. Reinforcers available for attending meetings.

I. Goods:
  1. Toys
  2. Stoves
  3. Refrigerators
  4. Furniture
  5. Clothing
  6. Rugs
  7. Kitchen utensils
II. Services:
  1. Assistance in negotiating an ADC grievance
  2. Assistance in locating a suitable house
  3. Assistance in negotiating house improvements with landlord
  4. Assistance in clearing up police or court problems
  5. Finding odd jobs for teen-agers
  6. Day camp scholarships
  7. Beauty and poise classes
III. Information:
  1. Additional ADC-grant benefits
  2. Benefits from other social service agencies
  3. Birth control information

---

attending meetings. This phase lasted for eight meetings.

During the fourth and final phase the counselor again accepted invitations to meetings and thereby made reinforcers available to members who attended meetings. The president of each group was notified of this at the beginning of the first month of this phase. This phase lasted for seven meetings.

RESULTS

The average number of ADC recipients who attended the first twenty-six meetings of the study is shown in Figure 1. These data show that an average of about three persons attended meetings during the first phase when the counselor was present but supplementary reinforcers were not contingent upon attending. No recipients attended during the last meeting of this phase. During the second phase, when supplementary reinforcers were given, attendance increased to an average of fifteen recipients per meeting. During the third phase, when supplementary reinforce-

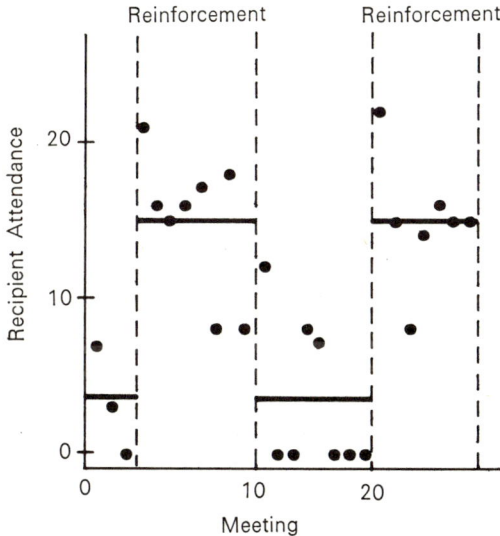

Figure 2. *Cumulative number of new members attending their first meeting when reinforcement was contingent on attendance (Reinforcement) and during periods when it was not.*

Figure 1. *Number of welfare recipients attending each of the first 26 meetings of the self-help groups. Recipients were given supplementary reinforcement during the periods labeled Reinforcement.*

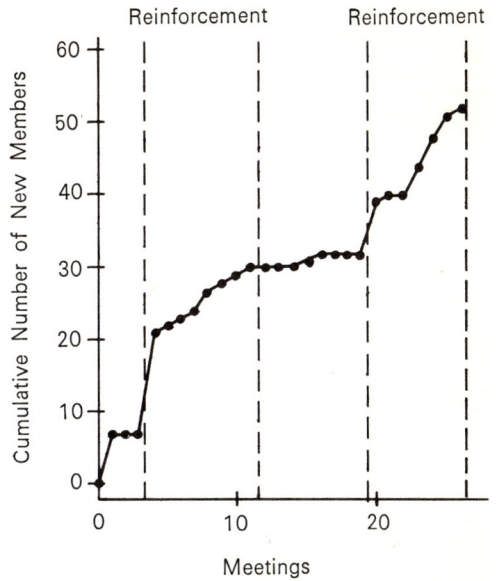

ment was not available because the counselor was absent, attendance averaged about three recipients per meeting. Finally, when supplementary reinforcement was again given (during the fourth phase), attendance increased and stabilized at an average of about sixteen recipients per meeting. These data show that more recipients attended meetings when supplementary reinforcement was available to them than when it was not.

Figure 2 shows the number of new members attending each of the 26 meetings. The data show that seven members attended the first meeting of the self-help groups when no supplementary reinforcement was contingent on attendance. The average rate of acquiring new members for the other 10 meetings when no supplementary reinforcement was scheduled was 0.2 per meeting; when supplementary reinforcement was scheduled the average was 2.8 for Phase 2 and 2.7 for Phase 4. A total of fifty-two members, or about 40 percent of the total persons on welfare were attracted to the groups during the course of the study. The data show, however, that members were attracted primarily when supplementary reinforcement was contingent upon attendance.

The data in Figure 2 suggest that the overall effect of supplementary reinforcement may have been to attract new members regularly, but not necessarily to keep them. Figure 3 shows the attendance rates for Phases 2, 3, and 4 for the twelve recipients who remained eligible for membership in the group for the entire study. Of the other nine members attending the first reinforced meeting, six moved from town, two dropped off of ADC, and one was dismissed from the club for violating the privacy of group members. The graph shows the number of those twelve who attended N percent of the meetings for a particular phase, for each of the three phases. Thus, during the first phase that supplementary reinforcement was available, six members attended between 80 and 90 percent of the meetings, three members attended between 70 and 80 percent of the meetings, and so on. As can be seen from the graphs, most of the members attended over 50 percent of the meetings when supplementary reinforcement was available. On the other hand, no members attended more than 30 percent of the meetings when supplementary reinforcement was not available. The trends for individual subjects are similar for ten of the twelve members, with only one member failing to show an increase during the final reinforcement phase. These data show that the reinforcement contingency maintained attendance among most of these twelve individual subjects.

Another method for exploring the ability of the supplementary reinforcement to both initiate and maintain attendance is to explore attendance of all fifty-two members between their first meetings and the time at which they become ineligible. If we define the failure to attend four or more consecutive meetings as "dropping membership" in the group, then only seven members voluntarily dropped out. An additional seventeen became ineligible for continued membership. Thus, some level of continued attendance was maintained in 86 percent of the total persons that experienced the contingency at least once. Further-

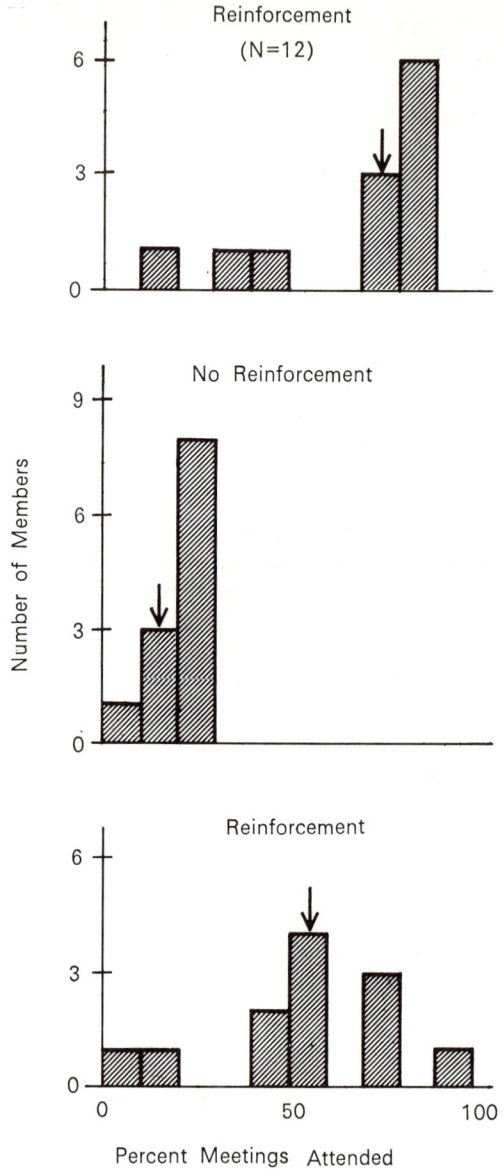

Figure 3. Percent of meetings attended by all (12) recipients who were members during these three periods. Arrows indicate mean percent of meetings attended during that condition.

more, counting all the time during which a person remained eligible from his first meeting attended, persons attended an average of 64 percent of all meetings scheduled. (During the periods of nonreinforcement, persons attended about 20 percent of all meetings.)

These data suggest that the use of supplementary reinforcement maintained a continued participation in the self-help groups among most persons who experienced the contingency.

One further question of interest is whether the involvement in one, highly structured self-help group generalizes. Do members tend to become involved in other civic activities? Unfortunately, data were kept on only one aspect of such generalization.

Figure 4 shows the number of civic groups attended by the presidents of the two self-help groups. While neither president participated in civic affairs before joining the group, they attended over ten new groups one or more times after joining. This participation included formal membership in the local O.E.O. governing board, the Model Cities Advisory Board, a citizen's advisory board, and a school integration committee. It included attendance at meetings of the city council, school board, and mayor's Youth Advisory Committee. The participation of the other members was not systematically observed, but there did seem to be some increase among them too.

DISCUSSION

The results indicate that more persons attended self-help group meetings when supplementary reinforcement was available than when it was not. The low rate when no supplementary reinforcement was scheduled, occurred whether the counselor was present (Phase 1) or absent (Phase 3). If the information and services provided by the counselor in these meetings is considered part of the supplementary reinforcement system (see Table 1), it is possible to conclude from this design that the absence of supplementary reinforcement leads to a low rate of attendance. Unfortunately the design does not definitively isolate the role of the counselor's social presence in the group meetings. Her presence in the first phase was not sufficient to maintain attendance, but possibly it would have been after a history of supplementary reinforcement. Furthermore, the presence of the counselor when supplementary reinforcement was scheduled leaves unanswered whether the attendance would continue at a high level if supplementary reinforcement could be scheduled by the group members themselves. Thus, the present experiment did not establish a procedure for developing and maintaining self-help groups unaided by outside personnel. It does clearly show that self-help groups can be aided in their formation and maintenance by a system of supplementary reinforcement delivered by a technical assistant to the group.

The present procedure did not lead to the involvement of all welfare recipients in self-help groups. In fact, strictly in terms of attendance, less than 20 percent participated in any one group meeting. However, the method was successful in maintaining the participation of most individuals who came into contact with the supplementary reinforcement. Few such individuals voluntarily dropped from the group (14 percent), while most individuals maintained a steady rate of attendance (64 percent attendance including those that dropped). Thus, the problem of generating greater involvement among all eligible recipients probably would involve devising procedures for getting them to sample the reinforcement at least once. Some extension of the reinforcement sampling procedures explored by Azrin and Ayllon (1968) might be suitable. At any rate, the present experiment seems to establish the success of the method

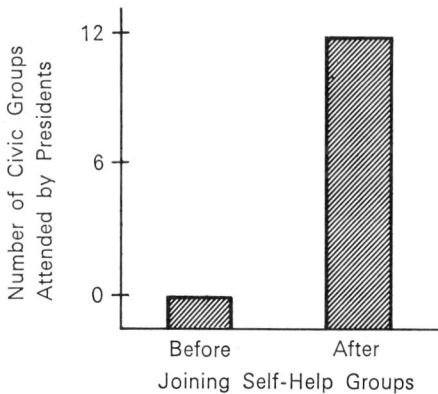

Figure 4. *Number of civic groups attended by self-help group members before and after joining.*

in maintaining attendance after that first sampling.

There is some evidence that participation in the self-help groups generalized to other forms of self-help; the attendance of the presidents at civic meetings increased from none before their membership in the self-help groups to about ten groups afterwards. Casual evidence also suggested that similar although less-pronounced increases occurred among other group members. It was also noted that an increased utilization of tutors for their children also occurred among group members. While evidence of generalization was not generated by an adequate experimental design, it is suggestive of such an effect. If such generalization does occur, it suggests that reinforcing attendance at meetings may have a kind of triggering effect leading poor persons to greater participation in controlling their own lives. Such a possibility clearly warrants further, and more careful, investigation.

Two features of the present procedures may be singled out for additional discussion: (1) the use of attendance as the target behavior; (2) the use of supplementary reinforcers.

The first major feature of the present procedure is the use of attendance as a target behavior. We see it as the first step in solving a difficult methodological problem: how to measure the success of a procedure in forming a self-help group. Previous approaches to this type of problem have relied on attitude scales and various subjective measurements (Hyman, Wright, and Hopkins, 1962) or "membership" (Clinard, 1966) which need not require participation. The use of attendance provides a directly observable approximation to "success" that can also have reinforcement contingencies applied to it. It suggests further approximations to defining a successful self-help group.

Thus, the use of attendance as a target behavior might be extended to group programs other than meetings; e.g., attendance at adult education programs, at projects that create income for the self-help groups, and at neighborhood rehabilitation projects. The attendance of a new member at one or more meetings also may be used to define recruitment, and the recruiter can be reinforced.

Thus, a simple behavior as attendance can be elaborated to a wide variety of projects within self-help groups, including even the growth of membership itself. Each added project would permit a closer approximation to a successful self-help group.

Attendance might be used as a target behavior with respect to programs outside the self-help groups as well. Thus, attendance at city council, school board, and urban renewal meetings provides a further elaboration of the success of self-help groups.

These examples suffice to suggest that attendance could be used to measure the participation of members not only in discussion meetings but also in a wide variety of projects within the self-help groups and between them and the broader community. Further, since it is an objective behavior, reinforcement contingencies could be specified to increase the attendance in these projects. Taken together, these elaborations of the present study would represent a significant approximation to community development goals within a behavior modification framework.

Further elaborations of the present work might take either or both of two directions. First, further specification of target behaviors might be undertaken when self-help group members meet together. Thus, different dimensions of attendance at group meetings might be specified, such as coming on time, paying dues, and bringing membership materials. Further specification might involve defining different roles within the meeting: taking attendance, recording dues payments and making a treasurer's statement, recording individual welfare problems on a checklist, making an agenda, recording minutes, and sending out notices of the next meeting. All of these target behaviors could be easily observed, and reinforcement criteria could be specified.

A second elaboration would involve measuring the effect of the self-help group in relation to the broader community. Thus, the effect of membership on the size of welfare benefits could be measured. The reassignment of recipients to new caseworkers, or even the termination of caseworkers could be determined. The size of the group's treasury and the size of its used-item stockpile could be additional measures. Membership in community groups such as War-on-Poverty and perhaps ultimately, the election to local office would provide further measurable criteria of the success of self-help groups.

The second major feature of the procedure is the use of supplementary reinforcers. One may think that the low-income individual lives in a subculture which displays feelings of despair, defeatism, and powerlessness (e.g., Harrington, 1962; Clinard, 1966). Consequently, community organizers sometimes emphasize the formulation of relatively minor initial goals that can be achieved immediately. This emphasis on quick success may be one way to increase the chance that the participation of the individual group member will be reinforced. The present procedure was an attempt to guarantee that members' participation would be reinforced by utilizing reinforcers that were not necessarily intrinsic to long-range group goals. These supplementary reinforcers allowed for the systematic scheduling of meaningful consequences that maintain individual participation until other naturally available reinforcers develop control. Such supplementary reinforcers may be imperative during the initial phases of an organization when it is not yet strong enough to guarantee group success.

Potential supplementary reinforcers can be readily obtained by organizers in almost any community. Such items as used clothing, furniture, appliances, and toys are readily available as donations from the more affluent members of the community who are "concerned" about poverty. Information about welfare policy regulations frequently can be obtained from a sympathetic caseworker or by accompanying a recipient to the welfare office to inspect the policy book. Other potential reinforcers such as tutoring services, free summer camp or day-camp scholarships, admission to recreational facilities, as well as arts and crafts workshops are often available without charge.

Greater flexibility in the management of supplementary reinforcers may be achieved through the use of a token system (Ayllon and Azrin, 1968). A self-help group might award a token to each member who attends a meeting. The members might then decide, for example, that a used refrigerator could be exchanged for forty tokens. Four tokens might be given to a person who brings a potential member to a meeting; five tokens might be given for attending a relevant public meeting (e.g., school board, city planning) and reporting back to the group. Such procedures would allow reinforcement contingencies to be attuned more sensitively to the needs of the group.

The use of contingency management to affect learning performance in adult institutionalized offenders

JOHN M. MCKEE

In recent years, behavioral science has made substantial contributions to problems of motivation. By providing effective tools to generate and maintain desirable behavior in many population groups, it has facilitated the efficiency of achieving objectives for guiding, teaching, or directing the work of others. One of these motivational tools is contingency management (CM). The term "CM," defined as the systematic arrangement of reinforcing consequences of behavior, is usually restricted to educational settings where the objective is to achieve increased student performance by manipulating the contingencies of reinforcement (Skinner, 1970). Homme, C'de Baca, and Cottingham (1968) restrict

Reprinted by permission of the author and the Rehabilitation Research Foundation.

This paper was presented September 1971, at a meeting of the American Psychological Association, Washington, D.C. Studies reported in this paper were supported by grants from NIMH and the U.S. Department of Labor.

the meaning of CM to managing or controlling the relationship of behavior and the consequences (reinforcing events) that follow it. According to their definition, the stimulus that controls the emission of behavior is not in the domain of CM. They illustrate the concept by the following paradigm:

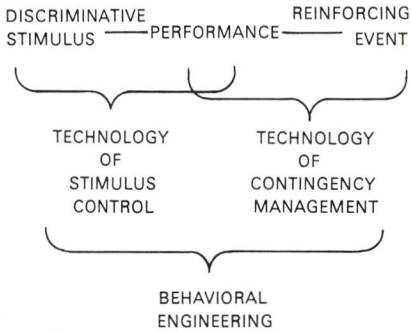

From "What Behavioral Engineering Is" by L. Homme, P. C'de Baca and L. Cottingham, *The Psychological Record, 18,* 1968. Reprinted by permission of *The Psychological Record.*

Figure 1. *Relationships between the three-term contingency and behavioral engineering.*

In actual practice, few experimenters separate stimulus control variables and deal exclusively with the right side of the operant paradigm. Such has been the case in the Draper CM studies. In fact, variables that are manipulated by the contingency manager in educational settings usually are quite complex and seldom pure or refined enough to be classified as one contingency without serving as another at the same time. For example, the contingency or performance contract is a favorite and quite useful instrument of the contingency manager. Its principal value lies in the fact that it can provide effective stimulus control over very complex behavior over a long period of time. Yet, the reinforcing consequence of contract completion puts it into the reinforcing-event category.

The purpose of this paper is to describe the development and application of CM techniques to the educational performance of a broad cross-section of adult male prison-inmates who, by most standards, are judged to

be at the lowest rung of the motivational ladder. It is a population group that has been genuinely "turned off" by public education which always has dealt them constant failure and rebuff, resulting in a mutual hostility and an avoidance of contact.

This same group of men have failed in more than education: They have failed in every major undertaking of their lives, including crime! As a success-deprived group, they have sought reinforcers in areas where they have been punished, including education, relationships with authority figures, and family relations. Needless to say, the typical prison has provided few opportunities to gain these reinforcers.

DRAPER EXPERIMENTAL PROJECTS BEGIN

Draper experimental and demonstration projects began in 1961. The focus was on providing quick and easy success in basic education through the use of programmed instruction (PI). Through a grant from NIMH in 1962, a "self-instructional school" was established in which PI materials comprised 95 percent of the curriculum. Reinforcers used to maintain learning behavior were largely social-staff approval, inspirational talks, visitors from the "free world," and student success.

Experience with PI soon generated questions on how to modify the operation of the self-instructional school. Two basic questions evolved: (1) How to more effectively tailor PI to meet individual deficiencies and (2) how to generate high levels of student performance. Response to the first of these needs resulted in the creation of an Individually Prescribed Instructional (IPI) System. The second need led to the development of effective contingency-management procedures.

One of the five major operations within the IPI System for basic education is managing the contingencies of reinforcement. Other key operations in the system are: establishing learning objectives, diagnosing the learner's relevant entry skills, prescribing modules of materials in the sequence the learner needs to attain his objectives or to remedy his deficiencies, and evaluating the learner's progress. After the student's learning objectives have been established, his deficiencies have been diagnosed, and his prescription has been developed, the student begins his assignments in weekly segments. As many segments or units are listed on the prescription as are required to bring the student up to a desired grade-average in all areas shown on a standardized achievement test. Each segment of work consists of what a student can be expected to accomplish in a given period of time. This unit of work is put into the form of a "contingency contract" which the student is expected to complete before the end of the week. If he finishes sooner than the estimated number of hours, he can accept another contract. The contingency contract requires a progress test for each module, and the student must score 85 percent or better on all module tests. Scores below 85 percent necessitate the assignment to an alternate module and its corresponding test. CM procedures used within the IPI System at Draper have been quite effective as a means of increasing efficiency in learning basic-education skills.

EXPERIMENTAL MANPOWER LABORATORY FOR CORRECTIONS

At Draper in 1968, the Department of Labor established an Experimental Manpower Laboratory for Corrections (EMLC) operated by the Foundation. The purpose of the lab is to conduct long-range research studies in correctional rehabilitation as it pertains to training prisoners for jobs, getting them employment, and keeping them in jobs. To accomplish these objectives, the lab does research on a wide range of problems. In addition, the lab seeks to perfect certain training systems in both basic education and vocational training. Developing an effective learning-model demands that considerable effort be spent on motivational research, with the point being that efficiency in learning is in high demand for prison inmates who must quickly make up educational time in order to compete effectively in the job market.

DRAPER STUDIES IN CONTINGENCY MANAGEMENT

Clark's Study (1966)

The first CM experiment at Draper was conducted by Hewitt Clark. He selected two inmate-subjects and attempted to increase their educational performance. Using a "reinforcing event menu" (Homme, 1966) listing high probability behaviors (Premack, 1965), Clark demonstrated that inmate-learners substantially increased their performance over their baseline measurements. Both Ss more than doubled their frame (PI) output during the CM phase, as compared to baseline performance (see Figures 2 and 3). Although significantly more tests were taken, test scores did not drop during the increased-performance period.

Clements and McKee (1968)

This study was designed in three phases. Sixteen volunteers ranging in age from 17 to 35 years served as subjects. Academic achievement level of the subjects varied from 7 to 12 grades. The environment for the study included a learning area and a reinforcing-event (RE) area in separate rooms. Phase I was a 3-week baseline period during which quantity and quality baseline measures of academic "productivity" were established.

In Phase II, the contingencies of reinforcement were managed by the experimenter. During each of the 14 weeks of this phase, a performance contract was used which specified the subject's daily output at approximately 20 percent greater than his average daily output during the immediately preceding week; such increases previously were agreed to by each subject. Upon completing a specified segment of work (e.g., a number of frames), the subject was allowed a 15-minute RE period. In Phase III, a 2-week self-management phase, each subject specified the amount of work he would do each day, the only limitation being that he contract for an output equal to or greater than his daily average under baseline conditions. During

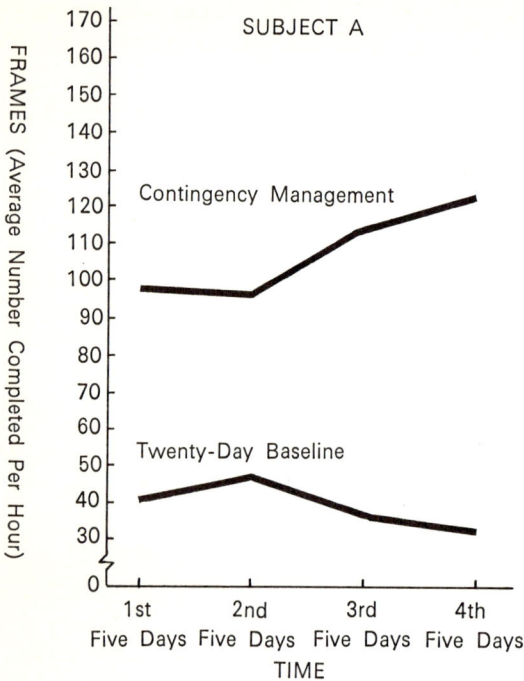

Figure 2. *Comparison of performance during baseline and contingency-management conditions.*

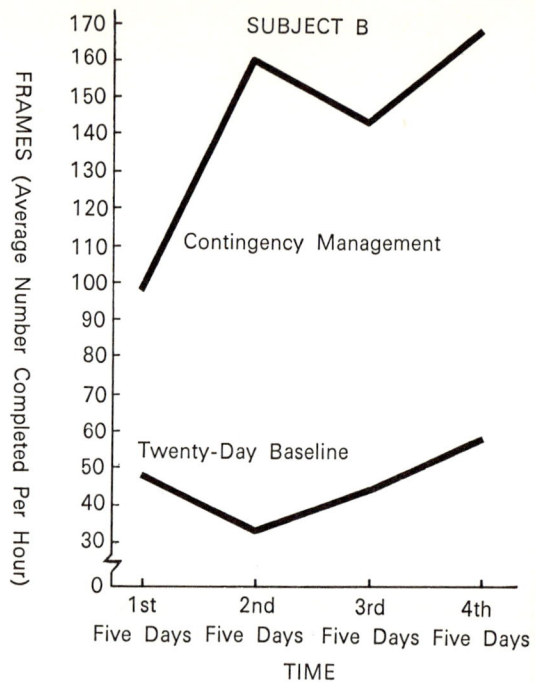

Figure 3. *Comparison of performance during baseline and contingency-management conditions.*

Table 1. *Summary of performance over six weeks.*

	Baseline (Phase 1)	E-management (Phase 2)				Self-management (Phase 3)	
	(3-wk. average)	1	2	3	4	5	6
Hours per day per man*	5.3	4.7	4.4	4.5	3.8	3.5	3.3
Frames per hour	61	77	92	102	134	125	126
Percent tests passed	71	70	88	70	90	81	85
Number of Ss	16	16	16	16	14†	13‡	13

* Includes RE periods, testing, reviews, etc.; 6 Ss were half-day students (A.M. or P.M. only.).
† One S dropped by request; one S released from prison.
‡ One S dropped by request.

From "Programmed instruction for institutionalized offenders: contingency management and performance contracts" by C. B. Clements and J. M. McKee from **Psychological Reports,** 1968, **22,** 957–964. Reprinted by permission of the authors and **Psychological Reports.**

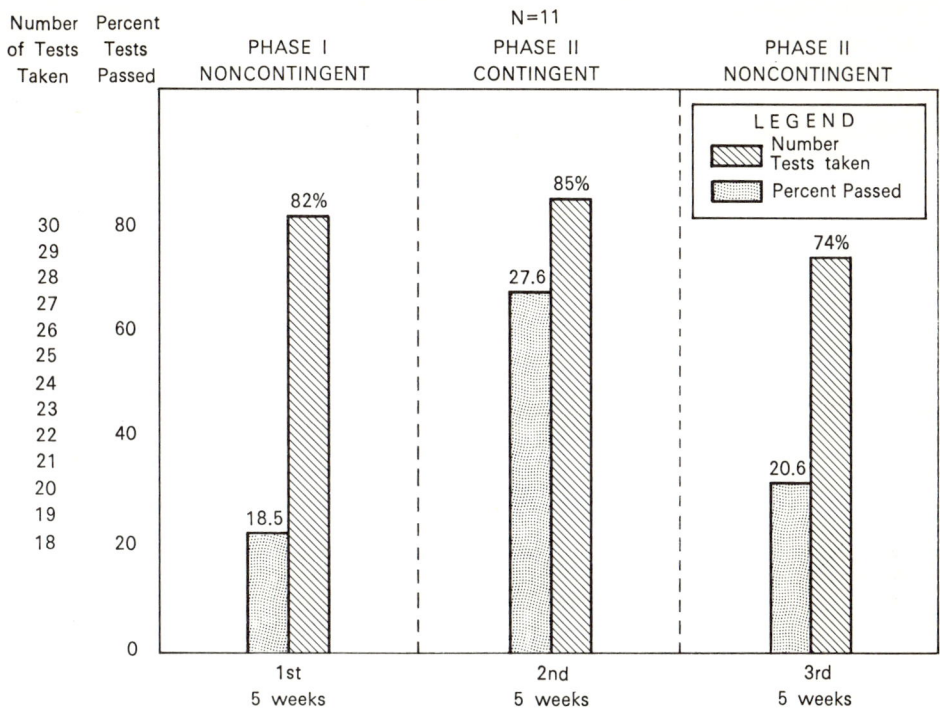

Number of Tests Taken	Percent Tests Passed	PHASE I NONCONTINGENT	PHASE II CONTINGENT	PHASE II NONCONTINGENT

LEGEND
Number Tests taken
Percent Passed

82%   85%
                        74%

18.5   27.6   20.6

1st 5 weeks   2nd 5 weeks   3rd 5 weeks

Figure 4. *Number of tests and percentage passed by phases for all Ss.*

all phases of the study, subjects were required to pass final exams on each programmed course before they could continue with new material.

Table 1 summarizes the performance over the 6 weeks of the experimental phases of the study. The increase for the last 3 weeks of Phase II averaged about 14 percent in frames per hour, but the increase in test-taking resulting from the increase in number of frames brought the task-oriented activity approximately to the proposed 20 percent increase. Though the frames-per-hour decreased from the experimenter-managed phase to the self-managed phase, the subjects' productivity remained well above the established minimum. The results supported the hypothesis that contingency-management techniques increased the productivity levels of offenders studying programmed materials. Additionally, subjects managed their own learning behavior. The implication that more was learned per unit of time was further supported by the superiority of test results during the ex-

perimental phases: an increase in the quantity without sacrificing quality.

Enslen's Study (1969)

Visible daily progress charts and monetary rewards for increased work were used in an attempt to increase the productivity of 11 prison inmates who studied programmed instruction. Each subject in the experiment agreed to accurately fill out his individual progress chart at the end of each day. All test scores were recorded, and completed units were represented by coloring a portion of a bar graph. Small amounts of money were awarded to those students who continued to perform outstanding work over a prolonged period. During the period in which the charts were used and the money was presented, there was a marked increase in the academic progress and output of the subjects as compared to both the baseline phase and post-chart phase.

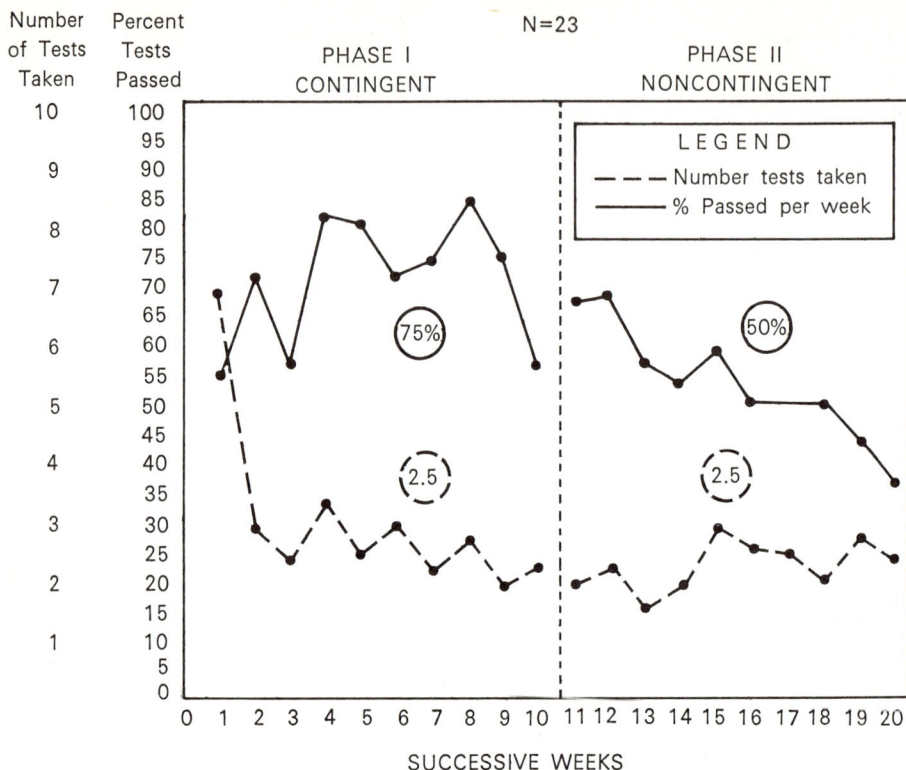

Figure 5. *Number of tests taken and percentage passed per week for all Ss.*

During the CM phase, there was a slight increase in the number of tests passed, but a substantial increase in number of tests taken (see Figure 4). This merely reflects the fact that the subject covered a great deal more PI material in the same period of time. During the 15 weeks of the experiment, the average grade level increased from 7.1 to 8.9 for the 11 Ss, an average gain of 1.8 grades for each subject.

Jenkins, McKee, Jordan, and Newmark (1969)

Another study, seeking to determine the relationship between learning performance and contingent money payments, addressed itself to the question of whether removal of a strong reinforcer contingent upon a student's behavior resulted in a decrease in desired performance levels. Twenty-three trainees in Draper's MDT program were subjects of this 20-week experiment. In Phase I of the experiment, money payments were contingent upon the trainees' learning performance as measured by: (1) number of tests taken and (2) percentage of tests passed. Trainees received $10 each week for satisfactory performance and were penalized at a rate not exceeding $2 per day for unsatisfactory performance. During Phase II, the last ten weeks, money payments were not contingent upon learning performance. Money payments were continued at the $10-per-week rate as in Phase I, whether performance was satisfactory or not.

Results indicated that 21 of the 23 Ss did not perform as well when money payments were no longer contingent upon their performance. The percentage of tests passed dropped markedly in Phase II, while the number of tests taken did not change (see Figure 5).

Recent Studies

The effect of CM procedures on the rate of learning (McKee, 1971). Few, if any studies have been conducted to determine the relationship between certain well-accepted learning variables as they interact with CM conditions. Therefore, it was important to study the interactions of learning rates, academic achievement scores, and IQ under controls afforded by PI and the procedures of CM.

Subjects included not only forty prison inmates from Draper but also 21 freshmen nursing students from Tuskegee Institute in Alabama who scored below the admission cut-off score on entrance tests and would not have been allowed to enter the nursing school were it not for a new academic upgrading. The initial mean grade-level achievement score for the prison inmates was 7.8; for the nurses, it was 10.5. For both groups the IPI System provided the stimulus materials and the process for obtaining the learning rates of the subjects.

The study compared the actual times which students took to complete the various modules with predetermined estimated times, allowing for a cumulative record of individual learning rates. Learning rates were analyzed to find out their relationships to initial reading level, initial grade level, final grade level, grade level change, and IQ.

Data collected from this study indicated a number of interesting and noteworthy conclusions. Analysis showed that grade-level change does not correlate even moderately with other measures (i.e., initial reading level, initial grade level, etc.). The extent to which a student changed his grade level appeared independent of initial as well as terminal grade levels. This finding was consistent in both the prison inmate group and the nursing student group. Perhaps the most significant outcome of this study was that of obtaining stable rates of learning in academic subject matter over a relatively long period of time. Motivation, provided by contingency-management procedures, was maintained at a consistent, if not optimum, level.

The arrangements and conditions of the study permitted reliable and valid correlation of learning rates with certain measures traditionally thought to be functionally related. For example, IQ, reading skill, and academic achievement are measures commonly believed to have a significant influence upon learning rate. But, it is interesting to note that two quite different samples—prisoners and college students—yielded similar results; according to the data, there is little cause-and-effect relationship in the idea that IQ is a cause of slow learning.

Figure 6 depicts three representative examples of high, medium, and low prison learners, as shown by cumulative records for three prison inmates. Both samples of prison and nursing-student subjects were distributed fairly evenly among the three groups, though the nursing students generally showed higher learning rates. Interesting, too, was the finding that stable learning rates were exhibited by all learners, with the exception of 3 *S*s, who showed an occasional acceleration or deceleration in their cumulative records.

OTHER RELEVANT DATA

CM procedures were also applied to vocational training at Draper in the MDT project. Courses in welding, refrigeration repair, barbering, and butchering were broken down into small tasks (modules) and time required for their completion was empirically derived from trainees going through the course. Then large segments of study were made self-instructional, and contracts were written with point value for completion of the modules to a specified criterion. The back-up reinforcer for these points was money.

The results of this individualizing shop training were twofold. First, trainees proceeded at their own rate through self-instructional modules, permitting an open-entry/open-exit training program. Second, trainees finished all required work without sacrifice of training quality much sooner than anticipated. The result was that the MDT project trained 30 percent more trainees than expected. A new project is scheduled to start at Draper, and the lab proposes to train 52

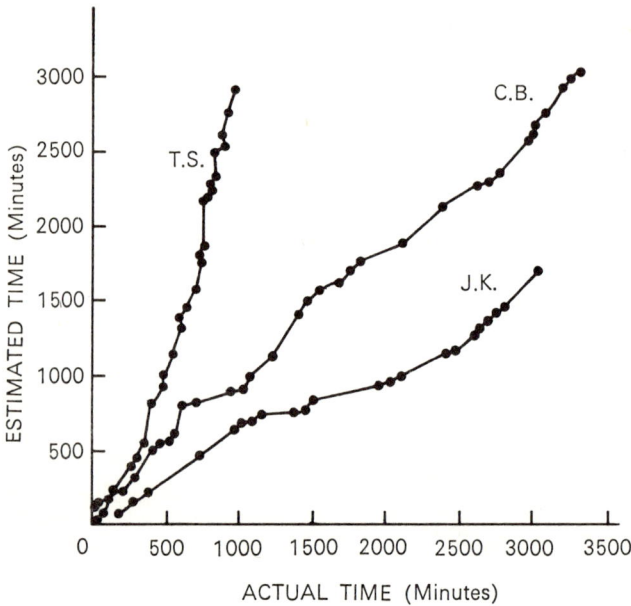

Figure 6. *Cumulative record of estimated and actual times by modules (representative records of three prison inmates).*

percent more students than the present program.

SPECIFIC CM TECHNIQUES EMPLOYED BY THE DRAPER PROJECT

The contingency-management materials and techniques that have been successfully employed by the Draper projects fall into two categories: the contingency or performance contract and progress plotters. The contract, aside from apparently being an effective stimulus control, permits the manager to administer points contingent upon contract performance and completion. These points usually have a "cash-in" value (back-up reinforcers) of either money, other tangible reinforcers, or privileges. Figures 7 and 8 are examples of CM devices and forms that are employed by the Draper MDT Project. Each is self-explanatory.

IMPACT

The studies presented in this paper sought to answer two important questions. The first is a theoretical one: Does the systematic arrangement of positive consequences for educational behavior (CM) significantly increase *S*'s performance? The second question is quite important from the standpoint of public policy: If the answer to the first question is positive, what implications does it hold for the awarding of "incentive allowances" to trainees in prison Manpower Development and Training programs? At present, prisoners receiving manpower training are paid allowances on a time-contingent basis. The results of the studies cited in this paper clearly show that performance-contingent pay to trainees is significantly superior in getting efficient and effective learning in both basic education and vocational programs.

EFFICIENCY QUOTIENT

Name of trainee: _____

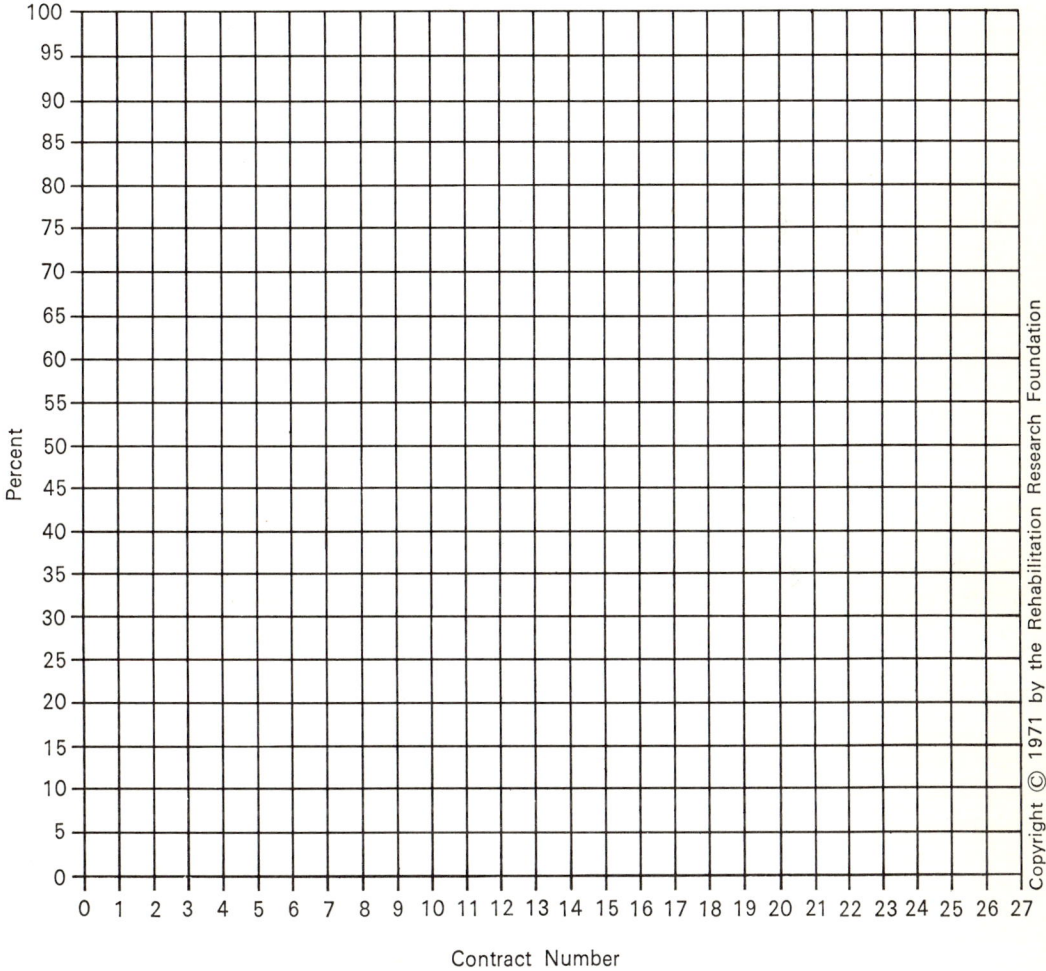

$$\text{Efficiency Quotient} = \frac{\text{Test Passed}}{\text{Test Taken}} \times 100$$

Figure 7.

POINT BANK ACCOUNT

Name: _____

Contract No.	Date	Points Earned	Points Used	Net	Total Accumulated

Figure 8.

Universal parenthood-training:
A proposal for preventive mental health

ROBERT P. HAWKINS

The perpetuation of a civilization depends on the younger generation's learning from the older generation. The new generation learns to behave in much the same way as did the old though not identically; otherwise cultural evolution would not occur. If a human infant is reared by Samoans, he behaves like a Samoan. If the infant is reared by Swedes, he behaves likes a Swede. This fact is made particularly evident when a human infant is reared by a nonhuman species and is then discovered and observed by humans (e.g., Itard, 1962). The human so reared behaves like a member of the species that reared it.

In the more complex cultures extant today the primary responsibility for child-rearing rests with two institutions—the home and the school. Of these two, the home probably has the most profound effect, at least in our society. The school is assigned more limited and specific teaching responsibilities than the home and is given a rather well-prescribed period of time in which to accomplish its assignment, namely approximately five hours per day, five days per week, 180 days per year for twelve years. The child spends most of his time at home, and the major portion of the task of developing responsible, productive, creative, moral, well-adjusted members of our society falls upon the home, which really means upon the parents. In fact, many of the behavior patterns that most profoundly affect the nature of adult-citizen patterns are laid down in the first five years of his life, before the school has any contact with him.

The Adequacy of Present Child-Rearing Practices

What kind of learning experiences, planned and unplanned, does a child receive while in the charge of his parents? Although there has been limited systematic study of the actual experiences children have in their home and neighborhood environments (such as Barker and Wright, 1949), it is possible to see what effects those environments have by looking at the behavioral characteristics of young children entering school. What one finds is that a distressing number of children have serious behavioral problems. For example, many children have disabling language deficits, lack certain conceptual behaviors essential in learning to read, are disinterested in learning academic kinds of skill, suffer anxiety when faced with any challenging task, are uncooperative and disobedient, or have little ability to get along with peers. These problems reduce the school's effectiveness in achieving its educational goals for the child and can even result in the school's having a detrimental rather than a favorable effect on the child.[1] They are likely to reduce the child's positive contribution to his society and the pleasure he gets from life in his society.

If one looks beyond the age of four or five, when the effects of home, school, and community experiences on the individual are combined, the data are even more distressing. According to the Task Force on Juvenile Delinquency (1967) one in every nine children will be referred to the courts by age eighteen. The report also estimates 10 percent (Eisenberg, 1961) to 33 percent (Co-

Adapted from "Universal Parenthood Training: A Proposal for Preventive Mental Health," by Robert P. Hawkins, *Educational Technology*, 1971, *11*(2), 28–35. Reprinted by permission of *Educational Technology Magazine*.

1 Elsewhere (Glasser, 1969; Leonard, 1968) it has been pointed out that the typical school environment itself is responsible for many of the difficulties children have in adjusting to school. It is said that the school has unrealistic structure, expectations, and methods in terms of its "livability" for children (even more, perhaps, for adults) and its effectiveness in achieving educational goals. The author's experience with "emotionally disturbed" children in schools has suggested that, in general, these conclusions are correct. Nevertheless, present-day school-life is only one of several difficult realities children must learn to cope with if they are to lead happy, constructive lives, and the home is in a favorable position to prepare them for many of these realities.

wen, Izzo, Mites, Telschow, Frost, and Zax, 1963) of the persons in our society are in need of psychological help. Although responsibility for this large number of maladjusted individuals cannot be placed solely on parents, it is probably fair to blame the home for a significant portion of the problem, because the home appears to determine the basic foundation for each individual's adjustment. It would seem reasonable to conclude that a large segment of American parents currently are failing in their responsibility to their offspring, to society, and to themselves.

Various programs and institutions are established to help parents become more effective in their child-rearing. Most of these are primarily remedial in nature (or at least intended to be remedial) rather than preventive. Child-guidance clinics, juvenile courts, family-service clinics, and other agencies devote considerable effort to helping parents correct problems of child behavior which the parents themselves create.[2] These and other similar agencies—such as the juvenile correction home, many special education programs, and Headstart programs—attempt to work directly with the child to remedy behavioral excesses and deficits created by inappropriate or inadequate learning in the home. All such remedial efforts are of limited effectiveness. A program oriented toward prevention would be more humane and less costly. It also could have the effect of preventing many of the minor behavioral problems that now do not come to the attention of remedial programs, but that still reduce the individual's satisfaction and productivity in life.

A preventive program might take one of three approaches. First, it might supplement the work of the parents. This approach is exemplified by the "Sesame Street" television series, which provides learning experiences for very young children who otherwise might not have comparable experiences. Such an approach seems very promising and practical; but it is likely to be limited in the kinds of behavior (skills, attitudes, concepts, etc.) it can teach, because it cannot reach children under age two, and it can provide only a two-dimensional visual and auditory experience of a nonindividualized nature. In addition, this type of televised appproach is more

appropriate for teaching new behavior than it is for correcting inappropriate behavior the child has already learned. Some of these limitations can be overcome by another form of supplementary approach that holds promise—the day-care program for very young children.

A second preventive approach is to place the task of all child-rearing in the hands of the better-qualified ("expert" may be too limiting a term) persons in the society. The Israeli practice of having certain members of a kibbutz do the child-rearing may be an example of such an approach.

A third approach would be to leave the responsibility of child-rearing with the parents, but take measures to assure that virtually all parents have the necessary skills and knowledge to do the job well. This is the approach that is suggested and discussed here; however, some combination of these three approaches may be possible.

Characteristics of a Preventive Program

Ideally, a preventive program oriented toward assuring the adequacy of parents' child-rearing skills and knowledge should reach every parent. It is difficult to know in advance which parents are going to do an inadequate job of child-rearing and, therefore, will have the greatest need for the preventive program. The ideal time to reach the parents would be early in their child's life or even before the child is born. The former may not be feasible, because there is no existing institution or program that has ready access to every parent of a newborn child and the ability to implement a program of training in child-rearing.[3] However, there is an existing institution that has access to virtually every person who will become a parent and has the ability to provide training. This institution is the school. Virtually every person

2 For a brief discussion of certain limitations in the approaches practiced by such clinics, and presentation of alternatives, see Hawkins, Peterson, Schweid, and Bijou (1966) and Ullmann and Krasner (1969).
3 The medical profession has access to nearly every parent but could not carry out adequate training.

who will be a father or mother attends school. In addition, the school already is recognized as an appropriate institution for education of this kind. If a widespread program is to be implemented, that would improve child-rearing and prevent the development of behavior patterns which interfere with a child's educability and general life-adjustment, a logical place for implementing it is in the education of parents-to-be.

Our schools already offer training in other "living skills" (as opposed to traditional academic skills). Young people are taught how to drive cars. Many of the boys are taught about shop tools and acquire some skill in using them. Many of the girls learn certain homemaking skills, such as sewing, shopping, cooking, and budgeting. Are any of these areas of knowledge and skill more important to our society than child-rearing? Certainly none of those areas of activity has as profound an influence on the nature of individuals within a society, the nature of the society as a whole, or the quality of life in that society as does the work of child-rearing. Even the commonly required courses in algebra, history, and English pale in value when compared with the potential value of training in child-rearing; yet child-rearing is not taught in our schools today.

Some educators will disagree. Some will say that a part of their high-school or junior high school course in homemaking is devoted to child-rearing or perhaps that they even have a whole course in child-rearing. There are two defects in such a defense of present curricula. First, though the great majority of youngsters will become parents, only girls typically take any course work in homemaking. Second, and much more important, the courses that do offer some content related to child-rearing only teach the student something (usually very little) *about* child-rearing; they do not teach the student *how* to rear children. The homemaking course may offer a sketchy description of the typical physical development expected of a child and an even more sketchy description of the typical behavioral development. There may even be a few vague guidelines offered about kinds of attitudes or techniques that are desirable or undesirable in child-rearing. While all of this content is relevant for child-rearing, it probably has little effect on the actual child-rearing behaviors of the students when they become parents. Certainly whatever effect it does have is unknown, for the educator never has the opportunity to observe the child-rearing behaviors of the students. All the educator observes is the verbal behavior of the student in the form of oral or written discussion or recitation.

An educator who wishes to produce certain complex behavior patterns in his student —such as algebra-problem solving, creative writing, cabinetmaking, automobile-driving, or child-rearing—must, ideally, meet at least three requirements. First, he must observe the actual behavior he wishes to produce, not some assumed verbal representation of that behavior. Second, the educator must observe the behavior in the actual setting where he hopes it will occur or in a setting closely resembling that one. Third, he must arrange for effective feedback to the student, so that appropriate behaviors are strengthened and inappropriate behaviors are weakened. These requirements are met adequately in driver education courses, for example, where the student does not just learn about cars, but actually is required to drive a real car on streets where many of the problems of driving occur naturally. His driving behavior in this realistic setting is observed, and appropriate consequences and cues are applied to improve performance to an acceptable level.

When these requirements are applied to the problem of teaching young people how to rear children, it means that the educator must see the student engage in child-rearing behaviors with real children and with child-rearing tasks resembling those faced by a parent. Doubtless there are many ways in which this problem can be solved, but one solution that appears particularly promising is to have a nursery school or day-care center as an integral part of every high school or junior high school.

The nursery school would serve as a laboratory in which every student would carry out certain exercises in working with children. This laboratory experience would be coordinated with reading, classroom discussion, and such activities as taking field trips, doing role-playing, and viewing films. Together the classroom and laboratory work would constitute a one-year course in child-rearing that would be required of every student, male or female. Thus every person who becomes a parent would have training, and even those who did not become parents would be better members of society because of their appreciation for children and parents.

The Nature of a Course in Child-Rearing

What should be the content of this course in child-rearing? Probably the content should cover at least three general areas characterized by the following three questions: What behavioral and physical development is it reasonable to expect of a child; what behavior (including traits, attitudes, knowledge, skills, and habits) should I develop in the child I am likely to have someday; and how can I develop these behaviors in my child?

To answer the question of how children typically develop, the student might be taught the usual progression or "stages" of physical and behavioral development that are commonly part of any course in child development. They should also learn about some of the kinds and degrees of deviation from these norms, perhaps through visits to programs serving various kinds of exceptional children.

To answer the question regarding what behavior should be developed in children, the teacher might provide reading on the opinions of a few experts and engage the students in open discussion of these and their own opinions. Ginott's (1969) popular paperback would be one appropriate reading, for it would introduce the student to some of the mental-health values that have evolved over the past century of clinical work with behaviorally disturbed individuals.[4] The group discussions would expose some basic values of the students and therefore would be rather emotional; but they would have the advantages of teaching the students to make child-rearing decisions consciously and rationally, rather than "by default," and of pointing out some of the long-term implications of certain

decisions. A beneficial by-product of the discussions would be the student's increased awareness and acceptance of values different from his own.

The question regarding how to develop the desired behavior patterns could be approached through a combination of reading, demonstration, and directly monitored laboratory experience with children. Probably the most valuable reading would cover the newly developing technology of teaching (see Skinner, 1968) and its application to problems in child-rearing (Harris, Wolf, and Baer, 1964; Hawkins, Peterson, Schweid, and Bijou, 1966; Allen and Harris, 1966; Hall and Broden, 1967). This technology is based on several decades of basic and applied scientific research about how behavior is established, strengthened, maintained, and weakened; and it has been demonstrated repeatedly that parents can learn and effectively utilize these principles in solving some common problems of child behavior (Wahler, Winkel, Peterson, and Morrison, 1965; Zeilberger, Sampen, and Sloane, 1968; Wahler and Erickson, 1969; Salzinger, Feldman, and Portnoy, 1970). No text available yet is designed specifically for high-school use, but Patterson and Gullion (1968), McIntire (1970), and Becker (1971) have written books for parents that deal with both theory and practice in a readable meaningful fashion.

Demonstrations might illustrate a basic teaching technique such as the fading of prompts, a particular method of teaching some skill such as counting, or a particular pattern of child behavior such as sound substitutions in the speech of three-year-olds. Another valuable demonstration would be videotapes or movies depicting desirable and undesirable parent behaviors. For example, a movie might depict a behaviorally disturbed child and his parents interacting, so that the student could see some of the ways in which parents inadvertently maintain maladaptive behavior. Another film could show a parent

---

4 Besides presenting this information about what behavior is desirable, the book also contains much wisdom regarding how to produce or avoid producing certain behavior patterns. The prescriptions derived from theories based on clinical experience would have to be evaluated in the light of more scientifically sound principles of behavior.

playing affectionately with a child or responding to vocalizations of an infant.

The laboratory aspect of the proposed course in child-rearing would take place in the nursery school or day-care center, where the course instructor and nursery-school teaching staff (not necessarily different individuals) would closely observe and supervise the student. In the laboratory the student would progress through a series of exercises designed to teach him to provide an environment conducive to the learning of healthy, socially constructive behaviors by his future child. The first exercise might be designed to teach the student some degree of facility at specifying and systematically observing behavior, as is illustrated in Patterson and Gullion (1968), Harris, Wolf, and Baer (1964), and Hall (1971). This is desirable because one of the first difficulties parents typically have in modifying any behavior pattern is in precisely identifying and describing the behavior and its severity. The next exercise could have the student develop a relationship with a child in which the student's attention and approval would be effective social reinforcers, and then their effectiveness could be demonstrated experimentally. Other exercises could involve extinction, punishment, discrimination-training, prompting, fading, shaping, and modeling. These basic behavior-control teaching techniques need not be learned separately but could be used in the context of teaching various desirable behaviors to the child, such as attentiveness, appropriate independence, intellectual curiosity, color-naming (and other concepts), language facility, and sociability. The emphasis of the laboratory experience would be on the students' learning to be personal and genuine, implement mental-health values, identify behavioral deficits and excesses, invent solutions to problems, indirectly promote learning by structuring situations where it is likely to occur, and directly promote learning by actively teaching the child.

Through close monitoring and supervision by the teachers, the student would receive frequent feedback about his performance and help in improving that performance. Obviously the nursery-school teachers would be trained in the application of behavioral principles as well as in the traditional aspects of nursery-school teaching.

It should be recognized that the proposed course in child-rearing might not prepare the students adequately for that portion of their parenthood when their child would be younger or older than the nursery-school child. If so, an infant day-care center could be added to the program, and arrangements could be made for the students to work with elementary-school children. These are logistical problems and certainly not overwhelming.

Universal Parenthood-Training— Now

Perhaps in a very primitive society the physical ability to reproduce was highly correlated with fitness for parenthood. Today this is not true, as will be attested by any child-guidance clinic staff member, juvenile-court judge, mental-hospital staff member, psychiatrist, teacher of the retarded, prison psychologist, pediatrician, or school principal. The number of grossly detrimental practices engaged in by parents, out of ignorance or misunderstanding, is tragic indeed. The cost in both human suffering and money is too great to allow us to continue ignoring the critical nature of the role played by parents in our society.

Parenthood-training is of such high priority that it is difficult to imagine an existing high-school course that could compare. Certainly many of the present school requirements are of very questionable relevance for a majority of the students. Among these are algebra, English grammar, and geometry. In addition, many other courses could be greatly abbreviated with very little loss to a majority of the students. By reducing or eliminating some of the less relevant (or less effective) course content, schools could make room in their curricula for the study of how to be a parent.

Admittedly the complexity of skills and knowledge involved in child-rearing is great, and it is not a traditional academic subject. But we now know enough about what kinds of behavior a parent should develop in his child and enough about the technology by which that behavior can be developed to begin to offer relevant and effective training in child-rearing.[5] If the schools are truly committed to preparing students for living in and contributing positively to our culture, there is no training that could be more relevant for the individual or the culture than training in parenthood.

5 As careful, scientific study of the effects of various parent behaviors progresses, it also may become feasible to begin certifying persons suitable for parenthood. By testing, in real-life situations, an applicant's behavior toward children of various ages and under various conditions, it should be possible to make very accurate predictions about his aptitude as a parent. Because of its profound ramifications, such a certification program would have to be developed very cautiously and with a wide spectrum of the society participating in the design and monitoring of the program.

8

IN SPECIAL EDUCATION

During the past twenty years or so, special education has come into its own. Special schools and classrooms have proliferated, and budgets have increased. Before special education facilities were available, problems such as "hyperactivity," "acting-out," and "dyslexia" were handled by the classroom teacher who often was poorly equipped to handle such problems. Special classrooms probably were regarded as a godsend. But, although they have made the work of many teachers easier, special education programs, on the average, have done little to improve the performance of the children they serve. Unfortunately, special education programs also consume large amounts of money that would be better spent on preventive programs.

A new approach to special education is described in the first paper in this section by Maryanne Q. Brown, a school psychologist. This approach tries to train teachers to deal with special education problems within their own classrooms. Brown describes some of the problems she encountered in instituting such an approach in a public school.

Even with good techniques, teachers find themselves unable to handle some children. These children are sent to special education classrooms; however, the aim should be to return the children as soon as possible to regular classrooms. This is the approach taken by the second paper presented in this section, by Hawkins. Hawkins' School Adjustment Program works with the teacher and obtains an objective description of the behaviors that make the child unacceptable in the regular classroom. In addition to specified nonacademic behavioral difficulties, the program concentrates on academic behaviors. The child in the special classroom lacks behaviors appropriate to an academic setting; many of his emotional and social problems may stem from inappropriate academic behavior. If the child is to ultimately function in a normal classroom, he must acquire new academic behaviors that will enable him to do so. Hawkins also describes the application of many basic techniques of behavior modification in the special education setting, including social reinforcement, token reinforcement, data-taking, and time-out.

Many of the children in special education programs have marked handicaps involving retardation or physical disabilities. Most of these children permanently require prosthetic environments. The approach taken in this section does not apply to them but rather to the special education problems encountered by most classroom teachers. Hopefully the approaches described here will not only be effective in helping problem children, but will also help divert resources to the ultimate answer to special education problems: prevention.

Nonreinforcement for teachers: Penalties for success

MARYANNE Q. BROWN

During this past year I worked in a school which housed all of the kindergarten and pre-kindergarten classes in the district, thirty-two to be exact. This school was staffed exclusively by experienced kindergarten teachers and was administered by a principal who had taught kindergarten for at least thirty years prior to her promotion to principal of the school. The teachers and administration operated within a framework that survived successfully with little change for many years. They viewed many of the children's problems and difficulties as stemming from difficulties within the children themselves, such as less-than-average ability, lack of motivation, and temperamental predisposition to mischief; another explanation used was poor parental-handling resulting from ignorance or permissiveness. Because the teachers saw the school psychologist as an outside agent who could either change the child, obtain help for the child, or remove the child from the classroom, I was quickly deluged with new referrals. Statements familiar to all school psychologists accompanied the referrals: "This child needs to be in a special class," or "if only the child's parents would take him for therapy. . . ." Both teachers and administrators approached behavior problems by focusing on the child and asking for some modification in his behavior or removal from the classroom, rather than considering a change in the system or routines within the classroom.

As a believer in learning theory, I viewed many of the problems displayed by the children as the logical outcome of some of the classroom practices. I was eager to demonstrate to the teachers that if they would change their timing or some of their methods they could produce the change in the child they desired, but the teachers were not very receptive.

Most of us feel threatened by new techniques and need to develop a sense of confidence with them before we can use them effectively. Teachers are no exception to this phenomenon. These teachers with many years of experience tended to feel most comfortable when operating within their familiar framework and were resistive to any suggestion of change. For example, early in the year one teacher experienced difficulty in keeping a little boy contained in her classroom. He repeatedly ran out of the room and then dared her to chase him. The chases usually resulted in several adults attempting to corner the child and tricking him or coercing him to return to the classroom—a most unsatisfactory solution to the problem and highly reinforcing to the child. In discussion of alternate ways of handling the situation, I suggested that the teacher should try to close her classroom door which was always left open. To this she replied that closing the door would be impossible since it would create a fire hazard, and she added that she didn't see why I didn't remove him from her class as former psychologists had with similar children who were "emotionally disturbed."

From the *Journal of School Psychology*, 1972 *10*(1). Reprinted by permission of the author and Behavioral Publications, Inc.

Presented at the annual meeting of the American Psychological Association, Washington, D.C., September 3, 1971.

In order to appear to be a "real" school psychologist in the eyes of these teachers, I found that before introducing any change, it was necessary to remove some of the most difficult children and to refer others for outside help. In the interim I waited for an opportunity to convince at least one of the teachers to try new methods, in the hope that if she were successful, others would be willing to emulate her. The time finally came when one of the teachers, Mrs. Smith, agreed to work with an acting-out boy, because his parents also agreed to cooperate. The teacher was to monitor his behavior at regular time-intervals during the day, and for each fifteen-minute period that he managed to conform to the classroom rules, Rodney was to receive a star on his chart. Each day the chart was to be sent home to the parents who were to reward him accordingly. As luck would have it, the teacher was absent several days during the next two weeks. This resulted in intermittent reinforcement of the bad behavior by a series of substitutes who had no interest in the program. It also confused the parents who did not understand why they did not receive information on a daily basis. By the end of two weeks there was no change in Rodney's behavior, and the teacher was discouraged and tired of the daily reports. I encouraged her to persevere with the program by making daily visits to her classroom and trying to reinforce her with praise. Finally, after almost one month, the child's behavior began to show dramatic improvement. The teacher showed considerable pride in her success and was able to continue to work with him alone. Unfortunately, during the period when no improvement was shown, the program was discussed in the lunchroom, and many of the teachers were convinced that it was not a good method. When success came, they decided it was a "fluke"—and I was back where I began.

As the school year progressed, a mounting number of children with behavior problems, which the teachers were unwilling or unable to deal with, were referred. Time and again, referral to a special class seemed to be the only viable solution to the problem. I knew I must be doing something wrong. Since, in changing the child's class I was able to select

the new teacher, the next time we had a serious problem I convinced Mrs. Smith that she could help the child by using the same behavior modification techniques that were so successful with Rodney. She accepted the child, an acting-out foster child who liked to set fires at home and at school. In a few weeks, with help from me and behavior modification, the child functioned on a very adequate level. Mrs. Smith was pleased and proud of her success, and soon the whole school knew the program was successful.

I was encouraged, but as usual more problems cropped up. Despite my reluctance, the principal always recommended that since Mrs. Smith did such a good job with the other children, she could solve this problem too. Mrs. Smith was a dedicated teacher whose self-confidence was bolstered by her recent successes, and she agreed to try to help several more problem children. Her class soon contained more problem children than any other class in the school. However, the knowledge of her success and praise from the principal were not enough reinforcement to overcome the exhaustion that arose from having new problem children enter her class every few weeks, particularly when she became aware that the other teachers found their work was reduced at her expense. Mrs. Smith received a lot of attention, but the tendency of the other teachers to find another problem child to send her, just as she managed to find a solution to the problem of the child she had received only two weeks before, became too aversive. Mrs. Smith perceived that she was being punished for success, while the other teachers were being rewarded for their inability to deal with difficult situations. Since every school has a number of children with behavior problems who must be carefully placed with a suitable teacher, often it is the most adequate teachers who receive more than their fair share of problems. It is understandable that after a period of years the most adequate teachers may begin to feel somewhat persecuted when year after year their class outnumbers other classes in terms of problem children.

When in good conscience I no longer could place any additional children in Mrs. Smith's class, I decided that the other teachers somehow would have to learn to deal with their own problems. I realized that in addition to the rewards the teachers received by having problem children removed from their rooms, I gave them a great deal of social attention for their behavior. Many teachers derive positive reinforcement from talking about their problems with administrators and psychologists, and these teachers were no exception. When I examined my daily schedule, I discovered that I spent an inordinate amount of time with only a few teachers, and they happened to be the ones who consistently could not deal with problems in their classrooms. I decided that rather than reinforce their complaining, I would try a new approach. Instead of attempting to deal with the immediate problems they regularly brought to me, I visited their classrooms only when I could see that everything was under control and the teacher was functioning adequately. One teacher in particular spent a great deal of time in my office. Mrs. Cooper's room was directly across the hall from my office, and I frequently heard her shouting at the children. Often there was a child standing outside her door, and sometimes she would drag a crying child to my office to tell me of his misdeeds. Mrs. Cooper always received some kind of attention for this behavior, even if I just listened to her. I started ignoring these outbursts when she brought a child to my office to get him out of her room; I told her I was busy, and she would have to take him back. If I saw a child standing outside her room, I took him back into the room and told the teacher he was ready to return. At the same time, I watched for those moments in the day when Mrs. Cooper had her class under good control and took these opportunities to praise her and the children. Occasionally, when I saw that she had the class working well, I would teach her class so she could take a short break. Previously, the only time I went into her room was when it was in its most chaotic state, and Mrs. Cooper learned from my behavior that there was always someone who would step in and help her in emergency situations.

This new approach had several almost immediate consequences. Mrs. Cooper's initial feelings of anger at having to deal with the emergency situations by herself began to dissipate as she received praise and attention from me for her more adequate behavior. This made her feel more competent in the classroom. I also repeated stories about Mrs. Smith's success with some of Mrs. Cooper's ex-pupils so that Mrs. Cooper might vicariously experience Mrs. Smith's reinforcement for a job well done. In any event, she began to express interest in the techniques Mrs. Smith had used to bring about such changes, and at one point she even asked to have a particularly troublesome child returned to her class so she could try again! This was a beginning, and as Mrs. Cooper became more adept at utilizing behavioral techniques, I found I had to spend less and less time with her and was able to work with a number of other teachers.

In conclusion, I learned that while the application of behavioral techniques as described in the textbooks was very straightforward, there were a host of contingencies which had to be carefully monitored and dealt with, such as:

1. Initial teacher resistance.
2. Unforeseen disruptions in carrying out a program, such as teacher absences or administrative decisions as to class placement for problem children.
3. Tremendous time commitment exacted from teachers and psychologists when undertaking such a program.
4. Constant checking of progress to avoid unforeseen aversive consequences.
5. Recognition that the same set of principles governs all our behavior, child and adult alike, and that attention should be given to bolster adequate performance, not inefficiency.

The School Adjustment Program: A model program for treatment of severely maladjusted children in the public schools

ROBERT P. HAWKINS AND J. ERIC HAYES

Public school classrooms for severely maladjusted children ("emotionally disturbed") are a recent development in this country, but already there are thousands of special education classes of this nature. The general approach used in these programs ranges from the psychodynamic strategies of Bettelheim (1950) and Redl and Wineman (1952), through the neurological strategy of Cruickshank (Cruickshank, Bentzen, Ratzeburg, and Tannhauser, 1961), to the behavior modification strategy (Whelan and Haring, 1966; Ross, 1967). In actual practice, most programs are probably eclectic; that is, they do not apply any one of the above strategies exclusively. This paper describes some of the characteristics of a program that consistently applies a behavior modification strategy and presents some research data from that program.

THE SCHOOL ADJUSTMENT PROGRAM OF KALAMAZOO VALLEY INTERMEDIATE SCHOOL DISTRICT

The School Adjustment Program (SAP) began in 1966 with two special education classrooms. Currently, the direct service portion of the program consists of ten special classrooms, a parent-training component, a prevention component that serves maladjusted children in regular classrooms, and a program-evaluation component. The ten SAP classrooms are located in ten separate school buildings in six different local school districts in Kalamazoo County.

The children served in the SAP classrooms currently range in age from five to fifteen. Each classroom serves an age-range of three or more years and an achievement-range up to approximately eight years. Each room has a teacher certified to teach emotionally disturbed children and an aide who serves as an assistant teacher.

The goal of SAP is to modify each child's behavior to the extent that he can return to (or, in some cases, attend for the first time) a regular classroom and make an adequate academic and social adjustment there and in the other facets of his life. Thus, the program is a treatment program as well as an academic educational program. Probably any treatment program (at least any that claims to be innovative) should devote approximately 20 percent of its resources to research, and, although that particular percentage has not been achieved in SAP, the SAP staff has collected a considerable quantity of data.

Generally, a treatment program should collect at least four kinds of data: (1) data descriptive of the subjects being treated, in this case the maladjusted children being served; (2) data descriptive of the general independent variable, the overall treatment program; (3) data regarding the general effectiveness of the program in producing behavioral change; and (4) data on effects of specific program characteristics or specific therapeutic techniques. As the data become more adequate (comprehensive, objective, quantitative, socially significant, specific, etc.) the information in them becomes more useful, and the program becomes more accountable and responsive to its own feedback. Interestingly, only the fourth kind of data typically is obtained by behavior modifiers, the data on effects of specific program techniques (e.g., Quay, Werry, McQueen, and Sprague, 1966; O'Leary and Becker, 1967; Hall and Broden, 1967; Kroth, Whelan, and Stables, 1970). But if the other three kinds of data are not obtained it is impossible for the outside observer to determine whether the program, as a whole, is worth imitating,

Reprinted by permission of the authors.

The program and research presented here were made possible by the support of Mr. Marland E. Bluhm and Mr. Vincent Farrell, successive directors of special education, Kalamazoo Valley Intermediate School District. J. Eric Hayes has succeeded Robert P. Hawkins as the Supervising Consultant and Coordinator of the School Adjustment Program.

and if it is, what its precise characteristics are. It will also be difficult for the program to continue improving beyond a particular point, because it does not have adequate feedback. In SAP all four kinds of data are being collected. Some of these data will be presented in describing the program and presenting one experimental analysis conducted within the program.

ASPECTS OF SCHOOL
ADJUSTMENT PROGRAM DESIGN

Behavioral Assessment

The term "diagnosis" is not popular among behavior modifiers because of its association with vague, mentalistic descriptions of behavior based on a medical model, often resulting from psychological tests of highly questionable validity, and typically having little relevance to the treatment undertaken. However, some form of assessment obviously must take place before behavioral objectives can be set and an appropriate intervention implemented.

For behavioral assessment in SAP we utilize no labels or classification scheme, but instead obtain simple descriptions of relatively specific behaviors and make those our behavioral objectives, or therapeutic goals, for the individual child. The most relevant diagnosis probably is a list of the child's behavioral excesses and deficits that originally caused him to be referred to SAP. We rely heavily on the referring teacher, principal, social worker, and others to produce such a list of behavioral objectives. At first the referring persons tended to give descriptions that were vague, incomplete, and described the child only in terms of hypothetical constructs (poor "self-image" was a common one). So we devised a "contract" to be filled out and signed by the teacher and principal before the screening meeting at which the child's admission to SAP is considered. This contract begins by saying: "When the following goals have been accomplished, this child will be considered ready to return to his regular classroom again." The teacher

and principal write in the behavioral objectives they wish to see achieved and sign their names at the bottom. They are provided guidance only by a form letter and a few examples of behavioral objectives from previous cases, for the most part written in terms of behaviors to be strengthened rather than behaviors to be eliminated. Although we often need to obtain clarification or further detail at the screening meeting, many sets of objectives are adequate without further modification.[1]

The following is a verbatim example of the behavioral objectives provided by one regular classroom teacher referring a child to SAP:

1. Classroom Conformity
   a. David should remain in seat during work periods.
   b. Make an effort to follow directions, attempt assignments, and complete assignments regularly.
   c. Refrain from disturbing the class with pencil tapping and mouth noises (blowing on arm or giggling).
   d. Stop interrupting class with irrelevant remarks.

2. Social Attitudes and Behavior
   a. Refrain from distorting the truth.
   b. Control temper (crying, name-calling, getting red in face, fighting) when children will not accept his fantastic tales.
   c. Refrain from saying things like: "No one at this school likes me."
   d. Abide by rules and display good sportsmanship when peers make an effort to include him in games.
   e. Learn to come in from playground when bell rings and be prompt for other scheduled changes. (He likes the added attention of having someone coming to look for him.)

---

1 Two other procedures that are helpful are observation of the child in his regular classroom by the prospective SAP teacher and/or one of the SAP consultants working in the program (J. Eric Hayes, Mary C. Hubbard, Peter J. Matz, Thomas I. Shikoski, or Steven H. Spiro) and the writing of anecdotes by the referring teacher to illustrate the child's problems. Both are standard assessment procedures in SAP.

f. Cease making frequent trips to the office to make unfounded reports about other children's actions.

g. Do routine things without prompting such as (1) taking off coat and going to his seat upon entering the room, (2) taking care of his other personal properties without having to be told.

h. Accept group instruction rather than requiring individual instruction.

This particular list required very little rewording, elaboration, or clarification at the screening-in meeting. One exception was that it was necessary to specify the behaviors being referred to in the last item when the teacher stated the child should "accept group instruction."

This diagnosis does not sound nearly as eloquent or insightful as saying the child has an "unresolved Oedipal conflict," "dyslexia," "cerebral dysfunction," "regressive fantasies," or "inadequate reality-testing." However, such diagnostic terms have limited usefulness in setting specific goals for treatment or in suggesting what kinds of treatment techniques to apply. Such diagnostic terms also have the characteristic of sounding like explanations for the observable behavior; but, as Skinner (1953) points out, they are usually fictional explanations founded on circular reasoning. The behavioral objectives given by teachers are realistic and relevant, and they help us determine what kinds of techniques to apply.

Terms such as "hyperactive," "shy," "hostile," and "irresponsible," are accepted in the list of behavioral objectives, despite their vagueness, so long as there is further specification. Even terms that seem to refer to hypothetical constructs, such as "attitude" or "self-concept," sometimes are accepted, provided there is an accompanying list of the observable behaviors that are the basis for assigning the particular description to the child.

The child's actual behavior in the referring classroom usually is not measured before the child enters the SAP program. Baseline data on the child's behavior in the regular classroom sometimes are taken for research purposes, and baseline data would be useful as part of an evaluation of the program. However, because of the wide range of behaviors listed by teachers, recording objective data on all target behaviors of all children would be impractical. A well-trained observer requires several full days to objectively define even a few behaviors, to become a familiar part of the classroom so that the behaviors are not changed by his presence, and to obtain an adequate baseline. Even if a comprehensive baseline were taken, it would be of little use to the SAP teacher since most of the target behaviors change immediately when the child enters a SAP room. This sudden improvement is common in special education programs, regardless of approach, and is called the "honeymoon period" because the improvement is usually temporary. In SAP it usually is permanent.

While the child is in SAP, his progress toward meeting his behavioral objectives is reevaluated every three months. Often the SAP teacher and her consultant think of additional behavioral objectives after becoming thoroughly acquainted with the child, and these are added to the progress evaluation form. If the program is not successful in modifying one of the child's behaviors, the SAP environment may be analyzed to identify the factors responsible.

Occasionally a SAP child may be treated in his regular classroom. In such cases, data are usually taken on baseline rates of the child's behavior, on environmental factors, and on changes in both the environment and the behavior.

Behavior Modification Programming (Treatment) in SAP

This paper will not offer any description of two treatment components of SAP: the informal parent-training groups, and the treatment of certain cases in the regular classroom rather than in the special SAP classroom. Both are valuable, recent additions to SAP, and both utilize the behavior modification approach. The aspect of treatment that will be presented is the program provided within the largest component of SAP, the ten special classrooms.[2]

The SAP classrooms differ from one another in many respects; in fact, teachers often are encouraged to try some particular strategy that is not in general use in the program. However, there are many commonalities among the SAP classrooms that are worthy of description.

Individual Therapeutic Programming

First, and perhaps of greatest significance, is the fact that therapeutic programming is individualized. The individualization is evident in several areas. First is the individualization of general difficulty level of academic assignments. The profound importance of this kind of individualization is familiar to all special educators, psychologists, social workers, and others who work with the individual child. Unfortunately, regular classroom teachers and their supervisors often fail to provide this basic kind of individualization and thus exacerbate or even create some of the severe adjustment problems that lead to a child's placement in a program like SAP. Also, unfortunately, many special education programs for maladjusted children "soft pedal" the child's academic instruction on the assumption that he needs relief from the pressure of academic work. Then the child falls farther behind academically and probably has greater difficulty adjusting to a regular classroom. Our approach is to teach the child to adjust to the demands of academic work. We cannot do this in a situation which does not make such demands.

The second kind of individualization is the setting of reinforcement criteria to solve specific academic problems within different academic areas. For one child, the teacher may emphasize the conditioning of a higher rate of reading, for another she may emphasize accuracy, and for yet another she may emphasize comprehension.

The third kind of individualization also relates directly to academic performance; it is the individualized programming for Requisite Antecedent Behaviors, or RAB's, as Stanley Sapon at the University of Rochester has called them (Reading Newsreport, 1969).

They are necessary behaviors if the child is taught academic skills in a group setting. We make certain adjustments to produce these RAB's in children who do not consistently exhibit them, but we do not find it advantageous to minimize structure for children with such problems or greatly reduce our expectations of such children on academic tasks (cf. Hewett, 1968). Generally we find that we produce consistent attentiveness, responsiveness to tasks, cooperativeness, and obedience to classroom rules simply by providing frequent, strong consequences for these behaviors and for their opposites. Nearly every child served by SAP has the appropriate RAB's in his repertoire, but in the regular classroom consequences have not been provided that are adequate to produce appropriate performance.

The fourth kind of individualization is in programming for nonacademic behaviors. It is evident from the list of behavioral objectives presented earlier that not all of the adjustment problems observed in an individual child are academic behaviors or even RAB's. Many SAP children present a variety of social and personal behavioral deviations that severely limit the reinforcers available to them currently and in their future. The following behavioral goals, extracted from several different cases, further illustrate such problems:

a. Tina should show emotion, when appropriate. She should laugh, get angry, show disappointment, show excitement, etc.

b. Michael should not use crude, profane language at inappropriate times and places.

c. Richard should seek social contact on his own initiative.

d. Gary should learn how to get more favorable social reactions from peers rather

2 The current teachers and their assistants whose dedication, enthusiasm, and cooperation make a program like SAP possible are: Sharon Biehl and Sue VanRavenswaay, Pam Bysiegal and Chuck Gladding, Narda Foreman and Dave Mosier, Grant Lenox and Debbie Brown, Karen McBratnie and Judy Hakes, Ron Morman and Ann Herman, Doris Mosier and Duane Trombley, Sharon Sharp and Sue Crossman, Jane Stinson and Dee Johnson, and Jayne Visser and Jean Musall.

than always being the target of teasing. (Here the actual behavior was not well specified, because it was difficult to specify what skills the child lacked, without extensive observation.)

e. Mike should look at persons to whom he is talking.

f. Leonard should stop emitting bizarre behaviors such as slapping his face, making odd vocalizations, sniffing people and objects (especially neckties), rolling on the floor at inappropriate times, giggling inappropriately, spinning around, etc.

g. Ron should learn appropriate grooming habits, especially cutting his extremely long fingernails and washing his hands regularly.

h. Mike should stop stealing.

In cases where we suspect that a child is inordinately fearful, or has some other undesirable emotional reaction, we believe that the problem can still be solved most readily by directly conditioning the operant behavior upon which such a conclusion is largely based. For example, with a child who appears to be afraid (respondent behavior) to assert himself, we might prompt successively more assertive responses (operant behavior), reinforce them, and then gradually fade the prompts. Typically, the judgment that fear is involved at all is gratuitous; the behavior observed is simply a low frequency of assertive responses. Thus the most parsimonious and, we feel, the most effective approach simply is to obtain assertive responses and reinforce them.

Contingent Attention and Praise

One of the primary generalizations we teach our SAP teachers is that attention is an almost universal reinforcer and that a teacher must be discriminating in its use. Considerable applied research literature supports this generalization (Harris, Wolf, and Baer, 1964; Hart, Allen, Buell, Harris, and Wolf, 1964; Harris, Johnston, Kelly, and Wolf, 1964; Allen, Hart, Buell, Harris, and Wolf, 1964; Hall and Broden, 1967; Hall, Lund, and Jackson, 1968; Madsen, Becker, Thomas, Koser, and Plager, 1968; Schutte and Hopkins, 1970). Therefore SAP teachers generally avoid looking at or talking to a child emitting an undesirable behavior such as inappropriate complaining about physical ailments, whining about the difficulty of assigned work, leaving the seat without permission, daydreaming, or various "clowning" behaviors. Because reprimanding a child verbally involves giving him attention and thus possibly reinforces a response one wishes to weaken, the SAP teachers very rarely reprimand a child. If the teacher wishes to weaken a response rapidly, she is likely to reinforce an incompatible response or apply some nonverbal punisher.

On the other hand, the teachers use a great deal of praise. This year we have had an observer record the frequency of teacher-dispensed verbal approval, so we could give a quantitative description of this important characteristic of the program. Verbal approval was defined in order to minimize the degree of subjective judgment required of the observer. With this definition we found that we were excluding a large number and variety of social reinforcers given by the teacher, perhaps as many as half of them in some of the classrooms, but it still provided an objective measure of a significant portion of the verbal reinforcers dispensed. The kinds of verbalizations that were excluded were primarily ones that had multiple meanings, such as "okay" and "alright," which often are used as cues to get the classes' attention but also are used extensively by some teachers as a form of verbal approval.

Data were recorded for forty-seven different sessions ranging in length from twenty minutes to sixty minutes. A total of more than thirty-four hours of data were collected. Data were recorded by both the teacher and aide (and student teacher, if one were present) together, so that the data represent the frequency with which verbal approval occurred audibly in the room, without regard to which teacher gave it or which child received it. The recording took place during various academic activities within the classroom. The teachers were told only that the observer could not tell them what behavior she was recording because it might cause the teacher to modify that behavior; thus there was an implication that a child's behavior was being recorded. The SAP teachers were accustomed to having visitors in the room; therefore it was reasonable to assume that the data were representative of the rate of dispensing verbal approval when observers were not present.

Interobserver reliability was checked on five occasions by having a second observer record the same data independently of the first. Independence of the data was assured by keeping the observers far enough apart and oriented in directions sufficiently different that the observers responded to the teachers' behavior and not to each other's behavior. The total number of occurrences of verbal approval recorded by one observer was divided into the total recorded by the other, always dividing the larger into the smaller. When multiplied by one hundred, this operation yielded a percentage of agreement. Over the five reliability checks, these scores ranged from 79 percent to 98 percent; the mean was 91 percent.

The lowest rate obtained on any single session was 8 approvals per hour and the highest was 185.[3] The mean rate of verbal approval for each room was based on as few as three and as many as twenty-four different sessions of observation; these means ranged from 39.3 approvals per hour to 94.3 approvals per hour. The mean of these averages was 60.0 approvals per hour, or exactly 1 per minute (remarkably). Thus it can be fairly stated that SAP teachers dispense frequent praise or verbal approval. The teachers try to develop friendly, accepting relationships with the children, not only because such relationships are themselves important for the child's development, but also because the teacher's approval is more likely to serve as a reinforcer and her disapproval as a punisher when such relationships exist.

Contingent token reinforcers. A token economy is employed in every SAP classroom, with poker chips serving as the tokens. We give tokens while desired behavior is occurring or immediately after it has occurred (cf.

Hewett, 1968). In addition, we dispense tokens for a wide variety of behaviors, depending on our behavioral objectives for the child and for the group. For example, tokens have been used to reward a profoundly withdrawn child for knocking the teacher's books off her desk (an assignment given to teach greater assertiveness), to reward another isolate child for initiating social interaction (Mosier, 1970), to reward a complainer for beginning a task without complaint, to reward a boy who had stolen tokens for going a prescribed period of time (we began with a thirty-minute criterion) without stealing, to reward a very shy boy for requesting help rather than crying when he had difficulty on an academic task, and to reward many children for such behaviors as reading expressively, working quietly, reading a line without error, participating in discussion, or ignoring a classmate who was being noisy.

Tokens are used liberally and are often paired with praise, pats on the back, or other social reinforcers. The tokens are dropped in small containers on the children's desks. This method produces a sound that makes it unnecessary for the child to look up momentarily to detect the receipt of a token, and we find that dispensing tokens is not disruptive to the child after his first hour or two in the classroom. This year we have measured the rate of token-dispensing, just as we measured the rate of verbal approval. The teachers sometimes dispensed several tokens at once, and the observer often could not tell how many were dispensed. Because we did not wish to ask teachers to tell us how many they were dispensing and thus reveal what we were recording, we actually recorded the frequency of the teachers' token-dispensing responses rather than the precise number of tokens dispensed. Reliability was checked by an independent, second observer on one occasion and was found to be 87 percent. Over sixteen sessions the mean frequency of token-

---

3 These and other data descriptive of SAP were taken by Peter Matz, Diane Hatfield, and Mary Collamer Hubbard. No data were obtained from one new classroom because the total enrollment was only six, which meant that attendance at any particular time of day was usually below six due to the fact that some children were attending regular classrooms part-time as a part of their phasing out.

dispensing in a classroom ranged from 32.6 tokens per hour to 102.0 per hour, with a mean of 62.1.

Contingent Token Withdrawal

On the same sessions in which token-dispensing was measured, token withdrawal was also measured. This consequence was used occasionally to weaken an inappropriate response. Reliability of these data was checked on one of the sixteen sessions and was found to be 100 percent. The frequency of token withdrawal in a classroom ranged from 0 per hour to 8.8 per hour with a mean of 2.0. This exemplified the general emphasis on reinforcement rather than punishment in SAP.

Contingent Time-out

Another consequence used as a punisher is time-out. Whelan and Haring (1966) were the first to describe the use of a time-out room for emotionally disturbed children in a school setting. In SAP this consequence is applied for one of four reasons: The response is potentially dangerous to someone in the group; the response is extremely disruptive; the response is likely to receive or is receiving social reinforcement from peers; or the response is very resistant to change by reinforcement procedures alone. Each SAP classroom has a $4' \times 4'$ booth in which the teacher can place a child immediately contingent on a response the teacher considers important to eliminate. The child usually stays in the booth approximately five to ten minutes and then is allowed out if he is being quiet. If the child has never been in the booth before, or if he has never tried to leave the booth without permission, the door may be left unlocked and ajar. After the time-out is over, the teacher records the incident on a special record sheet and indicates the total time spent in the booth. This year we took certain data from these sheets for the two SAP classrooms where time-out appears to be used most frequently (one teacher has not used it once in four months). The following table presents the data for six months from one classroom and seven months from the other. In both classes the most frequent reason for time-out is disruptive behavior (usually mild), and the second most frequent reason is refusal to work (including "daydreaming").

Consequences for School Behavior at Home

The last general SAP technique we will describe is based on research we conducted with seven underachievers in regular class-

Class	Month	Number of Time-outs	% Class Receiving Time-outs	Length of Time in Booth		
				Range	Median	Mean
#1	Sept.	18	55%			
	Oct.	41	64%			
	Nov.	40	80%	1 min.	12.5 min.	22 min.
	Dec.	18	60%	to		
	Jan.	8	50%	148 min.		
	Feb.	4	11%			
#2	Sept.	54	80%			
	Oct.	117	100%			
	Nov.	34	33%	2 min.	3 min.	4.5 min.
	Dec.	28	43%	to		
	Jan.	11	71%	60 min.		
	Feb.	24	71%			
	Mar.	37	75%			

rooms (Hawkins and Sluyter, 1970). We found that parents could readily modify significant school behaviors by providing consequences at home based on daily feedback from school. McKenzie, Clark, Wolf, Kothera, and Benson (1968); Cantrell, Cantrell, Huddleston, and Woolridge (1969); Kroth et al., (1970); and Bailey, Wolf, and Phillips (1970) obtained similar results. Therefore, all SAP teachers sent home daily reports on certain classroom performance and encouraged the parents to provide appropriate reinforcers. In some cases special report sheets were printed in order to solve some difficult problem of a particular child.

Experimental Research in the School Adjustment Program

Several studies were conducted as a part of the School Adjustment Program (Hawkins, 1967; Schwarz and Hawkins, 1970; Hawkins and Sluyter, 1970; Shikoski, 1971; Tough, Hawkins, McArthur, and Van Ravenswaay, in press) and a few were conducted within SAP classrooms (Hawkins, McArthur, Rinaldi, Gray, and Schaftenaar, 1967; Mosier, 1970). The study to be presented here also was conducted within a SAP classroom.[4] Its primary purpose was not therapeutic, though therapeutic change was an intended outcome. The primary purpose was investigation of a variable that could have considerable significance for the teaching of children with various learning problems.

The experiment was prompted by a decline in the reading performance of one SAP child. The teacher noticed that the child began making numerous errors in answering the oral comprehension questions that were asked daily after she had completed reading an assigned story. The teacher and the aide, a handsome young man who was new in the classroom, alternated working with the child, and both observed that she not only gave many incorrect answers but often gave answers that seemed bizarre because of their unrelatedness to the story or the question.

In observing the aide teaching the subject, it was noted that he was employing a pattern of teaching behavior that is very common for a teacher trying to give extra help and consideration to an individual child. When the child gave a correct answer, he praised her genuinely and then asked the next question, but when she gave an incorrect answer he patiently explained to her certain relevant aspects of the story and indicated why her answer was therefore incorrect. His response to an error was of much greater duration than his response to a correct answer. Because there was good evidence that attention itself can serve as a reinforcer and because we knew that for this child attention was a particularly powerful reinforcer, we suspected that the aide was reinforcing wrong answers by his long attention more than he was reinforcing right answers by his praise and brief attention. If this were true it would have important implications for the technology of teaching, especially of teaching exceptional children. We therefore decided to conduct an experiment to investigate this hypothesis.

Subject

The subject was a thirteen-year-old girl in one of the SAP classrooms. She had been referred to the program in third grade because of a history of bizarre behavior, hyperactivity, manipulativeness, and unmanageability at both school and home. Much of her bizarre behavior related to physical affection; she tried to touch, stroke, and kiss boys and even strange men. She also made grotesque faces, laughed at inappropriate times, and generally did and said a variety of strange things that resulted in active rejection by her peers. She had a history of seizures, some of which were suspected of being "faked." In approximately eleven months in SAP, the subject learned to be calm and orderly, work diligently, complete assignments, display an appropriate degree of affection, and have virtually no seizures. However, she still sought adult approval excessively, sometimes was manipulative, and had not made any friends (though she was no longer disliked).

4 This research was conducted with the able assistance of Doris B. Mosier and Joseph J. Vaal, Jr. The cooperation and enthusiastic support of Larry Lindeman, principal, also was essential.

Daily experimental sessions were conducted during the subject's reading period and started when she indicated that she had read the assigned story and was ready to answer comprehension questions. The sessions were approximately five to ten minutes in length. The teacher and aide alternated as instructors and asked the subject a series of approximately fifteen prepared, objective questions about the story. The instructors were asked to keep the difficulty of the questions comparable throughout the study and appeared to do so.

Data

The instructor also served as data-recorder. For each question he recorded whether the answer was right or wrong and the duration of his own verbal response to the answer. The latter was measured by starting a stopwatch when he started talking about the answer and stopping it when he finished. After the time was recorded, he reset the watch and asked the next question. From these records were calculated the percentage of errors made by the subject, the mean duration of teacher response to correct answers, and the mean duration of response to incorrect answers. Thus both the dependent variable and the independent variable were measured in each session. One of the experimenters frequently was present to assure that prescribed experimental and data-recording procedures were followed.

In order to determine objectivity of data recording, interobserver reliability was measured. On ten occasions, at least once in every phase of the experiment, a second observer recorded the same data as did the instructor and in the same manner. Interobserver agreement on the correctness data was determined by dividing the percentage of errors obtained by one observer by the percentage of errors obtained by the other observer, always dividing the smaller by the larger. This was then multiplied by one hundred, which yielded a reliability index called "percent agreement." The same method was used to calculate a reliability index for the mean duration of

teacher response to errors and the mean duration of response to correct answers. Reliability ranged from 84 percent agreement to 100 percent with a mean of 94 percent.

Procedure

The experiment was conducted in six phases, the first four constituting an ABAB experimental design. In all, four different patterns of teacher reaction were implemented as independent variables.

Phase I. The first phase consisted of consistently implementing the teaching pattern of the aide that was suspected of having produced the high percentage of errors from the child. This strategy appeared to offer more possibility of yielding understandable results than the usual procedure of measuring performance under relatively unspecified, unquantified, and variable baseline conditions. The instructors consistently gave longer responses to the subject's wrong answers to comprehension questions than to her right answers. This teaching pattern was called Teaching Condition 1.

Phase II. After forty-one sessions of Teaching Condition 1, Teaching Condition 2 was implemented. This condition was the reverse of Condition 1; the instructors consistently responded longer to correct answers than to errors. This was found to be a somewhat difficult and unnatural behavior pattern to emit, initially; it was easier to point out why an answer was wrong than why it was right.

Phase III. On session seventy-two, Teaching Condition 1 was again implemented. The instructors responded longer to errors than to correct answers.

Phase IV. On session ninety, Teaching Condition 2 was implemented again. The instructors responded longer to correct answers than to errors.

Phase V. Up to this point in the study the teaching pattern always involved differential response to right and wrong answers. On session 101, the instructors began responding

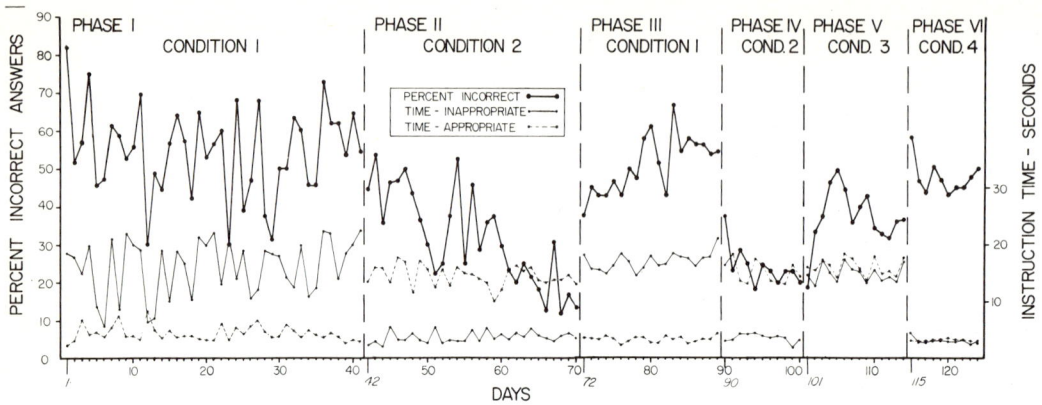

Figure 1. *Percent answers incorrect (heavy line) as a function of differential length of teacher response to correct (dashed line) and incorrect answers (solid, thin line). Note that ordinate represents both percent and time (in seconds).*

approximately the same length of time to right answers as to wrong ones. They gave a long response to either kind of answer. This was called Teaching Condition 3.

Phase VI. On session 115, Teaching Condition 4 was implemented. Like Condition 3, this consisted of equal duration of teacher response to correct and incorrect answers, but in Condition 4 both durations were short. This condition was in effect for ten sessions.

Results and Discussion

Data on both the behavior of the instructors and the behavior of the child are presented in Figure 1. During Phase I the instructors' mean duration of response to errors ranged from eight seconds to thirty-four seconds, with an overall mean (of these daily means) of sixteen seconds, while the mean response duration to correct answers ranged from three seconds to thirteen seconds, with an overall mean of five seconds.[5] The child's answers ranged from 30 percent incorrect to 82 percent incorrect, with a mean of 55 percent.

In Phase II the instructors' responses to correct answers averaged nearly the same as their responses to incorrect answers in the previous condition (mean, fourteen seconds), but showed less variability between daily means. Likewise, their mean response to incorrect answers, in Phase II nearly matched their response to correct answers in Phase I (mean, four seconds). Thus, in terms of duration, the instructors' responses in Teaching Condition 2 were nearly a perfect reversal of their responses in Condition 1. The child's percentage of errors gradually declined over Phase II, reaching a mean of only 14 percent on the last three sessions.

In Phase III the instructors' overall mean duration of response to errors was sixteen, exactly as in Phase I. Their responses to correct answers averaged three seconds during Phase II, somewhat less than in Phase I. The child's errors immediately increased under these conditions, finally reaching a level comparable to her performance in Phase I. She averaged 51 percent errors over Phase III.

The instructors' responses in Phase IV replicated those of Phase II very well. The

---

5 On session twelve the instructor, through a misunderstanding, accidentally reversed conditions, which may account for the change in the subject's performance on that day.

overall mean response to correct answers was fifteen seconds, and the overall mean response to errors was four seconds. The child's errors declined immediately and averaged 24 percent over Phase IV. Phases III and IV, then, replicated the results obtained in Phases I and II. The differential duration of teacher responses to errors and correct answers controlled the correctness of the child's performance within a rather wide range. When long responses followed errors, and short responses followed correct answers, the proportion of errors was high. When long responses followed correct answers, and short responses followed errors, the proportion of errors was low. This confirmed our original hypothesis regarding the cause of the subject's poor daily performance in reading and thus guided us in designing a solution to her reading problem.

However, we were curious whether the child's improvement under Teaching Condition 2 was a result of the decreased duration of attention following errors or the increased duration of attention following correct responses. We implemented Teaching Condition 3 to determine whether long responses to both kinds of answers would also produce a low proportion of errors. In Phase V the instructors' responses to errors and correct responses averaged sixteen and fifteen seconds respectively. The child's errors averaged 41 percent during this condition, higher than during Teaching Condition 2, but lower than during Condition 1. This suggested that the high percentage of errors under Condition 1 could be attributed only partially to the long duration of attention following errors.

In Phase VI the instructors' responses were all of short duration, averaging only three seconds for both right and wrong answers. Under this condition errors reached nearly as high proportions as during Teaching Condition 1, 48 percent. These results combined with those of Phase V suggested that both a long response to errors and a short response to correct answers contributed to the high percentage of errors in Teaching Condition 1, and the combination of the two (Phases I and III) tends to produce a consistently high percentage of errors.

The results could be accounted for by the hypothesis that, for this particular child, adult attention was a powerful reinforcer, but mild praise for correct responses (or simply feedback that an answer was correct) had only a slight reinforcing value (or at least a slightly more reinforcing value than being told her answer was wrong). Under such a hypothesis Teaching Condition 2 should be most conducive to a low percentage of errors, for correct answers would be receiving both kinds of reinforcers, the praise and the greatest amount of attention. Such was the case. Teaching Condition 3 should produce the next higher percentage of errors as correct answers and incorrect answers both received approximately equal duration of attention, but correct answers also received repeated praise as a result of the teachers' responding to correct answers for a longer period of time. For example, one long duration response to a correct answer, taken from a tape recording of a session, was: "Very good, Jane. It's good that you knew Hubert didn't go to school and that you knew why he didn't go to school. I'm glad that you are able to remember these details." The repetition of praise should reinforce correct answers more than one simple occurrence of praise and thus produce a lower percentage of errors under Condition 3 than under Conditions 1 or 4. Therefore, in Teaching Condition 3, one might expect a percentage of errors around 50 as a result of the equal duration of attention, which would be slightly lowered by the repeated praise for correct answers. Such was the case. Teaching Condition 4 should produce a slightly higher percentage of errors than Condition 3 because, whereas both correct and incorrect answers received an equally low duration of attention and the correct answers were praised briefly, there was not the repeated praise which was evident in Condition 3. Such was the case.

One additional experimental result should be reported. Comparison was made between the subject's performance for the teacher, a woman, and the aide, a young man. This was of interest because before admission to SAP, and for a period after her enrollment, the subject had appeared to be particularly eager to obtain male attention and affection. Comparisons were made between the child's performance for the aide and her performance for the teacher in Phases I and II. The aide was expected to produce the higher percentage of errors in Phase I and the lower in Phase II. Neither prediction was correct. In Phase I the subject made a mean of 55 percent errors when the aide acted as instructor and 53 percent errors when the teacher acted as instructor. In Phase II the subject made a mean of 31 percent errors for the aide and 32 percent for the teacher. These differences, though in the predicted directions, were too small to be of particular interest.

Following the end of the experiment the aide was quite convinced that he should praise the child heartily and comment at length about correct answers but give only brief feedback for errors. The child's reading comprehension, as judged by her answers to comprehension questions, improved greatly. In addition we learned that some seemingly natural methods for trying to help a child could be detrimental to the child. Allen and Harris (1966) found the same phenomenon in the case of a child who scratched herself excessively. Harris et al. (1966) found it in the case of regressed crawling in a nursery-school child. Allen et al. (1964) found it in the case of an isolate child. Hart et al. (1964) found it in the case of a child who cried excessively. Hawkins, Peterson, Schweid, and Bijou (1966) found it in the case of a child with tantrums (as had Williams, 1965).

The next question, then, had to do with the generality of the phenomenon. One brief replication of the first two conditions of the experiment was conducted with a boy in the same SAP classroom, and the results were similar. We attempted to replicate parts of the study with a third student in that classroom and obtained no effects resembling those reported here. Only continued research will answer the question of generality, but the primary fact remains that any teacher must be cautious in the dispensing of her attention; regardless of her good intentions she can actually be hurting the child she intends to help. A thorough awareness of behavioral principles can help prevent such unfortunate effects.

OTHER RESULTS OF THE SCHOOL ADJUSTMENT PROGRAM

The experimental research conducted at SAP has yielded evidence that the program has improved the behaviors of a number of children. Two other indices testify to SAP's success. First, approximately thirty-five children have been placed in regular classrooms during the five years of the program's existence. Only two of these children have been referred back to SAP. In both cases the screening-out procedures had not been followed properly. Second, at this writing in January 1973, 28.6 percent of the children enrolled in SAP classrooms in September 1972 have been placed in regular classrooms. As yet none has been returned to SAP.

GENERAL SUMMARY

We are convinced that a consistent, systematic, behavioral approach to the development and evaluation of treatment procedures for maladjusted children will yield increasingly effective programs for such children, whether these programs be in the schools, in hospitals, in clinics, in homes, or elsewhere. This developmental process is still in its infancy, but already programs adopting a consistent behavioral approach are meeting with remarkable success. It is our desire to contribute to the continued development of therapeutic technology and learn from the developments that take place elsewhere. We believe that the soundest single basis for developing effective behavior-change technology (though not the only source of worthy ideas) is the body of knowledge known as learning theory and the methodology of applied behavior analysis.

9

IN PERSONAL EDUCATION

For decades education has professed to serve the "whole" person. Indeed, the ultimate purpose of all education, even the teaching of academic skills, has been to make people effective and even happy. The papers in this section, however, deal directly with teaching people nonacademic behaviors for dealing with others and themselves.

Psychologists such as Maslow, Allport, and Rogers consistently have pointed out the value of "self-actualization." However, this goal has suffered from lack of objective definition and has not affected educational institutions. The first paper in this section, by Thoresen, attempts to define the goal in terms of "response capabilities." Thoresen suggests various behaviors that can be taught by educational institutions in order to help people become self-actualized.

Since Homme (1965) published a paper on "Control of Coverants, the Operants of the Mind," behavioral psychologists have taken an increased interest in covert behavior. The second paper, by Duncan, shows how precision-teaching techniques can be applied to behaviors such as selfishness and anger.

The final paper in this section, by Goetz and Baer, deals with behavior that might be labeled "creativity." Behavior modifiers often are accused of stifling creativity by introducing too much structured learning into children's school experience. The remedy usually suggested is to cut down on the structured learning of skills and let the child discover things for himself. It seems unlikely, however, that a less-skilled person will be more creative. Goetz and Baer describe another approach to enhancing creativity: They attempt objectively to define a creative behavior and to teach it using standard behavior modification techniques. Although their approach does represent only a beginning, it is an approach worth exploring.

As pointed out throughout this book, comprehensive behavioral education seeks ultimately to solve problems by preventing them. It tries to avoid academic failure by systematically and effectively teaching academic skills in such a way that the child will experience success. Similarly, it eventually may be able to solve personal and social problems by systematically and effectively teaching personal and social behaviors that are satisfying to the individual. The papers in this section represent some of the most recent attempts in that direction.

On developing personally competent individuals: A behavioral perspective

CARL E. THORESEN

As Western industrial culture expands, becoming larger in numbers and more technologically complex, the problems confronting the individual are accelerated. Paradoxically the affluence created in Western societies often fails to provide the individual with a more satisfying life. Cox (1969) observes that Western man has paid a frightful price for his opulence: "...while gaining the whole world he has been losing his own soul." Man, he believes, has been rapidly losing his capacity to behave in joyful festive ways—to express repressed and neglected feelings and to experience life more sensually. Man also has become trapped in the structure of everyday reality, failing to use fantasy ("advanced imagining") to see himself and others in new refreshing ways. To many, we live in a "putdown" society, one that ignores the individual and demands performances generally devoid of feeling and compassion.

The most pressing need in tomorrow's society of organized complexity and constant turmoil, according to Michael (1968, p. 34), will be for persons who are "...skilled in being human: in warmth, trust, openness, and compassion." Michael pessimistically observes that we have not even acknowledged as legitimate and worthy of concern the problems of how to develop personally effective individuals for today's—let alone tomorrow's—society. Dubos (1968) writes pejoratively of an "unbelievable future," unless we carefully begin to examine how the changes being made in our physical environments pervasively influence man's behavior both internally and externally. Dubos also argues that we must begin to provide the individual with skills and competencies to understand himself and to manage the many environments confronting him.

The message is abundantly clear. We must devote a great deal of effort to increase our understanding of how to help individuals function more effectively in a technologically dominated society. Contemporary changes in social and physical environments already control much of our behavior through technological devices. And such changes now produce "multiple crises"—problems pressing in at the same time demanding immediate action (London, 1970; Schwitzgebel, 1970). But the individual, the object of these manipulations, is ignored. He does not have the personal competencies to manage himself and his environment. Clearly we cannot continue to hope that the individual somehow will manage to adapt, to fit in, and get along.

We have assumed a tremendous responsibility in the process of becoming a highly industrialized, technologically managed culture, a culture that is generating its own future and starting to control its own evolution (Thiemann, 1970). A crucial part of that assumed responsibility has to do with deliberately fostering, rather than ignoring, the personal development of individuals. "Life in the lap of modern man is akin to fire in the hands of Prometheus. It is a dangerous theft and responsibility..." (Becker, 1967, p. 224). Can such a responsibility be successfully met? Perhaps. We might be successful if we begin to apply the principles and techniques of social behavior theory and practice to personal competence....

Personality as Response Capability

Personality theorists (e.g., Mischel, 1968; Wallace, 1966; Sechrest and Wallace, 1967) offer a behavior response-performance conception of personality. Wallace, for example, emphasizes "response-capability" and "re-

Published in Thoresen, C. E. (Ed.) Behavior modification in education. **72nd Yearbook of the National Society for the Study of Education.** Chicago: University of Chicago Press, 1973; and Thoresen, C. E., and McHargue, Michael, "Developing personally competent teachers." Stanford Center for Research and Development in Teaching, Research Memorandum, 1973.

Paper presented at the meeting of American Psychological Association, September 1970.

sponse-performance," and conceptualizes personality as developed abilities rather than as an essence, as energized traits, or as a hypothetical internal set of motives. The focus is placed on what the person does in specific situations rather than on what attributes the person has (Mischel, 1968). Individuals are viewed as having learned to respond in certain ways to specific situations with varying consequences. Some "growing-up" environments, for example, may provide effective human models of behavior with consistent and powerful positive consequences given for responding in certain ways. Other environments, however, may offer inadequate models and "double-bind" consequences (punished or ignored if you do and if you don't) for individuals. Every person is seen as gradually developing a response-capability to life which may be very effective or very ineffective, depending on the daily life-situations confronting him. . . .

Humanistic Behaviors

A prominent humanistic psychologist, Maslow (1969, p. 732), has observed that the most pressing problem confronting American society today is "to make the Good Person." Maslow and other humanistically oriented writers (e.g., Allport, 1963; Berne, 1964; Heath, 1964; Jourard, 1968; Landsman, 1968; Perls, 1969; Rogers, 1969) have written extensively about the optimally developed person, the "best" type of human being, using such terms as self-actualizing and fully functioning.[1] However, the discourse on the Good Person often has been, to paraphrase Sir Francis Bacon on writings of philosophers ". . . as stars, bright and sparkling, but giving little light because they are so high." Many agree that something much more tangible is needed than polemics and paperbacks. Calls for the "New Man," this person who is flexible, creative, spontaneous, and passionate, who ". . . has an Elizabethan quality—everything is possible, anything can be tried" (Rogers, 1968) generally fail to consider specific means of developing such individuals. How would an optimally mature or Good Person behave? And what is known

about the acquisition and modification of human behavior that might suggest methods of helping individuals act in these ways?

One way of answering these important questions is proposed here. First, an examination of humanistically oriented writers and a "translation" into response terms is offered. That is, what are the performances proposed by humanistic writers of a person who is optimally functioning? Second, it is suggested that research can be centered about selected response areas. These response areas then can serve as the basis for creating a program of inquiry on personal competence.

From the framework of personality as response capability, as discussed earlier, the daily life-situations and environments of a person are determining factors. Therefore a particular environmental setting is proposed: that of the primary-grade (K-3) elementary teacher. Developing an empirically based training system for the teacher of young children is of major import for several reasons: (1) The preschool and primary teacher exercises a very significant influence on the internal and external behaviors of young children directly (e.g., in the classroom) and indirectly (e.g., working with parents, peers, community representatives). (2) The personally competent teacher serves as a significant behavioral model for children and their parents. (3) Young children greatly benefit in a developmental-preventive sense from experiences that foster personal competence.

Internal and External Responses

The ideas expressed by humanistic writers about man center on activities taking place within the person: divergent thoughts, compassionate feelings and vivid perceptions, and actions with the environment, such as

---

1 The term humanistic is not used here in the limited denotation of the literary, critical-minded, individualistic Renaissance-type scholar (Blackham, 1968). Instead, those who have emphasized the undeveloped potentialities of contemporary man, especially in the areas of personal growth and social development, coupled with the negative effects of contemporary social, political, and economic environments on man are viewed as humanistic here.

verbal and nonverbal behavior with other persons, and physical actions with animate and inanimate objects. A key theme involves the "freedom" of choice—the individual making informed decisions coupled with assuming personal responsibility for his actions.

Humanistic ideas can be divided into internal and external response areas. The objective of such a division is to clarify these ideas and acknowledge that such a division is somewhat arbitrary since the human organism acts and reacts internally and externally simultaneously. The classification of internal and external response areas, however, is considered heuristic in facilitating the specific examination of several areas of research. Subsequent inquiry may lead to the addition, deletion, and combination of internal and external areas.

Some examples of internal responses derived from an initial investigation of humanistic writers are as follows:

1. Increasing the range and accuracy of self-observation and self-description of internal behavior (knows what is going on within);

2. Increasing perceptual accuracy and variety (can see things for what they really are, knows what others are experiencing);

3. Increasing frequency and variety of spontaneous responses (new and unusual thoughts and feelings);

4. Decreasing stress and tension responses within the body (experiences tranquillity—calmness in everyday life);

5. Increasing frequency of psychophysiological unity of autonomic and centrally mediated responses (experiences sense of unity within, puts it all together);

6. Increasing frequency and variety of fantastic responses (can alter state of consciousness, engages in rich fantasy);

7. Increasing frequency of using psychophysiological responses in situations as criteria (trusts own experience, reads himself and uses personal reactions to decide);

8. Decreasing frequency and variety of self-critical, negative covert responses (accepts oneself as worthy).

Some examples of external response areas suggested are:

1. Increasing range and accuracy of behavioral observation and analysis responses (knows what is happening with others around him);

2. Increasing frequency and variety of empathic responses (can communicate real understanding in different ways to others);

3. Increasing the variety of verbal and nonverbal social responses (can relate to others in many ways);

4. Increasing appropriate environmental stimulus cues by altering physical environments (makes things happen for himself and for others);

5. Decreasing the frequency of socially aversive, negative verbal and nonverbal responses (positive, accepting person);

6. Increasing frequency of positive verbal and nonverbal responses to animate and inanimate natural situations (good relationship with nature, feels close to nature).

Response areas such as these can provide the framework for a broad-spectrum research program that may incorporate already existing areas of social-psychological research as well as foster new areas of investigation. For example, the area having to do with reducing internal stress and tension responses relates to research work in self-attribution expectancy effects as well as to symbolic-counterconditioning research, such as systematic desensitization. Similarly, increasing external responses having to do with environmental stimulus cues relates to research in multimedia effects and the designing and altering of the physical environment (behavioral architecture) to encourage and discourage certain human performances. . . .

To Conclude

A tremendous amount of work lies ahead in initiating a system of inquiry designed to reflect a position termed behavioral humanism—the beginning efforts to synthesize areas of behavioral psychology with humanistic concepts. The development of a comprehensive training system for the preschool and primary teacher hopefully may provide one concrete means of improving the quality of human life in our technologically bewildering society. The teacher of young children possesses a tremendous potential for influencing the lives of the young. We need to prepare teachers who can behave as personally competent human beings—who can be instrumental in fostering the comprehensive growth of students as individuals.

The view from the inner eye: Personal management of inner and outer behaviors

ANN DELL DUNCAN

"Teacher, I sure get angry with my brother sometimes." "I don't want to try. I'm afraid I'll get it wrong." These are children's reports of the current state of their inner behavior, in a way the view from their inner eye. The investigation of thoughts, feelings, and inner urges which man experiences has intrigued mankind for centuries. Many great philosophers and scientists have employed the full power of the descriptive methods of their day in attempting to describe inner behavior.

We now are able to describe functionally and demonstrate empirically the personal management of a person's inner world. For the first time a behavioral approach has developed tools which permit sharing information about the thoughts, feelings, and inner urges of mankind striving to know itself. Just recently children and adults have begun to record, chart, and use precise personal-management tools to share their view of their own inner life directly with the rest of the world.

It has been difficult to find a concise term to describe looking at and changing oneself. At one time we used self-control to refer to self-application of behavior modification procedures (Duncan, 1969). However, it soon became evident that the term self was highly biased in our English language. Next we tried personal control. Yet, somehow control evoked images of robots—cold, mechanical 1984isms. With these management tools, people were able to develop an increase in empathy for themselves and others—a warm kindness too dynamic to be described by so mechanical a term. As a talented high-school student stated: "These tools let you make a choice about whether or not you want to do something." Hence, we have the current descriptive term: personal management.

The term inner behavior also has a history. Skinner (1953, p. 257) used "private event" when he stated: "We need not suppose that events which take place within an organism's skin have special properties. . . . A private event may be distinguished by its limited accessibility but not, so far as we know, by any special structure or nature." Other terms have been suggested such as "coverant" which is a play on the words covert and operant (Homme, 1965). However, the behavior under consideration certainly was not covert to the behaver, so we moved on in our search. Finally, the working term which seemed to be the most precise was inner be-

From *TEACHING Exceptional Children,* Spring 1971, 152-156. Reprinted with permission of The Council for Exceptional Children.

The author is indebted to Ogden R. Lindsley for his elegant strategies and compassion for all mankind. Appreciation is extended to the teachers and graduate students who facilitated this report but especially to Christine and Susan for sharing their inner life with the rest of the world.

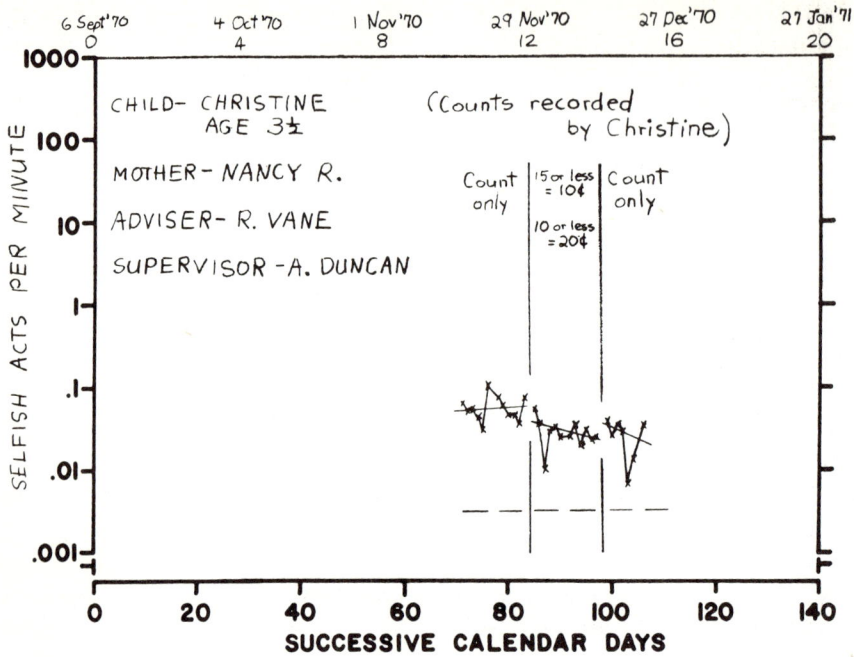

Figure 1. *Christine's selfish acts began decreasing.*

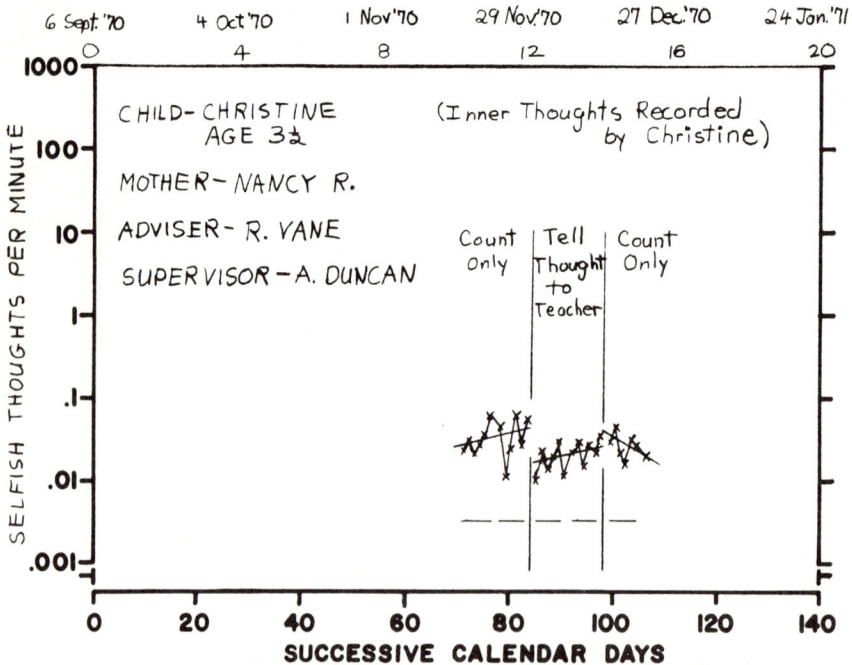

Figure 2. *Although Christine's selfish thoughts began increasing shortly after she started telling them aloud, overall they are lower in frequency than they were before this, and they began going down again when she went back to only counting them.*

havior—a behavior which occurs within the skin of the person. This term allowed a flexible and ready comparison with "outer" behavior, or those movements which could be observed by others.

The scientific dictum calling for observability has guarded the door to the inner world. The traditional approach states that in order for a behavior to be the subject of scientific investigation, several people must be able to observe and describe it in a similar fashion; in fact, one's total experiment must be reproducible using the same methods to produce similar results. This tradition has kept us from using our best methods to describe and change our thoughts, feelings, and urges —in short, our inner behaviors. The multitude of personal management projects which obey all the known laws of behavior, self-recording, and interreliability on similar pinpoints, have placed us on the threshold of a new era. Some of the youths of this new era are described in the report.

CHRISTINE'S SELFISH THOUGHTS AND ACTS

Christine was a 3½-year-old who attended nursery school. Ray Vane (project advisor) and her mother (project manager) talked about finding a child who would count inner and outer behavior. When Christine heard about the project, she volunteered. She chose to count her selfish acts and thoughts on two wrist counters while she was in school (300 minutes). She used one wrist counter for acts (outer behaviors) and the other for selfish thoughts (inner behaviors). She counted both concurrently.

Saying or Doing Something Selfish

When Christine first began counting, her selfish acts increased slightly (see Figure 1). After two weeks, she and her mother decided what they might do to decrease Christine's selfish acts. Christine selected her aim: If she did 15 or less selfish things, she would earn $.10; for 10 or less selfish acts, she

would earn $.20. Christine's selfish acts began their trek downward, and by the end of two weeks she had earned $2.00. Christine then decided to see if she could keep her selfish acts at a comfortable level without the incentive of a cash reward. For seven days she only counted her acts. Figure 1 shows how she succeeded.

Selfish Thoughts

Figure 2 shows that when Christine only counted the daily frequency of her selfish thoughts, they were lower than her selfish acts. The line drawn through her daily frequencies, however, shows that her selfish thoughts increased slightly more than her acts (compare the phases of Figures 1 and 2 before Christine tried to decrease her selfish acts).

To decrease the frequency of her selfish thoughts, she decided to report them aloud whenever they occurred. After she revealed each selfish thought, her nursery-school teachers chided her gently by saying something like "it's not nice to be selfish." After Christine began telling her thoughts, they immediately decreased sharply. Although they soon began increasing again, her overall daily frequencies during this phase of the project remained lower than when she only counted her thoughts. When she stopped telling her thoughts and only counted again, they increased slightly on the second day but began decreasing again (see Figure 2). Comparing Christine's outer and inner behavior charts (Figures 1 and 2) indicates she was more successful in decreasing her selfish acts than her thoughts.

SUSAN'S ANGRY OUTBURSTS AND ANGRY FEELINGS

Susan was a 12-year-old neighbor of a graduate student, Rachel Schulman, who served as Susan's project advisor. Susan chose to count inner and outer anger on two wrist counters for 500 minutes a day. In the beginning she noted that several of her angers were about her brother who was 10.

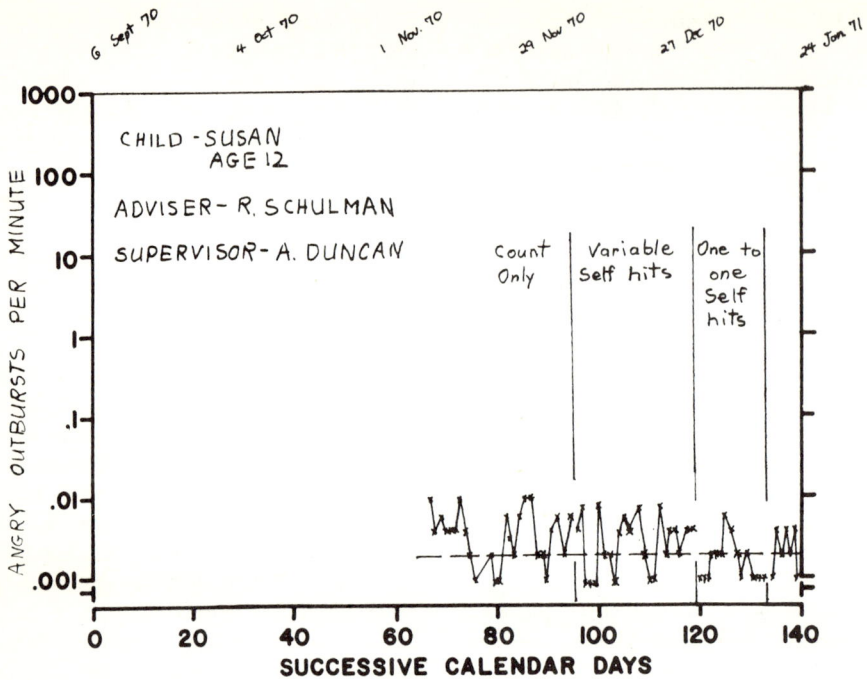

Figure 3. *Susan's angry outbursts.*

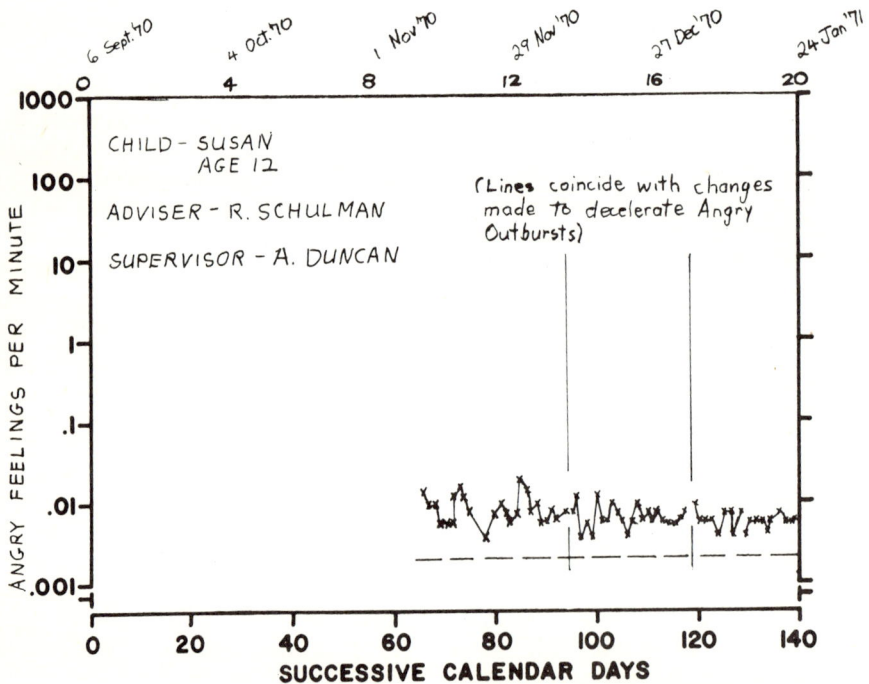

Figure 4. *Susan's angry feelings.*

During the first several days of only counting, there was a decrease in both outer and inner anger (see the "before" phases of Figures 3 and 4). During the fifth week in which Susan only counted, she decided to try to decrease her outbursts and see what happened to her inner angers. She hit herself on the wrist if she had an angry outburst. Three weeks later when Rachel (her project advisor) saw Susan's chart (Figure 3), she asked Susan if she were hitting herself every time she had an outburst, and Susan replied that she only hit herself occasionally. Rachel suggested that if Susan's outbursts did not decrease sufficiently, she might try one self-hit for every outburst. When she did, her outbursts decreased greatly. However, when she stopped giving herself one self-hit for each outburst, they increased slightly. Although Susan's angry feelings did not change much in overall frequency, by the end of the project her anger was less variable from day to day (see Figure 4).

DISCUSSION

These two youths have shared their inner and outer behavior charts with you. The success or failure of each project in reality is determined by the person himself. Thus we have Christine's success and Susan's moderate success.

The relevance for the classroom teacher is that there now is a means of (a) facilitating communication with a child in need, (b) checking out hunches (e.g., "I think he doesn't read well because he is anxious."), and (c) teaching a child a means of personal management which he can use to his advantage, not only in the classroom but for the rest of his lifetime.

Social control of form diversity and the emergence of new forms in children's blockbuilding

ELIZABETH M. GOETZ AND DONALD M. BAER

Virtually every nursery, preschool, and day-care center is equipped with a collection of blocks, usually incorporating a variety of shapes and sizes. Use of these blocks ordinarily is a frequent activity of the majority of preschool children, and such play is believed to be educational, contributing to the child's concepts of space, form, mathematics (cf. Cuisenaire rods), balance, leverage, and visual aesthetics. The possibility of this contribution does not appear to have been subjected to experimental analysis and verification, probably because the outcomes are not well specified in objectively measurable behavioral terms. Even without an empirical basis, though, it might be guessed that if blockbuilding were to yield such a contribution, the block play itself would need to be diverse rather than limited, repetitive, or stereotyped. If the guess is a good one, then diverse block play becomes a behavioral goal in itself. Significantly, it is one which readily can be given behavioral definition and thereby be subjected to experimental programming, e.g., by external reinforcement contingencies. If the guess is not a good one, the deliberate development of diverse blockbuilding may be taken as an experimental goal, so as to ask, if it is developed, what else results? The present study was undertaken to demonstrate the possibility of reinforcing

From *Journal of Applied Behavior Analysis,* 1973, *6.* Copyright © 1973 by the Society for the Experimental Analysis of Behavior, Inc. Reprinted by permission of the *Journal of Applied Behavior Analysis.*

A preliminary version of this study has been published in *A New Direction for Education: Behavior Analysis,* Vol. I, edited by G. A. Ramp and B. L. Hopkins (Lawrence: University of Kansas Printing Service, 1971). This research was supported in part by the University of Kansas Center for Research in Early Childhood Education, in association with the National Program for Research in Early Childhood Education, CEMREL, Inc., and the U.S. Office of Education. (Grant numbers OEC 3-7-070706-3118 and OEC 0-70-4152[607].)

an objectively specifiable aspect of children's blockbuilding which would yield results that might readily be labeled diverse or (less readily, no doubt) even creative. To the extent that such behavior is valued in itself, these procedures could contribute to an educational technology for its production; to the extent that the value of such behavior is questioned, these procedures could contribute to the experimental examination of any other results due to its deliberate development.

METHOD

Setting

The study took place in a university preschool classroom, specifically in the blockbuilding area of the classroom (characterized by a clear expanse of flat floor bordered by shelves containing the blocks). Each subject was invited by the teacher to play with the blocks in this area with her. An observer was stationed a few feet away. These invitations were made every few days and were invariably accepted. The blockbuilding session took place when the block area was free of all other children (they were engaged in a curricular activity outdoors). The session continued until the child said she was finished or until all the blocks available were used, their rearrangement was stopped, and the child agreed when the teacher asked, "Are you finished?" Usually, the child made a single construction per session. Occasionally, several separate constructions were made in a session, in which case all arrangements were considered in the data analysis of that session.

Subjects

The subjects of the study were three 4-year-old girls who had little in common other than an absence of well-developed blockbuilding skills. This deficit had been informally noted by the classroom staff during the months of school preceding the study and was formally examined in a baseline period at the outset of the study. Staff comments emphasized

that the girls' blockbuilding efforts were either devoid of construction (the blocks merely being laid out in like-shaped or like-sized groups) or primitive (characterized by repetition of the same structure, e.g., the same "castle" in every successive construction). One subject came from a low-income family; the other two represented highly enriched, intellectually and culturally stimulating family situations.

Behavior Definitions and Recording

Child behaviors. The basic child behaviors of blockbuilding were defined according to their products, block *forms*. In general, *form* referred to various uses of 2 or more blocks to create a specified shape or function. Specifically, 20 such forms were defined, as listed in Table 1. It will be noted that most of these forms could be constructed from a wide variety of blocks; only a few are defined in terms of specific pieces ("circle," "S," "X," and "interface"). It also should be noted that some of these definitions require that the block collection contain rectangular solids of various length-width-thickness ratios and arc-shaped and V-shaped pieces, as well as the more familiar cubes.

A *form-diversity* score was defined as the number of these 20 forms appearing at least once in any session's construction(s). A *new-forms* score was defined as the number of these 20 forms appearing in a given session's construction which had not appeared in any prior construction by that child (in previous sessions of blockbuilding) recorded within the study. The new-forms measure was not scored for the child's first block construction(s) on the first session of the study, in that all forms appearing on that session would have to be considered new. Instead, the number of forms appearing in the first construction(s) on the first session of the study was taken as the child's baseline of forms; new forms were scored starting from the second session's construction(s).

Recording of each construction was done photographically with a Polaroid camera. A series of photographs was taken of each session's construction(s), from all sides and

Table 1. *Definitions of 20 block forms.*

FENCE: any 2 or more blocks placed side by side in contiguity; if not contiguous, then any 3 or more blocks placed at regularly spaced intervals in a straight line.

STORY: any 2 or more blocks placed one atop another, the upper block(s) resting solely upon the lower.

RAMP: a block leaned against another, or a triangular block placed contiguous to another, to simulate a ramp.

PILLAR: any story in which the lowest block is at least twice as tall as it is wide.

POST: any story in which the lowest block is at least twice as wide and half as tall as the upper block(s).

TOWER: any story of 2 or more blocks, each of which is at least twice as tall as it is wide.

ROOF: 2 or more slat-shaped blocks placed flat and side by side atop at least 2 supports.

FLOOR: an inverted roof.

BALANCE: any story in which the upper block is at least 4 times as wide as the lower.

ELABORATED BALANCE: any balance in which both ends of the upper block contain additional blocks.

ENCLOSURE: any arrangement of fences which encloses an open area, with or without "gate."

SUBDIVISION: 2 or more enclosures in contiguity with at least 1 common fence.

ARCH: any placement of a block atop 2 lower blocks not in contiguity.

ADJUNCT: 2 or more forms connected by a fence; at least 1 of the forms must be an enclosure, subdivision, or roof.

CIRCLE: arrangement of 4 arc-shaped blocks in contiguity to form a circle.

"S": arrangement of 4 arc-shaped blocks in contiguity as 2 half-circles to simulate an S.

"X": arrangement of 2 V-shaped blocks in contiguity to simulate an X.

INTERFACE: arrangement of any 2 blocks with curved contours to fit precisely together, such as circle into hole of doughnut-shaped block, or half-circle into arch-shaped block.

SIMULATION: a construction of blocks which resembles a real-life object and is explicitly labeled by child as such; usually a building, boat, or swimming pool.

angles necessary for complete display of its structure. (The use of a Polaroid camera was considered important, in that each photograph could be examined for adequacy of exposure, focusing, scope, and clarity almost immediately; deficient photographs could be replaced or augmented by additional photographs before the construction was dismantled.) These photographs were taken after the child had left the setting. The camera was not in evidence during the blockbuilding, and the child presumably was unaware of the fact of photographic recording.

Two judges independently examined each series of photographs, counting the number of forms appearing at least once in the series representing the session's construction. Agreement in this counting of form diversity was 100 percent over all sessions of the study. The new-forms score was derived directly from these counts (comparing the identities of the forms found in a given construction to those found in all previous constructions). There also was 100-percent agreement between the judges on that score.

The duration of each session was recorded by the observer with a stopwatch. The session was defined as beginning when the first block was set down and as ending either when the child said she was finished or when the child replied affirmatively to a teacher question about completion.

Teacher behaviors. An observer silently watched the blockbuilding interaction from a few feet away and recorded teacher behavior and its contingency with the child's production of forms. Specifically, the observer recorded each successive new form built by the child in that day's construction, whether the teacher attended to that form production or not, whether her attention was enthusiastic and approving, and the duration of the session. These records were used primarily as a check on the teacher's efficiency in carrying out the social contingencies required by the experimental design, rather than as a direct measure of the child's behaviors in producing forms. (The photographs were likely to yield higher accuracy, since they could be examined at leisure many times over, whereas the observer was required to judge all block-

building behaviors immediately as they occurred.) In addition, the teacher kept similar
records, as the blockbuilding proceeded. Comparison of the teacher's records and the observer's showed agreement on 95 percent of
the events recorded over the study. The records also showed that 95 percent of the
teacher's attention was supplied in the contingencies required by the experimental design.

Procedures

Baseline: No reinforcement. During the first
3 to 5 sessions (varying with the subject), the
teacher sat by the child as she built with the
blocks, watched closely but quietly, and displayed neither criticism nor enthusiasm about
any particular use of the blocks. At the end
of each baseline session, the teacher expressed
her appreciation of the child's total effort
and conducted her back to the rest of the
classroom group (usually in the play yard
outside). She then returned to photograph
the construction(s). Baseline sessions were
continued until inspection of the child's
daily form-diversity scores showed a stable
enough level to justify experimental programming. The new-forms score was not
considered.

Reinforcement of different forms. After the
baseline sessions, the teacher began a program of social reinforcement of new forms.
In these sessions, the teacher remarked with
interest, enthusiasm, and delight every time
the child placed and/or rearranged blocks so
as to create a form which had not appeared
previously in that session's construction(s).
(However, the form might well have appeared in any previous session's construction[s]; it would be reinforced in this session
nevertheless.) In other words, the teacher
reinforced every first appearance of any form
within the current session but no subsequent
appearances of that form within that session.
The content of the teacher's remarks were
designed to accomplish descriptive reinforcement: That is, they often indicated the dimension to be reinforced, such as, "Oh, that's
very nice—that's different!" These proce-

dures were continued for 4 or 5 sessions until
clear evidence of increasing form diversity
was obtained, at which point the next experimental condition was implemented. (The
new-forms score was not considered.)

Reinforcement of same forms. Experimental control of the increasing form-diversity
score was attempted by reversal of the direction of the social reinforcement contingency
employed. Thus, for the next 2 to 4 sessions,
the teacher continued to display interest,
enthusiasm, and delight, but only at those
times when the child placed and/or rearranged a block so as to create a repetition
of a form already apparent in that session's
construction(s). (This form need not have
appeared in any previous session's construction[s]; so long as it had appeared earlier
in this session's construction[s], it would be
reinforced.) Thus, no first usage of a form in
a session was reinforced, but every second
usage of that form and every usage thereafter
within the session was. Again the content of
praise was descriptive: It specified the dimensions (sameness) being reinforced, such
as, "How nice—another arch!" These sessions were continued until a clear decrease in
form diversity was seen. (Again, the new-
forms score was not considered.)

*Resumption of reinforcement of different
forms.* To conclude the experimental analysis and leave each child with the desired
high level of form diversity, reinforcement of
different forms was resumed and continued
for 3 to 5 sessions, until high levels of form
diversity were seen. Procedures during this
condition were identical to those used in the
previous condition of reinforcement of different forms, i.e., only first appearances of
any form within the current session were
reinforced.

Number of blocks to be used. The first two
subjects, Sally and Kathy, were free to use
any number of blocks for each construction.
In fact, each girl tended to use a number of
blocks roughly correlated with her form-
diversity score across constructions. While the
correlation was not high, it did allow the
possibility that the increasing form-diversity

scores associated with reinforcement of different forms could represent a chance outcome of the increased opportunity to display different forms when using many blocks. Consequently, Mary's procedures were conducted as described above, but with one added element: Mary was told that she must use all of the blocks (53 in number) each session. Invariably she did.

RESULTS

Form Diversity

Each child's form-diversity score, for each experimental session, is shown in Figure 1. It is apparent that the social contingencies applied were effective in controlling the development of form diversity: Each child showed appreciable increases from her baseline (no reinforcement) levels during the two periods of reinforcement of different forms. During the interpolated condition of reinforcement of same forms, each child's form diversity decreased toward her baseline range.

New Forms

Each child's new-forms score, for all sessions subsequent to the first (which was used to define old forms for all later sessions), is cumulatively shown in Figure 2. That is, each bar represents the number of new forms displayed by the child in sessions since the first session. (The number of "new" forms seen in the first session is identical to the first point in each graph in Figure 1.) The increment each bar shows over the immediately preceding bar is the number of new forms that emerged in that session. Figure 2 shows that the emergence of new forms was largely restricted to periods in which different forms were being reinforced. Only three exceptions appear: Sally, in her second baseline session (first bar in Figure 2), showed 1 new form, and in her third session, another new form; Mary, in her second baseline session (first bar in Figure 2), showed 4. By contrast, Sally showed 9 new forms during periods of reinforcement of different forms, and

n—NO REINFORCEMENT
D—REINFORCE ONLY DIFFERENT FORMS
S—REINFORCE ONLY SAME FORMS

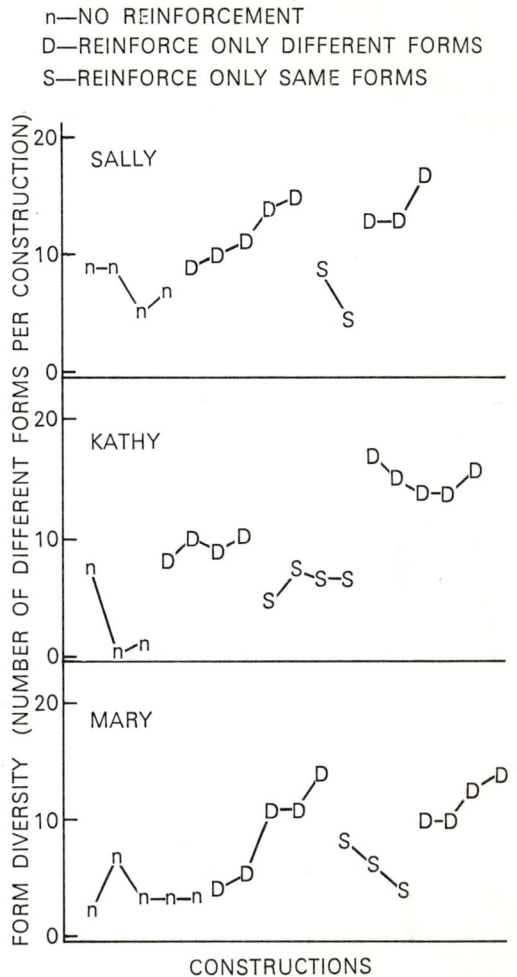

Figure 1. *The form-diversity scores of 3 children in the course of block-building training. Initial points, labeled as n's, represent baseline observations under conditions of no reinforcement; points labeled as D's represent scores produced when reinforcement was programmed only for different (nonrepetitive) forms; and points labeled as S's represent scores produced when reinforcement was programmed only for repetition of the same forms used previously that session.*

Mary displayed 14 during these periods. In Kathy's case, her 16 new forms emerged only during periods of reinforcement of different forms. In no child's study did new forms ap-

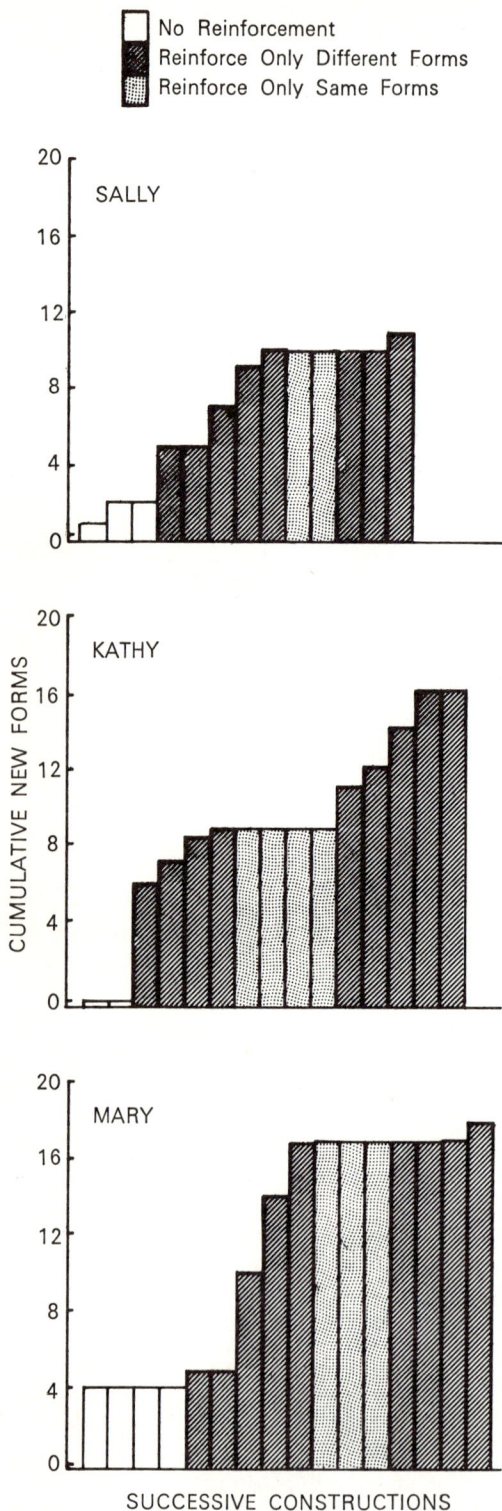

Figure 2. The cumulative number of new forms (forms never used before) produced by three children in the course of blockbuilding training. All scores represent cumulative increments above the score produced in the first session (not graphed). (The increment each bar shows over the preceding bar is the number of new forms produced in that session.)

pear during the period of reinforcement of same forms. On the average, across the three children, the rate of emergence of new forms during periods of reinforcement of different forms was 1.5 new forms per session; the rate of emergence of new forms during periods of baseline or reinforcement of same forms was 0.33 per session. These figures exclude the first baseline session, as required by the definition of the new-forms score.

Session Durations

The mean duration of blockbuilding sessions was 16 minutes in Sally's case, 19 minutes in Kathy's, and 9 minutes in Mary's. However, when Sally was being reinforced for different forms, her mean duration was 23 minutes; in conditions of baseline and reinforcement of same forms, her mean duration was 9 minutes. The comparable mean durations for Kathy were 22 minutes and 12 minutes, respectively, and for Mary, 10 minutes and 8 minutes. Thus, in general, performance during reinforcement of different forms required more time than during baseline or the reinforcement of same forms.

DISCUSSION

The three children of this study showed increasing form diversity when descriptively reinforced for creating different forms and showed decreasing form diversity when descriptively reinforced for repetition of similar forms. Thus the teacher's techniques implicit in descriptive reinforcement were functional in the analysis of this behavior of preschool children, as they have been in other studies (e.g., Baer and Wolf, 1968).

It will be recalled that two subjects, Sally and Kathy, were free to use many blocks or few for each construction, but that Mary was required to use all 53 blocks in each construction. Mary's results thus represent the number of different forms achieved per 53 blocks in each session and cannot simply represent a better chance to achieve many forms during the condition when different forms were being reinforced. The similarity of Mary's results to Sally's and Kathy's suggests that the same process operated in all three cases, independently of the number of blocks used per construction.

It seems clear that diversity of response, within this delimited sphere of activity, is readily modified by simple, everyday reinforcement contingencies. This is in agreement with the earlier demonstrations by Maltzman (1960), who performed a series of studies using verbal instruction and/or praise to increase original word associations in college students, and by Pryor, Haag, and O'Reilly (1969), who increased never-before-observed body movements in two porpoises, using food reinforcement. However, the Maltzman studies (1960) displayed their effects as changes in the mean scores of various subject groups, which is certainly valuable but nevertheless actuarial. Creativity could have its greatest meaning as a description of an individual's behavior. Pryor et al. (1969) showed a deliberate development of novel or original swimming gymnastics in each of its two porpoises but had difficulty maintaining objective, reliable measurement of these behaviors as they became increasingly original. In addition, the study did not offer an experimental analysis of the procedures necessary to this development. (Furthermore, creativity in the porpoise, while intriguing, is probably not analogous to any similar process in man or child.)

The generality of the ease of training displayed in the present study remains to be seen. Furthermore, whether or not to attribute the effect simply to a reinforcement mechanism remains to be seen as well. In this study, the content of the verbal reinforcement described the dimensions at issue, i.e., diversity as opposed to similarity of forms to be constructed. Analysis of the separate functions of description and reinforcement is still to be accomplished, although its value is more theoretical than applied. It is likely that the functions of description without praise and of praise without description are different in different children. In particular, it may well be supposed that for some children either will be sufficient without the other, but that for other children the mix of the two will be more effective than either alone. If so, then, for applied purposes, a package of the two probably is the best technique to apply to children in general. The present study, of course, testifies to the effectiveness of the package, not to its components.

It may be noted that the package was applied to form diversity directly, and only to form diversity. Change in the new-forms score and in session durations are thus collateral changes rather than direct results of the descriptive contingencies applied to each new (or each same) form. Nevertheless, these changes, taken together, suggest that children descriptively reinforced merely for form diversity within a session do display an emergence of new forms across sessions and take more time in their blockbuilding as they do so. The descriptive content of teacher praise specified "difference" (or "sameness") but did not include instruction in how to construct any form. For these reasons, the total pattern of behavior change seen in these three children might well be labeled "creative," pursuant to a discussion of the definitional problems inherent in the term.

It has never been easy to define creativity (cf. Crutchfield, 1965; Ghiselin, 1955; Guilford, 1959; Stein, 1953). However, one definition is attractive on face value and also lends itself to objective measurement and specific environmental programming. This definition equates creativity to novel or original behavior, i.e., behavior which the subject of study has not displayed before in his present setting, or behavior which his group, class, or culture has not displayed before in that setting (Maltzman, 1960; Pryor et al., 1969). The phrase, "not displayed before," implies a criterion of time: not displayed since when? Clearly, this definition of creativity confers maximum creativity on those behaviors which have never been displayed before—meaning never before within the limits of the observer's memory (or within the limits of his or his culture's recording system). Less creativity is suggested for behaviors which have not been displayed since more recent times, such as "since yesterday." Nevertheless, if the goal is to foster creativity through direct training, a lesser criterion of creativity may be necessary. To reinforce only those responses which have never been displayed before may result in an extremely thin schedule of reinforcement, which often will be an ineffective one. In the present study, the target of training was behavior not displayed previously in that session by the child. This short-term criterion of creativity allowed a realistic reinforcement schedule, and success with the short-term criterion was associated with a modest collateral development of behavior consistent with a long-term criterion, as evidenced by the new-forms score. Thus, it may well be that a short-term criterion, important on pragmatic grounds, may result in long-term outcomes of both pragmatic value and theoretical significance. Meanwhile, the definition of "creativity" is no less arbitrary than it has ever been, but one facet of that arbitrariness has been subjected to experimental analysis, within the obvious limits of this study.

10

IN COMMUNITY SETTINGS

An old cliché states that education should not be, and is not, limited to formal school settings; yet many opportunities for education outside the schools are neglected. The papers in this section discuss ways in which nonschool environments increase their educational value.

The first paper, by Screven, deals with learning in a museum. A traditional mission of museums, of course, has been to inform and stimulate its visitors. In that aim, museums are similar to classrooms. However, in the classroom the target population is a captive audience, and the teacher has relatively complete control over the presentation of antecedent and reinforcing events. In contrast, the visitor to a museum ambles through a situation in which he is free to stop, look, and listen at any time. The exhibits must attract and maintain the learner's behavior without any of the traditional classroom restrictions and must reinforce people with a wide range of ages, skills, and interests. Screven's paper presents one such attempt.

The second paper, by Chase, Williams, and Fisher, describes the establishment of less formal learning situations in the community. The authors' emphasis is on the role of the physical environment in learning, but they also point out that such environments must be reinforcing enough in themselves to maintain learning behavior. Exposure to many everyday environments can increase learning; incredible untapped resources exist that can be used to teach. As educators become more aware of these resources and are able to exploit them, not only increased learning, but an improvement in the quality of the environment will result.

Public access learning: Experimental studies in a public museum

C. G. SCREVEN

The experimental analysis of behavior and advances in programmed instruction and communications technology have raised interesting possibilities for utilizing "public access" settings (museums, zoos, botanical parks, shopping centers, etc.) as alternative learning environments in which substantive education might take place. The studies reported here concern some of these possibilities as applied to a public museum. They were conducted in cooperation with the Milwaukee Public Museum and represent an exploratory effort to see if the application of principles of behavior analysis might be helpful in facilitating learning within a public access environment. For other experimental efforts see Nicol (1969), Shettel (1968), and White (1967).

The museum has some unique and appealing features when compared with more formalized educational institutions (Lee, 1968; Screven, 1969, 1973). The museum is an *open* learning environment which, potentially at least, is an exciting alternative to the conventional, restrictive classroom. The museum visitor is in an exploratory situation, able to move about at his own pace and on his own terms. He may choose his own topics and establish the limits of his own inquiry, without coercion and arbitrary structures. Unlike formal schools, the museum is basically a "nonword" environment, filled with "things" and experiences often presented in real-life proportions.

But some features which give museums their attractive potentials pose difficulties which, if not met in other ways, will probably result in little actual learning for the average visitor. Museum populations are heterogeneous, varying widely in age, entering skills, interests, and reasons for being in a museum. Museum visitors are *voluntary* and must be "reached" while freely moving along corridors in more or less random fashion. The visitor seldom has specific objectives, much less an interest in devoting time and effort for substantive instructional ends. While he is free to stop, look, and listen, he is also free to ignore the relevant and attend to the irrelevant. Within displays, it is difficult to control the *order* with which a visitor will view certain materials. Therefore, it is difficult to develop concepts which build upon one another. The visitor's relationship to an exhibit usually is a one-way, nonresponsive affair. Discriminative responses are neither elicited nor selectively reinforced. Science museums sometimes provide buttons which can activate some part of a display, but, unfortunately, effective stimulus control usually is sadly lacking.

To complicate matters further, museum displays are put together by curators, artists, and other specialists who give much attention to accuracy and eye appeal, but little, if any, attention to the visitor behaviors (learning outcomes) to be achieved by the exhibit.

To the writer, however, it seems likely that many of these difficulties could be minimized or overcome through the application of behavior analysis and communications technology. This would require: (1) the specification of the behaviors to be produced by the exhibit; (2) an analysis of the behaviors and discriminative stimuli relevant to these objectives; (3) the use of some method for the pre- and posttesting of visitors; (4) provisions for some kind of visitor interaction and feedback in relation to discriminative elements of the exhibit (e.g., age, color, shape, etc.), and, when necessary, (5) provisions for some forms of positive reinforcers contingent on achievement of exhibit objectives. Precision and efficiency may also require some means of sequencing visitor responses.

Some possibilities for controlling information processing (and learning) activities in the public access environment include the use of programmed audio-cassettes, portable

Reprinted by permission of the author.

These studies were supported by a grant from the Office of Education of HEW, Project No. 7–0138, Grant No. OEG 3–7–070138–2882.

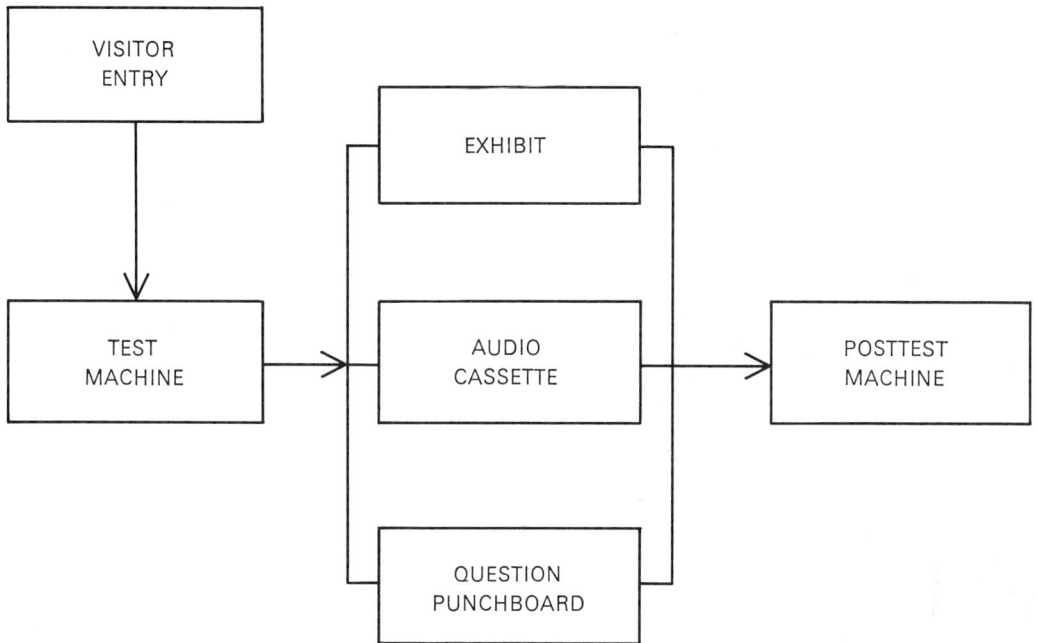

Figure 1. *Schematic diagram of the basic components of the testing and learning system used at the test exhibits.*

self-testing devices, public-access teaching machines, programmed interactive exhibits, and computer terminals at or near exhibits to program visitor uses of nearby exhibits.

The present paper presents some results using programmed audio-cassettes, portable punchboard answering devices, and a coin operated visitor self-testing machine which dispensed "expert" tokens for achieving mastery level performance.

The data to be reported involved two test exhibits at the Milwaukee Public Museum: a primitive man (skull) exhibit and an exhibit on animism and shamanism in a hall on religions. In these investigations, the exhibits were left unaltered in physical layout except for wooden letters (A, B, etc.) placed on top of each skull in the skull exhibit for identification purposes.

The basic components of the investigations are shown in Figure 1. The visitor first approaches a free-standing game like test machine and, in the process of playing it, answers a set of twelve criterion questions reflecting the instructional goal of the particular exhibit system. He then proceeds to the exhibit itself where he is exposed to one

of several possible exhibit learning systems which consist of up to three components shown in Figure 1: (a) the physical exhibit itself, (b) an individualized audio-cassette unit which directs his attention to relevant details in the exhibit, and (c) a portable punchboard questions device on which he responds to leading questions based on the exhibit objectives and receives immediate feedback. As shown in Figure 1, following exposure to the exhibit, the visitor returns to the test machine for a posttest.

The audio-cassette was a simple Norelco cassette "Carrycorder" worn by the visitor and listened to with earphones. A special circuit enabled the unit to be stopped automatically by a beep-tone recorded on the tape.

The punchboard device, shown in Figure 2, is being operated at the primitive man exhibit by a visitor. This simple response-feedback system is battery-operated and holds a sheet of printed questions answered by punching holes with the attached stylus as shown in Figure 2. The punchboard has a right-wrong circuit connected directly to the cassette recorder so that a correct answer automatically restarts the cassette after it stops for a question. Incorrect answers have no effect; thus, only correct answers lead to continuation of the tape. The punchboard also has a small display of lights on its front panel which comes on briefly with each correct answer.

Figure 2. *Punchboard and audio cassette being used by visitor at skull exhibit.*

The audio script consisted of brief statements about important exhibit relationships, directions as to how and where to look for specific details, and commands to answer punchboard questions. The tape automatically stopped at the end of each request to answer a question and restarted again only after the visitor answered the question on the punchboard correctly. For the studies reported here a total of 16 programmed questions carried the subject through the exhibit material (about 12 minutes).

Prior to use in these experiments, punchboard questions were tested with visitors in a series of preliminary tryouts and revised as necessary based on visitor errors. Analysis of visitor errors was based on the holes made

by the stylus in answering the questions. From these errors, both the audio script and the wording of questions were modified until error-rate fell below 5 percent for at least 90 percent of the visitors.

In order to test visitors prior to and following exposure to particular exhibit learning systems, a separate gamelike machine was used for testing purposes. A test machine is shown in Figure 3 with one of the primitive man test questions. The test machine stood near to the exhibit but not in visual contact. An Ectograph Kodak Carousel automatically presented 12 color slides representing 12 discrimination-type criterion questions reflecting the instructional objectives of the exhibit. The visitor pressed one of the 5 buttons (see Figure 3) directly under his choice for each question. The visitor received no

Figure 3. *Pre-posttest machine used in skull exhibit experimental studies.*

feedback for correct choices. After each choice, the next question was presented regardless of the correctness of the choice. A remote IBM card-punch machine recorded each answer along with the visitor's code number, age, and educational level. In the question shown in Figure 3, the visitor was asked to select the correct name of the circled skull shown in the context of the other skulls arranged by age. For the skull exhibit, objectives included naming each of the 5 skulls from pictures, ordering the skulls in terms of age, listing skull names by age, and selecting the older (or younger) of several skulls.

EXPERIMENTAL CONDITIONS

Pretest-posttest performance of museum visitors was compared under a variety of exhibit learning conditions with different types of audio, different response systems, and different motivational conditions. Because of space limitations, the results obtained for the four conditions representing the most important findings will be discussed. These four experimental conditions were as follows:

1. *M-condition.* Both the punchboard-response machine (Figure 2) and the cassette tape recorder were used to relate the visitor to the exhibit as diagrammed in Figure 1. Each visitor took the pretest on the test machine shown in Figure 3 and was then given the cassette tape and punchboard and sent to the exhibit where he worked under the direction of the audio tape, as described earlier. Upon completion of the 16 programmed questions on the punchboard, the visitor returned to the test machine and took his posttest questions.

2. *A-condition.* Only the cassette recorder was used, without the punchboard. The 16 questions, formerly asked on the punchboard were recorded on the tape. The visitor could answer the question only to himself. Each audio-question was followed by a 5-second silence followed by return of the voice with confirmation of the correct answer (the same confirmation given under the M-condition) and continuation of the program. Except for the questions, the audio script was identical to that used under the M-condition.

3. *E-condition.* The exhibit itself was used without either the cassette tape or the punchboard. Thus, the visitor was left entirely on his own to process whatever information he could from the labels and physical layout of the exhibit without guidance or feedback from the audio or the punchboard. Each visitor took the pretest on the test machine shown in Figure 3 and then was told to go to the exhibit, study it, and return for a test on the test machine.

4. *NP-condition.* The NP-condition was identical to the E-condition, except that the visitor was directed to the exhibit before taking the criterion test on the test machine. Thus, the visitor was exposed to the exhibit without prior knowledge of the instructional objectives obtained through the pretest.

RESULTS AND CONCLUSIONS

As noted earlier, the studies involved the voluntary "noncaptive" museum visitor who happened to be in the vicinity of the test exhibits involved. We were interested not only in what persons might learn from museum exhibits and under what conditions, but also whether the particular learning system would attract the passing visitor and motivate him to devote the time and effort required for learning to occur. The free-standing test machine shown in Figure 4 and the audio and response components used with the exhibit were highly effective in attracting and holding the attention of the younger visitors of intermediate and high-school age from widely different socioeconomic backgrounds. As visitors moved up above 18 years of age, however, they were much less effective in attracting visitors. Therefore, the 201 visitors involved in the present study had a median age of 14 years. The actual ages ranged between 10 and 38 years (persons below 10 years of age were turned away), but 75 percent of these subjects were between 11 and 17 years with from 4 to 12 years of schooling. Approximately 30 percent were from metropolitan disadvantaged neighborhoods.

Figures 4 through 7 summarize the results from the primitive skull exhibit obtained on pretests along with the posttest performance scores for two of the four experimental conditions described. These curves are frequency distributions showing the criterion test scores plotted against the percent of visitors obtaining these scores.

Pretest Performance

Mean pretest score for 201 visitors was 25.2 percent or about 5 percent above chance. As may be seen in Figure 4, the distribution of pretest scores is very similar to the chance distribution, showing only a small preexhibit knowledge of the subject matter on the primitive skulls. This pretest distribution has been obtained many times in other studies and has been highly stable across different times of the year, different days in the week, and different socioeconomic and age groups.

Posttest Performance under the Four Conditions

Figure 5 shows the frequency distribution of the posttest performances of 48 visitors exposed to the skull exhibit under the M-condition (punchboard and audio-cassette). As may be seen, the distribution of posttest performances compares very favorably with the distribution of the pretest performances of all 201 visitors. Over one third achieved a 92–100 percent posttest score, and over one quarter received a perfect score. Mean posttest performance for the group was 72.8 percent.

When the punchboard was removed and only the audio-cassette was used (A-condition), posttest performance (not shown) of the 49 visitors involved was almost identical to the M-condition (mean score = 72 percent). Thus, the availability of an overt response device does not seem to be necessary in achieving the high performance level

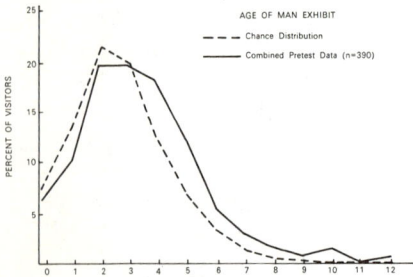

Figure 4. *Frequency distribution of pretest scores for skull exhibit (n = 201) compared with expected chance distribution.*

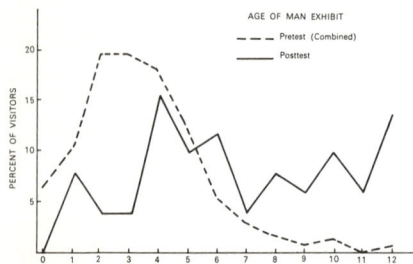

Figure 5. *Frequency distribution of posttest scores for M-condition (n = 50) at skull exhibit compared with pretest scores (n = 201).*

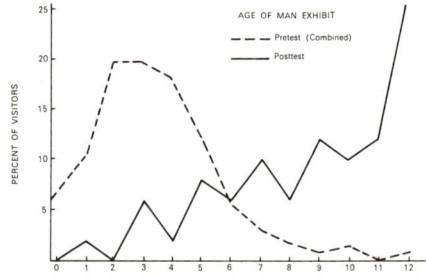

Figure 6. *Frequency distribution of posttest scores at skull exhibit for E-condition (n = 51) compared with pretest scores (n = 201).*

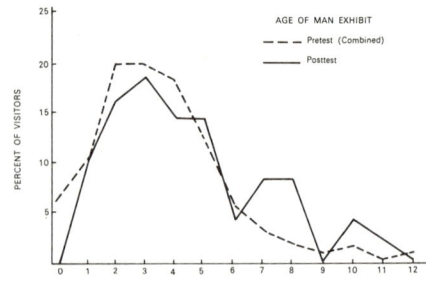

Figure 7. *Frequency distribution of posttest scores for E(NP)-condition at skull exhibit (n = 49) compared with pretest scores (n = 201).*

shown for the M-condition in Figure 5. However, the use of validated programmed questions was still involved but without the requirement of overt responding.

After taking the pretest, 51 visitors studied the exhibit without benefit of either the punchboard or audio-cassette (E-condition). Mean posttest performance, shown in Figure 6, dropped sharply to 57 percent with a sharp reduction in the number of 92–100 percent scores. Many subjects, however, still showed some overall improvement, although not as dramatic. These subjects had the benefit of the pretesting experience. While they received no feedback or other knowledge of how well they did on the pretest, the pretest experience provided important information about instructional objectives which apparently helped many visitors in "processing" relevant exhibit information.

The importance of this pretesting experience was substantiated by the results obtained for 49 subjects who studied the exhibit without taking the pretest (NP-condition). The frequency distribution of scores for these subjects, shown in Figure 7, closely approximates the distribution of pretest scores.

In conclusion, it appears that the use of programmed questions either with the punchboard device and audio-cassette, or with the audio-cassette alone, produced almost perfect performance in over one third of the subjects and significant learning in almost all of the visitors participating under these two conditions. These results occurred in spite of wide differences in age, schooling, and socioeconomic backgrounds.

Without the use of these technological aids at the exhibit, or the experience with the pretest prior to exhibit exposure, no relevant learning occurred. However, the pretest experience itself, without feedback and without further support except for the physical exhibit itself, was sufficient to produce some learning in many visitors and outstanding posttest performance in a few.

Retention

The delay between exposure to the exhibit and starting the posttest averaged about 2 minutes. To obtain information concerning retention of exhibit information over longer periods, a separate study was conducted with a separate group of 67 subjects. This study replicated the procedures and conditions described above but followed up the initial posttest with two additional test sessions approximately 2 days and 16 days later. Addresses and phone numbers were obtained at the end of the first posttest session when visitors were told they would be given the questions again at their homes. For home testing, an identical set of 12 criterion questions was prepared in a loose-leaf booklet arranged in identical format from the same colored slides used in the test machine. Of the original 67 visitors, 43 completed both the 2-day and 16-day posttest sessions. Mean posttest performance of the 43 subjects on the first, second, and the sixteenth days following exhibit exposure showed no statistically significant differences for any of the experimental exhibit conditions. Pretest and posttest distributions for these groups were essentially identical to those obtained for the same experimental exhibit conditions described earlier.

The results described concerned the primitive skull test exhibit. As indicated earlier, the experimental exhibit conditions described also were replicated in a second exhibit area on animism-shamanism. Pretest questions were constructed and yielded a distribution curve essentially the same as the pretest curve obtained on the skull pretest. Mean pretest performance was somewhat higher, reflecting greater preexhibit knowledge of the subject matter, but essentially the same shape. Posttest distributions for the four exhibit learning systems were essentially the same as those described earlier for the primitive skulls exhibit. Programmed questions for both audio plus punchboard and audio alone yielded very high scores for over one third of the subjects and a mean posttest performance of 75 percent. Studying the exhibit alone, but with a pretest, yielded lower but significant learning.

The fact that in all replications of the different exhibit conditions some visitors were able to learn, simply by having the pretest experience, opens up some interesting possibilities for relatively low-cost, automated "learning systems" for use in open-learning environments such as museums. One of these possibilities, called a "recycling" self-test system, will be reported here. The purpose was to provide some means by which visitors could test themselves on criterion questions, study the exhibit in terms of the framework provided by these questions, retest themselves on a comparable set of questions, return again to study the exhibit if necessary, retest themselves again, and so on. If visitors could effectively process the exhibit information on their own as the result of such repeated test experiences, this would eliminate costly programming of the exhibit itself and substitute the visitor's own information processing skills to reach the same end. Unlike the *E* condition, where visitors had only one exposure to the criterion (pretest) questions, the recycling system would allow slower and less skilled persons, through successive self-testing, to eventually "discover" those characteristics of the exhibit which were relevant to good test performance. This assumes, of course, that such visitors could be sufficiently motivated to repeatedly test their progress and attempt to achieve high test performance.

To evaluate such an approach, a coin-operated, "recycling" test machine was developed and tested (see Figure 8) in the Milwaukee Public Museum (Screven, 1973; Fazzini, 1972) and in the Milwaukee Art Center (Silberglitt, 1972). While several systems were tried, the self-testing procedure found to be most effective to date may be summarized as follows:

(a) The test machine (see Figure 8) is placed near (but not in) the reference exhibit area, where visitors may freely approach it as part of their normal exploratory activity. If they touch the machine, a projector turns on and a "come-on frame" invites them to insert 10 cents to test themselves on the nearby exhibit's topic. For a perfect score they are promised an "expert medal" (a gold colored token with "Museum Expert" printed on it).

(b) Inserting 10 cents provides 7 multiple-choice questions (from a pool of 50 to 60 criterion questions), which are interspersed with frames emphasizing that these ques-

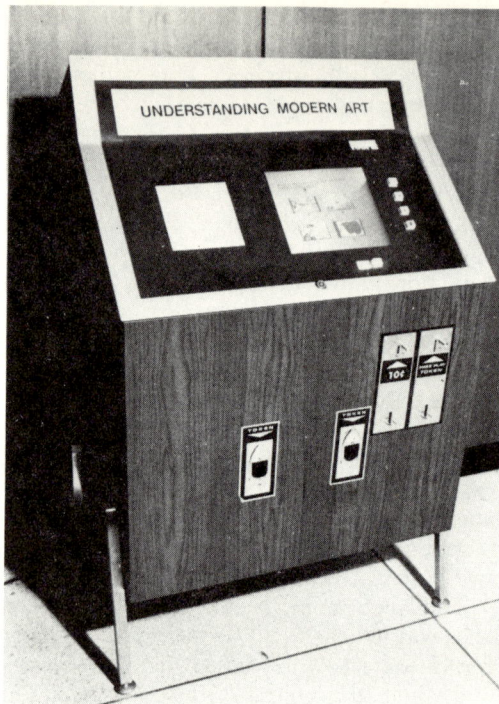

Figure 8. *Self-test coin game used for recycling applications in an art gallery. Cups in lower front dispensed free-play and "expert medal" tokens.*

tions will help clarify what to look for in the exhibit in order to improve their performance and perhaps win an "expert medal." The game ends with a final frame inviting the players to study the exhibit and return to better their score.
(c) Questions advance after each answer (regardless of correctness of choice) and correct answers receive feedback in the form of 100 points on a score counter.
(d) The machine dispenses a silver token (regardless of total score on the first game) with the message: "ONE FREE PLAY, STUDY THE EXHIBIT AND TRY AGAIN." Dispensing of free-play tokens on all later games is contingent on a score above chance.
(e) If, on any game, the player answers all 7 questions correctly, the machine dispenses the gold "expert medal" (token) which may be kept or used for replay.

Studies with over 600 visitors in the Milwaukee Public Museum and 50 visitors at the Milwaukee Art Center have been conducted to date. While further testing is needed to reach more definitive conclusions, some tentative results and conclusions include the following: (1) The self-test machine attracts visitors of all ages, but more males than females; (2) feedback does not affect scores on initial game but increases final score (last score before quitting) and total number of replays; (3) some feedback (e.g., advance of counter) is necessary, but additional supporting feedback (lights, bells, etc.) is redundant and does not affect final score, number of exhibit visits, etc.; (4) advance-on-correct mode is unacceptable in recycling procedure because it encourages use of the machine by itself without exhibit visits; (5) free-play tokens increase replays and final score level; (6) the "expert medal" increases frequency of high final scores and number of replays; (7) there is no relationship between age and final score; (8) over 60 percent of those winning "expert medal" continue playing; (9) visits to exhibits decrease and final scores increase with number of plays; and (10) in the Art Center application, independently measured posttest performance after use of recycling machine was comparable to posttest scores with programmed audio condition.

While tentative, these results are encouraging. One difficulty is maintaining exhibit visits with continued replays. It may be necessary to require exchange of the free-play token for a second token from the vending machine located at the reference exhibit.

There are, of course, other possibilities for facilitating visitor learning along the same lines. For example, self-check criterion question cards with chemical answer pens and feedback could be carried along on exhibit tours or dispensed at exhibits by coin-operated vendors. Visitors could, if they wished, turn in high-scoring cards for discounts, "expert tokens," or other positive reinforcers. Such test cards might also list appropriate learning objectives (what to compare, name, order, etc.) to aid in processing exhibit information and answering criterion questions on the test cards.

These studies also suggest the feasibility of using responsive (audio-visual) teaching devices as self-contained exhibits to augment nearby exhibits, provide background, orientation, etc. When we used self-test machines in an advance-on-correct mode, players tended to remain at the machines for repeated plays, and many managed to achieve mastery scores without visiting the exhibit. While this posed a problem when the purpose was to encourage learning from the exhibit, rather than from the machine, it suggests that machines might also provide, on their own, important historical, scientific, or artistic concepts coordinated with existing exhibit resources. A number of responsive audio-visual devices now on the market could be readily adapted for public access use in museums. Some existing programmed materials on a wide range of topics could be adapted for use in such devices to complement existing exhibits.

Perhaps the most flexible responsive system with the greatest potential for achieving some of the goals described in this paper is, of course, the computer. The computer could mobilize all of the resources of the museum for use by the individual visitor. It could not only provide direct instruction but could develop the visitor's abilities for inquiry and investigation using the museum's exhibits as a framework for such activities. Unlike the ordinary teaching machine, the computer could simulate scientific, artistic, social, or historical situations, helping the visitor to ask (as well as answer) questions, organize facts obtained from exhibits, apply principles illustrated in exhibits, predict consequences, discover defects, evaluate decisions, and so forth.

However, the use of computers in museums probably must be preceded by a less glamorous stage of experimentation, involving such things as programmed audio-cassettes, self-testing devices, etc. In any case, if the principles of behavior analysis, performance measurement, reinforcement, and stimulus control could be successfully applied to the vast educational potentials of museums, zoos, botanical parks, and other public access environments, "public-access education" may become a viable alternative to conventional public education.

Exercises in the design of learning environments

RICHARD ALLEN CHASE, M.D., D. MICHAEL WILLIAMS, AND
JOHN JACOB FISHER, III

In the second semester of the 1970-71 academic year, the department of design and environmental analysis, College of Human Ecology, Cornell University, offered a new course: Environmental Analysis: Human and Social Factors (DEA-150). The catalog description for the course was as follows:

"Introduction to the study of the relationships between the physical environment and man's behavior as an individual and in groups. Perception of space and effects of spatial arrangements on interactions between persons (social geography). Significance of man's capabilities and limitations in design of man-machine systems. Guidelines for analyzing environmental conditions."

This course primarily was designed by Professors Rose E. Steidl and Edward R. Ostrander with registration open to all students at the university; 190 students enrolled, representing all undergraduate years as well as graduate programs in architecture and engineering. The students' educational backgrounds showed concentration across a broad spectrum of specialty areas.

Dr. Richard Allen Chase and Mr. D. Michael Williams participated as guest professors for a section of this course and offered a two-week unit on "the design of learning environments." It is the purpose of this paper to review the design, execution, and implications of that experience.

EXERCISES IN THE DESIGN OF LEARNING ENVIRONMENTS

Orientation

We met our class for the first of four fifty-minute meetings (Wednesday and Friday mornings of two consecutive weeks) in a conventional classroom: a steep-sloped amphitheater with fixed seating. In preparation

for this introductory lecture and discussion, students had been asked to read a paper written by Stephen Carr and Kevin Lynch, "Where Learning Happens" (Carr and Lynch, 1968), and to review some recent efforts to construct catalogs of learning resources (Yanes and Holdorf, 1971; Last Whole Earth Catalog, 1971; Canadian Whole Earth Almanac, 1970; People's Yellow Pages, 1971; First Foundation Journal, 1971; Vocations for Social Change).

Lecture and discussion was used to consider the questions: What is learning; under what conditions does it occur; and how can the environmental designer increase the probability that learning will occur? A series of topics provided a framework for consideration of these questions. The principal topics considered are identified in the following discussion, with brief comments on each topic.

Topic 1: The importance of information in the design of learning environments. Learning requires the availability of information. Information can be created through architectural design, but it can also be incorporated into an environment in nonarchitectural forms. This concept is integral to the suggestions made by Thomas Vreeland that educational technology be located at drive-in learning centers and built into roving learning buses. Another example proposed by Cedric Price was that industrial storage structures be labeled with the names of the chemicals that they contain and that industries might arrange public demonstrations of their operations (Cannady, 1967). Carr and Lynch (1968) suggested modifications of the urban environment to include free transportation systems, elaborate systems of pathways and marked networks of educational tours, use of transparent containers that would allow general view of products being moved about, and broad dispersion of direct-access com-

Reprinted by permission of the authors.

puter systems, self-testing equipment, and environmental displays. The growth of concern about the character and quality of urban life provided the necessary condition for serious speculation about designing opportunities for learning within the infrastructure of the city (Cosby, 1965). The recent ambitious redesign programs of the Massachusetts Bay Transportation Authority included photomurals for underground station platforms that provide information about the neighborhood in which the station is located while a bridge mural in Arlington station tells passengers that they are near the public garden (Lukach, 1967).

Topic 2: Necessary and sufficient conditions for learning to occur. Although the provision of information within an environment is necessary for learning to occur, it is not a sufficient condition for learning. Learning occurs when information is selected and organized in a manner that is comprehensible, relevant, accessible, and, when used, has significant consequences for the life of the user. In order to more closely scrutinize the conditions under which learning occurs and the role that the environmental designer can play in increasing the probability that learning will occur, our orientation discussion moved to a closer examination of the behavioral consequences of environmental design.

Topic 3: Increasing the competence of environmental design by providing feedback about the performance of the designed environment. When objects and environments are designed and built by the people who use them, feedback about the design's competence to support specific behaviors is an integral part of the man-environment system. Modification of the emerging designed environment occurs because the user is also the designer, and when he becomes displeased with the relationships that are possible between himself and his environment, he changes the environment to rectify the discordance. The history of the development of tools and habitats reveals the participation of large numbers of anonymous designer-users who spontaneously and persistently contribute to the cumulative generation of competent designed environments. Bernard Rudofsky (1965) has collected many examples of anonymous and indigenous design efforts. Rudofsky (1965) writes:

"In orthodox architectural history, the emphasis is on the work of the individual architect; here the accent is on communal enterprise. Pietro Belluschi defined communal architecture as 'a communal art, not produced by a few intellectuals or specialists but by the spontaneous and continuing activity of a whole people with a common heritage, acting under a community of experience' [p. 3–4]."

Topic 4: Increasing the competence of environmental design by giving design authority to individuals whose histories allow them to be intimately familiar with the intended users' needs. Another way to achieve competence in environmental design is to grant considerable authority to a single individual or small group of individuals who are exceptionally well qualified to understand the requirements of the environment they are designing and are continuously informed about the performance of the resulting man-environment system. This requires that the designer be a participant in many of the functions of the designed environment which, in turn, requires that the system be appropriately modest in scale (Pushkarev, 1966, p. 100). Eighteenth- and nineteenth-century American colleges were, in just this way, largely influenced by the personalities and qualities of their presidents (Nye, 1963).

"The president of Princeton in 1802 presided at all college functions and ceremonies, taught the senior class, and held a regular ministerial post. At North Carolina, in addition to his other duties, the president examined each student every Sunday evening on the state of his religious beliefs. At Columbia the president was responsible for such things as purchasing books, providing coathooks for the classrooms, and taking attendance at faculty prayers. President Samuels of Vermont taught all classes offered at the college, supervised the construction of college buildings, and helped to chop down the trees to build them [p. 182]."

Topic 5: The consequences of increasing complexity of designed environments and increasing specialization within the design professions. As the scale and complexity of universities and other social institutions has enlarged, it has become the custom to delegate the authority for design of physical environments to architects, planners, and others whose training provides them with expertise in the specialty-areas relevant to design, materials, and building technology. However, these experts usually are not trained in the behavioral and biological sciences and are therefore at constant risk of producing environments which express the aesthetic values and meet the technical standards established by their professions, but fall short of providing a competent and humane container for the people who finally inhabit the designed-spaces not only with their bodies but with their interests, needs, and hopes for comfort, stimulation, and growth. One example of this dilemma is the high-rise dormitory complex built at the University of California Berkeley campus in the early 1960s. A design competition was held between several architectural firms, involving careful jury deliberation; a unanimous decision was reached by a jury of designers and university officials. However, students found the resulting facilities to be inadequate for study or social functions. As a result, occupancy rates began to fall, and investigations were initiated. An environmental-analysis study documented specific design failures that clearly were observable once the behaviors of students in these buildings were studied in a systematic manner.

Rooms were found to be too small, preventing sufficient separation of roommates and adequate surfaces for study materials. Social interaction was poorly accommodated by recreation and lounge areas, and much of it was displaced to the corridors, resulting in frequent distractions and interruptions for students who did attempt to study in their rooms. Rules concerning decoration of rooms, inspection of rooms, visiting privileges, times for meals, and dress for meals resulted in further deterioration of the morale of the

dormitory community (Van der Ryn and Silverstein, 1967).

Topic 6: An environmental design methodology that incorporates behavioral objectives. It is apparent to increasing numbers of people that contemporary design education and design methods must include significant information about the behavior of user-groups and ways in which this information can be integrated into environmental design and environmental management functions. We, therefore, presented our students with an outline of an environmental-design methodology consistent with these objectives as an antecedent to our exercises in the design of learning environments (see Table 1).

This methodology incorporates basic principles derived from the experimental analysis of behavior (Reese, 1966). It invites the designer to initiate the design process with a clear understanding of the behaviors that the design effort intends to support. This must be done not only in a general way; as many specific behaviors as possible should be identified. The designer of a learning environment knows that the design must make relevant information available. This is a general statement implying some understanding

Table 1. *Environmental design methodology.*

1. Define general behavioral objectives.
2. List specific terminal behaviors desired.
3. List relevant baseline behaviors for intended user groups.
4. Design the behavior modification plan intended to realize these terminal behaviors.
5. Design the physical facilities and the functional programs in a manner that optimally accommodates the behavior modification plan.
6. Construct the physical facilities.
7. Initiate the functional programs.
8. Monitor the behavioral consequences of the operating physical facilities-functional programs system, and compare these consequences with the terminal behaviors specified at the beginning of the project.
9. Modify the physical facilities and functional programs as indicated.

of the fact that learning behaviors require access to information. It is also necessary to know what type of learning is expected to take place before the environmental design effort can begin. Is the learning environment intended to support the acquisition of specific skills? If so, what skills: repair of automobiles, cultivation of plants, or cardio-vascular surgery? Even when this degree of specificity has been achieved, additional clarification of terminal behaviors is needed. One needs to list, for example, the specific skills that an automobile mechanic uses. In addition, it is necessary to know something about the baseline behaviors of the individuals who ultimately will use the designed environment. The same designed environment, intended to support the same behavioral objectives, may function competently for one group of users and fail in the case of another group with different behavioral histories. To avoid dysfunction in the ultimate relationships between an environment and its users, the environmental designer must know about the existing behaviors of the intended users of the environment. The designed environments, as a result, can avoid making demands that a particular group cannot meet and can sensitively accommodate existing behavioral styles.

The environmental designer is required to combine physical and program design, which are symbiotic components of a competent environment. The remainder of the steps in the methodology simply incorporate the traditional features of the experimental method used in the natural sciences into the design process. Continuous limited tests of the adequacy with which a designed environment meets the behavioral objectives appropriate to the needs of specific users should be conducted under laboratory conditions before full-scale execution of the environment is undertaken. The designer thereby assumes the responsibility for determining whether his hypotheses are correct instead of leaving his users to suffer the consequences of his errors. Once the designer assumes these responsibilities, his education is improved enormously by the addition of laboratory experiences, and he acquires the opportunity to repair design errors. This procedure represents formal acceptance of the simple feedback principle we

discussed earlier in the case of the anonymous designer-users who have produced so much good indigenous environmental design without ever having studied architecture (Rudofsky, 1965). Studer (1970) has done elegant theoretical work on the important role of feedback in environmental design methodology.

Topic 7: Utilization of the methodology for environmental design that incorporates behavioral objectives. We concluded our orientation lecture and discussion by presenting the first class assignment. Each student was invited to carefully study the design methodology outlined in Table 1. Then selection of a specific behavioral objective was to be made, followed by execution of a plan for appropriate modification of the behavior of a fellow student. The entire plan was to be written according to the outline in Table 1. The written plan and all materials necessary to the execution of the plan were to be brought to the next class which was to meet two days later in a large lounge in the student union building (Willard Straight Hall). Plans were to be modest enough so that they could be accomplished with another student in about ten minutes.

At the next meeting, the class would be divided into two equal groups. During the first twenty-five minutes, one half of the students would arrange themselves around the perimeter of the lounge room and hold their hands up to identify themselves as available "teachers." In this manner, spontaneous student-teacher pairs would be formed. These pairs could be changed as often as individuals considered it useful. "Teachers" would be asked to make written observations about the success of their behavior modification plans. After twenty-five minutes the students that had been "teaching" and the students that had been "learning" would reverse roles. All students were asked to design their own name tags to be worn at the next class meeting.

Students Teaching Students

The second class took place in a large lounge room prominently located on the

Figure 1. *The lounge in the student union building used for the "students-teaching-students" exercise. This picture was taken during the first five to ten minutes after the class started. Students with their hands raised are waiting to be approached by students wishing to learn what they have prepared to teach. Many students are wearing name tags designed for use during this class.*

ground floor of the student union building. Although all of the furniture normally occupying the center of the room had been removed, when we arrived students not in our class were occupying most of the seating that had been left along the walls. They soon were displaced by the students in our class who distributed themselves throughout the space (Figure 1). The students with raised hands (see Figure 1) are indicating their availability for teaching. Although the rules for this exercise suggested two person (student-teacher) groups, it was commonplace for small "observer" groups to form around sites of activity whether defined by single "teachers" with some interesting apparatus, student-teacher pairs at work, or small conversation groups. There was a great deal of conversation and movement facilitated by the use of name tags, barrier-free spaces, the shared common experience of an unprecedented class exercise

conducted in an unprecedented location, and an obvious general interest in social interaction with other members of the class community. The fact that this was a regularly scheduled class exercise seemed to provide a legitimation of interest in free-ranging social interaction between students. This exercise represented a balance of structure and lack of structure, of planned behavior and spontaneous behavior, of conformity to the organized culture of the university and nonconformity to that culture. Throughout this dialectical experience, there was a sense of comradeship, communion, and community (Turner, 1969; Dewey, 1946). For some, the departure from the conventional classroom and the generous mixture of experiential learning with more traditional didactic-learning exercises resulted in a feeling of confusion and a questioning of the purpose of the experience. There seems to be little doubt that for some students spontaneity and enjoyment are inconsistent with productive learning.

Figure 2 shows a number of "teachers" executing their designed learning exercises. Although at any one time they usually concentrated their efforts on a single individual, this picture makes clear that most of the teaching exercises served as foci for larger group formations. Sometimes the group consisted primarily of observers, and sometimes there was sufficient engagement of those who initially participated as observers to produce a small "class" of students with which the "teacher" worked simultaneously. The size and character of these groups constantly changed as students completed one teaching exercise and roamed about in search of another. Just as the size and boundaries of the groups constantly changed in a self-organiz-ing way, the relationship between our class as a whole and other students using the student union building for traditional purposes changed as well. The lounge we used was visible from the main entrance lobby of the building, and many students entering the building were diverted by the spectacle of our behavior. They approached, made enquiries, and were invited to join; many remained, not only as observers, but as participants. We estimated that at least one hundred students became participants in this fortuitous manner.

Most of the design exercises involved efforts to shape specific motor performances. This was appropriate to the requirement that there be explicit objective feedback about the extent to which the designed teaching exercise achieved its intended behavioral objectives. Many students had carefully written plans,

Figure 2. *The "students-teaching-students" exercise is now underway. This photograph shows many student-teacher pairs at work. In addition, it shows the variety of small groups that form around activity sites. In addition to the group that a student is closest to, attention also is directed to the activities of more distant groups.*

following the methodology outlined in Table 1, and kept correspondingly careful notes about the manner in which the behavior of each of the students taught corresponded to, or failed to correspond to, their expectations. The teacher determines the effectivenss of the teaching program by observing the emerging new behaviors of the student, and the student at any point can question the teacher about his progress. Direct feedback in communication systems not only increases the accuracy and usefulness of the information being communicated but also increases confidence and amity between those who are communicating (Leavitt and Mueller, 1966). Many of these designed teaching exercises involved crafts, games, paper construction, drawing and drafting techniques, and the use of tools and musical instruments. Students most often selected skills to be taught that were of great interest to them as well as being appropriate to the class assignment. Musicians brought their instruments, those who were accomplished in macrame, batik, and knitting made use of their skills in these crafts, and so forth. The selection of content for the designed teaching exercises, just like the design and use of name tags, gave individuals in the group information about each other.

The activity in the room was greater in amount and more varied in character than one usually encounters in a university classroom. The information density in the learning environment was vastly increased by allowing each student to function both as a student and teacher. This resulted in the instant creation of a faculty of 190. Allowing students to self-select what they would teach and inviting use of an explicit methodology for achieving specific behavioral objectives resulted in high levels of teaching competence. The vast stores of information about individual interests, skills, and life styles that remain private within the audience of the conventional classroom were utilized. This resulted in a radical alteration of the economics of information exchange in the classroom environment. Traditionally, most of the information delivered into such an environment issues from the authority figures running the class from the front of the room. Lateral com-

munication within the rest of the group is minimal, being sharply limited by most conventional fixed-seating plans and the traditional rules that govern communication patterns in conventional classrooms (Sommer, 1969; Hall, 1966; Richardson, 1970). In the case of our student-teacher pair exercise, once the class had started, there were no special authorities controlling the communication patterns. Each student was an authority, and teaching-learning relationships were negotiated directly by all members of the group. It was not necessary to announce midway through the class period that it was time for those students who had been teaching during the first half of the class to stop and allow the other students to assume teaching roles. This occurred spontaneously. Interest in the exercise remained high throughout the class period. Participation grew in intensity throughout the fifty-minute period and only fell sharply at the traditional time for changing classes. Some students remained beyond that time anyway. An increasing number of experiments in which students teach other students confirms the observation that this arrangement can produce sustained interest by both student and student-teacher, even when the students and student-teachers are very young (Martin and Pinck, 1966; Gartner, Kohler, and Riessman, 1971). Before leaving the room, each student submitted the papers on which plans for the designed learning programs and observations on the use of the plans were recorded. Instructions and materials for the next exercise on the design of learning environments were transmitted; this exercise was to be the creation of learning resources catalogs.

Catalogs of Personal and Environmental Resources

During the previous class, each student was given two ditto-master sheets. One sheet was to be used for one or more listings of a resource in the Cornell-Ithaca environment that was likely to be of interest to other students. The second page was used for listings of personal resources: Each student listed one or more things that he or she knew about, or knew how to do, and was willing to teach someone else. Information also was to be provided concerning the amount of time, material, and money that would be required of prospective students as well as how to get in touch with the person offering to teach. The personal resource listings represented an expansion of the exercises used during the last class in which students taught students. In this case more ambitious behavioral objectives could be selected, because there were no inherent limitations on time needed for learning, location of learning environments, or access to materials and equipment. All of these matters could be negotiated.

Completed ditto-master sheets were turned in during the third class, which met in the lounge of the student union building once again, but this time for purposes of general discussion of the second class in which students taught students. A volunteer task-group of approximately fifteen students printed and collated the ditto sheets that afternoon and evening. The objective was rapid assembly of complete separate catalogs of environmental and personal resources which would be distributed during the fourth and final exercise of the unit two days later.

This exercise was to make clear how much information of interest to a community remains unavailable because of limitations in the communication systems used by the community. Each member of the student community had explored the Cornell-Ithaca environment independently, and no matter how limited or how idiosyncratic any one exploration might have been, it surely must have generated information that would be of interest to some others who had not yet made the same discoveries. The larger the number of students consulted, the more thoroughly the environmental resources become mapped, and the more useful the composite information bank becomes to each member of the community. Since the information being requested is well known to each student, it is available on short notice and can be put on paper quickly. Theoretically, the master sheets could have been distributed at the beginning of a traditional fifty-minute class, collected ten minutes later, and with appropriate printing technology, reproduced, collated, stapled, and made ready for distribution as the students left the room at the end of the same class.

The same general principles apply to the catalog of personal resources. It is easily created because, once again, students make use of information that is well known to them. If entries are made by most of the members of a large group, the result is a substantial list of "short courses." This information is analogous to a conventional university course catalog. In our case it represented a "university" within a university; a listing of things that students were willing and competent to teach each other. The entries corresponded to the interests of the community because the "teachers" and the "students" were one and the same group, simply assuming different roles at different times.

The production of both the environmental resources and the personal resources catalogs continued the process of increasing the kinds and amounts of information made available to our class about its own members, since most of the catalog entries revealed the personalities of the individuals making the entries. The form of the communication was, in this regard, as important as its content. For this reason, no effort was made to "edit" the pages submitted. However, if sufficient time had been available, the addition of an alphabetized index would have increased the usefulness of the catalogs.

Representative catalog pages are shown in Figure 3. The personal resources catalog consisted of 158 pages (each submitted by a separate student), with 260 individual entries that were placed in 131 categories. The categories and number of entries in each category are listed in Table 2. The environmental resources catalog consisted of 143 pages (each submitted by a separate student), with 569 individual entries of information about the Cornell-Ithaca environment that were placed in 182 categories. The categories and number of entries in each category are listed in Table 3. The number of pages in each catalog was somewhat less than the number of students who returned ditto-master sheets, because some were incorrectly used, and there wasn't time to make corrections.

ENVIRONMENTAL RESOURCE

CHEAPEST GAS IN TOWN -
    WORKINGMAN'S FRIEND
        (ACROSS FROM CO-OP SHOPPING CENTER)
    REGULAR - 32⁹
    PREMIUM - 34⁹

    UNLESS YOU DRIVE A "FANCY RIG" YOU PROBABLY
    DON'T NEED "SUPER" GAS.
    A FILLUP AT THE WORKINGMAN'S FRIEND
    (15 gal) WILL SAVE YOU $1.05 COMPARED WITH
    THE COLLEGE-TOWN OR OTHER LOCAL BANDITS.

ICE-CREAM CONES -
    WHY PAY THE INFLATIONARY PRICES SWEEPING
    THOMPKINS COUNTY GO TO THE CORNELL DAIRY
    AND SAVE
    YOU GET 8⅓ (2 SCOOP) CONES AT
        PURITY ICE CREAM FOR $2.50.
    AT CORNELL, YOU GET 2 GALLONS
        OF ICE CREAM FOR THAT SAME $2.50
        (ENOUGH TO MAKE 50-75 CONES)
    THINK ABOUT IT. FOR A LITTLE BIT
    OF WORK, YOU GET A LOT MORE
    ICE CREAM!
    CORNELL DAIRY BAR - UPPER AG QUAD.

                        RUPERT STEINBERGER

I will help anyone learn to make
    BREAD
    THIS INCLUDES MANY TYPES OF BREAD, NORMAL WHITE
    BREAD, CUBAN BREAD AND FRENCH BREAD.

    I CAN DO THIS JUST ABOUT ANY SATURDAY OR SUNDAY
    IF YOU CHECKED WITH ME FIRST. ANY KITCHEN SUPPLIES
    WITH NORMAL SUPPLIES LIKE FLOUR, SALT AND MILK WILL
    DO. I WOULD RATHER DO IT IN MY OWN, BUT ITS YOUR
    CHOICE.

    BREAD TAKES OVER 6 HOURS TO RISE, MAKE, KNEAD
    AND BAKE SO ALLOW ALOT OF TIME FOR THIS ENTERPRISE.
    GET IN TOUCH WITH ME AT 273-1852. IF I'M
    NOT IN LEAVE A MESSAGE.

    CHRISTINE KORDA

Figure 3. *Representative pages from the catalogs which students created to share information about resources in the Cornell-Ithaca environment and things that they are willing to teach each other.*

Personal Resource
Be your own Auto Mechanic

Objective is to be able to fix minor
breakdowns and give proper general
maintenance to your automobile.

Design of plan is to set up a time
that instruction could be held. Supervision
would be given but it is important that the
student actually works so that he developes
the necessary skills.

Physical facilities needed are the car,
a simple set of tools and (if typical Ithaca
weather) a garage of some sort to protect
you from outside conditions

Contact.
Mark Goldfarb
572-5797

Lenore Tytelman

Environmental Resource

I would like to tell people about places in the Ithaca area
where design and construction materials can be had for low cost
or with maximum convenience.

At Cayuga Lumber they are generally pretty good about
allowing you to get small pieces of lumber or masonite out of
their remnant pile for no charge. They even offer to trim or
cut it to size for you.

A great deal of strange improvisational materials can be
found at Agway. (Their tubing in plastic is half price of
anywhere else.)

Ithaca plastics has a scrap pile of small pieces of plexi-
glass and other plastics if your needs are small.

Challenge Industries has a lot of miscellaneous junk that
could provide some useful things if you just have the patience
and insight to fish around.

Figure 3.

Table 2. *Categories of entries made in the Personal Resources Catalog and the number of entries made in each category.*

Categories	Entries
I. Instruction	
A-animal imitations	1
automobile repairs	3
B-badminton	1
basketball	3
batik	2
beaded flowers	1
billiards	1
book covering	1
boxing	1
bread baking	2
bridge	2
butterfly mountings	1
C-cake baking	1
calculus	1
camping techniques	1
candle making	6
canoeing	2
cards	1
change carbon arc on Fade-Ometer	1
chess	1
Chinese	1
clothing construction	3
collage making	1
cooking	7
crocheting	11
D-dice	1
diving	1
drafting	1
drawing	2
driving	1
E-embroidery	4
entertainment techniques	1
F-feather flower construction	1
fencing	1
finger painting	2
fishing	1
flat-pattern design	1
flute	1
flying	1
folk dancing	1
football	1
frisbee	1
G-gardening	2
German	1
golf	2
guitar	4
H-haircutting	1
house painting	1
I-ice-skating	1
ironing	1
J-judo	1
jug band instruments	1
juggling	1
K-karate	1
kite construction	1
knitting	7
knot tieing	1
L-leather craft	4
liquid acetate techniques	1
love	1
M-macrame	7
map reading	1
maple syrup making	1
mathematical games	1
metal craft	2
motorcycle riding	1
O-omelette making	1
P-painting	1
paper constructions	1
paper flower construction	2
papier-mâché	1
parallel parking	1
photograph mounting	1
piano	2
pigeon imitations	1
ping pong	2
place kicking	1
plexiglass techniques	2
pottery	2
print making	1
printing page layout	1
problem solving techniques	1
R-rifle	1
roulette	1
rug hooking	3
S-sailing	3
saxophone	1
scrimshaw	1
sewing	24
silk screening	2
singing	2
skate boarding	1
skiing and ski care	5
slide rule techniques	1
squash	2
swimming and water safety	12

T-tape recording	1
tennis	2
tie-dyeing	6
trampoline	1
trumpet	1
typing	2
V-violin	1
W-water polo	1
weaving	1
whistling	1
wine making	1
wood working	2
Y-yoga	1

| II. Services | |
| astrological charts | 2 |

clothes patching	1
exercise classes	4
flute concerts	1
haircutting	2
information exchange programs	1
kitchen facilities	1
rap sessions	2
saxophone concerts	1
transportation	1
III. Advice/Information	
Bahai Religion	1
clothes buying	1
communes and co-ops	1
course selection	1
diets/nutrition	1
Jesus	1

Table 3. *Categories of entries made in the Environmental Resources Catalog and the number of entries made in each category.*

Categories	Entries
I. Food	
A. Places to eat	
General	12
Chinese restaurants	2
Greek restaurants	2
Italian restaurants	2
Diners	10
Food trucks	6
Hamburger stands	3
Snack bars	8
Food specialties	
bagels	2
bakery goods	2
banana splits	2
brunch	1
cheeseburgers	1
chicken	4
clams	2
coffee	7
donuts	2
hamburgers	2
ice cream	4
milk shakes	1
onion rings	1
pizza	3
roast beef sandwiches	1
salad	3
spaghetti	1
submarine sandwiches	1
tea	2
yogurt	4
Bars	18
Coffeehouses	15
Dormitory dining plan	1
B. Shops (food)	
general groceries	8
apples	12
beer and liquors	4
bakery goods	4
bread	1
butterscotch brownies	1
candy	12
cookies	2
dairy products	7
donuts	3
eggs	2
ice cream	11
macaroons	1
meats	8
pretzels	1
soft drinks	2
tea	1
II. Stores	
general merchandise	5
antiques	2
appliances	2
art supplies	1

plays (free)	1
pool	1
record-listening rooms	6
skiing	5
squash	2
swimming	
outdoor (natural spots)	9
indoor (pools)	8
tennis	2
track	1
tray-sliding	1

VI. Places of interest

bird sanctuary	1
Cayuga Heights Cliffs	1
Cornell Game Farm	1
Cornell Observatory	2
Cornell Plantations and Sculpture Gardens	1
Corning Glass Factory	1
Eastern Artificial Insemination Co.	1
foundry	2
Garrett Clinic	1
graveyards	1
Historical Society	1
libraries (general)	14
art	3
music	1
museums	4
ornithology laboratory	1
science exhibits	1
wineries	1
zoo	2

VII. Services

automobile care	8
automobile mechanics course	1
birth control information	1
bulletin boards	2
bus	1
cabs	1
complaint column (in newspaper)	2
computer course	1
computer laboratory	1
craft shop	5
drivers' education course	1
drug information (Mainline)	1
legal aid	1
models	2
mystic	1
nursery school	1
photographers	2
planned parenthood information	2
pottery lessons	1

bar supplies	1
beads	1
bicycles	1
books	5
bricks (free)	1
bus tokens	1
candle wax	1
clothing (used)	1
coffee mugs	1
construction materials	1
dry ice	1
furniture	2
health needs	2
incense	1
laundry detergent	1
leather	1
leather scraps (free)	3
maps (free)	1
newspapers	3
note paper	1
pets	1
press lettering	3
records	2
sandals	1
shoes	2
silver jewelry	1
silver rivets	1
soapstone	1
sweaters	2
T-shirts	1
typing paper	1
water beds	1
yarn	1

III. Study areas

A. Indoors	31
B. Outdoors	9

IV. Retreat areas

A. Indoors (general)	8
lounges	4
meeting places	7
B. Outdoors (general)	37
flower gardens	1
Ithaca rapids	1
parks	21
rock garden	1
sculpture garden	3

V. Recreation and leisure

bird watching	1
bowling	2
canoeing	3
darkroom facilities	2
dancing (group)	1

film series	1
gymnasiums	2
hiking	1
ice-skating	3
macrame group	1
movie theaters	1
Ping-Pong	1
printers	2
ski information and services	1
typing	1
VIII. General	
check cashing service	6
church information	1
cider mill	1
communes	1
drinking fountain (cold water)	1
girls' schools	8
jobs	
registration committee	1

usher	1
kittens (free)	1
laundry facilities	7
lodging	3
meetings and seminars information	
art	1
bible study	1
Marx	1
rap sessions	3
music practice facilities	
general	1
guitar	1
harpsichord	1
organ	1
piano	2
parking areas	2
best streets to use	1
tunnels	3

Learning Party

The final exercise in the series on the design of learning environments consisted of a learning party open to the larger Cornell community and was designed to share, with that larger community, the essential elements of the student-teaching exercise and the catalog-construction exercise. The design and management of the learning party represented, in itself, a rather complex environmental design problem; it was solved by a task-group of approximately fifteen students, including several students from the school of architecture working with Michael Williams and Richard Chase. The learning party was scheduled to start at the regularly assigned time, and was to be accommodated in a television lounge, exhibit room, and adjoining corridor spaces in the student union building; most of the furniture was cleared from these spaces. An earlier plan called for the creation of a new inflatable environment in the open space in front of the student union building; however, difficulties concerning fire codes and the safety regulations of the department of buildings and grounds stood in the way of executing that plan.

On the morning of the party, members of the task-group arrived between one and two hours ahead of the regularly scheduled time for the start of class and modified the spaces by rearranging remaining furniture and making use of rolls of wrapping paper, masking tape, and corrugated boxes. A "path" was made of two-inch strips of masking tape which ran from the outside steps leading into the student union building, through the lobby, and to the area used for the party. Large signs with the words "learning party" accompanied by a brief description were placed at the entrance to the learning-party spaces; the signs could be clearly seen by everyone going downstairs from the main lobby of the building to the main cafeteria below (Figure 4). Each page of the Environmental Resources Catalog and each page of the Personal Resources Catalog was glued onto long sections of wrapping paper and taped on walls at eye level (Figure 5). Corrugated shipping cartons

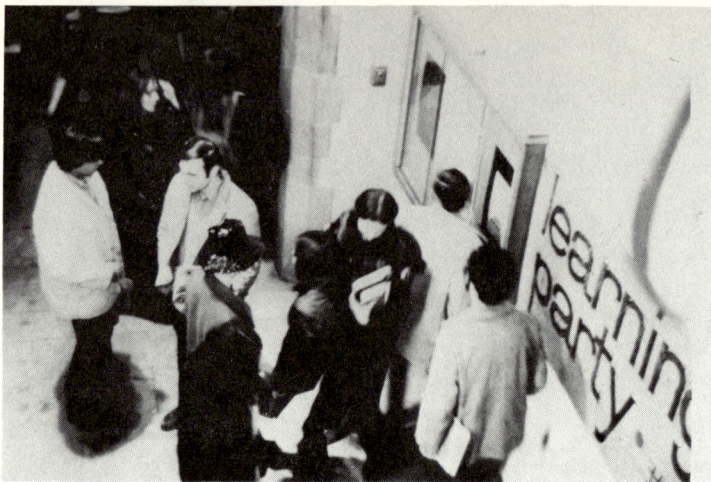

Figure 4. *Learning-party signs were placed just outside the area used for the learning party so that they could be seen by students moving from the lobby down the stairs to the main cafeteria.*

were covered with clean paper and piled in the middle of the floor of the TV lounge so that students could use them for support of materials needed for student-teaching exercises. Another wall was used for a display of information about the sponsors of the party: the department of design and environmental analysis and, more specifically, the class in Environmental Analysis: Human and Social

Factors. The duplicating machine and a supply of ditto masters were placed on a table. Most of the wall space in the exhibit room also was used for display of separate catalog pages glued to paper, but one wall was reserved for an information system with the title: "Will You Teach?" This system allowed visitors to fill out pages with information about things that they wanted to teach

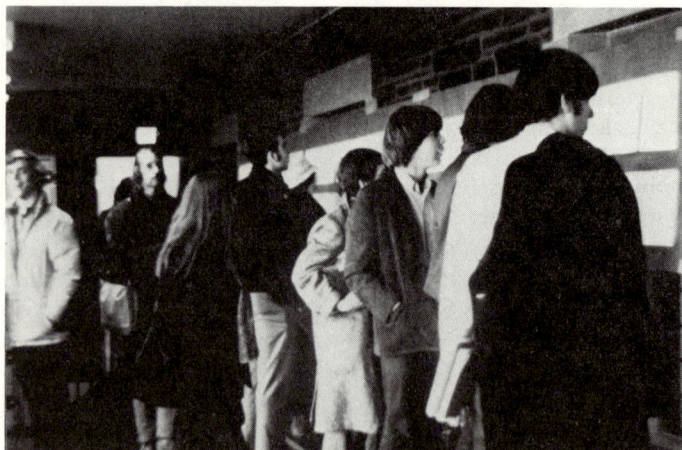

Figure 5. *The sections of wrapping paper with individual pages of Environmental Resources and Personal Resources Catalogs glued to them were taped on walls at eye level. As soon as they were in place, students studied the catalog pages with care, and many took notes on what they read.*

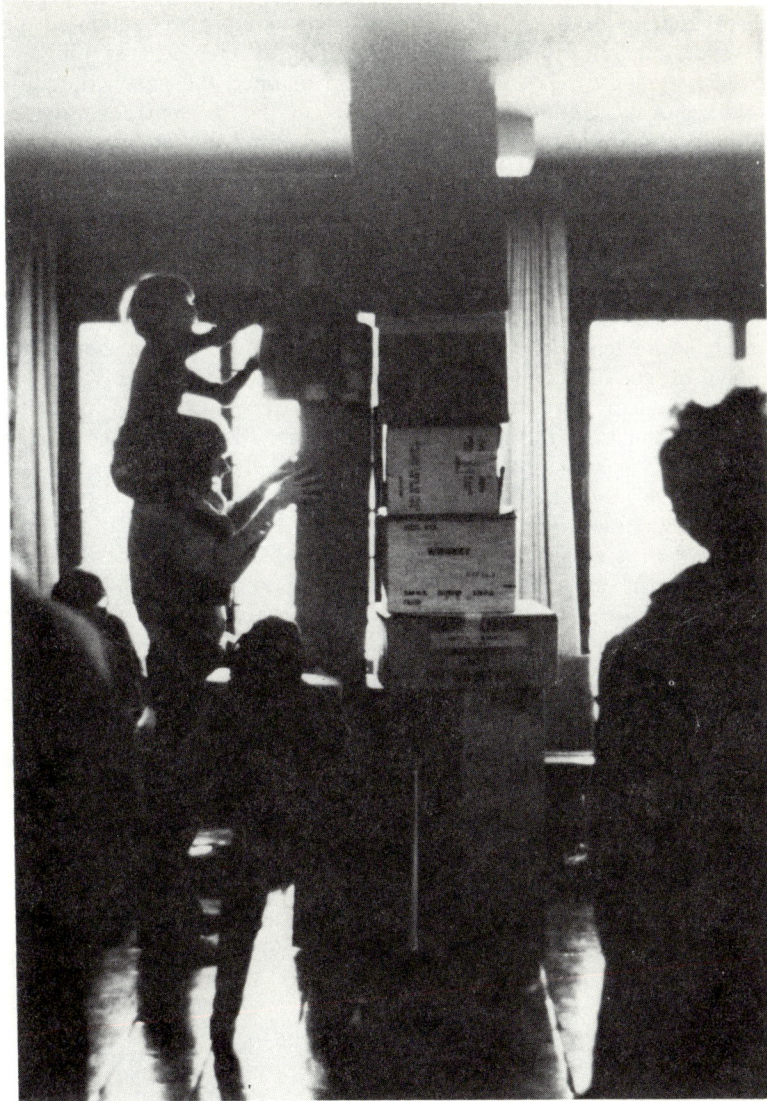

Figure 6. *Schoolchildren from a "free" experimental primary school in Ithaca arrived at the learning party early and used corrugated boxes intended for use in displays as play materials. They thereby created a "corrugated box playground" that persisted throughout the learning-party exercise.*

other students. This procedure was similar to the one used for compiling the Personal Resources Catalog. These pages were displayed immediately so that visitors could copy information from them.

As soon as catalog pages were taped to the walls, students on their way to the cafeteria began to read the pages. Almost everyone continued to read, moving from page to page; many took notes as they read. Additional students were directed to the area by the masking-tape path, the large signs on the wall, and leaflets about the party distributed at the main entrance to the building by visiting children. An invited group of children from a "free" experimental primary school in Ithaca arrived before the scheduled start of the party and began using the pile of corrugated boxes as play materials; the central area of the room was transformed into a playground (Figure 6).

A minority of the regular class-group had made arrangements to teach at the party, since that was an optional matter. However, most of the student teachers at the party had prepared more elaborate teaching programs, including displays of cooking and pottery-making, than we had seen at the first student-teaching exercise. By the time the full class arrived, many people were already using the spaces, and most of the class members behaved like the other guests and actively explored the displays of catalog pages, information about the sponsorship of the event, and additional student-teaching opportu-

nities. The collated catalogs were distributed to the regular class members.

The catalog-production display table was staffed by members of the task-group that had planned the party; they introduced visitors to the concepts underlying the catalog exercise and invited them to put information about environmental resources and personal resources on ditto masters, which were then promptly run off by machine. Periodically, five- to ten-page sets of these visitor-contributed catalog pages were collated, stapled, and handed out. Some of the catalog pages created by visitors are shown in Figure 7.

Hundreds of students who were not enrolled in our class visited throughout the morning. All of the spaces used for the party were filled to capacity most of the time. Many students listed things that they were willing to teach both at the catalog-production display and at the "Will You Teach?" information display board. All of the student-teaching exercises were actively subscribed,

Environmental Resources —
'Instant Packsack' from piece of Rope.
(Learned from "Eskimo, Baffin Is., Canada).

Materials: 1 piece ½" rope, 6 meters long.

Step ①: Lay out on Floor the rope (in a loop) underneath the object to be backpacked.

box to be carried

Step ②: Sit on Floor, lean against the box, and bring loop of rope over-head.

rope

Step ③: Feed Rope ends through the loop that crosses chest.

box → rope ends

Step ④: Rope ends can be held in hand for short hike, or tied in order to free hands.

MAIN-LINE

Main-Line is an independent group of Cornell students trained to provide drug information and aid in drug crises. A Main-Line volunteer will be available to talk with you on the phone or meet you in person. The Service is confidential, and if needed medical referral will be available.

Main-Line — 256-3888
office phone — 256-3893

We are now expanding our services to include all sorts of personal problems. Feel free to drop in and rap

Main-Line is now located in the back of Sheldon Court (the big brick bldg. on College Ave.)

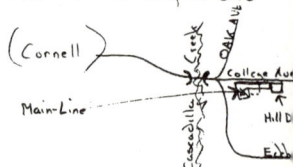

Figure 7. *Catalog pages contributed by visitors to the learning party.*

although the large numbers of spectators usually forced the student teachers to restrict their teaching to demonstrations with accompanying commentary.

As the number of people in the learning-party spaces increased, various people appeared who had not participated in the design of the learning party and represented special interests of their own. Several entrepreneurs set up table displays. One was used for the sale of jewelry, and another provided opportunities to sign up for bus trips. Representatives of the student radio station made arrangements to conduct interviews with members of the class while some faculty groups talked about the implications of the event for the design of other teaching experiences and the design of the freshman orientation program. Many visitors wanted to buy copies of the catalogs. Attendance and activity remained high for several hours after the scheduled termination of the event.

COMMENTARY

The series of exercises on the design of learning environments was designed with some common objectives in mind. Each exercise provided an opportunity to appreciate how much information is contained within a community but remains largely unavailable for general use because of the limitations of the communication systems being used. The environmental designer can modify communication systems in a way that makes large amounts of high-quality information relevant to the interests of large numbers of people readily available. The student-teacher, catalog, and the learning-party exercises all attempted to accomplish this objective. The deliberate modification of a group's communication systems is a powerful way of altering some aspects of the organization and function of the group. In our case the communication system was biased toward utilization of self-selected, self-organized, personalized information about members of the class community that would increase the probability of occurrence of a wide range of interpersonal encounters and social interaction among group members.

Game designers use three sets of variables to describe a game: players, resources, and rules (Shubik, 1964). In the case of our exercises, the players were always the same to begin with, although many exercises were designed to allow "visitors" to join the group. The resources available to the group were not supplemented in any significant way: The entire series of exercises was supported with a budget of $200.00, which was largely used to pay for printing supplies and services, wrapping paper, and masking tape. Many social and learning behaviors were generated by altering the rules by which members of the class relate to and make use of resources already available in their environment: in this case, largely the information available to each individual separately that usually was not shared with the group. This is an important lesson for the environmental designer. The ability to influence the ways in which resources in an existing environment are used can have consequences every bit as profound as the provision of new resources. Ideally, the creation of environmental resources and the design of rules that shape the relationships between people and environmental resources should be undertaken in the closest possible interrelationship. We had the advantage of working in this way in all of our exercises.

Each exercise prominently incorporated generalizing, regenerating, and self-organizing features. The first student-teaching exercise was held in view of regular visitors to the student union building, and when visitors volunteered to explore the new events, they were welcomed and given orientation and direct access to all available group privileges. The same can be said of the learning-party exercise. The catalogs were shared with the community as a whole, and visitors added entries to the catalogs. Execution of these exercises required a great deal of help from the regular caretakers of the Cornell environment. Space managers, custodians, security and safety staff, secretarial and technical staff, food service staff, and many others were approached by members of the task forces for collaboration and assistance in the execution of the exercises. Requests rarely were denied, and we must assume that requests were of a sort that engendered collaboration and affiliation.

All of the exercises allowed considerable freedom for the detailed aspects of performance. The general framework was determined by the course designers and the visiting professors; however, the framework was fashioned to demonstrate the enormous power of design decisions to evoke affiliative and cooperative behaviors within large groups. These behaviors can be shared by large numbers of people who are not part of the original group (generalizing features) and sustained well beyond the time and space limits of the original planned exercises (self-sustaining and regenerating features). Students made their own selections of the first student-teacher exercise (second class) and their own choices about whether they would teach at the learning party (self-organizing features). The group agreed to visitor-participation in all exercises, and both visitors and regular class students participated in the same direct patterns of negotiation concerning what they would share with each other and the manner in which they would share. The task-groups consisted of individuals who volunteered for substantial contributions of time over and above that required to meet the expected performance standards for the course, and, in addition, they largely determined their own patterns of specialization and division of labor. As would be expected, students in the school of architecture played a prominent role in the learning-party exercise, because that exercise involved designing on an architectural scale. In general, people volunteered for specialty assignments in accordance with well-established histories of interest and experience. This represents one of the self-organizing aspects of the exercise. Other examples of self-organizing activities were: the creation of a playground by visiting primary-school children from a pile of corrugated boxes intended for display; the establishment of independent entrepreneurial activity by the jewelry salesman and the travel agent; and development of incipient plans for more formal catalog-design efforts. The generalizing, self-sustaining, regenerating, and self-organizing features of the exercises do not represent independent, nonoverlapping aspects of the experiences we are describing. They are interdependent and closely related aspects of these experiences.

It is clear that our major investment of time and effort was made in the design and execution of the series of exercises reported in this paper. Our resources were limited, time was short, and we had the further disadvantage of being brief-visiting members of the Cornell community. For these reasons, objective quantitative evaluation of our own design efforts was not possible. We were forced to make our observations in an expedient manner, making use of our own and other photographs, verbal accounts, direct observations, and the written assignments turned in by the students. The result was, of necessity, a more anecdotal and subjective account of our experiences than we would have liked.

Design educators are developing an appreciation for the importance of integrating information about human behavior into every step of the design process, as well as the importance of incorporating laboratory exercises into the education of environmental designers. We feel that our experiences at Cornell illuminate some of the advantages of moving in these new directions.

A BEHAVIORAL TECHNOLOGY OF EDUCATION

m

11

BEHAVIORAL OBJECTIVES

Many techniques of behavioral education have been used in the programs already described: social, token, and behavioral reinforcement; contingency contracting; data-taking; specification of behaviors; and reinforcement of successive approximations, to mention some. The third part of this volume deals with some additional techniques that have emerged from behavioral education; however, "techniques" is perhaps too narrow a term. The areas treated in this part involve sweeping new approaches to education often included under the rubric of "educational technology."

Entire books and issues of journals have been devoted to each of the areas covered. Rather than undertaking the impossible task of presenting a comprehensive discussion of each topic, the editors have selected articles which will give the reader some idea of what does and can go on in this area. The articles selected represent a particularly worthwhile approach to the area even though some of the approaches are unusual.

The topic of the first section is behavioral objectives. The use of behavioral objectives has grown out of the notion, basic to behavior modification, that one must specify the terminal behavior one desires. The specification must be as positive as possible; it must pass Lindsley's well-known "dead-man" test. It also must be stated in terms of observable behavior. Words such as "understanding" and "appreciation" must be avoided in favor of words that describe what the learner will actually do. This simple idea of specifying terminal behavior has grown into the widespread use of behavioral objectives. Numerous books have been written and workshops held on the writing of behavioral objectives; in fact, objectives have been written on such wide-ranging topics as driver education, English composition, drawing, African history, and dental assisting.

The first paper in this section, by Short, gives an introduction to behavioral objectives. The second presents an example of using behavioral objectives in a program. The example used, by Lee, shows that behavioral objectives can be sensitive to the ultimate aims of the student as well as the instructor.

Measurable objectives for educational programs

JERRY SHORT

Not long ago, a reporter interviewed the director of one of the world's most successful family-planning and population-control programs. In the interview, the reporter asked the director about the main objective of the program. The director answered, "Well, I would say that the main objective is to establish family-planning concepts at all levels in the country." In his answer, the director described a general objective. It is typical of the type of general objective that is often used to describe a nation's overall educational goals or a teacher's overall objectives. Here are some other examples of general objectives:

> Our national goal is to educate effective citizens for the future.
> My main objective as a teacher is to develop individual students to their maximum potential.
> The goal of our educational system is to develop (1) the manpower skills needed for economic growth and (2) the conceptual skills needed for active participation in a democratic society.

These general objectives are useful starting points for planning educational programs, but they are no more than starting points. Before good educational programs can be designed and carried out, these general objectives must be converted into specific objectives.

Since the reporter realized the need for specific objectives, he continued his interview by asking the director to describe the objective in more detail. The director answered, "Well, during the first five years of our family-planning program, our objective is to contact 60 percent of the women in the target age group from 15 to 45 years old." This answer is more specific. It limits the objective to a five-year period and specifies the target group, but it is still not specific enough. The objective does not give a clear picture of what the program is attempting to do. More importantly, we do not know how to tell if the program is successful or not. In his answer, the director said, "Our objective is to contact 60 percent of the women in the target age group from 15 to 45 years old." But it is not clear what the director means by the word contact; he could mean two very different things. On the one hand, he could mean that women know the meaning of the term "family planning." On the other hand, he could mean that women are actively participating in family-planning programs. There is a great difference in these two interpretations. Although the director gave a more specific objective the second time than he did at first, he still did not give a measurable objective.

So the reporter asked another question. "What exactly do you mean when you say your objective is to contact people?" "Well, to be specific," the director answered, "I mean two things. First, I mean that someone has visited one of our clinics or hospitals and had an individual interview with a nurse or caseworker about family planning. In other words, our objective is to interview 60 percent of the target population during the next five years, but interviews are not enough. We want to achieve a high acceptance rate of family-planning practices among the women we interview. We want three-fourths of the people we interview to accept family-planning procedures. Acceptance means that they use some type of birth-control procedure to limit their families to two or three children, preferably two, and that they continue to come to local clinics at least twice a year for consultation, checkups, and medication."

Now the objectives of the program are clear; they are stated so that the director can use them to measure the success of the program. The director can do this by comparing the actual progress made in the program with the specific objectives of the program. In this way, he can tell if enough people are being

Reprinted by permission of the author.

interviewed and if the interviews are successful in getting the desired rate of acceptance.
If the program fails to meet its objectives,
he can take immediate action to improve the
program. In fact, during the first month of
the program, the number of interviews was
much lower than planned. The nurses often
had no one to interview because few people
voluntarily came to the family-planning clinics. Immediate corrective action was taken
to send the nurses where the people were in
community centers, factories, and homes, and
a new program was begun to contact couples
who had applied for marriage licenses. By
the end of the first year, this corrective action
had produced the desired results, and the
program was meeting its objectives.

Converting General Objectives to Measurable Objectives

The interview about the family-planning
program illustrates the difference between
general objectives and measurable objectives.
A measurable objective describes something
that can be observed; it describes the desired
outcome of a program in such a way that
most people can agree that the program is a
success or a failure. In contrast, a general
objective is usually vague and ambiguous.
People do not agree on what it means, how
to observe it, or how to tell if the objective
has been successfully met.

In the interview, the director and reporter
began by discussing a general objective and
then gradually converted it into a measurable
objective. Here are the stages in their development of the general objective into a measurable objective:

1. Establish family-planning concepts at all
levels in the country.
2. Contact 60 percent of the women in the
age group from 15 to 45 years old.
3. Conduct individual interviews about
family planning with 60 percent of the
women in the age group from 15 to 45.
Get three fourths of them to accept family-
planning procedures. Acceptance means
that they use some type of birth-control

procedure to limit their families to two or
three children, preferably two, and that
they continue to come to local clinics at
least twice a year for consultation, checkups, and medication.

Educators are often called on to convert
general objectives into measurable objectives.
A teacher interested in teaching "good citizenship" needs to convert this general objective into test items and situations that will
allow him to observe if his students actually
behave as good citizens. A teacher interested
in teaching students to "write effectively"
needs to convert this general objective into
ways of measuring his student's writing proficiency and their interest in writing. An
elementary-science specialist interested in
teaching "scientific attitudes" needs to convert this general objective into situations
where he can observe students approaching
new problems in ways that demonstrate they
have a scientific approach toward problem
solving.

The discussion described below is a typical
example. In it, a master-teacher (MT) guides
a student-teacher (ST) from a vague general
objective to a specific measurable objective.

MT (master-teacher):
　　What objectives for the preschool
　　program do you want to work on
　　this morning?
ST (student-teacher):
　　Let's start with math.
MT: What is your main objective in
　　mathematics?
ST: To teach number concepts.
MT: What do you want your students to
　　be able to do with number concepts
　　when they complete the preschool
　　program?
ST: Well, I want them to be able to un-
　　derstand number concepts from 1 to
　　10.
MT: That word "understand" is vague.
　　Can you give me an example of a
　　situation that you would use to de-
　　termine if a student really under-
　　stands number concepts?
ST: Let's see. I would give a student a
　　set of objects, like 10 coins, and ask

him to give me 7 of them, then 9 of them, and then 4, and so on.

MT: Does the student have to be able to read a problem or write his answer?

ST: No, I'll say the problem to him, and he can solve it by counting objects into sets.

In this conversation, the student teacher gradually converted a general objective into a specific measurable objective. These were the stages in developing the objective:

1. Teach number concepts.
2. The students should be able to understand number concepts from 1 to 10.
3. When a student is given a set of objects and asked for any number of objects from 1 to 10, he can correctly form a new set of objects containing the required number of objects.

In this sequence, the student-teacher began with a general objective which was difficult to measure. In the second item, she reduced the vagueness somewhat by specifying the range of numbers the student should be able to work with. In the third item, she described the objective in enough detail so that anyone could observe a student and tell if he could perform the objective correctly.

Summary. Two examples have been used to illustrate the difference between general objectives and measurable objectives. Both the family-planning example and the preschool example illustrate how a general objective can be converted into a measurable objective. Educators often need to do this. You may want to try doing it yourself at this point. If so, try to convert these two general objectives into measurable objectives:

Get students to understand some of the factors influencing great explorers like Columbus.
Allow primary students freedom of expression in art, and encourage their creativity in artistic self-expression.

These are difficult examples. Later, in the last section of this article, some measurable objectives are given for these two general ob-

jectives. You can compare your measurable objectives with those.

Other terms are often used to describe measurable objectives. These include terms such as behavioral objectives, learner objectives, instructional objectives, and terminal objectives. No important distinction between these terms is made in this article. All the terms emphasize the importance of (1) writing objectives that describe what a student should be able to do after he completes a learning experience, and (2) describing the desired behavior in detail so that it can be observed and measured.

Recognizing the Difference Between Measurable Objectives and Educational Methods and Materials

When student-teachers are first asked to write measurable objectives, they often write something else. They begin to write lesson plans, course outlines, and student assignments. All of these materials describe the activities of teachers and students *during* an educational event. In contrast, a measurable objective describes the desired behavior of students *after* completing an educational event. This distinction is not always clear to student-teachers who are often expected to prepare not only measurable objectives but also many other types of educational materials. The following conversation illustrates the problem; a master-teacher is working with a student-teacher.

MT (master-teacher):
    Let's work on the mathematics objectives for preschool students.

ST (student-teacher): OK.

MT: What is your main objective in mathematics?

ST: The main objective is to let the children play with many different objects and gain experience arranging them in sets of different numbers.

MT: That is not a measurable objective; you described an educational method. You told me what the students will do during instruction, but a measurable objective describes what the students will be able to do after the instruction is over. I want to know your measurable objectives. Can you be more specific?

ST: Well, I'll teach number concepts this way. For example, I'll hold up a card with a picture of 3 dogs on it, and I'll say "Here are 3 dogs; let's count them together."

MT: You are still describing a method of teaching number concepts. That is not what I want. An objective describes what a student does after he completes a lesson, not something a teacher does during the lesson. Before we talk about the way you plan to teach number concepts, I'd like to make sure I understand exactly what the students are supposed to learn.

ST: Well, they should learn number concepts from 1 to 10, the concept of sets and subsets, the distinction between numerals and numbers.

MT: No, that's not what I am talking about either. Now you are outlining the content and the subject matter. I'm not interested yet in (1) what you are going to teach, (2) how the student is going to learn it, or (3) what content you are going to cover. I want to know your objectives. What will a successful student be able to do when he finishes the pre-school program?

ST: You have me completely confused. I've told you how I would teach number concepts, what the students will do to practice number concepts, and the content I will cover. Don't you want to know any of that?

MT: Not yet. I want to get to methods, materials, and content later. First, I want to know your objectives. Let me put it another way. Suppose a student walked in here right now. How would you find out if he knew number concepts?

ST: Ask him.

MT: Ask him what?

ST: Well, I would give him a lot of objects, like a lot of coins, and ask him to give me 5 of them, or 8 of them, or 7. . . . Like that.

MT: Would you consider your preschool math program a success if all your students could do that when they were through?

ST: Yes.

MT: Well, now you've given me your measurable objective. Now I know what you want your students to be able to do after they complete the program. That's what I mean by measurable objective.

ST: I think I see what you mean.

At the end of the discussion, the student-teacher seems to recognize the difference between measurable objectives and other types of educational materials, but he probably does not see why the master-teacher made such a fuss about objectives. His next questions might be, "Now that I have the objective, what am I going to do with it, and how can I use it to help me teach a class?"

The Uses of Measurable Objectives

The student-teacher has a good point. At first, it seems that measurable objectives are not as useful as course outlines, curriculum guides, time schedules, textbooks, practice exercises, and other similar types of educational materials. These are the things that a teacher needs in order to run a traditional class in a traditional school on a day-to-day basis. But measurable objectives allow the teacher to be untraditional. They allow him to stand back from the rush of daily school activities and ask himself if these activities are of any value in helping students learn useful skills and concepts.

One advantage of beginning educational planning by specifying measurable objectives is that the objectives tend to free the educator from traditional approaches and allow him to think about alternative ways for students to learn objectives. In one innovative study (Mager and McCann, 1961), an instructor simply told his students what they were expected to learn (the measurable objectives) and dismissed them to learn the objectives on their own. They did, with the same success, but in half the time taken by students in a traditional course. On a larger scale, Project PLAN (Flanagan, 1970) combines measurable objectives with individualized student assignments. In each unit of this kindergarten-to-high-school program, each student knows the objectives he is supposed to learn and the activities he can perform to help him learn the objectives. Many other innovations in education, such as programmed instruction and other methods of individualized instruction, have been developed from a similar careful analysis of measurable objectives.

The concept of measurable objectives implies a certain concept of education. In this concept, the outcome of education is defined as a "change in a student's behavior." This is not a widely accepted concept of education; many people think of education as having no direct effect on a student's observable behavior. For example, a history teacher may be puzzled when he is asked to describe the measurable objectives of a lesson. He may answer that although he plans to talk about the economic conditions leading to war, he has no plans to change his student's behavior; he simply wants students to appreciate certain historical factors that lead to outbreaks of war. This teacher thinks of education as the presentation of theories, facts, and concepts; to him, education is essentially the presentation of ideas. This contrasts with the concept of education as the production of changes in student behavior.

Of course, education can be defined in either way and in many other ways as well. An educator should choose the concept that is most useful to him. For many educators today, the most useful concept of education appears to be the one which emphasizes observable changes in student behavior. It seems that this is the only concept that allows someone to evaluate education, and evaluation seems to be a necessary step in improving education.

An example may illustrate the relation between objectives and evaluation. There are many ways to teach history. Here are only a few of them.

Lectures to a group
History games for small groups to play
Textbook readings
Films
Jobs in government offices
Debates

How is a teacher to decide which method, or combination of methods, to use? In actual practice, a number of irrelevant things determine the teacher's decision. Which methods are the easiest for the teacher to use? Which methods are currently in fashion among the teacher's supervisors, administrators, and peers? Which methods produce the best superficial response from the class, i.e., responses from students such as silence, agreement, approval, smiling, taking notes, etc.? All of these factors probably determine which method the teacher chooses. However, none of these factors is capable of making any systematic improvement in the quality of education. The best educational methods are those that have the best effects on students. These effects can only be observed and measured by observing and measuring the students' behavior. Measurable objectives are a critical part of any observation and measurement scheme because they define the important behavior to be observed and measured.

Another example may illustrate this point. Suppose Teacher A drills her students on historical facts. In contrast, Teacher B assigns independent projects leading to understanding of relationships among historical facts. Which method is better? When we test for knowledge of historical facts, Class A does better than Class B, but when we test for ability to give historical relationships, Class B does better than Class A. The results show that one method achieves one objective, and the other method achieves another objective. Thus the entire evaluation process depends on the objectives we choose as the important desired outcomes of the educational process. Until these objectives are specified in measurable terms, it is impossible to evaluate educational methods and improve them.

In the example above, two educational methods were compared, but a comparison of this sort is an inefficient way to improve education. A better way is to start with a single method, evaluate it, and then revise it to make it better. For example, suppose a teacher wanted students to learn both of the objectives described above: to remember certain historical facts and to write reports illustrating certain types of relationships among other historical facts. She would plan her lesson, give it to some students, and then give the appropriate tests. After she scored the tests, she would analyze the mistakes and make revisions to improve the lesson. Then she would give the revised lesson to the same students or new ones and go through the testing and revision procedure again. This procedure usually is called a "tryout-and-revision" procedure, and several tryouts and revisions often are needed before a lesson is successful. In the example below, the teacher tries four different methods before she is able to meet her objectives. Each tryout of the lesson gives her new information for revising the lesson.

1. Original lesson: A long lecture. Results: Students failed to remember most of the facts and were not able to do the independent project.

2. Revision I: A short lecture and a list of facts for students to memorize. Results: Students remembered the facts but still were not able to do the independent project.

3. Revision II: The materials of Revision I and a new lecture on using the library. Results: Students remembered the facts but still were unable to do the project.

4. Revision III: The materials of Revision I and an individualized exercise giving the students practice in using the library to do independent projects. Results: Students remembered the facts and were able to do the project.

These revisions in educational materials led to improvements in educational outcomes; the revisions were possible because there were measurable objectives. Without these objectives, the teacher would not have realized that the original lecture was bad. The lecture could be evaluated only because the educational outcomes had been specified in advance.

Summary. Measurable objectives are useful for at least three reasons:

1. They emphasize the outcomes of education rather than the methods of education.

2. They suggest innovative methods for achieving the desired educational outcomes.

3. They make it possible to evaluate and improve educational methods through the process of tryout and revision.

Improving Educational Programs

Figure 1 illustrates a simple model for designing and improving any type of educational program. The program could be a family-planning program or a mathematics program, or it could be a national program or a program created by one teacher for a one-hour class. It could be a film, a lecture, an exercise, a self-instructional unit, or a textbook assignment. Regardless of the nature of the program, the general design, tryout, and revision process is the same.

Step 1 of the process is to specify the measurable objectives of the program. This step includes designing the actual tests, situations, and projects that can be used to measure student behavior. Measures of both knowl-

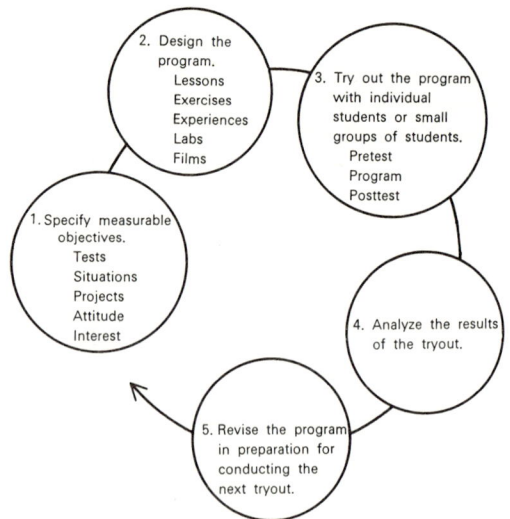

Figure 1. *A system for improving educational programs.*

edge and interest should be prepared since we sometimes achieve the undesirable result of teaching something well and at the same time teaching students to hate the general subject area. A program that is successful in teaching historical facts cannot be called a success if it also teaches students to hate history and avoid all further contacts with the area. In other words, a successful history program should not only teach certain facts and concepts but also increase the chances that later in life students will approach other history courses, history books, conversations about history, and historical places.

It may seem more difficult to measure this type of behavior than to measure knowledge of facts; it is certainly a less familiar process. One basic technique is to give students a choice of activities and record their choices. For example, a history teacher might schedule a free discussion period at the end of each class period and count the number of remarks that students make about history in comparison to other topics. If most students avoid talking about history—preferring to talk about dating, clothes, sports, etc.—the teacher will know that revisions are needed in the history program. If, on the other hand, the discussions are heated arguments about current events and recent history, the teacher can feel confident that the history program is not leading students to avoid history. Krathwohl, Bloom, and Masia (1964) have described many educational objectives relating to attitudes, interests, and feelings, and Mager (1968) has suggested many ingenious ways of measuring these types of objectives.

Step 2 of the process is to design a program which seems likely to achieve the objectives specified in Step 1. The word "program" is used to mean any experience planned for a student: a lecture, programmed text, a lab project, a discussion plan, an exercise, an exhibit, a field trip, a job in a work-study program, a film, or a TV program. In the designing of the program, two things should be kept in mind: money and time. It is best to begin by designing the least expensive program that is likely to succeed and that will require the minimum amount of the students' time. Although it is difficult to estimate final educational costs, it is not too difficult to estimate the comparative costs of educational methods. An objective that can be learned from a one-page diagram does not deserve to be presented as a motion-picture film in full color. Ideally, an educational program can be inexpensive, efficient, and easy to administer and still achieve its objectives.

Step 3 is the tryout step. It is a crucial step in designing good instructional programs. In recent years, tryouts have been emphasized as important experiences for student-teachers in micro-teaching exercises and as a critical step in the design of programmed instruction and other teaching materials. The purpose of a tryout is to test educational materials to see if they work. In tryouts of educational programs, it is important to measure changes in student behavior. This means it is important to know what students can do before the program as well as what they can do after the program. The measure of student behavior before a tryout is sometimes called a baseline or a pretest; without this measure, it is impossible to interpret the results of a tryout. The four graphs in Figure 2 illustrate this. Figure 2a shows an average posttest score of 70 percent. This tells us nothing about the program that preceded the test; if we had given a pretest, we would know more. Figure 2b shows one possible pretest-posttest result: In this case, the students did as well on the pretest as on the posttest. They already knew the objectives, and they did not learn anything from the program. Figure 2c shows another possible result: In this case, the students actually did better on the pretest than on the posttest. The program must have confused them. Figure 2d shows a desirable result: a pretest score of 20 percent and a posttest score of 70 percent. These examples show that without a pretest or baseline as a comparison point, it is difficult to interpret the results of a tryout.

Even experienced educators find tryouts valuable. In one study (Horst and Short, 1971), 24 experienced teachers wrote detailed lessons to teach sixth-grade students to convert temperature readings from Fahrenheit to centigrade scales. Most of the teachers considered this to be a simple learning task, but when the teachers conducted tryouts of their programs, they found that 2 of their 24

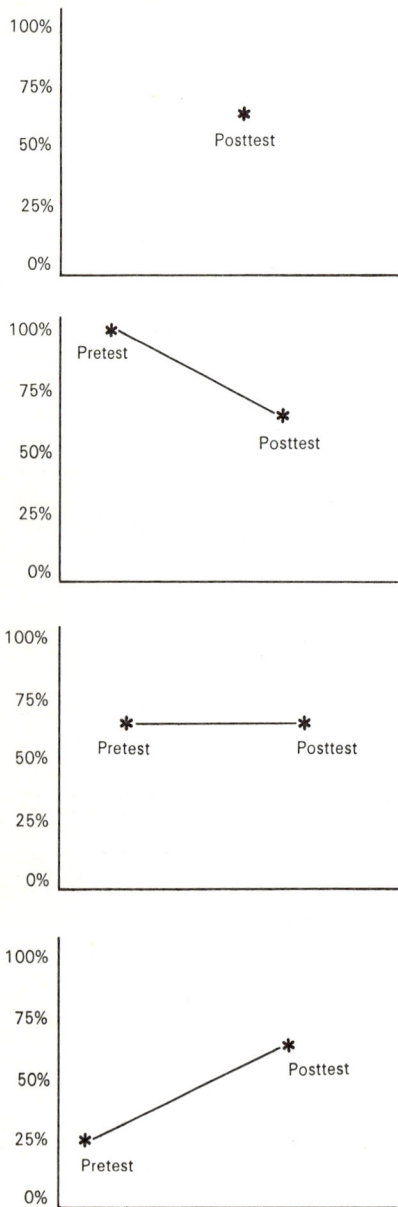

students already could make the conversions on the pretest. These 2 students did not need any instructional program. The other 22 students could not make the temperature conversions on either the pretest or the posttest; they did not learn from the program. Thus, most of the experienced teachers were not able to teach what they considered a simple task the first time they tried.

Step 4 of the process is to analyze the results of the tryout and make decisions about how to revise the program. Step 5 is to make the revisions in preparation for conducting new tryouts. Steps 3, 4, and 5 form a cycle that is repeated until the revised program meets its objectives. How often the cycle must be repeated depends on the skill of the educators and the complexity of the objectives they have set out to achieve.

Figure 3 shows the results of 4 tryouts and revisions of the same training course (Short, 1968). In all tryouts, the median pretest score was about 55 percent. With each successive tryout, the time required for students to take the course decreased from 20 days in Tryout 1 to 9 days in Tryout 4. At the same time, the students' mastery of the course objectives, as measured by the end-of-course test, improved from 80 percent to 92 percent. Figure 3 illustrates how the tryout-and-revision process can improve the effectiveness and efficiency of educational programs.

Summary. A five-step process or system like the one illustrated in Figure 1 is useful in improving the quality and efficiency of educational programs. The process has at least two unusual features: (1) The objectives and the procedures to be used in measuring them are determined before educational materials and methods are prepared; (2) these materials and methods then are used in a series of tryouts and revisions until they can produce the desired level of student mastery of the objectives.

Figure 2. *Illustrative test scores showing the need for a pretest or baseline measure in order to analyze the results of a posttest. The posttest scores are the same in each graph, but their meaning changes according to the pretest score.*

Ensuring the Relevance of Measurable Objectives

Measurable objectives are often good, but also they are often bad. Even the most carefully stated objective is worthless if it

	Number of Students	Median Training Time	Intermediate Criterion Tests			End-of-course Criterion Test
			1	2	3	
Tryout 1	8	20 days	92%	95%	99%	80%
Tryout 2	8	13 days	93%	98%	98%	91%
Tryout 3	16	9 days	95%	96%	98%	92%
Tryout 4	50	9 days	96%	94%	98%	92%

Figure 3. *The results of tryouts and revisions in developing an industrial educational program. Scores are median test scores (Short, 1968).*

describes a trivial or unneeded skill. Unfortunately, in converting general objectives to measurable objectives, it is easy to convert an important objective into a trivial one. For example:

General Objective—Understand some of the factors influencing great explorers like Columbus.

Specific Objective—The student will be able to list the following facts about Columbus: date of first arrival in America, location of landing, number of men with him, name of his ships, and length of largest ship.

Or another example:

General Objective—Allow primary students freedom of expression and encourage their creativity in self-expression in art.

Specific Objective—Fifth-grade students will be able to draw a rural landscape consisting of one barn, one road, and three hills in the distance.

The specific objectives in the examples above are bad because they are trivial and unimportant; they are poor translations. But there is no reason why a measurable objective should be any less important than a general objective. For example, the two general objectives could be converted into more relevant measurable objectives:

The student will be able to write an essay that (a) compares at least three similarities in the characters and motivation of three explorers and (b) contrasts at least one major difference in their characters and motivations. The student will be free to choose any explorers from any period of history.

The student will be shown a common object and told to express it freely and creatively in a drawing. The teacher will measure the success of her lesson by the diversity and differences in the drawings. If all the students draw similar pictures, the teacher will have failed.

Hopefully, these examples illustrate that it is not impossible to write measurable objectives that enhance the importance of a vague general objective. The solution is in carefully writing measurable objectives that do not reduce important skills and concepts to rote repetition of definitions, rules, and facts. Bloom (1956) and Gagné (1970) give many examples of measurable objectives involving complex skills and concepts such as problem solving, analysis, synthesis, and evaluation, and Flanagan, Shanner, and Mager (1971) have published a complete set of objectives for grades 1–12 in four areas (mathematics, language arts, social studies, and science) which again demonstrates the range and complexity of measurable objectives.

The value or relevance of an objective, however, is not determined by the way it is written but by its ultimate value to the student. Students often question why they need to learn something, and of what value it will be to them when they leave school. Students, even student-teachers, often complain that what they learn in school is of little use to them when they leave school. Rewriting an objective to make it specific and measurable does not solve the problem of determining if the objective is relevant to the student or not.

Some examples may help illustrate the point. Economists estimate that 70 percent of the people in many developing countries will continue to be involved in rural agricultural work for the remainder of this century. In these countries, is it more important for students to learn (1) to use modern agriculture methods or (2) to read? Our first reaction is that learning to read is clearly more important, but in some developing countries, children who are taught to read become illiterate again after they leave school because they have nothing to read and no apparent need to read. Perhaps learning to read in these areas is not really a more relevant objective than learning to farm. If there is only limited money for education, it is not entirely clear which objective should get priority, and experts disagree.

Schools teach many objectives which most of us never use again after we leave school. After we finish geometry, most of us never find the length of the hypotenuse of a right triangle or the area of a circle. After we finish English, most of us never differentiate between similes and metaphors, analyze the structural syntax of a sentence, or even write a research report with footnotes. After we finish history, most of us never discuss the five causes of the War of 1812 or the six causes of the great depression. Yet, once upon a time, for a few days or weeks in school, we could and did do these things. Why? Were they important and relevant then?

It is often said that the choice of objectives ultimately is a value judgment. The implication is that there is no advantage to being logical and scientific in approaching this decision. However, certain objectives have been selected and are being taught in schools today; someone has made decisions about the relevance of these objectives. The question is not whether value judgments of this type can be made, but how they can be made so that they represent more than the weight of tradition.

There seem to be at least two tests of the relevance of an objective.

1. Does the objective describe a skill or concept that a person is likely to need outside of school, either now or later in his life?
2. If it does not, then does the objective describe a skill or concept that a person needs to learn now, not for of its own value, but because it will help him learn other objectives that are useful outside of school?

These questions are much easier to ask than to answer. It is impossible to predict when a given bit of information will be important to an individual in the future. For example, in the movie *Lawrence of Arabia*, Lawrence gained the confidence of the Arab king by completing a quotation from the Koran; to Lawrence, this knowledge of the Koran was of great value. Since it was of value, perhaps memorization of the Koran in Arabic should have been added to the objectives of the British school system of the time. Or, perhaps, this objective should have been included only in the training programs of diplomats and advisors to Moslem countries. Or, perhaps, the choice should have been left to the individual student as it was in Lawrence's case.

It seems impossible to discard any educational objective because it may some day be useful to someone. Even the most obscure fact may mean the difference between life and death to some individual in some real-life adventure. But although we cannot say an objective is useless, we can evaluate its usefulness in comparison to other objectives, and this is all that is really needed. It is possible to get representative groups of people to rank the relevance of objectives and, in this way, to arrive at a more rational basis for including or excluding objectives in an educational program. The more information people are given about the objectives, the better their ranking should be. Ideally, they should not only consider the relevance of an objective but also consider the time and cost required for students to learn it. In this way, realistic decisions about which objectives to include in an educational program could be arrived at by a consensus of rankings and a pooling of value judgments based on maximum information.

Something of this sort was done for an industrial educational program (Short and Sands, 1965). Initially 500 objectives were identified. To teach all these objectives to everyone would have cost too much and taken too much time; some procedure was needed to establish a priority of objectives. People were identified who were familiar with the present and future needs of the industry, and they were asked to follow various procedures in ranking the relevance of the objectives. In this way, about 60 objectives were identified which almost everyone ranked as very important and relevant; the remaining objectives were chosen much less frequently and by only a small proportion of the group. Interestingly, the 60 high-priority objectives were not the objectives that traditionally had been taught in this setting.

A ranking procedure is useful in establishing the priority of objectives, but still better methods are needed. The equivalent of the industrial job-analysis perhaps can be applied to nonindustrial settings, such as families, communities, and political associations, to determine what people need to know in order to participate in these effectively. One of the greatest challenges in the field of education today is to develop better ways for determining the relevance of educational objectives, and, of course, the necessary first step in doing this is to describe objectives as measurable objectives. Then it is possible to consider priorities of objectives in terms of their relevance to the future needs of students.

Summary

1. Educational programs need measurable objectives.
2. Measurable objectives are useful because they
    a. emphasize educational results rather than educational methods.
    b. suggest innovative methods.
    c. provide a way of improving education.
3. Measurable objectives should be prepared before any other instructional materials are prepared. Objectives should determine the design of instruction and not the other way around.
4. A model for improving education requires measurable objectives and tryout and revision procedures.
5. The ultimate value of an educational objective is its relevance to the student after he leaves school.
    a. It is possible to rank the relevance of objectives and select the most relevant objectives for an educational program.
    b. Better methods are needed for determining the relevance of objectives.

Linguistics, communication, and behavioral objectives: A remedial curriculum

RICHARD R. LEE

Over the past four years, *The Speech Teacher* has reflected a growing interest in two directions of curriculum design: programs for the poor (Smith, 1966; Nash, 1969) and instructional programs specified in behavioral terms. Clevenger (1966) and, elsewhere, Kibler (1963) have presented the case for the use of behavioral objectives in program design; the specification of desired behaviors expedites learning. Baker (1967) has noted the lack of published material expressed in behavioral terms. Hawkins (1969) has reported a general speech program for disadvantaged

college students but not in behavioral terms. The program reported here, along with its rationale, is one more step in this established procedure of disseminating programs of consequence to those dealing with college-level students with histories of poor academic performance. Instruction is oriented toward linguistic behavior that is more basic than, and preparatory to, public address, oral in-

From *The Speech Teacher,* January 1971, *20*(1). Reprinted by permission of the author and the Speech Association of America.

terpretation, and the other traditional concerns of speech teachers. The program as described is intended to be illustrative rather than definitive, since curricula must be adjusted to vary with local conditions, individual needs, and feedback from evaluation instruments. It is axiomatic that behavior modification must start with a description of what behavior is to be modified.

There are several reasons for using linguistics to define what is to be taught to the guided-studies student (Campbell and Lindfors, 1969; Jacobs and Rosenbaum, 1968). For the scholar, it is a dispassionate, objective method of describing the differences among social dialects. For the layman, it is a framework for looking at speech in a way that forces a temporary suspension of affect. It also encourages the learner to monitor his own speech for specific features. Self-monitoring is a prerequisite for changing speech. Finally, performance feedback to the student is in neutral, specific terms that permit him to take responsibility for his own learning.

This particular curriculum is designed for a racially mixed junior-college guided-studies remedial program. The typical student joins the program as preventative insurance against failure in regular, transfer-credit courses. Typically, he has a history of poor high-school grades and test scores. He most likely comes from an economically poor family. His most careful speech is marked by frequent syntactic and phonological deviations from both Northern and Southern standard English in such locutions as, "They wasn't none" for "There weren't any" (McDavid, 1967; for a more complete description, see Davis et al., 1969). He also is ill at ease when talking in a heterogeneous group or in an interview. The program rests on several assumptions about the characteristics of the guided-study student and the design of remedial curricula, which are spelled out here.

First, it is assumed that the remedial junior-college student feels no strong need for speech instruction. Instead, this course and college itself are means to an end. The student's needs are an income, self-esteem, and possibly a draft deferment. In order for instruction to appear relevant, he needs to experience success in a worthy task, a sense of progress,

and esteem as a valid human being. His participation in the program, which does not count toward a diploma, indicates his awareness of his susceptibility to academic defeat. This is borne out by a high absentee and attrition rate.

There are special prerequisites to remedial instruction in speech which further differentiate the curriculum. First, the student must believe he can change his speech behavior and have the desire to do so. This in turn requires a desensitization of his defensive attitude about the way he talks. Independently both Golden (1960) and Labov (1966) have established that speakers of low-prestige dialects are aware that their own speech differs from standard English in some undefined way, a phenomenon Labov calls linguistic insecurity. The function of remedial instruction is to enable the student to modify his careful speech if he wants to, both in what he says and how he says it. At the same time, it is imperative that the choice be left up to him, since speech is social behavior and unlike science or mathematics, loaded with preferences and reactions. Simply by virtue of his college education, the instructor is likely to have different values from his students about the acceptability of many phonological and syntactic patterns, or the appropriateness of name-calling in public discussion. When social standards become academic standards, instruction takes on the cast of social coercion. The student needs to experience success at a worthy task, needs to feel a sense of progress, and must feel that he is esteemed as a valid human being.

There are several implications for the design of remedial curricula. First, elements of instruction are justified not by their transfer value to other courses, but to the degree to which they enable the remedial student to bring his own speech under scrutiny and control. Second, informational content in a remedial course is subordinate to affective considerations and justifiable only to the extent to which it serves them. The logical or psychological unity of the body of information in the curriculum is secondary to the coherence of activities which develop the student's ability to identify his characteristic patterns of verbal behavior. The use of behavior objectives is particularly important here, since they emphasize the learner's behavior rather than the instructor's.

Given time, feedback, and a noncoercive atmosphere, it is assumed that students will benefit from speech instruction if tasks are clearly delineated, if they are attainable, and if the reward system is direct and unambiguous. This implies that course objectives and performance criteria must be spelled out in detail from the outset, and that the achievement of specific goals, as distinct from the instructor's approval, is a primary source of motivation.

Another assumption underlying this curriculum is that, except for pathological aberrations, speech behavior is a manifestation of social attitudes, and that the use of one social dialect reflects an array of other social choices. As Labov (1963) has shown, pronunciation is directly related to an individual's social reference group. Convergence to the norm of standard English requires as a precondition the student's desire to change reference groups. Many remedial students are socially upward-mobile, but it is unreasonable and undemocratic to reward only the speech of the middle class. That is a social choice and must not function as a prerequisite for academic success.

Fourth, if social and regional dialects do in fact cause "communication problems," it becomes a problem for the student only when he defines it as such. Another more likely "problem" is his inability to control his interaction in group discussion or in a job interview. A major function of instruction is to provide him with precise feedback about his participation in group discussion, about his intelligibility to others in the class and about the linguistic choices he has made in his selection of a social dialect. *Evaluation of student performance is therefore based on three criteria: the accuracy with which he can assess his own oral language, his intelligibility, and the extent to which he communicates in a heterogeneous class.*

There is no ideal curriculum. Changes of class membership and instructors, and miscalculations of student capabilities demand that quantitative criteria be built into the curriculum to permit on-the-spot evaluation and to facilitate adjustments in its means and objectives.

A word should be said here about the form in which behavioral objectives are presented to the students. Kibler, Barker, and Miles (1970) distinguish between informational objectives, which specify the behavior to be demonstrated, and planning objectives, which also include the criterion and the conditions under which the behaviors are to be performed. Typically, a class is provided only the information objective, but we are dealing with remedial students who have a low tolerance for ambiguity, and so they are given the more complete planning objective. This eliminates all guesswork; the student knows what he must do, how well, and under what conditions. At first, students are skeptical that they have been given all of the performance information, because they recognize that the instructor has abandoned surprise as an evaluation tactic and the sanctions that derive from it. The curriculum below contains the same information given to the class.

I: Phonemic and Grammatical Description

Objective. The student must match a limited set of phonemic and syntactic differentia that distinguishes some social dialects in the United States.

G 1. I be here every morning.
        I'm here every morning.

D 2. /Bidnəs/ is bad.
        /Biznəs/ is bad.

E 3. He going home.
        He's going home.

H 4. You /shutn't/ do that.
        You /shudn't/ do that.

A 5. I /wen/ outside.
        I /went/ outside.

I 6. She's my /sistə/.
        She's my /sistər/.

J 7. They didn't have no money.
        They didn't have any money.

B 8. I asked him did he go.
        I asked him if he went.

C 9. He lazy.
        He's lazy.

F   10. That's John dog.
    That's John's dog.

These are features which may appear in the student's own careful speech. He will need the information for the following unit, but in the meantime the terminology permits a dispassionate discussion of social and regional dialects. This information performs a vital desensitizing function of the feelings that most people have about the funny way other people talk.

Prerequisites.   The ability to isolate sounds within a word, to assign consonantal grapheme-phoneme correspondences, to recognize slash-line convention for phonemes, and the sound value of schwa.

Criterion.   Given a list of eleven descriptors and a paired list of ten examples and ten nonexamples, the student should correctly match descriptors at 80 percent accuracy.

Pretest.   The student places the letter of the correct descriptor on the line to the left of the example.

    A.   Consonant cluster reduction
    B.   Inverted word order in embedded question
    C.   Missing linking verb
    D.   Stopped /z/
    E.   Deleted aspect
    F.   Deleted possessive marker
    G.   Invariant "be"
    H.   Unvoicing of voiced stop
    I.   Unconstricted /r/
    J.   Multiple negation
    K.   Double modal (distractor)

Instruction.   Instruction including pre- and posttesting lasts six hours. Instruction is limited to the identification of the first ten descriptors. Thus on the phonemic level, the student need only distinguish auditorially:

    1. stops from sibilants;
    2. vowels from consonants, and consonants from /r/;
    3. voiced from unvoiced consonants;
    4. vowel nuclei from consonant clusters;
    5. two degrees of /r/ constriction.

On the syntactic level, he need only distinguish:

    1. conjugations of "be" from all other verbs;
    2. contractions from full forms of verbs;
    3. question word-order from declarative order;
    4. cancellation of the auxiliary transformation for questions when embedded;
    5. the presence or absence of auxiliary "be" in progressive aspect;
    6. indefinite noun phrases from definite;
    7. multiple negation with indefinite noun phrases from single negation;
    8. the presence or absence of noun possessive /s/.

Posttest.   The posttest is a different form of the pretest with the same performance criterion. Some instruction may have to be given on the matter of isolating individual sounds within words. Some, but not all, of the technical vocabulary above is taught, depending on the receptivity of the class. The ten descriptors are taught as associates paired with several examples each.

II: Self-Analysis
of Oral-Reading Style

Objective.   To have the student correctly select which of two possible phonological or syntactic realizations he has employed in his reading of a passage. Most students have never heard their own voices on a tape recorder. This activity lets them form both general and specific evaluations of their own speech as someone else might hear them. The activity also demands self-monitoring of spoken language for specific features, which is a prerequisite for control. The mere feedback of the recording is often startling to students and motivating when they do not like what they hear.

Prerequisites.   Criterion performance on the Unit I posttest and the ability to read aloud.

Activity.   The student silently reads through an unmarked version of the passage on p. 269 and asks for help to decode any words which elude him. After reading the passage into a tape recorder, he listens to the tape, locates the points from a marked text, and identifies from a multiple-choice format which of two locutions or pronunciations he used. (The marginal letters are keyed to the ten descriptors in Section I.)

Instruction. The instructor demonstrates normal phonemic variation between reading and casual styles, i.e., /downtju/ *versus* /downča/ and the influence of social context upon lexical and syntactic choices, i.e., "Good morn-

Nobody Knows Your Name[1]

Paragraph one: Last year I we<u>nt</u> out for the basketball team, and I made out   A
 better than I expected. I wasn't too big, but I was quick on my feet, and my
 jump shot used to drop in when it counted. In the coach'<u>s</u> office, he told me   F
 himself I was a real help to the school.
Paragraph two: But you couldn't tell that to Eleanor. No matter if I did good or
 bad, she'd ask me afte<u>r</u> every game: "Why can't you be the man to put it in   I
 the basket?" I'd tell her, "Look, Eleanor, everybody can't be a star. I play the
 back cour<u>t</u>."   I
Paragraph three: "But all you do is put the ball in Lester'<u>s</u> hands," she said,   F
 "you must have passed it to Lester sixty times, and he missed it mo<u>st</u> of the time.   A
 Why don't you make the shots?" "It's easy enough to explain," I told her, "if
 you only know what's what. Lester is seven-foot-two; I'm five-foot-ten. He just
 twists his wrist and puts it in. He'<u>s</u> always in position, and <u>I'm</u> never near the   C,C
 basket."
Paragraph four: She woul<u>dn</u>'t see it, and I coul<u>dn</u>'t make her see it. I'd talk till   H,H
 I was out of breath, but <u>I</u> might as well have kept my mouth shut. It was always
 something.
Paragraph five: Then she tried a new line. "I know you're right," she said. "But
 what about my pride? I don't think any of my friends remember if you're a
 center or an end or a tackle. Nobody knows your name!"
Paragraph six: She made my blood boil. I said I was<u>n</u>'t going to ruin <u>a</u> game   D,J
 just to please her. And she said she wouldn't go ou<u>t</u> with me <u>any</u> more if I   J
 didn't score a lot of points.
 So I told the coach about it. He said, "Artie, everybody isn't a star. You're a
 good team man. It should be an easy game tomorrow night, so we'll keep setting
 you up."
Paragraph seven: The team really put me in bu<u>s</u>iness. I just hung under the bas-   D
 ket, and everybody passed me the ball. I pu<u>sh</u>ed the easy ones in, and nobody
 noticed when I missed. By the end of the game, I made thirty-three points. The
 whole school was cheering for me. Everybody was shouting my name.
Paragraph eight: Everybody, that is, but Eleanor. Finally I called her father on
 the phone. "I just made thirty-three points, Mr. Jones—but I can't find
 Eleanor." Then I asked him <u>if he knew</u> where she was.   B
Paragraph nine: Her father said, "Just a minute." Then he said, "She says she
 can't come to the phone right now. She'<u>s</u> watching television. But she asked <u>if</u>   E,B
 you would do it for her again next week—she can watch you then."
 Next year I'<u>m</u> going out for the swimming team—under water. Down there,   E
 nobody—but <u>nobody</u>—is going to know my name.

---

1 Adapted from an original passage by William Labov from A SOCIOLINGUISTIC DESCRIPTION OF DETROIT NEGRO SPEECH by Walter A. Wolfram, (Washington, D.C., 1969). Reprinted by permission of the author.

ing" *versus* "Hi," and "Gradually I worked up to foreman" *versus* "I worked up to foreman gradually." Average testing and instruction time is four hours.

Criterion. The criterion is 80 percent agreement with the instructor's scoring of the tape.

III: Large-Group Discussion

Objective. The objective is to bring the student's participation in group discussion to a quantitatively defined criterion. Operationally, participation is defined as the utterance of ideas related to a central topic of discussion. This activity serves two purposes. Typically, the remedial student is reticent about speaking out in class, yet this is often the only way to get certain kinds of information. Thus the activity helps develop a general academic skill. Too, uncertainty often expresses itself as hostility or withdrawal, behaviors which beget hostility or withdrawal. Instruction about supportive and punishing verbal behavior will help the student control his communication in a closely defined situation.

Pretest and criterion. In a twenty-minute discussion of a topic of general interest, such as "What's Wrong with America," which does not require specialized knowledge, each member of the class will make at least five oral responses of sentence length or greater that contain more than simple agreement or disagreement. ("That's right" and "You tell 'em" register only agreement.) The instructor contributes ideas for the first minute to start the discussion and reenters only if it stops for thirty seconds or more. Otherwise, he is busy tallying verbal responses.

Instruction. The instructor demonstrates communication reinforcers such as head-nodding, eye contact, and paraphrasing (Verplank, 1955). Keltner (1970) has summarized several factors which interfere with communication as "barriers and breakdowns." These are applicable to the analysis of discussion in large groups, particularly those which do not function as groups often enough

for clear-cut roles to emerge. With luck, the students verbalize anxieties about group discussion, such as the fear of ridicule or losing their train of thought. In a second discussion, half the class participates while the other half observes and records instances of reinforcing and punishing discussion behaviors. Instruction and testing time is three hours.

Posttest. The posttest is the same as the pretest with a different topic.

IV: The Job Interview

Objective. From memory the student describes in writing five features of verbal behavior and five features of nonverbal behavior that contribute to a good job interview for a semi-skilled job such as a retail clerk. If there is any utility in changing verbal behavior, it is most apparent in the job situation. The activity also affords an opportunity to present a behavioral model of the job interview and permits the class to ask an interviewer about his linguistic preferences. The instructor must maintain neutrality, but the real world of work does not (Smith, 1956).

Preparation. The instructor distributes the checklist below with the instructions to watch for these behaviors in the forthcoming interview.

Pretest. A trained interviewer stages a five-minute mock interview with a confederate, generally a verbal, well-poised student from a business class, playing the role of interviewee. Before the interview begins, the instructor explains that they will witness a good interview. The checklist focuses attention on the features that make it good. Then the interviewee exhibits the following nonverbal behaviors:

1. sits up straight in the chair;
2. keeps his feet on or near the floor;
3. looks at the interviewer for at least two minutes out of the five but not more than four;
4. acknowledges the interviewer's questions by nodding or smiling at the completion of a question;

5. keeps his hands immobilized in his lap or elsewhere for at least ten seconds between movements;

6. stands upon cue from the interviewer at the end of the interview.

In verbal behavior, the instructor-interviewee:

1. speaks with enough volume to be heard distinctly eight feet away;

2. fields open-ended questions about his background by speaking for at least ten seconds, but not more than sixty, between questions;

3. by his questions or statements, demonstrates that he has at least minimal information about the job he is applying for, or the range of jobs the store might have open;

4. admits to no direct work experience for the job, but pulls other experience from his background with tangentially related skills, such as extensive contact with the public;

5. responds with positive or neutral affect about past work experiences and supervisors;

6. corrects the interviewer, if necessary, by rephrasing a question or a statement, rather than openly contradicting;

7. follows the interviewer's lead in change of topics;

8. asks at least three questions about salary, work hours, or particulars about the job;

9. when asked about the future, describes interests that could be compatible with the company's range of operations, and an eventual job position that could be reached by promotion through the ranks;

10. allows the interviewer to initiate the topic of whether the job has been awarded, or when the interviewee will be contacted.

Criterion. After the check-sheets have been collected, the student describes in writing five verbal and five nonverbal behaviors listed above. Purely evaluative expressions ("He sounded educated") do not meet the criterion.

Instruction. The job interviewer presents a twenty-minute talk about what he likes to see in an applicant. The talk usually stresses physical appearance and mentions starting wages for unskilled and semi-skilled jobs, which raises the eyebrows and lowers the morale of many of the younger members of the class. The class then asks him his evaluation of the ten phonological and syntactic descriptors in Section I. Depending on the interviewer, some of these linguistic features will be said to be trivial and others important.

Following the question-and-answer period, the instructor, taking the role of interviewer, asks members of the class to respond authentically to the same open-ended questions asked by the professional interviewer. After each student response, the class orally evaluates the adequacy of the response and poses alternatives. Discussion should also point out common experiences that have transfer value to work situations, such as taking responsibility for younger siblings or persevering in an onerous task.[2] Approximate testing and instruction time is three hours.

Posttest. The instructor interviews a student for five minutes for a job of the student's choice. This is video-taped for later review by the student. Without the aid of the outline, the rest of the class writes out descriptions of his verbal and nonverbal behavior. Different students are interviewed until all members of the class can describe behaviors in wording similar to that of the check-sheet. Coaching of the slower members of the class by the more observant ones will prevent this activity from dragging on ad nauseum.

V: Intelligibility Training

Objective and Criterion. Ninety-five percent of the words pronounced in isolation shall be intelligible when spoken in a normal voice in a classroom to other students and identified from a multiple-choice format. Much of what has been called socially marked pronunciation is sloppy diction. One purpose of the activity is to bring specific, often idiosyn-

---

2 For the other side of the coin, interviewer behavior, see Keltner's chapter on interviewing (Keltner, 1970).

cratic, articulation lapses to the attention of the student. Such training probably does not transfer to casual speech, but it establishes a precondition for the modification of his very careful speech, the identification of weakly articulated or unarticulated phonemes. With some students, even their most careful articulation is insufficient to enable the listener to identify the spoken word from phonetically similar items. This particular barrier to communication can be made apparent to the speaker in a very direct and unambiguous way, and through the analysis of individual confusion patterns, the misarticulating speaker can begin to alter his careful speech in specific areas. The least capable articulators seem to have a global undifferentiated sense of dissatisfaction about their own speech. This activity lets them channel their dissatisfaction to an awareness of specific problems.

Each performance is a test and a drill. A student reads a list of twenty-four words in groups of three from the Multiple-Choice Intelligibility Test.[3] The rest of the class individually marks which of the four words they thought they heard. The self-scoring response protocols are returned to the speaker. From this he first calculates his own intelligibility score and then scans for recurring patterns of errors. These seem to vary among individuals. Performance time is about three hours, which can be interspersed in twenty-minute segments throughout the quarter.

Instruction. Although peer feedback is probably more important than formal instruction in changing performance, the instructor can point out the complex pre- and post-vocalic consonant clusters that contribute to the confusibility of these items. Some students have no trouble with this pronunciation task. As soon as they reach criterion, they are pressed into service to help the less articulate analyze the respondent protocols for problem patterns.

This program is neither a complete curriculum for a college speech course nor a panacea for the slow student. It is a start toward greater awareness and control of factors in verbal behavior. It does have transfer value into other parts of a remedial program. For instance, the linguistic information learned here applies to the analysis of spelling errors

arising from casual articulation and composition errors arising from dialect deviations from the syntax of literary English. The program also moves the student away from absolute reliance on casual spoken language—his kind, specifically—as the criterion for all language performance, spoken or written, casual or formal.

The program and the instructor are actively neutral about language values. Particularly in remedial speech, the role must be that of instructor and student, not parent and child. The program says implicitly that the business of instruction is to impart information and performance feedback. Rather than casting the instructor as an advocate of "good English," it assumes that the student knows about a better kind of speech performance than he practices. That knowledge needs to be made more precise and he must have the opportunity to check his performance in light of it. The program gives the adult student some information with which to discuss language differences and lets him ask a live job interviewer what the linguistic price of admission is into semiskilled jobs. The student draws his own inferences, based on his own aspiration. Finally, the use of explicit behavior objectives in this program is a keystone in the remedial program since it counteracts the ambient expectation of failure that most students bring in with them. After a few weeks, they often ask why the rest of the program is not set up the same way.

A total remedial program cannot be evaluated with the usual measures of instructional efficiency; the purpose of a remedial program is to remedy something, which in this case can be described as a whole set of academic work habits. A good remedial program will reward students sufficiently so that they will voluntarily come to class. A valid dependent measure is the rate of absenteeism from class. In relative terms, this curriculum has reduced absences about 80 percent when compared with a remedial speech curriculum which miniaturized the content of the basic public-address course. In absolute terms, only four students out of thirty-five missed class more

---

3 John Black, ed., *Multiple-Choice Intelligibility Test* (1963).

than once during a ten-week quarter. This speaks much more loudly than the verbalized enthusiasm of the students and the instructional staff. Instructor satisfaction derives partly from the modifiability of the curriculum. It is readily adjustable to feedback from student performance. No doubt the content will change somewhat over the next few years, but the principles of behavioral objectives expressed in linguistic terms will remain.

12

PROGRAMMED AND AUTOMATED INSTRUCTION

For many years, programmed instruction was *the* contribution of behavior analysis to education. Although it is still far from fulfilling its early promise, programmed instruction is alive, well, and growing. The first paper in this section is a program on programming by a noted expert, Susan Meyer Markle.

Many of the first programs were designed to be delivered to students automatically by a machine; the first teaching machines were simple delivery systems. However, as computers were developed and became highly sophisticated, educators envisioned correspondingly sophisticated, computer-administered educational programs. Unfortunately, most of the work done with computers to date has involved the automatic delivery of traditional academic drills. Few attempts have been made to fulfill early dreams of sophisticated branching programs geared to the individual student by the computer. The second paper in this section, by Ellison, discusses the state of the art in computer-assisted instruction and suggests some future directions.

Most programs for computer-assisted instruction have not been designed by people with a strong background in the analysis of behavior. The third paper in this section presents the result of one well-known behavioral psychologist, James Holland, and his associate, Judith Doran, applying their skills to the design of a computer-based instructional program. The program teaches classification of objects by their properties. In addition to presenting antecedent stimuli and verbal feedback, the computer dispenses tangible reinforcers. In scale, Holland and Doran's program is small when compared to massive programs developed, for example, at Stanford University and the University of Illinois. However, it may contain ideas, such as the incorporation of tangible reinforcement, useful to the larger programs.

A chronic problem with programmed and automated instruction has been lack of reinforcement for the learner. Skinner hypothesized that "being right" might be reinforcing enough to maintain students' behavior; however, "being right" also may be poor compensation for sitting in a sterile cubicle and working hard at a boring task. If teaching machines are to be widely used, they must be made as reinforcing or more reinforcing to the learner than traditional learning situations. The reinforcement may be extrinsic, as in Holland and Doran's program, or intrinsic. One of the best examples of intrinsically reinforcing automated instruction is well-designed educational television. Indeed, television, through such programs as "Sesame Street" and "The Electric Company," may turn out to be one of the most effective and economical teaching machines.

Educators must take care not to let programmed instruction, computers, and teaching machines become ends in themselves. Today there is more glamour in being called an educational technologist than a teacher. Computers carry almost mystical prestige. The new technology, however, must be evaluated solely on the basis of its results. Educators must embrace whatever works, whether it be the overmaligned and overrevered television set, or the latest, largest, and most fantastic production of the computer manufacturers.

The basic programming principles

SUSAN MEYER MARKLE

Programmers seek to solve educational problems by applying the techniques of behavior analysis. Most of us date the beginning of this application in 1954 with the publication of B. F. Skinner's article "The Science of Learning and the Art of Teaching." Unlike many other psychologists, Skinner saw a strong parallel between his activities in the laboratory and practices that would improve education. However apt the parallel may be, the fabled achievements in changing animal behavior in the laboratory did not lead to an immediate revolution in the schoolroom. If there was one great lie in the article, it was the statement in the concluding paragraph "There is a simple job to be done.... The necessary techniques are known." The years since 1954 have seen a gradual, often painful, growth in the technology of instructional design.

Historically, the first style of programming was the one called "linear," derived in part from Skinner's suggestions and in part from the characteristics of the first teaching machines (Markle, 1962). Although the term *linear* describes only one characteristic of the most popular early style of programming, many other characteristics crept in and were soon regarded as essential. Indeed, linearity —meaning that each student proceeds in a straight line through a fixed instructional sequence—is one of the less salient attributes

of what many people consider "Skinnerian programming" to be. When Schramm (1964) complained about the "hardening of the arteries" that he saw taking place in programming styles, it was not linearity *per se* that caused concern. Since each new convert to programming tended to imitate the programs he saw, a couple of bad apples in the barrel could spread their influence far and fast. Such imitation proved to be a sincere form of idiocy! And, as we shall see, much of the real activity in applying techniques of behavior analysis to education is, like the mass of an iceberg, below the surface and not visible in the final product. Copying the surface characteristics does not produce a program.

Since history may help in understanding where we are now, this program will begin with an early article by Skinner. Although written seven years after the first one, it makes very similar points. From this, you will get a good look at the basic principles which are still relevant.

THE THREE BASIC PRINCIPLES

The case for linear programming is presented

in the following article by Skinner. The sequence of frames that follow it are intended to start you thinking about the implications of what he has to say. As you read the article, keep the following study questions in mind.

(a) The way that teaching materials are designed implies a theory of learning. What is required, according to Skinner, to produce learning?

(b) What role do individual differences among students have in determining the design of a linear teaching sequence?

(c) What is Skinner's attitude toward errors?

No question in the succeeding frames on this text will require that you have memorized it. However, it is not advisable to treat it as "light" reading. No student of mine has ever found Skinner "light"!

"Obviously the machine itself does not teach. It simply brings the student into contact with the person who composed the material it presents. It is a labor-saving device because it can bring one programmer into contact with an indefinite number of students. This may suggest mass production, but the effect on each student is surprisingly like that of a private tutor. The comparison holds in several respects. There is a constant exchange between program and student. Unlike lectures, textbooks, and the usual audio-visual aids, the machine does not simply present something to be learned; it induces sustained activity. The student is always alert and busy. Like a good tutor, the machine insists that a given point be thoroughly understood, either frame by frame or set by set, before the student moves on. Lectures, textbooks, and their mechanized equivalents, on the other hand, proceed without making sure that the student understands, and they easily leave him behind. Like a tutor, the machine presents just that material for which the student is ready. It asks him to take only that step which he is at the moment best equipped and most likely to take. Like a tutor, the machine helps the student to come up with the right answer. It does this in part through the orderly construction of the program and in part with

techniques of hinting, prompting, suggesting, and so on, derived from an analysis of verbal behavior. Finally, the machine, like the private tutor, reinforces the student for every correct response, using this immediate feedback not only to shape his behavior most efficiently but also to maintain it in strength in a manner that the layman would describe as 'holding the student's interest. . . .'

A useful teaching machine will have several important features. Except in some kinds of stimulus learning, the student should compose his response, rather than select it from a set of alternatives, as he would in a multiple-choice scheme. One reason for this is that we want him to recall rather than merely recognize—to make a response as well as see that it is right. An equally important reason is that effective multiple-choice material must contain plausible wrong answers, which are out of place in the delicate process of shaping behavior because they strengthen unwanted responses. . . .

The student must pass through a carefully arranged sequence of steps, often of considerable length. The machine must be designed so that the student has to take each step and take it in the prescribed order. . . .

One of the great sources of inefficiency in modern education is due to our effort to teach a group of students at the same rate. We recognize that this is unfair to the student who is able to move faster, but we have no idea how much damage may be suffered by those who move slowly. There is no evidence that a slow student is necessarily unintelligent. . . . With properly designed machines and programs, a slow student free to move at his own normal rate of work may rise to undreamed-of levels of competence. . . .

Difficult as programming is, it has its compensations. It is a salutory thing to try to guarantee a correct response at every step in the presentation of a subject. The programmer will find that he has been accustomed to leaving much to the student, omitting essential steps, and neglecting relevant points. The responses made to his program may reveal surprising ambiguities. Unless he is extremely able, he may find that he still has something to learn about his subject. He will almost certainly find that he needs to learn a great deal more about the behavioral changes he is trying to induce in the student. His goal must be to keep refining his program until the point is reached at which the answers of the average child will almost always be right."[1]

The First Principle

1. In his article Skinner states "there is a constant exchange between program and student," and "the machine does not simply present something to be learned; it induces sustained activity."

In these and other statements, Skinner makes clear his position on one of the main necessities governing learning. In order for learning to occur, the student must _____ .

----

respond, or do something, or be active, etc.

---

2. From what Skinner says about "lectures, textbooks, and their mechanized equivalents," (refer to the text if you wish) would you say that *listening*, *reading*, and *watching* a film or TV presentation are responses of the sort that Skinner intends to have the student make?

The question asks what you would say. If you find yourself tending to say "yes," reread the first paragraph of Skinner's article. Note the emphasis on making sure that the student understands before he is allowed to go on.

---

3. A basic principle derived from the learning theory on which linear programming is based is:

In order for learning to occur, a response must be made by the learner. It follows that if we give a student two bits of information, both of which we expect him to learn, he should respond to:
(a) either of them
(b) both of them.

(b) both of them.

---

4. Suppose a student has been led to respond correctly to the question "What is the capital of France?" In psychological terms, we can say:

In the presence of the stimulus "capital of France," the student responds "Paris." Is this the same situation as that represented by the following?

In the presence of "Paris is the capital of what country?" the student will respond "France."

If your answer is "yes," go to item 4a.
If your answer is "no," go to item 4c.

4a. Your answer was "yes." When the sentence "Paris is the capital of France" is broken into a *stimulus* part and a *response* part, it can be made into several different combinations of stimulus and response:

"What country is Paris the capital of?" is one question to which the correct response is

"France."

"What is the capital of France?" is another question to which the correct response is

"Paris."

According to the principle of active responding, the student who has learned the answer to the first question has *not necessarily* learned the answer to the second question. The principle has been supported—often to the chagrin of program authors who assume that reading is an adequate response—by data drawn from all levels of student age and ability.

Minor wording changes (what we call "synonymous" phrasing) may be made without changing the stimulus-response relationship. One item is different from another whenever the stimulus is changed and a different response is asked for.

Are the following questions the same or are they different?

Q1. "What do you call the meaningful unit that goes in front of a root?"

> A1. "A prefix."
> Q2. "When a meaningful unit pre-
> cedes a root, it is a _____."
> A2. "prefix."

For any student for whom "precedes" =
"goes in front of," the items are the same.

4b. In the presence of the stimulus "The
particles that circle the nucleus are called
...," the student responds "electrons."
Is this the same situation as when in the
presence of "Electrons circle around the ...,"
the student responds "nucleus"?

4c. Answer to 4 and 4b: No.

Note. Although the question may seem obvious to you, the failure to discriminate that
such situations are different has led to criticisms of linear programs as being too repetitive (i.e., asking the student to do the same
thing over and over again), when in fact
they might not be. Go on to item 5.

----

5. According to the *principle of active responding*, the student learns only what he has
been led to do. Although "Madrid is the
capital of Spain" is a single sentence, it is the
answer to more than one question. Each of
the possible questions might be a terminal
frame (a test question) in a geography program.

To an unsophisticated reader who thinks of
the sentence as one sentence instead of as the
answer to several questions, a program based
on the principle of active responding will appear to be repetitive. Yet each question (1.
What is the capital of Spain? 2. What country is Madrid the capital of?) is different.
How would you describe the difference
between these two questions using the terms
stimulus and *response*?

You could say "Each question is a different
stimulus asking for a different response" or
"In the presence of different stimuli, the
student gives a different response" or you
could describe them by saying which is stimu-

lus and which is response in each case (Spain-
Madrid and Madrid-Spain).

----

6. Although much of what may appear to
the unsophisticated reader to be repetition in
a program turns out not to be, a programmer
may repeat himself—i.e., make use of review
items. When can you legitimately call some
item a review item? What characteristic must
it have?

It must ask for the same (or very similar)
response in the presence of the same (or
similar) stimulus as a previous item did.

Note. Changing the numbers in a mathematical problem and requiring the student to
repeat the same problem-solving process could
be said to be repetitive, especially if there
were no increase in complexity. Just where
the line is drawn between "same" and "different" will depend on many factors. What is
"the same" for a college student may represent an enormous difference to a first grader!

----

7. Programmers should keep in mind that
familiar maternal phrase, "How many times
do I have to tell you. ..." Putting words in
front of a student is no guarantee that he has
noticed them, much less understood them.
(Some sophisticated students look at the
blank first and then read backwards to find
the answer—a trick they have learned from
taking reading-comprehension tests. It sometimes saves a lot of reading!)

In this item, what information can be
ignored without affecting the answer at all?

> Electrons, which have a negative
> charge, circle around the nucleus,
> which has a positive charge. The
> center of an atom is called a
> [nucleus/electron].

The information about positive and negative
charges may be ignored.

----

8. Assume that the following item is an
introduction to the two key terms "prefix"

and "suffix." In what way does it *not* satisfy the principle of active responding?

> A prefix is a meaningful unit that goes in front of a root. A suffix is a meaningful unit that goes after a root. In the word "hopeless," the unit "less" is placed after the root, so it is a _____.

It includes two definitions and the student is only required to respond to the second one. (The item has other faults as well, to be discussed later.)

9. Suppose we take the above item and rewrite it in the form given below. Does it now appear to require students to attend to *both* definitions?

> Meaningful units that go in front of a root are called prefixes. Meaningful units that go after a root are called *suffixes*. Label the units in this word:
> UN BEAR ABLE
> _____ fix   (root)   _____ fix

Yes.

Research Note. The necessity to control what the student observes by requiring a response to anything we wish him to notice was learned "in the field," so to speak. Programmers working on practical problems verified the principle to their own satisfaction—enough to have it included in how-to books like this one. Controlled laboratory research has since provided firmer evidence. *If you are not interested in such basic research, skip directly to the next frame.*

A cogent technique for determining which parts of a frame could be skipped by students without increasing the number of errors they made was developed by Holland (1965). His "blackout technique," as its name implies, consisted of painting over the unnecessary content in the frame so that students could not read what was originally there.

Holland demonstrated that his judgments of what was unnecessary were correct by having two groups of students go through the two versions of the frames. If students made no more errors on the painted-out frames than they did on the original version, it followed that noticing the "unnecessary content" was not required in order to answer. Frames 7 and 8 above have asked you to make essentially the same kinds of judgments about the examples given in them.

Once we can show by the blackout technique that the content blacked out isn't necessary, we can go on to show that it isn't learned. Even when it is not blacked out, posttest questions asking for it will show that most students paid no attention and consequently didn't learn it. Several studies along these lines are reported in Holland's chapter (1965). A more recent exhaustive review of the research can be found in Anderson (1967).

10. There is no reason to hide the prejudice of your author until later in the program, so here goes.

An *active* response to all the content in a frame is obtained when the student is required to process all of it in order to respond. There is considerable evidence that active responding aids learning.

There is, however, a distinction between requiring active responding to each bit of information and requiring the student to give each response separately. In many lists of the "characteristics of programmed instruction" you will find the "principle of *small steps*" given as one of the necessary features. The word "small" has had unfortunate effects on the way some programmers have designed instruction.

On the following page is a frame from a program designed for medical technicians—adults who don't need to be fed in small bites. We'll call it one frame because confirmation of their responses is not presented until they have completed the whole frame. Glance at the following frame briefly. Do you agree that this could NOT be called a "small step"?

Now, inspect it carefully to answer this question. The student is to note five structures and three functions of a cell, and, with the

The drawing below represents the STRUCTURE of the cell. In this case it is an AMEBA, a unicellular animal.

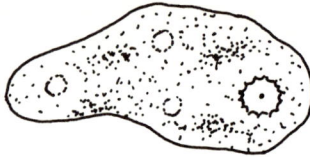

Using the following information, *you* draw arrows to and label the cell's STRUCTURES:

NUCLEUS—the most prominent structure in the cell

NUCLEAR MEMBRANE—the membrane surrounding the nucleus

CELL WALL—the membrane surrounding the cell

VACUOLE—cavity inside the cell

CYTOPLASM (endoplasm, ectoplasm)—material inside the cell

The drawings below represent FUNCTIONS of the cell (ameba).

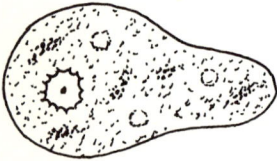

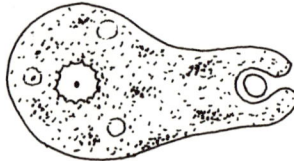

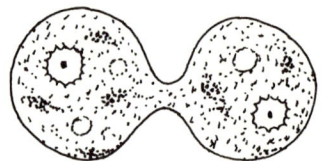

Using the information, *you* write in the FUNCTION represented by each drawing:

FEEDING—by surrounding food with pseudopodia
MOVEMENT—by thrusting of pseudopodia
REPRODUCTION—by binary fission

help of the descriptions given, match each of these with the appropriate illustrations. Activity we certainly have! Can you locate anything in the frame that the student is NOT required to attend to in order to complete the exercise? If so, what?

The first question asked for *your opinion.* Most people agree that this frame is a pretty big chunk.

If you could locate an unused bit of information, you probably selected the second sentence in the frame. The parenthetical "endoplasm, ectoplasm" also appears unnecessary to most people seeing this frame without the frame that preceded it. Looking at this frame by itself, you would be correct in assuming that students could ignore the material in the parentheses.

11. An active response is not necessarily a small response to a small bit of information, as you just saw. The "responses" near the end of a program on writing computer programs could ask the student to write such a program and debug it on a computer, a "response" which might take him an hour or more. At the end of an art-appreciation program, you might send the student out to spend an afternoon in the local art museum preparing a report on what he saw and felt. (This hasn't been done to my knowledge. But I still would call this a response—a very active foot-weary one!) Don't think of "active response" as a little twitch of the finger or writing a single word.

A further confusion about "active responding":

If you ask an arithmetic student to add a column of five numbers in his head and tell you the answer, you have an overt, observable response. Is this final sum the only response he made in doing the problem?

If you said yes, try to do it yourself. I think you will observe yourself responding to the sum of the first and second, then this sum and the third, and so on. (You are the only one who can observe this response, since it is covert.)

----

12. Covert responding is active responding. It isn't, of course, observable to anyone else. If a programmer is trying out some new frames, can he let the student respond covertly and still know that the frames are producing good answers?

No.

----

13. When the instruction is thoroughly tested, the programmer doesn't need to hear (or see) responses from everyone going through it. At that point, we can raise the question about overt versus covert responding. When does writing down an answer or saying it aloud help and when is it just a time-consuming nuisance? Research is still going on, and the answers are not all in (see Anderson, 1967). Common sense is one guide, of course. Which of these subjects would seem to require overt responding?

(a) student is learning how to write in script, after he has learned how to print letters.

(b) student is learning some basic terms in geography (all about mesas, peninsulas, etc.).

Common sense (mine, anyway) suggests that handwriting cannot be practiced very well covertly, although it might be possible to design a teaching sequence to do most of the teaching without having the student practice.

Research Note. Skip to the end of this section, if you are not interested. A fascinating example of this flying-in-the-face of "common sense" is found in a study by Evans (1961). Several youngsters who, on a pretest, could not form "good" numerals were taught to discriminate well-written numerals from poorly written ones by a sequence of multiple-choice responses (they picked the good one as the correct answer). Without any practice in writing them, the children wrote acceptable numerals on the posttest.

Moral: take common sense with a grain of salt.

End of subsection: Because this section is long, you may be running out of time. If so, this is a good place to stop. The next section will take up a second important principle.

The Second Principle

14. If a student must respond in order to learn, it may also be the case that the student will learn the response that he makes. According to this theory (with no further qualifications), what does he learn if he makes an error?

The erroneous response (we said nothing yet about telling him that he is wrong).

----

15. There are many inconclusive experimental demonstrations of the role of errors in learning; the relationships involved are com-

plex. There are subjects (and parts of almost all subjects) in which there are right answers and any other response is definitely incorrect. There are other situations in which several answers, even widely deviating ones, may all be correct. For the moment, we will ignore this latter type of situation.

Consider the following as applying to relatively simple responses such as correct spelling of a word, naming of an object, or solution of an arithmetical problem.

First, if a student responds "64" to the problem of "9×7," and he is not told that this response is incorrect, what response is he likely to give the next time he is asked the question? _____.

64.

_____

16. From this observation, then, we can derive the principle that, having made an error, the student should find out very soon that _____ in order to prevent his doing it again.

----

he is wrong (or equivalent).

_____

17. Carry the principle a step further. If a student writes "Misisipi" on a history test and his paper comes back with a red line under that word, does he now know how to spell it? _____.

No. He has many other possible spellings to try out on his teacher!

_____

18. From this observation, we can derive a further principle. Not only should the student's error be brought to his attention, but also he should find out _____ so that he will be right the next time.

----

what the correct answer is. (I did *not* say that he must be told—he may be required to look it up, but he should find it.)

_____

19. Carry the principle one step further, and you are in the Skinnerian camp:
Because "rhyme" and "rythm" (or is it

"rhythm"?) were frequently contrasted in discussions of poetry, I learned somewhere that their spellings also contrasted. As a consequence of this, I have so frequently misspelled and so frequently corrected the latter word that two responses of absolutely equal strength exist in my repertoire. Confronted with the task of spelling the word, the rule that has been adopted is: Write the word, erase it, and spell it the other way. Half the time this rule works. There is nothing unusual about this situation. "I can never remember whether it's an x or a y" is a common complaint. Under such conditions, what is the probability of choosing the correct response?

If the responses are absolutely equal in strength, the probability of choosing the correct one is ½ or 50-50.

_____

20. There seem to be times when an erroneous response, once made, is likely to recur although it is corrected. If every time an error is made the wrong response gets a little stronger, and then we correct it and the right response gets a little stronger, there is no way out. The probability of making the error remains high. If the effects of making an error are difficult to overcome, the programmer should _____.

(something like) not let errors occur, (or) see that the student is right the first time.

_____

21. The first principle derived from Skinner's theory—the principle of active responding—is carried to its logical extreme in linear programming. The student is to be led to make every response in the program that we can legitimately expect him to make when he is through learning. The second principle—correct responding on the first try—is also carried to its logical extreme. Although reading something is not considered an adequate type of response, Skinner has eliminated one type of question on the basis that a student might learn something by reading. What type of question is not allowed and why? (If your memory slips, see the second paragraph of Skinner's article, page 272.)

Multiple-choice, because the student might learn one of the plausible wrong answers.

---

22. The following is a definition of an error:

Error. A response not acceptable to the programmer. Programmers attempt to eliminate errors by revising the program. Erroneous responses may indicate: (a) a poorly designed item which fails to communicate and therefore needs to be rewritten; (b) a sequence in which prompts have been withdrawn too fast or inadequate practice given; (c) assumed previous knowledge which in fact the student does not have; (d) poor analysis of the subject matter, leading to a confusion not predicted by the programmer.

According to the criterion given here, does this definition imply that students should never be allowed to make responses that are in fact errors in the subject matter being taught?

No. The criterion is "not acceptable to the programmer." He might have a reason for getting some misconception out in the open —in order to show the student where the misconception would lead.

Note. The need to openly "punish" previous learning where it represents error is not universally agreed upon. For the time being, an open mind is recommended on this issue.

---

23. One of the essential features of Skinner's approach to a science of behavior is control of behavior. An investigator can be said to understand *why* some behavior occurs when he can make it occur (and prevent it from occurring) by manipulating some variable. Programmers following this line of thinking wish to *make* the student learn. To do this, they must control the student's responses.

Consider the following:

(a) If the programmer believes that learning is facilitated by permitting the misinformed student to give an erroneous response, is the programmer in control of the response when the student makes the error? _____.

(b) If the programmer predicts a correct answer to his "well-written" frame and the student makes an error, is the programmer in control of the student's response? _____.

(a) Yes (the error, which the programmer is trying to get out of the student, is "acceptable to the programmer").

(b) No (he has not produced the response he predicted).

---

24. In the development of a program, the programmer has to start somewhere. His first draft represents what he thinks is a reasonable order of presentation of the material. He includes what he thinks students may need and he excludes any material that he thinks students already know. Although, in the distant future, a perfect first draft may be produced, this has not yet happened.

The key to the effectiveness of the final product is the testing procedure. Many programmers prefer face-to-face testing with the first few students who go through a program. Talking to one student at a time can be a great deal more valuable than compiling errors from a large group. If the student does not understand a particular item, he can often say exactly what word or phrase is giving him difficulty. That phrase gets dropped and the item rewritten. If the student cannot solve some problem, he can often say exactly where his difficulty is. The programmer now knows that this source of difficulty will either have to be dealt with if it has not been or dealt with better if it has already been mentioned.

Eventually, of course, the program will be tested on a group of representative students. At this point the programmer should be ready to show that his program is in working order. If he gets a large number of errors from the group, he may be in trouble. Why? What data will be hard to get from the group?

It is hard to find out why the students made errors and exactly what they might need when they are not talking to the programmer.

---

25. A programmer writes a sequence that he thinks is adequate. He tries it out on a student. Parts of it do not work. So he rewrites these parts. Can he use the same student to test the second version? Why?

No. The student has already learned too much about the subject. (Or, put less elegantly, the programmer has already "ruined" the first student.)

---

26. The programmer's credo might be stated thus: "If the student errs, the programmer flunks." This statement has to be tempered with some common sense, of course. Even the best student makes a few careless mistakes. (Again, if you are talking with him, rather than reading his answer sheet, a careless error is easy to identify—the student readily recognizes what he should have done.) Truly errorless learning is probably unattainable and might be terribly tedious.

Any significant number of errors, however, is an indication that something is wrong and calls for revision of the sequence. Programmers argue about the figure—2 percent, 5 percent, 10 percent—that is permissible. In testing the first draft, however, the programmer may regard almost all errors as significant, depending on his discussions with his students. After revision, the second draft is tried on another student. If this second student makes a lot of errors and does not do well on a test, what should the programmer do (if he believes his own credo)?

Revise again.

---

27. After the first student has located some of the gross errors, the programmer rewrites the ineffective material and tries it again on a new "guinea pig." If it still doesn't work, he goes through the process again. What sort of rule of thumb does this suggest concerning how many students he will have to use in developing a programmed sequence?

(in your own words) He will have to keep trying until the sequence works with an individual student. The number of students

that he needs will depend on the programmer's skill.

Note. Nothing has been said about the "representativeness" of these individual students used in developmental testing. I, for one, prefer a slightly "unrepresentative" type of student at this point in the process. The student with high motivation to learn the material and with the gall to "tell the teacher off" whenever the sequence goes wrong is, for me, the easiest to work with. Some students simply cannot believe that a programmer blames himself for errors. If your student merely reports that he was careless each time he makes an error, the information is of little help. Other students have a hard time figuring out why they made mistakes or are too shy to say what they think. The student who tells you "I know what answer you expect here but ..." is the one you want! Learn from him.

---

28. Watch what happens to a program as it goes through the testing procedure. Some students in any group will lack some bit of information that is important for progress through the program. If a linear programmer is going to guarantee correct responses from almost all the students, what should he do about this bit of information if 30 percent of the students that he intends to teach do not have it?

Include it in the program or teach it. (He could, of course, take the easy way out and change his mind about whom the program was supposed to teach.)

---

29. When starting to write a program, programmers naturally make assumptions about what students know and do not know. Consider this one:

If a programmer assumes that students *do not* know something that they in fact do, he will put it into the program. If he assumes they *do* know something that they do not know, he will leave it out of the program.

When he tests the program, which of his

two erroneous assumptions will he find out about?

The second one. If they do not know something that he assumed, they will make mistakes. He will never find out by looking at the errors that he taught something that he did not need to teach.

---

30. The amount of practice that any one student needs in order to master some fact may differ considerably from the amount needed by another student. For any one individual, the amount of practice that he needs in one subject may be quite different from the amount that he needs in another. If the linear programmer is going to guarantee acquisition of some fact by all of his students, how much practice does he need to put in the program?

The amount required by the person who needs the most.

---

31. Errors by students will tell a programmer when he has [too much/too little] practice.

Too little (groans may tell him when he has too much!).

---

32. We can deduce that, on the average, the more a program is tested and adjusted to produce errorless learning, the [longer/shorter] it gets!

Longer. The answer is pretty obvious!

---

33. Among the early principles given as advice to programmers was the already mentioned principle of "small steps": The subject or skill to be acquired should be broken into "small" units easily digested by students. Historically, we may blame the resulting size-of-steps on two factors: first, the amount of space provided in some of the early teaching machines (you simply couldn't get more than thirty words in those small windows!) and second, on faulty design of frames. The idea

that learning can proceed with minimal errors is basic. So if you can't design good teaching exercises that enable the student to handle large amounts of material (as shown in Frame 10's example), then the only other solution seems to be that of making the steps so small that students can figure them out even if they are badly written.

In terms of what's "in" and what's "out," we can definitely say today that small steps are out. Does this mean that programmers have to abandon errorless learning as an ideal?

I think not. Instead we might give up the teaching techniques that necessitated small steps. Bad frames are out too!

Relevant Quote. "*The reader will recognize that 'errorless' learning is a conceptual convenience similar to the physicist's 'perfect' vacuum or the chemist's 'perfect' gas*" (Evans, 1965).

---

34. The theoretical necessity of guaranteeing mostly correct responding creates a dilemma for programmers. In the ordinary language and in statistical talk, the "average" person is in the middle of the distribution of some attribute.

If the "average" student in any grade level makes few errors on a program, then we would expect the "above-average" student to make no errors and the "below-average" student to make many errors.

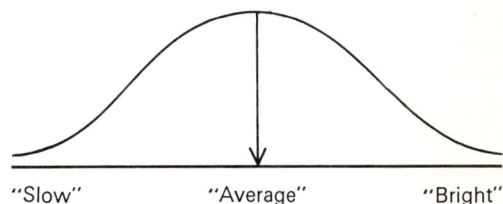

"Slow"   "Average"   "Bright"

But *(watch this logic, now!)*, the program is therefore NOT adequate for the below-average student. Our *average* student, who in the above diagram would be in the *middle* of the curve for his grade, becomes the *bot-*

tom of the population for which the program is any good.

Suppose we produce and thoroughly test a program in ninth-grade algebra until it performs well with all ninth-graders who score at the eighth-grade level or better in reading and have C's or better in arithmetic. (We're a bit below average on reading but are presumably at the average in arithmetic.)

(a) Will there be some students in a typical ninth-grade class who will make too many errors on this program?

(b) Who, in Skinner's sense, is the "average" child for whom this program is adjusted to produce a high percentage of correct responses?

(c) Is the student described in (b) above also the "average" student who can successfully take the program? (Consider all students who could succeed.)

(a) Yes—the below-average students will have trouble.

(b) The eighth-grade reader with C's in math.

(c) No. He is at the bottom of the distribution of students who can use the program successfully.

---

35. At some level of IQ, reading ability, previous training, etc., we would expect a program to "bottom out"; students would start making too many errors and show less than adequate performance on a test of what they had learned. In this case, the programmer is justified in stating that the program is not written for these students (and that he will not revise it to make it easy enough for them). If a program has a "floor," would you expect it also to have a "ceiling"? _____. How would you find out about this?

Yes. Certainly a program for seventh-graders would insult a college student even if he didn't know the subject matter.

There are many possible answers, such as "try another program that goes much faster and see if they learn as well from it," or "ask the students whether they're bored," and so forth.

---

36. In his article, Skinner notes that teaching a group of students at exactly the same rate is a great source of inefficiency in education. In proceeding through a linear program (linear = straight line), each student does every item. How, then, do students go at different rates?

(in your own words) Some do the items faster than others.

Note. Carried to its logical extreme (one frame for each possible response), the principle of active responding leads to a lengthy program. The problems dicussed above indicate that the second principle, minimal errors, also has a tendency to produce long programs.

Problem for consideration. (No answer is required at the moment.) Is the notion of bringing each student up to mastery at his own rate—that is, with maximum efficiency—simply an impossibility? Revision of existing frames is no solution to the problems of differences in previous knowledge or in rate of acquisition (amount of practice needed) for the material being taught. The need for a solution (but not necessarily *the* solution itself) will appear again and again in this program.

---

37. The only way to revise an item that leads to error is to break the idea into smaller steps. True or False?

False. Perhaps expressing it better or coming up with a more apt example would clear up the difficulty. In breaking some ideas down, we are likely to lose the whole picture.

Relevant Quote. "(The) student cannot fail. If he doesn't get where you want him to go, you have failed"* (Gilbert, 1960).

If you have to stop soon, stop here.

The Third Principle

38. Immediately after writing (or thinking or speaking) his response, the student proceeding through a linear program is provided

with "knowledge of results." He compares the answer that he gave with the correct answer provided by the programmer.

If he is correct, his response is "confirmed." If he is incorrect, he has at least read the correct response, which raises the probability (but does not guarantee) that he will give the correct response the next time he is asked a similar question.

Several experiments have been done with this variable—knowledge of results. The question often asked, "Is it necessary?" might better be phrased, "*When* is it necessary?" Consider the following:

(a) I ask you to guess which whole number I am thinking of that lies between 4 and 6. You respond. Do you need to have your response confirmed? _____. Why?

- -

No, providing we are using the same number system. The answer is completely obvious and you cannot really be said to be guessing.

Consider this situation:

(b) I ask you to guess which number I am thinking of that lies between 1 and 10. You respond. Do you need to have your response confirmed? _____. Why?

- -

Yes. You have no way of knowing what number I am thinking of, so you cannot evaluate your own response.

---

39. When the student is completely unsure of the correctness of his response, the teacher must provide "knowledge of results." When the student is completely sure (correctly so) of the correctness of his response, the teacher does not need to provide "knowledge of results." Does this latter case mean that learning can occur without knowledge of results? _____. What is the difference between the first and the second case here?

- -

No. In the latter case it is the student who provides himself with knowledge of results. The difference is in who provides it, not in whether it occurs or not (see Klaus [1965] and Gilbert [1962] for further argument on this subject).

40. For most of you, the following frame presents a new fact.

> Since aardvarks find uncles indigestible, they eat _____.
> (demonstration frame) Klaus

Figure out the answer to this "riddle." Do you need your response confirmed? _____. Why?

- -

Most people say "no," once they have figured out the answer. There is only one answer that "fits," and it obviously fits. Most riddles have this property—the answer may be difficult to get but you know when you've got it. (Those who pronounce "aunts" and "ants" differently are in trouble, of course.)

---

41. If you already know about aardvarks' appetites, you'll have to take the point made by the frame on faith. For those who do not know about aardvarks, it should be obvious that a student confronted with a new fact that he has just generated could [sometimes/never] provide himself with knowledge of results.

- -

Sometimes. (Frames of this type are rare, but such obviousness can also be brought about by clever sequencing.)

---

42. A program is supposed to proceed in logical fashion as it leads a student through a subject. There are rote drill aspects of many subjects in which we really can't say that an answer is supposed to seem "sensible," but if a subject has a structure—mathematics, for instance—we would hope that the answers required of students "make sense" to them. When you come up with an answer that makes sense to you, can you be fairly sure that you are correct? _____.

- -

Most would say "yes."

---

43. If the program in a machine (or out of a machine) asks the student to "take only

that step which he is at the moment best equipped to take," is it likely that the student will know that the response he is making is the correct one? _____.

Yes.

---

44. However,

(a) Is it possible for a student to be certain he is correct when he is in fact incorrect? _____.

(b) Is it possible for a student to be correct but to be uncertain that he is? _____.

(c) If thirty or more students are taking the same program, is it likely that the next step is *the* step for which all thirty are absolutely prepared? _____.

(a) Yes, it happens. (Answers to arithmetic problems are an obvious example—minor errors can occur without the student's feeling unsure.)

(b) Yes. For some "anxious" students, this happens frequently.

(c) No. It is unlikely that they are all alike. The step could be too big for some, who will therefore be unsure of their responses.

---

45. On the basis of the questions in the preceding frame, we may deduce that (a) a particular student may or may not need confirmation of his correct response or correction of his incorrect response on any particular frame in a program; and (b) that the program will be used by large groups of students who may vary in their reactions to any particular frame. Therefore, the programmer should provide knowledge of results on [every frame/those frames that he thinks are hard/those frames that his students missed in the trial of the program]. (Which?)

Every frame (unless his whole program reads like the "aardvark" frame!).

---

46. In an experiment by the author (Meyer, 1960) 16 eighth-graders completed a program with no immediate confirmation of

their responses. The group as a whole made significantly more errors and gained significantly less knowledge than a comparable group given knowledge of results in the usual way. However, two students in the "no-answer" group turned in an almost errorless performance and gained a great deal from pretest to posttest. How would you explain the data from these two students? (They did not cheat and their pretest scores showed they had much to learn.)

The best guess is that the program moved at a rate of progress that was right for them—they could take the next step correctly, and they knew that they were right.

---

47. If the "fit" between the size of the steps forward that the program asks for and the size of steps that an individual student can take happens to be good, this particular student may "know he is right" and do very well without ever having to check the correct answer. (Indeed many students can be observed doing just this—paying no attention to the answers.)

If the size of step in the program is too small for the student—that is, if he could have gone faster than the program allows, is he likely to do well without checking his answers?

Yes.

---

48. In any good program, the condition in which the student is guessing wildly (for example, "what number am I thinking of?") will not happen. (This does not mean that he won't be asked to guess, but his guess is left as a guess and not called wrong.) This was one condition under which it was necessary to provide knowledge of results.

For any particular student, what other *conditions* might arise in which he would need to be given knowledge of results even in a fairly good program?

(a) Whenever he is unsure of his response and needs it confirmed or corrected, and (b) whenever he is wrong but thought he was right.

Note. Pragmatically, most programmers adopt the conventional system of providing an answer or a model of kinds of good answers immediately after each frame, as you are experiencing in this program. Other solutions have been tried, such as having answers available if needed at the bottom of the page or back of the text. Certain kinds of teaching machines can "confirm" a correct answer by moving on to the next problem, without revealing the correct answer if the student errs —the machine simply waits.

An example of a program which provides no confirmation is *Child Management: A Program for Parents* by Judith M. and Donald E. P. Smith (1966). Here "frames" consist of presentation of material describing a general principle they are advising parents to adopt, followed by two or more "cases"— one of which illustrates the principle and the others of which do not. The reader is expected to be able to make the choices and to have the correctness of his choice as obvious as was the answer to the aardvark frame (presented in Frame 41). The answer to whether this procedure works is found, as always, in research with students, not in theoretical arguments. Each program is an individual case in itself.

Summary: Principles of Skinnerian Programming

The programmer's task is to create instructional materials which embody these principles:

1. Active Responding. The student learns what the program leads him to do.
An active response is not necessarily a small one nor is it necessarily (in the final version of the program) an overt one.

2. Minimal Errors. By good design of the instruction, and by repeated tryout and revision of the instruction, errors made by students in responding to frames and in exhibiting the final desired behavior are held to a minimum.
An error, as we defined it, is a response that the programmer did not expect or does not wish students to make.

3. Knowledge of Results. In some fashion, a student should be given such feedback on the adequacy of his response. This may be provided by skillful design, which leads a student to be right and be sure he's right, or by providing an answer as a guide to checking himself if he is unsure or in error. The status of confirmation as "the reinforcer" in the sense intended by Skinner and his colleagues is open to question.

* * *

Problems of applying computer technology to teacher education

ALFRED ELLISON

There is a real mystique about computer operations. The dazzling rapidity with which the computer spews forth its findings, the truly superhuman comprehensiveness of its capabilities, and the world-shaking ramifications of its application profoundly befuddle the uninitiated, who somehow or other are made to feel that understanding how computers might assist in instruction requires a particular kind of insight, an especial intel-

lectual brilliance, an habitual communion with esoteric engineering intricacies. Not so! What understanding CAI really requires is unmitigated optimism.

Once the educator became aware of the tremendous flexibility and comprehensiveness

From *Educational Technology,* 1970, *10*(11), pp. 35–39. Reprinted by permission of *Educational Technology Magazine.*

of the computer and its applications, there was little doubt that the future of education would be intimately tied to it. What has been in considerable doubt is the mode of operation and the kind of relationship which would exist.

When one concedes the inevitability of the use of the computer to support educational processes, the implications for teacher education need examination. This is particularly true if we expect teachers of today and tomorrow to be able to utilize this new instrument with confidence and purpose, without fear of either the instrument or of their own position. It seems reasonable to project that if we are to produce such a new generation of teachers, the computer must be intimately related to their own lives and their own education. This must happen at three different levels. First, the teacher needs to gain part of his own education through the medium of the computer. Courses exist now in several liberal arts content areas which show experimentation at this level. The courses in physics at Irvine and at Dartmouth, the course in economics at Stony Brook, the course in mathematics at Penn State, and several approaches to foreign language instruction come to mind immediately. Here is a start to solve the need of teachers-to-be to have part of their own instructional life experience in the liberal arts content attained through the medium of the computer. Second, the teacher needs to have some of his own professional education, the too often derided and underestimated "methods" courses, through the medium of the computer. The future of teaching a new kind of content may be dim indeed without such technological improvement. Third, the teacher-to-be needs to become familiar with the available programs for helping children learn at the elementary- and secondary-school level. He needs to know these programs so that he can apply them in his own teaching. To know programs and their possibilities, he should participate in developing new ones.

Experience at these three different levels needs to be provided if the next generation of teachers is not to be handicapped as the present ones are, so that they will not be fearful of this technological "monster," nor fearful of what it will do to their security. They need rather to be able to accept the tremendous challenge and opportunity for individualizing instruction which the computer enables us to reach for the first time.

How close are we to the fulfillment of this dream of applying computers to the solution of educational problems? Unfortunately, what we have at present is a dual failure: One is the awful problem of getting operational; the second has to do with the low quality of too many present approaches to CAI.

A journey across country examining CAI installations two years ago revealed two superior programs to a person eager to get started. One, a program in new mathematics at Penn State University, had been well standardized and tested in the field. The second was an inquiry-mode program developed at the University of Illinois. Of the two, specialized equipment was necessary for the second, which I preferred educationally, and it was not feasible to transfer it to another institution. However, the mathematics program was operating on standard IBM equipment, was written in a supposedly standard lan-

Reprinted by permission of Educational Technology Publications, Inc. Hal Money, cartoonist.

guage, and provided what seemed to be an ideal opportunity to become operational. Despite misgivings, I was very eager to get started; improvements could come later.

The Penn State math program was sound educationally and mathematically, and it had been developed on a federal grant; therefore, it was in the public domain. It seemed reasonable to assume that we could rent teletype machines, hook them up through data phones and telephone lines to the computer where the program was stored, schedule our students, and go into business. Thus the primary problem would be one of raising funds for the needed hook-up rather than development of hardware or software. I later learned that this was an incredibly naive assumption.

We have about five different computer complexes at New York University, which include most of the various generations of IBM equipment up through the model 360/50 and a huge CDC 6600 at our Mathematics Institute. Each group of people I spoke to as I went from one to another of the computer centers was most cordial and encouraging. With the availability of our own computers and personnel, the problem seemed a bit less frightening. However, two years later we still have not been able to get this program instituted. The problem has not been a financial one, because it would not have been very expensive. The point was never reached where the cost figures and a specific proposal could be taken to the dean.

The block, as nearly as I can understand it, is one of incompatibility of interfaces, or should we call it "incomputability" of computer components? I thought at first to tie into the computer where the program was stored. This was impossible; that computer was loaded and could not accept another time-sharing station. What then of storing the program in one of our computers? This was fine theoretically but practically not feasible. The program was written in a language our computers did not comprehend. Translating programs are still unavailable. Sadly, I confess, we are still not operating.

But this is not the only problem we face when we apply CAI to teacher education. We find a great failure at the conceptual level, as demonstrated by the comparatively few programs in existence which adequately account for the new kind of thinking about education which the computer makes possible. Most existing programs do not even attempt to fulfill the basic potential that the computer offers. We face a situation analogous to the early use of television, in which the most that could be done with the great potential of this great new medium was to show a teacher teaching a class, looking out of the video tube. Too often we merely translate the worst of current practice into new media. If the computer's application to education is to be limited to that of a glorified workbook or an automatic page-turner, it will be sad indeed. Too many existing programs are simply inadequate for the new tasks of education.

The situation in applying computers to use is closely related to the state of the art of programmed instruction as it has developed in the last decade. The research on PI for educational use was too often satisfied when no significant differences emerged between the material as programmed and its first-hand teaching by the instructor. This told us nothing about the quality of the instructor. How nearly the program came to accomplishing the objectives set up for it was important, but the quality of the objectives is simply not included in the evaluation scheme.

PI has gone through a number of different phases. There was a time, in 1961 and '62, when it appeared as if PI was the essence of the technological revolution for education. Many a school superintendent jumped on the apparent bandwagon, even if somewhat tentatively, to try out this new programmed instruction, by which it was claimed children could teach themselves as well as their teachers could teach them. Unfortunately, the willingness of the superintendent to try the programs did not affect their quality. Too many programs of this era were stupid at worst and insipid at best. Warehouses today are still loaded with materials put together by optimistic if somewhat careless or even ruthless publishers who seized on the bandwagon effect accompanying PI to produce a flood of materials of very doubtful quality. Superintendents who were stuck with their original enthusiasm were turned off by the quality of materials they received and the great gap between the promise and performance of PI. So much of this inferior material was produced that it not only clogged the warehouses but effectively acted to undo the positive attitudes about PI which had developed, so that even today, despite some outstanding examples of excellent programming, the field is in the doldrums. It exists as an exciting field of work mainly for its theoretical promise rather than the fulfillment of its original dream. And it is in the dream that we find an affinity to CAI.

The dream, most simply stated, is in the area of individualization of instruction and in concretely specifying the purposes of the teaching episode. PI provides a means by which, finally, children can proceed at their own pace to learn both content and skills prescribed. PI promised that instead of the constant time of exposure by a teacher presenting material to a class, we would achieve variability of exposure through the medium of self-pacing by children. By providing a wide variety of available materials we would finally come to achieving self-selection of problem areas to be studied. PI theorists indicated very clearly that among the requirements for good programs was the write-test-rewrite procedure: that programs had to be tested out on live populations and modified accordingly before they were acceptable. Today, most PI people insist that the population on which material was tried out should be identified, and the results published with the material, as a guide to the purchaser who could see whether or not the tested population was anything like the population he wanted to use the material with, and the level of success, together with the variations in that success, in the tested population. Accompanying all work with PI was the important idea of establishing specific objectives which the particular program was to accomplish. These were the promises of PI. What we got over the last decade was a progression of glorified workbooks, too often untested, unimaginative, and unstimulating. With the growth of CAI and the need for software, many of the PI experts moved into the vacuum. We got the same faults in programming CAI that we had in PI.

The major point to be emphasized and the basic problem has been the failure of conceptualization. Perhaps the wrong people have been developing the materials for use on the computer: on the one hand, engineers; on the other, PI practitioners. Perhaps we have been talking too much about instruction and not enough about education. The PI that has been most successful was that which taught definable skills, as demonstrated by the growth of PI in training programs in industry and in the armed forces. We see a similar phenomenon taking place with CAI in that skill-related training has provided its most effective utilization. Perhaps this is a function of the training of the people who have developed the programs which have been utilized.

I can best illustrate my meaning further by a chat I had several years ago with one of the top research men in CAI of one of the big computer companies. He was telling me with some glee about a mathematics program that had been developed for adolescents in a disadvantaged school district in the East. The program provided two numerals and an operation; the responder was to provide the answer. "Nine plus six," clicked out the computer's typewriter, and the answer "fifteen" was to come from the youngster. The program was arranged so that the problem combinations were repeated more frequently than the combinations receiving correct responses. Thus the youngster had more practice in learning to respond to the combinations which gave him trouble. In this respect it was certainly individual. My question to this gentleman was: "What is the theory of mathematics teaching on which this program is based?" He looked at me blankly. He simply did not understand the nature, the purport, or the meaning of the question.

I went after the information in another way. "Who did the program?" I asked.

"Oh," came the response, "a couple of my boys."

"What do you mean?" I pursued. "Who were they? What was their background?"

"Oh, they're engineers," was the answer, as if that solved all problems and settled all issues. This man had no idea that there was any ferment in the teaching of mathematics, that there was a revolution in the teaching of this subject in the 1930s, which—had it been successful—would have made the revolution of the 1950s unnecessary. These changes placed great emphasis on teaching *understanding* of meanings rather than mere mechanical response in teaching arithmetic. Here we had the anomaly of this most fantastic representation of twentieth-century mastery of technology, in its latest version representing fourth generation computers, being utilized to provide an antediluvian, outmoded, discredited approach to the teaching of mathematics. This research person's gleeful "It worked!" fell very dully on my ears, for his criteria for what working means were very different from that applied in current teaching of mathematics.

Another illustration, this one from the field of programmed instruction, may be helpful. At my request a course was set up in our division entitled "Programmed Instruction in Childhood Education." One of the outstanding people in the country in this field was the instructor. I asked about changing it to "Programmed Learning in Childhood Education" on the basis that instruction is what the teacher does, but learning is what the child does. Back of my question, of course, was the whole concept of how can we set up our materials so as to insure the child's learning—not merely our instruction of the child. He laughed and understood exactly what I meant, but indicated that the state of the art was not such as to insure that outcome. We retained the title.

It is time for us to rethink that popular title—computer-assisted instruction—and begin to reconceptualize this instrument from its primary use by the teacher to its primary use by the learner. This may lead to computer-assisted education. Let us pursue this idea.

In an instructional program the learner is told what to do, what he should know, when he should know it, and perhaps how he may use what he has learned. His success is measured on his ability to regurgitate the proper answers to the proper questions, which parallel the material presented. Education, however, goes far beyond this and presumes that the learner cannot only acquire the knowledge needed but can apply it in new and different situations. Material which is primarily factual can probably be adequately presented in an instructional mode. When it comes to the application of information, the use of those facts in new and different situations, we need to develop brand new approaches. This is precisely what has gone wrong with CAI. If it is the facts that we are interested in communicating, we have to live with the notion that these facts change, and not only is that change rapid, but facts are changing at an accelerating rate. The important contribution of the computer will not be, I venture to forecast, to teach those facts on a massive scale, nor to provide storage for programs which have this factual imparting as their primary purpose. Such programs can just as readily be mounted in other kinds of hardware, if they need hardware at all. Let us not forget that the computer itself can store the facts, keep them current, and reveal them in a retrieval system as needed. The user no longer needs to retain them for himself. The uniqueness of the computer, its speed, its flexibility, the vastness of its storage of materials, the quality of the responses it can provide, need to be

"OUR TEACHER REALLY FOOLED US TODAY... SHE ASKED US TO THINK."

placed at the disposal of the learner as he solves problems which are real to him.

Some Questions

I have a few questions about the development of CAI over these past few years, questions about some matters which block its use effectively in teacher education.

1. Why is it that the only program I found in an inquiry mode, that is, other than a linear or branching instructional program, was one worked out by Bitzer and Suchman at the University of Illinois? Nothing further seems to have been done with the inquiry mode. Why?

2. What has happened to the early efforts to give the computer a voice and make its voice responsive so that reading skill would not be a primary factor in determining the success of the student?

3. What came of the notion of giving the computer tremendous resources as an educational data bank?

4. What became of the potential of using the computer as a controlling mechanism as part of a larger program for numerous different audio-visual devices? In the earlier stages of its development, the computer was used to control a series of slides, tape recorders, video recorders, and cartridge-type film loops; also, it was used as an information-retrieval instrument. All of these have tremendous potential educationally. Why have they not been more adequately explored?

5. We are all using microfiche these days. With the latest "ultra-fiche" produced by National Cash Register, some three thousand pages of material are reproduced on a fiche of the standard four-by-six inch size that we have been using for sixty-four to ninety pages. The coordinates which would locate any one of these pages are simple x,y coordinates. Ten volumes of material could be adequately reproduced on a single fiche and access to any of these pages controlled by simple location of x,y coordinates. The computer-controlled reproduction of any of these pages in any desired sequence on a read-out screen or print-out is within the scope of the art today. Is anybody working with it?

6. What happened to simulation as a primary learning device? The computer offers storage and retrieval possibilities that are breathtaking. No one seems to care.

7. And when will the big companies do something about insuring the compatibility of program languages? Remember the time of competition between various systems of color television? Remember the early chaos about varying tape recorder speeds, the shift from wire to tape, and how standardization clarified that situation? There has been a corresponding confusion about current videotape recording differences in speeds and widths of tape. But there comes a time when the futile notion that each manufacturer holds that his own process is so superior that everyone will adopt it must give way to the notion that the primary good of the consumer is served by compatibility, and that the ultimate profit for the manufacturers lies in the direction of providing such compatibility.

To the Computer Makers

In the interest of applying computer potential further to the field of teacher education, let me close with a charge. To those who are working with traditional programs in CAI, a new concept of CAE must be developed, in which the material we present is not nearly as important as the learner's ability to make alternative choices, to raise intelligent questions, and to seek responses to them by calling for and applying available and pertinent data. Let us charge the companies involved in developing new generations of hardware to accept responsibility for the development and use of software for educational purposes; part of this responsibility is to either agree on a common language or to provide translators so that programs may be usable on more than one system.

Teaching classification by computer

JAMES G. HOLLAND AND JUDITH DORAN

In many applications of computer-assisted instruction, the instructional objectives can be taught with instrumentation much simpler than a computer. With the increasing availability and the decreasing cost of computers, it is important to explore those objectives which cannot be easily taught without a computer.

One instance in which the memory and decision-making capability of large computers can be useful is in teaching which requires the arrangement of sophisticated reinforcement contingencies. The capacity of the computer is required to determine whether the student has met the criterion for reinforcement.

Accordingly, we devised a computer-controlled program to teach young children classification skills. The instructional objective of the program was to increase the child's ability to classify on the basis of relationships that exist between and within classes. The child learns to classify according to perceptual qualities like color or shape, according to abstract qualities like fruit or animals, and according to use or function, like toys or clothes. The child also practices using the language concepts "all," "alike," "same," and "except." But the most interesting aspect, and the one which involves the most complex reinforcement contingencies, is that the child learns to classify a single collection of objects a number of different ways, beginning with any attribute he chooses and following any order he chooses.

Each array of objects was separately photographed and presented, with a 35mm random-access carousel projector (Kodak 950), on a touch-sensitive display, which is a computer interface device that transmits the location of the child's touch to the computer (cf. Fitzhugh and Katsuki, 1971). (See Figure 1.) The computer, a PDP 7/9, was programmed to control the contingencies associated with the various types of items. Appropriate messages were presented by a random-access auditory device (cf. Ragsdale,

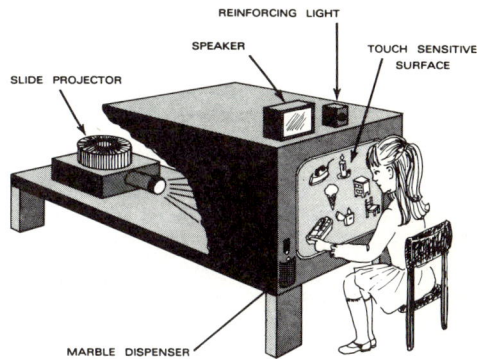

Figure 1. Child working on multiple-category item of the classification program.

1966 or Judd, 1969 for a description of the Westinghouse-designed CROWs).

The 160-item classification program began with simple identification of objects belonging to a single specified class and progressed to unprompted classifications for each of the several attributes in the array. Early items familiarized the child with the categories included in subsequent multiple-category items. To introduce a category, pictures of objects sharing a common attribute were displayed with a message identifying the attribute and asking the child to touch one or more additional exemplars in a second array at the bottom of the screen. Other items asked the child to touch the object that was different or to touch all the objects which belonged to a specified category.

From **Educational Technology,** December 1972, **12** (12), 58-60. Reprinted by permission of **Educational Technology Magazine.**

The research reported in this article was supported by the Learning Research and Development Center of the University of Pittsburgh, funded in part as a research and development center by the United States Office of Education, Department of Health, Education, and Welfare. Marcia Froimson Baum and Jacqueline W. Liebergott contributed to the development of the early versions of the classification program and Robert J. Fitzhugh devised the computer programming.

A multiple-category item is described in detail to illustrate the computer control of complex reinforcement contingencies. The child hears, "Touch all the things that are alike." If he fails to touch an object within fifteen seconds, the message is repeated. If he completes a category, e.g., touches all the things that are cold, a light flashes and the audio plays, "Find some more things that are alike." If he again selects the objects that are cold, he hears, "You already did that, try again." He may then touch all the things that are hot. If he stops without completing a category, after ten seconds he hears, "You didn't find them all, try again." After this category, he may touch all the furniture, or the wooden or metal objects, etc. If the child happens to make an invalid set, e.g., the chair and the lighter, he hears, "Those don't go together, try again." After each completed category, the light flashes and the audio plays, "Touch some more things that are alike." When all categories are completed (in this item, hot, cold, wood, metal, and furniture), the child is reinforced with a bell ringing, a light flashing, and a marble dispensing. The marbles can be exchanged for a toy at the end of the session. If the child fails to classify on some attributes, he is asked specifically to classify on the missed attributes, e.g., "Touch all the furniture," or "Touch all the things that are hot." After all the missed attributes are completed in this fashion, the original message is presented again, "Touch all the things that are alike," and the child starts again to classify the objects in a variety of different ways. The above example is not the typical case, however, because the child generally makes few mistakes; the error routines were the exception, not the rule.

The number of sets in the multiple-category items ranged from two to six. One group of subjects was required to complete all of these sets (the 100-percent-criterion group). Another group was not required to complete all of the possible sets. For this group, the number of sets required per item was the nearest whole number that did not exceed three-quarters of the total possible sets. The average was 62 percent of the sets.

The results demonstrated considerable success in reaching a low error rate and satisfactory improvement in the skill of multiple classification. The children completed the program in approximately five or six twenty-minute sessions. Overall average error rate per item for first opportunity responses was 11 percent (with a range from 4 to 24 percent). Average error rate for the multiple-category items was 20 percent (with a range from 5 to 30 percent). There were differences between subjects with the 100 percent criterion and those with the 62 percent criterion. For both groups of subjects there was a statistically significant improvement in posttest performance as compared with the pretest performance. In each case, the p value was less than .001. For the 100-percent-criterion group, performance improved from an average pretest score of 41 to an average posttest score of 84. For the 62-percent-criterion group, performance changed from an average pretest score of 30 to an average posttest score of 61. In both instances, the scores approximately doubled. Unfortunately, although group assignment was random, a sizeable difference occurred between the groups in pretest performance, tending to obscure comparisons between the two criteria. An analysis of covariance was used to adjust for this mismatching. The adjusted posttest mean for the 62-percent-criterion group was 63. This difference in posttest performance between the two groups favoring the 100-percent-criterion group is what one would expect; however, using an analysis of covariance, the difference fails to reach statistical significance. It seems likely that a larger n would demonstrate an advantage.

Success of the Program

In general, the results demonstrate that the program attained a reasonably low error rate and substantial improvement in posttest behavior. The success of the program is most striking when one remembers that the subjects were age six, and Piaget places this ability in his stage three, which begins at age nine or ten (Inhelder and Piaget, 1958).

The computer successfully managed reinforcement contingencies for this task, which would be difficult or impossible to arrange with our more simple devices or procedures. The only other procedure practical is a teacher who must monitor the behavior and determine whether the subject is always touching possible categories and remember whether the category was already covered. This would be done most imperfectly and would be prone to a great many errors and might, in fact, not be generally practical.

Some CAI programs which claim a basis in programming principles generate a need for the computer capacity largely by partially ignoring good programming practice. Thus, the drill and practice programs for math and spelling (cf. Suppes, 1966) use high error frequencies to differentially weigh items for drill. The high error rates are generated by a lack of programming and a lack of attention to the hierarchical structure of the subject matter. Others, such as the Stanford reading program (Atkinson, 1968), use a basic underlying linear program with remedial items on incorrect answers. There is work for the computer only to the extent that the defects of the program evoke errors on mainline items.

The present program, in contrast, attempts, with some success, to obtain a low error rate in a program in which the capacities of the computer are amply used in determining whether the subject has attained the condition for reinforcement. No doubt there are a number of other educational objectives which cannot easily be arranged without using the capacity of the computer, e.g., gaming and complex decision-making in simulated economic systems in business schools, simulated generations of plants and animals in genetics classes, and other chemical, physical, social, or historical situations in which the student supplies the parameters into the program (cf. May, 1970). Another promising application at the Learning Research and Development Center teaches spelling rules and heuristics with a computer program derived in part from the classification program described in this paper (cf. Block and Simon, 1972). However, such tasks seem all too rare in traditional academic education. For that reason, the present results, though encouraging, cannot be considered a particularly strong general endorsement of the application of computer-assisted instruction to educational tasks. However, perhaps in our schools we have taught only those things which have seemed feasible to teach. The opening of new possibilities in education via the computer may extend the things we will teach in the future.

13

STRUCTURING ANTECEDENT STIMULI

A criticism frequently leveled at behaviorally oriented psychologists is that they neglect "cognitive" factors. Cognitive factors have been the traditional domain of educators as they structure "antecedents." Antecedents are the books, programs, and presentations that direct learning behavior. Reinforcement may maintain (traditionalists say "motivate") learning, but antecedent stimuli control the form that learning will take.

Indeed, the primary emphasis in behavioral psychology has been on reinforcement. Discrimination has been extensively studied but in simplified situations. In the laboratory, questions of response topography have been sidestepped by using arbitrary, easily defined responses, such as a bar press or a key peck. However, Skinner, in his book *Verbal Behavior* and in his paper "An Operant Analysis of Problem Solving," made important contributions to a behavioral analysis of cognitive matters. The behaviorists' foray into education has forced them to come to grips with complex, human "cognitive" behavior.

Two similar behavioral approaches to antecedent stimuli are presented in this section. The first, by Becker, analyzes the presentation of antecedents that teach "concepts" and "operations." In Becker's scheme "concepts" parallel the discriminative behavior that occurs in laboratory situations, whereas "operations" appear to parallel response topographies, generally avoided in the laboratory but treated in more applied settings in terms of "response generalization." Becker presents some ideas for teaching concepts and operations to preschoolers. Engelmann's paper, in Section 3 of this volume, gives some of the impressive results of this approach.

The second paper, by Markle and Tiemann, reports some experiments on teaching more advanced concepts. These authors hold, as does Becker, that use of examples and nonexamples is valuable, if not essential, in the teaching of concepts. They study the effect on concept learning of using various kinds of examples and nonexamples, together with various descriptions of the concept.

Educators have rightfully stressed the importance of cognitive structure. However, as Markle and Tiemann point out, cognitive variables cannot be studied in a vacuum. Good experimental procedures are essential that will test out, in a realistic, behavioral context, assumptions about structuring antecedents. Behaviorists specialize in experimental procedures and analysis; they therefore should make a valuable contribution to the cognitive area of education.

Teaching concepts and operations, or how to make kids smart

WESLEY C. BECKER

In the first Banff International Conference on Behavior Modification, Dr. Richard Stuart, who is back again this year, presented a pointed and scholarly analysis of a host of current problems in the field of mental health (Stuart, 1969). His analysis of the role of poverty in "mental illness" pointed at deficiencies in basic life resources and in education as providing the clearest account of the development of behavior patterns that are rejected and punished by the middle-class establishment.

A corrective approach to such problems is to provide the basic necessities to all in one way or another and to change the educational institutions in directions that insure that all children, not just the privileged, learn or are taught. Dr. Stuart suggested the possible value of using TV to teach young children. "Sesame Street" is a current experiment in this direction, which has at least turned on a lot of adults. Dr. Stuart also suggested community centers for teaching parents basic literacy and to provide for other needs. But primarily, Stuart emphasized, and I must agree, that the major change has to occur in schools themselves. Schools historically designed for the advantaged have been adapted for the poor by adding the various special remedial programs after the children have already failed. In many cases not even special remedial programs are available. It is no secret that many remedial programs do little more than classify children as being retarded, emotionally disturbed, or socially maladjusted, or having a learning disability. Nor is it a secret that more often than not the label given a child leads to a self-fulfilling prophecy. The "stupid" child is presumed to learn at a "slower rate," thus, less is required of him. He is taught at a slower rate, and the early prediction of retardation is confirmed. The emotionally disturbed child is presumed not to be able to learn until his emotional disturbances are treated. Too often he too is prepared by the school to fail in mainstream society. Socially maladjusted children are placed in groups with a special teacher and, whether they are raising hell or not, are often given understanding and kindness as long as the teacher can take it but are not taught the basic skills in language concepts and reading needed to get back into an ordinary classroom. The "learning disability" child is often found to function delightfully in a one-to-one situation with his special teacher but still fails to perform in the classroom. Current remedial programs make it possible for nearly all *teaching failures* to be blamed on the child and for nearly all of these children to be shipped out of the classroom.

For those who see education as playing a major role in breaking the poverty cycle, Stuart correctly identifies two major changes required in current educational practices. The first is to provide more effective instruction; the second is the massive use of positive reinforcers to motivate children to behave and learn in school. I wholeheartedly agree, although the better the instruction, the less the need for unusual reinforcers. A third approach is to begin to teach children of the poor earlier.

During the past two years Siegfried Engelmann and I and a very valuable staff have been working with some five thousand poor children in eighteen parts of the United States under a program called Follow Through. This is a sequel to Head Start. We also have been teaching children labeled "educable retarded" by the public schools. Our uniform experience is that these children can be taught readily when effective reinforcers and teaching strategies are utilized. We see no reason why the mass of special labels and classes for problem children are needed except for those with very obvious impairments in vision, hearing, and motor functioning.

While it is too early to present final data,

From *An Empirical Basis for Change in Education* by W. C. Becker. © 1971, Science Research Associates, Inc. Reprinted by permission of the publisher.

This paper was first presented at the Banff International Conference on Behavior Modification, Alberta, Canada, May 1970.

the Follow Through program is probably the most significant experiment in educational change ever attempted and therefore merits mention in my introductory remarks. Follow Through uses funds from Title II of the Economic Opportunity Act and is administered by the Office of Education.

Engelmann and I are among fifteen to twenty sponsors selected to provide experimental programs to school districts with high percentages of children of the poor. Based on Engelmann's work with Bereiter (Bereiter and Engelmann, 1966) in teaching the disadvantaged and our own work in using behavior modification to motivate and teach disadvantaged children (Becker, Thomas, and Carnine, 1969), we teamed together to structure a kindergarten-through-third-grade program for poor children. The program has the following key features:

1. Classroom structure:
   One teacher and two aides for each twenty-five children. (Aides from the parent group where possible.) Small-group instruction in groups of three to eight. Academic goals given priority but not exclusively.
2. Teaching formats:
   Daily programmed lessons for direct instruction in language concepts, reading, and arithmetic by teachers and aides using prepared materials.[1] Science and social science added at level 2. Art and music designed to reinforce language program. Daily "take-home" sheets of skills learned in each area with instructions for parents.
3. Continuous monitoring:
   Progress of the children is monitored by testing (on the tasks taught) each month, by weekly reports of teaching, and by video tapes. Progress of the teachers and aides are monitored by video tape and consultants who supervise in-service training.
4. Parent involvement:
   Parents are provided with instructions on classroom teaching methods. Parents are provided with daily lessons to practice at home with their children. A course in child management based on be-

havior modification procedures is available to most parents (Becker, 1971). Parents are hired as testers, aides, and video clerks.

The key assumptions underlying the program are that children learn if they are taught, and that the only way to help disadvantaged children catch up is to teach them at a faster-than-normal rate *and to continue to do so.*

To insure that children are taught at a faster-than-normal rate, first it is necessary to have more manpower in the classroom. Aides are used because of cost considerations and because parents who have become teacher aides are likely to be better parents. The added manpower is needed because, if children cannot read well, they can be taught best by a person who can talk to them. By using daily lessons that program the teachers' and aides' behavior (about thirty minutes a day for each subject for each child), aides and teachers can be taught to start teaching our way with a week's preservice training. Continuing in-service training for about two hours a week is also required. The use of well-programmed materials makes it not only possible to use paraprofessionals, but also makes the teacher's use of her time more efficient. She is provided with programming sequences that work. She is taught how to *get* and *hold* attention (looking and listening), how to correct, and how to reinforce. The programmed materials help her to teach more in less time. The children proceed at a faster-than-normal rate. Efficiency is achieved in the moment-by-moment teacher-child interactions that constitute teaching. Engelmann, Thomas, and I have detailed a theory of teaching that encompasses behavior modification and spells out the details involved in efficient teaching interactions.[2]

However, in my opinion, the most important aspect of what we are doing involves the programming strategies embedded in Engelmann's programs. During the past year I have attempted to determine what it is that

---

1 Science Research Associates is publishing these materials under the trade name Distar™.

2 In W. C. Becker, S. Englemann, and D. R. Thomas, *Teaching: A Course in Applied Psychology* (Palo Alto, Calif.: Science Research Associates, 1971).

Engelmann does better than other people and place his procedures within a general framework of behavior theory. It is my major task to try to share with you some outcomes of this continuing analysis.

There are two focal points to this presentation. The first is a discussion of concepts and operations. The second is a discussion of some implications of Engelmann's viewpoint for programming.

CONCEPTS

For many, the explanation of a concept presented here will seem simple and obvious. At least we hope that will be the case *after* the presentation.

We begin with an operational test for the teaching of a concept. Consider the following diagram:

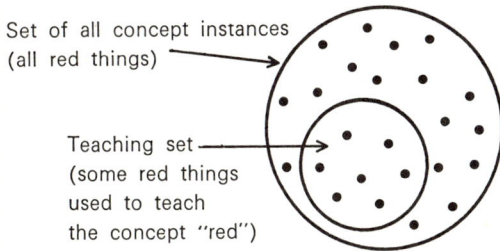

Set of all concept instances (all red things)

Teaching set (some red things used to teach the concept "red")

We have taught a concept when any or all members of the concept set are correctly identified (responded to), even though some were not in the teaching set. What is required to do this?

A Behavioral View

There is an area in the experimental analysis of behavior that provides some basis for specifying how stimulus events that precede a response can come to reliably control that response. The area is called *stimulus control of behavior* (control by preceding stimuli).

The basic paradigm is this:
a. In the presence of concept instances, reinforce one response consistently.

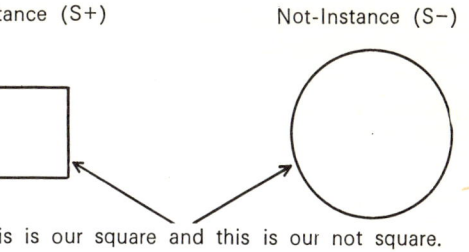

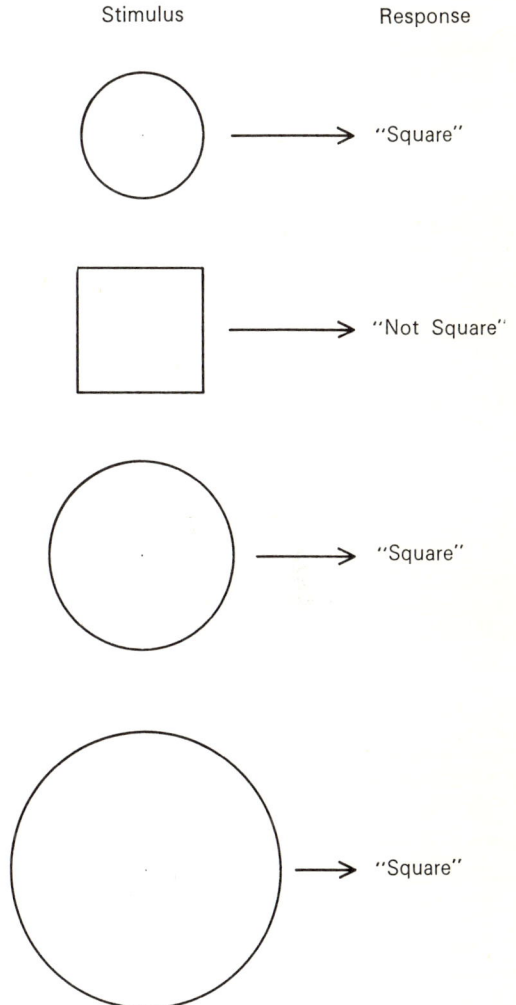

Instance (S+)   Not-Instance (S−)

This is our square and this is our not square.

Stimulus   Response

⟶ "Square"

⟶ "Not Square"

⟶ "Square"

⟶ "Square"

b. In the presence of not-instances, reinforce some other response or no response

We present the square and circle many times until the child always responds one way to the square and another way to the circle. Have we taught a concept? How can we tell? We can't look inside the head, so we must present some other stimuli and see how the organism responds.

Some tests. New members of the class and not-class are presented. (See fig. 3.).
We appear to have taught a brightness discrimination. We thought we were teaching squareness, but the child *could* respond correctly on the basis of size, brightness, *or* shape, and he responded to color. The teaching has to insure responding to critical concept characteristics. Let's correct that.

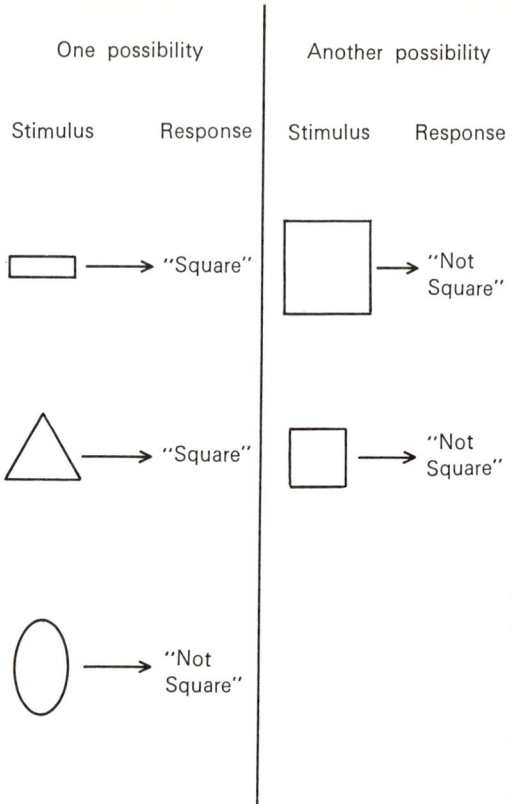

| One possibility | | Another possibility | |
| Stimulus | Response | Stimulus | Response |

We make S+ and S− so that they differ only in shape. We again train until there is consistent response to S+ and not to S−. Have we taught a concept? Let's test. (See right column.)
In the first case, the child learned a rule about corners but not about equal 90-degree corners and equal length sides. The second case was puzzling, so we asked the child what he was doing. He was responding to a smudge on the corner of the display square that wasn't on the display circle. The new squares did not have these cues.

Implication. To teach a concept it is necessary to insure that responding is controlled *only* by the *essential characteristics* of the concept. How do we do this?

   1. It is not possible to teach a concept through one instance and one not-instance. A set of instances and not-instances is required.

   2. The set should be constructed so that all instances share all essential concept characteristics and not-instances possess none of or only some of these characteristics.
   3. Within the set of instances or not-instances, it is necessary to vary stimulus characteristics that are not essential to instances or not-instances.

Concept learning involves a double discrimination. Two discriminations necessary to concept learning are: (1) the discrimination of relevant characteristics of instances (S+) from relevant characteristics of not-instances (S−); (2) the discrimination of relevant from irrelevant characteristics (Si) within instances or not-instances. (See top of p. 303.)
   Now what does all of this mean? Essentially it means, we *cannot teach a concept without teaching the relevant characteristics of other concepts from which the given concept is to be discriminated.* In other words, we cannot teach red without teaching not-red by

	Instance	Not-Instance
Relevant Characteristics	S+ ←(1)→	S−
Irrelevant Characteristics	Si	Si

(2) connects S+ to Si, and (2) connects S− to Si

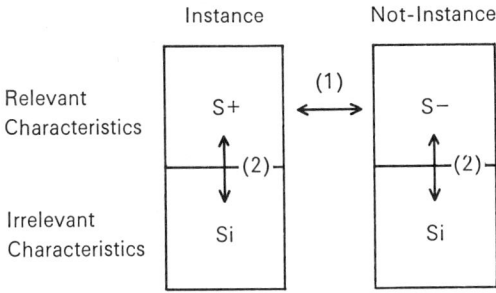

Note: S+, S−, and Si may be one characteristic or a set of characteristics.

including orange, blue, violet, and so forth in the not-set. We do not have to teach the discrimination of orange from blue to teach red. We only have to teach the discrimination of red from not-red colors. Furthermore, we cannot teach red without teaching that surface textures or patterns are not colors, that brightness differences or differences in shape or size of objects do not matter when we talk about red or any color. At some point in the teaching, *colors* as a set of concepts, or *color* as a higher order concept, have to be discriminated from patterns, textures, size, shape, brightness differences, materials, and positions. Even a concept as simple as red involves the teaching of a lot of discriminations.

The above ideas can be gleaned from the literature on stimulus control. However, in that literature

$S+ = S^D$ (Discriminative Stimulus)
$S− = S^\Delta$ (S − Delta)
Si is not labeled or is confused with S^Δ.

Also, the literature fails to explicitly recognize the double discrimination problem. In my opinion Engelmann adds significantly to this view.

Engelmann's Definition of a Concept

In his book *Conceptual Learning*, Engelmann (1969) defines a concept as *the set of characteristics shared by a set of instances in a given universe of concepts and not shared by other instances in that universe. Shared characteristics* refer to physically definable stimulus properties. *Instances* are the basic units the teacher would have to present to give examples of the concept. The *universe*

of concepts is the set of concepts from which a given concept is to be discriminated. The universe includes concepts whose characteristics can occur in the same instance with the concept under consideration, as well as concepts whose characteristics cannot occur in the same instance.

Engelmann's definition is procedural rather than functional. That is, a concept is defined in terms of the operations or procedures people would go through in identifying a concept in a given universe, rather than in terms of how stimulus events control the behavior of a person. From this approach, the first step is to determine logically (using induction and deduction) which characteristics are shared by a group of instances and *are not* shared by other instances in a given universe. The procedure required to identify essential concept characteristics is called *concept analysis*, or the logical analysis of concept characteristics. This approach should be familiar to every behaviorist. He uses logical analysis to determine his experimental design and specify the procedures to be followed (what is to be measured under what conditions). He uses functional definitions in talking about the generalizations that can be induced from his outcomes. In general, the experimental behaviorist, the teacher, and the programmer all use logical analysis of available information and procedural definitions in *designing* new experiments or programs; they use functional definitions in *evaluating* the outcomes of their efforts. The process of design requires the logical use of what is known; the process of evaluation requires an openness to the empirical facts to determine if the design was appropriate. Engelmann's definition of a concept is geared to the needs of the teacher or programmer who must look at concepts from the point of view of what has to be done to design efficient teaching programs. These programs are still subject to empirical evaluation of adequacy, but with a proper use of known knowledge from the start we will more quickly develop good programs.

Let's look at some of the implications of Engelmann's definition. This definition is important because it leads the teacher and programmer to look at *sets of concepts* and their structure in designing teaching strategies, rather than looking at *single concepts* one-by-one (as in the case of most other definitions of concept).

Engelmann's definition of a concept implies that a concept changes as the universe changes. Suppose we make up a universe that contains only dogs and horses. Our concept instances are dogs and the not-instances are horses. For S+ we note that dogs have *paws, small size, light weight,* a *bark,* and a *doglike configuration.* For S— we note that the not-instances have *hoofs, large size, heavy weight,* a *whinny,* and a *horselike configuration.* According to Engelmann's definition of a concept, we can change the concept of dog by changing the universe of concepts. For example, if we add mice to the universe, our concept of dog changes. Now *small size* and *light weight* are not characteristics that are shared only by all dogs (S+). If we add lions to the universe, our concept of dog changes again. Paws are no longer S+. If we include all known animals in the set of instances, our concept of dog would be quite different from the one obtained when the set of instances included only dogs and horses.

This definition of a concept allows the teacher or programmer to specify the essential discriminations that must be taught to avoid confusing concept instances with not-instances. These discriminations can be determined by a logical analysis of concepts within a given universe. (If the universe is not explicitly defined, the discriminations to be taught have to be based on estimates by the teacher or programmer as to what is most likely to be useful in an average child's en-vironment. Logical analysis of essential char-acteristics is only possible within a defined universe of concepts.)

Concept Analysis of Squareness

We want to teach the concept of square-ness within a universe of concepts that con-tains all *closed geometric figures* (circles, triangles, rectangles, and irregular closed fig-ures, and so forth). All of the figures can vary in size, color, position, and texture.

Concept instances and not-instances have the following characteristics. (See below.)

To teach the concept of squareness in this universe it is necessary to teach the discrimi-nation of S+ from S— characteristics, and S+ from Si characteristics. It is probably also important to teach the discrimination of S— from Si as a part of teaching the discrimina-tion of S—.

To test whether or not we have taught the concept of squareness within the defined uni-verse, we would use items like these. (See top of p. 305.)

Instead of trying to write programs adapted to each student's needs, it is possible to deter-mine the essential discriminations that must be learned in a given universe to be sure a concept has been taught and then program the teaching of those discriminations. If a child already knows some of the discrimina-tions, the program simply functions as a test, and the teacher moves on.

Engelmann's definition also calls attention to the fact that the teaching universe is a

	INSTANCES (S+)	NOT-INSTANCES (S−)
Relevant in (S+ and S−) Characteristics	Closed geometric figures with: a. 90-degree angles, and b. equal sides, and c. straight sides.	Closed geometric figures with: a. any other angle, or b. unequal sides c. curved lines, or irregular lines
	S+ ←——→ S−	
Irrelevant (Si) Characteristics	Si size color position surface texture	Si size color position surface texture

S+ | S−

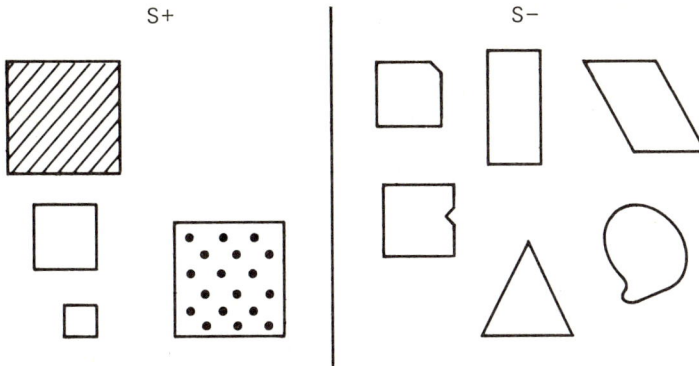

growing one. Initially, the programmer does not have to be concerned with all possible discriminations but just those concerning concepts already introduced. For example, in teaching sounds, we start with a universe of letters and their sounds. We select one letter *(m)* and a not-letter and start. "This is mmmmmm. This is not mmmmmm." Then we add a second letter *(a)*. A basic principle guides the selection of new sounds. We start with letters and sounds that are least similar to each other—that have the fewest common properties. If two letters *(like m and n, or d and b)* are very similar in shape or sound, the introduction of *one of them* is delayed as long as possible.

In deciding if two concepts are similar or not, we determine whether any properties are shared. For example, squares and rectangles are similar in that they are both closed figures that have four 90-degree angles and straight sides. Therefore, rectangles are more likely to be confused with squares than are circles. It is more important in teaching the concept "square" to be sure that the child is taught to discriminate rectangles from squares than circles from squares. This teaches an essential property of squares—namely, that squares have equal sides. Some concept differences are categorical, as above, and some concept differences are dimensional, as in the difference between the following *a* and *d:*

a   d

These letters differ only in the height of the stem. When analysis reveals that two concepts differ only in very small ways, we know we have to do something to be sure the dis-

crimination gets taught. The alternatives are: (1) we can focus directly on the difference in our program; or (2) we can exaggerate the difference by adding cues (for example, make the stem of the *d* especially long or make the

a this way [α]; and the *d* this way

[d]). Once the most basic discrimina-

tions have been mastered, we can introduce the more conventional discrimination requirements without overburdening the child.

CONCEPTS AND OPERATIONS

I next want to pursue the implications of this definition of a concept for teaching and talking about response mechanisms. The definition of an operation we are going to introduce is directly related to the concept of a *generalized response class* introduced by Baer and Sherman (1964). Both terms refer to operant behavior that functions beyond the situation in which it was taught.

Concepts are essential *stimulus* characteristics shared by a set of instances and not shared by other instances in a given universe of concepts. *Operations* are the essential *response* characteristics shared by a set of responses in a given universe of operations. *Instances* are to a *concept* as *individual responses* are to an *operation*.

Just as concepts are ordered into hierarchies, so are operations. The following illus-

Concept	Stimulus Instances
Color	A blue ball A red car A yellow banana A green tree A brown bear

Operation	Response Instances
Placing	Placing the box under the table. Placing the hat on the hook. Placing the tee in the ground. Placing the thread through the needle. Placing the fork beside the plate.

Concept	Stimulus Instances
Surface properties	A set of examples of pattern A set of examples of brightness A set of examples of color A set of examples of texture

Operation	Response Instances
Moving objects with hands	A set of examples of placing A set of examples of throwing A set of examples of pushing A set of examples of lifting

trate lower-order concepts and operations than those just presented.

Concept	Stimulus Instances
Blue	A blue truck A blue shirt A blue hat A blue book Blue Sky

Operation	Response Instances
Placing on	Placing the box on the table. Placing the table on the ground. Placing the hat on the head. Placing the book on the table. Placing the star on the chart.

The figure above illustrates higher-order concepts and operations than those presented first.

Concepts are taught through a set of instances (a program) designed to teach the range of instances, the range of not-instances, and the range of irrelevant stimulus characteristics. One response is reinforced in the presence of instances and another response in the presence of not-instances. Similarly, operations are taught through a set of tasks designed to teach the essential characteristics of the operation, the essential characteristics of

not-operations, and the irrelevant response characteristics. Correctly performed tasks are reinforced. Incorrectly performed tasks are not reinforced.

When we teach with properly designed sets of tasks, we have the basis for teaching both concepts and operations at the same time. For example, take the general task: *Move this object in relation to that object.* From this statement we can generate an endless series of tasks for teaching operations on objects *or* concepts about operations on objects *or* concepts about objects. For example:

Put the cup in the box.

Throw the ball at the desk.

Lift the dog up to the bed.

Usually, we would teach the object concepts prior to teaching the operations. If we require a child to perform many task responses on objects under conditions where the operations, the distance cues, the location of objects, and the objects themselves are varied, generalized response operations will be learned.

The significance of this analysis is that if we approach the teaching of operations as outlined above, we have the basis for building response systems that transcend our teaching. Task responses are instances of operations. If we teach a number of tasks for the same operation, there will come a point at which new tasks involving that operation are correctly responded to on first presentation. This means that the operation has been taught. This analysis directly parallels that for concepts. In concept teaching, we teach some instances in the concept set, and the rest are responded to correctly, if we have taught in the right way. In teaching operations, we teach some tasks involving that operation and the rest are responded to correctly on the test, if our teaching really teaches for operation.

It is important to discriminate between an operation and a concept about an operation. For example, when a child learns to plus (increase the members in a group), he is taught an operation. The teacher observing the behavior of a child who is plussing or not-plussing is observing instances or not-instances of the concept of plussing. What is an operation for the doer is concept for the observer. We have concepts of running and operations of running.

The paper by Baer, Peterson, and Sherman (1967) illustrated the process of teaching an operation called imitation, or looking at what someone else does and doing (approximately) the same thing. Imitating, following instructions, paying attention, responding on signal, and working for periods of time (persistence) are operations that are very important to the teacher. When children do not respond to the concept signals controlling such operations with the appropriate operations, the operations have to be taught, if the children are to succeed in school activities.

Essentially I am postulating that operations are established by a procedure equivalent to that used to establish concept control over behavior. In the case of concepts, the response is arbitrary.

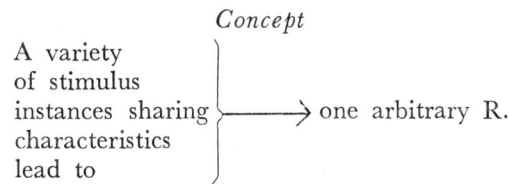

Concept

A variety
of stimulus
instances sharing ⎬⟶ one arbitrary R.
characteristics
lead to

In the case of operations, the controlling concept stimulus is arbitrary.

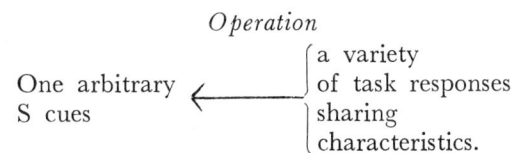

Operation

One arbitrary ⟵ ⎱ a variety
S cues ⎰ of task responses
⎱ sharing
⎰ characteristics.

As in the case of the term *concept,* the term *operation* is defined procedurally rather than functionally. On the basis of a logical analysis of the responses to be taught, a set of procedures that will very likely lead to teaching a given operation in a given universe is specified. This is done without testing to see whether or not the operation has been taught by presenting new instances of the class. In the behavioral-analysis literature, a "response" or a "generalized response class" is defined by the fact that more behavior is controlled by a given set of cues than that specifically taught. A generalized response class is defined functionally in terms of *the effects* of certain training procedures on behavior. The difference in these two positions is more one of emphasis than anything else. When Baer et al. (1964) *plan* a set of procedures that they believe will produce a generalized response class, they are talking about the procedures for defining an operation. When Becker and Engelmann (1971) talk about *testing* for having taught an operation, they are talking about a test for a functional generalized response class. In each case, one set of procedures is used for designing or planning, and another in evaluating or testing. Design is procedural; evaluation is functional. There is no reason that the term operation (or generalized response class) cannot be used both procedurally and functionally. In fact, there may be very good reasons for doing so, as long as one is clear in communication.

Our preference for the term operation rather than generalized response class, or just *operant response,* arises from the communication difficulties we have encountered in using the terms generalized response class or response. People do not readily see that you are not dealing with a given response but with what is common to a set of responses. The term operation more directly allows one to focus on those response characteristics shared by a set of responses. Also, use of the term operation may facilitate communication between Piagetians and behaviorists. We believe that the concept of an operation used by Piaget in his theory of development is entirely compatible with the one proposed here.

HABITS AND OPERATIONS

Concept teaching makes what is being taught relevant beyond the immediate classroom. Responses are tied not to specific stimulus instances as in simple discrimination training but to essential concept characteristics that go across instances. The teaching of operations has the same kind of power. The response mechanisms are not restricted to specific task signals or to specific task responses. They are response mechanisms under the control of concepts that can be used in large sets of tasks. Furthermore, operations can be combined in an infinite number of new ways to produce new task responses. All that is required is that each operation going into a new combination be under the control of a separate signal. When we have established such control, we can teach all sorts of skills by instruction. We can teach driving, flying, golfing, writing, and so forth. When we say "Turn left," or "Lift your foot off the gas," these tasks can be executed even if they have never been performed before.

Our language behavior illustrates the ways in which we can combine operations (in this case words) into new statements. The constraints on the ways in which we can put words together into statements—that is, the rules of grammar—are cross-statement concepts controlling operations, such as "Say nouns before verbs in declarative statements," or "A plural noun requires a plural verb."

Contrast these flexible response systems with habits. Many things are done more efficiently if they are done the same way each time. We all learn a variety of habits about how we brush our teeth, where we put our keys, how we eat, and so forth. A response gets "grooved," and we do it the same way each time. The trouble with habits is that if the conditions change current habits must be unlearned and new ones established.

Arithmetic

Let's take the habit or simple discrimination approach to teaching arithmetic. We have to teach number concepts, number names, and number symbols in some way.

Now we are ready to teach addition facts. It is possible to teach addition as a series of specific problems of this form.

Stimulus		Response
9+1	=	10
4+5	=	9
7+2	=	9
2+5	=	7

We can have the children practice their addition facts (with sums up to 10) until they have learned all problems of this form. Then we can move up to higher numbers and practice some more. We are teaching habits. In the presence of a particular stimulus instance, a particular response should be made.

Alternatively, we could break the task down into a series of concepts and operations, as Engelmann does in Distar, and teach the general case so that the child could solve any of forty problems (with sums up to 10) in the form $2+7 = \square$.

1. We teach the child to count to a number. This is a rote chain.

2. We teach him to use this chain to count objects. Counting objects is an operation for determining how many are in a group.

3. Symbol identification is taught using concept-teaching rules.

4. Given a numeral, the child is taught to make as many lines as the numeral stands for. This is also an operation.

5. The concepts of plus and equality are taught. Plussing is getting some more. Equality is a rule: "As many as we have on this side of the equal sign we have to have on the other side of the equal sign." The operation of counting is used to verify the equality rule. Now when a child is presented with a problem like this

$$4+5 = \square$$

he can solve it by putting five lines under the 5, and counting "four, five, six, seven, eight, nine." He touches each line as he counts it.

6. A little later, the lines are dropped and fingers are used in the operation. "We have four, and we plus five." (The children put out five fingers on the cue "and we plus five." Then they count, "Fouuurrr, five, six, seven, eight, nine," touching each of the five fingers as they count.

7. Still later the children are taught to count from a number to a number. They can now handle forty new problems like this.

$$4 + \square = 9$$

They just need to draw a line, or stick out a finger for each number they count after four until they get to nine, and they can produce the answer. With a slight variation on counting from a number to a number, they can also do forty problems of this form.

$$9 = 4 + \square$$

While this approach may take a little more time in building up the basic operations, the dividends are great, since the children can solve whole sets of new problems after going through just a few of them with the teacher. The basis has also been laid for solving algebraic equations. Note too that each example gives the child practice on the rote facts. At the end of each example he is trained to say the whole statement. "Four plus five equals nine."

Reading

Let's compare a hypothetical sight-reading program with the Distar reading-by-sound program. There is no doubt that we can teach a child to give responses to ten words faster than we can teach responses to ten symbols for sounds. It is easier to find words and word sounds that are markedly different from each other than it is to find ten letters and sounds that differ in many ways. However, by the time we have taught ten sounds and blending skills, we have the potential basis for reading-by-sound some 720 three-sound words, 4,320 four-sound words, and 21,600 five-sound words. Not all of these "words" would be real words, but the number of permutations of ten sounds is illustrated. By the time we have taught forty sounds, a basis has been established for reading a large percentage of the English language. Irregularities still need to be taught, but the child has skills with which to attack any new word. He has the basic operations for reading.

The strategy of teaching concepts and operations is a powerful one. Component opera-

tions are taught that can be *recombined* in any number of ways. In the Distar reading program, some of the operations taught are holding continuous sounds, switching to a new sound with no pause *(sssssssssssaaaaaaaammmmmmm)*, speeding up the sounds *(sam)*, and blending a stop sound *(t, p, b)* in with the next continuous sound *(taaaaaannnnnnn)*. Also, the child is taught to produce the sounds for any order of letters, even nonsense words. The combination of these operations is reading, for reading is a complex *operation* in which letters in space are converted to sounds in time. It should be evident that Engelmann's view of concepts and operations leads to considerable power in programming, since it leads one to look for sets of concepts and operations that can be taught using a common format.

PROBLEM-SOLVING BEHAVIOR

Problem-solving behavior involves the *operations* that can be used to solve sets of problem tasks. When a child is taught to read-by-sounds, he has been taught several problem-solving operations. The test for this teaching is the ability to solve problems that have not been taught. New combinations of the sounds that have been taught are read on first presentation. Similarly, to test whether we have taught the operation of adding two numbers with sums up to ten, we present number combinations that have not been taught to see whether the operation is correctly performed. Problem-solving behavior involves using *operations* that have been taught, often in *new* combinations or orderings, to solve problems that have not been seen before. All that is required is that *each operation in a new combination be under the control of a separate signal* that is available in the new context.

Problem-solving behavior also involves applying *strategies* for analyzing the nature of a problem to help determine which operations in which sequence will produce a solution. Strategies are rules for systematizing behavior in the face of a problem. Strategies will vary with different types of problems. For strategies to be useful, it is necessary that the *classes of problems* requiring different strategies be specified, or that the child be trained to test out a series of strategies for a new problem until he finds one that works.

If children are given training in a variety of problems and their solutions, the solutions become instances for deriving general procedures for operating on classes of problems. It is at this point in the educational process that a case can be made for teaching that uses the "discovery method." In teaching operations for *finding out something the child does not know*, the discovery method offers the possibility of *programming* repeated instances of various strategies to teach problem-solving operations.

At present a comprehensive analysis of problem-solving strategies has not been made. We can currently only illustrate the directions such an analysis might take. Consider the following concept identification task. The universe of possible concepts is restricted to groups of three geometric figures, each of which is a circle, triangle, or square. Concept instances and not-instances can vary in the type of figure found in any of the three positions. The problem is to find out, from as few instances as possible, what concept this is an example of.

1. ◯ ◯ △
2. ◯ △ ◯
3. □ ◯ ◯
4. ◯ □ □
5. □ ◯ □
6. □ □ ◯
7. □ □ □
8. ◯ ◯ △
9. ◯ △ ◯
10. △ ◯ ◯
11. △ ◯ △
12. △ △ ◯
13. △ △ △
14. □ □ △
15. □ △ □
16. △ □ □
17. □ △ △
18. △ □ △

◯ △ △

19. △ △ □
20. ◯ ◯ ◯
21. ◯ □ △
22. □ ◯ △
23. △ ◯ □
24. △ □ ◯
25. □ △ ◯
26. ◯ △ □

You are to select instances one at a time from the following test. After each selection, check the key below to find out if you have picked an instance or not-instance of this concept. Try to figure out the concept as you go along. The smart way to go about it is to select instances that change only one characteristic at a time (Bruner, Goodnow, and Austin, 1956). This will tell you what is essential to instances and not-instances. For example see top of p. 311.

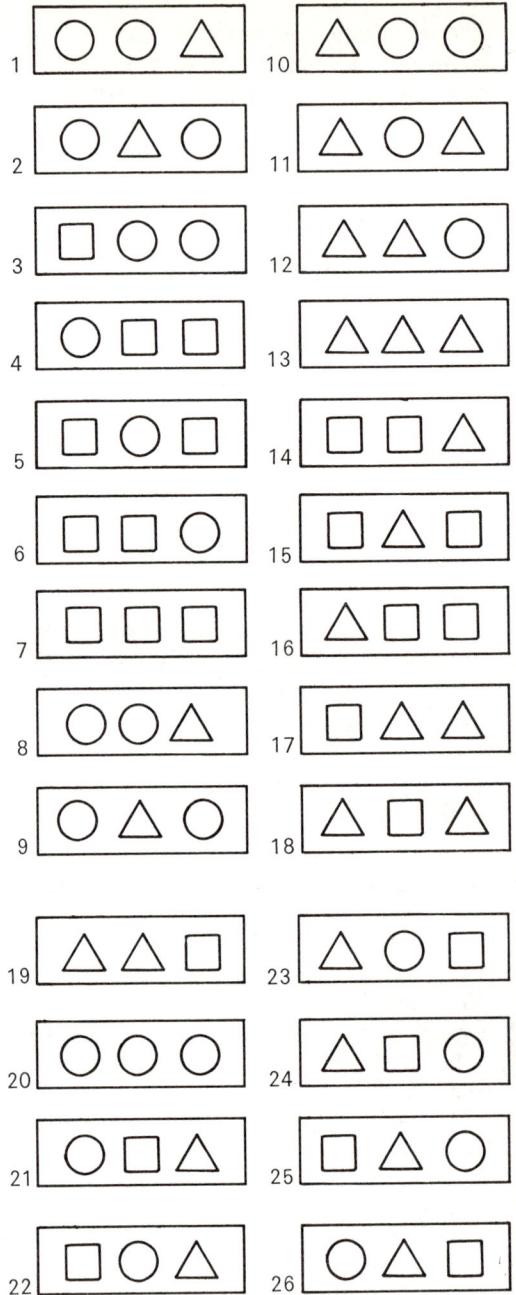

1. −	8. +	15. −	21. +
2. −	9. −	16. −	22. +
3. −	10. −	17. +	23. −
4. −	11. +	18. +	24. −
5. −	12. −	19. −	25. −
6. −	13. +	20. −	26. −
7. −	14. +		

1.

(+) You started with this.

2.

(+) Circle in position 1 is not important

3.

(+) Triangle in position 2 is not important.

4.

(−) Triangle in position 3 is essential.

5.

(−) Circle in position three is not important. (This eliminates the possibility that the concept is triangle *or* circle in position 3.)

Since nothing else is common to all three instances, the concept must be "triangle (only) in position three."

Note carefully the problem-solving strategy. Change only one thing at a time to identify the critical elements and to eliminate alternatives systematically. The principle involved in finding the solution to our concept-identification problem is the same as the one used in teaching concepts. To find out (or show) what is essential to some thing or process, change only one thing at a time. This same problem-solving strategy is the essence of the experimental method in science. To find out about causes, change one thing and check its effect, then change another, and so on. We can teach this strategy by presenting a number of concept-identification problems and

various solution strategies and allowing the children (with guidance) to compare strategies to determine the essential features. The strategy can then be extended to new sets of related problems. There are a number of such rules for solving problems that can be taught to children through the programmed presentation of sets of problem tasks that require common solution operations. Becker, Engelmann, and Thomas (1971) discuss some of these possibilities.

INTELLIGENT BEHAVIOR

Intelligent behavior involves various combinations of operations under the control of concepts. If we know how to teach concepts and operations, we know how to make people more intelligent. This is not to say that some people are not more readily taught than others or that genetics makes no difference. It is quite evident that genetics exerts control over the development of organisms as they constantly interact with an environment. The point to be made is that intelligent behavior does not come with the baby; it is learned. It is the product of *interactions* with an environment. If we as teachers know how to induce behavior that is considered intelligent, we know how to make people smarter than they were when they came to us.

SUMMARY

We have attempted to illustrate some of the potential gains to be derived from placing Engelmann's view of concepts and operations into the framework of general behavior theory. Concepts and operations are seen to be induced by quite analogous teaching processes. The principal difference is that in teaching concepts we primarily are concerned with stimulus events. The response forms are not essential. In teaching operations we are concerned with response events. The form of the stimulus events controlling the operations are not essential. Concept teaching involves a double-discrimination problem. Relevant characteristics of *instances* have to be discriminated from relevant characteristics of *not-instances,* and, within instances, *relevant* characteristics have to be discriminated from *irrelevant* characteristics. Restricting the definition of a concept to a given *teaching universe* leads to the specification of the discriminations that have to be taught by the teacher and programmer. Finally, we have suggested that intelligent behavior is essentially comprised of concepts and operations. Since we know how to teach such behavior, we know how to make kids smart.

Nowhere in this report have we attempted to deal with the rules for specific teaching strategies. Instead, we have focused our efforts on key concepts and rationales underlying Engelmann's approach. To know *how* to make kids smart, it would also be important to explore in detail what Engelmann has to say about teaching interactions (Engelmann, 1969; Becker et al., 1971).

Some principles of instructional design at higher cognitive levels

SUSAN M. MARKLE AND PHILIP W. TIEMANN

Instructional designers are becoming increasingly concerned with higher cognitive learning (Gagné, 1970; Merrill, 1971). Perhaps in the early years of programmed instruction our vision was narrowed by concentration on behaviors that could be easily described and measured, behaviors such as "the student will state the rule." Higher cognitive learning seemed to be an area in which terms were badly defined, and evidence that learning had occurred was hard to come by. Psychologists studying higher cognitive processes rarely talked to operant conditioners and to programmers who clung to operant conditioning as a way of thinking and talking about the world. Part of the dissatisfaction with early programmed materials may be attributed to the low-level objectives they embodied, objectives which did not satisfy educators who hoped for more, even though they themselves were inexperienced in defining in precise behavioral terms what it was they hoped for. When Gagné's *Conditions of Learning* appeared in 1965, higher cognitive learning gained a new importance. At the top of his learning hierarchy were concept learning, principle applying, and problem solving. He clearly implied that these were valuable behaviors toward which instruction should aim, although they were dependent upon mastery of the simpler behaviors such as discriminations and chains.

There is a vast literature of research on the learning of concepts. As is often true of psychological experimentation, the laboratory findings in concept attainment have been derived from a dominant research design of dubious relevance to the real world of instruction. The historical model is the research of Bruner, Goodnow, and Austin (1956). In this classic design, the individual learner is confronted with a thoroughly rational universe of pictured items in matrix form, containing all possible combinations of a very limited number of values of a limited number of attributes—each picture may have the attribute, color, with a value of red or green or blue. On the basis of one given example, the learner plays a game with the psychologist, selecting other specimens from the array and presumably thereby testing his hypotheses until he discovers the rule for class inclusion. Stating the rule, a rule such as "all members of the class are both blue and triangle," indicates mastery of the concept. While slight variations exist in experimental design, a great deal is known about what facilitates and what hinders attaining concepts under these conditions.

In a recent survey of over 250 studies based

Published in German as "Prinzipien für den Entwurf von Lehrmaterial für die höheren Stufen des kognitiven Lernens," in *Fortschritte Und Ergebnisse der Unterrichtstechnologie,* ed. by K. Weltner and B. Rollett. Berlin: Ehrenwirth-Verlag, 1972. Reprinted by permission.

Invited address to Lehrsysteme 72, International Congress for Instructional Technology, Berlin, Germany, April 5–8, 1972.

on this and similar research designs, Clark (1971) presented an insightful analysis of the major points of difference between this laboratory model and typical teaching practices. Of particular importance in the real world of instruction are three differences: first, in the way concept attainment is measured; second, in the total rationality of the experimental universe which cannot be duplicated in most real-world concept teaching situations; and third, in the obviousness of the attributes confronting the experimental learner. To take the favorite example from the real world of the very young child, would we ever check a child's mastery of the concept "dog" by asking him to list the attributes of "dogness"? Can we imagine, even at a major zoo, having such a neat matrix of the combinatorial possibilities to lay out before the child? Further, are the attributes that lead us to call an animal a dog obvious? What makes a dog a dog rather than a cat is not obvious to the young learner and is also very hard for adults to put into words. The teaching practices at the very young level differ in many ways from Bruner's model, but, like it, depend on instruction by examples and non-examples.

As we move into classroom practices as shown by the teaching methods displayed by teachers, textbooks, and other instructional media, we find an increasing tendency to verbalize about the concept to be learned. The verbalizing is intended to assist the learner in correctly classifying specimens that he might encounter. Even on "Sesame Street," a great deal of talking accompanies the presentation of examples and non-examples of concepts. In teaching the concept "pair," for instance, a puppet may hold up a pair of mittens and say that they match, and then hold up a sneaker and a shoe which, he points out, don't match and therefore do not make a pair. It is assumed that this verbalization aids the learner in attending to the relevant attributes or defining properties of the concept "pair."

If elementary education appears to rely heavily on lots of examples while using verbalization as a teaching aid, we might characterize the higher levels of education as the reverse—relying heavily on verbalization, with an occasional example as a teaching aid. This is almost a complete reversal of Bruner's laboratory situation, and we may question how many generalizations drawn from that research model apply directly. Gagné (1970), in a revised version of his hierarchy of learning types, has included a new category called the learning of defined concepts. He classified this type of learning as similar to principle learning and quite different from the process of acquiring concrete concepts of the "dog" and "pair" variety. In the defined concept type of instruction, the student is given the rule for class inclusion—the definition—and must apply it much as he applies a principle to instances in the real world.

Several key studies in recent years have explored the conditions under which defined concept learning takes place. In contrast to the early Bruner studies, the measure of concept attainment generally agreed upon is the student's ability to deal with examples and non-examples of the concept. A student who understands the instruction responds differentially to new examples and new non-examples not encountered during instruction. Being able to state the definition, which has been given to him in instruction, does not measure understanding.

At the simplest level, Anderson and Kulhavy (1972) demonstrated a high degree of learning from definitions. College students were given definitions of unknown concepts, difficult ones such as "atavistic" and "diluvial." With the one-sentence definition at hand, correct selection of examples in a multiple-choice situation was above 90 percent for almost all cases. Without the definition, selection was at chance level. Such findings would appear to support the time-honored text-and-lecture techniques of introducing new concepts by giving the rule. Verbalization at least can control some student behavior indicating understanding.

A behavioral measure of what is meant by "really understanding" a concept can be precisely defined (Markle and Tiemann, 1969). A single test item is not sufficient. Nor is a randomly chosen collection of items fully satisfactory, although such a collection provides an opportunity to quantify the number of correct responses and therefore to state that some students understand more than others do. Anderson (1971) surveyed the scanty or totally lacking information about test construction rationales provided in most articles in respectable American journals reporting experiments in educational psychology. His conclusion was strongly worded but justifiably so.

"Procedures currently in use for constructing and describing achievement tests are a mess. Conclusions about methods, variables, or procedures hardly can be taken seriously when you don't know what the test measures. Drastic action is indicated. Journal editors are admonished forthwith to reject papers unless they contain 1) a documented rationale for selecting the questions to be asked and 2) a fully explicated analysis of the relationship between the questions and the preceding instruction."

In testing for conceptual understanding, the relationship between the test items and the preceding instruction is firmly dictated by consensus among researchers that the items on the test must be new, in other words, not used in instruction. A good set of items will have further characteristics. In order to test for generalization across the total range of examples included in the concept, test items must cover the range identified by a thorough analysis of the concept. The number of examples the student can correctly classify is less important than the range of examples to which he can generalize. Discrimination of non-examples can be tested with equal precision when the analysis of the concept has identified the key critical attributes. We have defined a good non-example as one which shares all but one of the critical attributes which define the concept. Such a non-example requires of the student a fine discrimination at the boundary of the concept. In other words, each item selected for inclusion in the test of conceptual learning can be given a documented rationale, as proposed by Anderson, and the total test can also be rationalized in terms of the range of items sampled and the fineness of the discriminations sampled. With such a test, data from students provide a fine-grained analysis of the effects of teaching methods or research variables on student performance.

The variables which may affect student attainment of defined concepts are many. Since the definition of the concept is to be provided, the nature of the definition itself would contribute to student performance. We do not doubt that elegance of expression adjusted to the audience is one important variable. However, this variable, which we might call "communicability" or simply "good writing," is extremely difficult to quantify *a priori*. Another variable which can be more easily quantified is the completeness of the definition. A complete definition would cover all critical attributes of the concept and would also suggest the range of application by mentioning important irrelevant attributes. A second somewhat quantifiable variable is the use of technical terminology in a definition. In many subject matters, key concepts are often defined in terms of other concepts from the same discipline which are presumably mastered first or concurrently.

A further variable is exemplification. In textbooks, lectures, and dictionaries, one or more examples of the concept may be given. If more than one example is given, the range exemplified by the set of examples may be quantified. The provision of non-examples is still a rare practice, both in teaching and in the preparation of dictionary entries, but is a practice which many recent manuals on concept teaching strongly recommend (Engelmann, 1969; Markle and Tiemann, 1969). Traditional laboratory studies have failed to confirm the importance of providing non-examples as an instructional variable. Bruner (1966) stated: "Negative information is peculiarly unhelpful [p. 53]." Clark (1971), in his summary of laboratory studies, listed the provision of examples by themselves as the most effective teaching condition, with the provision of only non-examples as the least effective teaching condition. Despite the laboratory evidence, we have maintained the position that examples and non-examples are of equal importance in the teaching of real concepts. A well-selected set of teaching examples enables the student to generalize across the range of true examples included in the concept, and a well-selected set of non-examples enables the student to discriminate fine differences necessary to exclude similar specimens from membership in the class.

Support for the equal importance of examples and non-examples recently was provided by a study performed by Tennyson, Woolley, and Merrill (in press). The concept they chose to teach was the metrical concept, "trochaic meter," as exemplified in poetry selections. As a preliminary estimate of range, they asked naive students to classify a large number of examples and non-examples of the concept on the basis of a given definition. Some obvious examples were recognized by almost all students and therefore were termed high-probability examples. Some non-examples were equally obvious and were termed high-probability non-examples. Examples which were difficult to recognize were termed low-probability examples, and subtle discriminations which could not easily be made on the basis of the given definition produced low-probability non-examples. Thus, both range of examples and fine discrimination of non-examples were defined in their study on the basis of ratings by representative students rather than an *a priori* analysis of the concept.

Tennyson et al. (in press) hypothesized that different combinations of these high- and low-probability examples and non-examples would produce errors in concept attainment of a predictable sort. We (Markle and Tiemann, 1970) have proposed that restricting the range of examples will cause a student to undergeneralize, to accept on a test only the same limited range provided in instruction. Tennyson et al. (in press) produced precisely this effect by giving students instruction which included the definition and only high-probability examples and the subtle discriminations taught by the low-probability non-examples. We have also proposed that a poor selection of non-examples, in conjunction with a broad range of examples, will cause students to overgeneralize, to accept on a test non-examples as members of the class. Tennyson et al. (in press) produced this effect by providing instruction including the definition and a full range of high- and low-probability examples but only very high-probability non-examples. In other words, no

difficult discriminations were taught, and on the test these students did not succeed in making such fine discriminations. These two sets of results support the premise that non-examples have an important function in enabling students to really understand a concept.

Their study also demonstrated the effect of a particular kind of limitation on the range of examples, in which one salient but irrelevant attribute is always present. The attribute they chose to experiment with was Victorian origin of the selections. All examples of trochaic meter given students in this treatment were dated in the Victorian period, while non-examples were selected from earlier or later periods. Despite the definition directing attention to the meter of the examples as the critical attribute, students showed on the test what we call a misconception—they generalized correctly only to examples of trochaic meter written in the Victorian period. They rejected true examples from other stylistic eras and accepted some Victorian non-examples.

Tennyson's et al. (in press) data support the position that the selection of both examples and non-examples is an important item in effective concept teaching. A wide range of examples prevents undergeneralization, while a good selection of non-examples prevents overgeneralization. An outstanding feature of the design of their study is the precision with which they predicted the effects of each treatment on student performance. Had they, for instance, scored student performance simply on the basis of number of correct answers, no differences between groups would have appeared. The total number correct might be expected to be the same for the overgeneralizers, who score high on generalization and low on discrimination, as it would be for undergeneralizers, who score low on generalization and high on discrimination. In research on instructional variables and also in validation of instructional products, this level of precision in measuring the effects of treatments, we hope, will become increasingly common.

Tennyson et al. (in press) provided each group of students with the same definition but with a different selection of examples and non-examples. In their preliminary work, that same definition was used to quantify the probability status of the examples and non-examples. Since at least some examples and non-examples were given a low-probability rating, it is apparent that the definition by itself was not a sufficient teaching technique to lead students to generalize and discriminate as completely as an instructor would want. On the other hand, the high-probability ratings of examples and non-examples assigned by students indicates that they do indeed learn something from definitions, as the earlier study by Anderson et al. (in press) demonstrated.

We have been investigating some of the variables that should influence student mastery of a concept from a given definition. The concept we have been working with is "morpheme." There are several advantages to this concept as a research tool. First, stemming as it does from the science of linguistics, it is a well-defined concept. We expect agreement among subject-matter experts, the etymologists, on whether any given specimen in the language is or is not an example of the concept. There are borderline cases, but the universe of agreed-upon examples and non-examples is vast. In cases of doubt, we, as non-experts, could consult two sources prepared by experts (Partridge, 1958; Webster, 1961). Since few of our students have studied linguistics, the choice of "morpheme" offers another advantage, namely a large pool of naive subjects on which to experiment. And, unlike equally adequate well-defined concepts from other sciences, such as chemistry and physics, the concept applies to a universe of specimens with which our students are familiar, namely their own language. It is possible to illustrate a wide range of examples and non-examples without going beyond words known to the experimental subjects.

Our starting point was the definition provided in *Webster's Third New International Dictionary* (1961): "a meaningful linguistic unit whether a free form (as *pin, child, load, pray*) or a bound form (as the *-s* of *pins,* the *-hood* of *childhood,* the *un-* and *-er* of *unloader,* and the *-ed* of *prayed*) that contains no smaller meaningful parts." This definition mentions two critical attributes—(1) a

unit that has meaning and (2) indivisibility and one irrelevant attribute, expressed in the technical terminology of linguistics—free or bound. While nine examples are provided, the range exemplified by these selections is extremely limited when compared to the range of examples included in the concept. No non-examples are provided.

In an attempt to clarify Webster's definition, we generated three additional definitions which, along with Webster's, we tested in a pilot study. One of ours added a key irrelevant attribute, another rephrased the added attribute, and a third reworded Webster's critical attributes. While the main purpose of the pilot study was to refine our test items and explore dimensions of definitions, one intriguing finding might be worth mentioning. With fifty test items to be classified as morphemes or non-morphemes, one fourth of the subjects correctly classified less than half of the items, a performance below the level of chance. Admittedly the concept is a difficult one, all of the definitions suffered from incompleteness, and no group had any assistance from teaching examples. But the data support the contention of many of us that teaching simply by providing students with a definition of a concept can be an ineffective instructional practice.

With data from students on hand and our two source books (Partridge, 1958; Webster, 1961) serving as expert consultants, we completed our analysis of the concept. As shown in Table 1, the concept is defined by three critical attributes. Subclasses of examples to which students must generalize range across five irrelevant attributes.

Three treatments were based upon the attributes derived from analysis. Table 2 presents the statement of the three critical attributes in thirty-nine words, used as the total definition in one treatment; two further treatments each added statements of the three irrelevant attributes most likely to facilitate classification behavior.

One addition was expressed in technical terminology similar to that employed by Webster; the resulting definition was seventy-two words in total. The second addition translated these three irrelevants into non-technical terms, resulting in a considerable

Table 1. *Concept analysis of morpheme.*

	Attributes	
A morpheme is a linguistic unit which:	Critical	Irrelevant
1. carries a stable meaning from one construction to another, and*	X	
2. contributes that meaning to the construction in which it appears, and	X	
3. cannot be further subdivided into units having meanings related to that construction.	X	
4. Type of morpheme		X
a) free		
b) bound		
c) null (ϕ)**		
5. Syllabic length		X
a) less than one syllable		
b) one syllable		
c) two syllables		
d) more than two syllables		
6. Frequency of construction (Thorndike-Lorge Word List)		X
a) occurs at least once in one million words		
b) occurs less than once in one million but at least once in four million		
c) occurs less than once in four million but at least four times in eighteen million		
d) occurrence too rare to be listed**		
7. Type of remainder		X
a) free		
b) bound		
c) none		
d) both free and bound elements		
8. Location in construction		X
a) base		
b) prefix		
c) suffix		
d) infix**		
e) superfix**		

* Lack of critical attribute 1 can be apparent only when two different morphemes are presented at once. Discrimination on the basis of this critical attribute by itself was not tested by the experimental design.
** These values were judged to be beyond the scope of the study.

increase in verbiage to 102 words in total. Webster's definition as the fourth treatment expresses two critical attributes plus one irrelevant attribute in technical terms and is more efficient, a mere eighteen words. The first three definitions vary the independent variable of type of irrelevant attributes, that is, "none," "technical," or "nontechnical." The Webster's definition has been included as a reference point and varies primarily in

failing to express one of the critical attributes revealed by concept analysis.

In conjunction with the derived definitions varying the type of irrelevant attributes and the Webster's definition, we investigated a second independent variable, the effect of examples when provided with the definition. Additional treatments were constituted by providing these groups with a minimum rational set of examples, a set which illustrated

Table 2. *Definitions of morpheme provided.*

Definition of Three Critical Attributes Derived from Concept Analysis

A morpheme is a linguistic unit which carries a stable meaning from one construction to another, contributes that meaning to the construction in which it appears, and cannot be further subdivided into units having meanings related to that construction.

TREATMENTS—TYPE OF IRRELEVANT ATTRIBUTES

No Irrelevant Attributes: Derived definition of critical attributes only.

Technical Irrelevant Attributes: Derived criticals with following added.

It may be free or bound, base or affix, and may vary from a single phoneme to polysyllabic in length. The remainder of the construction, if any, may be one or more morphemes.

Nontechnical Irrelevant Attributes: Derived criticals with following added.

It may be a word or a unit that never stands alone; it may be a fundamental part of a word or a unit added to one; and it may be less than, equal to, or more than a syllable in length. The remainder of the construction, if any, may be one or more words, units that never stand alone, or combinations of these.

Webster's Definition: Provided by *Webster's Third New International Dictionary.*

A meaningful linguistic unit whether a free form (as *pin, child, load, pray*) or a bound form (as the *-s* of *pins,* the *-hood* of *childhood,* the *un-* and *-er* of *unloader,* and the *-ed* of *prayed*) that contains no smaller meaningful parts.

Table 3. *Minimum rational set provided to "with-examples" treatment.*

"The underlined portion of each of these constructions is a morpheme."

Example of Morpheme	*Rationale for Inclusion**				
bawd's	4b,	5a,	6c,	7a,	8c
dog-tired	4a,	5b,	6a,	7d,	8a
incontrovertible	4b,	5c,	6b,	7b,	8b
elephant	4a,	5d,	6a,	7c,	8a

---
* Rationale not provided to subjects.

each value of each irrelevant attribute. The set of examples provided is presented in Table 3. No group in the study was given any non-examples.

The combinations of irrelevant attribute treatments with or without examples resulted in six groups. Webster's definition, with our set of examples added to the nine it included, provided an additional group. College students, most in their third or fourth year, were assigned in a random manner to the groups and were given course credits for participation in the study. The dependent variables in the study were those of concern in any instance of concept learning, that is, correct classification of specimen items as examples or non-examples of the concept. Specifically, we were concerned with the amount of correct generalization to new examples and correct discrimination of new non-examples presented in the 50 test items, as listed in Table 4. These items, twenty-six examples and twenty-four non-examples, represent a revision of the pilot test items, structured to include samples of each kind of example and to balance the numbers of non-

Table 4. *Test examples and non-examples of morphemes.*

Examples

drop	4a, 5b, 6a, 7c, 8a	garbage	4a, 5c, 6a, 7c, 8a
comparison	4b, 5c, 6a, 7b, 8c	decapitate	4b, 5c, 6b, 7b, 8a
reactionary	4b, 5b, 6a, 7b, 8b	into	4a, 5b, 6a, 7a, 8a
followed	4b, 5a, 6a, 7a, 8b	handball	4a, 5b, 6a, 7a, 8a
scalawag	4a, 5d, 6c, 7c, 8a	beat	4a, 5b, 6a, 7c, 8a
manor	4a, 5c, 6a, 7c, 8a	postwar	4b, 5b, 6a, 7a, 8b
mother-in-law	4a, 5b, 6a, 7a, 8a	synonymous	4b, 5c, 6a, 7b, 8a
cupcakes	4b, 5a, 6b, 7a, 8c	roughage	4b, 5b, 6b, 7a, 8c
sandwich	4a, 5c, 6a, 7c, 8a	outlawed	4a, 5b, 6a, 7d, 8a
realize	4b, 5b, 6a, 7b, 8a	description	4b, 5b, 6a, 7d, 8b
I	4a, 5b, 6a, 7c, 8a	gangster	4b, 5b, 6a, 7a, 8c
undeserved	4a, 5b, 6a, 7b, 8b	microscope	4b, 5c, 6a, 7a, 8b
promoter	4b, 5b, 6a, 7b, 8c	youngster	4a, 5b, 6a, 7b, 8a

Non-Examples

dogmatic	Lacks 2 only	pumpkin	Lacks 2 only
bathtub	Lacks 3 only	everyone	Lacks 3 only
benefit	Lacks 3 only	to be	Lacks 3 only
feebly	Lacks 2 only	bi-lingual	Lacks 3 only
catsup	Lacks 2 only	door	Lacks 2 only
witches	Lacks 3 only	democratic	Lacks 3 only
meaningful	Lacks 3 only	back and forth	Lacks 3 only
ships	Lacks 1 and 2	hundred	Lacks 1 and 2
rearrange	Lacks 2 and 3	posterity	Lacks 3 only
billow	Lacks 2 only	spot	Lacks 1 and 2
underline	Lacks 2 only	mahogany	Lacks 2 only
fortunately	Lacks 2 only	activate	Lacks 3 only

examples lacking each critical attribute. More precise classification of the function of each individual test item will be discussed with respect to the study results.

Correct generalization to the total range of examples should be a function of the independent variables. The availability of stated irrelevant attributes should lead the student to ignore apparent differences between examples; for instance, given morphemes of different lengths, the student should correctly classify both short ones and long ones as "morphemes." We hypothesized that correct generalization by the group provided with the definition in nontechnical terms should therefore be superior to that performance by the group which had no ir-

relevant attributes stated and also superior to the group which had irrelevants stated in the technical terms of linguistics, a discipline the students did not know.

Figure 1 graphically presents the effect of the independent variables. The hypothesis failed to be confirmed. While the performance of the nontechnical group is not significantly different from the other groups, it most certainly shows a trend in the opposite direction from that we had hypothesized. Some students with the nontechnical, 103-word definition subsequently complained about the number of words and ideas in it. Their comments suggest that an actual teaching situation would require something more —perhaps more frames, additional exercises,

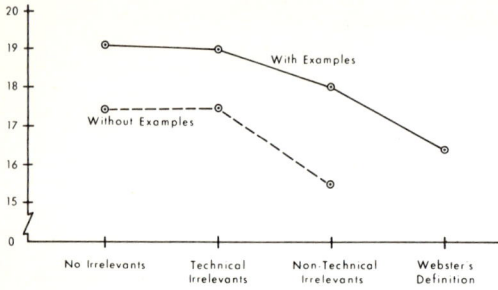

Figure 1. *Mean correct generalization to all examples (n = 26).*

or increased clarity through better organization or presentation—to enable learners to process such large quantities of information.

Figure 1 also presents the effect or examples on correct generalization. The provision of a full range of examples significantly improved generalization scores across all irrelevant attribute treatments ($F = 8.55$, $df = 1/131$, $p < .005$). Old-timers in programmed instruction may find this effect a confirmation of rules of frame-writing dating back to the early sixties. In the widely used RULEG system, the preferred design for an introductory frame was a statement of the rule or principle, followed by a fully worked example, followed by an example to be worked by the student (see Markle, 1964). If the RULEG prescription was valid for principles, it should also be valid for definitions because a definition is basically a rule for classification of a universe of specimens. It appears that teaching by example is as useful at this level of complexity as it has generally been found to be with concrete concepts at lower levels.

A second study, structuring a direct comparison between a group using only Webster's definition and another group using the same definition with our additional four examples, provides further evidence of the effect of examples. The addition of the full range of examples, although adding only four to the nine already included in Webster's definition, significantly improved generalization performance ($t = 9.58$, $df = 40$, $p < .001$). By analysis of performance subscores on various subset classes of examples, as shown in Table 5, we were able to pinpoint more precisely the effects of our additional four examples upon generalization. In the total test, for instance, there are eleven examples, such as *drop,* which are directly parallel in rationale to the ones provided by Webster's definition, e.g., *load.* On these eleven items, there was no significant difference in performance between the two groups ($t = 1.44$, $df = 40$). Equivalent performance is

Table 5. *Structure of subtests.*

		N
Free morphemes	All 4a examples	13
Bound morphemes	All 4b examples	13
One or less syllable morphemes	All 5a and 5b examples	18
Two or more syllable morphemes	All 5c and 5d examples	8
Common morphemes	All 6a examples	21
Rare morphemes	All 6b and 6c examples	5
Free remainder morphemes	All 7a examples	8
Bound remainder morphemes	All 7b examples	8
No remainder morphemes	All 7c examples	7
Other remainder morphemes	All 7d examples	3
Base morphemes	All 8a examples	15
Prefix morphemes	All 8b examples	5
Suffix morphemes	All 8c examples	6
Non-morphemes lacking CA#2	All "lacks 2" non-examples	13
Non-morphemes lacking CA#3	All "lacks 3" non-examples	11

predictable since both groups were given the same set of examples of this particular kind, a component of Webster's definition. On types of examples not illustrated by Webster, however, subscores were significantly different. For instance, Webster provides no examples longer than one syllable. On the eight test morphemes of two or more syllables, the group with the full range of examples illustrating long as well as short morphemes performed significantly better ($t = 2.61$, $df = 40$, $p < .01$). We analyzed eleven such subtests on various groupings of the examples. In all but one case, the effects were exactly as predicted: no difference in performance where Webster's examples illustrated the subset, and significant differences favoring the group with four additional examples where the test examples were outside the range provided by Webster's illustrations. These data support the findings by Tennyson et al. (in press) who confirmed that providing students with the full range of examples increases correct generalization.

The limited number of subjects available restricted our first study primarily to the effects of two independent variables, examples and irrelevant attributes, upon generalization performance; thus, within the experimental design, the effects of these variables upon discrimination performance are not clear-cut. We have hypothesized (Markle et al., 1969) that the most effective teaching technique for facilitating discrimination is the provision of the key set of non-examples, a treatment not included in this study. It is clear from the data that providing a full range of examples proved a more powerful variable controlling generalization than providing verbal descriptions of the full range of examples, that is, the statement of irrelevant attributes included in the definitions. We can argue that an equivalent result could be expected in variables controlling discrimination.

However, in the absence of illustrative non-examples, the statement of critical attributes provides some information on the basis of which discrimination decisions should be made for each specimen. Therefore, there should be no differences in total discrimination performance among the six groups which were provided with a complete statement of

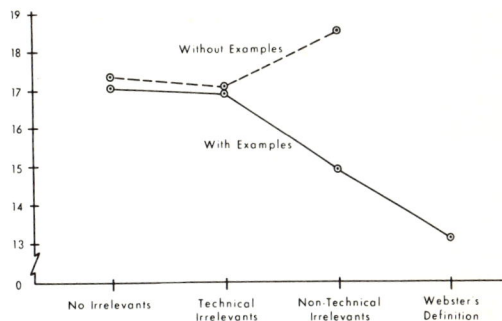

Figure 2. *Mean correct discrimination of all non-examples* ($n = 24$).

all three critical attributes. No significant differences in discrimination performance were observed with respect to the independent variables of examples and type of irrelevant attributes (respectively, $F = 3.71$, $df = 1/131$ and $F = 0.11$, $df = 2/131$).

One discrimination trend can be noted in Figure 2. Students provided with a full range of examples tend to overgeneralize, that is, to fail to discriminate as well as those students not provided with examples. The overgeneralization effect is consistent with the findings of Tennyson et al. (in press) and suggests that effective instruction requires the provision of both examples and non-examples, an issue which is the subject of future investigations.

One aspect of discrimination can be examined with the study data. The definition from Webster's fails to state one of the critical attributes at all, the second attribute in the concept analysis presented in Table 1. We, therefore, expected that students who were provided with Webster's definition lacking a critical attribute, and who thus lacked the basis for making discriminations, would fail to discriminate non-examples which lacked only this specific attribute. There were nine such non-examples on the test, and four non-examples which lacked the second critical attribute in conjunction with another. A planned comparison between the six groups provided with the definition derived from the concept analysis which possessed the critical attribute and the group provided with Webster's definition lacking this critical attribute indicated a significantly better discrimination performance by students possessing the statement of the critical attribute ($t = 6.50$, $df = 147$, $p < .001$), with this factor accounting for 31 percent of the observed variance across the planned comparison. Such a finding seems to confirm common sense in that we cannot expect a student to make fine discriminations on test items if he is not given the basis on which to make such discriminations. That basis would be either the verbalization of the rule for making the discrimination, in other words, the critical attribute, or the provision of model non-examples lacking only that critical attribute.

In their pioneer study of variables affecting concept learning, Tennyson et al. (in press) obtained their estimate of the range of examples and non-examples by having students classify specimens on the basis of a given definition, thus establishing the probability of recognition as "high" or "low" in terms of the resulting difficulty level of each item. A potential problem with such a technique became apparent from our data. The level of probability of recognition for a given specimen under one definition may radically change when the definition is changed. One test non-example, the *pump* in "*pumpkin*," was correctly discriminated by only 27 percent of the group using Webster's definition, while those students with statements of all critical attributes correctly discriminated at the 86 percent level, a shift from "low probability" to "high probability" according to Tennyson's level of difficulty technique. On the total set of twenty-four non-examples, there was a significant difference in ranking ($p < .0035$) by the difficulty level technique between students using the derived definition and students using Webster's definition when investigating with the Wilcoxon Matched-Pair Signed Ranks Test (Siegel, 1956).

A great deal of research remains to be done in delineating the variables which lead to efficient instructional design at the higher cognitive levels. We concur with Tennyson et al. (in press) that the initial studies reported here require replication with concepts drawn from many disciplines. Certain principles are emerging, however, from the preliminary studies. These studies confirm the value of analysis in determining the dimensions across which a universe of specimens may vary, a determination necessary to verbalize the concept definition accurately and to govern the selection of teaching and testing examples and non-examples. It is our hope that the frequently seen objective "the student will be able to define the concept"—which can be simply a measure of rote memory learning—will come to be replaced by a higher level objective of the form "the student will demonstrate real understanding as shown by correct generalizations across a full range of examples and by fine discriminations excluding a rational set of non-examples."

Addendum: Current Research in Progress

Two undergraduates (Thomas Jobling and Lydia Secrest) have completed a pilot study on the effects of both example and non-example treatments on generalization and dis-

Table 6. *Effects of example and non-example treatments on mean correct generalization ($n = 26$).*

Source	MS	df	F
Examples	111.91	1	11.09*
Non-examples	28.24	1	2.80
Interaction	19.24	1	1.91
Within	10.09	80	

* $p < .001$

Table 7. *Effects of example and non-example treatments on mean correct discrimination ($n = 24$).*

Source	MS	df	F
Examples	1.31	1	0.11
Non-examples	50.71	1	4.18**
Interaction	21.09	1	1.74
Within	12.13	80	

** $p < .05$

crimination performance. The definition used in their study was the statement of just the three critical attributes of the concept "morpheme" (see Table 2). One group in their study was given the definition alone. A second group was given the definition and three of the four examples from our minimum rational set (bawd's; dog-tired; elephant). A third group was given the definition and a rational set of non-examples (breathe; thing; paleface). A fourth group was given the definition and both sets of these examples and non-examples. Subjects were drawn from the pool of students in a beginning psychology course and randomly assigned to treatment groups. The test items were those used in the main study (see Table 4).

A summary of their data is presented in Tables 6 and 7. The data support the hypotheses mentioned in the main report: Examples significantly improve generalization scores, and non-examples significantly improve discrimination scores. We plan to rerun the study with an improved set of non-examples, since the non-example "thing" is not directly parallel to those in the test which lack only critical attribute two (non-examples such as "pumpkin" and "catsup").

14

TECHNIQUES FOR THE MODIFICATION OF GROUP BEHAVIOR

"We will all go out for recess just as soon as the entire class is quiet." Most of us can recall that kind of contingency from our elementary-school experience, and reflection also will probably suggest that the technique was very effective. Friends who perhaps were something less than model students themselves were suddenly urging—no, insisting—that everyone quiet down so that recess could get under way.

The intuitive feeling that use of group contingencies is a powerful modification procedure is well documented by the two articles in this section. The study by Schmidt and Ulrich probably is first in the literature to treat a group as a single responding organism. Other studies have reported the use of group contingencies, e.g., the "good-behavior game" devised by Barrish, Saunders, and Wolf, which is included in Section 15 of this volume. In those instances, however, individual behavior was recorded and then summed to ascertain the group's performance. In the portion of the Schmidt and Ulrich study that studied noise level, no individual data were recorded. A sound-level meter measured the simultaneous performance of the entire group to determine if the reinforcement criterion had been met.

The second article, by Hamblin, Hathaway, and Wodarski is an extremely important contribution to the literature. It affords a direct comparison of the relative effectiveness of individual versus group contingencies on cooperative behaviors in an applied setting—with truly dramatic results. The findings are nothing short of thrilling for those of us who are products of an educational system which fostered a cruel, destructive competition. For example, one of the editors, while in graduate school, was ill for a week and missed three class sessions; when he returned to class, he asked a fellow student to loan him his notes. He was told "no" in a very matter-of-fact way with the explanation that it was common knowledge the professor graded on a curve; loaning his notebook might help produce a high score and therefore reduce his own chances of getting an "A." The technology for obviating that kind of inhumanity is available and must be implemented at all levels of the education process.

Effects of group contingent events upon classroom noise

GILBERT W. SCHMIDT AND ROGER E. ULRICH

A number of studies clearly indicate that the systematic application of operant conditioning techniques has been highly effective in modifying a variety of behavioral problems (Ullmann and Krasner, 1965; Krasner and Ullmann, 1965; Ulrich, Stachnik, and Mabry, 1966). Thus far, the application of these techniques has been used primarily within special educational settings and with individuals rather than groups. The present study investigated the utilization of operant principles in a regular public-school classroom using the combined behavior of a group of persons as the dependent variable.

EXPERIMENT I: CONTROL OF PUPIL-PRODUCED NOISE

The first experiment investigated a group control procedure designed to suppress excessive classroom sound. The class was allowed a 2-minute addition to the gym period and a 2-minute break contingent upon maintaining an unbroken 10-minute quiet period as monitored on a decibel meter. Direct contingencies were not placed on other classroom behaviors.

Method

Subjects

A class of 29 fourth-grade elementary students, 14 boys and 15 girls, was selected because of excessive noise during their free-study period. This was a regular public-school class with most of the children coming from lower-middle- and middle-class backgrounds.

Apparatus

The experiment was conducted in a typical classroom equipped with desks and facilities for 29 students. A General Radio Corporation model 710-A sound-level meter was used to measure the sound intensities during all phases of the experiment. An SRA electric timer with a buzzer was used to signal the time periods. A whistle was used as a signal to the pupils when they had exceeded the sound intensity limits. A stopwatch attached to the clipboard, which held the data sheets, indicated the time intervals used in recording the data.

Observation Procedures

The basic data for the study consisted of the decibel (db) readings from the dial of the sound-level meter. The observer recorded the data from a position in the rear center of the room. Recording was done on sheets of paper attached to a clipboard. Readings were taken every 3 minutes on the minute during the baseline phase and every 1 minute on the minute during the experimental and reversal phases. The change to 1-minute interval recordings was to increase the sensitivity of measurement during the experimental, reversal, and follow-up phases. Frequent reliability checks were accomplished by having 2 observers simultaneously record individual sessions. Reliability, in this case, reflected the degree to which 2 observers obtained the same average decibel reading during 20-minute observation periods. The smaller score was divided by the larger score. The interobserver reliability was found to exceed 95 percent in all cases.

From *Journal of Applied Behavior Analysis*, 1969, *2*(3), 171–79. Copyright 1969 by the Society for the Experimental Analysis of Behavior, Inc. Reprinted by permission of the authors and the *Journal of Applied Behavior Analysis.*

This paper is a report of a study conducted jointly by The Behavior Research Laboratory at Western Michigan University and the Kalamazoo Valley Intermediate School District, Albert Bradfield, Superintendent. In addition to the above-named institutions, the project received support from other sources: (1) The Extramural Research Fund, State Department of Mental Health, Lansing, Michigan, and (2) Kalamazoo County Mental Health Board.

Procedure

The study was conducted during a free-study period that occurred daily, Monday through Friday, sometime between 9:00 A.M. and 11:00 A.M. It was during these periods that the class had been noted to be excessively noisy. The sessions recorded ranged in duration from 40 to 60 minutes, depending upon completion of the morning's activities.

For purposes of this study, the entire class of 29 students was treated as a single responding organism. The decibel intensity readings are a total of the noise produced by the entire class.

After the 10-day baseline period recordings and before the first experimental phase, the teacher informed the pupils of the procedures by which they, as a group, would earn extra gym time. They were told the following:

"A timer will be set at 10 minutes and be allowed to run to zero, at which time a buzzer will sound. Each time the buzzer sounds, you (the class) will receive 2 extra minutes added to your gym period, and a 2-minute break to talk, ask questions, sharpen pencils, or whatever before beginning the next 10-minute period. If, however, you become too noisy at any time during the 10-minute period, Mr. _____ will blow a whistle to let you know and reset the timer back to 10 minutes regardless of how many minutes have gone by."

During the reversal phase, the students were told simply that the previous conditions were not in effect. Data were taken without explanation to the students during the follow-up.

It was arbitrarily decided that the noise-level limit be set at 42 db. Thus, the experimenter constantly maintaining the sound-meter dial would sound the whistle and reset the timer for each class-produced noise that exceeded 42 db. A 42-db limit proved reasonable since the room without students registered between 36 and 37 db. Sound levels near 42 db were found to be generally acceptable to the teaching staff.

Results

The data for all phases of the experiment are presented in Figure 1. Each point on the graph represents the average sound-level reading for one session and the vertical lines denote the mean deviation of the sound. The ordinate indicates the sound-level reading in decibels of sound intensity, and the abscissa denotes the session with the vertical lines separating the various phases of the experiment. The first phase represents data collected before any contingencies were placed on the classroom sound level, the first experimental phase shows the results of Phase I conditions, the reversal phase is the return to noncontingent conditions, and the second experimental phase is the reinstatement of sound contingencies.

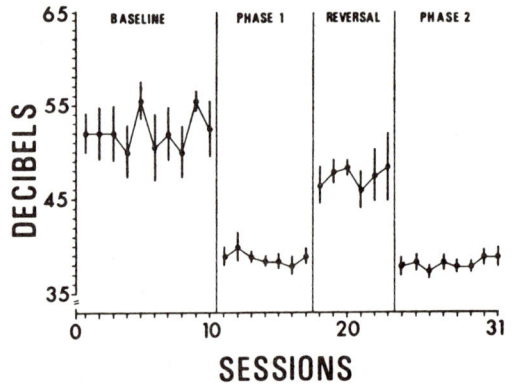

Figure 1. *The effects of sound-control procedures on the classroom noise level. Each point represents the average sound-level reading for one session with vertical lines denoting the mean deviation.*

Evidence of the degree of suppression of sound intensity can be seen by comparing the average sound-level readings of the baseline, experimental, reversal, and second experimental phase of the study. The mean readings of the 10 sessions of baseline data in decibels were 52, 52, 52, 50, 55.5, 50.5, 52, 50, 55.5, and 52. The first session of the experimental phase shows an immediate drop from the preceding mean baseline reading of 52.5 to a mean of 39 db, a drop of 13.5 db in sound intensity. The mean 39-db reading indicates that the students were producing little extraneous noise, since the classroom without the students present registered a sound level between 36 and 37 db. The other readings during Phase I averaged 40, 39, 38.5, 38.5, 38, and 39 db per session. During the reversal period, when the baseline conditions were again put into effect, an immediate increase in sound intensity per session averages of 46.5, 48, 48.5, 46, 47.5, and 48.5 db occurred. Although intermediate to the baseline and experimental phases, these readings more closely approximate baseline. During Phase II, when the sound contingencies were again in effect, the sound level lowered to averages of 38, 38.5, 37.5, 38.5, 38, 38, 39, and 39 db per session. As was true in Phase I, this drop was immediate with no apparent transition or gradual reduction of sound level during the first or subsequent sessions.

Figure 2 provides examples of readings taken during individual sessions. The top por-

tion of the figure represents readings taken every 3 minutes during Sessions 1, 4, 7, and 10 (baseline). Phase I of Figure 2 shows the recordings taken each minute during Sessions 11, 13, 15, and 17 while Sessions 18, 20, 21, and 23 represent samples of the reversal phase. Sessions 24, 26, 29, and 31 show recordings taken from the second experimental phase. These sessions are typical of each phase and show that the sound levels were uniform throughout each session as well as throughout each session within the phase. The sessions shown in Figure 2 are the first session, two intermediate sessions, and the last session of each phase.

Discussion

The results of Experiment I show that, under certain specific circumstances, control and suppression of sound-intensity levels can be accomplished in a regular elementary-

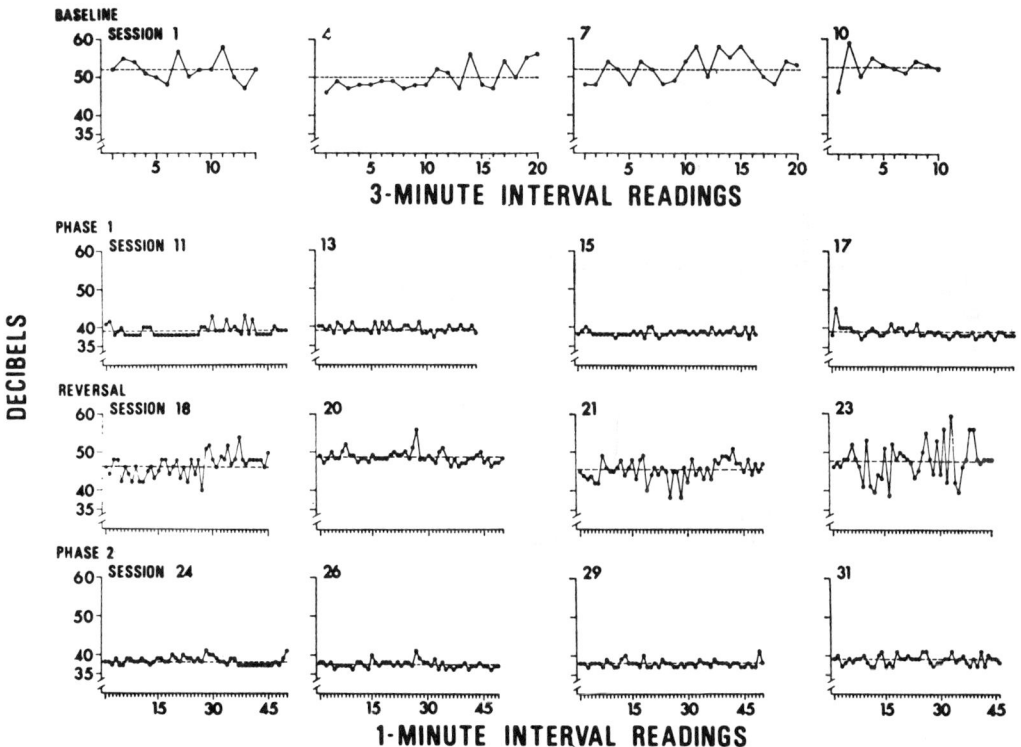

Figure 2. *Typical examples of sound-level readings taken during individual sessions of all four phases. Dotted horizontal lines indicate mean reading for each session.*

school classroom. The immediate increase of sound intensity during the reversal and its immediate suppression with reinstatement of reinforcement contingencies strongly indicate that the contingencies, in effect, were the crucial variable. While the additional gym time, as well as the 2-minute breaks, may have been reinforcing for most students, it need not have been so for all. Peer consequences in the form of threatening gestures, arm-moving, and facial expression were observed being directed at more noisy members of the class. These expressions also were directed at special teachers and the school nurse who were observed entering the room during the quiet periods. Such behaviors on the part of certain students may have had some effect on maintaining quiet.

Quay, Werry, McQueen, and Sprague (1966) pointed out that the economics of public schools require the development of group techniques that will allow children to be handled by as few adults as possible. They further point out that it is crucial at this state that the techniques developed on an individual basis be extended to group situations. The present experiment provided an example of a technique that allows for handling a group as an individual responding organism. In developing methods that are both economically feasible and practical for application to the entire classroom, group procedures such as described here probably hold the most promise of success and acceptance by concerned teachers.

The apparent effectiveness of this technique in suppressing out-of-seat behavior and disturbing antics further suggests its application in the control of individual behavior problems. It also may be helpful in promoting increased learning because studying is generally quite compatible with quietness.

EXPERIMENT II: CONTROL OF NOISE AND OUT-OF-SEAT BEHAVIOR AND ITS EFFECT UPON TEACHER REPRIMANDS

In the previous experiment, the teacher noted that the children seemed to be better behaved in relation to their out-of-seat behavior. In this study, data were collected not only on sound level, but on out-of-seat behavior and teacher reprimands as well. During Phase I, contingencies were placed on sound level only with 2 minutes additional gym period allowed for each unbroken 5-minute quiet period. No breaks between quiet periods were allowed. During Phase II, special contingencies of a 5-minute loss of gym time were levied on individuals who exceeded the sound level or were found inappropriately out of their seats. Teacher reprimands were recorded throughout all phases. Follow-up phase data were recorded the following school year.

Method

Subjects

A class of 28 second-grade elementary students, 13 boys and 15 girls, was selected for this experiment, again due to excessive noise and other behaviors conflicting with ongoing small reading groups. The children were from the same locale and background and attended the same school as the subjects of Experiment I.

Apparatus

This experiment was conducted in a regular classroom very similar to that described in Experiment I. The apparatus for Phase I was the same as that used in Experiment I.

In Phase II, a common household interval timer with a bell signal was used to control out-of-seat behavior.

Observation Procedures

Sound-level data were recorded by an observer in the rear center of the classroom monitoring the decibel readings dial as in Experiment I. Sound intensities were recorded every minute on the minute throughout all phases.

In addition, every minute on the half minute, the observer recorded the number of students inappropriately out of their seats at that moment. Inappropriate out-of-seat behavior included any student found out of his seat and not directly enroute to or from the reading materials table.

Every teacher-initiated reprimand to the class at large was indicated by an X recorded beneath the 10-second interval space in which it occurred. The teacher was unaware that a reprimand was defined as any statement such as "sit down" or "be quiet, it's too noisy in here" when not directed at one individual as the recipient. Points at which reinforcement or punishment for sound level occurred were similarly indicated on the data sheets. A "D" was used to indicate the point at which the out-of-seat bell sounded and the number of those punished indicated by the number following it.

Interobserver reliability checks were made on the sound-level data by having two observers record readings from the sound meter dial for 20 minutes. Reliability was calculated by dividing the largest mean reading into the smallest. These checks yielded interobserver reliabilities in excess of 99 percent. Reliability checks were performed for teacher reprimands by having 2 observers record the number of reprimands occurring over a 30-minute period. The larger number was then divided into the smaller number, yielding interobserver reliabilities of 100 percent. Interobserver reliabilities were also 100 percent for out-of-seat tallies by a similar procedure. Two observers recorded the number of students out of their seat every minute on the half minute for 20 minutes. These tallies were totaled, and the largest total was divided into the smallest total.

Procedure

This experiment had 5 phases. All phases, including the follow-up phase, were conducted during a morning reading class from approximately 8:30 to 9:30 A.M., Monday, Tuesday, Thursday, and Friday. The teacher reported that the excessive noise and the problem of keeping the students at their respective desks without giving each of them her full attention made this particular period especially troublesome to her.

During these periods, small groups of students attended 20-minute teacher-led reading sessions held in the rear corner of the class-room. The corner in which these groups were held was partitioned off on one side by a cardboard divider, with the end facing the class left open. If the teacher's voice was loud enough to register on the sound-intensity meter, the minute reading was taken when she paused or terminated her speech. This seldom occurred.

During the 13 baseline sessions, the data were recorded as previously indicated. There were no direct experimenter-induced contingencies in effect throughout this phase.

Phase I. Directly before the first session of Phase I, the teacher read the following message to the class:

"The class has been too noisy and disruptive during the time that I am working with the reading groups, so we are going to let you earn extra time in the gym by being extra quiet. Mr. _____ will set the timer clock for 5 minutes. Each time the 5 minutes are up, a buzzer will sound and you will have 2 minutes extra added to your gym period. The room captain will put marks on the board to show how many extra minutes you have earned. If you become too noisy, Mr. _____ will blow the harmonica and set the timer back to the start of the 5 minutes without the buzzer ringing."

These procedures were adhered to throughout Phase I without contingencies being placed directly on out-of-seat behavior. The sound-intensity limit used was arbitrarily set at 42 db as in Experiment I. Thus, the harmonica was blown, and the timer reset for sound intensities exceeding the 42-db limit, except when reading groups were changing. During these interludes, readings were not taken because of necessary noise created by moving chairs.

Phase II. Directly before the first session of Experimental Phase II, the teacher informed the class of the following procedure and changes. They were informed that they now would have to earn all of their gym period by the method used in Phase I. Under the Phase II conditions, however, the class was allowed to earn 3 minutes for every unbroken 5-minute quiet interval. Further, individual pupils who alone created noise in excess of the 42-db limit, such as by yelling across the room or slamming a door, were required to write their names on the blackboard. For each such infraction, they lost 5 minutes of their individual gym time.

To control out-of-seat behavior, an interval timer with a bell device was continuously set at varied intervals. Each time the timer bell rang, any students discovered out of their seat and not enroute to or from the reading material were also required to place their names on the blackboard and forfeit 5 minutes of their gym time. During the first sessions, the timer interval averaged approximately 5 minutes. This interval was lengthened, reducing the number of bells per session, until it was phased out by the last 4 Phase II sessions.

During the reversal phase, all conditions were returned to baseline with no contingencies placed upon either the classroom as a whole or upon individuals. The gym period was again established as 15 minutes in length with no extra time available.

The follow-up data were recorded over 5 sessions during October and November of the following school year. Conditions were the same as those of baseline, the only major difference being a different teacher.

Results

Figure 3 (top graph) presents the sound-intenstity data for all phases of the experiment. As in Experiment I, the class as a whole was treated as a single responding organism with each point on the graph representing the average sound-level reading for 1 session. The vertical axis indicates the sound-level readings in decibels, and the horizontal axis denotes the session with vertical lines separating phases of the experiment. The dotted lines indicate the sessions during which the sound meter was malfunctioning. During these sessions, conditions did not change because the experimenter estimated sound level and acted accordingly.

The degree of suppression of classroom sound level is evidenced by a comparison of

the baseline sound-level means with those of the sound-level mean during Phases I and II and reversal phase of the experiment. It can be seen that this was an immediate drop of 12 db. The level during reversal tended to be slightly higher. The number of timer resets that occurred during Phase I averaged 13 per 45-minute session, while during Phase II, only 3.86 punishments were levied per session.

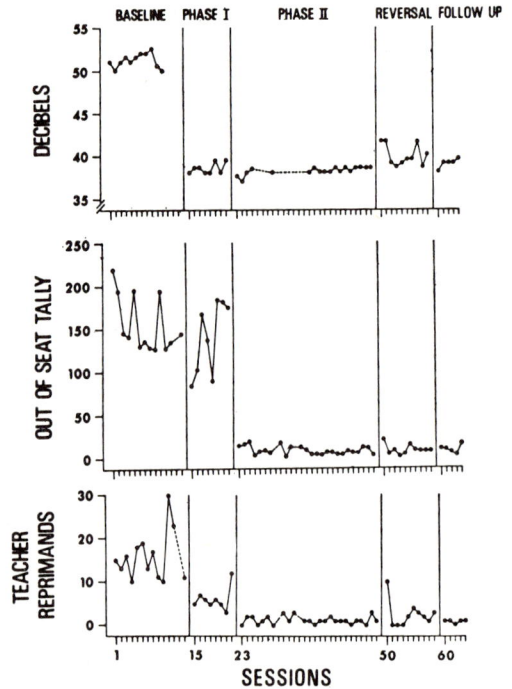

Figure 3. *Top: each point represents average sound-level reading for one session. Middle: each point represents cumulative tally of out-of-seat behavior per 45-minute session. Bottom: each point indicates the number of teacher reprimands directly to the class per 45-minute session. Dotted lines without points represent equipment malfunction.*

Figure 3 (middle graph) represents the cumulative out-of-seat tallies recorded every minute on the half minute. Each point on the graph represents the cumulative tally per 45-minute period. The ordinate represents the accumulated tally for each 45-minute session, and the abscissa denotes the session. Each point represents the summation of these tallies for the first 45 minutes of each session. Sessions 30 and 34 were omitted because they were less than 45 minutes in duration. Figure 3 (middle graph) shows that many of the students were out of their seats during the baseline period with little change occurring during the Phase I condition. During Phase II, an immediate and very substantial drop is noted in out-of-seat behavior. This level was maintained throughout the Phase II and reversal sessions. Individual sound-level readings for Phases I and II are similar to those shown for Experiment I. Figure 3 (bottom graph) shows teacher behavior in terms of number of reprimands directed to the class at large per 45-minute session. The ordinate represents the actual number of reprimands per session, and the abscissa denotes the session number. As can be seen in Figure 3 (bottom graph), teacher reprimands were highest during baseline with a considerable reduction during Phase I. Phase II data show drastic reduction over the baseline level. A slight increase was noted during reversal, especially the first reversal session. Again, sessions 30 and 34 were eliminated because they were less than 45 minutes.

Discussion

The results of Experiment II, consonant with the results of Experiment I, again clearly indicate that under certain specific circumstances, control and suppression of sound-intensity levels can be demonstrated in the elementary-school classroom, in this instance, even with younger second-graders. Although the data indicate substantial sound-level reduction in Phase I, the average number of timer resettings, relative to the average number of resettings in Phase II (13 to fewer than 3) indicates that greater numbers of infractions were occurring, usually between decibel recordings. This in part may have been due largely to less disciplined individuals rather than the group as a whole, since these occurrences largely dropped out with the institution of added individualized contingencies in Phase II. The sound data further indicate that the method is feasible without allowing time-out periods as frequently or of the un-

structured type used in Experiment II. This finding suggests that the longer-term reinforcer of accrued gym time in itself may be sufficient to maintain more quiet behaviors.

The technique used here for control of out-of-seat behavior is a simple one that a teacher alone could easily operate or could allow another student to operate. Its effectiveness with these relatively young students implies possible wide application. The present data further suggest that it can be gradually discontinued without loss in effectiveness. This may be because behaviors incompatible with being out of one's seat have been sufficiently strengthened.

The reversal phase, while showing some increase in unwanted behaviors, was still relatively stable at low levels. This may be related to the length of the experimental control phases. The 10 reversal sessions were taken over the last 3 weeks of school.

During the follow-up phase the next school year, the class was being taught by the same teacher who had previously had them as first-graders. It was her opinion that they were very much improved in conduct, particularly in regard to noisiness and being out of their seats. Her impression was supported by the follow-up data. Thus, it appeared that the changes effected in the previous school year were lasting, at least over the summer and following fall.

It is unlikely that the observer's presence influenced the class's behavior during the follow-up phase, since he appeared to be able to enter any classroom at the school without arousing the students' interest or attention. Further, the teacher's impression was that the class did not behave any differently when the observer was not present. Without reliability data, these subjective opinions must be presented in a guarded manner.

The teacher during the follow-up phase, however, had had two years' experience and had been enrolled in the in-service training course in behavior modification for teachers, and thus inadvertently may have been able to exercise increased controls over the class's behavior. She was not yet, however, using any defined behavioral control techniques for this class during or before the follow-up.

While the effects of the changes in procedure in Phase II were effective in gaining control of the classroom noise level and out-of-seat behavior, the fact that both the revised sound-control contingencies and institution of the timer for control of out-of-seat behavior were simultaneous makes the assessment of the effect of each move difficult. Changing these conditions at different times would allow a cleaner analysis of the effects of each condition.

EXPERIMENT III:
AFFECTING AN INDIVIDUAL'S
OUT-OF-SEAT BEHAVIOR DURING
GROUP CONTROL PROCEDURES

This experiment followed the behavior of 1 individual student through all phases of Experiment II. Emphasis was placed on the student's excessive out-of-seat behavior, which was her only noted problem. This behavior was greatly reduced with the institution of a variable-interval timer and bell. Whenever the bell rang, every student inappropriately out of his seat lost 5 minutes of his gym period.

Method

Subject

The subject of this study was a 7-year-old girl in the second-grade class used in Experiment II. She was chosen for her excessive out-of-seat behaviors which were deemed a problem by the classroom teacher. Other undesirable behaviors, such as talking, etc., were minimal.

Procedure

Data for all phases of this study were collected simultaneously with Experiment II data. The subject's data were very discrete and easily observable, since out-of-seat was defined as any occurrence whenever she was not in contact with the seat portion of her chair. A reliability check indicated reliability of 100 percent between 2 observers over a 20-minute period. Recordings were taken on a 10-second interval basis. At the end of any 10-second interval, the observer marked a box on the sheet divided into 6 boxes per minute (1 per 10-second interval) and 5 minutes per line. An O was placed in each box if the subject left her seat at any time during that 10-second interval. A line was placed in the box if she was seated in any manner or permissibly out of her seat (teacher permission for leaving seat or going to and from reading materials).

The observation sessions varied in length, with the shortest being 20 minutes. Most were near 30 minutes. Observations were omitted while she attended her reading group. The procedures and apparatus are those described in Experiment II.

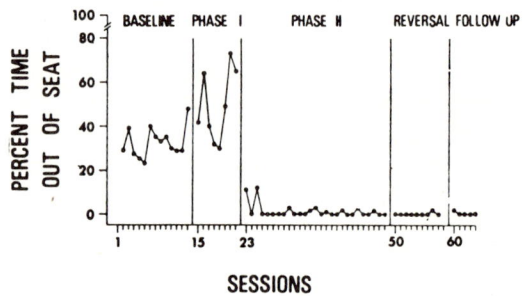

Figure 4. Each point indicates the percent of time the subject was inappropriately out of her seat during the observation period.

Results

Figure 4 indicates the percent of time the subject was inappropriately out of her seat during the observation period. The baseline data indicate a relatively high and consistent rate of out-of-seat behavior (compared to other students). During Phase I, this rate of out-of-seat behavior increased. During the first session of Phase II, the subject was discovered out of her seat on one occasion and for the remainder of the session remained seated. The subject's out-of-seat behavior was virtually eliminated. As indicated by the reversal, it maintained itself at an even lower rate after the contingencies were removed. The follow-up data indicate that the change had been maintained.

This study represents the behavior of one individual within the class under varied experimental and baseline conditions. The experimenters' somewhat subjective impression suggests that the high degree of suppression of undesirable behavior probably was not as marked in many of the other more deviantly behaving individuals.

At present, the experimenters can offer no explanation for the rise in out-of-seat behavior in Phase I, since the low rate of talking was not significantly altered throughout the experiment. The rapid and highly effective suppression noted in Phase II strongly suggests that the specific interval timer contingencies were responsible for the behavior change.

The maintenance of this low rate of out-of-seat behavior in part may have been the result of reinforcement of the incompatible behaviors required in completion of work. The teacher reported a higher rate of work completed by the student. Praise and better grades (sometimes leading to further reinforcement) followed this.

Perhaps the most valuable contribution of the tactics of behavior control utilized in this study is in terms of preventing the occurrence of problem behavior. With an understanding of the variables which, when manipulated, can eliminate nonadaptive classroom behavior, teachers will be in a position to program their classrooms so that the probability of such behavior occurring is minimized by the strengthening of more desirable behaviors compatible with educational goals and good adjustment. In cases where maladaptive behaviors do arise, they often could be dealt with before they were allowed to reach critical proportions.

Further, such tactics used effectively in eliminating and controlling behavior problems may have the added advantage of freeing the teacher so that he might have more time to do a better job of teaching. In order to accomplish this successfully, these tactics more often must be applied to students as a group, rather than as an individual. These studies show that group-control procedures are possible in terms of economic feasibility and practicability.

Group contingencies, peer tutoring, and accelerating academic achievement

ROBERT L. HAMBLIN, CRAIG HATHAWAY, AND JOHN WODARSKI

Accumulated research indicates that behavior modification procedures help inner-city children with various behavior and learning problems including deficient verbal, reading, and arithmetic behaviors (cf. Hall, Panyan, Rabon, and Broden, 1968; Hamblin, Buckholdt, Ferritor, Kozloff, and Blackwell, 1971; Reynolds and Risley, 1968; Staats and Butterfield, 1965; Wodarski, Hamblin, Buckholdt, and Ferritor, 1971; Wolf, Giles, and Hall,

Prepared under the auspices of CEMREL, Inc., a private nonprofit corporation supported in part as a regional educational laboratory by funds from the U.S. Office of Education, Department of Health, Education, and Welfare. The opinions expressed in this publication do not necessarily reflect the position or policy of the Office of Education, and no official endorsement by the Office of Education should be inferred.

1968). At CEMREL we have found training teachers to modify and control disruptive behavior easier than training them to accelerate academic achievement. In part, this is because disruptive behavior apparently is of greater concern to most teachers and hence this behavior is controlled more effectively than achievement. The logistics involved in modification of disruptive behavior are also easier. In most classrooms only 4 or 5 children are disruptive enough to require much in the way of behavior modification; in contrast, the teacher may need to accelerate the academic performance of at least half the class.

Reinforcement procedures, to be most effective in accelerating academic achievement, require an individualized curriculum which allows each child to proceed at his own speed. There are, of course, individualized curricula available, but even with these materials many children need remedial tutoring. Many experiments show that students can effectively tutor one another; however, if the teacher uses individual reinforcement contingencies precious little tutoring occurs. Individual contingencies tend to atomize students, to let them stand or fall alone, by themselves.

Bronfenbrenner and Condrey's (1970) studies of Russian education suggest that, when children are schooled under *group contingencies*, tutoring by peers occurs spontaneously and as a result academic achievement is facilitated. Wolf et al. (1968), Hamblin et al. (1971), and Hamblin and Hamblin (1972) have used group contingencies in a limited manner with various types of children with good preliminary results. However, using a group contingency for the acceleration of academic achievement represents a relatively unworked field of scientific investigation.

The purpose of this paper is to present briefly two experiments designed to investigate the relationship of several group and individual contingencies to academic achievement. The purpose of the first experiment, by Hathaway and Hamblin, was to compare the effect on academic achievement of the average, high, and low performance group contingencies with the effect of two types of individual contingencies, for performance and for attendance.

To most people group contingencies suggest a situation where members of a group are reinforced on the basis of the average performance of all of the group members. For example, if the members of a group averaged 50 percent on a test, the members might receive 5 tokens each (if 10 is the maximum), or if they averaged 90 percent on a test they might receive 9 tokens each. Such a procedure, in which the responses of *all* group members are averaged and reinforced is called an *average performance group contingency*.

Alternatively, group members may be reinforced on the basis of the high performances in the group. Thus, if the top 3 scores on a test by members of a group averaged 80 percent, all members of the group might receive 8 tokens; if the top 3 performances averaged 98 percent, then each member of the group might receive 10 tokens. This procedure is called *high performance group contingency*.

Finally, group members may be reinforced on the basis of the low performances in the group. If the bottom 3 scores on a test by members of the group averaged 50 percent, then each member might receive 5 tokens, or if the low performance score averaged 70 percent, 7 tokens. This is referred to as *low performance group contingency*.

The reinforcement of an individual in proportion to his own performance is called an *individual performance contingency*. When an individual's performance is ignored, he is reinforced simply for being present; this is referred to as an *individual attendance contingency*.

Experiment I studied the effects of average, high, and low performance group contingencies and individual performance and attendance contingencies on academic achievement.

Method

One class of fourth-grade pupils (n=38) at an inner-city school in St. Louis was divided into 5 experimental groups (three with an n of 7, one with 8, and one with 9). All of the pupils were black and lived in tenements near the Pruitt-Igoe Housing Project.

The 5 experimental groups were subjected to each of the contingencies defined above for a 3-week period in a different, randomly assigned order to allow experimental comparison and to control for order effects.

There were 3 dependent variables in the experiment: gain scores on weekly math, reading, and spelling pre- and posttests. Assignments in each of these subject-matter areas, using the regular curricula materials provided by the school, were given by the teacher to all of the groups on a weekly basis. Curricular materials involving new ideas, concepts, or principles were introduced by the teacher to the class as a whole; past materials also were reviewed.

The assignments given to prepare the students for the tests did not preclude the students' helping one another, and, as part of the instruction given for each assignment, the students were reminded that they could discuss assignments and teach one another in preparation for the tests. At the time each assignment was given, each group was also reminded of the potential consequences of the contingency in effect at the time.

At the beginning of the week the groups were pretested on the materials and at the end of the week, posttested. The tests were made up by the teacher and the experimenter and were constant across groups. Gain scores on these tests were calculated for each of the students; student progress in each of these subjects was gauged using a standardized score—the student's own score divided by the average of the entire class. Thus, a gain score of 1.0 indicated that a student made average progress in the subject matter under consideration. The performance of the students on their daily assignments and on both the pretest and the posttest, not the gain score, was reinforced using points and material back-ups—mainly food, toys, and sundries.

Results

The results for the experiment are summarized in Figures 1, 2, and 3. They represent the average gains in performance in

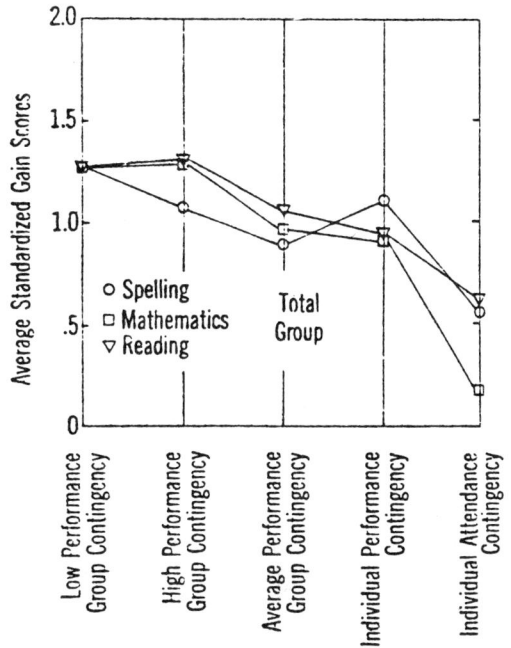

Figure 1. *Average standardized gain scores in spelling, mathematics, and reading for the total experimental groups under five contingency conditions.*

math, spelling, and reading for (1) the average of all performances in all 5 groups and under all 5 contingencies, (2) the top 3 performances, and (3) the bottom 3 performances.

Figure 1 shows how the groups as a whole performed under the various conditions. These data are presented in Figure 1. The gain scores show that overall improvement was best under the low performance (1.5) and the high performance group contingency conditions (1.4), was average under the average performance group contingency (1.0) and the individual performance contingency conditions (1.0), and was worst under the individual attendance contingency (.5).

In Figure 2 the performances of the most gifted students, as gauged by the average of the 3 high performances each day, was highest under the high performance group contingency condition (1.5); was average under the lower performance group contingency (1.0), the average performance group con-

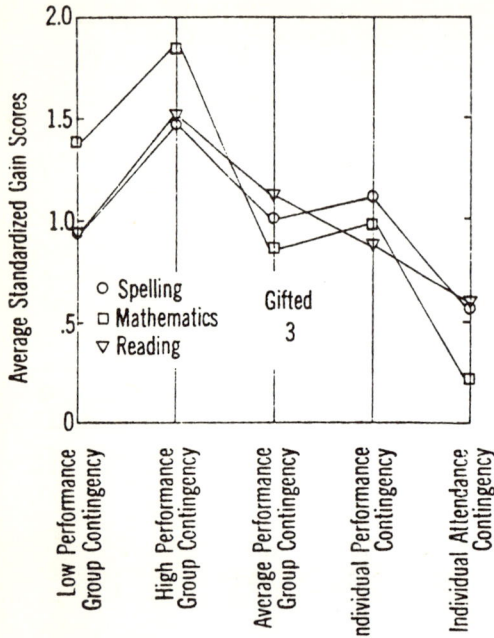

Figure 2. *Average standardized gain scores in spelling, mathematics, and reading for the three most gifted students in each experimental group under five contingency conditions.*

tingency (1.0), and the individual contingency conditions (1.0); and was lowest under the individual attendance contingency conditions (.5).

Figure 3 shows the gain scores of the 3 slowest students in each group. In contrast, these gain scores were highest under the low performance group contingency condition (1.9), were average under the average performance group contingency (0.9) and the individual performance contingency conditions (1.0), and were lowest under the individual attendance contingency (0.6) and the high performance group contingency conditions (0.6).

Discussion

The overall gain scores indicate that on the average the children learned the most either under the low performance group contin-

gency or the high performance group contingency conditions. The data also indicate, however, that differential performances are maximized under the high performance group contingency condition: The slower students perform their worst and the gifted students perform their best.

The low performance group contingency seemed to foster a kind of egalitarian excellence that was not equaled under any of the other contingencies investigated in this experiment. The gifted students did about as well as they did under individual performance or average performance group contingency, and the slower students did three times better than they did under the high performance group and the individual attendance contingencies. The high performance group contingency apparently fosters excellence among the elite more than any other contingency, but it does so at terrible cost to the slower students.

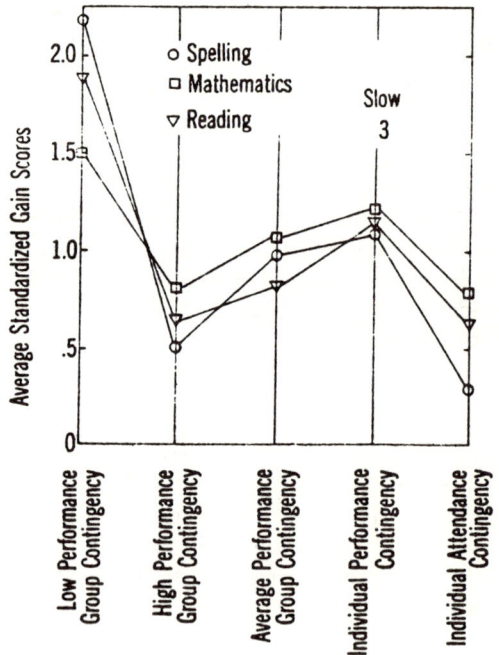

Figure 3. *Average standardized gain scores in spelling, mathematics, and reading for the three slowest students in each experimental group under five contingency conditions.*

The individual attendance contingencies, which wrought havoc with the academic performance of all students is the contingency in effect for all material reinforcers in the traditional school system. What goodies that are available are generally given to all students simply for being present.

While these results are provocative, the experiment leaves a number of questions unanswered. Most important, why should the slower students do better under low performance group contingencies? Classroom observation indicates that the gains of the slower students seem to be largely due to the fact that under the low performance group contingency the gifted students spent a considerable amount of time teaching or tutoring the slower students.

EXPERIMENT 2

The second experiment (Wodarski, Hamblin, Buckholdt, and Ferritor, in press) measured the amount of spontaneous peer tutoring to see if, in fact, it might account for the unusual gains made by the slower students. Various mixes of contingencies also were tried to determine if some combination of low performance group contingencies and individual performance contingencies might not be more optimal than the 100 percent low performance group contingency.

Method

Two classes of fifth-grade pupils (n=60) at another inner-city school in St. Louis were divided into four experimental groups. All of the pupils were black and lived in the Pruitt-Igoe Housing Project.

Before the experiment began, the pupils went through a pilot period of observation to determine the adequate level of problem difficulty. This pilot period also provided an opportunity for the children to adapt to the presence of an observer.

There were four experimental contingencies. Under 100 percent individual contingency, each student received a dollar *in play money* for each problem he worked correctly.

Under 100 percent low performance group contingency, the number of dollars each pupil received each day was determined by averaging the bottom four scores earned by his experimental group. Under the 67 percent individual/33 percent group contingency, each pupil received 67 cents for every problem he worked correctly and 33 cents for the average of the bottom four scores of his group. Under the 33 percent individual/67 percent group contingency, each pupil received 33 cents for every problem he worked correctly and 67 cents for the average of the bottom four scores in his group that day. The play money was used once a week to buy a variety of material reinforcers—edibles, toys, and sundries—that student representatives helped choose for the store.

The 4 experimental groups each spent 14 consecutive days under each of the 4 reinforcement conditions; they moved through those conditions in a different, randomly assigned order.

The 40 mathematics problems assigned to the pupils by their teacher each day were randomly selected from a pool of 4820 consecutively numbered problems from Laidlow Brothers, *Lennes Essentials of Arithmetic,* pupil activity textbooks for Grades 4, 5, and 6. The problems were stratified to insure equal numbers each day at each grade level.

Peer tutoring was allowed every other day. When tutoring was allowed the students were simply told that, if they chose to do so, they could tutor another student in their group once they had finished their own assignment.

An observation form was used to determine the rates of peer tutoring, studying, and disruptive behavior. Peer tutoring behaviors were defined as informal helping patterns exhibited between pupils which might increase the academic performance of the pupil receiving help. Studying behavior was defined as any behavior which was directed toward completion of the problems assigned by the teacher. Disruptive behavior was defined as any behavior by a pupil which prevented another pupil from working on his assignment. Ten randomly chosen pupils were observed each day in each experimental group of 15 pupils; children with the next random numbers were observed if one or

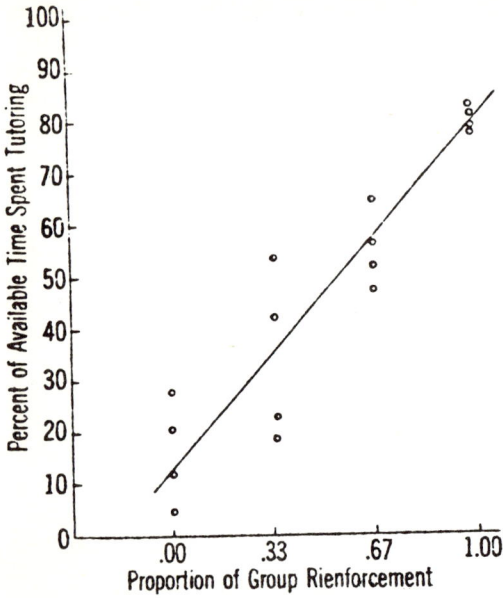

Figure 4. *Least squares regression line for the percent of the available time spent in peer tutoring against the proportion of group reinforcement composing each contingency:* $r^2 = .88.$

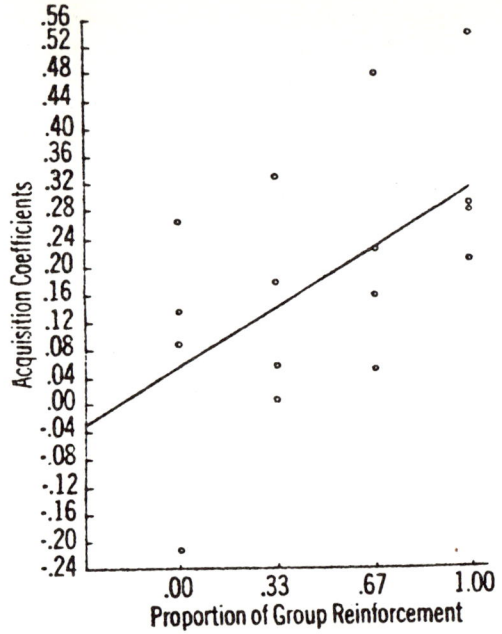

Figure 6. *Least squares regression line for the bottom four performances plotted against the proportion of group reinforcement composing each contingency:* $r^2 = .28.$

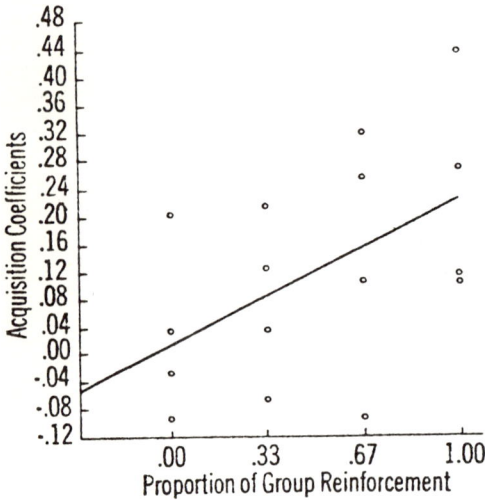

Figure 5. *Least squares regression line for the coefficients for the whole group plotted against the proportion of group reinforcement composing each contingency:* $r^2 = .25.$

more of the sample children were absent. To insure reliability throughout the experiment, 24 checks were executed on the observer ratings. The mean reliability ratio, defined as the number of agreements on each 10-second observational interval divided by the number of agreements plus the number of disagreements, was .96.

Results

As the proportion of low performance group contingency increased, the rate of disruptive behavior decreased ($r^2 = .10$), and the amount of time spent studying increased ($r^2 = .19$). Most importantly, the amount of peer tutoring also increased ($r^2 = .88$), as may be noted in Figure 4.

The acquisition data are plotted in Figures 5, 6, and 7. A preliminary check of the data indicated that there was no significant difference in performance on the peer tutoring

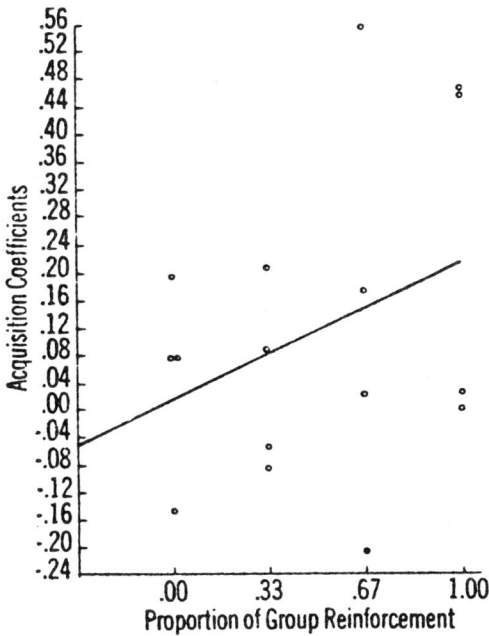

Figure 7. Least squares regression line for the top four performances plotted against the proportion of group reinforcement composing each contingency: $r^2 = .10$.

and non-peer tutoring days. Hence, these analyses include both sets of data. Note the average acquisition rate increased as the proportion of low performance group contingency increased ($r^2=.25$). The data also indicate that the acquisition rate of the slower students, the average of the 4 low performances, increased ($r^2=.28$) as did the acquisition rates of the most gifted students, the average of the top 4 performances ($r^2=.10$).

During the experiment, the experimenters wrote down all of the comments the children made about each of the reinforcement contingencies. The data in Table 1 are clear-cut —an early stated preference for the individual contingency and an early stated aversion to the group contingency. The children evidently did not feel strongly enough to persist in their comments however, since there were none during the third week.

Discussion

The data again indicate that low performance group contingencies accelerate learning

	100% Individual			67% Individual 33% Group			33% Individual 67% Group			100% Group		
	Week			Week			Week			Week		
	1st	2nd	3rd	1st	2nd	3rd	1st	2nd	3rd	1st	2nd	3rd
Positive Comments:												
Group I	5	2	0	1	3	0	0	1	0	0	0	0
Group II	4	0	0	2	1	0	0	0	0	0	0	0
Group III	7	1	0	2	0	0	0	1	0	0	0	0
Group IV	4	1	0	1	0	0	0	1	1	0	2	0
Mean	5	1	0	1.5	1	0	0	0.75	0.25	0	0.5	0
Negative Comments:												
Group I	0	0	0	3	1	0	4	0	0	4	2	0
Group II	0	0	0	4	1	0	4	3	1	3	1	0
Group III	0	0	0	0	0	0	2	0	0	5	2	0
Group IV	1	1	0	1	0	0	3	0	0	3	2	0
Mean	0.25	0.25	0	2	0.5	0	3.25	0.75	0.25	3.75	1.75	0

At top: Mix of Contingencies

Table 1. Number of unsolicited comments by the children about the Reinforcement systems according to mix of contingencies and experimental group.

more than do individual performance contingencies. However, as adjudged by the explained variance, the primary effect of the low performance group contingency was the acceleration of spontaneous peer tutoring. Hence, the differential in learning rates is apparently a weaker, second order effect, a by-product, of the differential in peer tutoring. As in the first experiment, the data show that the slower students were benefited more by the low performance group contingencies than were the more gifted students. Even so, the gifted students tended to do slightly better on the low performance group contingencies than they did on individual contingencies.

At first some students did object to being placed on the low performance group contingency; they seemed to share what may be a cultural bias toward individual contingencies. Even so, these students seemed to adapt rather quickly. We also have observed in oral presentations of this experiment that low performance group contingency strikes a raw nerve in some adults. As one put it, it seems to involve the enslavement of the gifted. If so, it is an enslavement which produces no long-term complaints from the participants and under which all benefit, even the gifted, possibly more than they would under an individual contingency. (After all, in this situation the gifted learn to teach, a very precious skill.) Hence, the data suggest that a try-and-see attitude is appropriate.

CONCLUSIONS

In general, experimental results have shown that biological learning mechanisms mediate behavioral adaptation most quickly in environments where there are (a) strong reinforcers for the adaptive response in question, where there is (b) quick and (c) consistent feedback (reinforcement or process cues predictive of later reinforcement), and where (d) the individual is able to work in the environment at his own pace, i.e., where he is neither rushed nor slowed down by environmental response (cf. Hamblin et al., 1971). In manipulating these variables to decelerate a behavior the operational problem is often quite simple—i.e., do nothing in response to the behavior in question. However, in designing a classroom learning environment to accelerate acquisition rate, it is usually necessary to do something new to optimize all four factors discussed. In a classroom this usually implies an instructional system with several components: (a) individualized curricula, (b) a token reinforcement system with powerful back-ups contingent on tests which gauge acquisition of subject matter dealt with in the curricula, and (c) a teaching procedure which. allows self-pacing and yet provides quick and consistent feedback.

To date, the major difficulty in putting together such an instructional system for the typical classroom has been to find a teaching procedure which allows self-pacing and which effectively and feasibly provides quick and consistent feedback. It would appear from present data that spontaneous peer tutoring, which evidently occurs maximally under low performance group contingencies, may be such a teaching procedure. There may be problems with group contingencies, but the experimental results are most encouraging and suggest that such contingencies deserve serious investigation and consideration for the acceleration of academic achievement.

15

TECHNIQUES FOR THE REDUCTION OF PROBLEM BEHAVIORS

Perhaps the aspect of behavior modification most immediately attractive to teachers has been the technology developed to handle problem behaviors. The techniques are explicit, usually not too difficult to administer, and dramatically effective. Examples of some basic techniques for the control of problem behaviors are given in this section.

The first paper, by McArthur and Hawkins, demonstrates treatment of a candidate for special education in a regular classroom. The techniques used, reinforcement of desired behaviors and time-out for some undesired behaviors, can be applied by classroom teachers to the treatment of other, less severe behavior problems. Even in severe cases, such as the one described, use of auxiliary personnel, such as data takers and token dispensers, to effect changes in the regular classroom may be preferable to sending the child into a special education situation. McArthur and Hawkins' data also indicate that, in some cases at least, behavioral treatment of problems will succeed where drug treatment and psychotherapy have failed.

As teachers know, entire classes can be disruptive. Ingenious methods have been devised to deal with problem behaviors on a group level as seen in the previous section where Schmidt and Ulrich described the use of a meter to monitor the noise level of an entire class. The second paper in this section, by Barrish, Saunders, and Wolf, describes another method. They divide the class into two teams who play a game. Thus the method utilizes both group contingencies and the positive feelings most children have about games. For back-up reinforcers, classroom privileges and enjoyable activities are utilized. These "behavioral reinforcers" are available to almost every teacher.

The third paper in this section, by LeBlanc, Busby, and Thomson, deals with the most difficult problem a teacher is likely to face: aggression. Aggression is a special problem because it is caused by a wide variety of stimuli besides reinforcing ones. Because aggression can be destructive, the need to control it is greater than any other problem behavior. Brown and Elliott (1965) have reported some success in controlling aggression by reinforcing incompatible behaviors, but many aggressive behaviors are too severe to await gradual reduction through differential reinforcement. Punishment effects a swift reduction in behavior; however, the aversive stimuli involved in punishment can themselves cause aggression. In addition, the use of physical punishment to control aggression models the very behavior to be eliminated. Nevertheless, one technique used with some success is mild punishment, such as time-out. The paper by LeBlanc, Busby, and Thomson describes the use of time-out techniques to control aggression in a preschool child.

Although behavior modification is sometimes pictured as rigid and authoritarian, its techniques for controlling problem behaviors are usually more positive than traditional methods. Praise has been found to be more effective than disapproval; enjoyable interludes can be added to a student's day and at the same time be used to reinforce desirable behavior. Even in dealing with aggression, the mildest possible punishment may be, in the long run, the most effective. Behavior modification, then, may not only make the teacher's life easier and more pleasant but may free the student from some of the more aversive means of classroom control.

The modification of several classroom behaviors of an emotionally disturbed child in a regular classroom

MOIRA MCARTHUR AND ROBERT P. HAWKINS

Every schoolteacher occasionally has a pupil who persistently breaks the class rules. The behavior exhibited by such a child reduces the teacher's general effectiveness and distracts the other children's attention. The teacher sometimes reprimands the rule-breaking child when he is engaging in a disruptive behavior. Although the teacher generally intends such a reprimand to function as a punisher, it may actually be a reinforcer (even though the child immediately ceases his disruptive activity, thereby reinforcing the teacher's behavior of reprimanding and perpetuating a vicious circle). In the long run the reprimanding may increase the rate of the disruptive behavior. Madsen, Becker, Thomas, Koser, and Plager (1968) demonstrated such an effect by experimentally strengthening standing-up behavior by increasing the use of commands to sit down. A decrease in standing-up behavior was produced when this behavior was ignored, and sitting was praised.

With a rule-breaking child, the dispensing of social reinforcers contingent on disruptive behavior often is combined with an unresponsiveness to desirable behavior. It is likely that such a child is unable to secure reinforcement for his schoolwork, since his academic skills are usually inferior to those of his classmates. These conditions may combine in the classroom environment so that of all the behaviors the child emits, the disruptive behaviors produce the greatest net amount of reinforcement.

Several researchers have recently become interested in applying techniques based on behavioral principles to the modification of classroom behaviors in the public school. The first to report the successful application of such techniques in the educational setting were Zimmerman and Zimmerman (1962). These authors reported that unproductive classroom behaviors were eliminated in two emotionally disturbed boys through the systematic application of social reinforcement and extinction procedures by the teacher. Haring and Whelan (1965); Hewett (1967);

Reprinted by permission of the authors.

The experimental results presented here are from research being conducted under the sponsorship of the Kalamazoo Valley Intermediate School District. This report is based on a thesis by the senior author submitted to Western Michigan University in partial fulfillment of the requirement for the M.A. degree.

Quay, Werry, McQueen, and Sprague (1966); and Whelan and Haring (1966) provided detailed accounts of their special classrooms for disturbed children based on behavioral principles.

Only recently, however, have studies been reported which contain objective data to substantiate subjective impressions about the efficacy of such techniques in the classroom. For example, Becker, Madsen, Arnold, and Thomas (1967) presented the modification of the deviant behavior of several children through contingent teacher attention and praise; Hall, Lund, and Jackson (1968) strengthened study behavior with contingent teacher attention; Thomas, Becker, and Armstrong (1968) controlled the task-relevant behaviors and certain disruptive behaviors of schoolchildren by manipulating the dispensing of teacher approval and disapproval; and Surratt, Ulrich, and Hawkins (1969) increased the studying behaviors of four first-grade children by using response-contingent light onset and offset.

The present study was designed to demonstrate the efficacy of certain operant conditioning techniques in the modification of several classroom behaviors of a seriously disturbed, disruptive child. A second aim of the study was to evaluate the feasibility of treating grossly maladaptive behavior in a regular public-school classroom rather than in a special classroom. Perhaps many behavior problems could be more efficiently modified within the regular classroom for several reasons: (a) In the special education room the child typically is presented with numerous models exhibiting inappropriate behavior, and the experimental evidence regarding imitation indicates that a model's undesirable behavior is an S^D for undesirable behavior in the observing child (Bandura, Ross, and Ross, 1963). (b) With appropriate training, the normal youngsters in a regular classroom might serve as very effective modifiers of a classmate's deviant behavior, thus acting as ever present therapists. (c) The problem of eventually generalizing the improved behavior of the treated child from the special classroom to the regular classroom is eliminated. (d) The regular classroom teacher can

be an integral part of the modification procedure and may, therefore, learn techniques whereby adaptive behavior patterns may be maintained. A third aim of this study was to assess whether intensive treatment during part of the school day would have any effect on the child's behavior during the rest of the day. This question would be of practical interest to school personnel, such as the school social worker, who might consider working with a child intensively and directly for a portion of the school day, but might not be willing or able to work with the child all day.

METHOD

Subject

The child in this study was an eight-year-old second-grader named Ronnie. Prior to and during the study, Ronnie was a student in a regular school classroom. He had been referred to the school adjustment program, a special education program for emotionally disturbed children (Hawkins, McArthur, Rinaldi, Gray, and Schafetnaar, 1967), as a result of long-standing disruptive classroom behavior and poor academic achievement. He was not admitted to the program because enrollment in these special rooms had reached its capacity. During four years at school, including a repeat of first grade, Ronnie had exhibited numerous disruptive behaviors. In his second-grade classroom, the boy engaged in one or more of the following behaviors during the greater portion of the day: talking or shouting without permission; uttering sundry distracting noises, such as barks, meows, and burps; walking or crawling about the room or hallway; and disturbing other children by poking them, wrestling with them, or taking things from them. Ronnie's teacher described him as being belligerent, disobedient, and destructive. His antics repeatedly disrupted most classroom activities and were being imitated by a few peers.

Ronnie's academic skills were considerably

below those of his classmates. During class periods he seldom attended to the teacher or to his work and rarely worked on any of his assignments. His reading skills were minimal; he could give the phonetic sounds for only a few letters of the alphabet. When administered the Metropolitan Achievement Test, Primary II, prior to the study, he refused to attempt the Word Knowledge, Word Discrimination, Sentence Reading, Story Reading, and Spelling Sections of the test. His arithmetic skills also were below his grade level (1.3, second percentile, Metropolitan Achievement Test).

Prior to the experiment, different drugs had been prescribed in attempts to alleviate the child's problem behaviors both at home and at school. Ronnie had been placed on 20 mg. of Ritalin, three times per day for three months preceding the experiment, and on 50 mg. of Mellaril twice a day for one month prior to the experiment. The type of medication and/or dosage had been altered several times, as the drugs did not satisfactorily improve his behavior either at home or at school.

Before the experiment Ronnie and his mother had been seeing a child psychiatrist for three months. They continued to see him every two weeks throughout the experiment. Both the mother and the psychiatrist reported that this treatment was meeting with little success. The psychiatrist described Ronnie as the most severely disturbed of the children that he was currently treating.

Informal observation in the classroom indicated that much of Ronnie's disruptive behavior was followed by peer attention. When Ronnie exhibited disruptive behaviors, some of his classmates usually would respond to him by looking at him, laughing at him, commenting on his behavior, speaking directly to him, or imitating him. The teacher ignored most of Ronnie's antics, but when his behavior became particularly annoying she sometimes would reprimand him or threaten to send him to the principal's office. Generally, she failed to carry through on these consequences or was unable to do so because the child refused to leave the room. In contrast, the boy's occasional appropriate behaviors consistently passed unnoticed.

Data Recording

One observer was in the classroom during the afternoon and another during part of the morning. The observers were instructed not to respond to the children while in the classroom. They recorded instances of out-of-turn vocalizations, out-of-seat behavior, and attention to his work or to the teacher. The frequency of these behaviors was measured by recording for each successive ten-second interval, whether or not the particular behavior occurred during that interval (Allen, Hart, Buell, Harris, and Wolf, 1964). Stopwatches were used to time ten-second intervals. These three behaviors were recorded daily during two morning activities and three afternoon activities (except that on some days a particular activity was not scheduled). During two afternoon periods, spelling and number study, the child's productivity was measured by the number of letters or numbers written per minute. During the experimental phases of the study, the afternoon observer also recorded the number of tokens the child received daily.

In order to assess interobserver reliability, on three afternoons during the study a second observer independently recorded the same behaviors. Reliability assessments occurred once during baseline, once during experimental phase I, and once during the second baseline phase. The observers positioned themselves in the room so that one observer could not see or hear when the other scored a response. Reliability on any one category of behavior was indicated by an "agreement ratio," obtained by dividing the smaller score by the larger score. "Agreement ratios" ranged from .75 to 1.00.

Baseline. During the baseline condition, the observers refrained from advising the teacher in any way and had no interaction with the child. For nine afternoon and fourteen morning sessions, the observers recorded instances of out-of-turn vocalizations, out-of-seat behavior, and attention to work or the teacher; and they obtained productivity data from spelling and number study.

Experimental Phase I. Experimental procedures began in the tenth afternoon session and were used only in the afternoon. However, data collection continued in both morning and afternoon sessions. Potential reinforcers such as candy, praise, and poker chips exchangeable for material items were made contingent on classroom behaviors, but only token deliveries were recorded. In the first experimental session, the child was informed of experimental contingencies and shown items for which he could exchange poker-chip tokens. Initially, reinforcement contingencies were arranged such that enough tokens could be earned to purchase an item every one to two days. Gradually, token-reinforcement frequency was reduced and exchange "prices" raised so that it took several days to earn enough to make a purchase. Reinforcement was administered by an experimenter seated at a small table beside Ronnie's desk. The teacher was asked to ignore all disruptive behaviors but otherwise to interact with the child as she had formerly.

During the first few sessions, social, candy, and token reinforcers were dispensed whenever Ronnie was sitting quietly in his seat. When a response was reinforced, the contingency usually was stated; e.g., "Ronnie, this is for sitting in your seat like a good boy." Praise was paired with the candy and token reinforcement in an attempt to strengthen its properties as a conditioned reinforcer. Usually, only one chip was given at a time, but if the child made some unusual response that the experimenter particularly wished to strengthen or if he was doing exceptionally well on all behaviors, he was given several chips at a time. Chips were delivered by placing them in a container in front of the boy.

During the first two experimental sessions, Ronnie continued to leave his seat frequently. In an attempt to gain control of the behavior, a five-minute time-out from positive reinforcement (TO) was introduced in session 12. The experimenter left the room for five minutes contingent on the child's leaving his seat. In session 15, the TO procedure was changed: The assistant placed the poker-chip rack on the floor and turned away from the child for five minutes. If at the end of five minutes the child was seated and quiet,

the poker-chip rack was replaced, and the session continued. If the child was still out of his seat at the end of five minutes, another five-minute TO was begun.

By session 16, the child was seated and quiet during most of the session, and token reinforcement contingencies were shifted to attentive behavior and correct academic responses, which included the behaviors of being seated and quiet. Instructions and prompts for academic responses were given frequently, so that correct responses would occur and be reinforced. This extra stimulus support gradually was reduced as the study progressed.

The frequency with which token reinforcers were dispensed was initially high. In the beginning sessions of experimental phase I, the child received an average of slightly more than two chips per minute. By the end of experimental phase I, he was receiving slightly more than one chip per minute. No count was taken of the frequency with which praise and candy were dispensed.

Second Baseline Phase. When desirable and stable changes were observed in Ronnie's afternoon behavior, the second baseline phase was introduced in order to assess whether these changes were a function of the experimental manipulations or of some other factor. During this phase, the experimenter was not present in the classroom and asked the teacher to treat the child in the same manner as she had in the baseline phase. On the evening prior to the first session of the second baseline, the child's mother told him that the experimenter would no longer be able to help him. After eight sessions, when the effects of this procedure were evident, the second baseline phase was terminated.

Experimental Phase II. Following the second baseline phase, the terminal conditions of experimental phase I were reintroduced, and one new variable was added. The teacher was instructed to reward Ronnie's classmates for ignoring him when he engaged in disruptive behavior. The teacher was to dispense tokens exchangeable for toys, games, and parties to the whole class contingent on their all ignoring Ronnie's disruptive behavior. However, this new procedure was not consistently implemented. The teacher found it difficult to observe Ronnie's behavior and that of his peers, dispense tokens, and give instructions to the class all at the same time. The result was that the teacher dispensed one to three poker chips per afternoon contingent on the good working behavior of the whole class, rather than on their success in ignoring Ronnie's undesirable behavior. Because the experimenter was too occupied in working with the child, she was unable to instruct the teacher more adequately.

During experimental phase II, token reinforcement was made contingent on the child's working behavior, attentive behavior, answering correctly, and hand-raising. The rate at which the tokens were dispensed was decreased as Ronnie's behavior improved. By session 33 the tokens were being dispensed at an average frequency of approximately one every three minutes. This rate did not change appreciably during the remainder of the experiment.

Experimental Phase III. On session 38, a new procedure was introduced. On two afternoons a week the experimenter took the child from the room and tutored him in reading and arithmetic in order to raise the level of his academic skills, thus allowing the experimenter's stimulus support in the classroom to be faded out. No data were secured on those afternoons. The same data as before still were taken on the remaining three afternoons of the week. His arithmetic assignments were constructed so that he could successfully obtain the right answers with minimal assistance. The reading material used was *Programmed Reading* (Buchanan, 1968), Primer and Book I. Tokens, candy, and social reinforcement were still contingent on working behavior and correct responses.

Experimental Phase IV. On session 41, a revision was made in the morning procedure, because very little generalization of the afternoon effects had been noted. Ronnie was given brief individual morning assignments prepared by the experimenter; he was no longer expected to do the work assigned to the other children, since these assignments

continued to be far beyond his current skills. The teacher presented the individualized assignments to him and gave him a certain number of chips when he finished a set of assignments. The teacher also corrected his seat work and handed it back to the child when she handed back the other children's morning work. Although this phase included twenty-one morning sessions, only nine appear on the graphs because the morning observer was available only two days a week during this phase.

Afternoon Treatment

The behavioral data collected during the afternoon treatment portion of the day are presented in Figures 1 through 4, with each afternoon designated as one session. Figure 1 shows the percentage of time that Ronnie spent out of his seat. Each point represents the total percentage of time in one afternoon that Ronnie was out of his seat during the three activities in which the data were recorded: spelling, number study—group instruction, and number study—individual assignment. During the baseline phase of the study, the child spent a mean of 32.2 percent of the time out of his seat. During the first two sessions (10 and 11) of experimental phase I, the percentage of out-of-seat behavior decreased. On session 12, when the TO procedure was introduced, the percentage rose to 77 and remained high on session 13. On session 14, the TO procedure was modified, and a concomitant decrease in the percentage of out-of-seat behavior was noted. The behavior stabilized at below 1 percent.

The percentage of out-of-seat behavior increased during the second baseline phase, when the experimenter ceased coming to work with Ronnie. The mean percentage of out-of-seat behavior during this phase of the study was 47.9. With the resumption of experimental procedures in experimental phase II, the amount of time Ronnie spent out of his seat declined immediately to a near-zero percentage and remained there until the

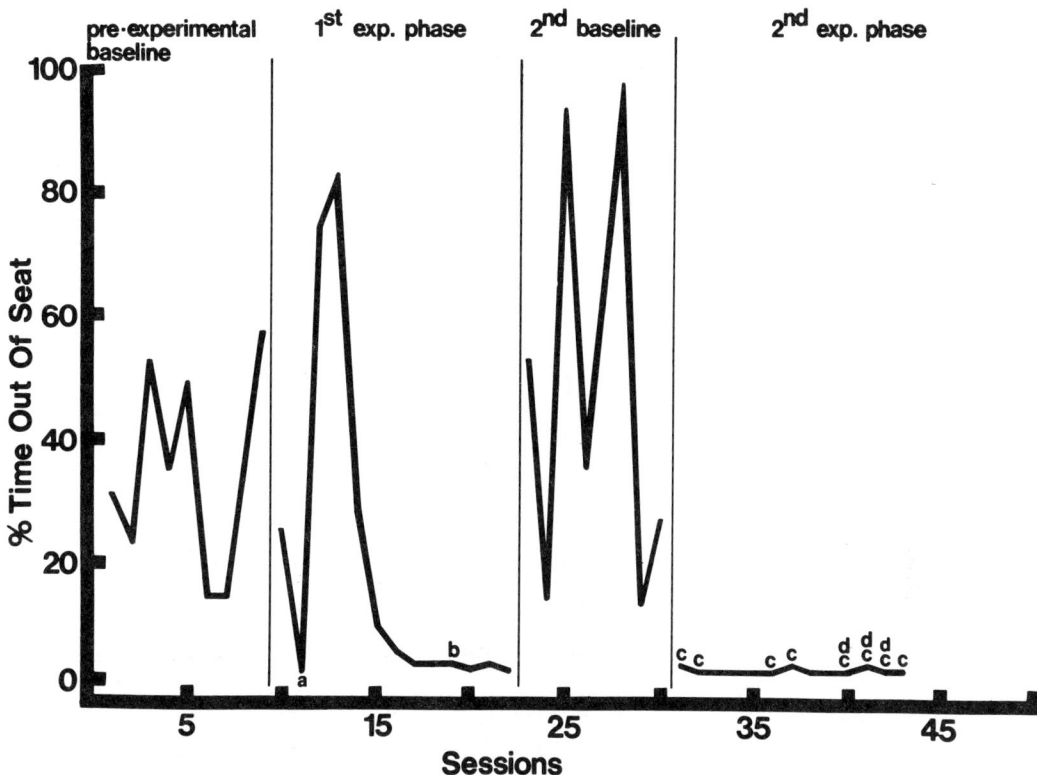

Figure 1. *The effect of experimental contingencies on out-of-seat behaviors during after-noon activities. Letters beside data points indicate drug and dosage changes.*

termination of the experiment at the end of the school year.

Several drug changes occurred over the course of the experiment. Two of these changes were made by Ronnie's psychiatrist in attempts to reduce the boy's hyperactivity at home. Ronnie's daily dosage of Ritalin and Mellaril was .doubled on session 11. This event is indicated by an *a* on all figures. A 25 mg. daily dosage of Tofranil was added to Ronnie's medication by his psychiatrist on the day of session 19 and is denoted by a *b* on all figures. Additional drug changes were made by the intentional omission of Ronnie's usual medication on several occasions. On some afternoons, marked *c,* during experimental phase II, the experimenter, with the permission of the child's psychiatrist, had the teacher omit the child's afternoon medica-

tion; and on the three sessions marked *d,* Ronnie's mother had failed to give the child his Tofranil, because he was ill.

Figure 2 indicates the percentage of time that Ronnie vocalized out of turn during the afternoon activities. During 8 of the 9 baseline sessions, vocalizing out of turn occurred more than 20 percent of the time. During the first three sessions of experimental phase I, the percentages of this behavior were 40, 9, and 13 percent respectively. From sessions 13 to 22, vocalizing out of turn remained below 10 percent. During the second baseline phase, the percentage of time that the child displayed this behavior increased but did not reach the levels observed during the initial baseline phase. The mean percentage of vocalizing out of turn for this phase was 20.5 percent. Following the introduction of ex-

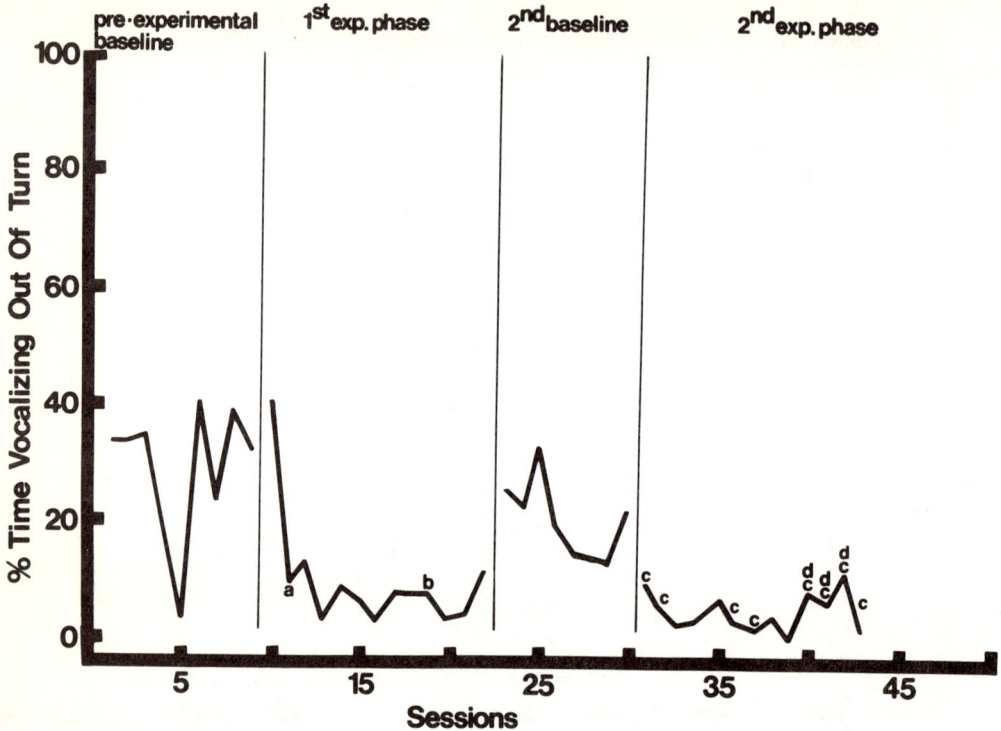

Figure 2. *The effect of experimental contingencies on talking out of turn during afternoon activities. Letters beside data points indicate drug and dosage changes.*

perimental phase II conditions, the inappropriate vocalizing remained below 10 percent for all sessions except one.

Figure 3 depicts the percentage of time that Ronnie attended to his work or to the teacher during the afternoon session. This behavior was very infrequent during the baseline phase (below 15 percent). During experimental phase I, the behavior increased gradually, and by session 19 it was consistently evident more than 50 percent of the time. This gradual rise probably was a function of the gradual shifting of reinforcement contingencies. While Ronnie's simply being in his seat was adequate to produce frequent reinforcers early in experimental phase I, in later sessions it was necessary that Ronnie also be attending to his work before reinforcers would be presented.

The return to baseline conditions resulted in a decrease in attentive behavior. During this phase attentive behavior occurred an average of 9.3 percent of each session, which nevertheless was a better level of performance than was seen during the initial baseline phase. With the reintroduction of reinforcement procedures on session 31, the amount of attentive behavior increased and remained above 69 percent for the remaining sessions of experimental phase II.

Measures of Ronnie's productivity were secured daily in two afternoon activities: number study and spelling. Only those data collected for number study will be presented, because these results closely resemble those obtained during spelling. Figure 4 illustrates Ronnie's rate of working arithmetic problems. His productivity was extremely low during baseline (0-0.7 numbers per minute), rose during experimental phase I (0-3.0 numbers per minute), dropped during second baseline (0-0.7 numbers per minute), and increased immediately during experimental phase II (0.8-5.3 numbers per minute). During the

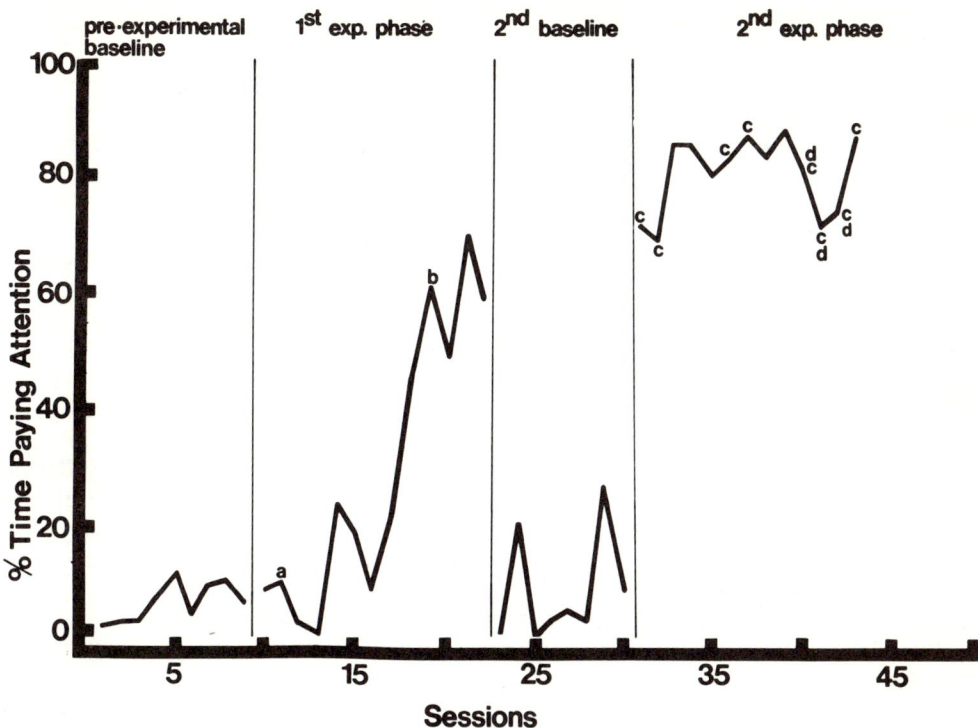

Figure 3. *The effect of experimental contingencies on attentiveness to afternoon academic activities. Letters beside data points indicate drug and dosage changes.*

last three sessions of experimental phase II, his rate decreased somewhat, probably because of a change in the nature of the workbook assignments. These assignments had become much more difficult for all children in the classroom.

During experimental phase II, Ronnie was taken from the classroom on two afternoons per week and given tutoring by the experimenter in reading and arithmetic. No data were recorded on these afternoons. These sessions were instituted in order to increase the child's academic skills and allow the experimenter to fade out prompts given in the classroom for academic work. It was not possible to objectively determine the effects of this tutoring, for the behaviors being recorded during the afternoon could not be expected to reflect any change. The experimenter, however, did feel that this bi-weekly tutoring made it possible to fade out stimulus support for correct answers on afternoon

classroom work more rapidly than would have been possible otherwise.

Morning Generalization Data

Figures 5 and 6 present some of the data secured during the morning activities to test for generalization of the behavioral changes produced by the afternoon treatment procedures. The collection of these generalization data was begun a few days later than the collection of afternoon data. The data in Figure 5 begin with session number 5, and those in Figure 6 begin with session 4.

Of the three behaviors recorded during three morning activities, the only behavior which evidenced any change attributable to the experimental manipulations was vocalization out of turn during individual seat-work activity. These data are presented in Figure 5. The conditions of experimental phase I appear to have had no reliable effect on the vocalizations. However, with the second introduction of nearly the same conditions in experimental phase II, vocalizations showed a gradual decline, eventually falling below 5 percent. This was the only change in Ronnie's morning behavior that appeared to be a generalization from the afternoon. However, another improvement in Ronnie's morning behavior is evident in Figure 5 that is not attributable to afternoon procedures. During experimental phase IV, when Ronnie's morning seat work was individualized, the amount of vocalization was maintained below 5 percent in all sessions.

Though the afternoon procedures affected only one behavior during one activity in the morning—the vocalization represented in Figure 5—the morning procedure introduced in experimental phase IV succeeded in improving two additional morning behaviors. The first was Ronnie's attentiveness to his work during morning individual seat work; the second, his out-of-seat behavior during the same activity. Individual seat work was the activity in which individualization of assigned work and reinforcement for completed assignments was introduced during experimental phase IV. Because of the secondary importance of these data, only the data on attentiveness will be presented. Figure 6 shows the percentage of time that Ronnie paid attention to his work during the morning individual seat-work activity. The experimental manipulations introduced in the afternoon treatment effected no change in this morning behavior. The mean percentages in each phase are indicated by dashed lines in Figure 6 and vary little from one phase of the experiment to another. However, with the introduction of experimental phase IV conditions, a marked increase in attentive behavior was observed.

The subjective observations of members of

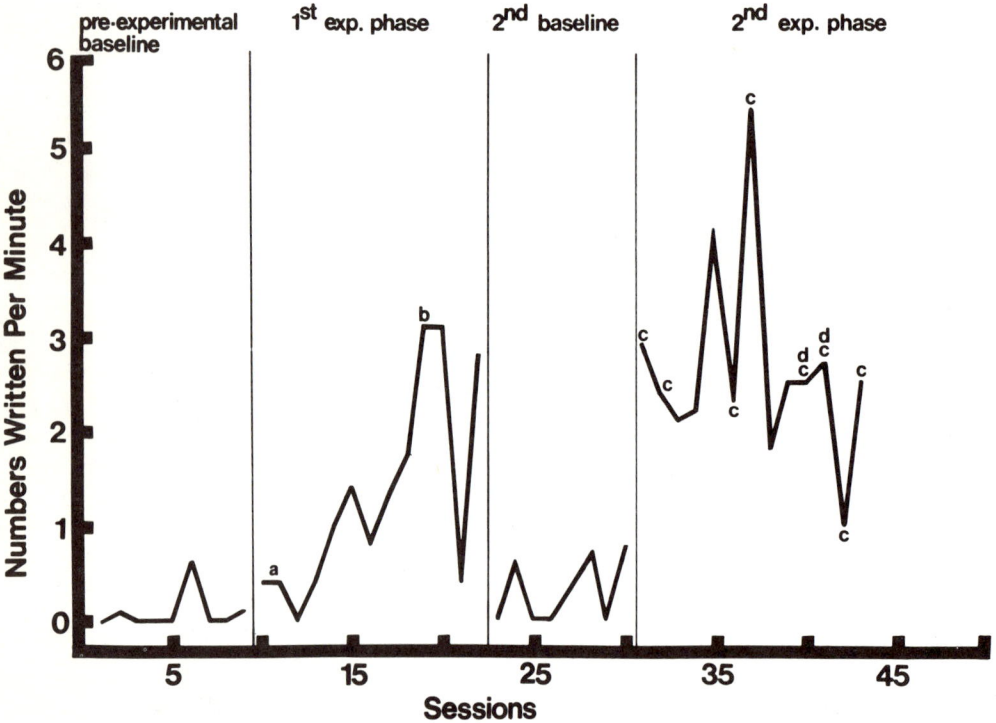

Figure 4. *The effect of experimental contingencies on academic productivity in arithmetic. Letters beside data points indicate drug and dosage changes.*

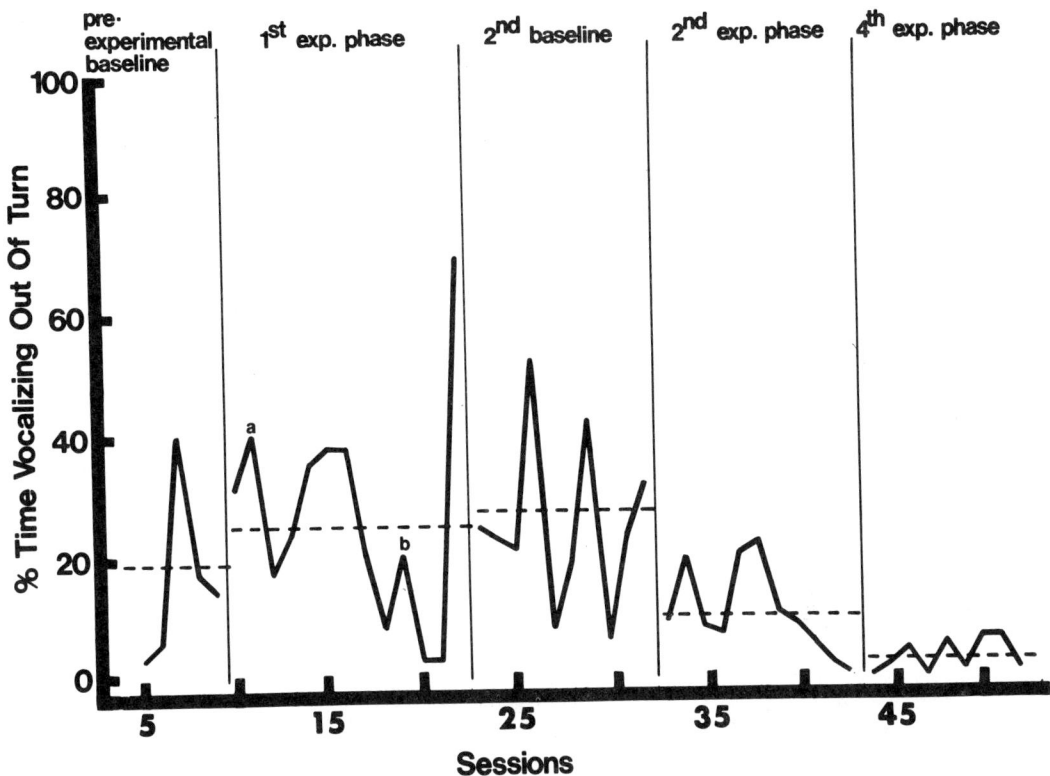

Figure 5. *The effect of afternoon contingencies (in experimental phases I and II) and adjustment of morning reading assignments (experimental phase IV) on talking out of turn during the individual seat work in the morning. Recording of these morning data was begun on day 5 of the experiment. A dashed line indicates the mean of each phase. Letters indicate drug and dosage changes in effect during the morning.*

the school faculty served as an additional source of evidence regarding Ronnie's overall progress. Favorable reports regarding Ronnie's manners, motivation, and general school deportment were received from his teacher, his principal, and the school social worker.

DISCUSSION

This study demonstrates the possibility of treating the behavior problems displayed by the emotionally disturbed child within a regular public-school classroom by employing a special therapist for the child. Due to the end of the school term, this study was terminated before control of his behavior had been transferred to the child's teacher. This

probably would have been a fairly simple behavioral engineering problem if Ronnie's academic skills were first raised to the level of other children in the class.

Treatment of the emotionally disturbed child within the environs of the regular public school traditionally has been conducted outside the classroom by a school social worker, counselor, or other such specialist. Such an approach is limited by the fact that the behaviors of which the maladjustment consists may not occur or even be possible except in a classroom or at least a peer-group setting. In addition, if the specialist succeeds in producing more adjustive behaviors, they may not generalize to situations outside the specialist's office. The procedures described in the present study may suggest alternative

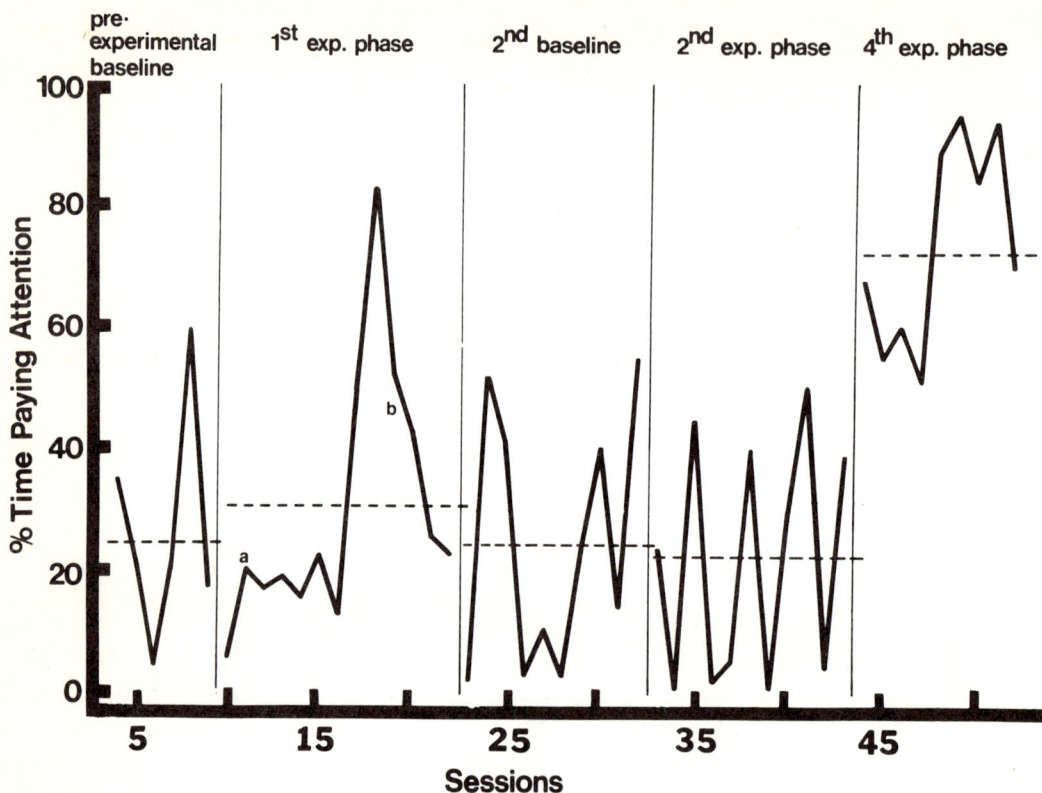

Figure 6. *The effect of afternoon contingencies (in experimental phase I and II) and adjustment of morning reading assignments (experimental phase IV) on talking out of turn during the individual seat work in the morning. Recording of these morning data was begun on day 4 of the experiment. A dashed line indicates the mean of each phase. Letters indicate drug and dosage changes in effect during the morning.*

therapeutic techniques for specialists dealing with maladjusted schoolchildren.

The fact that there appeared to be little or no generalization of afternoon effects to the morning is interesting and illustrates the fact that generalization from one setting (such as a specialist's office) to another, or even from one time of day to another, cannot be assumed. Instead, generalization must be programmed for, as is illustrated by the results of experimental phase IV. Some generalization or response induction may have occurred for which no objective data are available, because various faculty members reported improvements in behaviors for which no new consequences had been programmed.

It is interesting that the drug changes showed little or no effect on the behaviors

recorded. Only a more systematic manipulation of the drugs over longer periods of time and under various stimulus conditions would reveal the actual effectiveness of these drugs for this child and the interaction between the contingencies and the drugs.

This experiment was concluded at the end of the school year. It appeared that due to the time limitation, there had not yet been adequate programming to assure Ronnie's success in a regular classroom without special treatment procedures. His academic skills, though markedly improved, were still far below those of his peers. Also, behavioral improvements had not been generalized to the whole school day. Nevertheless, when Ronnie began third grade the next year in a regular classroom, he was a much better adjusted child than he had been in his three years in first and second grades. In arithmetic, the only area in which his academic skills had been brought up to grade level during the experiment, he sat quietly and completed any part of his assignment that did not require reading. In other skill areas, he often attempted to do his work, even though it was much too difficult for him. He showed an interest in being involved in class activities, whereas he formerly had not. However, as the year progressed, Ronnie's adjustment in

third grade gradually deteriorated, perhaps because his academic deficiencies prevented him from obtaining the social reinforcement that most children received for the myriad of appropriate behaviors that terminate in correct academic responses. He subsequently was admitted to a special education classroom for emotionally disturbed children, where work was adjusted to his level of proficiency and consistent reinforcement was programmed for both academic and nonacademic behavior. His adjustment in this setting was very good.

Good behavior game: Effects of individual contingencies for group consequences on disruptive behavior in a classroom

HARRIET H. BARRISH, MURIEL SAUNDERS, AND MONTROSE M. WOLF

Researchers have recently begun to assess the effectiveness of a variety of behavioral procedures for management of disruptive classroom behavior. Some investigators have arranged token reinforcement contingencies for appropriate classroom behavior (Birnbrauer, Wolf, Kidder, and Tague, 1965; O'Leary and Becker, 1967; Wolf, Giles, and Hall, 1968). However, these token reinforcers often have been dependent upon back-up reinforcers that were unnatural in the regular classroom, such as candy and money. On the other hand, several investigators have utilized a reinforcer intrinsic to every classroom, i.e., teacher attention (Zimmerman and Zimmerman, 1962; Hall and Broden, 1967; Becker, Madsen, Arnold, and Thomas, 1967; Hall, Lund, and Jackson, 1968; Thomas, Becker, and Armstrong, 1968; Madsen, Becker, and Thomas, 1968). Even so, at least one group of investigators (Hall et al., 1968) encountered a teacher who apparently did not have sufficient social reinforcers in her repertoire to apply social reinforcement procedures successfully. The present study investigated the effects of a classroom behavior management technique based on reinforcers natural to the classroom, other than teacher attention. The technique was designed to reduce disruptive

classroom behavior through a game involving competition for privileges available in almost every classroom. The students were divided into 2 teams and disruptive behavior by any member of a team resulted in possible loss of privileges for every member of his team.

METHOD

Subjects and Setting

The study was conducted in a fourth-grade classroom of 24 students. Seven of the students had been referred several times by the

From *Journal of Applied Behavior Analysis,* Summer 1969, *2*(2), 119-124. Copyright © 1969 by the Society for the Experimental Analysis of Behavior, Inc. Reprinted by permission of the authors and the *Journal of Applied Behavior Analysis.*

This study is based upon a thesis submitted by the senior author to the Department of Human Development in partial fulfillment of the requirements for the Master of Arts degree. The research was supported by a Public Health Service Fellowship IFI MH-36, 964-01 from the National Institute of Mental Health and by a grant (HD 03144) from the National Institute of Child Health and Human Development to the Bureau of Child Research and the Department of Human Development, University of Kansas.

teacher to the school principal for such problems as out-of-seat behavior, indiscriminate noise and talking, uncooperativeness, and general classroom disruption. Further, the school principal reported that a general behavior management problem existed in the classroom. According to the teacher, she frequently had informed the class of the rules of good classroom behavior.

Definition of the Behavior

One and sometimes 2 observers visited the classroom for approximately 1 hour each Monday, Wednesday, and Friday. Observation took place during the last half of the reading period and the first half of the math period. During both of these periods, similar types of activities such as individual assignments, oral lessons and discussion, chalkboard work, and short quizzes were assigned to the students; only the subject matter varied —i.e., reading or math. Recording was discontinued during the brief transition from the reading to the math period.

Observers sat at the side of the classroom and avoided eye contact and interactions both before and during recording. Observers used recording sheets similar to those used in other studies (Hall et al., 1968). These were divided into rows of squares for each behavior. Each square represented an interval of 1 minute. If any child in the classroom emitted the behavior, a check was made in the row assigned to the behavior, in the square representing that particular interval of time. Teacher attention to inappropriate behavior was marked in the corresponding square by an asterisk.

Inter-observer agreement was analyzed by having a second observer periodically (at least once during each of the experimental conditions) make a simultaneous but independent observation record. Agreement was measured by comparing the 2 records for agreement, interval by interval. The percentage of agreement between the 2 records was calculated (number of agreements × 100 ÷ the total number of intervals). In addition, by indicating teacher attention to inappropriate behavior by an asterisk, intervals could

be compared asterisk against check in the appropriate square to yield a percentage of agreement between the observer and the teacher during the phases that the game was in effect.

While the behavioral definitions were constructed by the experimenter, they were formulated with the help of the principal and the classroom teacher on the basis of what they considered to be the disruptive classroom behaviors.

Out-of-seat behavior was defined as leaving the seat and/or seated position during a lesson or scooting the desk without permission. Exceptions to the definition, and instances not recorded, included out-of-seat behavior that occurred when no more than 4 pupils signed out on the chalkboard to leave for the restroom, when pupils went one at a time to the teacher's desk during independent study assignment, and when pupils were merely changing orientation in their seat. Also, when a child left his seat to approach the teacher's desk, but then appeared to notice that someone else was already there or on his way and consequently quickly returned to his seat, the behavior was not counted. Permission was defined throughout the study as raising one's hand, being recognized by the teacher, and receiving consent from her to engage in a behavior.

Talking-out behavior was defined as talking or whispering without permission. It included, for example, talking while raising one's hand, talking to classmates, talking to the teacher, calling the teacher's name, blurting out answers, or making vocal noises such as animal-like sounds, howls, cat calls, etc., all without permission.

Introduction of the Game

Immediately after the reading period and before the math period in which the system was initially used, a presentation closely following the points listed below was made by the teacher to her class. She explained that: (a) what they were about to do was a game that they would play every day during math period only; (b) the class would be divided into two teams; (she then divided the class by rows and seats of the center row); (c) when a team or teams won the game, the team(s) would receive certain privileges; (d) there were certain rules, however, that the teams had to follow to win. These rules were based on the behavior categories as previously defined. (1) No one was to be out of his seat without permission (except that 4 pupils were allowed to leave their seats without permission in order to sign out on the chalkboard to leave for the restroom). Permission could be obtained only by raising the hand and being called on by the teacher. (2) No one was to sit on top of his desk or on any of his neighbors' desks. (3) No one was to get out of his seat to move his desk or scoot his desk. (4) No one was to get out of his seat to talk to a neighbor. This also meant there was to be no leaning forward out of a seat to whisper. (5) No one was to get out of his seat to go to the chalkboard (except to sign out for the restroom), pencil sharpener, waste basket, drinking fountain, sink, or to the teacher without permission. (6) When the teacher was seated at her desk during study time, students could come to her desk one at a time if they had a question. (7) No one was to talk without permission. Permission could be obtained again only by raising the hand and being called on by the teacher. (8) No one was to talk while raising his hand. (9) No one was to talk or whisper to his neighbors. (10) No one was to call out the teacher's name unless he had permission to answer. (11) No one was to make vocal noises. (e) Whenever she saw anyone on a team breaking one of these rules, that team would get a mark on the chalkboard. (f) If a team had the fewest marks, or if neither team received more than 5 marks, the team(s) would get to wear victory tags, put a star by each of its members' names on the winner's chart, line up first for lunch if 1 team won or early if both teams won, and take part at the end of the day in a 30-minute free time during which the team(s) would have special projects. (g) The team that lost would not get these privileges, would continue working on an assignment during the last half-hour of the day, and members would have to stay after school as usual if they did not do their work during the last half-hour period. (h) If a team or teams had not received more than 20 marks in a week, it would get the extra weekly privilege of going to recess 4 minutes early.

Whenever the experimental conditions were changed, point "a" was again presented to the class by the teacher with a new explanation about when the game would be played. All the above points were presented before the initial use of the program and then once again after a week-long period of achievement testing during which time the game had not been in effect. The victory tags were commercially prepared circular convention tags. Each tag was of the same color and was threaded with a uniform length of wool yarn of a contrasting color. Tags were worn around the neck. They allowed the teacher to easily identify the winners during the rest of the day. The star chart consisted of a 22-inch by 28-inch piece of white poster board labeled "Winners." The chart was divided into 2 portions designated "Team One" and "Team Two" and ruled off with team members (names) by dates (month and day). The stars were commercially manufactured with gummed backs. The special projects consisted of educational activities in the areas of science or arts which were done as a team or individually.

During the first period in which the game was applied, the teacher stipulated that the team with the fewest marks, or 10 or less, would win. The criterion for the second observed session, and for all other sessions except the last one, was set at 5 marks or fewer. The last session was also the last full day of school. The teacher expected the children to be very excited, and she wanted to be sure that both teams would win, since she had treats planned for the special project period. For this session the criterion was the fewest marks, or 8 or less.

Experimental Phases

The experimental design included both reversal and multiple baseline phases. The data were recorded separately during the reading and math periods providing the 2 baselines. The study was divided into 4 corresponding phases. A session in 1 class period corresponded to a session in the other class period in that they were recorded consecutively and on the same day.

Math-baseline, reading-baseline. For 10 sessions, the normal (baseline) rates of out-of-seat and talking-out behaviors of the class were recorded during the math and reading periods. The teacher carried out her classroom activities in her usual manner.

Math-game₁, reading-baseline. During the second phase, the game was introduced during math but not during reading.

Math-reversal, reading-game. In the third phase, the game was introduced during reading and withdrawn during math.

Math-game₂, reading-game. Lastly, the game was reintroduced in math period and remained in effect during reading period. Both periods were treated as one extended period, thus using the same initial criteria of the least number of marks, or 5 or fewer marks.

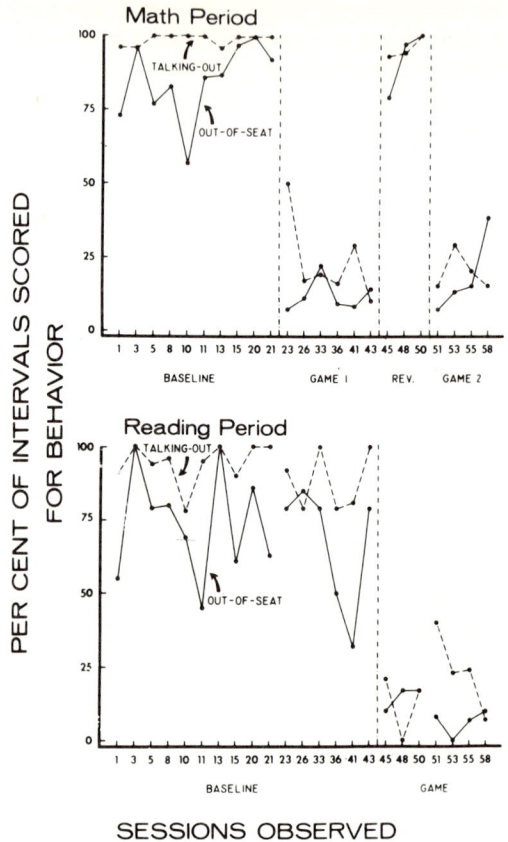

Figure 1. *Percent of 1-minute intervals scored by an observer as containing talking-out and out-of-seat behaviors occurring in a classroom of 24 fourth-grade school children during math and reading periods. In the baseline conditions the teacher attempted to manage the disruptive classroom behavior in her usual manner. During the game conditions out-of-seat and talking-out responses by a student resulted in a possible loss of privileges for the student and his team.*

RESULTS

Figure 1 shows the extent to which out-of-seat and talking-out behaviors were influenced by the game. These data indicate that the game had a reliable effect, since out-of-seat and talking-out behaviors changed maximally only when the game was applied. In the math and reading baselines, the median interval scored for talking-out was approximately 96 percent and for out-of-seat it was approximately 82 percent.

When the game was applied during math period, there was a sharp decline in the scored intervals to medians of approximately 19 percent and 9 percent respectively. Meanwhile, during reading period where the game was not applied, talking-out behavior remained essentially at baseline levels, and out-of-seat behavior declined somewhat.

During the third phase, the game was withdrawn during math period, and the baseline rates of the behaviors recovered; in the

same phase during the reading period, the game was introduced for the first time, and a decline in the percent of scored intervals for both behaviors resulted. Finally in the fourth phase, the game was applied during math and reading periods simultaneously. The disruptive behaviors again declined during math and continued low in reading.

Both teams almost always won the game.

In the 17 class periods that observations were made, both teams won on all but 3 occasions, or 82 percent of the time.

The reliability of the measurement procedures was analyzed during the reading and math periods on 6 occasions. Three different reliability observers were used. Agreement for out-of-seat behavior ranged from 74 percent to 98 percent and averaged 91 percent. Agreement for talking-out behavior ranged from 75 percent to 98 percent and averaged 86 percent.

Agreement between the observer and the teacher was measured during each class period that the game was played. Agreement about the occurrence of out-of-seat behavior ranged from 61 percent to 100 percent and averaged 92 percent. Agreement about the occurrence of talking-out behavior ranged from 71 percent to 100 percent and averaged 85 percent. Thus, the levels of agreement between the observer and the teacher, and the observer and the reliability observers, were approximately the same.

DISCUSSION

The game significantly and reliably modified the disruptive out-of-seat and talking-out behavior of the students. The experimental design, involving elements of both multiple baseline and reversal strategies, demonstrated that the effect could be replicated across subject-matter periods and that the game had a continuing role in maintaining the reduced level of disruptive behavior. On the other hand, no analysis was carried out to determine the roles of the various components of the game. An analysis of exactly what components contributed to the effectiveness of the procedure is left to future research.

As in the present study, the subject-matter periods of the typical school day lend themselves perfectly to a multiple-baseline experimental design. Simultaneous baselines of the behavior of 1 student or of an entire class can be obtained simultaneously in 2 or more subject-matter periods. The modification technique then can be introduced successively into each of the periods. If in each instance there is a change in behavior (and the behavior during the remaining baseline periods remains essentially unchanged), the investigator will have achieved a believable demonstration of the effectiveness of his technique. And he will have done so without having depended upon or required a reversal of the behavior (Baer, Wolf, and Risley, 1968).

Some problems arose which should be noted. The preparation of the special projects required the time and ingenuity of the teacher. This sometimes placed an extra burden on her, since she also had to prepare regular lessons. Another problem that perhaps was not as serious concerned teacher observation of behaviors. No signaling system was used. The teacher had to become alert to out-of-seat and talking-out behaviors in addition to continuing to conduct regular classroom activities. Spotting the target behaviors did not appear to be difficult for the teacher except when she faced the chalkboard or talked with individual students.

The greatest problem with the game involved 2 students who, before the study began, had been referred to the principal on a number of occasions for disruptive behavior. Both were on the same team and consistently gained a number of marks for their team. Usually they engaged in talking-out behavior. In most instances only 1 of the students was involved. In 1 session, 1 of these students emphatically announced that he was no longer going to play the game. Both the other children and the teacher expressed the opinion that it was not fair to penalize further an entire team because 1 member would not control himself. The teacher, therefore, dropped the student from the game, and the marks that normally would have been imposed on the entire team were imposed just on him. During the free time, he also refused to work so he was kept after school. The same individual-consequence procedure was used for 1 or both students on 6 occasions. Each time, the marks that they had accumulated were subtracted from the team score. It is possible that the numerous peer comments that appeared to be directed toward these students may have served as social reinforcement for their disruptive behavior. It is important to note, however, that when the students were dropped from their team the observer continued to record their behavior as before.

Some reactions to the program were gathered from the children, teacher, and school officials. The program apparently was popular with students and school officials. Every professional involved in the study who directly observed the classroom situation during the game stated that, in general, the students seemed to enjoy playing the game. The teacher stated that some students went so far as to request that the game be played every period. After the last session in which the game was played, the teacher requested that each child briefly write whether he or she liked or disliked the game and why. Of the 21 comments turned in, 14 indicated that they liked the game and 7 indicated that they did not. Of those who indicated that they liked the game, some made comments such as: "I like the game because I can read better when it is quiet," "I liked it cause it was fun," "You give us free time," "I like the morning game because it helps keep people quiet so we can work," and, "I like the team game because we win all the time." Of those who indicated that they disliked the

game, some made comments such as: "No, I hate being quiet," "I didn't like it because you didn't make good rules," "Because when your team loses the team that won will make fun of your team," and "It's not fair because we have the guys that talk a lot." The teacher stated that she was pleased with the method because "it was an easy program to install since it did not change any of the rules or daily activities in the classroom." All of the back-up reinforcers, with the possible exception of the victory tags, naturally occurred in the classroom setting. Only the structure of the free-time period at the end of the day changed, but it, of course, involved projects of an educational nature.

While gamelike techniques are certainly not new to the classroom (Russell and Karp, 1938), an experimental analysis of their effects on behavior is unique. It may follow that an understanding of the mechanisms of the game, e.g., peer competition, group consequences *vs.* individual consequences, etc., together with research designed to enhance the significance of winning, by pairing winning with privileges, could lead to a set of effective and practical techniques of classroom behavior management based on games.

The functions of time-out for changing the aggressive behaviors of a preschool child: A multiple-baseline analysis

JUDITH M. LE BLANC, KAREN HANEY BUSBY, AND CAROLYN L. THOMSON

Punishment appears sometimes to permanently eliminate behaviors. This phenomenon can pose problems when using an ABA (reversal) design. For example, in the setting of the present study, the University of Kansas Child Development Preschool Laboratory, time-out has been used on several occasions to eliminate aggressive behavior; subsequent removal of the time-out contingencies did not result in a return of the behavior to its original baseline level. Thus, the role of time-out in decreasing aggression was not clearly demonstrated. The multiple-baseline experimental design can be effective in analyzing the

effectiveness of punishment techniques which may produce these "irreversible" changes in behavior. Undesirable behaviors such as high-rate aggression frequently consist of many behavioral components which may serve as the independent response classes necessary for

Reprinted by permission of the authors.

Portions of this paper were presented at the annual meeting of the American Psychological Association, Washington, D.C., September 1971. This research was in part supported by NICHHD Grant HD00247 to the Bureau of Child Research at the University of Kansas and by NIMH Training Grant MH11739 and NICHHD Grant HD02528 to the Department of Human Development, the University of Kansas.

a multiple-baseline design. The fact that teachers and others who work with children resist reversing undesirable behaviors is one more reason for using a multiple-baseline design. The purpose of the present study was to analyze the effectiveness of time-out as a punishment technique for reducing undesirable behavior and to examine the permanence of behavioral change effected by the application of this technique.

METHOD

Setting and Subject

The setting was a preschool classroom in the Department of Human Development Preschool Laboratory at the University of Kansas. The class consisted of 16 children, a supervising teacher, and 2 student teachers. The class was in session for 3 hours each morning. Data were recorded during a 70-minute period of the preschool day which was allotted to indoor and outdoor free play. During this time the children were allowed to participate in the activity of their choice.

The subject was a 4-year-old male. Upon entering preschool, he yelled and screamed at his peers, called them names, hit them, took objects from them, and threw materials. Once tranquilizers were prescribed to control his behavior but were discontinued prior to the onset of the study.

Behavioral Definitions and Recording

Three categories of aggressive behavior were manipulated in this experiment: 1) physical attacks on children (attacks), 2) name-calling (name-calling), and 3) making demands of children (demands). Attacks included shoving, hitting, kicking, or choking peers or throwing them to the ground. Name-calling included any derogatory name addressed to either adults or children, and demands consisted of verbal statements such as, "Give me that!" or "Shut up!" and rough removal of materials from other children. A

subcategory of demands (demands 2) was incorporated into the study on the twentieth day. Not all the subject's demands were inappropriate, e.g., demands emitted in the defense of the subject's property. Further it seemed desirable to allow the subject to contact peer contingencies resulting in response to his demands. Therefore, demands 2 (which ultimately were manipulated) consisted of those socially inappropriate demands which were initiated by the subject or those which resulted in another child crying, not responding to the subject, or pulling away from him. The total category of demands (i.e., both the appropriate and inappropriate demands) was then referred to as demands 1.

The dependent variables of the 3 aggressive behaviors and the independent variables of time-out and teacher attention to nonaggressive behavior were recorded in 10-second intervals by a trained observer using a stopwatch and clipboard. Although the procedures were implemented throughout the entire preschool day, data were formally recorded for only the 70-minute free-play time.

General Procedures

Two types of time-out were used to decrease the aggressive behaviors. One consisted of removing the child from the play area subsequent to an aggression and placing him on a chair with instructions to remain until told he could return to play. This was referred to as chair time-out. If he refused to sit in the chair or left it before the end of 1 minute, when permission was granted, he was placed in a small, empty, but lighted room, and the door was closed. This was referred to as room time-out. He remained in the room for a period of 3 minutes after the door was closed or 3 minutes from the end of his last tantrum or audible cry.

The teachers attempted to keep their attention to nonaggressive behavior constant across conditions. Thus, the effects of time-out were not confounded by increased and/ or decreased teacher attention to nonaggressive behaviors which were incompatible with aggressive behaviors.

INAPPROPRIATE BEHAVIORS

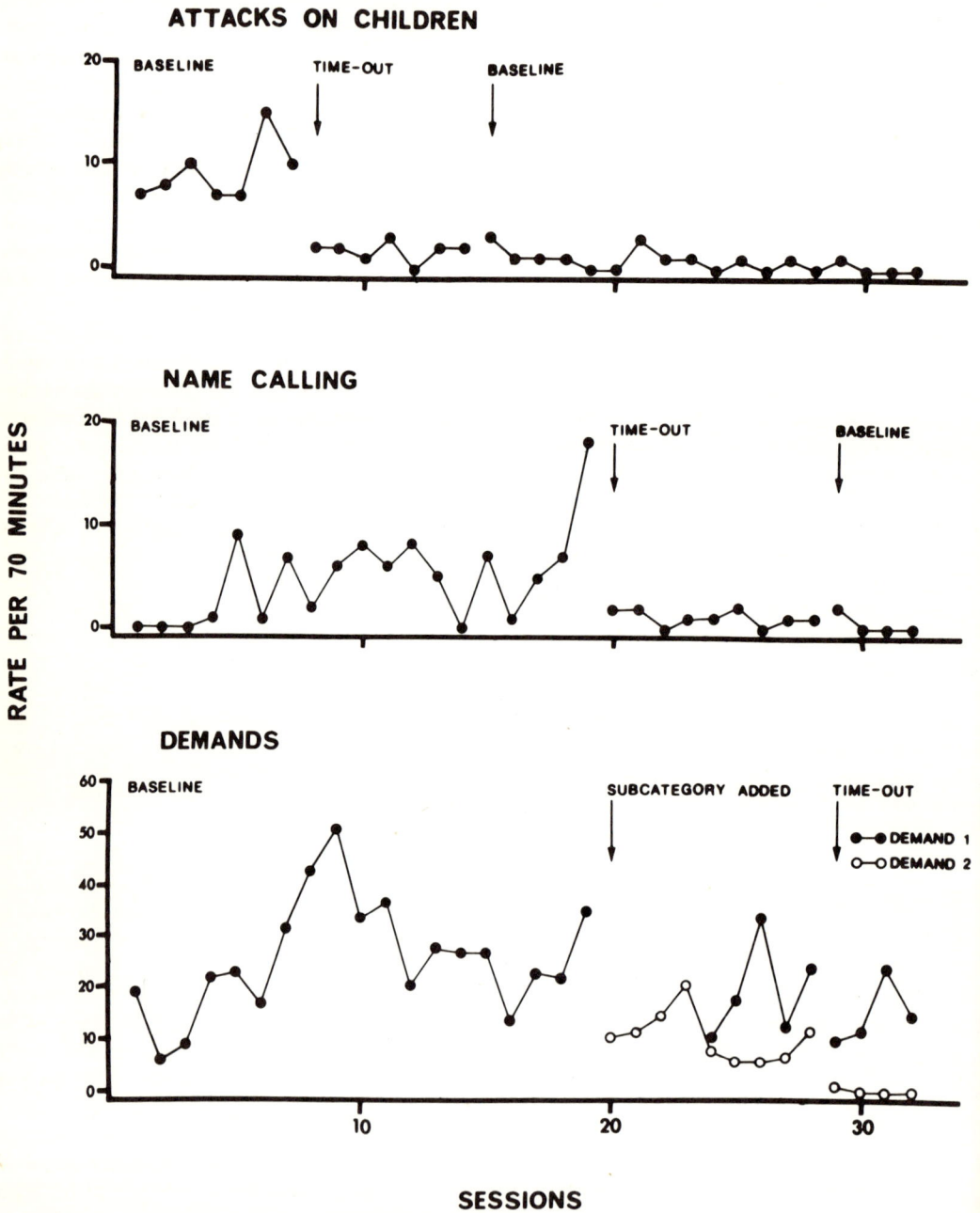

Figure 1. *Occurrence rate per 70 minutes for the 3 categories of aggressive behavior: attacks, name-calling, and demands. The data represent the occurrences of each of the behaviors during the 70-minute observation period.*

Design

Following a baseline period, during which the teachers treated the subject's aggressive behavior by admonishing him or protecting his peers, time-out was implemented for attacks on peers but not for name-calling or demands. Time-out was then removed for attacks throughout the remainder of the study. After the return to baseline for attacks, time-out was implemented for name-calling only. Demands and attacks, if they occurred, did not result in time-out. The behavioral subcategory, demands 2, was added during this condition. On days 20 through 23, the observer did not record the original behaviors deleted from the total category of demands. Thus, on those days there were no data for demands 1. The final condition consisted of the application of time-out for demands 2. Name-calling and attacks, if they occurred, did not result in contingent time-out during this final condition.

Therefore, the sequence of implementing and removing contingent time-out for both attacks and name-calling provided a programmed ABA design within a multiple baseline. That is, there was a baseline, manipulation of contingent time-out, and a programmed return to baseline conditions for both of these 2 behaviors. There was no programmed reversal (or planned removal of time-out) of the manipulation for demands 2. However, functionally a reversal occurred the last 2 days of the study because demands 2 behaviors did not occur, and thus no time-out was required.

Removing contingencies once implemented in a multiple-baseline design is not a usual practice. However, for purposes of determining how permanent the effects of time-out might be, systematic reversals were programmed for the behaviors in this study.

TIME OUTS

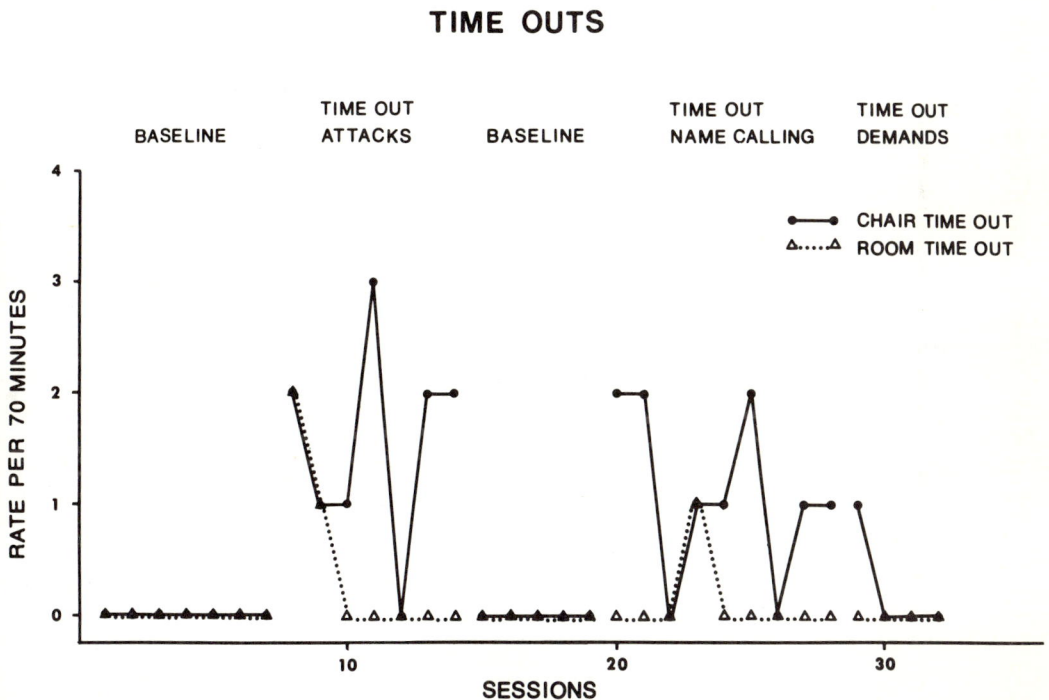

Figure 2. *Occurrence rate per 70 minutes of room time-out and chair time-out. The data represent the occurrences of time-out during the 70-minute observation period.*

The 3 graphs in Figure 1 indicate the rate of aggressive behaviors in each of the 3 categories per each 70-minute period. When chair and room time-out were contingently applied to attacks, this behavior immediately decreased to near zero while name-calling and demands 1, which were not being manipulated, remained at their previous levels. When the time-out contingency was removed for attacks on the fifteenth day of the study (i.e., baseline conditions were again in effect for all behaviors), attacks did not increase to their original baseline level. Instead attacks remained at a near-zero level throughout the remainder of the study even though time-out was never again contingently applied. During the 5-day return to baseline conditions for attacks, demands 1, and name-calling, which had no previous contact with contingent time-out, remained the same or increased slightly.

When time-out was contingently applied to name-calling, it was immediately reduced to a near-zero level. During this condition, attacks remained low, and behavioral occurrences in the new subcategory of demands (demands 2) was high. When time-out was contingently applied to demands 2 and removed from name-calling, the behaviors in demands 2 immediately decreased, and attacks and name-calling continued to remain at near-zero levels.

The total number of chair and room time-outs which occurred each day of the experiment are presented in Figure 2. During the manipulation of attacks, room time-out was paired with chair time-out 3 times; twice the first day and once the second day. During the manipulation of name-calling, only 1 pairing of room with chair time-out occurred.

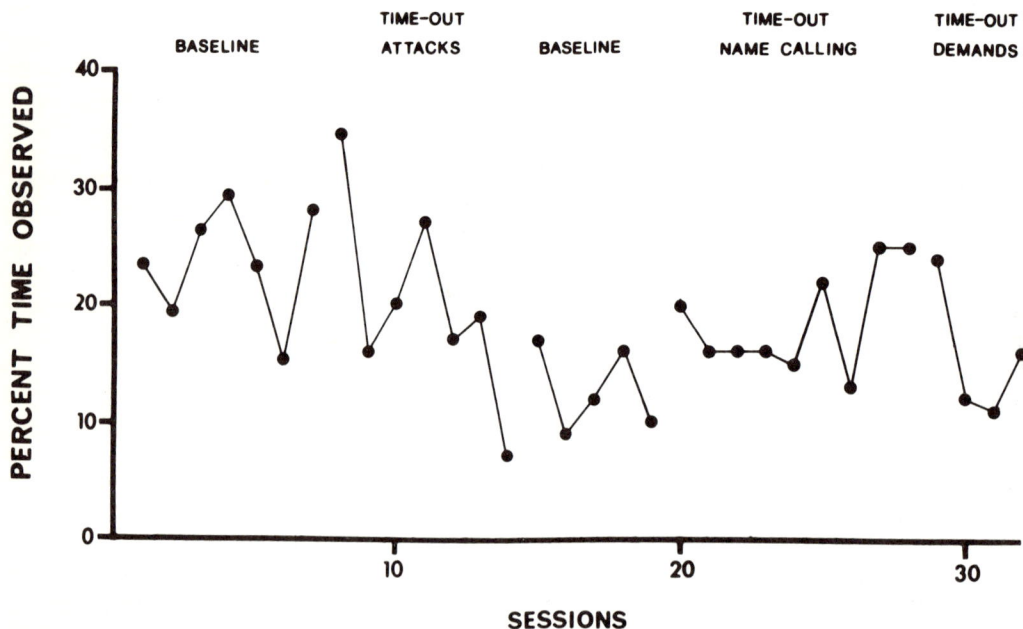

Figure 3. The percentage of time teachers attended to the student's appropriate behavior was calculated by dividing the number of intervals of teacher attention contingent upon appropriate behavior by the number of 10-second intervals in the 70-minute observation period.

During the last manipulation (time-out for demands 2), no pairing of room time-out with chair time-out occurred. In addition, each time the time-out procedures were implemented to decrease another behavior, fewer chair time-outs were required to effect this change. Time-outs which occurred at times other than when data were recorded also decreased across conditions.

Figure 3 shows that teacher attention to nonaggressive behavior remained somewhat constant across all experimental conditions. When time-out for attacks was implemented, teacher attention to nonaggressive behaviors increased slightly at first but decreased across sessions. However, increased attention for nonaggression did not occur with the implementation of time-out for name-calling or demands 2.

DISCUSSION

Time-out was an effective procedure for reducing 3 categories of this subject's aggressive behavior. Although reversals were programmed for 2 of the 3 behaviors, the rate of these behaviors remained low throughout the remainder of the experiment. The third manipulated behavior was not programmed for a return to baseline conditions, but the last 3 days of the study were functionally such a return. During the last 3 days, none of the previously manipulated behaviors occurred, thus requiring no implementation of either room or chair time-out.

The effectiveness of both room and class time-out apparently increased across time; more room and chair time-outs were required for the first manipulated behavior (attacks) and fewer for each of the succeeding behaviors. Also, no pairing of chair with room time-out was required to decrease the third manipulated behavior. Perhaps the subject began discriminating the inevitability of room time-out as a consequence of leaving his chair. Thus, once chair time-out was imposed, he could stay there quietly, choosing to reinforce himself for doing so by being allowed to return to his play rather than to further punish himself by not sitting quietly and thus going to the time-out room.

The multiple baseline with programmed reversals used in this study provided a method for examining the permanence of behavioral change within the environment in which change occurred. This seeming permanence was best demonstrated in the last 3 days of the study when none of the manipulated behaviors occurred.

The design aspects involved in the manipulation of demands 2 posed some interesting considerations. Because demands 2 was first recorded during the manipulation of name-calling, its baseline was not separately recorded and graphed from the outset of the study. Thus, the baseline for demands 2 was not as extensive as is typical in multiple-baseline designs. Nevertheless the effectiveness of time-out in reducing aggression remains clear. The manipulation of demands 2 provided a second replication demonstrating the effectiveness of the time-out procedures for reducing this child's aggressive behavior, and a sufficient baseline of this behavior was obtained during the manipulation of name-calling. The behaviors in the subcategory, demands 2, were also shown to be in a separate response class from the total demands category (demands 1) by the fact that only demands 2 was reduced to a near-zero level when time-out was implemented while demands 1 remained at a higher level.

Perhaps the seeming permanence of change once a behavior was manipulated was due to avoidance. The adults in the child's environment who were imposing time-out as well as the actual procedures involved in the time-out, perhaps became discriminative stimuli that signaled the child not to engage in certain behaviors. For example, when time-out was implemented for demands 2, perhaps the subject was reminded that he should not engage in any of the 2 previously manipulated behaviors. However, this rationale for the permanence of behavioral change is weakened somewhat by the fact that the programmed return to baseline subsequent to the manipulation of time-out for attacks (the first manipulated behavior) resulted in no occurrences of attacks even though time-out was not contingently applied to any behaviors. Further, no time-outs occurred during the last three days. At least for a short period of time, time-outs were not needed to "remind" the subject not to engage in the previously manipulated behaviors.

Perhaps a more reasonable explanation for the seeming permanence of behavioral change is that other events within the child's environment, such as attention from peers, were reinforcing the subject's nonaggressive behavior. If so, time-out merely became a vehicle through which the child came into contact with these other contingencies. There were no data to support this assumption, but the teachers did report that the other children were more willing to play with the subject subsequent to the decreases in his aggressive behaviors.

In summary, time-out was demonstrated to be an effective technique for reducing this subject's aggressive behaviors. Programmed returns to baseline demonstrated the seeming permanence of this behavioral reduction since the behaviors did not reverse. Further, fewer applications of both room and chair time-out were necessary to effectively reduce each target behavior with succeeding manipulations in the multiple baseline.

16

ASSESSMENT, ACCOUNTABILITY, AND PERFORMANCE CONTRACTING

Perhaps the first law of behavior modification states that "behavior is controlled by its consequences." Relatively few consequences for poor performance accrue to public schools as institutions or to the individuals that constitute the schools. The schools have a captive audience; most parents are either financially unable or unwilling to remove their children from public schools and place them in private schools, and often good private schools are not readily available. In most districts, children are not allowed to transfer to other public schools. In addition, many teachers are tenured, and increases in pay result from seniority and taking university courses, rather than output in the classroom. Even results of standardized tests, in the past, have not been available to the public.

Proposals for accountability in the public schools have stemmed from this lack of consequences, but unfortunately, many proposals for accountability have a punitive or authoritarian air that has alarmed school personnel. Accountability proposals have implied that educators have the behaviors necessary to improve their performance; all they lack is incentives. However, many teachers may not have the behaviors necessary to perform well. They may have received inadequate training, or many face a difficult situation for which effective educational techniques have not been developed. Applying consequences to an organism that lacks prerequisite behaviors does no good. If teachers truly do not "know" how to do any better, threatening them with postponed raises or professional humiliation will only create turmoil.

Besides the negative feelings of teachers, accountability faces another problem. Basically it is the problem of defining the behaviors for which educational systems will be held accountable; thus educators interested in accountability must become embroiled in the area of assessment, or evaluation. The first paper included in this section, by Moxley, describes two approaches to evaluation. The first, "norm-referenced" evaluation, includes standardized testing, traditional classroom examinations, and grading on a curve. When norm-referenced evaluation is used in accountability programs, progress is usually measured by improvements in scores on standardized tests. The second type of evaluation discussed by Moxley is "criterion-referenced." In criterion-referenced evaluation, goals are set—perhaps in the form of behavioral objectives—which every student is expected to achieve. An accountability program would be judged successful insofar as students met the criteria. Moxley discusses the advantages of criterion-referenced evaluation. If accountability is to become a reality, a form of criterion-referenced evaluation must be developed that will have the advantages of availability and standardization, now peculiar to norm-referenced evaluation.

The second paper in this section, by Offenberg, gives an example of one constructive direction accountability can take. Offenberg describes the use of accountability in the development of a program; however, constructive account-ability could also be used to revise or maintain existing programs. First, objec-tives of various levels of generality were set, and then teachers observed the children directly and recorded their meeting the objectives. On the basis of these data, revisions were made in the objectives and the curriculum. In this program accountability data were used, not simply to mete out incentives but to improve instruction. Similarly, accountability data could be used to focus on areas in which teachers need further training. Incentives also could be used; however, incentives should be used in addition to programs that will enable personnel to obtain the incentives offered.

Performance contracting has been a fashionable means of seeking account-ability. In performance contracting, a group of educators, usually a private corporation, contracts with a school system to achieve specific educational goals in return for specific monetary payment. Recently, the Office of Economic Opportunity conducted an extensive study of performance contracting and obtained negative results: Performance contractors were no more effective than traditional school personnel in educating very low-achieving children. This re-search is described in the third selection in this section, by Page. Page concludes that the failure of performance contracts in the OEO study represents a general failure in the application of psychology to education. Whether or not this con-clusion is warranted, the results do show that the contingencies involved in performance contracting are not sufficient, in themselves, to guarantee im-provement in education.

A source of disorder in the schools and a way to reduce it: Two kinds of tests

ROY A. MOXLEY, JR.

Typically, when people feel attacked or disturbed, they look for a "who" to blame. The assumption is that disorder is generated by "disorderly" people. Such a concrete, specific, localized source of disorder presents a target that permits concrete, specific, localized responses—like a punch in the nose. The trick then lies simply in identifying the "who" to hit.

Now, this is not the only way to seek the source of a disorder. The source may also be sought for in a "what." What things, what situations, what conditions produce disorder? The difficulty here lies not just with identifying the source but with providing adequate responses. Man needs to do something to reduce the disorder. And it's a little more difficult to respond to a "what" which may be abstract, general, and not constrained to a localized name. The target of a response is selected for its visibility and what you can do to it, among other considerations, such as what it can do to you.

The "whats" can be made visible by making critical discriminations, the kind that prefers "flammable" to "inflammable" as a contrast to "noninflammable." For example, tests may be distinguished as being either *norm-referenced* (based upon relative rankings between individuals) or *criterion-referenced* (based upon mastery of a specified performance) by listing some of the critical discriminations between them.

One of these discriminations is that the virtually exclusive use of distribution rankings or norm-referenced measures of evaluation has been a source of disorder in learning, a disorder that can be reduced by using measures with an absolute or criterion reference. Put another way, disorder can be reduced if more "grades" are given that indicate complete or incomplete as opposed to A, B, C, D, or E.

Consider two ways of evaluating a student's achievement, two ways of measuring what he has learned. One way provides information on the relative ranking of individuals, how many problems one person can solve relative to how many problems other people can solve. How many solved more, how many solved less? The other way of testing provides information on the attainment of an absolute standard of performance, whether a person can satisfactorily solve a particular kind of arithmetic problem, write a particular kind of essay, drive a particular kind of car, produce $1.75 at the ticket window. Has he achieved that mastery? How many steps away is he? Although this distinction has been nicely formulated by Glaser (1963) in terms of norm-referenced measures (standardized tests) and criterion-referenced measures (mastery tests), there has been a conspicuous lack of published response to it, despite, or more likely because of, the far-ranging implications.

Note that we are considering two distinct instruments of measurement. Attention is directed to two distinct sources of disorder, two distinct sources of variability. Correspondingly, these instruments channel data through two distinct media of information, and the adjustments to these sources of information produce rather distinct viewpoints.

VARIABILITY

Variability in the Individual

The selection of a norm-referenced measure rather than a criterion-referenced measure is dependent upon the existence and maintenance of variability in a group of individuals. Any time a teacher distributes grades of A, B, C, D, and E, as they are now

From **Teacher and Technology Supplement**, March 1970. Reprinted by permission of the author and **Educational Technology Magazine**.

employed, he is basing that distribution upon the variability in the group of individual performances.

And those who are makers of standardized tests make an equivalent assumption. Furthermore, they are supported by the extensive and powerful technology of statistics.

"Statistical experimental design takes variability as its starting point for the evaluation of data. Variability may be measured, and even used as a datum, but it cannot be eliminated without destroying the experimental strategy ... The major alternative is that of treating variations as examples of orderliness, rather than of capriciousness, in nature. Such an approach, if successful, will severely circumscribe the doctrine of natural variability. In order to treat any given instance of variability as a manifestation of an orderly process, we must not only identify the source of the variability but also control it" (Sidman, 1960).

Variability in the Environment

The selection of a criterion-referenced measure looks for variability in the environment. There are a couple of arguments for looking in this direction. One, if you view the evolution of more complex living organisms as the development of increasingly powerful systems for reducing disorder, then man stands out as a more orderly system than any other in his environment. Hence, it is then reasonable to see man as a standard of orderliness to which the variability of his environment is compared. This is as opposed to assuming the environment, or teaching method, as the standard of orderliness for the measure of man's disorder, i.e., variability. A question of your opinion of man: How successfully do you think he was designed? Two, the more practical argument is that it's simply more useful to attend to the variability in the environment. You can do something to change the environment, to reduce the disorder in it. But what can you do about man's hereditary makeup? Perform brain surgery

on him? Give him pills? Pound some sense into him? It may be more useful to assume most humans could learn most responses in the human repertoire, given the appropriate environment and enough time.

There's a curious little twist to the above, a kind of chicken-and-the-egg question as to what follows from what. Does the use of a criterion-referenced instrument, in itself, impose an orderliness on man's behavior? Further, does the use of a norm-referenced instrument impose a disorderliness on man's behavior?

CONSTRUCTING TESTS

Norm-referenced Tests

You construct the test "so as to maximize the discriminations made among people having specified backgrounds and experience. Such tests include items which maximize the likelihood of observing individual differences in performance along various task dimensions; this maximizes the variability of the distribution of scores that are obtained. In practical test construction, the variability of test scores is increased by manipulating the difficulty levels and content of the test items" (Glaser, 1963).

Notice the nature of the manipulation process. You avoid and/or reject items that everyone gets correct, as well as items that everyone gets incorrect. You are transforming similarities among individuals into differences.

Criterion-referenced Tests

You construct the test "so as to maximize the discriminations made between *groups* treated differently and to minimize the differences between the individuals in any one group. Such a test will be sensitive to the differences produced by instructional conditions. For example, a test designed to demonstrate the effectiveness of instruction would be constructed so that it was generally difficult for those taking it before training and generally easy after training. The content of the test used to differentiate treatments should be maximally sensitive to the performance changes anticipated from the instructional treatments. In essence, the distinction between achievement tests used to maximize individual treatment or group differences is established during the selection of test items" (Glaser, 1963).

Notice that in this manipulation of the testing instrument, you are transforming the differences into similarities. You seek items everyone gets wrong before instructional treatment and correct afterwards. The premium is on those items that everyone answers correctly after treatment, those items that enable everyone to score 100 percent.

METHODS OF INSTRUCTION

Norm-referenced Tests

The focus of attention is not on the differences between methods of instruction. An improved method is likely to skew the normal bell-shape curve into a J-shape, unless you unskew it again by manipulating more differences into the test. You don't want people getting 100 percent.

Criterion-referenced Tests

The focus of attention is on the differences between methods of instruction, between treatments, between *groups*. It is "desirable to retain test items which were responded to correctly by all members of the posttraining group, but which were answered incorrectly by students who had not yet been trained. In a test constructed for the purpose of differentiating groups, items which indicated substantial variability within either the pretraining or posttraining group would be undesirable because of the likelihood that they would cloud the effects which might be attributable to the treatment variable" (Glaser, 1963).

Norm-referenced Tests

You are able to accept vague objectives, to increase variability, since a definite, concrete, highly visible target may be hit by too many students. This also avoids the disturbing feedback which a highly visible, public target may receive. You avoid criticism of your instruction. If someone says, "You have a poor method for doing this," you reply, "I wasn't trying to do this, I was trying to do that."

Criterion-referenced Tests

You need to specify the objectives, the behavior, the conditions, the criterion of acceptability. You seek to make a precise statement on the distinction between a state of non-mastery and a state of mastery. What exactly do you want mastered? It should be highly visible, highly recognizable. And it must bear the test of exposure to feedback, like any public record.

Minimal group requirements will be sought. Excessive and irrelevant requirements will be avoided, because they will not be supported by the immediate receiving system, and because they will obstruct the group achievement of the criterion. These are difficult requirements. Not just any objective will survive.

USEFULNESS OF OBJECTIVES

Norm-referenced Tests

The usefulness, application, or generality of a norm-referenced test extends from a sample ranking to a population ranking, from one ranking correlated to another ranking. You replicate rankings. If your rankings are anchored to specific criteria, well and good, but the use of norm-referenced tests are not dependent upon it. Although you may seek to use norm-referenced tests to discriminate between the effects of instructional treatments, they are not designed for such a discrimination. They're designed to discriminate between individuals.

Criterion-referenced Tests

Among the constraints on the objectives for criterion-referenced tests are the receiving systems that maintain or use this behavior. A specific behavior has been replicated with a high proportion of frequency. You generalize that when the conditions reoccur, you expect a re-replication of the behavior. If you can specify all the relevant variables, if you can match these specifications with their equivalence in a receiving system, you have a useful and powerful generalization. However, gaining control over all of the relevant variables does not come easily. It only comes after a successive discrimination of treatments, after increasing discrimination between the methods of instruction.

THE PRODUCT

Norm-referenced Tests

What, then, is the output of norm-referenced measures? It is this. You have selected the survival of the "fittest" individuals. You have selected those with superior internal control, those with superior genes, will-power, discipline, intelligence, qualities recognized by the fruit of their performance.

That performance is high grade-getting behavior, the production of pleasing images, usually symbolic images, often mirror images; copies from the instructor, from books, from other student copies; accurate reports of the thoughts of others, occasionally reduced and transformed, but not too much transformed. They must be recognizable. The "fittest" is he who gives supporting feedback, who produces the images that reduce dissonance, uncertainty, disorder. In whom? The student? No, the instructor. Do you find that curious? Naturally, such a dependency upon different instructors for confirmation of responses can be a bit confusing, especially when objectives are so vague that you have trouble recognizing exactly what you've done, much less determining how it corresponds

with your other observations. The origin of superstitious behavior in students. The student indeed has accomplished a heroic task and is fit to join the ranks of heroes, along with his instructor who performed similar tasks before him.

Criterion-referenced Tests

What, then, tends to survive in criterion-referenced measures? Well, all the individuals tend to survive but only the "fittest" *processes*. In this "natural selection," the "fittest" method is the one that leads most directly from criterion to criterion, from mastery to mastery, step by step, with the least production of disorder. There is no need for maintaining variability. In this way, the underlying continuum of achievement becomes more and more delineated from the background of noise, of unpredictability. The network of sequences tightens, the steps are reached more quickly, distances are covered in less and less time. And the difference between preinstruction and postinstruction over any given period of time becomes greater.

FANCIFUL ANALOGIES

Norm-referenced Tests

The survival of the fittest "who." The following is a representation of many a story, including the old Russian folktale, "Go to 'I do not know where' and bring me 'I do not know what.'"

The voice of authority (e.g., a king, a father, a teacher) requests a task. He offers reward for success, punishment for failure. The task is obviously difficult because of the many instances of punishment and singularly few instances of reward. With a little aid, such as superhuman strength, the hero achieves the task, i.e., he survives where others fail. Whereupon he is quite likely to be betrayed. The request-maker may add another requirement or change his mind altogether, or some other excuse or pitfall intervenes. Of course, if he's really a hero, he survives and gets his reward.

"In primitive literature, the hero is often the man who can whip everyone else in the group in open combat. He controls with the techniques of the bully.... A later type of popular hero is the cheat, who outwits the strong man by misrepresentation and deceit ... it was natural that some special honor should accrue to the individual who arises above his faulty intellectual and ethical training and is wise and good in spite of it. At times, men have been almost entirely occupied in deciding what is right, intellectually and morally. A world in which education is so successful that one who is naturally right in both these senses is criticized, because it provides no heroism in transcending an inadequate environment. One might as well criticize fireproof buildings, because the world is thus deprived of brave firemen" (Skinner, 1961).

Criterion-referenced Tests

The survival of the fittest "what." It might be worthwhile pointing out that there is more than one situation in the world today where the concept of the fittest "who" tends to be a bit irrelevant. Not all people who provide services treat their clients this way. Your doctor doesn't tell you to go out and find a solution for your problem, to cure your own ailment. He doesn't tell you that all you need is to exercise a little will-power and discipline, and you can cure that cancer of yours (at least all doctors don't).

CONCLUSION

Items for a norm-referenced test are selected to establish differences among individuals in meeting group objectives. Items for a criterion-referenced test are selected to establish similarities among the individuals in meeting group objectives and to meet the minimal requirements for the immediate receiving systems. The underlying issues involve variability, replication, reward, and control. Norm-referenced measures raise questions.

They depend upon internal variability, focusing on the differences in individuals. They are loosely connected to individual replication. Success is attributed to students who reward the instructor. Criterion-referenced measures indicate answers. They depend upon external variability, focusing on the differences in instructional methods. They are tightly connected to individual replication. Success is attributed to the method that rewards the student.

If you assume that environmental control leads to more punishment for individuals, you are likely to prefer norm-referenced measures. If you assume that environmental control leads to more rewards for individuals, you are likely to prefer criterion-referenced measures.

Then there's the computer analogy. In computer programming, if the computer is in error, you don't blame the computer; instead, you make the programmer accountable. It's his responsibility to see to it that his instructions can be followed; otherwise his instructions are inadequate and need to be revised. Incidentally, the use of computer-assisted instruction is most useful in courses that would employ criterion-referenced measures. If you're going to gear your instruction around norm-referenced measures, why bother with a computer, why bother with media, why bother ...

I have tried to trace a source of disorder in the schools to a "what" not a "who": not to bewildered students, nor to beleagured teachers, who both somehow still manage to reduce disorder in spite of the system, but to a method of evaluating achievement. The exclusive use of norm-referenced measures may not be the sole source of disorder, but I put it to the reader that it is a major source of disorder. And this does not mean that the alternative is the complete abandonment of norm-referenced measures; everything's good for something. Rather, the alternative is the use of criterion-referenced measures. I hope you will also be able to see some specific and concrete responses you can make, and I don't mean a punch in the nose.

The effect of internal accountability on the development of a bilingual program

ROBERT M. OFFENBERG

In a recent paper, Moktus (1971) described the new role of a Reverend Dogood, who had entered into a contract which made him accountable to his congregation, and included performance objectives for evaluating his performance. The objectives in the contract he had entered into included: "Ninety percent of the congregation will be able to recite the Ten Commandments with less than 10 percent error," and "The illegitimacy rate will decrease by 10 percent per year for ten successive years." Absent were objectives referring to salvation, because they could not be expressed in performance terms. The implication of this tongue-in-cheek presentation was that in making the reverend accountable, the church's role was changed and was somehow less than it was before.

In this paper, I will attempt to show that the Philadelphia bilingual program, *Let's Be Amigos,* funded under Title VII, was indeed changed, as we of the program staff came to grips with the problem of building in accountability. Whether this Philadelphia program, like Reverend Dogood's church, is worse off than it would have been without accountability will ultimately be judged by those who read the full evaluation report. I do not think so.

The changes which resulted from coming to grips with the problem of accountability fall roughly into two categories as I see them:

1. A new set of role relationships between members of the project staff and the evaluator developed. The change resulted during development of objectives in performance terms.
2. Change in the program itself came about as a result of the application of the new evaluation role and the application of Title VII guidelines to the specification of the program.

Before focusing on these points, I feel the need to clarify the meaning of the term "accountability." One viewpoint, advocated by Barro (1970) and many others, implies that there will be a reward system (performance incentives, performance contracting) which holds individuals directly responsible for the outcome of a program. I believe that this view is appropriate when a program is fully developed, i.e., when it has reached the *summative* evaluation phase, but is not an appropriate view for programs in the process of development.

In the context of a developing program, where it is expected that initial results will be less than ideal, accountability in my view means that data are gathered to provide feedback for program improvement. Dissemination of evaluation findings to the public and to community advisory groups is for the purpose of discovering ways in which problems can be remedied. In essence, the community and advisory groups are not being asked to determine whether the program staff "did the right thing," but are being asked to assure that the program staff takes action based on *formative* evaluation data.

It is in this latter context that I wish to explore the impact of becoming accountable on the development of the program with which I am associated. The data which I will present are from the evaluation report of the first year (Offenberg, 1970) supplemented with my personal recollection of "how it happened." I will begin with my perception of my role as "internal" project evaluator.

CHANGES IN THE EVALUATOR'S ROLE

Hemphill (1969) has made a distinction be-

From **Education,** 1972, **93**(1), 73-79. Reprinted by permission of the author and **Education.**
   Paper presented at the 79th annual convention of the American Psychological Association, September 7, 1971.

tween the educational *researcher* and the educational *evaluator*. The researcher is an independent individual, whose goal is the increase of knowledge of the education process. He conceives of a project, makes the major decisions at choice points, and draws his conclusions. The educational evaluator, on the other hand, provides a service to a client by providing data on the successes and failures of an existing educational program.

My experience as an evaluator of Title VII Bilingual *Let's Be Amigos* suggests that the "internal-evaluator" role has elements of both the "evaluator" and the "researcher" roles, because the requirements of an adequate evaluation—the requirements of the accountability model of USOE—make demands which alter the project plans. This gives the "internal evaluator" some influence on the decisions made in the development of the program.

The planning stage of the project was the first place where the accountability demands and the evaluator role made changes apparent. For the Philadelphia bilingual program, *Let's Be Amigos*, this planning stage covered the time period beginning with acceptance of a preliminary proposal by the Office of Education, continuing through the writing of the full proposal, which was funded but accompanied by a request for revisions, and ending with the preparation of a revised proposal document. This phase was completed a few months after the program had already become operational.

From the beginning, the project staff assumed that the objectives of the program were of primary importance and so were the main focus of attention. During the proposal-preparation period, the project staff and the project evaluator had to move from generalized, socially meaningful, but unoperationalized goal statements to specific program objectives stated in performance terms. The sequence of development seems to be systematic enough to warrant the hypothesis that similar development might be found in other programs aiming at similar levels of specificity.

First, broad goals were stated. Some of these related directly to the operation such as "to begin teaching each pupil in the program

in his mother tongue, and then introduce a second language gradually." Other goals were more general, such as "to foster bilingualism in the community." Goals of the first type eventually became project objectives. Goals of the second type eventually appeared as long-range goals which served more as a philosophical frame in which the project could be viewed than as elements in a concrete plan.

It was at this point that the unique role of the internal evaluator became manifest. I, as evaluator, participated in drawing distinctions between program-specific goals and broader philosophy by playing a devil's-advocate role, challenging other staff members to tell how I or any outsider could observe the program outcomes implied by a goal statement. Those objectives whose outcome could not be observed within the context of the project became parts of the philosophical framework; those where specific goals could be developed evolved into project objectives. Thus, the interaction between the evaluator (with his concept of the demands of evaluation) and the policy-making project staff resulted in changing the project by drawing attention to behaviors and products which could be observed within the program.

This change was somewhat like the change in Reverend Dogood's church when accountability was introduced there. However, it did not mean abandonment of the philosophical frame as implied in that story, because the frame remained in our program's long-range goals. As the staff made its decisions about behaviors to be specified as objectives, this frame served as a guide. It was especially important when it was discovered that not all possible program outcomes could be observed.

CHANGES IN THE PROGRAM

After the program objectives were separated from the framework, each of them was further refined through one of three procedures: (a) preparation of microobjectives, (b) selection of existing materials, namely, tests or criterion measures, or (c) if there was not sufficient information to state a true performance objective, stopgap development of inferences about correlates to the desired behaviors.

Developing Objectives from Microobjectives

For the earliest grade levels, where something close to a "zero" starting point could be assumed, and where there was a high level of expertise in the staff, this phase resulted in developing lists of specific behaviors; e.g., "The pupil should be able to count to ten in his mother tongue and in his second language" and "He should be able to name the members of the nuclear family in his second language." These bits of behavior were unified enough so that dichotomous evaluation could be made: Someone could respond "yes" or "no" to whether the pupil performed each behavior bit.

Once a list of these behaviors (we called them microobjectives) had been agreed to by the project staff, specification of the related objectives for pupil performance became a relatively easy task. Calling on their experience with English-speaking pupils, the staff found it relatively easy to specify the performance levels which pupils should attain by year-end.

This process resulted in objectives which contained specification of (a) a general description of the behaviors to be exhibited by the pupils, (b) a list of microobjectives which specify the unitary behaviors which would be observed, (c) an observation method, e.g., teachers' checking off the date when they observed the pupil's success in performing the behavior either in a one-to-one testing situation or as part of an ongoing class activity, and (d) a criterion in terms of the percentage of the behaviors a given part of the pupil group should be able to master, e.g., 90 percent of the pupils to be able to carry out at least 75 percent of the microobjectives.

This approach produces one of the clearest kinds of evaluation in the program. Figure 1 shows the finding for one of the bilingual model school component's objectives: "sec-ond-language skills in the kindergarten." At the time when these observations were made, it was anticipated that the typical microobjective would be mastered by 68 percent of both Anglo and Latino pupils. The mastery level was, in fact, 50.2 percent for the Anglo pupils, and 81.3 percent for the Latinos. Thus, the second-language skills were mastered more slowly than program-planners anticipated by Anglo pupils and more rapidly by Latino pupils.

We see now that this Anglo-Latino difference in performance could have been anticipated because Latino pupils are immersed in an English-speaking environment to a much greater extent than Anglo pupils are immersed in a Spanish-speaking one. When this difference became apparent in the finding, two major changes were made for the second year of the program's operation:

1. Latino pupils were expected to continue to show mastery of all the second-language skills, but expectations for Anglo pupils were lowered on an interim basis from a 90 percent year-end criterion to 80 percent.
2. To improve the second-language learning rate of Anglos, additional curriculum-development resources were provided in this subject area. The aim of this resource allocation was the preparation of a course of study for Anglo pupils learning Spanish in kindergarten through second grade. The materials have been written and will be used during the 1971–72 school year.

Developing Objectives from Existing Materials

In contrast to those goals of the program for which microobjectives could clearly be stated, some goals were best able to be stated in terms of existing textbooks or tests. These materials were selected to be comprehensive enough for the project staff to agree that good performance on them would be a fair representation of the skills which needed to be mastered. Once the textbook or measure was selected, it was necessary to work with the program staff to develop the teaching strategies, the measure (if the objective was

Objective 2.2 (Second Language)

1. Self-identification (First and last name).
2. Answers "How old are you?"
3. Answers "Where do you live?"
4. Identifies family members in pictures.
5. Answers questions about family member roles.
6. Ans. "Who is he?/She?" about fellow students.
7. Ans. "Who is the principal?"
8. Ans. "Who is the nurse?"
9. How do the doctor and nurse help us?
10. Identifies the crossing guard.
11. Identifies the milkman.
12. Identifies the policeman.
13. Identifies the fireman.
14. Identifies the mailman.
15. Discriminates auditory stimuli.
16. Discriminates tactile stimuli.
17. Discriminates tastes.
18. Discriminates smells.
19. Identifies at least six colors.
20. Obeys "Sit!"/"Stand!"
21. Obeys "Come here!"
22. Obeys "Give me!"
23. Obeys "Show me!"
24. Obeys "Put away!"
25. Obeys "Be quiet!"
26. Obeys "Look!"/"Listen!"
27. Obeys "Get the ____!"
28. Obeys "Walk!"
29. Obeys "Run!"
30. Obeys "Jump!"
31. Uses "Good morning," "Good afternoon".
32. Uses and answers "How are you?"
33. Uses, "Please."
34. Uses "Thank you"/"Your welcome."

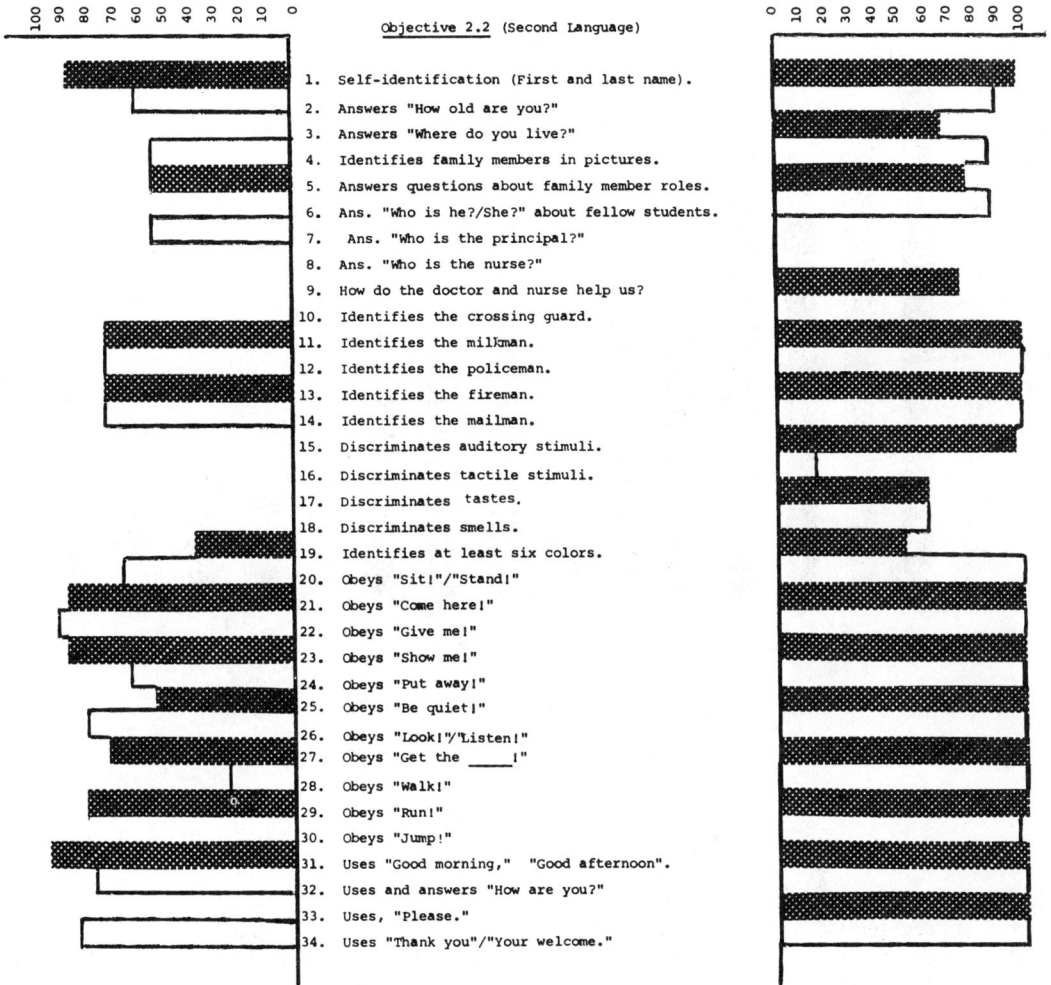

Figure 1. *Performance of Anglo and Latino kindergarten pupils on the second language objective.*

based on a textbook), or the materials (if the objective was based on a measure).

An example of this approach, in which an objective was built on an existing textbook, is found in an interim report on reading. The performance objective developed was that 90 percent of Latino pupils in the first grade would be able to read aloud correctly 80 percent of the sight vocabulary included in the preprimer and primer texts of the Laidlaw Reading Series (*Camino de la Escuela* and *Aprendemos a Leer*). A similar objective was also stated for the Anglo pupils with reference to the Bank Street Readers which they were using, but it is the Latino pupils' performance which concerns us here. It was felt that, by mid-year, pupils ought to be reading the preprimer at about the criterion level. For assessing this objective, a simple word-calling test was prepared in which each word introduced by the preprimer appeared. The words were written in manuscript in the order in which they had been introduced in the reading textbook. Pupils were tested individ-

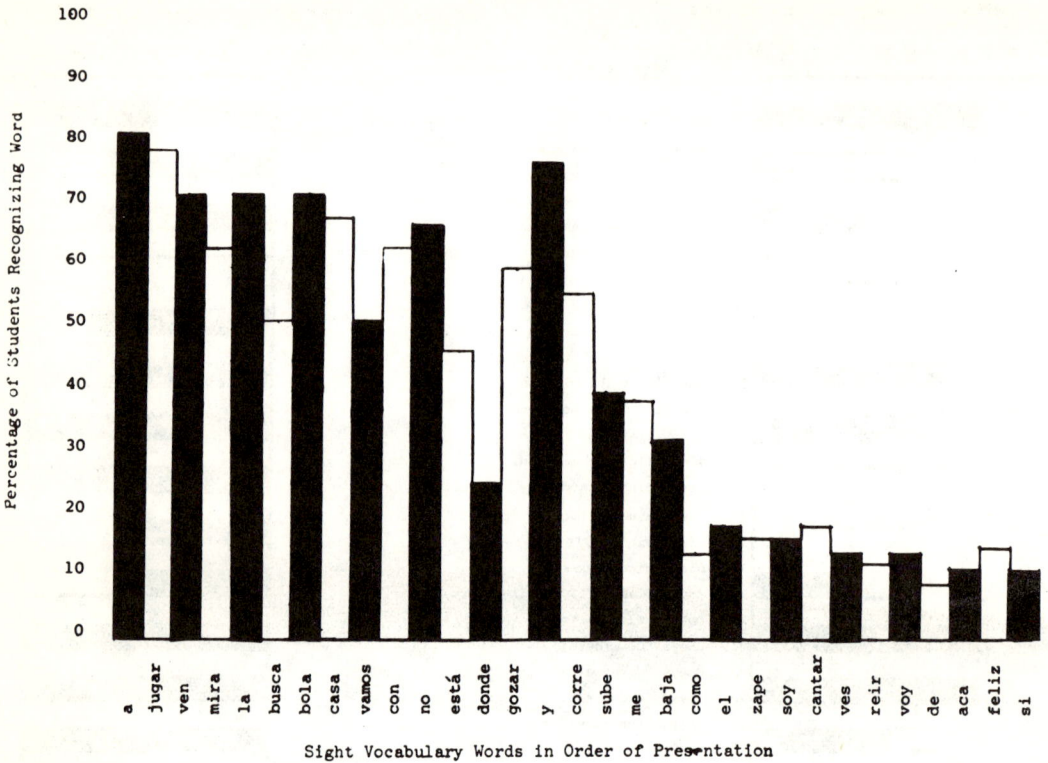

Figure 2. *February Reading Test, Latino children, pre-primer level.*

ually, to see whether 90 percent of the pupils could indeed read 80 percent of the vocabulary appearing in the preprimer.

The data for the Latino pupils in Figure 2 show the number of pupils able to read each word. As can be seen, the first fifteen words could be read at about the expected rate, but material from the end of the textbook was mastered by only a few pupils. The findings for the Anglo pupils, while not quite up to the anticipated criterion, showed a much higher mastery rate. This led to exploration of the texts and teaching methods on the part of the program staff. Some interesting conclusions were drawn from them:

1. The Spanish reading text, while introducing a vocabulary about as large and judged by the staff to be about as difficult as that of the English reader, was nearly three times longer.

2. The team-teaching plan in use required that both Anglo and Latino pupils work in the reading area for about the same number of hours per week.

These two facts resulted in the Latino pupils' being exposed to fewer new words in a given time than Anglos, and so resulted in slower mastery of sight vocabulary. The project staff considered a variety of alternatives, including accepting the slower-than-anticipated learning rate and changing the teaching plan to include more reading time for Latinos. It was ultimately decided that the Laidlaw text had so much repetition and had such frequent reentry of new material, that it could be used selectively. Some "stories" could be skipped if all new material in them was reentered later in the text. At year-end, reexamination of reading skills showed that they grew at a more rapid rate after adoption of the change without any apparent loss of level of quality of pupil performance.

These two examples of the development of objectives from a broad goal did not involve any traditional experimental design, but rather compared performance of the target group against an expert-developed criterion. However, one should not think that objectives developed by the approaches used necessarily avoided more traditional designs. The *Let's Be Amigos* program has included them where appropriate base lines were available: readiness of kindergarten pupils for first grade, speaking skills of pupils in their mother tongue, grades earned, attendance, classroom discipline, and during the second year of operation, performance on a standardized reading test. In deciding whether a more traditional design was to be used or not, the main factor which guided us was the existence or nonexistence of an appropriate comparison group. These two examples were chosen because they contributed to change in the program operation.

Developing Stopgap Objectives for Later Refinement

The third possible outcome of curriculum development occurred in the project component aimed at fourth-to-twelfth-grade Spanish-speaking children. We call this component "Arriba." The target group is pupils who have already had experience in either mainland or Puerto Rican schools. The attempt to develop performance goals for this component resulted in the realization that clear-cut goals could not yet be developed. Information about the changes in attendance, report-card grades, classroom behavior, and pupil reactions on questionnaires was available, and objectives in these areas could be developed. But the staff's ultimate concern was for academic skills.

The great heterogeneity of the pupil population for this component made specification of academic skills difficult. Among the problems apparent at the time when the proposal was being written were two important ones: (a) It was not clear how literate the pupils were in either English or Spanish, and (b) it was not clear how spotty the previous schooling of the target group had been, although it was believed that some pupils had missed some years of school. These problems resulted in a decision to hold specification of academic-skills performance objectives in abeyance.

During the first year, teachers were provided with whatever existing Spanish-language materials were obtainable and were asked to develop teaching strategies as well as they could, as the background of their pupils became clear to them. Supervisors served as consultants to these teachers, helping them to develop lesson plans as they were needed. The second year of operation, for which evaluation is now being completed, saw development of curricular units. They were prepared by teams consisting of curriculum specialists and teachers who had had the experience of direct contact with the program participants during the first year. These units include objectives and criterion-referenced tests. During the coming year, we hope to be able to assess these units through teacher comments and through pupil performance on the tests, thus bringing the "Arriba" component for older children into line with the rigorous level of specification of the rest of the project.

SUMMARY

I have tried to indicate the ways in which an attempt at building internal accountability has affected a program's operation. I believe that one can point to at least three ways:

1. The need to specify in detail the program strategies and outcomes shifted the project staff's attention from broadly stated social goals to concrete program outcomes.
2. The need to specify program outcomes and processes made it clear to the staff that there were parts of the program where they had insufficient background data. This resulted in their setting up mechanisms for acquiring the necessary background. We

anticipate that this process will lead to as vigorous a program specification as the parts where the staff had better information at the onset.

3. The development of concrete outcome specifications into objectives resulted in the collection of data which were useful in allocating resources and developing remedies where the original program plan was insufficient for the task.

How we ALL failed in performance contracting[1]

ELLIS B. PAGE

Educational psychologists little realize, so far, how our world has changed. Some of our most valued practices and assumptions have been put to a massive test, almost without our awareness, and have fared badly indeed. When we really grasp what happened, we possibly will never again feel quite so secure in our profession.

What happened was the extraordinary experiment conducted by the Office of Economic Opportunity (OEO). The subject was, at first glance, just one of many educational gimmicks currently on the scene: "performance contracting" (PC). Yet also on the block, because of the way the experiment was designed, were some common practices and beliefs about: (1) compensatory education; (2) the design of educational experiments; (3) the selection of suitable criterion tests; (4) the contributions of behaviorism to the schools. These are near the heart of our professional concerns, and those involved are our colleagues and brothers. And brothers, we have problems.

* * *

The OEO study of performance contracting is, quite possibly, the most impressive *experiment* ever conducted in education. As such, it has no competition from such massive nonexperimental researches as Project Talent, National Assessment, and other status studies. In fact, it has very little competition at all, when one realizes how it was put together, and what a range of important subjects and situations it sampled.

The earlier trials of performance contracting, though flawed by poor controls and even by scandal, enjoyed such remarkable "success" that many believed that PC, in some form, might well be *the* solution to educational inequality. Among the believers were officials in OEO, who had smarted with the criticism that in Texarkana there was "teaching to the test," and who resolved to make, at last, a demonstration of PC which would be beyond reproach. Their faith was impressive (OEO, 1971):

> "Staff visited Texarkana and saw great promise in performance contracting as a means to *help poor children achieve the same results from classroom effort now achieved by nonpoor students* [p. 3, italics added]."

There in a phrase is the soul of compensatory education: Poverty did the harm, and schooling will undo it all and make it right again.[2]

It was not just the OEO who believed this; it was a vast number of contractors as well. If the contractors are now accused of overselling their product, it is unfair; they obviously believed their own claims. There were at least fifty companies bidding on work in 1971. Thirty-one of them bid on this major

From *Educational Psychologist,* 1972, 9(3), 40-42. Copyright © 1972 by the American Psychological Association, and reproduced by permission.

1 Thanks are given to Charles Stalford of the OEO, to Jason Millman, and to Bruce Rogers for their own opinions and comments. The present writer did a short consulting assignment with OEO concerning this project, but had no part in the design or analysis of the study. And this article is based on sources which are publicly available. Naturally, no one else should be considered party to the opinions or conclusions expressed here.

2 The official current position of the OEO, notwithstanding such quotes as given, is that it was not *promoting* PC as a solution but was *testing* it as one promising effort. And the rigor of the test surely lends weight to this position.

PC experiment, and six unlucky companies won the bid. It was a punishing experience for all six, and three or four are now out of the business. If there was a major deception, then it was deep in the heart of our profession.

Listen to the OEO's description (OEO, 1971) of the "relatively simple" system of PC:

—"A contractor signs an agreement to improve students' performance in certain basic skills by set amounts.

—The contractor is paid according to his success in bringing students' performance up to those prespecified levels. If he succeeds, he makes a profit. If he fails, he doesn't get paid.

—Within guidelines established by the school board, the contractor is free to use whatever instructional techniques, incentive systems, and audio-visual aids he feels can be most effective. He thus is allowed more flexibility than is usually offered a building principal or a classroom teacher [p. 2]."

Does this sound familiar? It should. It is at least implied by our behaviorist doctrine of the past several decades. It is main-line, established reinforcement theory put into action. Programmed instruction was strongly related to it, and behavior mod seems to have the action right now. One of its main assumptions is the crucial nature of *motivation*. And this problem may be overcome by incentives (OEO, 1971): e.g., "trading stamps, that they would use for gifts, and free time during the class period that they could use to read magazines, listen to records, or other recreational activities [p. 3]." Some of the anticipated gains would be "better overall performance . . . accountability . . . dropout prevention . . . integration . . . individualization of instruction [pp. 5–6]."

To be important, an experiment must seek generality, and this remarkable experiment had it built into the design. The six PC contractors reflected the most persuasive and varied practices in applied psychology. Each hired company would apply its principles in three different school systems (eighteen in all), widely separated throughout the U.S., across six grade levels (1–3, 7–9), and across

every major low-achieving ethnic group, from poor urban Anglos to Alaskan Eskimos. There was to be, furthermore, generalization across the two most important educational skills: reading and arithmetic. Over 25,000 students would participate, and over six million dollars would be spent.

Many intervention studies report glowing results to the newspapers but upon examination are lacking in even the most primitive controls. But the OEO had been burned and determined that this study was to be, within its realm of political possibility, a model of experimental practice. It came very close. The eighteen participating districts were carefully chosen, and the subjects, both E and C, were from the worst-performing schools in the districts. And from each school, for each grade, the 100 students furthest behind their grade levels would serve as Ss. The resulting composite of subjects is very representative of the target population.

Precisely at this point of assignment to the E and C groups, where most wide-scale studies flounder, the OEO likewise relaxed from the best research practice. Assignment of schools to treatments was very complicated in so widespread a study, where at least 100 E students were sought in each grade at each site, and where some schools obviously would not supply enough potential Ss. Therefore a number of compromises were made. But the most serious lapse from rigor, at least in theory, was permitting nonrandom considerations of cooperativeness, political considerations, and apparent need to decide which school was E and which C.[3] This resulted in a slightly abler group, on the average, for C schools as judged by the pretest.

As irritating as this compromise is to the professional psychometrician,[4] it is surely not

---

3 According to Battelle (1972): "Generally speaking, the most deficient school or schools were selected as the experimental school(s) and the next most deficient as the control schools. In large districts where there was sometimes a substantial choice of schools, the selection was affected by the presence or absence of other special programs in them, the receptivity of individual schools to being included in the experiment, and the relative efficiency with which the required number of experimental and control subjects could be accumulated in them" [p. 8].

4 As Campbell and Stanley (1963) noted, randomization is the *only* all-purpose method of achieving pretreatment equality.

fatal to this study. Battelle brought sophisticated attention to creating regression models which, under reasonable assumptions, adequately accounted for these group differences in the tests of main effects. This is a study which, because of its results, many would like to belittle or set aside. But with the widely heterogeneous Ss making up both E and C groups, with the broad generality of tests employed for contractual and evaluation measures, and the variety of experimental techniques applied, there is no justifiable claim that the E methods had substantial effects which were not evident in the analysis. The breadth of design weakens competitive hypotheses.

Even more than the other generality in the design, the distinctive achievement was in the criterion testing. Texarkana had left scars, and there would be, in this large PC study, no "teaching to the test" if OEO could help it.[5] These results were to be unassailable. The procedures were not simply those of ordinary good practice; they were virtually unprecedented.

To construct special tests would have been expensive, complicated, and questionable, and the decision was made to use most of the major, currently published tests in reading and arithmetic. These were to be given in an elaborate double-blind, with the identity of pretests and posttests kept secret from everyone: contractors, teachers, and even students.

Furthermore, any attempt by the contractors to discover the identity of the test would be sufficient cause for the termination of the contract. And even the instructional content was to be spot-checked to make sure that no testing material was used in the conduct of instruction. Finally, tests were to be administered by outsiders, so that there would be neither identification of tests, nor aid to the students in taking them. And the evaluation of all the data was to be done by a responsible and disinterested corporation. In short, there was rare rigor and generality in the criterion testing, perhaps without parallel in large-scale research.

One remarkable feature of the design was the elimination of the usual upward drift caused by regression. The students were chosen *before* the pretest on the basis of *other* data. Whatever general upward shift would occur from selection would already have happened *for the pretest itself*. No upward change in the posttest general mean, then, would come as an unearned gift to the contractors. And the OEO had thus avoided one more of the most common artifacts in educational research.

* * *

Even with all this control, the OEO, the school systems, and the PC contractors went enthusiastically into the following arrangement: *Essentially, and in most cases, payment was to be made only for a student who gained one school year of growth between the fall pretest and the spring posttest.*[6] Note, the design eliminated ordinary upward regression, teaching of the test, and biasing of the evaluation—all three of them the bane of sound inference, but the comfort of those determined to report favorable results. What was left was essentially improvement in the actual, general, *transferable* skills of reading and arithmetic.

How much improvement should one ordinarily expect in a year of schooling? From the lowest-achieving youngsters, given the usual instruction, one would expect perhaps .7 of a year—surely *not* a full year's growth. For as we know, in school ability the weak usually become weaker. That is, they maintain their relative position in standard deviations below the mean, and this means a greater and greater lag behind their abler classmates.

Given these warning signs, *why* did contractors, schools, and the OEO sign the contracts, and move so happily on toward their fates? The answer is inescapable: They *really believed* that the lagging pupils were dis-

---

5 Such test-teaching is difficult to control. In another study, one PC contractor held the position that the target *domain* of content was precisely the *six reading tests* which might be employed as criterion tests! Thus he developed a drill device to teach the vocabulary *from those tests*, and maintained that this was acceptable practice, despite the objections of testing experts.

6 Since the contractual arrangements were based on the E group's own progress, regardless of the controls, the biased assignment to E and C would not importantly affect payment.

advantaged only in their prior experience; that the public schools were terribly ineffective teachers; and that the application of the usual psychological principles would cause extraordinary leaps in achievement.

* * *

When the results were finally released, the shock was severe. The pupils fell far short of the year's gain required by contract, and the contractors were immediately in deep financial danger. And the OEO was in deep embarrassment. It had achieved a rare kind of research rigor, yet the testing results were shattering. It was apparent that the hopes for PC which led to the contracts had been wildly optimistic.

There were educational scientists, of course, who believed that many gains claimed by compensatory education during the past decade resulted, in fact, from just such artifacts as the OEO was, at last, controlling: regression and practice effects, teaching to the test, biased analyses of data, and confusion of item samples with item domain. For such skeptics, it was no surprise that the contractors suffered loss, or that the target pupils failed to achieve a year in a year.[7]

Nevertheless, there is a deep shock for almost every educational psychologist who looks seriously into the data. The outcome is not simply that the PC enthusiasts were optimistic, but that *there was no detectable effect of the experiment.* In the words of the OEO (1972):

"[T]he difference in gains was remarkably small in all ten of the grade/subject combinations for which this analysis is appropriate.[8] In half of the ten cases, there was no difference at all between the gains of the experimental and control groups. In four of the cases there was a difference of as much as two-tenths of a grade level. These overall differences are so slight that we can conclude that performance contracting was no more effective in either reading or math than the traditional classroom methods of instruction. ...[T]he performance of students in the experimental group does not appear disappointing just because students in the control group did unexpectedly well. In fact, neither group

did well. In only two of the twenty possible cases was the mean gain of either the control or experimental students as much as one grade level. ... In all cases, the average achievement level of children in the experimental group was well below the norm for their grade, and in all cases, in terms of grade equivalents, the average slipped even further behind during the year. ... [There] is no evidence that performance contracting had differential results for the lowest or highest achieving students in the sample. ... Not only did both groups do equally poorly in terms of overall averages, but also these averages were very nearly the same in each grade, in each subject, for the best and worst students in the sample, and, with few exceptions, in each site. Indeed, the most interesting aspect of these conclusions is their very consistency. This evidence does not indicate that performance contracting will bring about any great improvement in the educational status of disadvantaged children [pp. 17–24]."

No matter how these data are revolved (and more elaborate analyses are forthcoming), the essential conclusion will remain, and it seems a severe blow to certain of our professional illusions. Many of us have believed, implicitly, something like this: Applied psychology has certain powerful behavioral skills. We understand task analysis; input repertory; stimulus shaping; response elicitation; the provision of reinforcement; the arrangement of repetition, sequencing, looping; concept formation; the practicing of transfer. These are important ingredients in learning, and as psychologists we understand these things much better than traditionally trained teachers. If we as a profession are given the support, the students, the autonomy, we can make incalculable improvements in education. This belief has been one cornerstone of our faith in ourselves.

Now the OEO has provided what may be the first really solid test of its truth—whether

---

7 Recently, a study very popular with the press has raised the IQs of disadvantaged pupils by "an average of over 30 points." A detailed analysis may be found in Page (1972).
8 "Gain" scores were difficult to calculate or rationalize for the first-grade work.

the present, state-of-the-art, garden-variety, applied psychology can in fact contribute to the most important learnings in the schools. We will not make those statements so casually in the future. Our skills in training do *not* seem the immediate solution to our problems in education.

There are arguments to be raised, of course, some with validity. These PC contractors had materials and programs that were far from ideal. This is only a limited test of one year's duration. This study compared a well-bred horse (teaching) with the *first* automobile (PC). The tests are perhaps biased toward the conventional methods of teaching. We have not seen the affective changes. Perhaps the higher-order interactions . . .

Yet this experience with performance contracting, painful as it is, should be squarely confronted. It may cause us to reexamine many of our practices and assumptions about school learning and its evaluation. We have much to reappraise. It will be exciting to see how, in the next few years, we cope with this threat to our professional confidence.

17

PRECISION TEACHING

In the previous section, a case was made for criterion-referenced assessment procedures. Perhaps the best-known criterion-referenced evaluation system is that used in "precision teaching." The reader has already seen precision teaching at work in two papers that appeared earlier in this volume, Pennypacker's "How I Spent My Christmas Vacation" and Duncan's "Personal Management of Inner and Outer Behaviors." The present section deals directly with precision teaching.

In the first paper, five-year-old Stephanie Bates explains how to use a precision-teaching chart. The second paper is an interview with Ogden Lindsley, the originator of precision teaching. In it, Lindsley gives part of the rationale for the development of precision-teaching techniques. The interview also conveys some of the flavor of Lindsley and of his impact on education. The third paper, by Gaasholt, shows how precision teaching can be used to record the behavior of the teacher, to discover the effect on students' behavior of prompts and praise from the teacher, and to choose the correct level of curriculum for students.

Many criterion-referenced data-keeping systems are available to the educator. Although their proliferation does not hinder their usefulness to the individual classroom teacher, it does limit their usefulness in areas, such as accountability, in which standardization is preferred. Perhaps, as Lindsley suggests, precision teaching will ultimately develop into a criterion-referenced evaluation system that also will be standardized. In any case, precision teaching provides a useful data-taking system for the teacher and a good example of criterion-referenced evaluation.

"...and a child shall lead them": Stephanie's chart story

STEPHANIE BATES AND DOUGLAS F. BATES

Hello! My name is Stephanie Bates. I am 5. I go to kindergarten. I would like to show you how to use a chart.

This is a chart. You use it to write down how many times in a day you help your mother, how many words you can read in a minute, and how many times the teacher has to tell the boys to stop running and making noise.

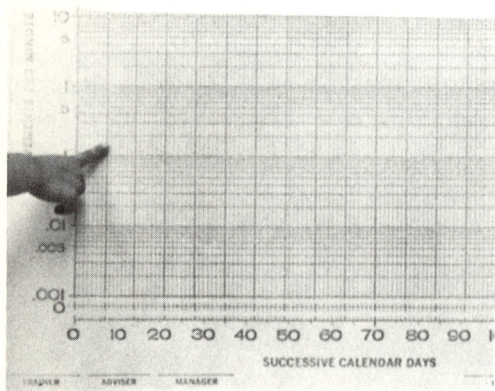

The chart has heavy, thick lines and light, skinny lines. The lines that go up and down are day lines. See this Sunday line going up

and down and the Monday line right next to it. Do you see another Sunday line? The big heavy lines are Sunday lines. They are day lines.

Do you see all the Monday, Tuesday, and Wednesday lines, and Thursday lines, and Friday and Saturday lines? They all go up and down like Sunday lines but are skinny. They are day lines too. All up and down lines are day lines.

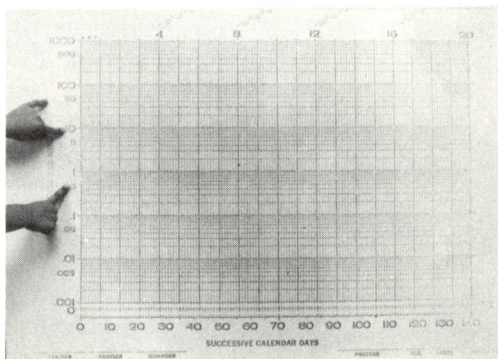

These lines go across the chart. They tell you how many times you do something. They tell you how often you can do something. I would like to teach you a new word. The new word is frequency. Frequency is how many times you do something in one minute. We use frequency on this chart to say how many times we do something in 1 minute, 10 minutes, 100 minutes, or a whole day. These lines that go across the chart are frequency lines.

See where the one line is that goes across. Dot number 1 is on the 1 line. The line that goes up and down through dot number 1 is the Monday line. Dot number 1 means I did something 1 time in 1 minute on Monday.

From *TEACHING Exceptional Children*, Spring 1971, *3*(3), 110-113. Reprinted with permission of The Council for Exceptional Children.

PHS Grant #NB05362 of the Bureau of Child Research, University of Kansas.

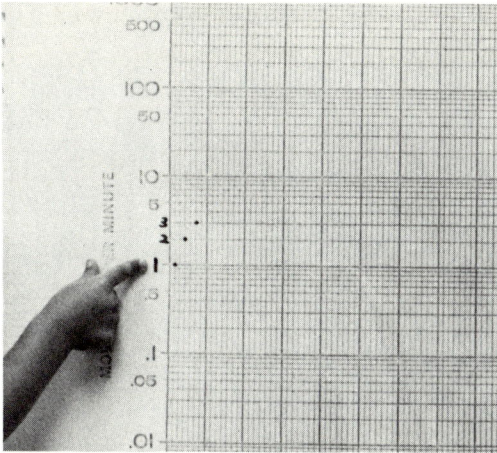

Dot number 2 is on the 2 line. The line that goes up and down through it is a Wednesday line. Dot number 2 means I did something 2 times in 1 minute on Wednesday. Dot number 3 is on the 3 line and also on a Friday line. Dot number 3 means I did something 3 times in 1 minute on Friday.

Now look at the frequency lines again. The lines that go across the chart are frequency lines. Look how the frequency lines are in groups. I made curves on this chart to show where the groups are. We call each group a cycle. There are 6 cycles on the chart.

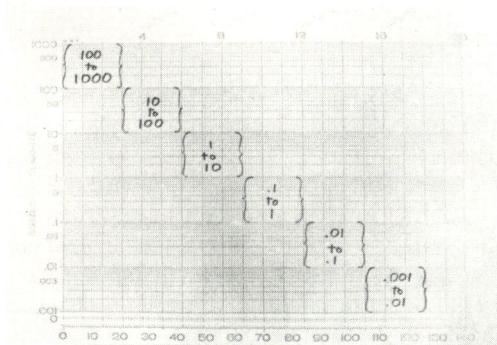

Now look at the numbers on the left side where the frequency lines are. The numbers tell us how often we do something. Let's look at the cycle from 1 to 10 and tell what each frequency line means. When we count

up from 1 the lines mean 1, 2, 3, 4, 5, 6, 7, 8, 9, 10 times a minute.

In the next group of frequency lines, the line above 10 is 20. In that cycle the lines mean 10, 20, 30, 40, 50, 60, 70, 80, 90, and 100 times a minute. The next cycle of lines means 100, 200, 300, 400, 500, 600, 700, 800, 900, and 1000 times a minute.

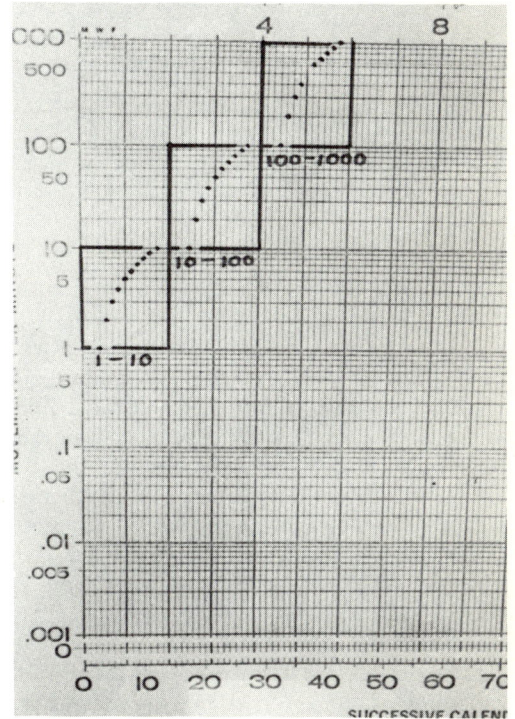

The bottom half of the chart is for the things that happen less than one time in one minute. The numbers for these lines are decimal fractions. I don't know what decimal fractions are yet, so my daddy has shown me another way to talk about the bottom half of the chart. But it still means the same thing.

Look at the bottom cycle that goes from .001 to .01. It tells how many times something happens in 1000 minutes. The next to the bottom cycle is from .01 to .1. It tells how many times something happens in 100 minutes. The next cycle up, .1 to 1, tells how many times something happens in 10 minutes.

See the other dots that I have put on this

Bates & Bates: Stephanie's chart story **385**

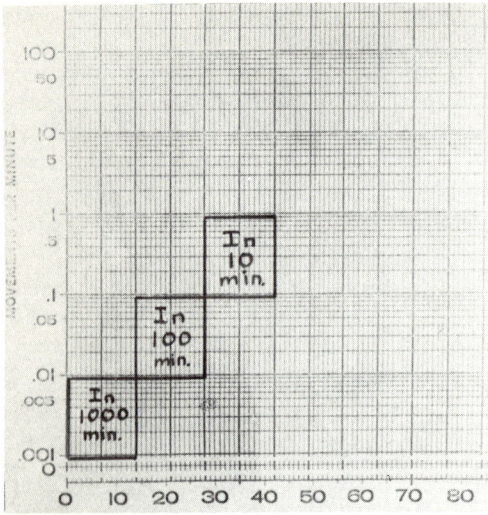

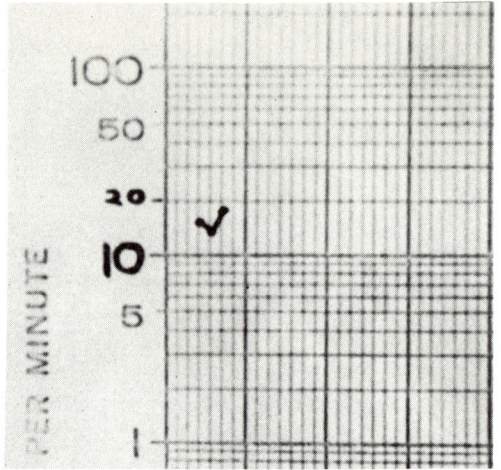

next chart? Can you guess what the dots mean?

All of the dots are on Wednesday lines. They show how often I did something on Wednesdays. That number 1 is on the 1 line in the 10 minute cycle. Line number 1 in the 10 minute cycle is the same thing as the 10 line in the 100 minute cycle. Dot number 1 means I did something 1 time in 10 minutes. Dot number 2 is on the 2 line in the 100 minute cycle. That means I did something 2 times in 100 minutes.

Dot number 3 is on the 3 line in the 1000 minute cycle. Dot number 3 means I did something 3 times in 1000 minutes. Dot

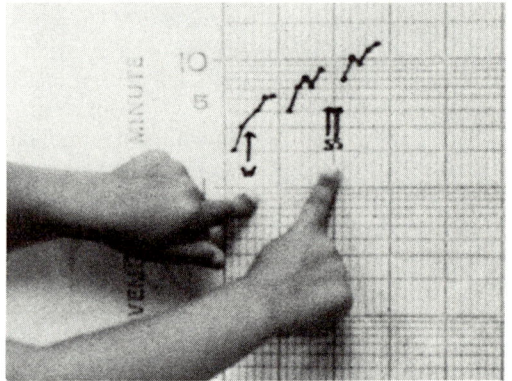

number 4 means I did something 4 times in 100 minutes. Dot number 5 is on the 5 line in the 10 minute cycle. Dot number 5 means I did something 5 times in 10 minutes.

Sometimes when you want to put a dot on the chart, there is not a frequency line where you want to put it. What would you do? You would put it in the place you want it between the 2 closest frequency lines. Look at the place where I put the dot on the Wednesday line. It means I did something 15 times in 1 minute.

Now we have learned the things that are most important about charting. I would like to say them over again so you don't forget them when you do your own charts.

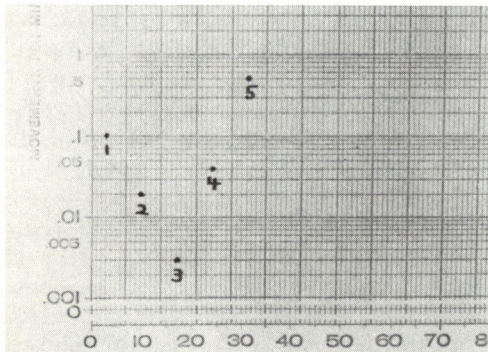

There are 140 days on this chart. The big heavy lines that go up and down are Sunday lines. The light lines that go up and down are Monday and Tuesday and Wednesday and Thursday and Friday and Saturday lines. The lines that go up and down are all day lines.

The lines that go across are frequency lines. Frequency is how often you do something. These frequency lines tell how many times you do something. This chart can show when you do something 1000 times in 1 minute or 1 time in 1000 minutes. One thousand minutes are about the same as 1 day.

You can show how many times you do something by putting a dot on this chart where the frequency line and the day line cross. Sometimes you have to put a dot between two frequency lines, but you still put it on the right day line.

There are 6 frequency cycles on this chart. They are .001 to .01, .01 to .1, .1 to 1, 1 to 10, 10 to 100, 100 to 1000.

You can show three different kinds of days on this chart: Charted Days, Ignored Days, and No Chance Days. A Charted Day is when you count something. You show a Charted Day by putting a dot on the chart in the right place.

A No Chance Day is when you can't do what you are counting. Just leave the chart blank. An Ignored Day is when you can do something but you don't count it. Connect the dots on each side of Ignored Days.

Now take your chart and a pencil. Write in your name where it says protége or behaver. Write how old you are where it says age, and then write what grade you are in where it says label. Then where it says movement write something you do that you want to change. Start to count how often you do it so you can put it on the chart. Then you'll have a picture of whether you're really changing.

Thank you for letting me tell you about charting. Have fun using it. Bye. Be good.

Precision teaching in perspective: An interview with Ogden R. Lindsley

Precision teaching is a new technique in special education. Ogden R. Lindsley shaped and developed the idea in response to the needs of exceptional children as reported to him by the teachers of these special children. In this interview, conducted by Dr. Duncan, Dr. Lindsley described the origins of precision teaching, the difference between behavior modification and precision teaching, and the present and future implications of precision teaching for special and regular education.

Dr. Lindsley, we've heard a great deal about precision teaching, but we would like some answers to some questions, like where did precision teaching come from?

First, let me emphasize that precision teaching came about because of children in special

education classrooms. If it had not been for these students communicating their needs to their teachers and the teachers sharing ideas with us, we could not have developed precision teaching as beautifully and quickly as we did.

In 1965, here at the University of Kansas, we decided to see if collecting daily frequency records of students' performance would be useful to classroom teachers. This idea of recording frequency of performance came from learning research. Dr. B. F. Skinner was the person who developed frequency to measure behavior. But Skinner's work was based on laboratory research, and we wanted to see if recording daily frequency would be of any help in monitoring instruction and evaluat-

From *TEACHING Exceptional Children*, Spring 1971, *3*(3), 114-119. Reprinted with permission of The Council for Exceptional Children.

ing curriculum and teaching in special and regular classes. So in 1965 we started having teachers record students' performances. Our first problem was that it was too much work for most teachers to record 2, 3, or 4 different daily frequencies on each child, especially if they had 12 to 30 students.

Then about 1968 many of our creative teachers began to involve the students in recording. We found that this was the answer to our economic and time problems—having the students record their own behavior. Now our kindergarten and first-grade children are recording and charting their daily classroom performances on Standard Behavior Charts. These records of performance are turning out to be very useful in curriculum design, behavior change, and handling discipline problems.

Is precision teaching different from or the same as behavior modification?

The thing they have in common is that the first people to use both originally were trained in the same academic discipline—operant conditioning. This was developed by Fred Skinner at Harvard and Fred Keller at Columbia and some of their associates and students. The thing that makes them different is that behavior modification stresses the change procedures that were originally used in laboratory operant conditioning. It focuses on the use of extrinsic rewards or reinforcement with tokens or candy to bring about change.

Precision teaching on the other hand uses the measurement procedures that operant conditioning originally used but relies more on traditional change procedures that teachers and students invent and select. We're finding in precision teaching that the most effective ways of improving behavior, when we measure behavior frequency, tend to be curricular. They consume less classroom time and don't rely on synthetic rewards or some form of punishment to change behavior. In other words, in precision teaching we try to get the child doing more successful classroom work by making curricular changes which involve him in the learning process, rather than trying to jack up a dull curriculum with rewards for doing boring tasks.

Precision teaching involves daily recording of the frequencies of different classroom performances on a standard chart. This permits teachers and students to project the outcome of the procedures they are using. Standard charts facilitate sharing data. Behavior modification tends to use procedures like reward and punishment in new and more controlled ways to affect instruction. The child's performance is usually measured by the teacher and does not necessarily include frequencies or the use of a standard chart. In behavior modification, measurement tends to be used to determine whether the reward system was effective or should be altered.

What implications do you think precision techniques have for exceptional children?

If we accept the fact, which most teachers do, that every child is different, then *every* child is exceptional. In the past we've labeled children as exceptional, or we've used specific labels like retarded or learning disabled. These children have dropped out of the bottom of a normal class. The gifted child has popped out of the top of a normal class. Gifted and learning disabled students are retarded by the curriculum assigned them in the average classroom. The gifted child is not stimulated to perform to his ultimate; the retarded child can't perform to the average. Through individualized planning, we can give every child his own curriculum. In special education this is practically a necessity if we are to help students reach their educational goals and become functioning citizens.

Precision teaching gives the child, the parent, and the teacher a recording technique, a tool to select curriculum materials and involve the child in this selection. This makes it highly probable that you will find a curriculum that will be best for Tommy for October and one for February. If you tried 2 or 3 different curricular materials at the same time and made them as different as possible and involved the child in selecting his materials, you would probably soon find the best curriculum for him. If you try 3 each day and separately record his improvement on each, within 2 to 3 weeks (or in an extreme case, 4 weeks), both the child and teacher can see which of the curricula he shows the most improvement on and which one he should stay with to gain most educationally. Once you pick the best one, then choose a new curriculum as "insurance." You may find that it is even better. In this way every child can be working on different curriculum materials at a different acceleration, and we can have a constant record for the child and teacher that shows with which set of materials the student improved the most for that month.

Another built-in advantage is that precision teaching gives an ever ready, on-going report system to the parents. In addition, if teachers share with parents the techniques which succeed in the classroom, parents may be more willing to share home techniques with teachers.

Why is it important to chart daily frequencies of classroom behaviors? Don't children improve anyway?

There are hundreds of ways of improving a child's behavior; every child is unique and different. The problem is not to discover a new universal teaching method. I don't think one will ever be discovered. The problem is to use the excellent teaching methods we already have with the children that they will work best with.

We discovered in our original work that to benefit from Skinner's greatest discovery (the use of frequency as a measure of behavior), frequencies had to be recorded in the classroom. Then we found that we had to make a standard chart, because without guidance and structure daily charting was just too complicated and consumed too much time for most teachers. Most teachers and students made charts as unique as their personalities. When we tried to share those charts in in-service training meetings, we spent all of our time trying to figure out each others' charts. When teachers made their own charts it took as long as 28 or 30 minutes for a teacher to make her chart clear to the other 20 or 30 teachers. The Standard Behavior Chart increases communication at least 10 times, since it only takes 2 to 3 minutes to share a project. Also since equal percent gains get equal distance on the standard chart, you can project the future course of behavior by drawing a straight line through the middle of the daily frequencies you've charted. The direction of this line shows whether the frequency of performance is increasing, decreasing, or remaining the same.

The 6-cycle design of the chart provides an adequate range of behavior. Behaviors which occur once a day as well as those which occur as frequently as 1000 times per minute can be charted. This feature of the standard chart insures that the types of behaviors teachers would tend to measure are not biased by the nature of the chart.

Once teachers learned how to chart, it was clear that teacher- and child-invented change procedures were more fun, more effective, and less expensive than many reinforcement, reward, or punishment procedures that we might advise from a theoretical or academic point of view. It's very clear that what teachers need most is a way of comparing and evaluating the daily effects of the teaching procedures they already know, rather than advice on new ways of changing the behavior of students.

Where do you think precision teaching goes from here?

This is probably the most important question you have asked me. Around 1962, we recognized that future education desperately needed some way to handle unique differences among students. We needed some way to determine which curriculum format fitted which child best. So we set a strategy for the future. Probably one of the biggest advantages in the development of precision teaching is its future orientation.

The funny anachronism that faced us in the 1950s in human learning research was that the method which Skinner had developed to assess general laws of behavior also was the most appropriate one to study individual differences, and those studying individuals were using methods only appropriate for groups. Right now we have a similar problem where the most dynamic, and I think, the most efficient and exciting learning trends and ideas are those coming out of Piaget,

Neill's Summerhill, and the British Open School. However, the evaluation methods used for these new classroom ideas and theories are ones which *by design* can pick up only similarities and general trends among people. So a pay-off area would be to take these highly unique and different types of open classrooms and use precision-teaching techniques to monitor the improvement and growth of each child, working on his own custom tailored curriculum program. A beautiful wedding would be that of the best techniques for monitoring the performance of students with the best programs for maximizing dynamic curriculum and individual learning.

Measuring the frequency of behavior was developed to record the *outer* behavior of people. Recently we have been charting inner behaviors like success, thoughts, anxiety feelings, joy, love, and compassion. How many times a day do you feel compassionate? How many ecology thoughts did you have today? Charting may be one of the few sensitive techniques that we have to keep track of these inner thoughts, feelings, and urges. It could be that precision teaching will ultimately provide man with the most good and the most help by being applied to his inner behaviors. It is one of the few ways to chart and change inner behaviors. Thus, some future strategies include using precision teaching to monitor students in open dynamic classrooms and letting them chart their own social interaction and self-concepts.

Another use would be to accelerate the ability of students in our regular classrooms who are getting 90 to 100 percent correct every day and are nowhere close to their educational potential. With precision-teaching charts we can show that some students have been in school 4 years, received straight A's, and are bored to tears. They have never shown any acceleration or improvement on their charts, which means the school has taught them nothing. They have simply performed at the top of their class. Those students should be put on a curriculum which could allow them to make a high frequency of errors. This may sound strange, because we as teachers are generally pleased when our students make few errors. The errors, however, would show that a student is challenged and working towards improvement. In addition, a special curriculum could be selected for a child gifted in math but in nothing else. Then he could stay in his regular school activities, but he could be working on college math because his charts showed that was the only math that was challenging to him.

We can use these charts on daily classroom performance and improvement to design curriculum packages. Each child possibly could have 10 curricular choices. They all could be recorded on the standard charts. No students would ever be reading the same material each week; they would change to the curriculum alternative that they showed the most improvement on.

One problem will have to be solved to make this process work. We will have to learn to treat errors as learning opportunities, as a beautiful man named Caleb Gattegno does. We want to constantly increase the difficulty of the material so that errors are present and can be used not as social stigmata but as *opportunities to learn.* The whole idea is to challenge the myth that children have to be right most of the time, since this idea slows down the learning process terribly. By taking the onus from errors we may find that children dare more and try more.

It is essential for creative people to be allowed to make mistakes. Most creative people I have known are different from all the people around them, for they don't know when to quit. For them every failure is a success, because they then know how not to fail that way again.

Is there anything else you would like to add?

Yes, There's a lot of confusion about precision teaching. People think it's a new teaching approach, a new type of learning or reinforcement theory. In the past most new ideas about classroom instruction have literally been "approaches" or theories involving goals. *Precision teaching is not an approach;* it is an easy, inexpensive system of monitoring daily improvement—not performance, but improvement. Improvement is acceleration; performance is frequency of occurrence.

The difference is an important one, especially in view of all the talk we're hearing about raising teachers' salaries on the basis of how well the children in their classes perform. For example, if a teacher uses standard achievement tests with a group of children who are good achievers, it's not too difficult to get their performance up to criterion. The teacher can then qualify for a raise based on teaching output, measured by children's achievement test scores. The problem, however, is that if a teacher is assigned children who have great difficulty learning, the teacher would have an awful time getting the children up to criterion before the end of the semester.

You would have a very different situation if the teacher were being evaluated on the children's improvement or acceleration, that is the *change* or improvement in the frequency with which a particular behavior is performed. Then the teacher who had the most underachieving children would have the greatest opportunity to show pupil improvement. This kind of evaluation would directly reward a teacher for improving the behavior of children, not for trying to get them to reach some standard level of performance. In short then, precision teaching entails recording the acceleration or change in frequency of wanted behaviors or the deceleration of unwanted behaviors, as opposed to simply recording level of performance.

I'd again like to underscore that precision teaching is *not* an approach to classroom instruction. Any teacher who is now comfortable with her style of teaching, her hard learned way of communicating with her students, and the unique way she expresses her love for her students would not substitute precision teaching for what she is doing. She simply *adds* precision-teaching techniques to her current style in order to become even more efficient. Precision-teaching tools are designed to improve and refine current teaching methods and materials. That's a confusion I find in a lot of teachers. They fear that if they try this new thing they will have to temporarily put aside or abandon their trusted teaching skills. Precision teaching simply adds a more precise measurement instrument to present teaching, making teaching more economical, more effective, more enjoyable, and more loving.

Precision techniques in the management of teacher and child behaviors

MARIE GAASHOLT

Parent-teacher conferences and report cards require teachers to evaluate pupil progress. Unfortunately, these appraisals often are inadequate because the observation periods are too short, the tests imprecise, and the goals undefined (Zimmerman, 1969). Lack of time, heavy class loads, and inadequate materials too often result in the acceptance of less than precise measuring techniques and evaluation.

Important as the measurement of pupil performance is the evaluation and measurement of teacher performance. Yet, systematic evaluations of teacher performance as it influences pupil performance are rarely carried out. Precision teaching, a system of continuous and direct recording of a pinpointed movement (Lindsley, 1969), is a technique whereby teachers can efficiently and economically evaluate both pupil performance and their own instructional endeavors. Precision teaching involves five basic steps:

1. Pinpointing a pupil behavior.
2. Recording this behavior daily, comput-

From ***Exceptional Children***, October 1970, ***37***, 129–135. Reprinted with permission of The Council for Exceptional Children.

ing the rate (number of responses over elapsed time), and charting it on a 6-cycle behavior chart.

3. Recording teacher behavior in relation to pupil behavior.

4. Analyzing data to decide what change in teacher performance might affect pupil performance, if a pupil performance rate needs to be changed.

5. Making only one change in teacher performance at a time and then reevaluating.

METHOD

Children and Setting

Six or 7 children were referred to the Engineered Learning Project (ELP) experimental classroom every 8 weeks. The ELP, a unique teaching situation (Walker, Mattson, and Buckley, 1969), is sponsored by the Department of Special Education, University of Oregon. The students, of average or above average intelligence, were behavior problems in their respective classrooms. Twenty-five children (24 boys and 1 girl) in grades 3 through 7 received instruction during the 1968–69 school year. All the children were below grade-level in one or more subjects, as indicated by the Gates-McKillop Reading Test, Stanford Diagnostic Arithmetic Test, and daily performance rates.

The goal of the project was to alter teacher defined deviant behaviors of the students. Within this primary focus, the instructional goals were to pinpoint each child's deficit areas and to teach the needed skills as effectively as possible while searching for materials and motivators which could be used in the regular classroom.

Charting

Performance rates were charted on equal proportion 6-cycle chart paper with units ranging from .001 to 1000 over 6 logarithmic cycles (see Figures 1–6). This standardized chart is specifically designed for recording broad ranges of behavior, a great advantage when two very different behaviors are being charted. A teacher concerned with a behav-

ior, e.g., temper tantrums, which might occur only once a day and a teacher concerned with oral reading rates which could occur at a rate of 200 words per minute could use the same type of chart paper to record either behavior.

Data Collection

Direct observation of academic behavior was made by the teacher, the teacher aide, and the students. Students recorded their start and stop times, while either the teacher or the teacher aide recorded and charted the rate on the 6-cycle chart paper.

Since the children attended the ELP classroom for only 8 weeks, immediate daily feedback was needed if the teacher's classroom planning was to be effective. The following teacher questions were typical: "Should Robert advance to 3-place multiplication, or does he need additional instruction and practice on basic facts and 2-place multiplication problems?" "Will Mark read better if I say 'good' for every 3 sentences he reads correctly?" "Am I giving equal instruction, time, and effort to each child?" By direct recording and charting, the teacher had a firm basis for the decisions she would have to make in program planning.

TEACHER-PUPIL INTERACTION

It is generally assumed that help and encouragement will accelerate pupil performance. However, without data, teachers have no way of knowing how often interaction occurs between pupil and teacher or whether the contact is pupil- or teacher-initiated. To obtain such data, a sheet of paper taped to each child's desk was used to record the times a teacher or teacher aide went over and spoke to the child. The sheet also indicated whether the contact was student- or teacher-initiated and noted in which subject area it occurred.

Figure I shows the teacher-pupil interaction data for 1 group. The vertical lines indicate the range of teacher interactions with the 7 pupils, while the short horizontal lines show the daily median or middle rate. These pupil-teacher interactions were recorded daily for 166 minutes. The record floor at .006 on the chart was determined by dividing 1 by the time of the observation $(1 \div 166 = .006)$. The record floor indicates the time of the observation period and indicates the lowest rate (other than zero) at which a behavior could occur.

As illustrated on the figure, the first day's range extended from .1 to .3 with a median at .2. Multiplying these rates by the observation time determines frequency of interaction. On the first day the range of interaction was from about 17 to 50 with a median of 33. These data indicated that over a 22-day period the range of interactions remained about the same, but the median rate of interacting had decelerated.

When the individual data were analyzed, it was revealed that on some days 1 child was asking for and receiving teacher attention at a rate 8 times higher than the other 6 students. When the pattern persisted on the fourth day, it was decided to cut down on teacher-initiated contacts, and this decision was successfully implemented.

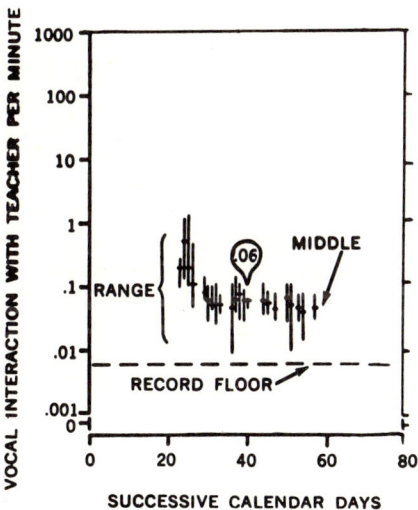

Figure 1. *Range and middles of interactions between teachers and seven students during individualized instruction periods.*

The data also revealed that 1 child rarely received any teacher attention. What little interaction was made was initiated by the student. Although it was decided to pay more attention to the pupil and a conscious effort to give him equal time was made, the chart showed that the previous pattern recurred.

When the teacher-pupil interaction records of various groups of children were compared, it was obvious that variation was great between groups and among individuals within groups.

EFFECT OF TEACHER BEHAVIORS ON PUPIL PERFORMANCE

Filling out an IS Description is the first step of a teaching plan. The IS Description is a list of the environmental components which could have an influence upon the behavior, the specific effects of which have not been determined. With a lesson plan based on an IS Description (Lindsley, 1969), teacher behaviors, like instruction or verbal praise, are specified and therefore can be independently measured. The IS Description has two sides, one describing acceleration and the other, deceleration. The following is an explanation of a child's reading session planned on the IS Description:

1. Program: The activity was scheduled between 9:30 and 10:00 A.M. The child's oral reading rate was sampled for 2 minutes.
2. Programmed events: The classroom events used to elicit Mark's reading responses were the book *Smashup* and verbal instructions such as "Remember to look at the ends of the words" and "Try not to repeat so many passages today."
3. Movement cycle: Oral words read correctly was the behavior to be counted.
4. Arrangement: The ratio between the movement cycle and the arranged event was 3 to 1, the first number referring to the movement cycle, the second to the arranged event.
5. Arranged event: After Mark read three sentences correctly, the teacher said "Good!"

The program and programmed events for

the deceleration portion of Mark's IS Description were identical to the acceleration side. Incorrect words were counted, rated, and charted as the movement to decelerate but no arranged event, hence, no arrangement, was contingent on that behavior.

Consistency in following a lesson plan is important but often difficult to maintain. Therefore, the teacher's responses, which formed the programmed and arranged events for the child, were monitored. For example, if the teacher said "good" after 3 correct sentences, her response was counted as correct. If the teacher failed to say "good" or said "good" regardless of the number or the quality of the sentences that the pupil read, her response was incorrect and so tallied. Teacher errors declined from 3.0 per minute the first 5 days to zero the last 5 days during the charting.

Since teacher errors were reduced, the project was considered successful. However, the function of the change on pupil progress could be determined only by consulting the student's chart. These latter data indicated that as the teacher adhered more closely to her teaching plans, the pupil's correct reading rate accelerated.

In a similar project, "teacher helps" and a pupil's oral reading rate were simultaneously measured. Teacher helps consisted of teacher statements such as "Think hard" or "What's the beginning sound?" or pointing to a particular word or to part of a word. These data revealed that for a period of about 5 weeks the median rate of teacher helps in a 30-minute reading period was 1 per minute. During this same time, the boy's median correct oral reading rate was about 15 per minute. During the final phase of the project, when the teacher attempted to reduce the helping rate, her median rate was zero and the pupil's 45. Apparently, teacher helps were hindering the boy's performance.

An analysis of the teacher's actions indicated that some helps like "come on" were program events (preceding or not contingent on pupil behavior) whereas others such as pointing to a mispronounced word were arranged events (followed by or contingent on pupil performance). On the teacher's IS Description or plan sheet she had not included coaxing as a programmed event or pointing as an arranged event. She had written out a plan but had not followed it consistently. This information would not have been available without measurement of teacher behavior.

SETTING PROFICIENCY LEVELS IN MATH

Teachers have many questions which are not answered by curriculum guides or teacher manuals: "Should the student be able to do basic facts (add, subtract, multiply, and divide) at 10, 30, or 60 answers per minute before advancing to more difficult problems?" "Will acquisition of new material vary when different proficiency levels are used?" "How can classroom data indicate when a child is most likely to succeed at a new task?"

In an attempt to find answers to such questions, performance rates of 2 children in the ELP classes were examined. To obtain these data the pupils were provided with a ditto sheet of 60 problems involving 1 or 2 movements. A sum requiring 1 written numeral, $2 \times 3 = $ ——, was counted as 1 movement, while a solution requiring 2 written numerals, such as $6 \times 9 = $ ——, was considered 2 movements. Five different dittos containing a mixed arrangement of the same 60 basic facts were used daily. To avoid positional memorization, no child received the same ditto 2 days in succession.

Both students, Robert and Sam, began on multiplication facts where the multiplier and multiplicand were from 0-5. According to Robert's chart (Figure 2) his correct and error rates throughout the first 17 days generally accelerated. His median correct rate was 7 and his median error rate was .2 answers per minute.

In the second phase of the study more difficult problems were programmed. The multiplication program throughout this phase included problems whose multipliers and multiplicands were from 6 to 9. The data throughout this phase also revealed that correct and error rates were generally accelerated. It may be additionally observed, however, that an immediate correct rate drop and error rate increase were noted when the more difficult materials were scheduled. These performance changes continued to be noted as Robert was advanced to successively more difficult materials. Probably, Robert's initial correct rate of 7 and error rate of .2 were not proficient, since he experienced more and more difficulty as he was advanced to more difficult material.

Sam's performance on multiplication facts is illustrated by Figure 3. As noted throughout the first phase of 10 days when the 0-5 type problems were scheduled, his median correct rate was 20 and his median error rate, zero. When the more difficult problems were scheduled throughout the second phase, his correct median rate rose to 30 per minute, while his error rate remained generally at zero.

When still more difficult multiplication problems were subsequently scheduled, Sam's performance continued to improve. Unlike Robert, Sam probably reached a proficiency level on the first set of multiplication facts,

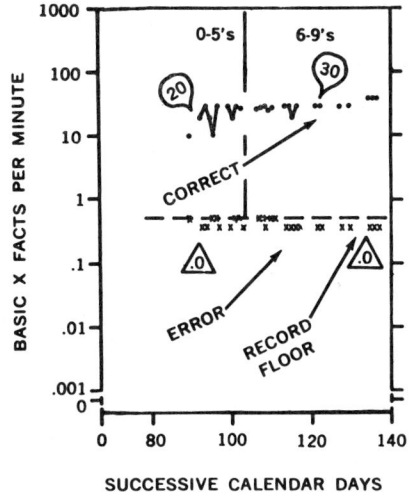

Figure 3. *Sam's correct and error rates of basic multiplication facts. During the first phase a proficiency level had been reached. In the second phase, when more difficult problems were scheduled, his performance continued to be satisfactory.*

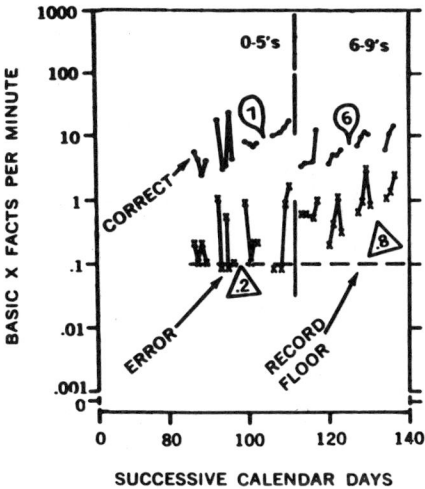

Figure 2. *Robert's correct and error rates of basic multiplication facts. He had not reached a proficiency level in the first phase. Correct rate decelerated while error rate accelerated when the second phase (more difficult problems) was begun. The x's on the record floor indicate a rate of one, those x's placed immediately below the record floor indicate a zero error rate.*

since his rates on successive problems were always satisfactory.

One way to set a proficiency level in math is to have children write numbers for 1 minute. If the numbers are correctly formed and the child has worked efficiently, the number writing rate indicates the highest possible response rate (Haughton, 1969). Basic facts rates may be set just below the written number rate since the goal is complete mastery; however, solving complex problems may produce a slightly lower performance rate.

Multiple digit problems require more movement cycles per problem than 1 or 2 digit basic facts problems. The problem 608×2, for example, has 5 movements when all written numbers and the process of carrying to the tens place are counted. All movements must be counted to give equal credit for performance on more difficult problems. When all movements are tallied, a fairly consistent digit per minute rate is maintained whether complex problems or basic facts are involved.

SETTING PROFICIENCY LEVELS IN WRITING

This project attempted to set reasonable proficiency levels for cursive writing, and to assess the effects of student self-charting on individual writing rates. According to studies by Kunzelmann (1969), some pupil performance rates are about half that of adults. With this information in mind, the teacher calculated her own writing rate for several days. She observed that her rates were about 100 letters per minute, and she therefore established a writing rate of 50 letters per minute as a proficiency level for her pupils.

To obtain the pupils' writing rates, a mimeographed sheet containing paragraphs of cursive writing, penmanship paper, and pencil were distributed each day. At the signal, everyone, including the teacher, wrote as quickly and as neatly as possible for 1 minute. Then everyone corrected his own paper by circling any incorrectly formed letters. A brief discussion concerning the formation of letters occasionally preceded this correction period. Although not all the children had reached the assumed proficiency level, every child, on the twelfth day of the project, was given his correct and error charts and told how to chart his own rate.

In the first phase, before self-charting was introduced, the middle group rate was 28 correct letters per minute and was accelerating. After student charting began, the middle rate was slightly higher. The data suggest that charting may have hindered the rate of cursive writing, since, as a group, performances during the second phase were decelerating (see Figure 4).

A further analysis of the relationship between proficiency level and charting was possible when the rates of individual students were examined. Mark's middle rate for the first 11 days was 53, slightly above the assumed proficiency level. After he began to chart, his middle rate continued to rise to 60 words per minute. Mark's self-charting therefore could be interpreted as an aid to his writing rate (see Figure 5).

On the other hand, Robert's chart showed a middle rate of 17 for the first 10 days, considerably below proficiency level, but ac-

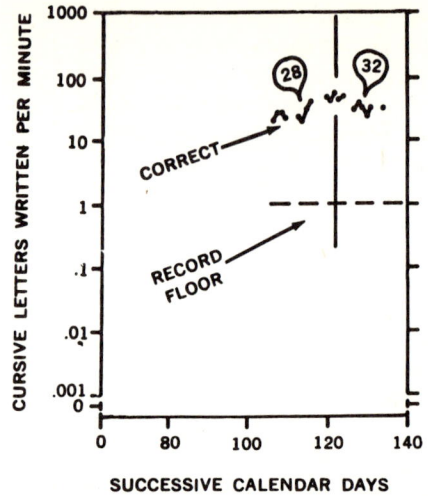

Figure 4. *This group summary contains the students' daily middle (median) rates before and after the students began charting their own writing rates.*

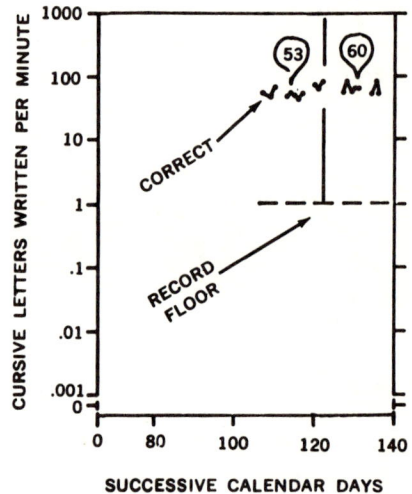

Figure 5. *Mark reached proficiency level of writing cursive letters during the first phase. His writing rate continued to accelerate after personal charting.*

celerating. When self-charting was initiated, Robert's rates decelerated sharply, indicating that self-charting may have hindered a con-

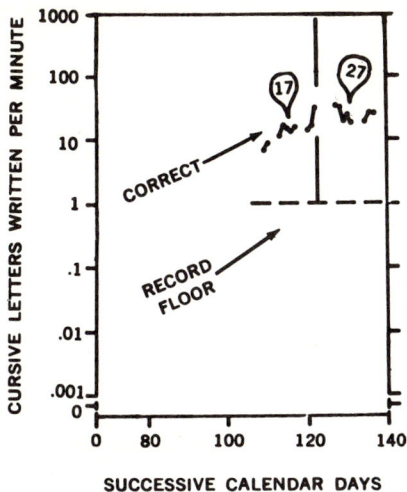

Figure 6. *Robert did not reach proficiency level of writing cursive letters in the first phase. After personal charting was initiated in the second phase his rates begin to decelerate.*

tinued acceleration of his writing rate (see Figure 6).

These writing data, like those in math, seem to indicate that when a child has reached a proficiency level, new tasks and program events are less likely to cause a rate decrease, and some new program events, such as self-charting, may actually increase the rate. When the behavior is in the acquisition stage, new program events may slow down acceleration.

CONCLUSIONS

A thorough study of performance data can improve teaching skills. This study suggested the following conclusions: (a) Teacher behavior differs with different children. Direct recording immediately clarifies these trends, allowing teachers to give parents and administrators interaction data objectively and accurately, and measures the effectiveness of attempted alterations of teacher or pupil behavior. (b) What a teacher plans and what she does often differ. When planning is based on an IS Description and the teacher's performance is recorded, possible strengths or weaknesses in the plan and the implementation show up. (c) The attainment of a proficiency level before altering events seems necessary for optimum growth. A child should not struggle with new tasks until he is proficient in basic ones.

THE FUTURE OF BEHAVIORAL EDUCATION: ISSUES AND POSSIBILITIES

IV

18

SOME ISSUES IN BEHAVIORAL EDUCATION

The preceding parts of this collection have presented a picture of behavioral education as it exists today. This last part deals with the future of behavioral education, both in terms of social and ethical pitfalls that must be avoided and in terms of some positive possibilities that the future affords. The papers presented in this section explore social and ethical issues.

The first paper, by O'Leary, Poulos, and Devine, discusses an important reservation teachers often express when introduced to behavior modification techniques. Since behavior modification makes contingencies explicit and uses reinforcers such as candy, toys, and special privileges, some teachers fear that behavioral procedures will make children overly sensitive to the contingencies and reinforcers; the learning behavior that the procedures are designed to maintain might then be obscured. These teachers feel that students may become greedy and materialistic. O'Leary, Poulos, and Devine thoroughly discuss these and other issues attendant upon the use of tangible reinforcers in the classroom.

The second paper, by McIntire, explores some of the dangers educational institutions face when they use behavior modification. For example, the teachers and administrators may be tempted to use behavior modification more to serve their own convenience and survival than to serve their students. Such dangers are not peculiar to behavior modification but are aggravated by its relative effectiveness. McIntire gives some guidelines that will help educational staff to use behavior modification primarily for the benefit of their students.

The third paper, by Holland, analyzes power relationships in American society. Holland defines power as holding contingencies over others who have no reciprocal control. He points out that the wealthy and powerful in this country hold such contingencies, and he contends that they use them to perpetuate their own position at the expense of less powerful people. Because the less powerful have relatively little money and legally sanctioned aversive control at their disposal, people who want to change society may resort to illegal aversive consequences, such as rioting.

The reinforcement systems of American society, according to Holland, are based on the competitive acquisition of material things and special privileges. He pictures an alternative society in which access to and control over reinforcers would be equally distributed. Although many behavioral psychologists would like to work toward a less materialistic, egalitarian society, Holland presents evidence that their science is in fact being used to perpetuate the present social order. Whether or not everyone agrees with Holland's political views, everyone can agree that similar analyses of the place of behavior modification in large-scale social institutions and events will be necessary to prevent the blind use of behavioral psychology for goals that psychologists themselves might condemn.

Behavioral psychologists have always recognized that their science could be misused, but in the past they have dismissed most laymen's fears as excessive or irrational and have devoted themselves primarily to building their technology. Now these same psychologists are expressing fears and examining dangers. Although continual vigilance and action will be necessary to direct behavior modification toward humanistic goals, the fact that behavioral psychologists, such as those whose work is included in this section, are willing to keep watch and perhaps take action promises a positive future for behavior modification.

Tangible reinforcers: Bonuses or bribes?

K. DANIEL O'LEARY, RITA W. POULOS, AND VERNON T. DEVINE

The use of tangible or concrete reinforcers, such as candy or prizes, is often a crucial aspect of behavior modification programs, and the effectiveness of such reinforcers in changing the behaviors of diverse populations has been well documented (Ayllon and Azrin, 1968; Hopkins, 1968; O'Leary and Drabman, 1971; Risley and Hart, 1968). It is noteworthy, however, that the prospect of utilizing tangible reinforcers is frequently met with highly divergent reactions. Parents, teachers, and ward personnel often raise objections to concrete reinforcers which are sufficiently strong to prohibit or seriously jeopardize their use. On the other hand, novice behavior modifiers too often avidly seek the power of concrete reinforcers without considering the possible problems associated with tangible reinforcement and without searching for more subtle yet equally important factors which may control the behavior of the client. In fact, due to an apparent but mistaken simplicity, token programs, which utilize tangible reinforcers, are probably one of the most misused therapeutic procedures developed within the behavioral framework.

Previous attempts to deal with objections to concrete reinforcers have been limited in scope or have dealt with these objections only as a side issue. Because of the frequency and intensity of the objections to tangible reinforcers, further examination of the objections appears warranted. It is hoped that an examination of the objections to tangible reinforcers will prove instructive not only to those people who have a great deal of skepticism about their use but also to those behavior modifiers who use them too enthusiastically. This paper will focus on a number of such objections after first discussing several definitions of bribery—an issue intimately related to the objections to tangible reinforcers.

Concrete Reinforcers and Bribery

Parents and administrators frequently state that the dispensing of concrete reinforcers is tantamount to giving bribes. However, close

From *Journal of Consulting and Clinical Psychology,* 1972, *38*(1), 1–8. Copyright © 1972 by the American Psychological Association, and reproduced by permission.

scrutiny of the definitions of bribery and attitudes toward the use of tangible reinforcers reveals a considerable amount of inconsistency and ambiguity. For instance, as many people have noted, parents who balk at giving concrete rewards to their children for schoolwork on the grounds that such a procedure is bribery do not regard their paychecks as bribery. Teachers who feel uneasy about trinkets or candy as incentives for achievement regard merit raises in salary for themselves as legitimate. Similarly, teachers who feel that the use of trinkets or candy as reinforcers is ill-advised freely use stars for the same purpose. Even in the professional literature, the issue of bribery is cloaked with ambiguity, since such literature contains various definitions of bribery which not only differ from one another but also frequently differ from those definitions used in ordinary discourse. For example, note the following variations in the definitions of bribery taken from recent psychological or psychiatric literature:

"giving a gift to prevent misbehavior" (Bakwin and Bakwin, 1967, p. 276).

"With adults we talk about bribery where someone is paid to do something illegal. . . . With children bribery usually refers to the situation where the child *will not do* something and parent says 'O.K., Mary, I'll give you a dime if you'll do the dishes.' Mary was supposed to do something. When she failed to do it, mother upped the ante to get her to do it. *That is bribery"* (Becker, 1969, p. 49).

"in bribery, pay is given before the act. . . . [In contrast] reinforcers . . . are only given *after* a desired behavior has occurred" (Schaefer and Martin, 1969, p. 202).

"To bribe means to influence dishonestly, to pervert the judgment or to corrupt the conduct of a person in a position of trust by means of some reward" (Meyerson, Kerr, and Michael, 1967; Ross, 1967). [This definition used by both Meyerson et al. and Ross is consonant with Webster's (1967) dictionary definition of bribery.]

Although some of these definitions of bribery point to important issues concerning the actual *use* of tangible reinforcers, they are idiosyncratic, with the exception of the latter definition, and only serve to confuse the issue of bribery. Furthermore, when one is dealing with the general public—as behavior modifiers are—one should use definitions consistent with those used by the public.

According to the primary dictionary definition, a bribe is a "price, reward, gift, or favor bestowed or promised with a view to pervert the judgment or corrupt the conduct, especially of a person of trust (as a public official)" (Webster, 1967). A tracing of the word bribery from the sixteenth century to the present clearly denotes immorality through its historical associations with stealing and corruption—especially of public officials (Oxford, 1959). This primary definition clearly is not applicable to tangible reinforcers when they are used in intervention programs for establishing behaviors such as self-care in hospitalized patients or speaking and reading in children. That is, unless one considers self-help, reading, or speaking as corrupt, one cannot regard the use of concrete reinforcers for their establishment as bribery. In short, procedurally, the use of concrete reinforcers is neutral; only when one considers the social desirability of the behaviors being changed does the issue of bribery arise.

When the primary definition of bribery is considered, the distinction between concrete reinforcers and bribes is cogent and valid. However, this distinction breaks down when the secondary, more general definition of a bribe is used. A bribe, according to this secondary meaning, is "something that serves to induce or influence to a given line of conduct" (Webster, 1967). One finds the following examples in Webster of bribery given to illustrate its secondary meaning: "Using bribes of candy to get a small child to go to bed" and "bribes offered to new readers ranged from cameras to flannel trousers, E. S. Turner." Thus, bribery when used in its secondary sense is an appropriate label for the dispensing of concrete reinforcers. It should be noted, however, that the acceptance of the similarity of reinforcement to bribery, in the second sense, recognizes only that reinforcement is an influencing process. The use of tangible reinforcers to build behaviors such as self-help skills or speech should be regarded as bribery *only* in the sense that there is a definite aim to influence these behaviors which are generally evaluated as beneficial for the client. However, the problem with using the term bribery—even when used in its secondary sense—is that it elicits strong, emotional responses due to its association with the primary definition of bribery and its immoral denotations. Consequently, those persons using tangible reinforcers to build behaviors such as self-help skills or speaking should continually emphasize to those who raise the issue of bribery that the use of concrete reinforcers should *only* be regarded as bribery in the sense that there is a definite aim of changing said behaviors.

Objections to the Use of Tangible Reinforcers

In addition to the strong reactions to the word bribery because of its immoral connotations, there are a number of other attitudes or beliefs which lead to resistance to the use of tangible reinforcers; they range from philosophical objections to objections based on the behavioral effects of using tangible reinforcers. These objections will now be considered.

1. *One should not be reinforced for something which is a requirement of one's general daily living.* Thus, reinforcers should not be dispensed to the student for reading or to an adult for making a bed, since reading is a general requirement of a student and since making one's bed is the requirement of most adults (or adult women). This approach places a strong emphasis on duty and responsibility, and its flavor was described by Tharp and Wetzel (1969) who quoted a principal as saying "I will not reward a child for doing his moral duty!" This view is also reflected in the feelings of ward personnel who strongly assert that patients should make their beds without concrete reinforcers because it is the normal, responsible thing to do. Unfortunately, exhortation and preaching

has not been effective in treatment, and this plea to one's responsibility provides a relatively weak aid in modifying behavior. The temporary use of extrinsic or "crutch" reinforcers may be called for in those instances where the person has not learned to do his moral duty. Had he, he would not be a subject of our ministrations.

2. *One should engage in an activity because of intrinsic, not extrinsic, rewards.* When applied to learning tasks, this view is reflected in the assumption that children should engage in such tasks because of the self-satisfaction inherent in their completion. Kilpatrick, a student of Dewey, had contempt for rewards and honors because he felt that extrinsic interests held dim prospects for producing desirable attitudes and ideals (Tenenbaum, 1951). Neil (1959) stated,

"The danger in rewarding a child is not as extreme as that of punishing him, but the undermining of the child's morale through the giving of rewards is more subtle. Rewards are superfluous and negative. To offer a prize for doing a deed is tantamount to declaring that the deed is not worth doing for its own sake. . . . A reward should, for the most part, be subjective: self-satisfaction for the work accomplished [pp. 162–163]."

While few would argue against the merit of "intrinsic" satisfaction, unfortunately, for some individuals, completing or even working on tasks is not self-satisfying. Tangible reinforcers have been successfully used to enable such individuals not only to complete educational tasks but apparently to enjoy their completion (O'Leary and Becker, 1967). It is difficult if not impossible to determine when engaging in a task is intrinsically reinforcing, but mastery of certain tasks, satisfaction in finding answers, and discovery of new things are examples of behavior which appear to be reinforcing in their own right. If a teacher or hospital attendant builds certain skills over a long period using tangible reinforcers, he will be able to maintain such skills later by using praise, and finally a behavior such as reading may be engaged in without praise from others. The factors responsible for the maintenance of the reading are complex and may not be limited to intrinsic reinforcers. Furthermore, the use of tangible reinforcers is certainly not always necessary. However, for those individuals who find academic tasks such as reading only minimally reinforcing, or in some cases actually punishing, the use of tangible reinforcers may be very valuable in building "intrinsic" reinforcers.

3. *A reinforcement program will teach greed and avarice.* Neil (1959) said that parents who tell their children that when they learn to read they will get a scooter are using a procedure which leads to a "ready acceptance of our greedy, profit-seeking civilization [p. 164]." Ginott (1965) noted that "some parents have been so conditioned by their children that they do not dare come home from a shopping trip without a present. They are greeted by the children, not with a 'hello' but with a 'what-did-you-bring-me' [p. 56]." Montessori (1967) wrote that "extrinsic rewards would flatter basic sentiments such as gluttony, vanity, and self-love [p. 61]." These objections to the use of tangible reinforcers seem well taken, and they seem to be increasingly important with older children and adolescents. Because of the possible development of greed, it is wise to use natural reinforcers such as privileges, recess, ward passes, or weekend visits to one's home wherever possible in a token program, and where extrinsic reinforcers are used, one should withdraw them as quickly as possible.

4. *The recipients of tangible reinforcers will learn to use tangibles to control others.* Bushell, Wrobel, and Michaelis (1968) mentioned that bright children aged 3–6 who were in a token program were observed hiring the services of one another, and it seems quite possible that the recipients of reinforcers will model the methods of the token dispenser (parent, attendant, or teacher). That is, the recipient of the reinforcers may learn to control others by promises of gifts, material goods, and services. While this concern is not to be taken lightly, it should be noted that most token programs ideally move from positive concrete reinforcers to positive social reinforcers. Thus, they provide a model for influencing others which is far superior to the aversive control anecdotally observed in

classes for disruptive children, psychiatric hospitals, and detention homes (O'Leary and Drabman, 1971).

5. *Rewarding a child for being good will teach him to be bad.* Baruch (cited in Ginott, 1965) described a boy who said, "I get what I want by keeping mother thinking I'll be bad. Of course, I have to be bad often enough to convince her she is not paying me for nothing [p. 55]." This problem is also reflected in the point made by Becker (1969) who regards bribery as upping the ante or reward for a child who has failed to do something that he should have done. Though the present authors do not accept that definition of bribery, the procedural aspects of that definition are important to note. The present authors have not seen children display bad behavior in order to receive tangible reinforcers, but if reinforcers are repeatedly given *after* disruptive behavior of an individual, it is entirely possible that the individual will learn that his *bad* behavior leads to prizes. Such a procedure would be a misuse of a tangible reinforcement and clearly should be avoided. This general objection would only occur where a token program is started and stopped repeatedly, and this is generally not the case, or where a parent misuses tangible reinforcers by saying to a crying child, "Stop crying, and I'll buy you some ice cream." In the latter case, the child might learn to display bad behavior so that when he stops he will receive ice cream.

6. *The dispenser comes to rely almost exclusively on concrete reinforcers, thereby losing or failing to develop more desirable means to control behavior.* More specifically, it is felt that teachers using token reinforcement will rely on the back-up reinforcers instead of focusing on academic programming and their own interpersonal or social skills to establish or maintain appropriate behavior. Similarly, it is possible that if a parent starts a token program in the home without proper consultation, the parent will regard the token program as a panacea and will ignore critical aspects of his or her own behavior and their effects on the child. The person responsible for the implementation of a program should stress that back-up reinforcers are powerful *primers* of behavior which should be paired

with and gradually replaced by praise and approval. Supervision is a necessary part of any token program—whether it be to monitor such events as the giving of an insufficient amount of praise by attendants or the changing of the criteria for reinforcement in the shaping process. As Kuypers, Becker, and O'Leary (1968) emphasized,

"A token program is not a magical procedure to be applied in a mechanical way. It is simply one tool within a larger set of tools available to the teacher concerned with improving the behavior of children [p. 108]."

Since withdrawal of the concrete back-up reinforcers is usually a procedural goal of token programs, there must be continuing emphasis on variables that will help maintain the behavior when the back-up reinforcers are withdrawn.

7. *The token program will have adverse effects on other individuals such as siblings, fellow patients, or classmates.* When tangible reinforcers are given exclusively to some but not all individuals in the environment, it is entirely possible that those excluded will feel unjustly treated or even adopt "being bad" as a strategy for obtaining reinforcers. The senior author has seen five-year-old children react negatively when a single child in a class is placed on a token program. Adverse effects on others can sometimes be alleviated by explaining to others that the recipient of the token program needs special help and that an increase in the good behavior of the child on the token program has favorable consequences for everyone. Structuring the program so that others share in the reinforcers earned by the recipient is another possible solution. In the case of a nine-year-old hyperactive boy, the child shared his candy rewards with his classmates thereby prompting interest and help from them in regard to his failure to sit still (Patterson, 1965). The procedure of peers sharing reinforcers must be used cautiously, however, since peers might try to use threat or physical force to coerce the recipient to perform for their benefit. An alternative procedure might be a private contract with the recipient which spells out the behaviors for which he can be privately reinforced. A home-based program (Bailey, Phillips, and Wolf, 1970) in which appropriate behavior is tallied at school but reinforced at home is still another alternative. Such a program would involve having a child carry a card with a note or checks about his behavior; the teacher would check the card, and the child would give the card to his parents for receipt of his prize.

8. *The behavior change will be limited to the situation in which the token and back-up reinforcers are given or to the duration of such reinforcers.* In fact, with populations requiring special treatment if reinforcers *other* than the token and back-up reinforcers are not made contingent upon appropriate behavior, when the token program is withdrawn, the appropriate behavior *will* decline (Ayllon et al., 1968; Birnbrauer, Wolf, Kidder, and Tague, 1965; Bushell et al., 1968; Kuypers et al., 1968; O'Leary, Becker, Evans, and Saudargas, 1969). On the other hand, where reinforcers which are natural to the classroom or hospital ward, such as frequent praise and special activities, are substituted for reinforcers extrinsic to the treatment facility such as candy, cigarettes, and prizes, it appears that a token program can be withdrawn without a loss of appropriate behavior (Graubard, Lanier, Weisert, and Miller, 1970;[1] O'Leary et al., 1971; Walker, Mattson, and Buckley, 1969). While it is likely that the natural consequences of some behavior such as talking (Lovaas, 1966) are sufficiently powerful to maintain these behaviors once they are primed by tangible or concrete reinforcers, in many instances it is necessary to program generalization of behaviors like any other behavior change (Baer, Wolf, and Risley, 1968).

9. *Behaviors in situations not supported by tangible reinforcers will be adversely influenced.* This objection proposes that the recipient of tangible reinforcers will come to expect payoff for *all* appropriate behavior

---

1 The Graubard et al. (1970) study used a control in which delinquent students who had been reinforced for a number of problems correct, as well as appropriate social behavior, were later reinforced for an academically irrelevant behavior such as appearing in class with clean hands. Such a control might produce different results than a complete withdrawal of extrinsic reinforcers.

and will not perform without it; for example, a child receiving reinforcers for completing homework assignments may refuse to do chores which he previously finished without concrete payment. In contrast to the ninth objection which states that the beneficial changes in behavior during the token program will decrease or not be influenced at all when the token program is withdrawn, this objection clearly points to the negative effects a token program will have when the program is in effect for only a portion of the day or for only a few behaviors. A number of studies do not support this contention that behavior in situations not supported by tangible reinforcers will be adversely affected (Kuypers et al., 1968; O'Leary et al., 1969), and it is the authors' opinion that if the problem arises, it is transitory or can be dealt with effectively. In a recent study, Meichenbaum, Bowers, and Ross (1968) found that the appropriate behavior of delinquent female adolescents decreased during the morning when a token reinforcement program utilizing money as a back-up reinforcer was instituted in the afternoon. The girls told the Es "If you don't pay us, we won't shape up." As Meichenbaum et al. (1968) state, "Clearly the girls were manipulating the psychologists into initiating payment in the morning class and were offering appropriate behavior in the morning class as the possible reward [p. 349]." Consequently, the token program was put into effect in the morning. Clients such as delinquents and adolescents deprived of goods or money may attempt to gain as many material reinforcers as they can by various manipulative ploys. Responses to such ploys should be made cautiously, however, lest one simply reinforce manipulative behavior which may be incompatible with the goals of the program, for example, more cooperative and democratic behavior and gradual elimination of back-up reinforcers. If one envisioned such problems, one could make participation in the token program contingent upon some level of appropriate behavior during a portion of the day or week when the token program is not in effect. Alternatively one could respond to such a ploy by simply stating unequivocally the behaviors encompassed by the token program. However, if it is likely that the increase in appropriate behavior will be particularly large in a token program encompassing behavior throughout the day, one may wish to build a token program throughout the day even if it were requested by the clients. In short, one must weigh the likely increase in appropriate behavior that would result if a full-day program were put into existence versus the possible adverse side effects of reinforcing manipulative behavior of the clients or patients.

10. *The use of tangible reinforcers combined with a system of if-then statements is essentially self-defeating because "our very words convey to him that we doubt his ability to change for the better." "If you learn the poem" means "We are not sure you can"* (Ginott, 1965). In many cases there is real doubt that an individual can perform certain behaviors, but a token program should be established so that it is very very likely that the individual will exhibit desired behaviors which will eventually result in the requisite skills to perform a terminal behavior such as reading a poem. Related to this criticism concerning the use of tangible reinforcers is the problem of continual prompting of behaviors with if-then statements. Some people regard the contingent use of tangible reinforcers as a procedure in which if-then statements are repeatedly made to an individual. That is, *if* you do such and such, *then* you will receive a certain thing. In most token programs there are instructions concerning the desired behaviors and their corresponding payoffs, and it is likely that a number of if-then statements are made during the token program. Particularly, since a token program must be constantly changing to be effective, there must be instructions and certain if-then statements concerning these changes. However, these if-then statements should be minimized as the token program progresses, since society will not incessantly prompt the behavior of our clients. Furthermore, it is the authors' opinion that continual reiteration of if-then statements may become highly aversive to the recipient of tangible reinforcers. To appreciate this opinion, one need only imagine himself in a situation in which a person who controls key reinforcers for him (employer, husband, wife, or lover) repeatedly stated

that only if certain behaviors were exhibited would affection or material goods be granted.

11. *The use of token and back-up reinforcers interferes with learning.*

"The performance of elementary schoolchildren on a two-alternative discrimination task has been found to be significantly poorer under a reinforcement condition in which a material reward (candy) was given for each correct response than under a symbolic reward condition ('right' spoken by the experimenter or a light signal)" (Spence, 1970, p. 103).

Though this study by Spence was not related to token reinforcement programs, the results of this study were said to provide some support for the hypothesis that inferior performances of material reward groups in certain experiments are brought about by the distracting effects of the reinforcement procedures. On the basis of pilot work now being conducted with Head Start children, it appears to us that with young children the receipt of tokens and back-up reinforcers may initially be distracting, but after the first week of an educational program, the interest of the children receiving tokens is maintained better than those children who simply receive the instruction with praise for correct answers. Thus it appears that the decision to use tangible rewards—particularly with young children—may depend on the length of the particular program. If the educational program is relatively short—lasting only several hours or several days—the use of tangible rewards may be ill-advised. On the other hand, the disadvantages of the distracting effects of the tokens and/or back-up reinforcers may be greatly offset by the sustained interest obtained by their use where a program is put into effect for several weeks or more and then gradually withdrawn.

DISCUSSION

The behavior modifier wishing to use concrete or tangible reinforcers to change behavior is challenged frequently by people who assert that the behavior modifier wishes to use bribery. When such objections occur, it is probably wise to emphasize that the use of concrete reinforcers is not bribery in the sense that the reinforcers are used to induce corrupt or immoral behavior. One might also add that tangible reinforcers are definitely intended to influence the behavior of others; in this instance, tangible reinforcers can be regarded as bribery but only according to the secondary definition of bribery. It should be noted that tangible reinforcers such as food are used by almost all parents to influence the behavior of young children. Thus, if one regards bribery in its secondary or general influence sense, almost all parents have used bribery to some extent, and it should be emphasized that this latter definition of bribery does not refer to the "immoral" use of tangible reinforcers. It is probably also wise to discuss the natural development of secondary reinforcers with those people who question the use of tangible reinforcers to change behavior. Most children of school age and most adults have outgrown the need to receive tangible reinforcers for appropriate behavior. Praise and affection are but two of the strong secondary reinforcers which gain influence over a child's behavior as a result of being paired with tangible reinforcers. Unfortunately, due to poor learning experiences or perhaps biological deficiencies, praise and affection do not acquire reinforcing value for some people. A treatment program in which tangible reinforcers are paired with social approval can be used to build the reinforcers which have become effective for most people as a result of their natural development.

In addition to aiding in the possible development of social reinforcers, tangible reinforcers as primers may have several immediate positive effects. They may serve as a concrete demonstration to the recipient that he can succeed—no small accomplishment to an individual who has experienced persistent failure. Tangible reinforcers may also prompt an individual to engage in behaviors which he previously avoided, thereby creating the opportunity for increased skill or task-related satisfaction. Furthermore, in some situations, an immediate change in behavior may prevent an impending dire occurrence such as expulsion from school, demotion on a job, or firing. Most important, in order to have long-range effects, a token program should be used to teach people to display behaviors which will be maintained by the natural reinforcers from people in the schools, hospitals, or communities in which they reside.

Despite some of the more apparent advantages of a program using tangible reinforcers, the behavior modifier should seriously face questions raised by skeptics of token programs. Many of these questions have only begun to receive research attention. Attention to such questions should prove helpful not only in considering *whether* a program

using tangible reinforcers should be used but also *how* to implement such a program. The authors here recommend that token programs using tangible extrinsic reinforcers should be implemented *only after* other procedures of prompting and reinforcing with natural reinforcers have been tried. However, where other methods fail, a token reinforcement program may prove very valuable, and if tangible reinforcers are used as primers of behavior, they may prove a bonus to the mental health personnel who find their clients "unmotivated," "lazy," or "resistant to treatment."

Guidelines for using behavior modification in education

ROGER W. MCINTIRE

Skinner (1971) in *Beyond Freedom and Dignity* has suggested the application of behavioral technology to the systematic control of human behavior. Such a proposal brings forth two justifiable objections. First, people fear giving Skinner or his followers the privilege of selecting which behaviors will be controlled and of selecting ultimate behavioral goals. Second, people fear that controlling measures will be coercive; that they will rely on aversive stimuli.

In many ways, society already selects behavioral goals for its members and uses coercive measures to enforce those goals. It's true that in dealing with adults, social agencies may be reluctant to dictate goals and to use obviously coercive measures to enforce them; however, in dealing with children, we adults blatantly select goals and often substitute aversive consequences for Skinnerian positive reinforcement. Our children are already beyond freedom and dignity, but we'd like to retain a little for ourselves.

In our attempts to control children we must develop guidelines for selecting behavioral goals and selecting methods for control. Such guidelines will make us more humane in our treatment of children. Our schools, in which we attempt to control children, provide models for social design; they illustrate what can happen when we disregard the dangers inherent in systematic, institutional control of behavior. They also serve as laboratories for the development of control strategies that are ethically satisfying.

INSTITUTIONAL GOALS VS. INDIVIDUAL GOALS

Most schools today profess to move the individual toward goals that will enhance his happiness and effectiveness. This moving of the individual toward his own goals is held up as the prime institutional goal of education. Favorite educational phrases such as "broadening of experience" and "development of intellect" reflect this goal. Some schools are so oriented toward individual goals that they encourage the student, however unprepared, to set his own goals. Others blatantly set goals for the student on the basis of what is "good for him." In either case, education professes to consist of giving the student the behaviors he will need to reach his individual goals.

Reprinted by permission of the author.

But in actuality, the schools have a number of other institutional goals. These include keeper of parental morality, daytime baby-sitter, organizer of the PTA, and depository for young potential workers in order to keep the job market clear. The schools become agents for the enforcement of adult goals. To some extent these goals may overlap with individual goals. It may be better for the individual to conform to adult morality, to spend all day in school, and to remain in school during early adulthood. In other instances, it may be better for the individual to experiment with behaviors not acceptable to adults. For example, a more open approach to sexual behavior may make individuals happier and more effective. However, the idea of children being involved in sexual behavior makes most adults very uncomfortable, and the schools enforce the adult point of view. It may be better for some children to attend school part of the day, or at odd hours; however, schools are scheduled for the convenience of adults. It may be better for some teen-agers to work rather than go to school. As a result, adults would lose jobs, so children are kept in school as long as they can possibly stand it.

Schools also set behavioral goals that are convenient to their everyday operation, sometimes without regard to the actual needs of children. For example, schools ordinarily allow "no talking in line or in class" even though social and verbal behavior are most important skills to practice. Mostly for the convenience of school personnel, children are taught to accept rules and decisions made by others, not to make their own rules and decisions. They are taught that they must defer to adult authority, and that they have few rights of their own. Many high schools are just as rigid as grade schools. No effort seems to be made to shape the decision-making and self-control skills children will need when they become adults.

A related problem is the obsession of schools with conformity. Certain clothes and hair-styles are forbidden; certain conduct is outlawed. Too frequently conformity extends into intellectual areas. Objective discussion of topics such as communism, abortion, and drugs is avoided. When such topics are not avoided, many students are taught only what society wants them to believe. Again, students are not shaped into making their own decisions regarding their appearance, behavior, and opinions. Later, when young people emotionally embrace the latest political philosophy, adults innocently complain that the young are simply unfit to make rational decisions.

In summary, here is a first guideline: When there is a divergence between the goals of institutions and of the individuals served by the institutions, goals should be selected that serve the individual. Obviously, when small sacrifices in individual goals are necessary for the survival of the institution, they should be made. However, institutions should be prepared to sacrifice convenience, inertia, and inappropriate *raisons d'être* when they do not serve the institution's true clientele.

SETTING INDIVIDUAL GOALS

Even when we propose to set individual goals above institutional ones, we are left with the problem of determining individual goals. In the case of children, especially, we have been willing to dictate individual goals. As people get older, our willingness to specify their goals declines, until we have the "free" adult who supposedly is able to specify his own goals. Actually, because children have limited behavioral repertoires and environments, it is relatively easy to specify children's goals. As people get older, the task of goal specification becomes more difficult, and it is ultimately given over to the individual. It is not so much that we advocate behavioral control for young people and freedom for adults; it is merely that we are confident in our selection of goals for the young, and not so confident in selecting goals for adults.

Teach Individuals to Set Their Own Goals

Wherever possible, people should select their own goals. The individual is most responsive to the contingencies that determine his own welfare and is more likely to disregard divergent institutional goals. Many "modern" educational proposals allow and, in fact, demand that children select their own goals. However, the solution should not be to transfer to children the systematic ignorance adults now exercise in selecting goals. Rather, techniques for effective individual goal selection must be developed and systematically taught to children. Self-selection of goals must be faded in as part of our educational system. Self-selection skills could include the ability to recognize and evaluate alternatives, the ability to foresee distant consequences, and the ability to evaluate one's own current behavior in order to set achievable goals.

Here, then, is a second guideline: Individual goals are best set by the individual himself, when that individual has been properly equipped to set his goals.

Make Goals Explicit

At times the institution must set goals for the individual. In such cases an explicit statement of the goals provides an ethical safeguard. The statement must include an objective description of the behaviors the person is to end up with. Lakin (1969), in his discussion of ethical issues in sensitivity training states that, "it is imperative for the trainer to be first of all clear about his own intentions and goals." When dictation of goals is necessary, the cards should be placed on the table. Here, then, is guideline number three: Make goals explicit.

Make Goals Relevant

Goals set by the institution must be relevant to the individual. Often, in an attempt to skirt ethical issues, trivial or irrelevant goals are set. For example, a therapist cannot deal with a hospitalized alcoholic's problem by setting up a token economy program that makes sure he gets to dinner on time, that his bed is made, and that he has gone to his job assignment. Experience with opportunities to drink is the most relevant behavioral practice, and it shouldn't be ignored just because the staff can more conveniently run a

token economy. Similarly, our social studies programs are not going to teach good citizenship by concentrating on the natural resources of southern Illinois or the fact that Ponce de León hoped to find the fountain of youth in Florida. Thus guideline number four: Make goals relevant—behaviorally relevant.

Avoid Conformity

In setting goals for individuals, we must be careful to avoid the tendency for institutions to enforce conformity. A psychologist may consider himself a liberal in the sense that he remains uninfluenced by the Department of Defense, but it may require another intensity of courage not to be influenced by an unreasonable Puritan ethic of his university administration, of the APA, or the nondefense granting agencies. In each professional activity the psychologist must ask, "Am I helping an institution impose a behavioral goal which assumes an unreasonable amount of conformity?" Already there are many reports concerning programs which impose conformity through behavioral techniques. For example, Ayllon and Azrin (1968) in *The Token Economy* report successful attendance at religious services, and counter conditioning studies claim success in treating a cleanliness obsession (Wolpe, 1964), frigidity (Lazarus, 1963), and sexual deviations (Stevenson and Wolpe, 1960).

To summarize, then, some guidelines for selecting goals:

1) Whenever possible teach and allow the individual to select his own goals.
2) Make goals explicit.
3) Make goals relevant.
4) Avoid goals that simply enforce conformity.

SELECTING STRATEGIES

A second area of concern, when people contemplate the control of their behavior, is that the strategies chosen will be aversive. Properly designed positive reinforcement strategies are in themselves reinforcing. Although they are effective, people are more likely to feel "happy" or even "free" under their control. However, the more popular method of controlling behavior relies on punishment or the threat of punishment. Such strategies of "aversive control" are usually, in themselves, aversive and, therefore, even the "powers-that-be" are unhappy with this strategy. When people strongly object to behavioral control, they usually have in mind some sort of aversive control. But even some strategies of positive reinforcement are aversive, as, for example, when a very large amount of work is necessary in order to obtain reinforcement.

Neither the control of behavior through positive reinforcement nor control by aversive consequences is new in education. Incentives such as grades, scores, gold stars, and recess have long been used, and all of us have experienced some of these in our younger days. Nor are social reinforcers, such as praise or blame, strangers to the classroom. However, rewards are generally available only to the better students, those who need them least. Only when a student meets very high standards does strong positive encouragement occur. Lesser students draw attention only by their errors. Students at the top are controlled positively, students at the bottom are controlled negatively. The punishment of low-performing students also is less systematic and more emotional because the performance reflects upon the teacher. Punishment is more predictable by the emotional behavior of the teacher than by student behavior. So the student who wishes to avoid punishment learns to watch the teacher's behavior for signs of exasperation more than he learns to watch his own behavior for signs of success or failure. The unplanned use of punishment then can produce a scheming student and privileges for the already successful student. Consequences, therefore, as they are now used in the classroom, may be described as privilege by halo and punishment by exasperation.

Use Good Techniques of Positive Reinforcement

To be truly positive, schedules of reinforcement must not require heavy, fixed work loads. Egyptian slaves may have been rewarded occasionally with rest periods and food, but only (one presumes) after incredible amounts of work. Also, the reinforcing value of the reward must not depend on an unreasonable amount of deprivation. It is one thing to give a food pellet to a food-deprived monkey, and another thing to give a banana to a reasonably satiated monkey. Similarly, making lunch contingent on classroom performance is quite different from reinforcing seat work with a snack.

One shortcoming of positive reinforcement as used in the classroom has already been mentioned: neglect of shaping procedures, or arbitrarily high response criteria. When reinforcement is used in the laboratory, a shaping procedure is used; the initial behavioral criterion is defined in such a way as to guarantee that a successful performance will immediately occur and, therefore, an opportunity for early reinforcement. Ordinarily, in the classroom, this line is drawn very high, and only those students who can make that first jump are adequately supported for their performance.

Here, then, are some guidelines for using positive reinforcement strategies:

1. Make sure reinforcement is frequent and does not depend excessively on deprivation states.
2. Make sure the behavioral repertory of your student is adequate to obtain reinforcement even on his first try.

Minimize Aversive Control

Most of the traditional techniques overtly used to control children have relied on punishment or threat of punishment. Again, this may be one reason why adults fear the application of scientific control to adults themselves; they consider "control" to be synonymous with aversive control. Because organisms appear to find aversive control techniques in themselves aversive, educators should minimize the use of punishment. The alternative, of course, is to use correct techniques of positive reinforcement, already mentioned.

Aversive stimuli, however, are effective controllers of behavior. When faced with a behavior such as aggression or extreme classroom disruption that cannot be gradually reduced, educators often must use aversive stimuli. However, they should use it by design, not by exasperation. They should use the mildest punishment possible; time-out is a favorite mild punishment that can be used in educational settings. Loss of positive reinforcers, as in a token economy, is another. Punishment must also be consistent.

A response-cost technique may at times be a useful substitute for punishment; it might also be called the "red tape" method. For example, a teacher may have in class a child who is constantly raising his hand and asking questions, most of which are irrelevant and merely attention seeking. The teacher knows she can eventually reduce the behavior by increasing competing academic responses. However, in the meantime, she is having difficulty proceeding with the lesson. Also, she is going nuts. So she asks the child to write out his questions noting the origin of each (text, lecture, etc.). The procedure does not forbid the child to ask questions, but by adding a mildly aversive aspect to the situation, it does get the number of questions down to a level that is reinforcing to the teacher. Here are some guidelines in using aversive control:

1) Minimize its use.
2) Use the mildest punishment possible.
3) Use it consistently.
4) Consider substituting response-cost techniques for punishment.

Minimize Rules

Educational settings have traditionally featured too many rules, particularly punitive rules. Rules help stultify the school atmosphere. As Charles Silberman (1971) has written, most public schools are

"grim, intellectually sterile, and show a preoccupation with order and control, a slavish adherence to the time table and lesson plan, the obsession with routine qua routine, (the schools have) absence of noise and move-

ment, joylessness and repression, (and) the universality of formal lecture or teacher dominated 'discussion' in which the teacher instructs an entire class as a unit, the emphasis on the verbal and deemphasis on the concrete, the inability of students to work on their own, and the dichotomy between work and play."

Also, schools are supposed to move students away from reliance on institutional rules. They cannot meet this goal and proliferate their institutional rules at the same time.

I'm afraid at times, in speaking to PTA's, I have given the impression to teachers and parents that they should use more "good rules." Now I'm terribly sorry to have given that impression. I would rather they examined the rules now in effect and reduced the number of inefficient and punitive rules. Often we behavior modifiers hold that the reason good behaviors are not occurring is that there are too few clearly stated positive incentives. In fact we could state a huge number of positive incentives and make things worse if we are just adding excessive positive rules to excessive negative rules. Also, rules do not include the shaping necessary to insure that people have a chance to obtain the incentives. Flatly laying down rules with no concurrent shaping is likely to deteriorate behavior, not improve behavior.

Here is another guideline: Decrease the overall quantity of rules by eliminating punitive and unnecessary ones.

INSTITUTIONALIZATION

The scientific control of social behavior, like less systematic methods of control, will necessarily involve social institutions. I have already mentioned the effect institutionalization can have on goals: Goals are set that serve the institution, rather than its clientele. Another form of institutionalization occurs in the clientele themselves; the example usually given is patients in state hospitals. As hospitalization continues, the patient becomes apathetic, passive, and lacking in enthusiasm for and responsiveness to his environment. He even lacks the desire to leave that environment.

Seligman, Mier, and Geer (1968), in their discussion of learned helplessness, describe similar behavior in experimental animals. They present to the animal uncontrollable and unpredictable shocks. After such a history, the animal cannot solve a simple avoidance problem. He will not even try, because, in the past, aversive stimuli such as those connected with the avoidance problem have not been under his control. Similarly, in institutionalization, the patient's lack of responding may come from his inability to influence his environment.

Over the past year, I attempted to construct several behavior modification programs at a state hospital. In the process of working with the staff and obtaining the necessary approval, it became apparent that staff as well as patients can become institutionalized. The staff member learns through bitter experience not to make waves. So, in most token economy programs, we reinforce self-care behaviors instead of loving or sexual behavior. We keep the sexes segregated, even though we know that integration of the sexes would not only benefit affectionate social behavior but self-care behavior as well. Again, the welfare of the client is being sacrificed to a form of institutionalization.

We psychologists must continually examine our behavior for signs of institutionalization.

Schools are famous for squelching the enthusiasm of teachers with their "up-the-down-staircase" policies. In education, as in other areas, we may become institutionalized and unresponsive to ethical problems, and we may blindly enforce institutional goals to the detriment of the student. Through our own "learned helplessness" we may give up on some of the ethical issues discussed above.

Our society is desperately in need of help. It has tried self-analysis and found it too painful. Perhaps it has now opted for suicide by revolution. If the revolution comes, the blame will be placed on those who were aware of the behavioral principles but misused them. It will be we who are to blame, we who could have remedied the problems, not the "establishment" which has proved to us over and over again that it doesn't know what changes to make or how to make them.

We must begin, in education and throughout our society, to counteract institutionalization, to reduce the excessive use of punishment and of rules, to use positive reinforcement in a shaping procedure. From the determinist's view, freedom and dignity are not possible. But if our science is applied with consideration, our society could be both productive and content.

Political implications of applying behavioral psychology

JAMES G. HOLLAND

In recent years, there has been a steady growth in the application of the science of behavior. All applications, whether described as programmed instruction, behavior therapy, or behavior modification, reflect the same underlying principles. All involve a behavioral analysis of the situation and the arrangement of reinforcing consequences dependent upon (or contingent upon) the desired behavior; these relationships between behavior and its consequences are generically termed contingency management.

"Behavior therapies" are used in the treatment of a variety of problems from alcoholism to a long and growing list of phobias. In

Copyright © 1974 by James G. Holland. Reprinted by permission of the author.

This article is based on a paper presented at the Second Annual International Seminar on Behavior Modification, January 1972, in Mexico City. Much of the time for the preparation of this paper was made possible by the Learning Research and Development Center supported in part as a research and development center by funds from the Office of Education, Department of Health, Education, and Welfare. The opinions expressed in this publication do not necessarily reflect the position or policy of the Office of Education, and no official endorsement should be inferred.

work with autistic and severely retarded children, capabilities have been elevated to levels not thought possible only a few years ago. On mental hospital wards daily activities of patients have been managed through application of principles of reinforcement in procedures that have come to be called "token economies." The tokens or points act as reinforcers for specified behaviors and are exchangeable for goods and services. Recently economists also have expressed interest in using token economies as an experimental laboratory for economics.

Another area of most rapid adoption of behavior modification procedures is in prisons and juvenile detention centers; behavior modification can increase the possibility of rehabilitation. Within prisons behavior therapy has been used with individual prisoners, and reinforcement procedures, including token economies, have been implemented to manage the behavior of groups of prisoners. Such model prison programs are found across the country, and the Bureau of Prisons is currently planning a large research center to investigate further use of behavior modification in prisons.

In the schools from preschool through higher education, examples of behavior management principles for controlling classroom behavior are visible as well as principles for the design of curricular materials and the individualization of instruction. However, the army and industry have been the heaviest users of programmed instruction, and now experimentation in industry includes the use of behavior modification procedures in management.

The various uses of the science of behavior in modifying or managing human behavior show mixed results. Many instances are spectacular successes, others at best qualified successes, and some would have to be judged failures. But like other efforts which are based on scientific findings and which use scientific method in their development, a steady increase in the management of behavior is likely as the failures are discarded and the successful techniques are improved. Once developed, little training is needed to apply the procedures and, moreover, they often can be automated.

It is just such an increase in use of behavior modification principles that Skinner (1971) calls for in his recent book, *Beyond Freedom and Dignity*. He argues that much of the discontent in our society results from the use of aversive control. Behavioral technologists can aid design of reinforcement contingencies using positive reinforcement; hence, discontent will lessen because people will be doing what they "want."

While the behavioral scientist feels the flush of success, there are growing objections from those who view these accomplishments with alarm. The critics are the people who Skinner labels the writers of the literature of freedom and dignity. I believe that behind their concerns there are problems which merit every bit of the concern expressed. It is unfortunate, even dangerous, however, that the issue is drawn along invalid lines. Some argue for free will and speak against the proposition that all behavior follows certain fundamental laws which enable the manipulation of behavior. Others claim that, at least, if behavior were left alone by the managers, there would be basic personal freedom. In rebuttal, the scientist presents evidence of the lawfulness of behavior and reports of success in the clinic, in the school, and in prison rehabilitation. Surely such lawfulness speaks for deliberate design in the control of human affairs rather than leaving accidental contingencies in force.

It is possible to accept both the facts of behavioral science and the aims and values of those who speak against exploitative manipulation of behavior. Indeed, most behavioral scientists probably share these values with their critics. Even so, these same scientists seldom question the broader social or political implications of their work. In the design of culture and in the use of behavior management in the today's society, how will be this work ultimately be used? Into what shape will society evolve when today's decision-makers increasingly use behavior modification? Does contingency management automatically establish some of the worst features of our society as a by-product? On the other hand, are there alternative societal values and structures, however different, however revolutionary, that we need move toward? Given a completely different set of goals for society, what role might contingency management play in the formation and maintenance of such a society?

There is a real and critical basis for the resistance to the increased use of the experimental analysis of behavior in the design of social control systems. The danger is all the greater because the techniques of behavior modification do work, notwithstanding the critics' claim that they are ineffective. Problems of how behavior management should be used arise not in the science but in the social order of which the behavioral scientist is a part. In a radically different equalitarian society, there would not only be a role for the design of deliberate behavior change, but the successful transition from the present society to a revolutionary society requires such planned change. However, the form that behavior modification would take in revolutionary societies, while reflecting the same underlying laws of behavior, would be quite different in the nature of reinforcers and in the way contingencies would be set and assessed.

Those familiar with Skinner's (1948) earlier Utopian society, Walden Two, may imagine the consequences of Skinner's suggestion to be politically radical since Walden Two was a society involving social and material equality with little or nothing in the way of elitist hierarchies. But Walden Two had a hypothetical founder, Frazier, who created the society. When behavioral principles are recommended to those in authority in today's society, the implications are quite different, and the results are likely to be quite conservative. Persons with authority to manage others, whether nationwide or in small groups in classrooms, prisons, etc., are increasingly looking to the behavioral technologists to further their present objectives. The use of behavior modification then relates directly to existing power relationships. Often the psychologist, like other scientists, sees himself as totally uninvolved in the application of his work, and, indeed, the science theoretically can be used in the context of any culture. But whether the psychologist is concerned or not, the growing use of contingency management in our society most often is in the service of our present elite.

The relationship between the psychologist and the recipient of behavior modification often is not the traditional one of professional to client. The person or group of persons whose behavior is being modified may be controlled for the benefit of yet some other person or group. It seems clear that in our present social system the people who determine whose behavior is to be changed and toward what end are those in established positions of power. The science will be at the service of those who command the means to use it. One illustration is the U.S. Army's use of a behavior management system for basic training (Datel and Legters, 1970). At Fort Ord, a token-economy reinforcement system covers all aspects of basic military training from barracks inspection, standing formations, rifle-range training, to various objective test performances. Officers and noncoms punch designed areas on the trainee's card when reinforcement criteria are met. The points accumulated are exchangeable for privileges, such as attending a movie or getting a weekend pass, and the highest third get a promotion and raise in pay at the completion of the eight weeks of training.

Thus behavior modification serves power by creating a better army. One may applaud the replacement of the traditional aversive control by positive reinforcement, and it certainly must seem more humane to the trainee, but it was not done for the purpose of humanity. It was done to make a better army. The developers, Colonel Datel and Colonel Legters, readily learned that aversive control generates countercontrol and that a more effective army could result from the introduction of positive reinforcement. The form of the contingency management used by them legitimates an elitist structure which is typical of many token economies. The trained cadre, the drill sergeant, the platoon sergeant, and the officers hand out the points. The behavior management system itself takes on the characteristics of the elitist structure it serves. But the important point is the relationship between the person the system is operating upon and the person or institution the behavioral techniques really serve. The reinforcement system was not designed for the soldiers; it was designed for those who run the army. The army is the client, but the individual soldier is the one who receives the treatment. As such, the ultimate worth of the system will depend on the evaluation of the army's mission, not on the effect on the soldier.

The fact that these techniques serve those in power can be unequivocally illustrated by the use of behavior modification in foreign pacification programs. Here the resources for using the techniques exist on a gigantic scale compared to the occasional worthy use in mental hospitals at home. A survey among experts in weapons systems conducted by the Rand Corporation (Gordon and Helmer, 1964) projected the behavioral control of mass populations as a major weapons system. Most of these experts expected it to be reality by 1980; that's good old American know-how beating by four years the English masters of *1984*. In what amounts to an outright lobby to get free-flowing money the military will spend on counterinsurgency, a panel on "Defense Social Sciences and Behavioral Sciences" was formed under the sponsorship of no less than the National Academy of Sciences. The opening of this report clearly indicates how some psychologists eagerly solicit the chance to use behavioral science to manipulate behavior on behalf of the military establishment.

"The DOD mission now embraces problems and responsibilities which have not been previously assigned to a military establishment. It has been properly stated that the DOD must now wage not only warfare but 'peacefare' as well. Pacification, assistance, and the battle of ideas are major segments of the DOD responsibility. The social and behavioral sciences constitute the unique resource for support of these new requirements and must be vigorously pursued if our operations are to be effective. Hardware alone will not win modern wars without effective use of manpower in foreign environments, an understanding of the dynamics of cultural change, and a perception of the varying needs, attitudes, and ethics of other peoples. The problems presented by this broadening of mission demand the attention of all the dis-

ciplines included under the social and behavioral sciences, operating in a multidisciplinary, coordinated manner."[1]

Crude versions of contingency management have been used for some time in our pacification programs. A chapter on military psychology from a general psychology textbook (Walters, 1968) describes a case study in a so-called Token Civic Action Program which included the use of candy to reinforce village children and a lottery to reinforce retention of propaganda leaflets. A number of other contrived efforts to use trivial positive reinforcement are included in the so-called pacification of the village. Fortunately, these procedures are primitive and probably relatively ineffective. But as the science improves, the people of future Vietnams will not fare so well. One hardly can argue that the recipients of behavior modification are served by these manipulations.

A yet more odious and obvious example is found in a research proposal prepared in 1967 by the American Institutes for Research which requested and received more than a million dollars to work on problems of counterinsurgency in Thailand. The proposal (American Institutes for Research, 1967) describes the dependence of the nature of appropriate reinforcers on a subject's past history and present circumstance and gives the following practical suggestion:

"The offer of food in exchange for certain services affords a convenient example. If this has in the past been a strong stimulus, it can probably be weakened by increasing local agricultural production. If it has been a weak or neutral stimulus, it can probably be strengthened by burning the crops [p. 7]."

Nor are the benefits of this research to be limited to Thailand. The report (American Institutes for Research, 1967), continues:

"The potential applicability of the findings

---

1 This quotation from the "Report of the Panel on Defense Social Sciences and Behavioral Sciences" was reproduced in *The Washington Report*, 1967, *3*, edited by Michael Armine and published by the American Psychological Association. The report of the panel was not made public.

in the United States will also receive special attention. In many of our key domestic programs, especially those directed at disadvantaged subcultures, the methodological problems are similar to those described in this proposal, and the application of the Thai findings at home constitutes a potentially more significant project contribution [p. 34]."

For whose benefit are they planning to manipulate the reinforcing value of food—for the army and the American imperialists—and whose behavior is to be modified?

Closer to home, one of the stories circulating among operant conditioners is about a visit made by Ronald Reagan, governor of California, to a hospital ward at Patton State Hospital in California. There he watched with interest the token reinforcement system used to control the ward behavior of psychotic patients. Reagan, who has a long history of fighting what he considers "welfare handouts," was impressed by what he saw at Patton State and commented that this was the kind of giving that he was in sympathy with because "it was given for doing something." The story is usually told with some glee at the fact that the liberal psychologist seems to have deceived Reagan. But I think Reagan may be the more perceptive one in this case. The token economy, in this instance and in many other instances, follows an elitist system and seems to legitimize that form. Moreover, while I know those conducting behavior management programs on hospital wards and in prisons, etc., will take issue with me, the decisions as to what behaviors should be reinforced very often depend upon the creation of ward behavior that pleases hospital personnel. "Big Nurse" of Kesey's (1962) *One Flew Over the Cuckoo's Nest* simply adds tokens to her arsenal. Although making beds, sweeping the floor, and keeping the place neat may be valuable behaviors to the patients themselves, they more clearly reflect what Big Nurse desires. It is questionable whether nurses walking around handing out tokens do much to establish personal self-esteem in the patient. Again, the question is whether the real client is the hospital establishment or the patient.

In the schools we also find this dilemma.

A psychologist used reinforcement procedures in what he called "survival training" for young kindergarten children who were to enter conventional schools (Risley, 1971). The phrase "survival training" suggests a psychologist helping a client struggle in an oppressive system. But reading on, one finds that the so-called survival training consisted of teaching children to line up and sit quietly and avoid engaging in talking or other behavior which the teacher might consider disruptive; in other words, the student learned to do what the school establishment demanded. All this was gained through positive reinforcement rather than through aversive techniques, but it seems more like capitulation than survival.

In any contingency management system involving many people, it is difficult to determine when contingencies have been met. This limits the more stringent applications to confined, supervised situations such as classrooms, hospital wards, and prison cell blocks. However, modern technology has increased the ability of governmental or other authorities to extensively control the activities of a much larger population. The combination of the development of modern surveillance techniques, the use of computers, and further, the creation of large data banks considerably extend this possibility.

A psychologist recently has described preliminary work on a special belt which allows two-way voice communication both to monitor a subject's voice and simple physiological data and to give feedback to the subject (Schwitzgebel, 1969). The belt can work in the community over a limited broadcast range, and attempts to remove the belt can be determined. This device might be useful in monitoring people with medical problems as diabetes or epilepsy, but it also could be used to monitor the movements and activities of parolees. It is easy to imagine the belt's introduction as a liberal alternative to preventive detention. It is estimated that it would be technically feasible to monitor several hundred individuals in a single city wearing such belts.

Other developments in the technology of secret surveillance already are used extensively by agencies of the federal and local governments and by numerous private companies (cf. Westin, 1970). Coin-sized radio transmitters easily planted in briefcases, pockets, cars, and elsewhere can track an individual's movements. Very small radio transmitters can transmit conversations over short distances while the radio pill can be substituted in bottles of antihistamines and, when swallowed, enable tracking of a person throughout the day. TV camera monitoring has become commonplace in apartment elevators, lobbies, subway cars, prison cell blocks, stores, and even on street corners. Moreover, there are techniques for hiding TV cameras in rooms including the use of fiber optics which can transmit images around corners. Techniques perfected by the military enable surveillance even in darkness. Surveillance of speech over long distances requires antennae, and there are ingenious devices for hiding antennae in the seams of clothing and in the thread which stitches a coat. Receivers can be concealed in belts and belt buckles. Microphones and transmitters come disguised as a variety of common objects including water coolers, desk sets, clocks, and ashtrays. Also a variety of techniques have been perfected for bugging rooms that the agent cannot enter.

Another development of a rapidly growing technology which can increase the determination of reinforcement or punishment contingencies is the data bank. The government is already pooling the information available on every citizen—information on taxes, social security, census, the draft, applications for federal jobs, etc. Other computerized information exists in other segments of society, and, theoretically, with the rapid development of computer technology, this data could easily be drawn upon and further combined. This additional information includes credit, insurance, medical, educational, and library records. Moreover, it is projected that we will move to a "cashless" society in which the credit card will be used in all purchases, and salary will be automatically credited to accounts. As such, an individual could be tracked across the country as he traveled, rented cars, checked into motels, and made various purchases. The future potential for large-scale contingency management in these systems seems impressive indeed.

All examples of behavior modification described in this paper benefit someone higher in an elitist hierarchy than the recipient of the procedure. All use some form of direct material reinforcement, and some use competitiveness. All mimic the elitist form in that the system is run by people of special status.

What role could behavioral psychology play in a new revolutionary society? Let us suppose that the goal of the revolutionary society is that every citizen is equal in his status and in his access to material needs, with no possibility of one group amassing wealth at the expense of others. Stress is on group wisdom; individual accomplishment is valued if it contributes to group accomplishment not individual gain. Here the old reinforcement systems of competition, accumulation of wealth, and assent in the elite system of power are replaced by altruism, pride in work, and cooperation. Behavior leading to the development of separate managerial, intellectual, or academic classes would not be reinforced.

To succeed, reinforcement systems would have to change; revolution requires the remaking of man. Reich (1970) in his book, *The Greening of America*, has suggested that the new counterculture in the United States constitutes just such a revolutionary change. Another example is China's cultural revolution which was an apparently successful attempt to rid society of continued or new forms of elitism. Intellectuals and managers were reeducated and now engage in manual labor a part of the time. Students entering the university are not from an entrenched middle or upper class; they are nominated by their fellow workers in participatory meetings in which discussion centers around who might best use the education to serve society. If the success of revolution depends on the changing of man, the changing of values, or better, the changing of the nature of each individual's reinforcement system, surely there must be an important role for a science of behavior modification. However, a serious problem remains, i.e., identifying how the science can be used.

While most behavior modification work is counterrevolutionary, there are a few examples that may have merit as systems that are compatible with a new society. One example is found in Skinner's (1948) *Walden Two* in which an egalitarian society is described in which managers have no special status. A work-credit system with interesting properties as a societal token economy is also employed. The total work pool is constantly reassessed and "work credits" are divided up among the jobs. The principle of assigning credits is in the reverse order of the empirically determined desirability of the job. That is, an undesirable job earns more credits than a desirable job, and someone choosing the undesirable job might need to work only an hour a day while someone choosing the most enjoyable work might work four hours a day. There is a premium on improved techniques and no need for "making work" because the more efficiently tasks are done, the lower the total work pool and the better it is for everyone. Although this is a fictional society, the work-credit system currently is being used in an experimental community called Twin Oaks near Lyons, Virginia.

A second example of a system with compatible revolutionary values is a system developed by Fred Keller (1968) for conducting college courses. Along with the reading, lab work, movies, or other source materials, there are questions or exercises prepared for the student. The answers are reviewed and discussed by other students who previously completed those units. Although some lectures and demonstrations are given by the instructor, they are relatively infrequent and are not required. The critical conduct of the course, completing one's own units and monitoring one's peers, is in the hands of the students. Thus, the elitism of conventional classrooms is lessened.

A third example involves a deliberate effort to use reinforcement principles in the struggle for social justice. A token economy (using "freedom money") was used in reinforcing welfare recipients for activities in organizing and working for welfare rights (Miller and Miller, 1969). Although the originators of the system initially arranged reinforcement for such things as attendance at meetings, as the activities got under way the group took over the task of determining the criteria for reinforcement and in dispensing reinforcers.

A fourth and last example involves a greater change and is less compatible with traditional behavior modification. At Mendocino State Hospital in California, alcoholic "patients" become "students" of behavioral psychology (Rozynko, Flint, Hammer, Swift, Kline, and King, 1971). The view was developed that the patients could alter the determining conditions and work with their individual "hang-ups." Individually, the students identified the situations that created anxiety for themselves and prepared a graded series of these instances to be administered by a fellow student. Together the students worked on methods of coping with the situations, and administered the desensitivity procedures. Conditions were created to increase self-esteem and deal with the types of social situations which had caused difficulty. In short, a reinforcing community of peers was established which changed the values, attitudes, and social behavior of its members.

Conclusion

The use of contingency management by a group of peers who are themselves the object of the behavior modification is possible but rare. Most cases involve manipulation of behavior by trained personnel who oversee the behavior management system for the benefit of some third party. Those who apply behavior principles are dealing with the very core of power relationships among people and cannot be considered politically neutral. The choice is whether the science is to serve the elite or the people who are the object of management procedures.

19

SOME POSSIBILITIES IN BEHAVIORAL EDUCATION

The preceding section raised some issues that must be faced in the future by behavioral education. This last section presents some possibilities. The first paper, by Graubard, Rosenberg, and Miller, discusses an experimental approach to some of the problems raised in the preceding section. The experimenters worked directly with the subjects of behavior control techniques and taught them skills that can make that control reciprocal. Unfortunately, the behavior of people who exercise control over "deviants" can include both inappropriate labeling and inadvertent maintaining of undesired behavior. To the extent that deviant people can modify the behavior of their controllers, they will be on their way to being their own therapists, teachers, or controllers. The article by Graubard et al. also illustrates a crucial point in the long-standing controversy between those who feel that techniques for the control of behavior should be developed and applied and those who fear that development. In fact, techniques for control of behavior probably will continue to grow. Rather than trying to stifle that growth, those who fear abuses of behavior control should help promote the widest possible dissemination of the techniques. With dissemination can come effective countercontrol procedures; the paper by Graubard et al. provides a concrete illustration of this process of dissemination and countercontrol.

This section, and the book, ends with a discussion, by Pennypacker, of the problems surrounding the developmental stage characterized as "youth." Pennypacker points out that our society delays an individual's participation in adult contingencies of reinforcement far beyond the age of physical maturity; many of the problems associated with "youth" may be due to this delay. Young people, for example, may lack "realism" because they have not been exposed to realistic contingencies in their families or their schools. At present the educational system operates inefficiently and keeps young people in an artificial educational atmosphere much longer than necessary. Behavioral education could provide solutions to the situation described by Pennypacker. By making education more efficient, it could prepare young people to cope with the real world at an age much closer to biological maturity. In addition, it could be used to introduce more realistic contingencies into the educational system itself. Whatever the exact solution, some alternative to keeping young people in behavioral limbo must be found. Reform of our educational system must be a major part of that alternative.

Student applications of behavior modification to teachers and environments or ecological approaches to social deviancy

PAUL S. GRAUBARD, HARRY ROSENBERG, AND MARTIN B. MILLER

This paper describes how social deviance and maladaptive behavior can be alleviated through the use of behavior modification techniques. In the four experiments reported here a novel approach was taken: The "normals" were treated to increase their tolerance for deviant behavior.

This approach was developed as a result of our concern at seeing individuality and creativity suppressed in "exceptional" children, who were expected to conform to rules of the dominant culture. These children are often the tragic victims of our society. Under the mantle of "helping," society has stigmatized these children with labels such as "mentally retarded," "psychotic," and "schizophrenic." They have been subjected to loss of privacy, to public ridicule, to involuntary detention in training schools and hospitals, and to loss of prestige and privileges. In many cases, this "help" also leads to physical abuse (James, 1969). This phenomenon is also compounded by racism and class bias. In our opinion, it is no accident that special education classes, child guidance clinics, mental hospitals, and training schools are filled with youth of minority-group status far out of proportion to their actual numbers in the population.

For an understanding of our approach, first imagine that a child has absented himself for thirty-seven days of an eighty-day school term. If he is referred to a guidance counselor or clinical psychologist, the medical label (which usually tends to preempt all others) can be applied to him. He will be viewed and designated as "school phobic," "emotionally disturbed," or "sick" to some degree. A dean of discipline or probation officer would label and treat the same child as a "juvenile delinquent," "incorrigible youth," or "youth in need of supervision." Other citizens might view this absentee behavior as "wrong" and would recommend moral lessons dealing with the rewards of virtue and respect for diligence. In contrast, some members of a counterculture might define this same truancy as heroic behavior to be encouraged, as it seems to violate an oppressive law.

Thus, the problem of maladaptive behavior (or what is popularly called emotional disturbance) can be reasonably interpreted in the language of psychopathology, of learning theory, or of social deviancy. The social deviancy model, long popular in anthropology, has seen little use in the field of applied behavior analysis. This is unfortunate, as it is a model which carries many implications for both understanding and ameliorating behavior problems.

In her study of comparative cultures, Benedict (1934) noted the ease with which people that would be considered abnormal in America were functional in other cultures. It did not matter what kind of "abnormality" she looked at—those which indicated extreme instability or those which were more in the nature of character traits like sadism or delusions of grandeur—there still were well described cultures in which these abnormals could function at ease and with honor. These people apparently functioned without danger or difficulty to their society. If one agrees that given behaviors are not good, bad, healthy, or pathological in themselves, and that any component of behavior is either adaptive or maladaptive for a specific culture, then "nonnormative," "pathological," and "social deviant" become equivalent terms. Use of this conceptualization demands examination of: (1) the specific behavior; (2) the perceiver of the behavior; and (3) the effect of the behavior upon the perceiver.

Theories and methods generated by the field of ecology are of great value here, as they view man within the ecosystem or context of his environment. Ecologists do not conceptualize or treat "emotional disturbance." They attempt to describe behavior

Reprinted by permission of the authors.

which is a mismatch between surroundings and individuals or groups. The implication is that behavior, behavior analysis, and planning strategies to reduce conflict can be conducted only in the originating habitat. It is the "goodness of fit" of behaviors to specific environments that must be scrutinized. Rabkin and Rabkin (1969) say that it is the interface (described as the meeting of two social systems, including the context or background of their encounter) and the clash between cultures that is in need of change when clinical intervention is requested. The behavior of neither the behaver nor the perceiver in isolation from this interface is the target. The behaver, whether a member of either minority or majority groups, should be considered with reference to culture-specific factors. This is particularly true if we take the pluralistic ideals of our society and the rights of minority groups seriously. In our opinion, aberrant behavers constitute a minority group as meaningful as groups composed of ethnically different members of the population. In the field of mental health, we usually find one group—usually that within the dominant, established culture—which labels the behavior of individuals from another group as disturbed. Those so labeled usually come from a political or social minority. Both Szasz (1970) and Rhodes (1969) discuss the political underpinnings of mental-health labeling in current society.

The treatment of "social deviants" by "normals" cannot be extensively documented here. The theme of cruelty to underdogs runs through the social history of Western society and is extensively detailed in our literature (e.g., Chekhov's *Ward Six*, 1965) and the harrassment of "deviants" can be seen on any playground as "normal" children torment a "different" child. Thus, if we work with the "goodness of fit" model, to change the behavior of "normals" may be of equal importance to changing the behavior of "deviants." Change in the interface between conflicting groups is the most significant factor. The behavioral literature is replete with examples of how behavior modification has been used to change the behavior of the social deviant (e.g., any issue of *Journal of Applied Behavior Analysis*). There are few examples in the literature where deviants, as part of a planned process of change, were taught to modify the behavior of normals.

We feel that it is necessary to teach deviants to change other people, not only for self-protection, but also because the positive use of power leads to self-enhancement and positive feelings about the self. If children are to be more than recipients of someone's benevolence, they must learn how to operate on society, as well as to accept being operated upon. Moreover, our clinical data indicated that in the process of learning to change others, the "deviant" changes his own behavior and receives feedback and reinforcement for this change.

The four experiments described in this paper took place in an agricultural community in the San Joaquin Valley in California. "Anglos" comprise the predominant group within the town, although there is a large Chicano population and a small black community. Each experiment describes a special application of our approach. These experiments are reported as representative of our method, and we assume a much wider spectrum of possible applications than is illustrated here.

EXPERIMENT I: CHILDREN-MODIFIED TEACHER BEHAVIOR

This experiment took place in a school which had a reputation for being hostile to the special education program in general and towards adolescent minority-group children in particular. Experience had shown that it was extremely difficult to reintegrate special education children into the mainstream of that particular school; it was felt that many regular class teachers scapegoated special education children. Supervisors' directives that all children, including special education children, were to be treated equally had little effect.

The goal of the special education program was to reintegrate its members into regular classes of the school. The children spent more time with each of the regular class teachers than any professional consultant or administrator could and had the greatest personal interest in changing their teachers. They were, therefore, expected to exert the most influence over their teachers, if given an effective technology.

Method

Subjects. Seven children with an age range of 12 to 15 were selected as behavior engineers. Two children were Caucasian, 2 were black, and 3 were Chicanos. Each engineer was assigned 2 clients (teachers), and each had the responsibility of accelerating praise rates and decelerating negative comments and punishment by the teachers.

Procedure. The class day in the school was organized into seven 43-minute periods. Special education children met with a special class teacher 3 periods a day and were integrated into the regular classes for 4 periods daily.

Instruction and practice in behavior modification theory and techniques were given during 1 period a day by the special class teachers. Initially, instruction was on a one-to-one basis, but later the whole class worked together on practicing their newly learned skills. The children were told that they were going to participate in an experiment. Scientific accuracy was stressed as being extremely important, and students were directed to record all the client-teacher's remarks during the pilot period of 2 weeks. Through consensual validation of the class and special education staff, these comments were sorted into positive or negative groups.

Techniques taught to the children included making eye contact with teachers and asking for extra help, and, further, children were taught to make reinforcing comments such as: "Gee, it makes me feel good, and I work so much better when you praise me," and "I like the way you teach that lesson." They also were taught to use reinforcing behavior such as sitting up straight and nodding in agreement as teachers spoke. These techniques and phrases were used contingent upon teacher performance. The pupils were

also taught to perform the "Ah-Hah" reaction (so notably described by Fritz Redl) as follows: When a pupil understood an assignment, he was to ask the teachers to explain it once again. In the middle of the second explanation the student was to exclaim "Ah Hah! Now I understand; I could never get that point before."

Pupils also were taught to break eye contact with the teacher during a scolding, to ignore a teacher's provocation, to show up early for class, and to ask for extra assignments. These techniques were explicitly taught and practiced repeatedly. Simulation techniques and role playing were employed. Video tapes were used extensively so that other children could monitor their performance and, under both class and teacher promptings, adjust those factors that were targets for change.

Reliability. Each of the 7 students was observed in action. At various times, an observer-aide unobtrusively recorded his own version of positive and negative contacts within the teacher-student interface. These records were compared later with those of the student-participants for the same observation periods. On positive contacts from teacher-clients, the range of correlations between student and observer records was very narrow, from a low of .815 to a high of .980. The mean correlation across 7 student-observer combinations is .942. On negative contacts, the range of correlations is from .453 for 1 student-observer combination to 1.00 for 2 such combinations. These perfect correlations reflect the fact that students often were observed well into the experiment, during preiods when negative contacts by teachers were few, often zero. Therefore, agreement between students and observers in the absence of negative contact for such periods is quite high. The average over the 7 student-observer combinations is .957.

An interesting sidelight was that at the beginning, when procedures were piloted, the observer-aides consistently differed from the children in the number of positive comments made. Closer monitoring revealed that the aides were more accurate in recording, as often the special education children were unable to recognize conventional phrases of praise as such. Therefore, they consistently underestimated the amount of praise that was given to them. Teachers were experimentally naive.

Results

Data were collected during a 9-week period. With 7 student-engineers, each with 2 teacher-clients, there were, in effect, 14 replications to examine. An ABA design was employed: The first 2 weeks were considered baseline weeks and were followed by 5 weeks of intervention. During the last 2 weeks, students were instructed to stop all reinforcements, thereby applying extinction.

Data on positive contacts by each teacher-behavior engineer during the 9 weeks were cast into a repeated-measures analysis of variance. One data point was used per student-teacher combination for each week (the average number of positive contacts during the week for that combination). The results of that ANOVA are summarized in Table 1.

The results are fairly straightforward. There is no significant interaction between weeks and teacher replications and no significant overall effect for teachers. There is a very marked effect for weeks (which we shall return to in our discussion briefly), and as might be expected, a significant effect for subjects.

A similar analysis on negative teacher-as-client contacts is summarized in Table 2. In

Table 1. *Analysis of variance for positive contacts in student-teacher shaping as a function of weeks and teacher replication.*

Source	df	ms	F
Subjects (S)	6	113.83	4.84**
Weeks (A)	8	975.88	41.49**
Teacher Rep. (B)	1	6.00	1.50
A × B	8	6.00	1.68
A × S	48	23.52	
B × S	6	4.00	
A × B × S	48	3.58	

** $p < .01$

Table 2. *Analysis of variance for negative contacts in student-teacher shaping as a function of weeks and teacher replication.*

Source	df	ms	F
Subjects (S)	6	211.50	7.06**
Weeks (A)	8	562.75	18.80**
Teacher Rep. (B)	1	8.00	9.64*
A × B	8	1.25	.48
A × S	48	29.94	
B × S	6	.83	
A × B × S	48	2.60	

* $p < .05$
** $p < .01$

most respects, the effects here are similar to those for positive contacts. The exception is a significant effect for Teacher Replications which, though reliable, is quite small in magnitude.

Figure 1 shows a plot of average frequency of positive contact, and of negative contacts over the nine weeks of the experiment. For positive contacts, there is a significant jump from week 2 (a baseline week) to week 3 (the first week of treatment). There is a general improvement in frequency of positive contacts throughout the next 4 weeks, all intervention weeks. With week 8 (the first week of extinction), there is a marked and significant drop in positive contacts by teacher-clients. By week 9, the frequency of positive contacts has fallen to below the base rates for weeks 1 and 2, although this is not statistically significant.

The results on negative contacts are fairly analogous to those for positive contacts. Indeed, they appear to be mutually dependent, until we examine the extinction weeks, 8 and 9. Here, although there is a significant increase in negative contact from the last week of treatment (week 7) to the first week of extinction (week 8), the frequency of negative contacts does not increase significantly between weeks 8 and 9. Also, negative contacts during extinction are still significantly fewer than for weeks 1 and 2, the baseline weeks. It clearly can be seen that children are able to modify teacher behavior, at least temporarily. However, the teacher-clients ap-

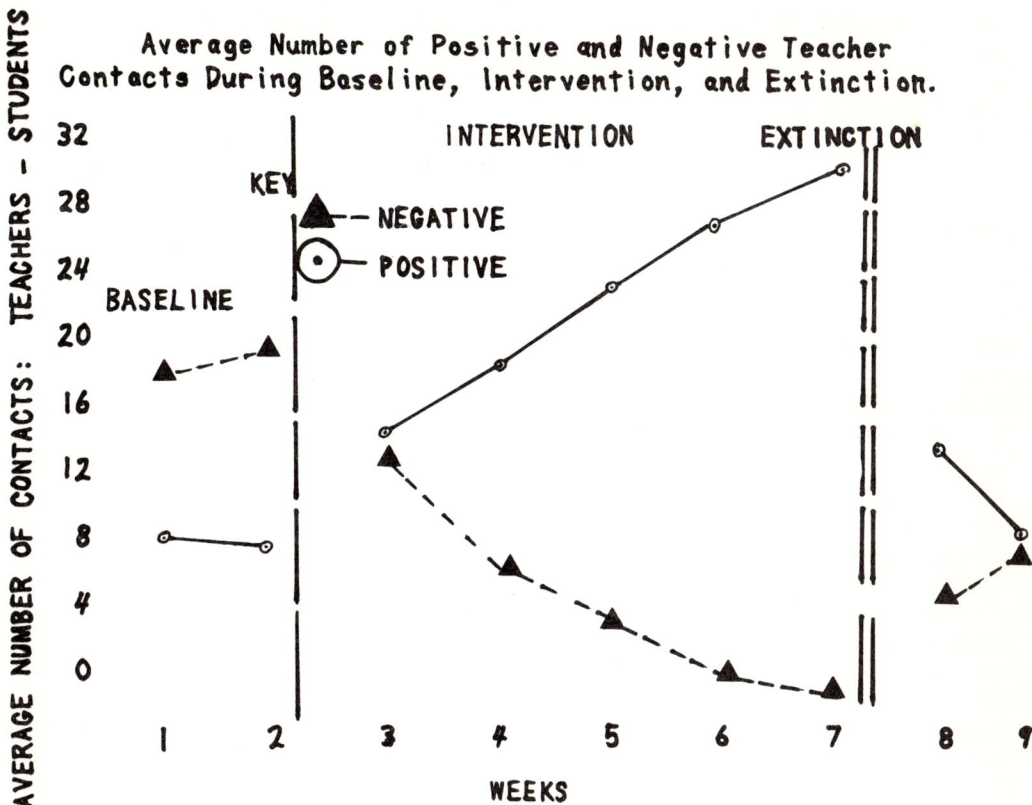

Figure 1. *Average number of positive and negative teacher contacts during baseline, intervention, and extinction.*

pear to be quite dependent on a maintained reinforcement schedule for positive contacts; this is less the case for negative contacts, at least as far as these data can show us. Of course, the frequency of negative contacts might have increased to base-rate levels or even beyond in subsequent weeks, but these data are beyond the scope of the present analyses. Nevertheless, we might hazard a guess that teacher-clients did learn to be less punitive with training, and that this training held to some extent even when the reinforcements were withdrawn. It does appear, however, that teachers, like most people, are backsliders and need a high level of reinforcement to maintain particular kinds of new behaviors.

A number of ethical questions are raised by this experiment, not the least of which is the surreptitious observation of teacher behavior by aides in order to establish a reliability coefficient. This was felt to be justified by the necessity for scientific validation of the procedure. The observations were in no way used as evaluation of teacher performance. These data will not affect teachers retaining jobs or getting increments, nor will the data contribute to any of the rewards or punishments established by the school system. Data concerning teachers and children are confidential; our interest is in exploring the consequences of particular management techniques, not in specifying or evaluating individuals.

The procedures used seemed to be effective within a very short period of time. The children's labor contributing to effective change was free; and it is certainly less costly to employ pupils, using reinforcements readily available in the classroom, than it is to pay clinical personnel within the traditional medical model to change behavior.

EXPERIMENT II: CHANGING TOLERANCE FOR NOISE

The second experiment consisted of increasing teacher tolerance to noise. One of the most basic issues of teacher-pupil interaction is the complaint that children are too noisy. Our approach was not to attempt elimination of the noise problem by producing more quiet children. Rather, we wanted to promote teacher readiness to accept the children's spontaneous noise level. Given our ecological approach we felt the significant factor was elimination of conflict in this aspect of the interface between teacher and students.

Method

Subjects. We chose 4 classrooms for this experiment that were highly controlled by the teachers in charge. The classes selected were staffed by teachers in the district with the highest amount of personal investment in developing a contingency management program along the lines suggested by Hewitt (1967). One of the 4 teachers was the first teacher in the district to develop an engineered and structured classroom. This teacher had been a consultant to various districts throughout the state in training new special education teachers in the use of an engineered classroom. None of the 4 teachers was likely to prefer an increase of tolerance to classroom noise level as each had received considerable recognition for skill in modifying the behavior of deviant children and maintaining a quiet, well-controlled, structured classroom. The teachers' ages ranged from 37 years to 58 years old, with a mean age of 46, and their years of teaching experience ranged from 12 to 21 years with a mean of 17.

Procedure. After baseline reading (to be explained), the special education supervisor praised each teacher generally for competence and specifically for tolerance of noise and for

freedom of self-expression allowed to the children. The supervisor then asked each teacher's permission to use his classroom as a model. The stated purpose was to provide an opportunity for other teachers to observe how much freedom of self-expression and behavior a good teacher permits students. Visitors, including the superintendent of the district, were brought in, and the students' freedom of self-expression and behavior were underscored by the supervisor as being worthy of emulation.

Decibel recordings were surreptitiously taken by aides and were checked for reliability by having 2 observers corroborate the readings. Perfect agreement between observers was reached. The decibel readings were taken by hiding a tape recorder in a briefcase and bringing it into the classrooms. Recordings were taken during the same activity and at the same time of day in each instance.

Results

Audio tapes were replayed into a decibel counter, and the 5 highest readings were averaged for one data point. The first of the 5 weeks was a baseline week, and the analysis of variance was used to measure changes. Since 4 classes were used, the experiment was replicated 4 times. The results of this analysis are summarized in Table 3.

Table 3. *Analysis of variance of changes in noise level over 5 weeks.*

Source	df	ms	F
Replications	3	33.67	1.82
Weeks	4	664.75	35.93**
Residual	12	18.50	

** $p < .01$

Figure 2 is a plot of the 5 weekly averages for the 4 classrooms combined. It shows a systematic increase in noise level over weeks, as we hoped it would. Not only was there a dramatic change in the level of noise tolerated, but the classroom did become freer.

It is not at all unusual for reform-minded

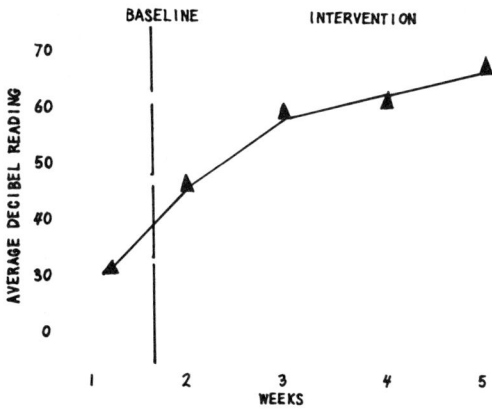

Instances Selected

Figure 2. *Average noise level and combined classrooms as a function of directed praise to teachers.*

people to enter schools in an attempt to bring in innovative programs. Too often they fail because teachers are viewed as "obsolete," "rigid," and "maintainers of the status quo!" These assumptions are communicated to the teacher, and consequently teacher resistance prevents the reform, no matter how good or well intentioned. This experiment demonstrates that teachers can change and change quite radically. In this case, observers of high prestige—supervisors and superintendents—used rewards such as praise, reinforcement, and modeling. They communicated the good job the teachers were doing to others. In short, the positive aspects of the teacher's performance became an underlined focus. In essence, this is what the children in the previous experiment did. Significant change was effected in the present case, also.

EXPERIMENT III:
DEVIANT CHILDREN CHANGE NORMALS

The third experiment consisted of training special education children (officially designated as emotionally handicapped) to modify the behavior of "normal" children. This was again done using the rationale of the social deviancy model and the need the experimenters felt to change the interface between children who were clashing. We observed that often the "normal" children scapegoated the

special education children, using derogatory terms such as "retards," "rejects from the funny farm," and "tardos." A popular game for the normal children was "Saluggi": Bigger children would throw one child's cap around while the unfortunate owner ran around vainly trying to reclaim his property. Being teased, ignored, and ridiculed were part of the social roles thrust upon the special education children.

Method

Our work with the special education children consisted of individual counseling by 2 resource teachers. We explicitly explained and illustrated operant theory to the children. The counseling consisted of one 30-minute session per week which lasted for a 9-week period. The special education children were asked to list those children who made school unpleasant for them. They specifically described the behavior of the children whose behavior they wanted to change and those children they wished to spend more time with.

Among the things counted were the number of hostile physical contacts that took place on the playground with their "arch enemy," if that was the problem, or the number of snubs or hostile remarks directed toward each child. Positive contacts with particular children were recorded and quantified if the special education child's goal was to increase such interactions. The data collection was done by the special education children and handed in each day to their counselors.

Procedure. The behavioral engineers were taught the following methods: (1) *Extinction*, or walking away from the chase-the-cap game, breaking eye contact with the provocative children, and ignoring negative remarks. (The children received primary reinforcers such as candy from their counselor for each instance in which they succeeded.) (2) *Reinforcement* or explicitly sharing toys or candy or giving compliments to those children who made positive contact with the behavior engineers. (3) *Reinforcing* incompatible responses, by first initiating and reinforcing the children participating in active ball games, etc. (4) *Setting contingencies* such as helping the children with homework, crafts, and school activities was also used.

Reliability. As with the student-to-teacher study, observers in the peer-to-peer experiment unobtrusively checked and recorded positive and negative comments by peer-clients. On positive contacts by peer-clients the correlation between the 6 student trainers and their observers ranged from .570 to .984. The average correlation across student-observer combinations is .824, rather low as reliability coefficients should go, but given the inherent difficulties in making surreptitious observations in playgrounds and classrooms, the best we could get.

The reliability for negative comments are about the same as for positive comments, ranging from .435 to .957, for an average of .876. In the peer-to-peer study each of the 6 students as behavior engineers had 3 client-peers who entered treatment on a staggered baseline, as schematized in Figure 3.

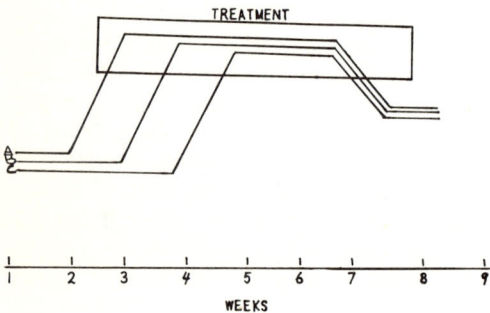

Figure 3. *Schematic of design in Experiment 3.*

Client A enters treatment after 2 baseline weeks; Client B after 3 weeks; Client C after 4 weeks. Reinforcements are subsequently withdrawn during 2 extinction weeks for all clients. Since there are 6 student-trainers, each line (A, B, and C) applies to 6 different client-peer combinations.

Results

Data were cast into separate analyses of variance, one for each frequency of positive

Table 4. *Analysis of variance for positive contacts in peer-to-peer shaping as a function of weeks and treatment-entry conditions.*

Source	df	ms	F
Subjects (S)	5	81.00	5.08**
Weeks (A)	8	571.75	35.89**
Entry Cond. (B)	2	202.50	4.47*
A × B	16	15.44	1.73†
A × S	40	15.93	
B × S	10	45.30	
A × B × S	80	8.95	

† $p = .064$
* $p < .05$
** $p < .01$

Table 5. *Analysis of variance for negative contacts in peer-to-peer shaping as a function of weeks and treatment-entry conditions.*

Source	df	ms	F
Subjects (S)	5	665.40	12.76**
Weeks (A)	8	1321.88	25.36**
Entry Cond. (B)	2	129.00	1.46
A × B	16	34.69	1.33
A × S	40	52.13	
B × S	10	88.50	
A × B × S	80	26.08	

** $p < .01$

and negative contacts by client-peers. Table 4 shows a summary of ANOVA for positive contacts.

If the staggered baseline has a reliable impact, we would expect significance for the interaction between weeks and treatment—entry conditions, the A×B interaction term. The interaction is significant with a probability of .06 (which we take seriously enough).

Figure 4 shows a plot of positive contact frequencies over the 9 weeks of the experiment for client-peers in the 3 different entry conditions. Things turn out pretty well according to plan with the exception that the difference between week 2 (the last baseline week) and week 3, the first treatment week for A-type clients, is not significant.

The corresponding differences between the last week of baseline and the first week of

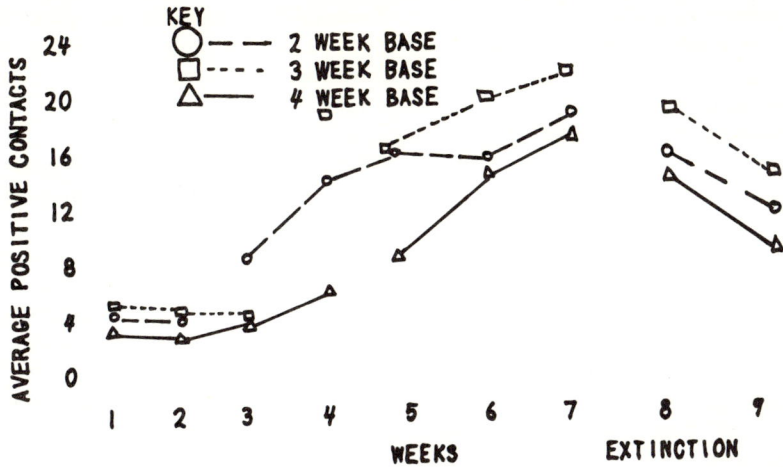

Figure 4. *Average of position contacts by teachers as a function of student-delivered reinforcement.*

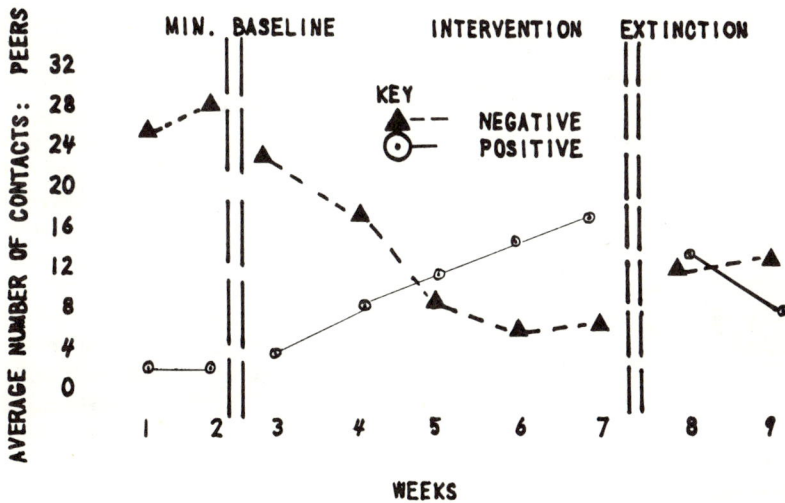

Figure 5. *Average number of positive and negative contacts by peers as a function of treatment.*

treatment for B- and C-type clients are significant drops in positive contact frequencies. These drops are still well above the baseline rates for all 3 client groups. This can be contrasted to what happened to the teacher-clients who fell back to their base rates during extinction of positive contacts.

Table 5 shows the ANOVA for negative contacts in the peer-to-peer shaping.

Here, we must dismiss the weeks-by-entry-conditions interaction term as nonsignificant. There is, however, a clear effect for weeks.

Figure 5 shows average positive and negative contact frequencies contrasted for all 18 client-peers combined, ignoring the staggered baseline conditions.

Notice that negative contact rate shows a systematic drop with treatment beginning with week 3, which actually reflects only a third of the client-peers in treatment. Extinction in weeks 8 and 9 yields an increase in frequency of negative contacts, but once again, these averages are still different from any of those for baseline weeks.

We note that, at least with reference to positive contacts, the students—as behavior engineers—are able to manage a fairly subtle posture, gradually bringing in a new client in successive weeks of treatment. They are doing about as well in exercising control over human behavior as many a graduate does in a Ph.D. thesis or professionals who charge $50 an hour, for that matter.

Our conclusions from this data are that deviant children can change the behavior of "normal" children, and that hostile physical contacts, instances of teasing, etc., were considerably reduced. Moreover, approach behaviors, such as invitations to parties, invitations to play in ball games, etc., were considerably accelerated. At no time did any teacher intervene with the normal children and encourage or limit their behavior. Behavior modification appears to be a powerful tool which can give "deviant" children the social skills and power to change the behavior of others toward them. While the "deviant" children undoubtedly changed their own behavior, the important thing remains that they did dramatically change the behavior of others toward them.

EXPERIMENT IV: CHANGING THE PERCEPTIONS OF NORMALS TOWARD SPECIAL EDUCATION CLASSES AND CHILDREN

This experiment was initiated because, despite the gratifying academic progress made by children in special education classes (e.g., Rosenberg, Graubard, and Miller, 1971), we were concerned with the loss of prestige and concomitant harrassment that they were sometimes subjected to. It has been recognized by special educators for the past decade that the normal child shuns contact with the special child and avoids going into or near the special education classroom, and attempts to change this have been largely unsuccessful (Lilly, 1971). Placement in a special class for the "emotionally disturbed" or "retarded" may become a self-fulfilling prophecy and be experienced by the child as defeating.

One reason for the stigma often attached to the special education room is its isolation from the mainstream of regular education. It was the goal of this project to make special education classrooms a focal point of positive attention for the entire student body and school and to have the special education classrooms become places visited more frequently by regular students than any other place in the school.

Method

We wanted to change the perception of the special education children in the eyes of "normals." This was done by instituting a whole set of contingencies as part of the special education program. Various kinds of reinforcing activities took place in the special education classrooms and were sponsored by the special education students. These activities included wrestling, boxing, fishing derbies, crafts classes, pottery, listening to music, ice-skating, and other exciting trips. These activities were available to regular students only if they participated in these activities with special education students; in many cases they were available to regular students only at the invitation of the special education student.

We took a pool of children who had been referred to special education classes because of "peculiar mannerisms," low academic status, and "inappropriate behaviors and social skills," and randomly assigned one group to treatment, while the other group remained untreated.

Results

We examined 2 indices of changes in the acceptance of the special education children by normals. One was more or less traditional, the other relatively unusual, as well as unobtrusive. The first of these indices was the

Table 6. *Analysis of variance on sociometric ranking for special and regular class children (n=10 per group).*

Source	df	ms	F
Subjects (S)	19	77.22	1.58
Spec. vs. Reg. (B)	1	585.00	11.94**
error (b)	18	49.00	
Within Ss	20		
Pre vs. Post (A)	1	141.00	1.77
A × B	1	198.00	10.21
error (W)	18	19.39	

** $p < .01$

Table 7. *Analysis of variance on visitor rate over weeks as function of special treatment.*

Source	df	ms	F
Replications	3	6716.33	4.04*
Weeks	7	7197.29	4.33**
Residual	21	1663.86	

* $p < .05$
** $p < .01$

sociometric status of children labeled "disturbed" who were in the special privileges group as compared with status of similarly labeled children who were not in the special privileges group. We considered sociometric status for 10 children in each group. Fortunately, we had sociometric data on the children before introduction of the special privileges conditions as well as for some months afterward, and we took a pre-post measure (Lilly, 1971). The summary of the analysis of these data is shown in Table 6.

The sociometric averages, pre and post, for the two groups are plotted in Figure 6. Most notably, the significant interaction between pre- versus post-status and groups highlights the significant improvement in sociometric status for the special class students (revealed inversely in Figure 6; i.e., the higher the average, the lower the sociometric standing). Differences between the 2 groups on the premeasure are not significant. However, while the special group shows a sharp improvement in sociometric status in pre-to-post effects, the control group shows a nonsignificant drop in status.

The second index considers the visitor rate in 4 special classes which were given the privileges specified earlier. We examined the number of visitors to each such classroom for 3 baseline weeks and then for 5 subsequent weeks after the introduction of special privileges. Table 7 gives a summary of the ANOVA on these data, with classes as repli-

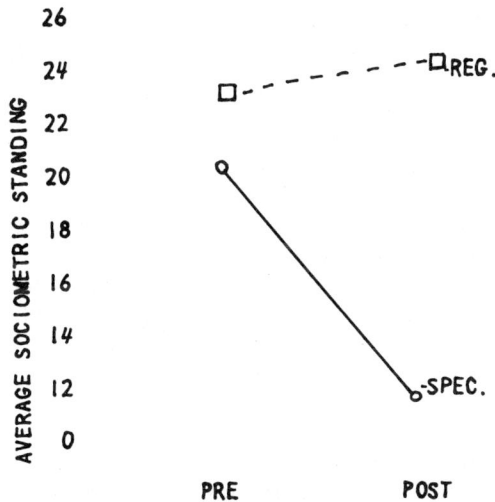

Figure 6. *Pre- and post-sociometric standings of target children and controls.*

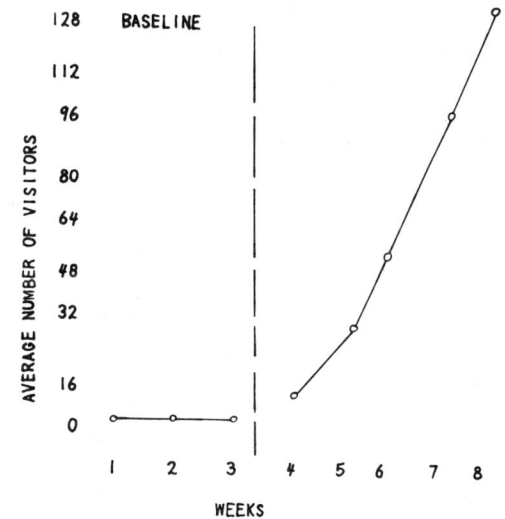

Figure 7. *Average number of visitors to Special Projects Center as a function of treatment.*

cations considered over the 8 weeks taken into account in analysis.

Figure 7 presents the weekly visiting-rate averages graphically. There is a significant effect for replications, i.e., all classes do not share the same rate of visitation. Most particularly, there is a clear-cut and dramatic increase in the number of visitors who came into the special classes when contrasted with rates during the baseline period, and these classes did, in fact, become the most popular in the school.

GENERAL SUMMARY AND CONCLUSION

The main implication of these four studies is that socially deviant groups can readily change the behavior of those groups who generally exercise the most control over them. The program that was implemented in this school also shows that it is possible to diffuse power, even political power, in a way that is not usually available to those from minority groups. Currently, establishment groups, such as teachers, normals, and high-status children, retain control over the power structure within the schools. It has been demonstrated that this control may be neutralized by developing the capacity to change others' behavior in those groups usually regarded by society as being in need of change. This is particularly important, as several observers (e.g., Sloane, 1971; Madsen, 1970) have noted, that when research or pilot programs are terminated teachers tend to revert to normal or baseline conditions. Therefore, so crucial a variable as power or the issue of behavior control must be dealt with if the "deviant" is to be released from the not-too-tender mercies of power groups such as clinics, schools, and courts.

We feel confident that the lives of the individual children involved in these studies have been helped. We wonder in the long run what such diffusion of power might bring.

The challenge of youth

HENRY S. PENNYPACKER

"Youth" has been defined as a new psychological stage of life occurring after adolescence and before adulthood. It is a new stage of life in the sense that it has emerged fairly recently in those cultures which, for a variety of reasons, do not require all of their members to assume the full status of adulthood when they have achieved complete physical growth and sexual maturity. Let us glance briefly at the biological and behavioral mechanisms of human growth and development and see if we can illuminate some of the principles of human behavior which we can apply to the problems of youth.

We begin with some hard biological facts. Every member of virtually every animal species goes through a fixed series of rather clearly definable maturational stages: Infancy, childhood, adolescence, and adulthood are the four stages which have most generally been used to describe these periods of the human's life. We are well aware that, in the biological sense, adulthood is reached when reproduction can occur, and the genetic material of the species is transmitted to yet another generation.

What is the importance of behavior to this whole cycle? It is clear that the organism must first of all survive for a considerable period of time if these various maturational stages are to unfold. Further, the organism must survive the influence of a tremendously complex set of circumstances and their interrelationships we call the environment. The interface between the organism and its environment—the details of the contact between a living creature and the world around it—is what, in the most general sense, we mean by behavior. For example, a young predator, like a mountain lion, must successfully learn the skills and complex behaviors of hunting and killing prey, or he will perish before he becomes even a year old. A mountain lion who, for whatever reason, fails to display the correct combination of innate and learned behavior patterns that produce food does not earn the opportunity to transmit this deficiency into the gene pool of the species, since he does not survive to maturity and does not reproduce.

The process of maturation, then, may be seen to be dependent upon adaptation to the environment through basically behavioral means. Thus, as the environment—both internal and external—changes, behavior must change in order for adaptation to occur. If the environment changes and the behavior remains rigid and fixed, the organism is not likely to survive. In this sense, the maturational stages may be thought of as programmed changes in the internal environment to which the organism must adapt by appropriate modifications of his behavior. Such modification of behavior largely comes about through the effects the behavior has on the environment. In other words, behavior may be said to be a product of its consequences, defined as changes in the internal and external environment. This principle operates very clearly in the case of the human organism.

The behavioral capabilities of the human infant are extremely limited. His most effective means of producing change in his environment is vocal. He cries when he is hungry or uncomfortable, and there soon appears a parent, who, in order to stop the crying, feeds or otherwise attends to the infant. This arrangement suffices until sufficient neurological development has occurred for locomotion to begin. Now the infant is able to move about in his environment—each movement producing environmental changes. These changes may be extremely pleasurable, or they may be painful. In any case, the importance lies in the fact that they are *caused* by the infant's behavior and serve as the basis for all learning about the effects of what he does and what happens to him.

As language develops, the infant, whom we now call the child, learns that he can exert some control over the social environment—his parents, siblings, peers, and animals—through his verbal behavior in essentially the same manner that he was able to exert control over his material environment by his motor behavior. It is at this stage that socialization starts, and children begin to learn the regular and predictable effects of their behavior upon other peoples' behavior. The social customs and practices of the culture are acquired in this way.

With language in the case of the human, another important capacity is acquired at about this time: the ability to arrange and react to postponed consequences for one's behavior. Closely related, and equally dependent upon language, is the ability to generate private, personal consequences for one's own behavior. A five-year-old who tells himself that he is a good boy when he clears the table of the dinner dishes is displaying this capacity. Through these two capabilities—the ability to tolerate delays of consequence occurrence and the ability to generate one's own consequences—comes the capability for what we call self-management or self-control. Thus, as a child matures, he becomes able to generate long and complicated sequences of behavior whose payoffs are quite remote. He can, for example, work long and hard in a school course although the final grade and the promotion to the next level may be deferred by a matter of weeks or months. He is similarly able to engage in interpersonal relationships such as dating and courting which may have no payoff at all in a substantive sense, save that which he can provide for himself. In other words, his behavior may be sustained by the thought that "he is doing the right thing" or "we will get married when we graduate from high school." In any case the importance of self-management to human behavior cannot be overemphasized. Almost all of our social and cultural institutions depend upon this capacity for their existence.

In the scheme we have outlined, by the time the individual has passed puberty and is capable of reproduction, ideally he has acquired the skills of self-management which would entitle him to membership in the adult society. Most importantly, he should be able to postpone the most powerful of all gratifiers

—copulation—until he has been able to so arrange the environment that the consequences of that behavior—parenthood—will not be chaotic and aversive. In order to do this, a young male traditionally has gotten a job, saved some money, and was generally able to provide for his offspring. The female learned the skills of homemaking or, less frequently, those of a commercial career before assuming the responsibility of matrimony and parenthood. In either case, the ability to manage one's own behavior to this extent and the ability to reproduce occurred nearly coincidently. It can in fact be argued that culture and society have evolved with respect to the means for reproducing this coincidence. That is, those cultural or societal forms which retard the development of self-management skills and therefore suffer from the chaos of ubiquitous premature parenthood—high incidence of broken homes, divorce, illegitimacy, and welfare excesses—will be altered to reduce these burdensome sources of collective unhappiness.

The emergence of the stage of life called youth may be exactly the product of what we have been talking about. That is, advanced Western cultures have begun to defer the necessary conditions and opportunities for adult self-management until sometime after the maturational capacity for reproductive behavior has been achieved. If one argues that the necessary and sufficient conditions for adult self-management skills to be developed and maintained occur only as a result of full participation in adult behavioral patterns with no modulation of consequences, it follows that only by coming into contact with the fully operating contingencies and their implied responsibilities does an individual develop the capability for successful parenthood, not just successful procreation. We have created the stage of life we call youth because, in our opinion, we have permitted our adolescents to attain physical maturity without the corresponding behavioral and psychological maturity which both biological and cultural analysis tells us is necessary for the stability of the society and the well-being of its members.

To say that we have created this stage of life is not to say that we have wrought a biological miracle. It is simply to say that we have allowed certain of our institutions to develop to an extent where they no longer complement man's development but may impede or contradict it. Since these institutions are essentially man-made and since man is constantly seeking ways of improving the quality of his life through modification of his institutions, we may be hopeful that the discomforting emergence of the youth culture may stimulate an intelligent analysis and reevaluation of those societal and institutional practices which may be held responsible.

It seems to us that our institutionalized educational structure is the central villain in this bio-social melodrama of which youth is the principal victim. In our society at least, we have permitted and encouraged the formal educational process to extend well beyond that point in an individual's growth where he might otherwise be ready to assume full participation in the adult society. Earlier, we stressed the acquisition of self-management skills as being essential to successful participation as an adult member of the community. We pointed out that these skills are probably not developed fully until the individual is allowed to come into contact with the real and complete contingencies of economic survival. The formal educational institutions of our society do not, in any meaningful way, permit individuals to experience these contingencies. As Lipset (1970) points out in a recent article in the *American Psychologist,* college students have dispensable jobs. That is, the consequences of doing or not doing what a student does are not particularly noticeable in the social fabric at large. A student strike simply does not have the consequences, either for the student or for the economy, of an airline strike or a steelworkers' strike. Just as their jobs are dispensable, their payoffs for performing these jobs are relatively trivial, at least as measured by the standards of the adult society around them. Small wonder then, that students create more meaningful payoffs, and that their payoff systems are often strangely different from those of the adult society. These individuals have the biological and psychological maturity to behave in accordance with the powerful payoff system of the affluent society around them, but, because of their role as students, they are prohibited from partaking of this system. With their greater leisure and intellectual development, they quite naturally create payoff systems of their own which support behavior patterns which do not always closely resemble those of the larger society. It is these often startling differences between the behavioral patterns and the payoff systems of youth and those of the society at large which creates the problem. The transition from youth to adulthood is extremely difficult and painful in direct proportion to the difference in payoff contingencies between the two stages.

A solution, then, may be stated in terms of modifying the structure of our educational institutions to permit full participation in the contingency system of the adult world at the point in time when the individual is biologically and psychologically prepared to do so. How is this to be accomplished in a society whose very affluence and complexity seems to demand more and more formal education? Two answers come readily to mind. The first involves streamlining our present educational procedures and making them more efficient. Evidence is rapidly mounting that an effective, scientifically based educational technology can greatly increase the efficiency of education from nursery school to graduate school (Skinner, 1968; Johnston and Pennypacker, 1971). Thus, it may be possible to accomplish in fifteen years of an individual's life that which now takes twenty-five years, leaving the individual fully trained to function as an adult at the conclusion of his adolescent years. The development of this technology, while having already begun, will be gradual, however. Meanwhile the problems of youth are rapidly growing more acute, both for individuals in that age group and for the society around them.

A more fundamental means of coping with these problems through revision of the role of educational institutions has been proposed in a startling and refreshing utopian novel, *The Troika Incident* (Brown, 1970). Brown essentially proposes the direct solution that we have been hinting at all along—let people participate fully in the contingencies of adult economic life as soon as they are physically able. This means permitting young people to do important work of which they may be uniquely capable, and it means paying them well for their accomplishments. Such activities as social work, teaching, exploration, and development of barren or inaccessible regions like the Amazon jungle and the ocean floor obviously require the combination of idealism and stamina that is uniquely characteristic of young people. There can be no doubt that work of this type is also of real economic value and should be rewarded in those terms, not in terms of token compensation and "inestimable educational opportunity" that characterizes such programs as the Peace Corps and VISTA. In addition, higher education should and would then become accessible to adults of all ages. A young person of, say, seventeen might opt to spend five years working on a game preserve in Africa before entering the university to pursue studies in zoology. He would, in principle, be able to earn and save enough during those five years to finance his education, and he would not be stigmatized for entering the university at twenty-two or twenty-three years of age. Indeed, some of his classmates might be coming back for the third or fourth time and be preparing for yet another career change or major advancement. The point is very simple: The energy and idealism of youth could and should be channeled through differential payoff into pursuits which benefit both the youth and the society in which he lives, not pursuits which serve to isolate him and place him at odds with the culture he must some day enter. By removing the formal timetable from the educational process and recognizing that education is a lifelong business anyhow, the zest and idealism of youth may be preserved and rekindled throughout the remaining years of the individual's life.

But what of reproduction? Are we suggesting that people oscillate between periods of formal education and productive work, somehow squeezing out time to raise a family in between? The answer is no, as Brown (1970) points out, because our technology has all but freed us from the nearly inevitable consequences of reproductive behavior—unwanted children. We are technologically capable, in other words, of letting the powerful reinforcers inherent in sexual behavior function to reward desirable forms of productive behavior without burdening the individual behavers or the society at large with the unwanted consequences of their behavior. We must recognize and act upon the potential for social advancement inherent in our ability to separate the pleasurable and reproductive functions of sex. The youth of today have clearly recognized this separability, and they are properly critical of the adult society which continues, in spite of the evidence, to pretend that it does not exist. But in the enthusiasm of their discovery, young people have overlooked the power of sexual fulfillment to reinforce the development of stable and meaningful interpersonal relationships which are necessary for responsible and productive citizenship just as they are necessary for effective parenthood. A young person today, therefore, is in a position to build deep and enduring interpersonal relationships cemented by the mortar of *appropriately delayed* sexual gratification and uncomplicated by unwanted children. The fact that he rarely uses sex in this fashion, but rather appears to tend toward indifferent promiscuity, serves only to underscore the fact that the society at large has failed to provide an effective environment for the development of such behavior.

Parenthood may now be chosen and need no longer be endured as the almost inevitable consequence of connubial enjoyment. The implications of this fact are indeed staggering. Brown (1970) suggests that many people will *choose* to become parents, after perhaps a number of alternating career and educational sortees. By using sex appropriately as the terminal event in the molding and shaping of meaningful interpersonal relationships, the individual may be expected to exercise unprecedented wisdom in the selection of a mate for reproductive purposes. The social consequences of such wisdom could be enormously beneficial. Social burdens presently produced by illegitimacy as well as by divorce and remarriage would be reduced. Finally, the list of benefits would include an elevated standard of living in those regions of the globe where ignorance and superstition combine to keep the birthrate well above the level manageable by an undeveloped economy.

These and other changes are within our grasp. Our technology and our affluence have created this possibility. They also have created a generation of individuals—our youth—who are causing pain to themselves and to the adult society of which they are not yet a part. If through their existence, there exists the potential for a better world—a world in which youth is not a separate stage of life but a recurring and important facet of adulthood—then the suffering will not have been wasted. Youth will disappear as a separate stage in life and be replaced by youthful maturity, an indispensable ingredient of adult life.

REFERENCES

A

Abbott, M., Howard, K., & Walter, T. Sullivan school project: Final report. Unpublished manuscript, University of Michigan, **1969.**

Acker, L. E. (Ed.) Behavior modification and ideal mental health services. *Proceedings of the 1st Banff Conference on Behavior Modification,* University of Calgary, **1969.**

Ackerman, J. M. *Operant conditioning techniques for the classroom teacher.* (6th ed.) Albany, Oregon: Linn County Mental Health Clinic, **1969.**

Addison, R. M. & Homme, Lloyd E. The reinforcing event (RE) menu. *National Society for Programmed Instruction Journal,* **1966,** *5,* 8–9.

Allen, K. E. & Harris, F. R. Elimination of a child's excessive scratching by training the mother in reinforcement procedures. *Behaviour Research and Therapy,* **1964,** *4,* 70–84.

Allen, K. E., Hart, B. M., Buell, J. C., Harris, F. R., & Wolf, M. M. Effects of social reinforcement on isolate behavior of a nursery school child. *Child Development,* **1964,** *35,* 511–518.

Allen, K. E., Henke, L. B., Harris, F. R., Baer, D. M., & Reynolds, N. J. Control of hyperactivity by social reinforcement of attending behavior. *Journal of Educational Psychology,* **1967,** *58,* 231–237.

Allport, G. W. *Pattern and growth in personality.* New York: Holt, Rinehart & Winston, **1963.**

American Institutes for Research. *Counterinsurgency in Thailand.* (A research and development proposal) Pittsburgh: Advanced Research Projects Agency, **1967.**

Amidon, E. & Flanders, N. *The role of the teacher in the classroom.* Minneapolis: Paul S. Amidon and Associates, **1963.**

Amidon, E. & Giammatteo, M. The verbal behavior of superior elementary teachers. In E. Amidon & J. Hough, (Eds.), *Interaction analysis: Theory, research, and application.* Reading, Massachusetts: Addison-Wesley, **1967.**

Amidon, E. J. & Hough, J. B. *Interaction analysis: Theory, research, and application.* Reading, Massachusetts: Addison-Wesley, **1967.**

Anderson, R. C. Educational psychology. *Annual Review of Psychology,* **1967,** *18.*

Anderson, R. C. "How to construct achievement tests to assess comprehension." Unpublished manuscript, **1971.**

Anderson, R. C. & Kulhavy, R. W. Learning concepts from definitions. *Journal of Educational Psychology,* in press.

Atkinson, R. C. Computerized instruction and the learning process. *American Psychologist,* **1968,** *23,* 225–239.

Atkinson, R. C. The computer is a tutor. *Psychology Today,* **1968,** *1,* 57–59.

Attneave, F. *Applications of information theory to psychology.* New York: Henry Holt and Company, **1959.**

Ayllon, T. & Azrin, N. H. Measurement and reinforcement of behavior of psychotics. *Journal of the Experimental Analysis of Behavior,* **1965,** *8,* 357–383.

Ayllon, T. & Azrin, N. H. *The token economy: A motivational system for therapy and rehabilitation.* New York: Appleton-Century-Crofts, **1968.**

Ayllon, T. & Michael, J. The psychiatric nurse as a behavioral engineer. *Journal of the Experimental Analysis of Behavior,* **1959,** *2,* 323–334.

Azrin, N. H. & Ayllon, T. Reinforcer sampling: A technique for increasing the behavior of mental patients. *Journal of Applied Behavior Analysis,* **1968,** *1,* 13–20.

Azrin, N. H. & Lindsley, O. R. The reinforcement of cooperation between children. In L. Krasner & L. P. Ullman (Eds.), *Case studies in behavior modification.* New York: Holt, Rinehart & Winston, **1965.**

Azrin, N. H. & Holz, W. C. Punishment. In W. K. Honig, (Ed.), *Operant behavior: Areas of research and application.* New York: Appleton-Century-Crofts, 1966.

B

Baer, D. M. Effect of withdrawal of positive reinforcement on an extinguishing response in young children. *Child Development,* 1961, *32,* 64–74.

Baer, D. M. Laboratory control of thumb-sucking by withdrawal and representation of reinforcement. *Journal of Experimental Analysis of Behavior,* 1962, *5,* 143–159.

Baer, D. M., Peterson, R. F., & Sherman, J. A. The development of imitation by reinforcing behavioral similarity to a model. *Journal of the Experimental Analysis of Behavior,* 1967, *10,* 405–416.

Baer, D. M. & Sherman, J. A. Reinforcement control of generalized imitation in young children. *Journal of Experimental Child Psychology,* 1964, *1,* 37–49.

Baer, D. M. & Wolf, M. M. The entry nito natural communities of reinforcement. Paper presented at the meeting of the American Psychological Association, Washington, 1967.

Baer, D. M. & Wolf, M. M. The reinforcement contingency in preschool and remedial education. In R. D. Hess & R. M. Bear (Eds.), *Early education: Current theory, research, and practice.* Chicago: Aldine, 1968.

Baer, D. M., Wolf, M. M., & Risley, T. Some current dimensions of applied behavior analysis. *Journal of Applied Behavior Analysis,* 1968, *1,* 91–97.

Bailey, J., Phillips, E., & Wolf, M. M. Modification of predelinquents' classroom behavior with home-based reinforcement. Paper presented at the meeting of the American Psychological Association, Miami, September 1970.

Bailey, J. S., Wolf, M. M., & Phillips, E. L. Home-based reinforcement and the modification of predelinquents' classroom behavior. *Journal of Applied Behavior Analysis,* 1970, *3,* 223–233.

Baker, E. E. Aligning speech evaluation and behavior objectives. *Speech Teacher,* 1967, *16,* 158–160.

Bakwin, H. & Bakwin, R. *Clinical management of behavior disorders in children.* Philadelphia: Saunders, 1967.

Bandura, A. Behavioral modification through modeling Procedures. In L. Krasner, & L. P. Ullmann (Eds.), *Research in behavior modification.* New York: Holt, Rinehart & Winston, 1966.

Bandura, A., Ross, D., & Ross, S. A. Vicarious reinforcement and imitative learning. *Journal of Abnormal and Social Psychology,* 1963, *67,* 601–607.

Barker, R. G. & Wright, H. F. Psychological ecology and the problem of psychosocial development. *Child Development,* 1949, *20,* 131–143.

Barrish, H., Saunders, M., & Wolf, M. Good behavior game: Effects of individual contingencies for group consequences on disruptive behavior in a classroom. *Journal of the Experimental Analysis of Behavior,* 1969, *2,* 119–124.

Barro, S. M. An approach to developing accountability measures for the public schools. *Phi Delta Kappan,* 1970, *52,* 196–205.

Battelle Memorial Institute. The Office of Economic Opportunity experiment in educational performance contracting. (Research report) Columbus Laboratories, January 1972.

Becker, E. *Beyond alienation.* New York: Braziller, 1967.

Becker, W. C. *Parents are teachers.* Champaign, Ill.: Research Press, 1971.

Becker, W. C. *Teaching children: A child management program for parents.* Champaign, Ill.: Englemann-Becker Corporation, 1969.

Becker, W. C., Engelmann, S., & Thomas, D. R. *Teaching: A course in applied psychology.* Palo Alto, Calif.: Science Research Associates, 1971.

Becker, W. C., Madsen, C. H., Jr., Arnold, C. R., & Thomas, D. R. The contingent use of teacher attention and praise in reducing classroom behavior problems. *Journal of Special Education,* 1967, *1,* 287–307.

Becker, W. C., Thomas, D. R., & Carnine, D. *Reducing behavior problems: An operant conditioning guide for teachers.* Urbana, Ill.: Educational Research Information Center, 1969.

Benedict, R. *Patterns of culture.* New York: Houghton Mifflin, 1934.

Bereiter, C. & Engelmann, S. *Teaching disadvantaged children in the preschool.* Englewood Cliffs, N.J.: Prentice-Hall, 1966.

Berelson, B. & Steiner, G. A. *Human behavior.* New York: Harcourt Brace Jovanovich, 1964.

Bergan, J. R. & Caldwell, T. Operant techniques in school psychology. *Psychology in the Schools,* 1967, *4,* 137–141.

Berne, E. *Games people play.* New York: Grove, 1964.

Bettelheim, B. *Love is not enough.* New York: The Free Press, 1950.

Bijou, S. W., Peterson, R. F., & Ault, M. H. A method to integrate descriptive and experimental field studies at the level of data and empirical concepts. *Journal of Applied Behavior Analysis,* 1968, *1,* 175–191.

Birnbrauer, J. S. Generalization of punishment effects: A case study. *Journal of Applied Behavior Analysis*, 1968, *1*, 201–211.

Birnbrauer, J. S., Bijou, S. W., Wolf, M. M., & Kidder, J. D. Programmed instruction in the classroom. In L. Krasner & L. P. Ullmann (Eds.), *Case studies in behavior modification*. New York: Holt, Rinehart & Winston, Inc., 1965.

Birnbrauer, J. S. & Lawler, J. Token reinforcement for learning. *Mental Retardation*, 1965, *2*, 219–235.

Birnbrauer, J. S., Wolf, M. M., Kidder, J. D., & Tague, C. E. Classroom behavior of retarded pupils with token reinforcement. *Journal of Experimental Child Psychology*, 1965, *2*, 219–235.

Blackham, H. J. *Humanism*. Baltimore: Penguin, 1968.

Block, K. K. & Simon, D. *Computer-assisted spelling*. National Science Foundation, 1972.

Bloom, B. S. (Ed.) *Taxonomy of educational objectives: The classification of educational goals*. Handbook 1. *Cognitive domain*. New York: McKay, 1956.

Bloom, B. S. Twenty-five years of educational research. *American Education Research Journal*, 1966, *3*, 211–221.

Blough, G. O., Marshall, J. S., Bailey, J. B., & Beauchamp, W. L. *Science is discovering*. Glenview, Ill.: Scott, Foresman, 1968.

Blough, G. O., Marshall, J. S., Bailey, J. B., & Beauchamp, W. L. *Science is experimenting*. Glenview, Ill.: Scott, Foresman, 1968.

Boudin, H. M. Behavior modification techniques in the ripple effect. Unpublished master's thesis, University of Toronto, 1967.

Bowlby, J. *Child care and the growth of love*. Baltimore: Penguin Books, 1953.

Branch, R. C. & Sulzbacher, S. I. Rapid computation of rates with a simple nomogram. *Journal of Applied Behavior Analysis*, 1968, *1*, 251–252.

Brethower, D. M. Classroom management: A total management system for a classroom. Unpublished manuscript, Reading Improvement Service, University of Michigan, 1969.

Brison, D. W. A non-talking child in kindergarten: An application of behavior therapy. *Journal of School Psychology*, 1966, *4*, 65–69.

Bronfenbrenner, U. & Condry, J. *Two worlds of childhood: U.S. and U.S.S.R.* New York: Russell Sage Foundation, 1970.

Brown, E. R. & Shields, E. Results with systematic suspension: A guidance technique to help children develop self-control in public school classrooms. *Journal of Special Education*, 1967, *1*, 425–437.

Brown, James Cooke. *The troika incident*. New York: Doubleday, 1970.

Brown, P. & Elliott, R. Control of aggression in a nursery-school class. *Journal of Experimental Child Psychology*, 1965, *2*, 103–107.

Bruner, J. S., Goodnow, J. J., & Austin, G. A. *A study of thinking*. New York: Wiley, 1956.

Bruner, J. S. *Toward a theory of instruction*. Cambridge, Mass.: Belknap Press, 1966.

Buchanan, C. D. *Programmed reading*. St. Louis: Webster Division, McGraw-Hill, 1968.

Buell, J., Stoddard, P., Harris, F., & Baer, D. M. Collateral social development accompanying reinforcement of outdoor play in a preschool child. *Journal of Applied Behavior Analysis*, 1968, *1*, 167–173.

Bushell, D. & Jacobson, J. The simultaneous rehabilitation of mothers and their children. *Boston Association for the Education of Young Children Reports*, 1969, *1*, 85–90.

Bushell, D., Wrobel, P. A., & Michaelis, M. L. Applying "group" contingencies to the classroom study behavior of preschool children. *Journal of Applied Behavior Analysis*, 1968, *1*, 55–61.

C

Campbell, D. T. & Stanley, J. C. Experimental and quasi-experimental designs for research on teaching. In N. L. Gage (Ed.), *Handbook of research on teaching*. Chicago: Rand McNally, 1963.

Campbell, R. N. & Lindfors, J. *Insights into English structure: A programmed course*. Englewood Cliffs, N.J.: Prentice-Hall, 1969.

Canadian whole earth almanac. Toronto, Ontario: New Press, 1970.

Cannady, W. (Ed.) *New schools for new towns*. New York: Educational Facilities Laboratories, Inc., 1967.

Cantrell, R. P., Cantrell, M. L., Huddleston, C. M., & Woolridge, R. L. Contingency contracting with school problems. *Journal of Applied Behavior Analysis*, 1969, *3*, 215–220.

Carlsen, C. S., Arnold, C. R., Becker, W. C., & Madsen, C. H. The elimination of tantrum behavior of a child in an elementary classroom. *Behavior Research and Therapy*, 1968, *6*, 117–119.

Carnine, D., Becker, W. C., Thomas, D. R., Poe, M., & Plager, E. The effects of direct and vicarious reinforcement on the behavior of problem boys in an elementary-school classroom. Unpublished manuscript, University of Illinois, 1968.

Carr, S. & Lynch, K. Where learning happens. *Daedalus*, 1968, *97*(4), 1277–1291.

Cataldo, M. F. & Risley, T. R. The organization of group-care environments: The infant day-care center. Paper presented at the meeting of the American Psychological Association, Honolulu, September 1972.

Cattel, P. *The measurement of intelligence of infants and young children*. New York: The Psychological Corp., 1940.

Charlesworth, R. & Hartup, W. W. An observational study of positive social reinforcement in the nursery-school peer group. In *Research Bulletin*. Princeton, New Jersey: Educational Testing Service, 1966.

Chekhov, A. *Ward six and other short novels*. New York: Signet Books, New American Library, 1965.

Clark, D. C. Teaching concepts in the classroom: A set of teaching prescriptions derived from experimental research. *Journal of Educational Psychology*, 1971, *62*, 253–278.

Clark, H. B. *Contingency management and programmed learning materials*. (Unpublished study report) Elmore, Alabama: Rehabilitation Research Foundation, 1966.

Clark, M., Lachowicz, J., & Wolf, M. A pilot education program for school dropouts incorporating a token reinforcement system. *Behaviour Research and Therapy*, 1968, *6*, 183–188.

Cleary, A. & Packham, D. A touch-detecting teaching machine with auditory reinforcement. *Journal of Applied Behavior Analysis*, 1968, *1*, 341–345.

Clements, C. B. & McKee, J. M. Programmed instruction for institutionalized offenders: Contingency management and performance contracts. *Psychological Reports*, 1968, *22*, 957–964.

Clevenger, T., Jr. Some factors involved in classroom procedures for the acquisition of verbal concepts. *Speech Teacher*, 1966, *15*, 113–118.

Clinard, M. *Slums and community development*. Toronto: Collier-Macmillan Canada, Ltd., 1966.

Coch, L. & French, J. R. P., Jr. Overcoming resistance to change. *Human Relations*, 1948, *1*, 512–532.

Cohen, H. L. M.O.D.E.L.—Motivationally oriented designs for an ecology of learning. Paper presented at the meeting of the American Educational Research Association, February 1967.

Cohen, H. L., Filipczak, J. A., & Bis, J. S. *CASE Project: Contingencies applicable for special education*. Washington, D.C.: U.S. Department of Health, Education, and Welfare, Office of Juvenile Delinquency and Youth Development.

Cohen, H. L., Goldiamond, I., Filipczak, J., & Pooley, R. Training professionals in procedures for the establishment of educational environments: A report on the CASE Training Institute (CTI). Silver Spring, Md.: Institute for Behavioral Research, 1968.

Cohen, S. I., Keyworth, J. M., Kleiner, R. I., Libert, J. M., Brown, W. L., Lessey, B., McGowan, M., McGuckian, J., Roebuck, E., Turner, P., & Wagner, D. The support of school behaviors by home-based reinforcement via parent-child contingency contracts. In E. Ramp and B. L. Hopkins (Eds.), *A new direction for education: Behavior analysis*. Lawrence, Kansas: Project Follow-thru, 1972.

Cosby, T. *Architecture: City sense*. New York: Reinhold, 1965.

Cowen, E. L., Izzo, L. D., Mites, H., Telschow, E. F., Frost, M. A., & Zax, M. A. Preventive mental health program in the school setting: Description and evaluation. *Journal of Psychology*, 1963, *56*, 307–356.

Cox, H. *The feast of fools*. Cambridge: Harvard University Press, 1969.

Cruickshank, W., Bentzen, F., Ratzeburg, F., & Tannhauser, M. *A teaching methodology for brain-injured and hyperactive children*. New York: Syracuse University Press, 1961.

Crutchfield, R. S. Creative thinking in children: Its teaching and testing. In H. Brim, R. S. Crutchfield, and W. Holtzman (Eds.), *Intelligence: Perspectives*. New York: Harcourt Brace Jovanovich, 1965.

Cummings, J. D. The incidence of emotional problems in school children. *British Journal of Educational Psychology*, 1944, *14*, 151–161.

D

Datel, W. E. & Legters, L. J. The psychology of the army recruit. Paper presented at the meeting of the American Medical Association, Chicago, June 1970.

Davis, A. L. *Language resource information for teachers of the culturally disadvantaged*. Washington, D.C.: U.S. Office of Education, 1969.

Dewey, J. *The public and its problems*. Chicago: Gateway Books, 1946.

Doke, L. A. & Risley, T. R. The organization of day-care environments: Required versus optional activities. *Journal of Applied Behavior Analysis*, 1972, *5*, 405–420.

Doll, E. A. Preschool attainment record. Circle Pines, Minn.: American Guidance Service, 1966.

Doll, E. A. The vineland social maturity scale. Circle Pines, Minn.: American Guidance Service, 1965.

Dubos, Rene. *So human an animal.* New York: Scribner, 1968.

Duncan, A. D. Self-application of behavior modification techniques by teen-agers. *Adolescence,* 1969, *16*(4), 541–556.

E

Ebner, M. An investigation of the role of the social environment in the generalization and persistence of the effect of a behavior modification program. Unpublished doctoral dissertation, University of Oregon, 1967.

Eisenberg, L. The strategic deployment of the child psychiatrist. *Journal of Child Psychology and Psychiatry,* 1961, *2,* 229–241.

Eldred, D. M. & Brooks, G. W. *Use of programmed instruction with disturbed children.* Waterbury, Vermont: Vermont State Hospital, 1966.

Engelmann, S. *Conceptual learning.* San Rafael, Calif.: Dimensions Press, 1969.

Engelmann, S. & Bruner, E. C. *Distar reading.* Chicago: Science Research Associates, 1969.

Enslen, J. E. Contingency management: Monetary rewards for progress charts as motivators for inmates using programmed instruction. (Unpublished study report) Elmore, Alabama: Rehabilitation Research Foundation, 1969.

Essay Productions. *Essay on war.* Chicago: Encyclopaedia Britannica Educational Corp., undated.

Evans, G. W. & Oswalt, G. L. Acceleration of academic progress through the manipulation of peer influence. *Behavior Research and Therapy,* 1968, *6,* 189–195.

Evans, J. L. Multiple-choice discrimination programming. Paper presented at the meeting of the American Psychological Association, New York, September 1961.

Evans, J. L. Programming in mathematics and logic. In R. Glaser (Ed.), *Teaching machines and programmed learning, II: Data and directions.* Washington, D.C.: National Education Association, 1965.

F

Fazzini, D. The museum as a learning environment: A self-motivating, recycling, learning system for museum visitors. Unpublished doctoral dissertation, University of Wisconsin-Milwaukee, 1972.

Ferster, C. B. Arbitrary and natural reinforcement. *Psychological Record,* 1967, *17,* 341–347.

Ferster, C. B. & Perrott, M. C. *Behavior principles.* New York: Appleton-Century-Crofts, 1968.

First foundation journal. Minneapolis, Minnesota: Foundation, Inc., 1971.

Fitzhugh, R. J. & Katsuki, D. The touch-sensitive screen as a flexible response device in CAI and behavioral research. *Behavior Research Methods and Instrumentation,* 1971, *3,* 159–164.

Flanagan, J. C. How instructional systems will manage learning. *Nation's Schools,* 1970, *86*(4).

Flanagan, J. C., Shanner, W. M., & Mager, R. F. *Behavioral objectives: Science, social studies, mathematics, language arts; A guide to individualizing learning; Primary, intermediate, secondary.* Palo Alto: Westinghouse Learning Corporation, 1971.

Flanders, N. A. Some relationships among teacher influence, pupil attitudes, and achievement. In E. Amidon and J. Hough (Eds.), *Interaction analysis: Theory, research, and application.* Reading, Massachusetts: Addison-Wesley, 1967.

Flanders, N. A. Intent, action, and feedback: A preparation for teaching. *Journal of Teacher Education,* 1963, *14,* 251–260.

Flanders, N. A. *Teacher influence: Pupil attitudes and achievement.* Minneapolis: University of Minnesota Press, 1960.

G

Gagné, R. M. The analysis of instructional objectives for the design of instruction. In R. Glaser (Ed.), *Teaching machines and programmed learning, II: Data and directions.* Washington, D.C.: National Education Association, 1965.

Gagné, R. M. *The conditions of learning.* New York: Holt, Rinehart, & Winston, 1970.

Gallimore, R. Variations in the motivational antecedents of achievement among Hawaii's ethnic groups. Paper presented at the meeting of the East-West Conference, Honolulu, March 1969.

Gallimore, R. & Howard, A. *Studies in a Hawaiian community: Na Makamaka o Nanakuli.* Bishop Museum, Pacific Anthropological Record 1, Department of Anthropology, 1968.

Gallimore, R., Tharp, R. G., & Kemp, B. Positive reinforcing function of "negative attention." *Journal of Experimental Child Psychology,* 1969, *8,* 140–146.

Gartner, A., Kohler, M., & Riessman, F. *Children teach children: Learning by teaching.* New York: Harper & Row, 1971.

Ghiselin, B. *The creative process.* New York: New American Library, 1955.

Gideonse, H. D. Research development and the improvement of education. *Science,* 1968, *162,* 541–545.

Gilbert, T. F. Mathetics: The technology of education. *Journal of Mathetics*, 1962, *1*(1). (a)

Gilbert, T. F. Mathetics: II. The design of teaching exercises. *Journal of Mathetics*, 1962, *1*(2). (b)

Gilbert, T. F. On the relevance of laboratory investigation of learning to self-instructional programming. In A. A. Lumsdaine and R. Glaser (Eds.), *Teaching machines and programmed learning*. Washington, D.C.: Department of Audiovisual Instruction, National Education Association, 1960.

Giles, D. *Progress report: East side youth project.* Detroit: Neighborhood Service Organization, December 1969.

Ginott, H. *Between parent and child.* New York: Macmillan, 1965.

Giradeau, F. L. & Spradlin, J. E. Token rewards in a cottage program. *Mental Retardation*, 1964, *2*, 345–351.

Glaser, R. Instructional technology and the measurement of learning outcomes: Some questions. *American Psychologist*, 1963, 519–521.

Glasser, W. *Schools without failure.* Evanston, Ill.: Harper & Row, 1969.

Gnagey, W. J. Effects on classmates of a deviant student's power and response to a teacher-exerted control technique. *Journal of Educational Psychology*, 1960, *51*, 1–9.

Golden, R. I. *Improving patterns of language usage.* Detroit, 1960.

Goldiamond, I. Programs, paradigms and procedures. In H. L. Cohen, I. Goldiamond, J. Filipczak, & R. Pooley (Eds.), *Training professionals in procedures for the establishment of educational environments: A report on the CASE Training Institute (CTI).* Silver Spring, Md.: Institute for Behavioral Research, 1968.

Gordon, I. J. *Baby learning through baby play.* New York: St. Martin's Press, 1970.

Gordon, T. & Helmer, O. *Report on a long-range forecasting study.* Santa Monica, Calif.: Rand Corporation, 1964.

Graubard, P. S., Lanier, P., Weisert, H., & Miller, M. *An investigation into the use of indigenous grouping as the reinforcing agent in teaching maladjusted boys to read.* (Project report) Washington, D.C.: United States Office of Education, Bureau of Education for the Handicapped, 1970.

Grotberg, E. H. Learning disabilities and remediation in disadvantaged children. *Review of Educational Research*, 1965, *35*, 413–425.

Guilford, J. P. Traits of creativity. In H. H. Anderson (Ed.), *Creativity and its cultivation.* New York: Harpers, 1959.

H

Hall, E. T. *The hidden dimension.* New York: Doubleday, 1966.

Hall, R. V. *Behavior modification: The measurement of behavior.* Merriam, Kans.: H & H Enterprises, 1971.

Hall, R. V. & Broden, M. Behavior changes in brain-injured children through social reinforcement. *Journal of Experimental Child Psychology*, 1967, *5*, 463–479.

Hall, R. V., Lund, D., & Jackson, D. Effects of teacher attention on study behavior. *Journal of Applied Behavior Analysis*, 1968, *1*, 1–12.

Hall, R. V., Panyan, M., Rabon, D., & Broden, M. Instructing beginning teachers in reinforcement procedures which improve classroom control. *Journal of Applied Behavior Analysis*, 1968, *1*, 315–322. (a)

Hall, R. V., Panyan, M., Rabon, D., & Broden, M. Teacher applied contingencies and appropriate classroom behavior. Paper presented at the meeting of the American Psychological Association, San Francisco, September 1968. (b)

Hamblin, J. A. & Hamblin, R. On teaching disadvantaged preschoolers to read: A successful experiment. *American Educational Research Journal*, 1972.

Hamblin, R., Buckholdt, D., Ferritor, D., Kozloff, M., & Blackwell, L. The humanization processes. New York: Wiley, 1971.

Hammerlynck, L. A. Direct observation of student behavior to validate teacher reports. Paper presented at the meeting of the Canadian Psychological Association, Calgary, Alberta, June 1968.

Hammerlynck, L. A., Martin, J. W., & Rolland, J. C. Systematic observation of behavior: A primary teacher skill. In L. A. Hammerlynck & J. W. Martin (Eds.), *Education and training of the mentally retarded*, in press.

Haring, N. G. & Whelan, N. G. Experimental methods in education and management. In N. S. Long, W. C. Morse, & R. G. Newman (Eds.), *Conflict in the classroom*. Belmont, California: Wadsworth, 1965.

Harrington, M. *The other America.* Baltimore: Penguin, 1962.

Harris, F. R., Johnston, M. K., Kelley, C. S., & Wolf, M. M. Effects of positive social reinforcement on regressed crawling of a nursery-school child. *Journal of Educational Psychology*, 1964, *55*, 35–41.

Harris, F. R., Wolf, M. M., & Baer, D. M. Effects of adult social reinforcement of child behavior. *Young children*, 1964, *20*, 8–17.

Hart, B. M., Allen, K. E., Buell, J. S., Harris, F. R., & Wolf, M. M. Effects of social reinforcement on operant crying. *Journal of Experimental Child Psychology*, 1964, *1*, 145–153.

Hart, B. M., Reynolds, N. J., Baer, D. M., Brawley, E. M., & Harris, F. R. Effect of contingent and non-contingent social reinforcement on the cooperative play of a preschool child. *Journal of Applied Behavior Analysis*, 1968, *1*(1), 73–76.

Hart, B. & Risley, T. Establishing use of descriptive adjectives in the spontaneous speech of disadvantaged preschool children. *Journal of Applied Behavior Analysis*, 1968, *1*, 109–120.

Hart, B. M. & Risley, T. R. The use of preschool materials for modifying the language of disadvantaged children. *Journal of Applied Behavior Analysis*, in press.

Hartup, W. W. Friendship status and the effectiveness of peers as reinforcing agents. *Journal of Experimental Child Psychology*, 1964, *1*, 154–162.

Hathaway, C. Use of group contingencies in a public school classroom. Doctoral dissertation, Washington University, in preparation.

Haughton, E. Personal communication, 1969.

Hawkins, R. B. A speech program in an experimental college for the disadvantaged. *Speech Teacher*, 1969, *18*, 115–119.

Hawkins, R. Personal communication, April 1971.

Hawkins, R. P. The public school classroom as a behavioral laboratory. Paper presented at the meeting of the American Psychological Association, Washington, D.C., September 1967.

Hawkins, R. P., McArthur, M., Rinaldi, P., Gray, D., & Schaftenaar, L. Results of operant conditioning techniques in modifying the behavior of emotionally disturbed children. Paper presented at the meeting of the International Council for Exceptional Children, St. Louis, Mo., March 1967.

Hawkins, R. P., Peterson, R. F., Schweid, E., & Bijou, S. W. Behavior therapy in the home: Amelioration of problem parent-child relations with the parent in a therapeutic role. *Journal of Experimental Child Psychology*, 1966, *4*, 99–107.

Hawkins, R. P. & Sluyter, D. J. Modification of achievement by a simple technique involving parents and teacher. Paper presented at the meeting of the American Educational Research Association, Minneapolis, Minn., March 1970.

Hawkridge, D., Chalupsky, A., & Roberts, A. *A study of selected exemplary programs for the education of disadvantaged children*. Palo Alto, Calif.: American Institutes for Research in the Behavioral Sciences, 1968.

Heath, R. S. *The reasonable adventurer*. Pittsburgh, Pa.: University of Pittsburgh Press, 1964.

Hemphill, J. K. The relationship between research and evaluation studies. In R. W. Tyler (Ed.), *Educational evaluation: New roles and new means*. Chicago: National Society for the Study of Education, 1969.

Hendershot, C. H. *Programmed learning: A bibliography of programs and presentation devices*. Bay City, Michigan: Hendershot Associates, 1967.

Hewett, F. M. Educational engineering with emotionally disturbed children. *Exceptional Children*, 1967, *33*, 459–467.

Hewett, F. M. *The emotionally disturbed child in the classroom*. Boston: Allyn & Bacon, 1968.

Hill, W. F. Sources of evaluative reinforcement. *Psychological Bulletin*, 1968, *69*, 132–146.

Holland, J. G. Research on programing variables. In R. Glaser (Ed.), *Teaching machines and programed learning, II: Data and directions*. Washington, D.C.: National Education Association, 1965.

Holland, J. G. & Skinner, B. F. *The analysis of behavior*. New York: McGraw-Hill, 1961.

Holmes, D. S. The application of learning theory to the treatment of a school behavior problem: A case study. *Psychology in the School*, 1966, *3*, 355–359.

Homme, L. A behavior technology exists—here and now. A version of this paper was presented at the meeting of the Aerospace Education Foundation, Washington, 1967.

Homme, L. Contingency management. *Newsletter* (Section on Clinical Child Psychology, Division of Clinical Psychology, APA), 1966, *4*.

Homme, L. Control of coverants, the operants of the mind. *Psychological Record*, 1965, *15*, 501–511.

Homme, L. *How to use contingency contracting in the classroom*. Champaign, Illinois: Research Press, 1969.

Homme, L., C'de Baca, P., & Cottingham, L. What behavioral engineering is. *Psychological Record*, 1968, *18*, 425–434.

Homme, L., Csanyi, A. P., Gonzales, M. A., & Rechs, J. R. *How to use contingency contracting in the classroom*. Champaign, Illinois: Research Press, 1969.

Honig, W. K. *Operant behavior: Areas of research and application*. New York: Appleton-Century-Crofts, 1966.

Hopkins, B. L. Effects of candy and social reinforcement, instructions, and reinforcement schedule-learning on the modification and maintenance of smiling. *Journal of Applied Behavior Analysis*, **1968**, *1*, 121–130.

Horst, D. P. & Short, J. G. *Evaluation of a workshop in individualized instruction.* Singapore: Regional Innotech Center, **1971**.

Hunt, D. E. Adolescence: Cultural deprivation, poverty, and dropout. *Review of Educational Research*, **1966**, *36*, 463–473.

Hyman, H., Wright, C. R., & Hopkins, T. K. *Applications of methods of evaluations.* Berkeley: University of California Press, **1962**.

I

Inhelder, B. & Piaget, J. *The growth of logical thinking from childhood to adolescence.* New York: Basic Books, **1958**.

Itard, J. M. G. *The wild boy of Aveyron.* New York: Appleton-Century-Crofts, **1962**.

J

Jacobs, R. A. & Rosenbaum, P. S. *English transformational grammar.* Massachusetts: Blaisdell, **1968**.

Jacobson, J., Bushell, D., & Risley, T. Switching requirements in a Head Start classroom. *Journal of Applied Behavior Analysis*, **1969**, *2*, 43–47.

James, H. *Children in trouble: A national scandal.* New York: David McKay, **1969**.

Jenkins, W. O., McKee, J. M., Jordan, S., & Newmark, Z. M. Contingent monies and learning performances. (Unpublished study report) Elmore, Alabama: Rehabilitation Research Foundation, **1969**.

Johnson, N. A., Davis, J., & Lindsley, O. R. Teacher recorded performance rates of emotionally disturbed children. Unpublished manuscript, University of Kansas, **1968**.

Johnson, N. J. A. Daily arithmetic performance compared with teacher ratings, IQ, and achievement tests. Unpublished manuscript, University of Kansas, **1967**.

Johnston, J. M. & Pennypacker, H. S. A behavioral approach to college teaching. *American Psychologist*, **1971**, *26*, 219–244.

Jourard, S. M. *Disclosing man to himself.* Princeton: Van Nostrand, **1968**.

Judd, W. A. The development of an on-line laboratory for CAI and other behavioral research (1964–1968). *Technical Report Series.* Pittsburgh: University of Pittsburgh, Learning Research and Development Center, **1969**.

K

Kale, R. J., Kaye, J. H., Whelan, P. A., & Hopkins, B. L. The effect of reinforcement on the modification, maintenance, and generaliza-

tion of social responses of mental patients. *Journal of Applied Behavior Analysis*, **1968**, *1*, 307–314.

Kanfer, F. H. & Phillips, J. S. A survey of current behavior therapies and a proposal for classification. In C. M. Franks (Ed.), *Behavior therapy: Appraisal and status.* New York: McGraw-Hill, **1969**.

Keller, F. S. A programmed system of instruction. *Educational Technology Monographs*, **1969**, *2*, 1–26.

Keller, F. S. Goodbye teacher.... *Journal of Applied Behavior Analysis*, **1968**, *1*, 78–89.

Keltner, J. W. *Interpersonal speech-communication: Elements and structures.* Belmont, California: Wadsworth, **1970**.

Kesey, K. *One flew over the cuckoo's nest.* New York: Viking, **1962**.

Kibler, R. J. Developing behavioral objectives for undergraduate speech instruction. Paper presented at the meeting of the Speech Association of America, Denver, **1963**.

Kibler, R. J., Barker, L. L., & Miles, D. T. *Behavioral objectives and instruction.* Boston: Allyn & Bacon, **1970**.

Kirk, J. Elementary-school student teachers and interaction analysis. In E. J. Amidon & J. B. Hough (Eds.), *Interaction analysis: Theory research and application.* Reading, Massachusetts: Addison-Wesley, **1967**.

Klaus, D. J. An analysis of programing techniques. In R. Glaser (Ed.), *Teaching machines and programed learning, II: Data and directions.* Washington, D.C.: National Education Association, **1965**.

Koenig, C. H. Precision teaching with emotionally disturbed pupils. Unpublished manuscript, University of Kansas, **1967**.

Kounin, J. S. & Gump, P. V. The ripple effect in discipline. *Elementary School Journal*, **1958**, *59*, 158–162.

Krasner, L. & Ullmann, L. *Research in behavior modification.* New York: Holt, Rinehart & Winston, **1965**.

Krathwohl, D. R., Bloom, B. S., & Masia, B. B. *Taxonomy of educational objectives: The classification of educational goals.* Handbook 2. *Affective domain.* New York: McKay, **1964**.

Kroth, R. L., Whelan, R. J., & Stables, J. M. Teacher application of behavior principles in home and classroom environments. *Focus on Exceptional Children*, **1970**, *1*, 1–10.

Kunzelmann, H. Research and interpretation. Paper presented at the Precision Teaching Workshop, Eugene, Oregon, August **1969**.

Kuypers, D. S., Becker, W. C., & O'Leary, K. D.

How to make a token system fail. *Exceptional Children*, 1968, *35*, 101–109.

L

Labov, W. The social motivation of a sound change. *Word*, 1963, *19*, 273–309.

Labov, W. *The social stratification of English in New York City*. Washington, D.C., 1966.

Lakin, M. Some ethical issues in sensitivity training. *American Psychologist*, 1969, *24*, 923–928.

Landsman, T. Positive experience and the beautiful person. Presidential address presented at the meeting of the Southeastern Psychological Association, April 1968.

Last whole earth catalog. New York: Random House, 1971.

Lazarus, A. A. The treatment of chronic frigidity by systematic desensitization. *Journal of Nervous Mental Disorders*, 1963, *136*, 272–278.

Leavitt, H. J. & Mueller, R. A. H. Some effects of feedback on communication. In A. G. Smith (Ed.), *Communication and culture: Readings in the codes of human interaction*. New York: Holt, Rinehart & Winston, 1966.

Lee, R. S. The future of the museum as a learning environment. Paper presented at the Conference on Potential Applications of Computers in Museums, IBM Corporation, 1968.

Leib, J. W., Cusack, J., Hughes, D., Pilette, S., Wertner, J., & Kintz, B. L. Teaching machines and programmed instruction. *Psychological Bulletin*, 1967, *67*, 12–26.

LeLaurin, K. & Risley, T. R. Infant day care: An introduction. Paper presented at the meeting of the Kansas Psychological Association, Overland Park, April 1971.

LeLaurin, K. & Risley, T. R. The organization of day-care environments: "Zone" versus "man-to-man" staff assignments. *Journal of Applied Behavior Analysis*, 1972, *5*, 225–232.

Lennes, N. J. & Traver, L. R. *The Lennes essentials of arithmetic, 4, 5, & 6*. River Forest, Illinois: Laidlaw Brothers, 1964.

Leonard, G. B. *Education and ecstasy*. New York: Delacorte, 1968.

Lilly, M. S. Improving social acceptance of low sociometric status, low achieving students. *Exceptional Children*, 1971, *37*, 341–347.

Lindsley, O. Direct measurement and prosthesis of retarded behavior. (Rev. ed.) *University of Oregon Curriculum Bulletin*, 1969, *25*.

Lindsley, O. R. Experimental analysis of social reinforcement: Terms and methods. *American Journal of Orthopsychiatry*, 1963, *33*, 624–633.

Lindsley, O. R. Theoretical basis of behavior modification. Paper presented at the school of education, University of Oregon, Eugene, May 1967.

Lindsley, O. R. Procedures in common described by a common language. Paper presented at the University of Kansas Ninth Annual Institute for Research in Clinical Psychology, July 1968.

Lipset, S. M. American student activism in comparative perspective. *American Psychologist*, 1970, *25*, 675–693.

Lloyd, K. E. Performance of undergraduate students on multiple contingency management systems. Manuscript submitted to *Journal of Applied Behavior Analysis*, 1969.

Lloyd, K. E. & Garlington, W. K. Weekly variations in performance on a token economy psychiatric ward. *Behavior Research and Therapy*, 1968, *6*, 407–410.

Lloyd, K. E. & Knutzen, N. J. A self-paced programmed undergraduate course in the experimental analysis of behavior. *Journal of Applied Analysis*, 1969, *2*, 125–133.

London, P. *Behavior control*. Evanston: Harper & Row, 1970.

Lovaas, I., Schaeffer, B., & Simmons, J. Building social behavior in autistic children by use of electric shock. *Journal of Experimental Research in Personality*, 1965, *1*, 99–109.

Lovaas, O. I. A program for the establishment of speech in psychotic children. In J. K. Wing (Ed.), *Early childhood autism*. London: Pergamon Press, 1966.

Lovaas, O. I. & Simmons, J. Q. Manipulation of self-destruction in three retarded children. *Journal of Applied Behavior Analysis*, 1969, *2*, 143–157.

Lovitt, T. C. & Curtiss, K. K. Academic response rate as a function of teacher and self-imposed contingencies. *Journal of Applied Behavior Analysis*, 1969, *1*, 49–53.

Lukach, J. M. *Design in transit*. Boston, Massachusetts: Institute of Contemporary Art, 1967.

Lumsdaine, A. A. Educational technology, programmed learning, and instructional science. In E. R. Hilgard (Ed.), *Sixty-third Yearbook*, National Society for the Study of Education. Chicago: University of Chicago Press, 1964.

M

MacDonald, W. S. Responsibility and goal establishment: Critical elements in Job Corps program. *Perceptual and Motor Skills*, 1967, *24*, 104.

MacDonald, W. S., Gallimore, R., & MacDonald, G. Contingency counseling by school personnel: An economical model of intervention. *Journal of Applied Behavior Analysis*, 1970, *3*, 175–182.

Madsen, C. Address presented to Symposium on Behavior Analysis in Education, University of Kansas, 1970.

Madsen, C. M., Becker, W. C., Thomas, D. R., Koser, L., & Plager, E. An analysis of the reinforcing function of "sit-down" commands. In R. K. Parker (Ed.), *Readings in educational psychology*. Boston: Allyn & Bacon, 1968.

Madsen, H., Jr., Becker, C., & Thomas, R. Rules, praise, and ignoring: Elements of elementary classroom control. *Journal of Applied Behavior Analysis*, 1968, *1*, 139–150.

Mager, R. F. *Developing attitudes toward learning*. Palo Alto: Fearon Publishers, 1968.

Mager, R. F. & McCann, J. *Learner-controlled instruction*. Palo Alto: Varian Associates, 1961.

Malott, R. W. Contingency management in an introductory psychology course for 1000 students. Paper presented at the meeting of the American Psychological Association, San Francisco, 1968.

Maltzman, I. On the training of originality. *Psychological Review*, 1960, *67*, 229–242.

Markle, S. M. *Good frames and bad*. (2nd ed.) New York: John Wiley, 1969.

Markle, S. M. Teaching machines versus programmers. *Audiovisual Communication Review*, 1962, *10*(4).

Markle, S. M. & Tiemann, P. W. Problems of conceptual learning. *Journal of Educational Technology*, 1970, *1*, 52–62.

Markle, S. M. & Tiemann, P. W. *Really understanding concepts: Or in frumious pursuit of the jabberwock*. Chicago: Tiemann Associates, 1969.

Marshall, J. S. & Beauchamp, W. L. *Science is learning*. Glenview, Ill.: Scott, Foresman, 1968.

Marshall, J. S., Challand, H. J., & Beauchamp, W. L. *Science is exploring*. Glenview, Ill.: Scott, Foresman, 1968.

Martin, M., Burkholder, R., Rosenthal, R., Tharp, R. G., & Thorne, G. L. Programming behavior change into school milieux of extreme adolescent deviates. *Behaviour Research and Therapy*, 1968, *6*, 371–383.

Martin, W. T. & Pinck, D. C. (Eds.), *Curriculum improvement and innovations: A partnership of students, school teachers, and research scholars*. Cambridge, Massachusetts: Robert Bentley, Inc., 1966.

Maslow, A. H. Toward a humanistic biology. *American Psychologist*, 1969, *24*, 724–735.

May, R. E. A landmark year for computers. *Computers and Automation*, 1970, *19*, 26–28.

McDavid, R. I., Jr. A checklist of significant features for discriminating social dialects. In E. L. Evertts (Ed.), *Dimensions of dialect*. Champaign: National Council of Teachers of English, 1967.

McIntire, R. W. *For love of children*. Del Mar, California: Communication Research Machines, 1970.

McKee, J. M. Contingency management in a correctional institution. *Educational Technology*, 1971, *11*(4), 51–54.

McKee, P. & Harrison, M. L. *English for meaning*. Boston: Houghton Mifflin, 1968.

McKenzie, H. S., Clark, M., Wolf, M. M., Kothera, R., & Benson, C. Behavior modification of children with learning disabilities using grades as tokens and allowances as back-up reinforcers. *Exceptional Children*, 1968, *34*, 745–752.

McKerracher, D. Alleviation of reading difficulties by a simple operant conditioning technique. *Journal of Child Psychology and Psychiatry*, 1967, *8*, 51–56.

McMichael, J. S. & Corey, J. R. Contingency management in an introductory psychology course produces better learning. *Journal of Applied Behavior Analysis*, 1969, *2*, 79–84.

Medley, D. M. & Mitzel, H. E. Measuring classroom behavior by systematic observation. In N. L. Gage (Ed.), *Handbook of research and teaching*. Chicago: Rand McNally, 1963.

Meichenbaum, D. H., Bowers, K. S., & Ross, R. R. Modification of classroom behavior of institutionalized female adolescent offenders. *Behavior Research and Therapy*, 1968, *6*, 343–353.

Merrill, M. D. (Ed.) *Instructional design: Readings*. Englewood Cliffs, N.J.: Prentice-Hall, 1971.

Meyer, S. R. Report of the initial test of a junior high school vocabulary program. In A. A. Lumsdaine & R. Glaser (Eds.), *Teaching machines and programmed learning*. Washington, D.C.: Department of Audiovisual Instruction, National Education Association, 1960.

Meyerson, L., Kerr, N., & Michael, J. L. Behavior modification in rehabilitation. In S. W. Bijou & D. M. Baer (Eds.), *Child development: Readings in experimental analysis*. New York: Appleton-Century-Crofts, 1967.

Michael, D. N. *The unprepared society: Planning for a precarious future*. New York: Basic Books, 1968.

Millenson, J. R. *Principles of behavioral analysis*. New York: Macmillan, 1967.

Miller, K. & Miller, O. Maintaining attendance of welfare recipients in self-help programs by supplementary reinforcement. Paper presented at the meetings of the American Psychological Association, Washington, D.C., September 1969.

Miller, L. K. & Miller, O. L. Reinforcing self-help group activities of welfare recipients. *Journal of Applied Behavior Analysis*, **1970**, *3*, 57–64.

Miller, L. K. & Schneider, R. The use of a token system in project Head Start. Paper read at the meeting of the American Psychological Association, San Francisco, **1968**.

Miller, L. R. A note on the control of study behavior. *Journal of Experimental Child Psychology*, **1964**, *1*, 108–110.

Miller, S. M. Dropouts—a political problem. In C. W. Hunnicutt (Ed.), *The school dropout*. Syracuse Univ. Press, **1964**.

Miller, S. M. School dropouts. *New Society*, **1963**, *2*, 12–20.

Mischel, W. *Personality assessment*. New York: Wiley, **1968**.

Mithaug, D. E. & Burgess, R. L. The effects of differential reinforcement contingencies in the development of social cooperation. *Journal of Experimental Psychology*, **1968**, *6*, 402–426.

Moktus, J. Accountability and the Reverend Dogood. *NEA Journal*, March **1971**, 57.

Montessori, M. *The discovery of the child*. Notre Dame, Ind.: Fides Publishers, **1967**.

Mosier, D. B. Operant conditioning techniques applied to low rate self-initiated conversation and eye-contact. *School Applications of Learning Theory*, **1970**, *2*, 49–54.

N

Nash, R. L. Teaching speech improvement to the disadvantaged. *Speech Teacher*, **1967**, *16*, 69–73.

Neill, A. S. *Summerhill: A radical approach to child rearing*. New York: Hart, **1959**.

Nicol, E. H. *The development of validated museum exhibits*. (Final Report, H.E.W. Contract OECI 6-050 245-1015, Project No. 5-0245) **1969**.

Nolen, P. A., Knuzelmann, H. P., & Haring, N. G. Behavior modification in a junior-high learning disabilities classroom. *Exceptional Children*, **1967**, *34*, 163–168.

Nye, R. B. *The cultural life of the new nation, 1776–1830*. New York: Harper & Row, **1963**.

O

Offenberg, R. M. *Title VII project let's be amigos: Evaluation of the first year, 1969–1970*. Philadelphia: The School District of Philadelphia, **1970**.

Office of Economic Opportunity. *An experiment in performance contracting: Summary of preliminary results*. (OEO Pamphlet 3400–5) Washington, D.C.: February **1972**.

O'Leary, K. D. & Becker, W. C. Behavior modification of an adjustment class: A token reinforcement program. *Exceptional Children*, **1967**, *33*, 637–642.

O'Leary, K. D., Becker, W. C., Evans, M. B., & Saudargas, R. A. A token reinforcement program in a public school: A replication and systematic analysis. *Journal of Applied Behavior Analysis*, **1969**, *2*, 3–13.

O'Leary, K. D. & Drabman, R. S. Token reinforcement programs in the classroom: A review. *Psychological Bulletin*, **1971**, *75*, 379–398.

Osborne, J. G. Free-time as a reinforcer in the management of classroom behavior. *Journal of Applied Behavior Analysis*, **1969**, *2*, 113–118.

Oxford (shorter) English dictionary. (3rd ed.) London: Oxford University Press, **1959**.

P

Page, E. B. Miracle in Milwaukee: Raising the IQ. *Educational Researcher*, **1972**, *1*(10), 8–15.

Painter, G. *Teach your baby*. New York: Simon & Schuster, **1971**.

Parker, D., Covell, H. M., La Forge, P. J., Paternoster, L. M., Quinn, T. J., & Fisher, L. E. *The SRA reading laboratory*. Chicago: Science Research Associates, **1959**.

Partridge, E. *Origins: A short etymological dictionary of modern English*. New York: Macmillan, **1958**.

Patterson, G. R. A community mental health program for children. In L. A. Hammerlynck, P. O. Davidson, & L. E. Acker (Eds.), *Behavior modification and ideal mental health services*. Calgary, Alberta, Canada: University of Calgary, **1969**. (a)

Patterson, G. R. An application of conditioning techniques to the control of a hyperactive child. In L. P. Ullmann & L. Krasner (Eds.), *Case studies in behavior modification*. New York: Holt, Rinehart & Winston, **1965**.

Patterson, G. R. Parents as behavior modifiers in the classroom. In J. D. Krumboltz & C. Thoresen (Eds.), *Behavioral counseling: Cases and techniques*. New York: Holt, Rinehart & Winston, **1969**. (b)

Patterson, G. R., Ebner, M., & Shaw, D. Teachers, peers, and parents as agents of change. In A. Benson (Ed.), *Behavior modification in the schools*. Eugene: University of Oregon Press, **1969**.

Patterson, G. R. & Gullion, M. E. *Living with children: New methods for parents and teachers*. Champaign, Ill.: Research Press, **1968**.

Patterson, G. R. & Harris, A. Methodological problems in observation procedure. Paper presented at the meeting of the American Psychological Association, San Francisco, **1968**.

Patterson, G. R., Hawkins, N., McNeal, S., & Phelps, R. Reprogramming the social environment. *Journal of Child Psychology and Psychiatry*, 1968, 8, 181–196.

Patterson, G. R., Jones, R., Whittier, J., & Wright, M. A behavior modification technique for the hyperactive child. *Behavior Research and Therapy*, 1965, 2, 217–226.

Patterson, G. R., Shaw, D. A., & Ebner, M. J. Teachers, peers, and parents as agents of change in the classroom. In A. M. Benson (Ed.), *Modifying deviant social behaviors in various classroom settings*. Eugene, Oregon: University of Oregon, 1969, No. 1.

Patterson, G. R. & White, G. D. *It's a small world: The application of "time out from positive reinforcement."* Oregon Research Institute, undated. Mimeo.

People's yellow pages; a directory of alternatives in San Francisco. San Francisco: The People's Yellow Pages Collective, 1971.

Perline, I. H. & Levensky, D. Controlling maladaptive classroom behavior of the severely retarded. *American Journal of Mental Deficiency*, 1968, 73, 74–78.

Perls, F. S. *Gestalt therapy verbatim*. LaFayette, Calif.: Real People Press, 1969.

Phillips, E. Achievement place: Token reninforcement procedures in a home-style rehabilitation setting for pre-delinquent boys. *Journal of Applied Behavior Analysis*, 1968, 1, 213–223.

Premack, D. *Reinforcement theory in Nebraska symposium on motivation 1965*. Lincoln: University of Nebraska Press, 1965.

Pressman, H. Schools to beat the system. *Psychology Today*, 1969, 2, 58–63.

Pryor, K. W., Haag, R., & O'Reilly, J. The creative porpoise: Training for novel behavior. *Journal of the Experimental Analysis of Behavior*, 1969, 12, 653–661.

Pushkarev, B. Scale and design in a new environment. In L. B. Holland (Ed.), *Who designs America?* New York: Doubleday, Anchor Books, 1966.

Q

Quay, H. C., Werry, J. S., McQueen, M., & Sprague, R. L. Remediation of the conduct problem child in the special class setting. *Exceptional Children*, 1966, 32, 509–515.

R

Rabb, E. & Hewett, F. M. Developing appropriate classroom behaviors in a severely disturbed group of institutionalized kindergarten-primary children utilizing a behavior modification model.

American Journal of Orthopsychiatry, 1967, 37, 313–314.

Rabkin, J. & Rabkin, R. Delinquency and the lateral boundary of the family. In P. S. Graubard (Ed.), *Children against schools: Education of the delinquent, disturbed, disruptive*. Chicago: Follett Educational Corp., 1969.

Ragsdale, R. G. The learning research and development center's computer-assisted laboratory. *DECUS Proceedings*, 1966, 5, 65–68.

Ray, R. S., Shaw, D. A., & Patterson, G. R. *Observation in the school: Description of a coding form*. Eugene, Oregon: Oregon Research Institute, 1968.

Redl, F. & Wineman, D. *Controls from within*. Glencoe: The Free Press, 1952.

Reese, E. P. *The analysis of human operant behavior*. Dubuque, Iowa: Wm. C. Brown, 1966.

Reich, C. A. *The greening of America*. New York: Random House, 1970.

Research and Development Center (D. E. P. Smith, Dir.) Minutes: Staff meeting. Ann Arbor: University School, University of Michigan, undated. Mimeo.

Reynolds, N. J. & Risley, T. R. The role of social and material reinforcers in increasing talking of a disadvantaged preschool child. *Journal of Applied Behavior Analysis*, 1968, 1(3), 253–262.

Rhodes, W. C. The disturbing child: A problem of ecological management. In P. S. Graubard (Ed.), *Children against schools: Education of the delinquent, disturbed, disruptive*. Chicago: Follett Educational Corp., 1969.

Richardson, E. The physical setting and its influence on learning. In H. M. Proshansky, W. H. Ittelson, and L. G. Rivlin (Eds.), *Environmental psychology; man and his physical setting*. New York: Holt, Rinehart & Winston, 1970.

Risley, T. Learning and lollipops. *Psychology Today*, 1968, 1, 28–31, 62–65.

Risley, T. R. & Baer, D. M. *Operant conditioning: "Develop" is a transitive, active verb*. Lawrence, Kansas: University of Kansas, undated. Mimeo.

Risley, T. R. & Hart, B. Developing correspondence between the nonverbal and verbal behavior of preschool children. *Journal of Applied Behavior Analysis*, 1968, 1, 267–282.

Risley, T. R., Hart, B., & Doke, L. A. Operant language development: The outline of a therapeutic technology. In R. L. Schiefelbusch (Ed.), *The language of the mentally retarded*. Baltimore: University Park Press, 1971.

Risley, T. R., Reynolds, N. J., & Hart, B. The disadvantaged: Behavior modification with disadvantaged preschool children. In R. Bradfield

(Ed.), *Behavior modification: The human effort.* Palo Alto: Science & Behavior Books, 1970.

Risley urges "survival training" for preschoolers. *Report on Education Research,* 1971, *3,* 6.

Rogers, C. *Freedom to learn.* Columbus: Merrill, 1969.

Rogers, C. Mental health problems in three elementary schools. *Educational Research Bulletin,* 1942, *21,* 67–79.

Rogers, C. The person of tomorrow. Commencement address presented at Sonoma State College, California, June 1968.

Rosenberg, H., Graubard, P., & Miller, M. B. A comparative cost and achievement study of regular and special classes, in preparation.

Rosenthal, R. & Jacobson, L. Teachers' expectancies: Determinants of pupils' IQ gains. *Psychological Reports,* 1966, *19,* 115–118.

Ross, A. O. The application of behavior principles in therapeutic education. *The Journal of Special Education,* 1967, *1,* 275–284.

Rozynko, V. V., Flint, G. A., Hammer, C. E., Swift, K. D., Kline, J. A., & King, R. M. An operant behavior modification program. Paper presented at the meeting of the Western Psychological Association, April 1971.

Rudofsky, B. *Architecture without architects.* New York: The Museum of Modern Art, 1965.

Russell, D. H. & Karp, E. E. *Reading aids through the grades.* New York: Bureau of Publications, Columbia University, 1938.

Ryan, J. J. Factors associated with pupil-audience reaction to teacher management of deviancy in the classroom. *American Psychologist,* 1959, *7,* 378.

S

Salzinger, K., Feldman, R. S., & Portnoy, S. Training parents of brain-injured children in the use of operant conditioning procedures. *Behavior Therapy,* 1970, *1,* 4–32.

Schaefer, H. H. & Martin, P. L. *Behavioral therapy.* New York: McGraw-Hill, 1969.

Schmidt, G. W. & Ulrich, R. E. Effects of group contingent events upon classroom noise. *Journal of Applied Behavior Analysis,* 1969, *2,* 171–180.

Schramm, W. Programed instruction today and tomorrow. In W. Schramm (Ed.), *Four case studies of programed instruction.* New York: Fund for the Advancement of Education, 1964.

Schroer, P. & Johnson, N. J. A. The effects of curtailed and delayed lunchtime upon fifteen sixth-grade pupils' arithmetic performance. Unpublished manuscript, University of Kansas, 1968.

Schutte, R. C. & Hopkins, B. L. The effects of teacher attention on following instructions in a kindergarten class. *Journal of Applied Behavior Analysis,* 1970, *3,* 117–122.

Schwarz, M. L. & Hawkins, R. P. Application of delayed reinforcement procedures to the behavior problems of an elementary-school child. *Journal of Applied Behavior Analysis,* 1970, *3,* 85–96.

Schwitzgebel, R. L. A remote instrumentation system for behavior modification: A preliminary report. In R. Rubin & C. M. Franks (Eds.), *Advances in behavior therapy, 1968.* New York: Academic Press, 1969.

Schwitzgebel, R. L. Behavior instrumentation and social technology. *American Psychologist,* 1970, *25,* 491–499.

Scott, J. P. A time to learn. *Psychology Today,* 1969, *2,* 46–48, 66–67.

Screven, C. G. *Experimental studies of learning in a museum. Vol. 1. Studies on museum behavior.* Washington, D.C.: Office of Museum Programs, Smithsonian Institution, 1973.

Screven, C. G. The museum as a responsive learning environment. *Museum News,* 1969, *4,* 7–10.

Sechrest, L. & Wallace, J. *Psychology and human problems.* Columbus: Merrill, 1967.

Seligman, M. E. P., Mier, S. F., & Geer, O. H. Alleviation of learned helplessness in the dog. *Journal of Abnormal Psychology,* 1968, *73,* 256–262.

Semmelroth, C. How to tell a well-managed classroom when you see one. Paper presented at the meeting of the Council for Exceptional Children, Denver, Colorado, April 1969.

Sherman, J. A. & Baer, D. M. Appraisal of operant therapy techniques with children and adults. In C. M. Franks (Ed.), *Behavior therapy: Appraisal and status.* New York: McGraw-Hill, 1969.

Shettel, H. H. Strategies for determining exhibit effectiveness. (USOE Final Report, Contract OEG 6-10-213, Project V-011) Pittsburgh: American Institutes of Research, 1968.

Shikoski, T. Modification of pants-wetting behavior. *School Applications of Learning Theory,* 1971, *3,* 19–25.

Short, J. G. *Strategies of training development.* Pittsburgh, Pa.: American Institutes for Research, 1968.

Short, J. & Sands, H. R. *The development of a method for determining fundamental performance objectives.* Pittsburgh, Pa.: American Institutes for Research, 1965.

Shubik, M. Game theory and the study of social behavior: An introductory statement. In M.

Shubik (Ed.), *Game theory and related approaches to social behavior*. New York: Wiley, 1964.

Sidman, M. *Tactics of scientific research: Evaluating experimental data in psychology*. New York: Basic Books, 1960.

Siegel, S. *Nonparametric statistics for the behavioral Sciences*. New York: McGraw-Hill, 1956.

Silberglitt, B. The use of audio and prosthetic devices to improve and evaluate exhibit effectiveness. Unpublished doctoral dissertation, University of Wisconsin-Milwaukee, 1972.

Silberman, C. E. Report on the Nation's Public Schools. Commissioned by the Carnegie Corporation, Chicago, Illinois.

Skinner, B. F. *Beyond freedom and dignity*. New York: Knopf, 1971.

Skinner, B. F. Contingency management in the classroom. *Educate*, 1970, *3*, 20–25.

Skinner, B. F. *Science and human behavior*. New York: Macmillan, 1953.

Skinner, B. F. *Science and human behavior*. New York: Appleton-Century-Crofts, 1953.

Skinner, B. F. Teaching machines. *Scientific American*, 1961, *205*(5).

Skinner, B. F. Teaching science in high school—what is wrong? *Science*, 1968, *159*, 704–710.

Skinner, B. F. The control of human behavior (1955). In *Cumulative record*. New York: Appleton-Century-Crofts, 1961.

Skinner, B. F. *The technology of teaching*. New York: Appleton-Century-Crofts, 1968.

Skinner, B. F. *Verbal behavior*. New York: Appleton-Century-Crofts, 1957.

Skinner, B. F. *Walden two*. New York: Macmillan, 1948.

Skinner, B. F. & Krakower, S. *Handwriting with write and see*. Chicago: Lyons and Carnahan, 1968.

Sloane, H. Address presented at the symposium on Behavior Analysis in Education, University of Kansas, 1971.

Sloggett, B., Gallimore, R., & Kubany, E. A comparative analysis of fantasy need achievement among high and low achieving male Hawaiian Americans. *Journal of Cross-Cultural Psychology*, 1970, *1*, 53–61.

Smith, D. E. P. & Smith, J. M. Teacher's manual for the Michigan language program. Ann Arbor, Michigan: Ann Arbor Publishers, 1968.

Smith, D. H. Teaching speech to the culturally disadvantaged. *Speech Teacher*, 1966, *15*, 140–144.

Smith, E. C. Industry views the teaching of English. *English Journal*, 1956, *6*, 122–128.

Smith, J. M. & D. E. P. Smith. *Child management: A program for parents*. Ann Arbor, Mich.: Ann Arbor Publishers, 1966.

Sommer, R. *Personal space*. Englewood Cliffs, N.J.: Prentice-Hall, 1969.

Spence, J. T. The distracting effects of material reinforcers in the discrimination learning of lower and middle class children. *Child Development*, 1970, *41*, 103–112.

Spitz, R. A. & Cobliner, W. G. *The first year of life*. New York: International Universities Press, 1965.

Staats, A. W. Development, use, and social extensions of reinforcer (motivational) systems in the solution of human problems. *Progress in behavior modification: Programs and results*. Honolulu, 1969.

Staats, A. W. *Learning, language, and cognition*. New York: Holt, Rinehart & Winston, 1968.

Staats, A. W. & Butterfield, W. H. Treatment of nonreading in a culturally deprived juvenile delinquent: An application of reinforcement principles. *Child Development*, 1965, *36*, 925–942.

Staats, A. W. & Staats, C. K. *Complex human behavior*. New York: Holt, Rinehart & Winston, 1963.

Staats, A. W., Minker, K. A., Goodwin, W., & Landeed, J. Cognitive behavior modification: Motivated learning and reading treatment with sub-professional therapy technicians. *Behavior Research and Therapy*, 1967, *5*, 283–300.

Stein, M. E. Creativity and culture. *Journal of Psychology*, 1953, *36*, 311–322.

Stevenson, I. & Wolpe, J. Recovery from sexual deviations through overcoming nonsexual neurotic responses. *American Journal of Psychiatry*, 1960, *116*, 737–742.

Stevenson, M. B. & Fitzgerald, H. E. Standards for infant day care in the United States and Canada. *Child Care Quarterly*, 1971, *1*, 89–110.

Stuart, R. B. A guide to behavior modification. Ann Arbor, Michigan: University of Michigan, 1969. Mimeo. (a)

Stuart, R. B. Assessment and change of the communicational patterns of juvenile delinquents and their parents. In R. D. Rubin (Ed.), *Advances in behavior therapy: 1969*. New York: Academic Press, 1970. (a)

Stuart, R. B. Behavioral contracting within the families of delinquents. Paper presented at the meeting of the American Psychological Association, Miami Beach, Florida, September 1970. (b)

Stuart, R. B. Critical reappraisal of selected mental health programs. In L. A. Hammerlynck, P. O. Davidson, and L. E. Acker (Eds.), *Behav-*

ior modification and ideal mental health services. Calgary, Alberta, Canada: University of Calgary Press, 1969. (b)

Stuart, R. B. *Trick or treatment: How and when psychotherapy fails.* Champaign, Ill.: Research Press, 1970. (c)

Studer, R. G. The dynamics of behavior-contingent physical systems. In H. M. Proshansky, W. H. Ittelson, and L. G. Rivlin (Eds.), *Environment psychology; man and his physical setting.* New York: Holt, Rinehart & Winston, 1970.

Sulzbucker, S. I. & Houser, J. E. A tactic to eliminate disruptive behaviors in the classroom: Group contingent consequences. *American Journal of Mental Deficiency,* 1968, *73,* 88–90.

Suppes, P. The uses of computers in education. *Scientific American,* 1966, *215,* 206–221.

Suppes, P. & Suppes, J. *Sets and numbers.* (Rev. ed.) New York: Singer, 1962.

Surratt, P. R., Ulrich, R. E., & Hawkins, R. P. An elementary student as a behavioral engineer. *Journal of Applied Behavior Analysis,* 1969, *2,* 85–92.

Szasz, T. S. *The manufacture of madness: The comparative study of the inquisition and the mental health movement.* New York: Harper & Row, 1970.

T

Task Force on Juvenile Delinquency, The President's Commission on Law Enforcement and Administration of Justice. *Task Force Report: Juvenile Delinquency and Youth Crime.* Washington, D.C.: U.S. Government Printing Office, 1967.

Tate, B. G. & Baroff, G. S. Aversive control of self-injurious behavior in a psychotic boy. *Behavior Research and Therapy,* 1966, *4,* 281–287.

Tenenbaum, S. *William Heard Kilpatrick.* New York: Harper & Row, 1951.

Tennyson, R. D., Woolley, F. R., & Merrill, M. D. Exemplar and non-exemplar variables which produce correct concept classification behavior and specified classification errors. *Journal of Educational Psychology,* in press.

Test, L. The relative effects of an individual and a group reinforcement contingency system on the learning behavior of culturally-deprived juvenile delinquents. Unpublished doctoral dissertation, University of Hawaii, 1969.

Tharp, R. G. & Wetzel, R. J. *Behavior modification in the natural environment.* New York: Academic Press, 1969.

Thiemann, H. Changing dynamics in research and development. *Science,* 1970, *168,* 1427–1431.

Thomas, D. A., Nielsen, L. J., Kuypers, D. S., & Becker, W. C. Social reinforcement and remedial instruction in the elimination of a classroom behavior problem. *Journal of Special Education,* 1968, *2,* 291–302.

Thomas, D. R., Becker, W. C., & Armstrong, M. Production and elimination of disruptive classroom behavior by systematically varying teacher's behavior. *Journal of Applied Behavior Analysis,* 1968, *1,* 34–45.

Tiktin, S. & Hartup, W. W. Sociometric status and the reinforcing effectiveness of children's peers. *Journal of Experimental Child Psychology,* 1965, *2,* 306–315.

Toffler, A. *Future shock.* New York: Random House, 1970.

Tough, J., Hawkins, R. P., McArthur, M. M., & Van Ravenswaay, S. Modification of enuretic behavior by punishment. *Behavior Therapy,* in press.

Turner, V. W. *The ritual process: structure and anti-structure.* Chicago: Aldine, 1969.

U

Ullmann, L. & Krasner, L. *A psychological approach to abnormal behavior.* Englewood Cliffs, N.J.: Prentice-Hall, 1969.

Ullmann, L. & Krasner, L. *Case studies in behavior modification.* New York: Holt, Rinehart, & Winston, 1965.

Ulrich, R. E., Louisell, S. E., & Wolfe, M. The Learning Village: A behavioral approach to early education. *Educational Technology,* 1971, *11*(2), 32–45.

Ulrich, R., Stachnik, T., & Mabry, J. *Control of human behavior.* Glenview: Scott, Foresman, 1966.

Ulrich, R. E., Surratt, P. R., & Wolfe, M. Accelerated training programs in underprivileged environments. *Michigan Mental Health Research Bulletin,* 1969, *3,* 40–42.

Ulrich, R. E., Wolfe, M. M., & Bluhm, M. Operant conditioning in the public schools. *Behavior Modification Monographs,* 1968, *1*(1).

Ulrich, R. E., Wolfe, M., & Cole, R. Early education: A preventive mental health program. *Michigan Mental Health Research Bulletin,* 1970, *4*(1).

V

Van der Ryn, S. & Silverstein, M. *Dorms at Berkeley; an environmental analysis.* New York: Educational Facilities Laboratories, Inc., 1967.

Verhave, T. *The experimental analysis of behav-*

ior. New York: Appleton-Century-Crofts, **1966**.

Verplank, W. S. The control of the content of conversation: Reinforcement of statements of opinion. *Journal of Abnormal and Social Psychology*, **1955**, *51*, 668–676.

Vocations for Social Change. Canyon, California: Vocations for Social Change, Inc.

W

Wahler, R. G. Child-child interactions in free field settings: Some experimental analysis. *Journal of Experimental Child Psychology*, **1967**, *5*, 278–293.

Wahler, R. G. & Erickson, M. Child behavior therapy: A community program in Appalachia. *Behaviour Research and Therapy*, **1969**, *7*, 71–78.

Wahler, R. G., Winkel, G. H., Peterson, R. F., & Morrison, D. C. Mothers as behavior therapists for their own children. *Behaviour Research and Therapy*, **1965**, *3*, 113–124.

Walker, H. M. & Buckley, N. K. The use of positive reinforcement in conditioning attending behavior. *Journal of Applied Behavior Analysis*, **1968**, *1*, 245–250.

Walker, H. M., Mattson, R. H., & Buckley, N. K. Special class placement as a treatment alternative for deviant behavior in children. In F. A. M. Benson (Ed.), *Modifying deviant social behavior in various classroom settings*. (Monograph Series 1) Eugene, Oregon: University of Oregon, Department of Special Education, **1969**.

Wall, W. D. *Education and mental health*. Paris: UNESCO, **1955**.

Wallace, J. An abilities conception of personality: Some implications for personality measurement. *American Psychologist*, **1966**, *21*, 132–138.

Walsh, J. F. & O'Connor, J. D. When are children disturbed? *Elementary School Journal*, **1968**, *68*, 353–356.

Walters, H. C. *Military Psychology: Its use in modern war and indirect conflict*. Dubuque, Iowa: Wm. C. Brown, **1968**.

Ward, M. H. & Baker, B. L. Reinforcement therapy in the classroom. *Journal of Applied Behavior Analysis*, **1968**, *1*, 323–328.

Wasik, B. B., Senn, K., Welch, R. H., & Cooper, B. A. Behavior modification with culturally deprived school children: Two case studies. *Journal of Applied Behavior Analysis*, **1969**, *2*, 181–194.

Webster's third new international dictionary. (Unabridged) Springfield, Mass.: G. & C. Merriam, **1967**.

Weikart, D. P. Relationship of curriculum, teaching, and learning in preschool education. In J. C. Stanley (Ed.), *Preschool programs for the disadvantaged: Five experimental approaches to early childhood education*. Baltimore: The Johns Hopkins University Press, **1972**.

Weiner, H. Some effects of response cost upon human operant behavior. *Journal of the Experimental Analysis of Behavior*, **1962**, *5*, 201–208.

Werry, J. & Quay, H. Observing the classroom behavior of elementary school children. Paper presented at the meeting of the Council on Exceptional Children, New York City, April **1968**.

Westin, A. F. *Privacy and freedom*. New York: Atheneum, **1970**.

Westinghouse Learning Corporation. *The impact of Head Start, an evaluation of the effect of Head Start on children's cognitive and affective development*. Vol. 1, Text and Appendices A-E (PB 184 328). Washington, D.C.: Clearinghouse for Federal Scientific and Technical Information, U.S. Department of Commerce/National Bureau of Standards, June **1969**.

Whelan, R. G. & Haring, N. G. Modification and maintenance of behavior through systematic application of consequences. *Exceptional Children*, **1966**, *32*, 281–289.

White, H. E. The design, development, and testing of a response box, a new component for science museum exhibits. (Contract OE6-10-056, Project 3148) USOE, **1967**.

Wiener, N. *The human use of human beings*. Garden City, New York: Doubleday, Anchor, **1956**.

Wike, E. L. *A statistical primer for psychology students*. New York: Aldine-Atherton, **1971**.

Williams, C. D. The elimination of tantrum behavior by extinction procedures. In L. P. Ullmann and L. Krasner (Eds.), *Case studies in behavior modification*. New York: Holt, Rinehart & Winston, **1965**.

Wodarski, J. S., Hamblin, R. L., Buckholdt, D. R., & Ferritor, D. E. Effects of individual and group contingencies on arithmetic performance. *The Psychological Record*, **1972**.

Wodarski, J., Hamblin, R., Buckholdt, D., & Ferritor, D. Individual consequences versus different shared consequences contingent on the performances of low achieving group members. *Journal of Applied Social Psychology*, in press.

Wolfe, M. M., Giles, D. K., & Hall, R. V. Experiments with token reinforcement in a remedial classroom. *Behaviour Research and Therapy*, **1968**, *6*, 51–64.

Wolfe, M., Risley, T., & Mees, H. Application of operant conditioning procedures to the behavior problems of an autistic child. *Behaviour Research and Therapy*, **1964**, *1*, 304–312.

Wolfe, M., Ulrich, R., & Ulrich, C. Administrative hurdles blocking preventive mental health programs for children. *Michigan Mental Health Research Bulletin*, **1970**, *4*(2), 44–48.

Wolpe, J. Behavior therapy in complex neurotic states. *British Journal of Psychiatry*, **1964**, *110*, 28–34.

Wood, W. S. The Lincoln Elementary School projects: Some results of an in-service training course in behavioral psychology. *Educational Technology Monographs*, **1968**, *1*, 3–26.

Woody, R. H. The use of electro-encephalography and mental abilities tests in the diagnosis of behavioral problem males. Unpublished doctoral dissertation, Michigan State University, **1964**.

World without words. *Reading Newsreport*, **1969**, *3*, 26–31.

Y

Yanes, S. & Holdorf, C. (Eds.), *Big rock candy mountain: Resources for our education*. New York: Dell, **1971**.

Z

Zax, M., Cowen, E., Rappaport, J., Beach, D. R., & Laird, J. D. Follow-up of children identified early as emotionally disturbed. *Journal of Consulting and Clinical Psychology*, **1968**, *32*, 369–374.

Zeilberger, J., Sampen, S. E., & Sloane, H. N., Jr. Modification of a child's problem behaviors in the home with the mother as therapist. *Journal of Applied Behavior Analysis*, **1968**, *1*, 47–53.

Zimmerman, C. Classroom academic feedback and elementary administrator and staff behavior. Unpublished doctoral dissertation, University of Oregon, **1969**.

Zimmerman, E. H. & Zimmerman, J. The alteration of behavior in a special classroom situation. *Journal of Experimental Analysis of Behavior*, **1962**, *5*, 59–60.

Zimmerman, E. H., Zimmerman, J., & Russell, C. D. Differential effects of token reinforcement on instruction-following behavior in retarded students instructed as a group. *Journal of Applied Behavior Analysis*, **1969**, *2*, 101–112.

94

1 2 3 4 5 6 7 8 9 10 11 12 13 14 15 16 17 18 19 20 21 22 23 24 25   82 81 80 79 78 77 76 75 74